Director® Shockwave® Studio Developer's Guide

About the Author

James Newton is the author of many behaviors found in the Library Palette that shipped with Director 7.0, Director 8.0, and Director 8.5. He is Technical Director of OpenSpark Interactive Ltd, a Scottish company that produces customized tools for multimedia development. James is chairman of the British Director Users' Group DUG UK (http://www.duguk.org/) and, with Emmanuel Beuque and Christophe Leske, is co-founder of the French Director Users' Group, Director Hors Piste (http://www.director-fr.com/). He is an Authorized Training Provider for Macromedia Director and contributes regularly to a number of Director-oriented mailing lists.

Director® Shockwave® Studio Developer's Guide

James Newton

McGraw-Hill/Osborne

New York Chicago San Francisco
Lisbon London Madrid Mexico City
Milan New Delhi San Juan
Seoul Singapore Sydney Toronto

McGraw-Hill/Osborne
2600 Tenth Street
Berkeley, California 94710
U.S.A.

To arrange bulk purchase discounts for sales promotions, premiums, or fund-raisers, please contact **McGraw-Hill**/Osborne at the above address. For information on translations or book distributors outside the U.S.A., please see the International Contact Information page immediately following the index of this book.

Director® Shockwave® Studio Developer's Guide

1234567890 CUS CUS 0198765432

Book p/n 0-07-213263-9 and CD p/n 0-07-213264-7
parts of
ISBN 0-07-213265-5

Publisher	Brandon A. Nordin
Vice President & Associate Publisher	Scott Rogers
Acquisitions Editor	James Schachterle
Project Editor	Jody McKenzie
Acquisitions Coordinator	Tim Madrid
Technical Editor	Emmanuel Beuque
Copy Editor	Rachel Lopez
Proofreader	Linda Medoff
Indexer	David Heiret
Computer Designers	Carie Abrew and Kelly Stanton-Scott
Illustrator	Michael Mueller and Lyssa Wald
Series Design	Roberta Steele
Cover Series Design	Greg Scott
Cover Illustration	Eliot Bergman

This book was composed with Corel VENTURA ™ Publisher.

Contents at a Glance

Contents

Acknowledgments

I am indebted to Jakob Hede Madsen for showing me how to use Lingo to understand Lingo. Without the penetrating insight he has shared with me since I was a newcomer to Director, I would have passed by many of the ideas and techniques covered in this book. Jakob's intelligent and creative coding has always been an inspiration to me.

I am most grateful to Emmanuel Beuque for his painstaking work as technical editor. His attention to detail has undoubtedly made this a better book. Any remaining errors are mine.

Special thanks to Charlotte Thibault for the original artwork she created especially for this book, and for her cheerful encouragement at all times.

Kouki kouki to Sébastien Portebois for his undying determination to find bugs in my code, his suggestions for simplifying my algorithms, and his contribution to Chapter 12.

The influence of Pim van Bochoven and Mark Reijnders is evident throughout the book. Their OSControls Xtra and top-class technical support for it have saved me many hours of work and ensured that the interfaces for the tools movies have a truly professional look.

Many thanks to Werner Sharp for his patience in helping me understand the intricacies of Imaging Lingo and the use of inks, and for permission to quote his explanations.

A big thank you to Rebecca Lovelace for taking me to task on uncounted points of detail and for her positive feedback on each of the chapters.

Many thanks to Karina Steffens for providing a reality check on the user friendliness of my mathematical explanations, for providing the inspiration for Chapter 5, and for the original photographs used in the movies for Chapters 3 and 14.

Thanks also to Mike Chausovsky for permission to use his paintings in the Imaging Lingo section and the Gallery movie.

I am grateful to Roy Pardi both for his refreshingly direct criticism and for raising a number of points I otherwise would have overlooked.

To Danny Kodicek I owe the pleasure of developing a set of routines for virtual origami. His advice on the finer points of vector mathematics has been a great help.

I very much appreciate the encouragement and support I received from Daniel Devolder, Gretchen McDowall, and Vahé Kassardjian. Their contribution of demonstration versions of a number of well-crafted xtras adds value to the accompanying CD-ROM.

Thanks also to Irv Kalb, Benoît Pereira da Silva, Darrel Plant, Kerry Thompson, Arnauld de la Grandière (dit Nonoche), Murielle Lefèvre, Frédéric Durieu, Alan Levine, Robert Walch, and Bruno Sébarte for their feedback on the draft version of this book.

Most of all, I would like to thank my wife and family for supporting me ungrudgingly during the long hours and months I worked on this book.

Introduction

A lion who imitates a lion is an ape.

—Victor Hugo

Director Shockwave Studio is show business in a box. Your clients and consumer end users expect to be surprised, challenged, even moved by the content you create. Director Shockwave Studio is a database by any other name. Your business clients expect your applications to be sturdy, ergonomic, and flexible.

Director Shockwave Studio is a different product in the hands of each developer. No one else needs to produce quite the same content that you do. No one else is faced with quite the same development issues that you are. Director Shockwave Studio is a wealth of solutions in search of an original problem. The very richness of Director and the Lingo language can be overwhelming. To get the most out of Director, to bring the power of Director to bear on your unique development situation, you need to focus your attention on a particular set of features. That is what this book and the subsequent editions will help you to do.

This volume concentrates on two specific areas: Imaging Lingo and 3D Lingo. It provides a three-pronged approach to learning:

- Practical exercises through which you build a project step by step from scratch. The immediate purpose of each exercise is to deal with a particular aspect of Director in context.
- Meta-Lingo experiments in which you use Lingo to explore how Lingo works. The broader purpose of these experiments is to encourage you to transfer these meta-Lingo techniques to those other areas of Director in which you have a specific interest.
- Tool movies, which demonstrate the principles of a particularly complex Director feature, and which you can use to create scripts automatically. You can use these tool movies both as they stand—as development time savers—and (if you have the courage to investigate them on your own) as a source of advanced coding techniques.

Who Should Read This Book

This book assumes that you already have some knowledge of Macromedia Director. If you have read the Using Director manual which comes with Director, and have already taken the time to get familiar with the Lingo programming language, you should be ready for this book.

How This Book Should Be Read

While writing this book I have imagined you in two situations. In the first you are sitting in front of your computer, actively experimenting with the Lingo code I present. In the second you are comfortably seated in an armchair with your computer unplugged, or less comfortably standing at a bus stop, with no access to a computer. Your requirements depend on which situation you find yourself in. I've written this book so that it reads well in either case.

Using Your Computer

The files on the CD-ROM are an essential part of the book: They bring the Lingo code to life. You will learn a great deal by working through them and adapting them for your own projects. The code is more complete and more fully commented than the extracts of code I include in the text. You'll also want to add the tool movies to your Xtras folder, so that you can use them at any time when you are working on a project.

Before you start, I recommend that you run the AddXtras.exe projector on the CD-ROM. This application will automatically add the tool movies and a couple of useful xtras to your Director application.

Using Your Head

You also need to get a broader picture of how to get Director to work for you. From time to time you need to switch your computer off and just juggle with ideas. To help you do this, I have included numerous code extracts and screenshots so that you can read the text without interruption, and visualize the effects described.

What Is In This Book

This volume covers Imaging Lingo and 3D Lingo. Each of these is a subject in its own right. Coupled together, they offer great potential. Using Imaging Lingo you can create dynamic textures for your 3D models. You can use the `image` property of your Shockwave 3D members as a source for the `copyPixels()` command.

Imaging Lingo

Examples for the Imaging Lingo part have been written using Director 8.0 and tested in Director 8.5. Where there are differences between the two versions, these are noted in the text. New features, such as the undocumented `floodFill()` command, are activated if the example movies are played in Director 8.5.

Movies such as Copyxels.dir and InkTest.dir give you immediate insight into how the more complex features of Imaging Lingo work and help you choose the parameters you need to use to get the results you want. You will find ready-made behaviors for exploiting the `draw()` and `fill()` commands and step-by-step explanations of how to build transitions and other dynamic imaging effects such as goo. You will learn how to use the `image` properties of Text, Flash, and Vector Shape members to produce impressive compound images quickly and efficiently.

3D Lingo

The 3D part requires Director 8.5; it does not require you to have access to any third-party 3D design software. All the movies featured in the book are created using Lingo alone. You are not expected to have any prior knowledge of 3D concepts. The 3D part starts from the very beginning: You will learn how to reinvent the wheel, how to create fire (virtually speaking), and how to deal with primitives. As your understanding of vectors and transforms develops, you will be able to tackle more refined issues such as origami, the oriental art of paper folding, and space flight.

Director 8.5 provides a powerful set of 3D Lingo commands but little in the way of a visual interface to help you understand the effect of these commands. There are a number of tool movies in the 3D part of the CD-ROM which fill the gap. You can use these movies in a window to improve your productivity, or open them on the Stage to study their construction.

- **Lathe.dir** This movie enables you to create lathed objects, making up for the absence of such a tool in Director itself. The movie outputs behavior scripts;

simply drop one of these scripts on a Shockwave 3D member in a different movie to recreate the lathed shape.

- **Shaders.dir** Used as a movie in a window, the Shaders.dir movie enables you to build your own textures and shaders for your own movies, and to output the scripts that recreate these textures and shaders. Opened on the Stage, you can use the movie to understand the concepts involved.
- **gForce.dir** This movie is both an aid to understanding and a concept you can develop into a customized game. It includes a behavior that you can use to create a wide range of automatic camera movements, and shows you how to write a script that will write a script.
- **SnapShot.dir** Use this movie in a window to manipulate the camera in your own movies on the stage. You can seek out the best vantage point and zoom, dolly, pan, and lock the camera to track a given object. Best of all, you can take snapshots of the stage from different viewpoints and compare the results.
- **fpsMeter.dir** Used in a window, this movie gives you an accurate idea of the performance of the movie on the stage. It gives you both the instantaneous frame rate at any given moment and the average frame rates over a variety of different periods. You are likely to find this tool invaluable for all your projects; not just those which use 3D.

Whether you have the time to study the details or are under pressure to produce impressive work to a tight deadline, this book provides you with the tools and concepts you need.

Conventions Used In This Book

We have used several conventions to make it easier to read the book. You can identify code listings by their font. Following is an example.

L 1-1

```
property myMember

on beginSprite(me)
  myMember = sprite(me.spriteNum).member
  me.mCreateWorld()
end beginSprite
```

If a line of code is split across two lines, you will see the \ character:

L 1-2

```
  tFaceList = [\
[1, 3, 4], \
[1, 2, 3], \
[1, 4, 3], \
[1, 3, 2] \
]
```

When you are supposed to press a key or a combination of keys, they will be identified like this:

COMMAND-S (Macintosh) / CTRL-S (Windows)

Steps you need to follow will be presented as numbered list.

1. Create a new movie with a white stage and set the palette to System - Win.
2. In the Paint window, create a large rectangle using dark red—rgb("#800000").
3. Choose dark cyan—rgb("#008080")—and draw a smaller rectangle inside the dark red rectangle.

Beyond the Book

A printed book is one great medium for sharing knowledge. It sits quietly in the palm of your hand and lets you skim through its pages for the information you want. The Internet is another great medium. It provides instant updates and a sense of community. To get the best of both worlds, I have set up a web site where you will find the latest versions of the movies available on the CD-ROM, and where you can join a mailing list to swap ideas with the other readers of this book.

Come and find us all at http://nonlinear.openspark.com/.

PART I

Imaging Lingo

OBJECTIVES

- Investigate the commands and image properties associated with image objects
- Gain insight into how Director deals with color and alpha channel information
- Experiment with dithering
- Develop anti-aliased drawing routines
- Use quads for 2D distortion and simulated 3D effects
- Exploit inks to the full
- Isolate colors and split images into separate color channels
- Use Text, Flash, and VectorShape members as sources for images
- Build your own transitions

CHAPTER

1

Imaging Lingo Concepts

IN THIS CHAPTER:

The painting is a flat surface covered with colors assembled in a certain order.
—Maurice Denis

Imaging Lingo enables you to create and manipulate bitmap images on-the-fly. For Shockwave projects, this can help you reduce download time: instead of downloading large images, you can simply provide a template and construct the images on the user's machine. A template can consist of Flash members and Vector Shapes, smaller bitmaps, and a sprinkling of Lingo. You can use it in your projects to add real-time graphics effects similar to those achieved by Kai's Super Goo and simulated 3D effects.

The Paintbox behaviors, shipped with Director 8.0 and up, use Imaging Lingo to provide all the features you would expect of a simple paint program, and Darrel Plant's Animation > Sprite Transition behaviors provide customizable visual effects. Both these sets of behaviors can offer insights into the mechanics and potential of Imaging Lingo.

Imaging Lingo was introduced in Director 8.0, when Director engineer Werner Sharp realized that the C++ code used by the Director player to display sprites on the stage could be exposed to Lingo relatively painlessly. Imaging Lingo is fast and powerful; the five chapters in this part of the book show you how to exploit the power and optimize the speed.

This chapter quickly introduces you to the concepts and the possibilities of Imaging Lingo. Chapter 2 discusses color and how Director deals with it. Chapter 3 goes into the details of the pixel manipulation commands for Bitmap members. In Chapter 4, I extend the discussion to other member types. Chapter 5 adds the fourth dimension of time and gives you practice with using imaging Lingo for Transitions.

For a graphic representation of what Imaging Lingo can do, test the various movies in the Imaging\ folder on the CD-ROM that accompanies this book. The effects used in each movie will be explained in the following chapters.

Look, No Sprites!

Colorect.dir

On the CD-ROM that accompanies this book, you will find a number of movies in the folder Imaging\Concepts\. Before we get into the specifics of the Lingo techniques that are going to be discussed in this chapter, open the movie Colorect.dir and run it. For reasons you will appreciate later, you will need to ensure that the Loop playback button is selected in the control panel. Take a moment to play with the movie. Simply click the black canvas and drag the mouse while holding the mouse button down. Click the palette chips to change the color.

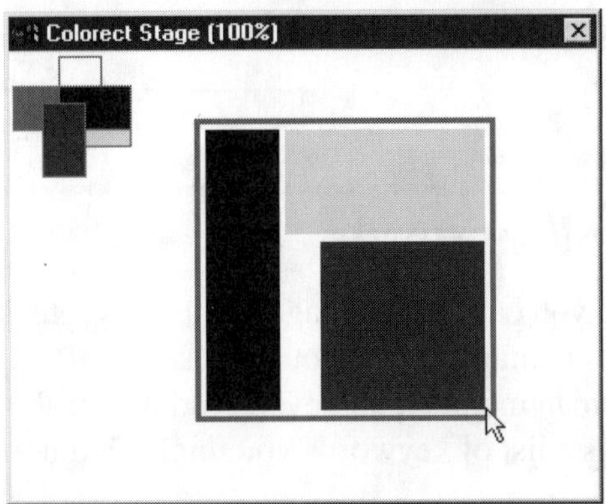

When you click a paint chip, notice how it passes in front of the others. Notice how the palette always appears in the foreground—you can't paint over it. The rectangles you paint leave no trails; when you shrink the rectangle in any direction, the area behind the rectangle reappears as before. Click the last rectangle you painted. You now can move it around with the mouse, as long as you hold the mouse button down. If you change colors before moving on the rectangle, the rectangle changes color to match. Take a look at the Score window. What do you see?

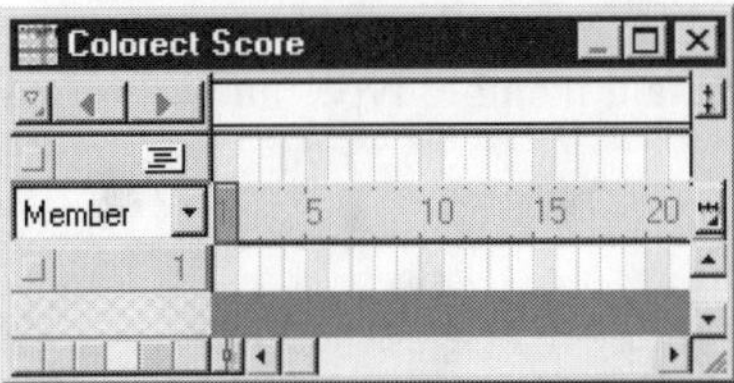

Nothing. The movie uses no sprites. The sprite channels all are empty. Now open the Internal Cast window.

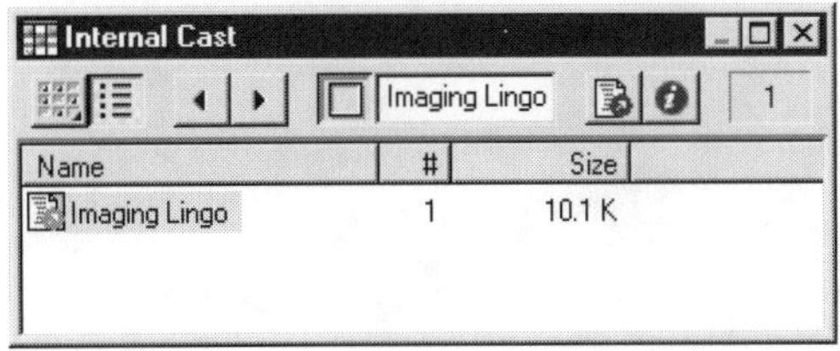

You might be surprised to discover that this movie contains a single movie script and nothing else. Yet you have been manipulating colored rectangles by changing their shape, size, position, and locZ. Where do these shapes come from? The answer is that the shapes are created at runtime using Imaging Lingo, as discussed in the following section.

Imaging Lingo Keywords

Using Imaging Lingo, you can create images on-the-fly, stock them in RAM, and manipulate their pixels in many ways. You can use ink effects and quad distortions, save the result in a bitmap member, and even send it over the Internet using the Multiuser Xtra. Here is a list of keywords you might find useful when working with Imaging Lingo.

NOTE

You will find many of these words listed in the Lingo Dictionary *by Macromedia in the "Bitmaps" section of Chapter 1, "Lingo by Feature."*

The terms here appear in the order in which I deal with them. Only the first six are used in the Colorect.dir movie. You will find concrete examples of each of these terms as you work through this part of the book.

`rgb()`
`image` (property of certain member types and of the stage)
`fill()`
`rect()`
`duplicate()`
`copyPixels()`
`image()` (function that returns a new image object, not connected to any member)
`quad`
`getPixel()`
`setPixel()`
`color()`
`hexString()`
`setAlpha()`
`extractAlpha()`
`useAlpha`
`alphaThreshold`
`depth`
`palette`
`puppetPalette()`

```
paletteIndex()
dither
draw()
floodFill()
createMask()
createMatte()
picture
```

TIP

In some cases the information I give here will expand upon the entries in the Lingo Dictionary. *You might find it helpful to annotate your copy of the* Lingo Dictionary *as you work through this chapter. Starting with Director 8.5, the online help is provided in HTML format. If you edit a centralized set of online help files, you can make your annotations available to your co-workers.*

Shapes on the Stage

Before looking at the scripts of the Colorect.dir movie, let's start with some hard code. Here are two simple handlers that create shapes on the Stage:

```
on redSquare
  square = rect(60, 20, 260, 220)
  red = rgb(255, 0, 0)
  (the stage).image.fill(square, red)
  updateStage
end

on blueCircle
  square = rect(50, 10, 270, 230)
  blue = rgb(0, 0, 255)
  options = [#color: blue, #shapeType: #oval]
  (the stage).image.fill(square, options)
  updateStage
end
```

Both handlers start by defining a bounding rectangle and a color. I'll explain how Director handles color in detail in Chapter 2; for the moment, please take the `rgb()` function on trust. The key line in each handler is the one that uses the `fill()` command. As you can see, the `fill()` command accepts several types of syntax. Note that to draw an ellipse you have to define a rectangle and then use a list of options to indicate that Director should fill the rectangle with an oval shape. Test the different properties that can be used in this options list: `#shapeType`, `#lineSize`, `#color`, and `#bgColor`. Check the *Lingo Dictionary* or turn to Chapter 3 for more details.

Director 8 introduced a new `image` property, which offers direct access to the pixels. Bitmap, Flash, and Vector Shape members also have an `image` property. Soon you will be using the similarly named `image()` function to create a raw image and stock it in a variable.

In the preceding code, the expression `(the stage).image` gives you access to the pixels on the Stage itself. Actually, no: it gives you access to the pixels in the offscreen buffer for the Stage. As you shall see, Director keeps a copy of what will appear on the screen in a separate block of the computer's memory. Using the `fill()` command, you change the information in this buffer. You then need the `updateStage` command to copy the information from the buffer onto the screen. When a movie is running, the screen is updated automatically each time the playback head enters a new frame. For the moment, let's work with the movie stopped, so that all steps in the process need to be explicit.

Create a new movie, open the Script window, and type the two handlers quoted in the preceding code into it (`on redSquare` and `on blueCircle`). Don't bother to run your movie, it contains no sprites and would stop as soon as you start it. However, you can type the following commands into the Message window, as shown in the next illustration, while the movie is halted:

```
redSquare
blueCircle
```

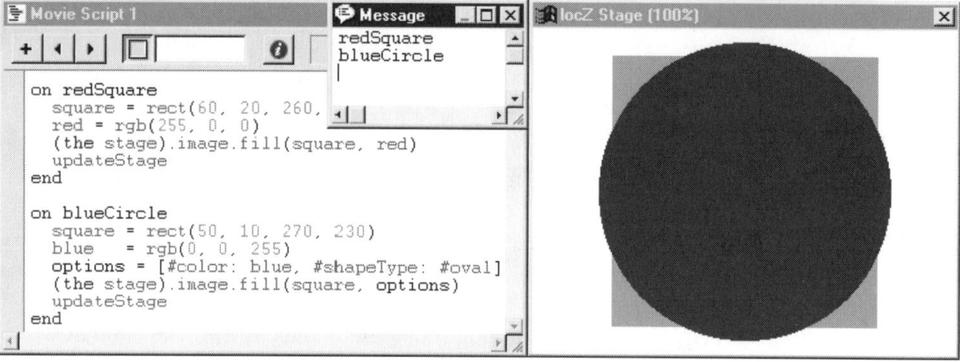

Other Shapes with Quads

You can create even more interesting shapes by using a quad as the destination area, rather than a rectangle. A quad is a list of four points: each point defines the corner of an arbitrary quadrilateral shape (see the beginning of the "CopyPixels" section of Chapter 3 for more details). In the following example, two of these points coincide; thus, the quad forms a triangle.

```
on yellowTriangle
  left = point( 50, 35)
  right = point(270, 35)
  bottom = point(160, 235)
  triangle = [left, right, bottom, bottom] -- triangular quad

  yellow = rgb(255, 255, 0)
  square = image(200, 200, 8) -- square image is blank
  square.fill(square.rect, yellow) -- square image is now yellow

  (the stage).image.copyPixels(square, triangle, square.rect)
  updateStage
end
```

Add this handler to your script; then type the following into the Message window:

```
yellowTriangle
```

The following illustration shows how the Stage appears after the `yellowTriangle` handler is executed.

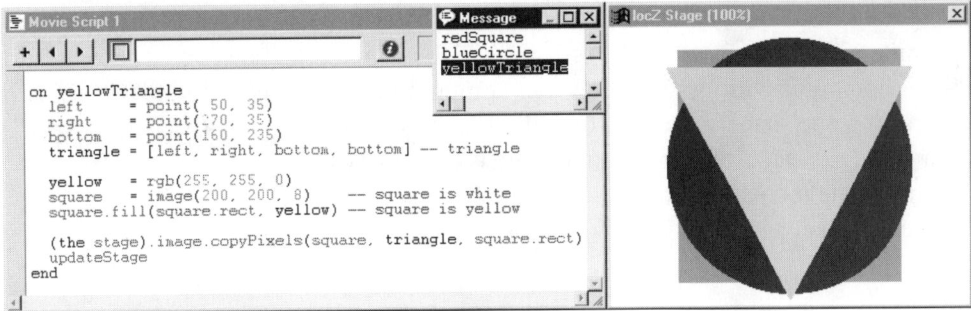

Image Objects and copyPixels()

Note the `image()` function, which enables you to create a new image out of nothing, directly in the computer's memory. All the pixels of the new image are white by default. (To test this, comment out the line that fills the square image with yellow.)

Note also the `copyPixels()` command. We can't use `fill()` to color a triangular area. Instead, we create a temporary square image and deform it by limiting it to an area defined by the quad "triangle." `copyPixels()` is a very powerful command. For instance, you can use a list of parameters to modify the way the copy is carried out. You can thus manipulate the following:

- **#ink and #blendLevel** Ink effects and transparency.
- **#color and #bgColor** Used to colorize areas (the exact effect of these values depends on the ink. See the "color and bgColor" section of Chapter 3 for details.
- **#maskImage and #maskOffset** The image used to define which areas of the source image to copy and which to ignore.
- **#dither** Used to prevent an image breaking up into flat areas of color when a low resolution version is created.
- **#useFastQuads** Used with distorted images when performance is more important than image quality.

Simulating locZ

locZ.dir

A sprite's `locZ` determines the order in which its image will be copied onto the Stage compared with those of the other sprites. You can easily simulate this effect by redrawing one shape in front of the others. Because we are using areas of a single, flat color, we can determine which shape is clicked by testing the color under the mouse at the moment it is clicked. (In the Colorect.dir movie, I use a list of rects to achieve the same result.)

Add the following lines at the beginning of your Movie Script. The globals should be declared at the very top of the script before any of the handlers that use them:

```
global red    -- initialized in the redSquare() handler
global blue   -- initialized in the blueCircle() handler
global yellow -- initialized in the yellowTriangle() handler

on mouseUp
  colorUnderMouse = (the stage).image.getPixel(the mouseLoc)
  case colorUnderMouse of
    red:    redSquare
    blue:   blueCircle
    yellow: yellowTriangle
  end case
end
```

You'll also need to draw the shapes on the Stage automatically and to prevent the movie from stopping as soon as it starts. Add the following handlers to do this:

```
on startMovie
  redSquare
  blueCircle
  yellowTriangle
end

on exitFrame
  go the frame
end
```

You'll find the full script in the movie named locZ.dir in the Imaging\Concepts\ folder on the CD-ROM. Run your movie again and click any part of a shape that is not covered by the foremost shape. The shape you click is redrawn in front of the others.

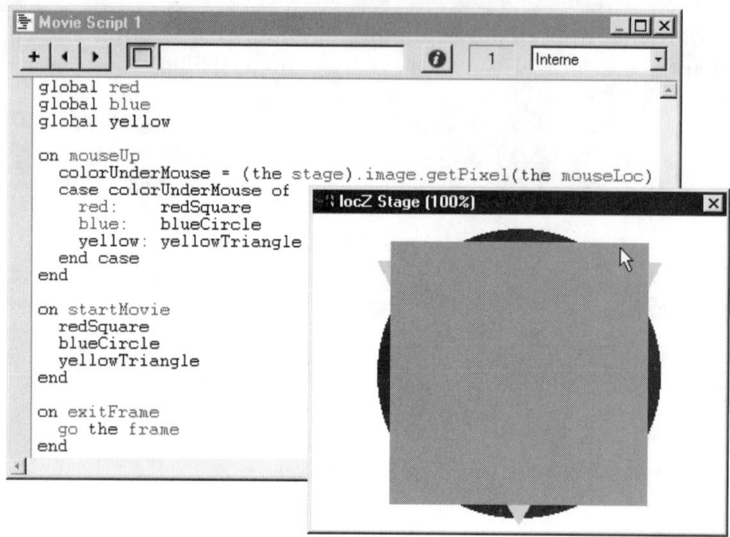

Screen Buffer

When you move a sprite across the Stage, the background reappears, unchanged, in the wake of the sprite. Director must hold in its memory any part of the background that is hidden by a sprite, or it would not know what to show once the sprite has moved on. To do this, Director reserves a block of memory known as the *screen buffer,* where it stocks the entire image of the Stage before it displays it on the screen.

To imitate the sprite's independence of the background, you are going to create your own screen buffer. This is a very memory-hungry step. The dimensions of the stage must be multiplied by the screen's color resolution. Try this in the Message window:

```
put the stage.rect.width*the stage.rect.height*the colorDepth/8/1024&&"Ko"
```

If your Stage is 800 × 600 pixels and the screen has a resolution of 32 bits, this represents almost 2MB. Because Director already monopolizes a memory block of this size, it is not usually good practice to grab the same amount of memory for your scripts. If you do, ensure that you release the memory block as soon as possible.

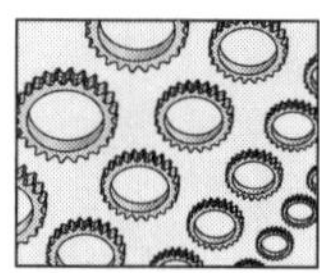

NOTE

In the DrawFill.dir movie that you will meet in Chapter 3, you will discover a more efficient technique. This uses a buffer whose size adapts to suit the size of the changed area on the screen.

A Two-Tiered Image

Buffer.dir

Here is a stripped-down version of the script used in the Colorect.dir movie. It enables you to draw a series of red rectangles on the screen. (In this simplified version, you have to drag from the top left to the bottom right.) You can find this script all ready for you in the Buffer.dir movie in the Imaging\Concepts\ folder:

```
global gStartH     -- the mouseH on mouseDown
global gStartV     -- the mouseV on mouseDown
global gRect       -- rect of the shape currently being drawn
global gStageImage -- copy of (the stage).image before painting

on mouseDown()
  -- Start to draw a new rectangle
  gStartH     = the mouseH
  gStartV     = the mouseV
  gRect       = rect(0, 0, 0, 0)                 -- dummy value
  gStageImage = (the stage).image.duplicate() -- current state
end mouseDown

on exitFrame()
  if the mouseDown then
    -- Restore the area that was modified the last time round
    (the stage).image.copyPixels(gStageImage, gRect, gRect)

    -- Remember which area is about to be changed
    gRect = rect(gStartH, gStartV, the mouseH, the mouseV)

    -- Draw the rectangle with its new dimensions
    (the stage).image.fill(gRect, rgb(255, 0, 0))
  end if

  go the frame
end exitFrame
```

Run the Buffer.dir movie, click the stage, and drag down and to the left; the red rectangle gets bigger. Without releasing the mouse, drag up and to the right; the red rectangle gets smaller. It doesn't leave a trace. How is this done?

The last line of the `mouseDown()` handler creates a copy of the current image of the Stage in the global `gStageImage`. As you hold the mouse down and drag it, the main part of the `exitFrame()` handler is executed repeatedly. The zone previously hidden by the current rectangle is restored first; the colored rectangle then is drawn on top. The screen is not refreshed between these two actions. There is no `updateStage` command, and Director waits for the next frame before it redraws the Stage. As a result, the user sees only the result of the two actions; the Stage image changes only once.

Also note the `duplicate()` function, which is used on the image of the Stage. For Lingo, an image is a *pointer,* which means it contains the address in the computer's memory where the pixel information is stored; it doesn't contain the pixel information itself. If two variables contain the same memory address, both can be used to manipulate the same pixels. When you change the pixels defined at the memory address, the pixel data returned by both variables will automatically reflect the change. It is as if two doors open into the same room.

As a test, comment out the use of the duplicate function:

```
gStageImage = (the stage).image --.duplicate()
```

Now run the movie again. Once you have colored a patch of the Stage red, it stays that way. Setting the variable `gStageImage` directly to `(the stage).image` means the pixels addressed by `gStageImage` will change continually to reflect the changes on the Stage. This is the reason we had to make a separate copy of the current state of the Stage using the `duplicate()` function. Additionally, this is where that massive extra chunk of memory is commandeered. To use the same metaphor, the `duplicate()` function here creates a whole new room; and then tells us where to find the door.

Over to You

The Colorect.dir movie offers a richer set of features. The Imaging Lingo script is constructed in a more rigorous fashion than the handlers you have studied in this chapter, and it is well commented. You could try to complete the two simplified scripts you have studied here using the Imaging Lingo script for inspiration. You could even add your own features: a choice of shapes (line, oval, quad, and so forth), an Undo button, or a button to replay the creation.

This chapter has shown you a glimpse of the possibilities of Imaging Lingo. The following four chapters go into the subject in much greater depth.

CHAPTER

2

Understanding Color

IN THIS CHAPTER:

Colorless green dreams sleep furiously.

—Noam Chomsky

In the handlers on Chapter 1, I used the `rgb()` function, but didn't explain it. To understand this function and the other methods Director uses to describe colors, you'll need to know a little about how the human eye sees color and a little about how computers think. There are three standards you should know about: 8 bit, 16 bit and 32 bit. We will discuss these in the order that makes them easiest to understand.

In the Eye of the Beholder

The human eye is complex. One simple way of describing how it works is to imagine that it contains receptors for three specific wavelengths of light: red, green, and blue. According to this model, all the colors we can see can be described as a mixture of these three colors in varying proportions. Points of color sufficiently close together are not resolved into separate images; they appear to merge into a single color.

This model is not entirely accurate but it is simple. Creating colors on your computer screen simply means creating points with varying intensity of red, green, and blue. If all colors are at their maximum intensity, the result will appear as white. If there is no light at all, the result will appear black.

Each point of light is known as a *pixel,* or PICTure ELement. A group of pixels often is called a *bitmap* (I'll explain *bits* in the next section). Technically, a bitmap is a group of black-and-white pixels. A more appropriate term for a colored image would be *pixelmap,* but bitmap has been universally adopted.

Binary, Bits, and Bytes

Defining a color thus becomes a case of determining how much red, green, and blue are required. Computers know nothing of color. They know only about the states of their *transistors.* A transistor is a miniature switch that has two states: on or off. By convention these states are referred to as 1 and 0; the system of counting with ones and zeros is known as the *binary system.* Humans count on their fingers; the word "digit" comes from the Latin word for finger, and "decimal" comes from the Latin word for ten. Computers use bits, or BInary digiTS to count with.

The number 2 pervades all computer logic. Data is handled more rapidly if it can be treated in powers of 2: 2, 4, 8, 16, 32, 64, and so on. You should be familiar with the word *byte*, which means a group of 8 bits. A group of 8 bits can represent any binary number from 00000000 to 11111111. The first number obviously is zero; the second can be understood as 128+64+32+16+8+4+2+1 = 255. Depending on which transistors are set to 1 or 0, a byte can have any of 256 distinct values. Think of 0 as being the first of these values.

RGB

To describe a color on a computer, one convention is to allow for 256 different values for red, green, and blue. For each given value of red, there can be 256 different values of green. For each distinct red/green combination, there can be 256 different values of blue. That makes 256 × 256 × 256 = 16 ,777, 216 different colors. This turns out to be a very efficient system: the computer can work fast with one byte of information per color, and the human eye cannot easily distinguish between two colors that differ by only one bit of one data. Both humans and computers can work optimally with this system.

Lingo provides you with a ready-made object for describing colors. You will find details on this in the *Lingo Dictionary* under the entry "color()." Let's start with the `rgb()` function, which enables you to express a color in this form,

```
rgb(red, green, blue)
```

where `red, green,` and `blue` all are integers between 0 and 255.

An RGB Color Picker

Chooser.dir

To help you visualize this, I've made a movie with three sliders, whose values can vary between 0 and 255. You'll find this in the Imaging\Colors\ folder: it's called Chooser.dir. Open the movie and run it; then test what happens when you vary the proportions of the different primary colors. As you drag one of the slider thumbs, note how the color gradient of the other two slider bars changes.

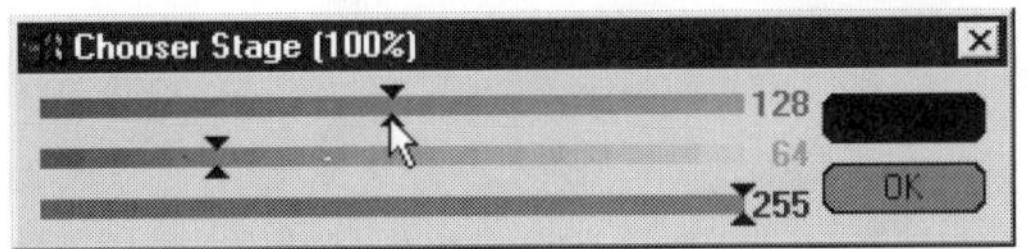

The main behavior (Color slider, member 12) is fairly complex because it deals with both moving the slider thumb and changing the color gradient of the other slider bars. To clarify things, let's just look at the handler that uses Imaging Lingo. Following, you will see a simplified version of the `createGradient()` handler. The definitive version of this handler is called each time you move one of the sliders to a new position.

```
on createGradient(colorObject, redGreenOrBlue, bitmapMember)
  -- <colorObject> should have a format similar to rgb(0, 0, 0)
  -- <redBlueOrGreen> should be a symbol: #red | #blue | #green
  -- <bitmapMember> can be void or a member created by this handler

  if ilk(bitmapMember) <> #member then
    bitmapMember = new(#bitmap)
    bitmapMember.image = image(256, 1, 32)
  end if

  bitmapImage = bitmapMember.image --.duplicate()

 ms = the milliseconds
  case redGreenOrBlue of
    #red:
      repeat with i = 0 to 255
        colorObject.red = i
        bitmapMember.image.setPixel(i, 0, colorObject)
      end repeat
    #green:
      repeat with i = 0 to 255
        colorObject.green = i
        bitmapMember.image.setPixel(i, 0, colorObject)
      end repeat
    #blue:
      repeat with i = 0 to 255
        colorObject.blue = i
        bitmapMember.image.setPixel(i, 0, colorObject)
      end repeat
  end case
```

```
  -- bitmapMember.image = bitmapImage
  put the milliseconds - ms&&"milliseconds"
end createGradient
```

The preceding version is slow; it takes a significant fraction of a second to update a single slider. Create a Movie Script with this scriptText, and call it from the Message window, as shown here:

```
createGradient(rgb(0, 0, 0), #red)
-- "81 milliseconds"
```

The millisecond value you see depends on the configuration of your computer.

Two lines are (partially) commented out. Remove the comment characters before the expression `.duplicate()` in line 11 and before the third last line; then run the handler again:

```
createGradient(rgb(0, 0, 0), #red)
-- "5 milliseconds"
```

Suddenly it is much faster, but it produces exactly the same effect. This is because the first version worked directly on the member. Each time a pixel was changed, the bitmap member was refreshed. In the second version, extra time is taken at the beginning to create a copy of the member's image and at the end to set it to a new value. In between, the handler works on an independent image that exists only in the computer's memory and is unattached to any member. In tests on Windows, I find that this makes it 12–20 times faster. On Macintosh, the speed increase is 3–4. Your results are likely to vary.

An Alternative Approach Without Imaging Lingo

Gradient.dir

You can achieve the same effect in even better time. Instead of using Lingo's `setPixels()` command, you can get Director to use the underlying C++ code. To do this, you must use a Vector Shape member using the `#gradient fillMode`. The Gradient.dir movie in the Imaging\Colors\ folder compares these three techniques by executing each 100 times. Consult the Vector Gradient Movie Script (member 3) for the details of the vector technique. Here are the results it gives on my machine:

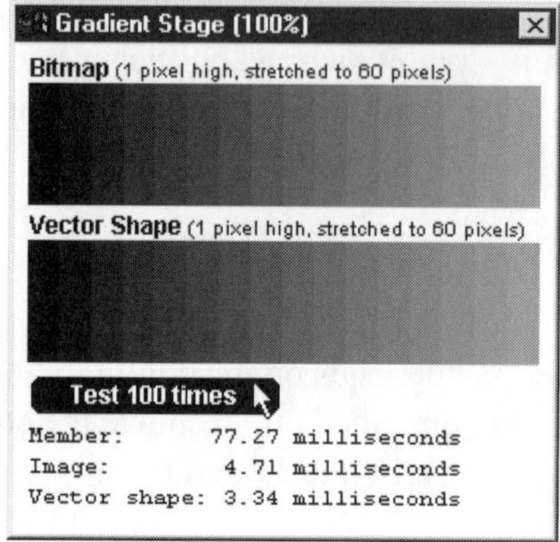

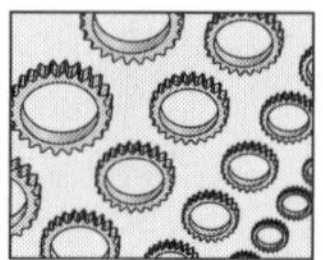

NOTE

Vector Shape members in Director 7.0.2 and 8.0 are surrounded by a border, which might be visible to the top and left of the member. This has been corrected in Director 8.5.

Hexadecimal Notation

The binary system is great for computers; however, humans find it difficult to read. The hexadecimal system provides a reasonable compromise. Whereas the decimal system uses 10 digits (0–9), hexadecimal uses 16. The letters A–F are used to signify the numbers 10–15. For example, the number 43 is equal to 32 + 11. In hexadecimal, that would be written 2B: 2 × 16 + 11 × 1. Thus the numbers 0–255 can be written using only two hex-digits: 00–FF. You'll see colors described in hexadecimal notation in the field at the top of Director's pop-up color palette:

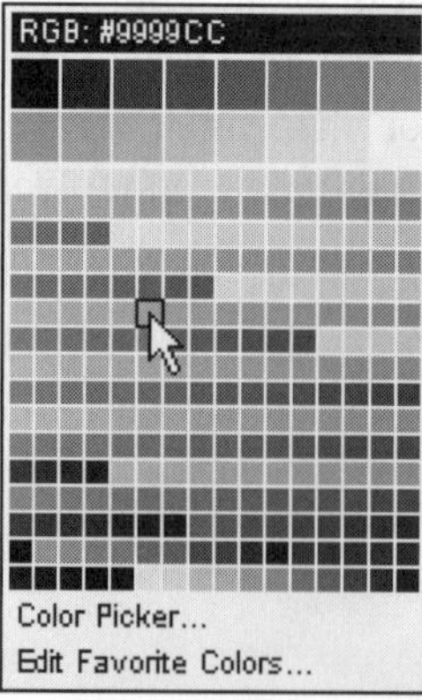

You can convert an rgb color to hexadecimal notation using the under-documented hexString() function:

```
put hexString(rgb(0, 43, 255))
-- "#002BFF"
```

You also can create a color object using a hexadecimal string:

```
slateBlue = rgb("#9999CC")
put slateBlue
-- rgb( 153, 153, 204 )
```

TIP

If you need to convert decimal numbers to hexadecimal numbers and back (for a hex editor, for example), the fastest technique I know is to hijack the color commands:

```
on hex(aDecimal)
  return rgb(aDecimal, 0, 0) -- char[1..2])
end hex

on decimal(hexString)
  return rgb(hexString).blue
end
```

Note that this works one byte at a time: numbers less than 0 or greater than 255 will provoke unexpected results.

Raw Integer Color Values

The computer processor can't understand either rgb color objects or hexadecimal strings directly. It first has to convert these into ones and zeros. For the setPixel() function only, you can simplify the process for the processor by giving it 1s and 0s in as pure a form as possible: as an integer.

You can discover the integer value of a color using the getPixel() function if you use #integer as an optional additional parameter:

```
put (the stage).image.getPixel(100, 100, #integer)
-- 5913189
```

You also can work it out for yourself, from the red, green, and blue values of a color object:

```
rgbValue = (the stage).image.getPixel(100, 100)
put rgbValue
-- rgb( 90, 58, 101 )

put (rgbValue.red * 256* 256) + (rgbValue.green * 256) + rgbValue.blue
-- 5913189
```

Raw integer values are difficult for a human to decipher. Does the number `5913189` evoke a plum color to you?

One advantage to using the integer value for a color is that is offers access to the alpha channel data for that pixel. The alpha channel is described in the next section.

The Alpha Channel

The data for red, green, and blue takes up 24 bits, or three bytes. Computers work fastest in powers of 2, so it makes sense to code a single color over four bytes, or 32 bits. If you consider that colors are opaque like oil paints, the extra 8 bits are not used for anything. They simply allow the computer to deal with the data in 32-bit chunks.

But why should all colors be opaque? If you work in watercolors, you can add colors in layers, where each layer modifies the color of the layers underneath. The extra 8 bits of a 32-bit chunk can be used to define the opacity of a given pixel. Like the color values, the opacity value can be any number between 0 and 255. Because opacity information has no color, it is conventional to present it as a grayscale image: 255 is shown as black and defines fully opaque pixels; 0 is shown as white and defines fully transparent pixels. The actual color of a fully transparent pixel is arbitrary because the pixel in question is not visible.

Alpha channel information only has meaning when used in layers. Sprites appear in layers, each in its separate channel. Imaging Lingo can be used to build up image information in layers in the image object you are working on. When a given pixel in a given layer is semitransparent, the color of the pixel on the layer behind is mixed with the color of the pixel in question. The precise mix depends on the alpha channel value. An alpha channel value of 55 would take 200 parts of the color from the layer behind and 55 parts from the pixel in the new layer to make a total of 255 parts, and display the resulting mix. If you move a variegated background behind a semitransparent sprite, the processor will need to calculate the result of the same foreground color mixed in the same proportions with a changing background color each time the sprite's image is refreshed.

It can be useful to visualize the alpha channel information for an image separately from the image itself. The command `extractAlpha()` will return the alpha channel data for a given 32-bit bitmap member in the form of an 8-bit grayscale image of the same dimensions. You also can use `setAlpha()` to apply an 8-bit image to a 32-bit bitmap member. However, this will have no effect unless the `useAlpha` property of the member is set to `TRUE`.

Using the Alpha Channel

Here is a simple experiment to discover how the alpha channel works. In a new movie, create a new bitmap member in cast slot 1. Choose a dark color with a fairly high palette index, such as 216, and draw an arbitrary shape. Ensure that the depth of the bitmap is set to 32 bits. (Use the menu Modify | Transform Bitmap…, if necessary.) Place your bitmap member on the Stage. Set the name of the image to 32 bit. Now duplicate the image in member 2. Type the following in the Message window:

```
put member(1).image.setAlpha(member(2).image)
-- 0
```

The result of zero indicates that the command has failed. The `setAlpha()` command is very particular. It will fail if

- The host image is not 32 bit.
- The alpha channel image is not 8 bit (as is the case here).
- The alpha channel image is not exactly the same dimensions as the 32-bit image.

TIP

This last criterion can prove awkward. For example, if your alpha image uses a gradient that diminishes to 0 on one edge, the alpha image might be automatically trimmed along that edge, and thus be one pixel short of its original dimensions. Therefore, it is a good idea to check that the `setAlpha()` command returns `1 (TRUE)` indicating that all the commands succeeded. Setting the alpha image's `trimWhiteSpace` option to `FALSE` also can be useful in this situation.

Change the name of member 2 to 8-bit, set its depth to 8 bits (see Figure 2-1), and try again. Even though the 8-bit image is not grayscale, the command should work, as shown in Figure 2-2.

Type the following in the Message window:

```
member(2).image = member(1).image.extractAlpha()
```

The image of member 2 should become dark gray. Although you set the alpha channel with a colored image, its palette was converted to `#grayScale` automatically. Choose the Bucket tool and set the ink to gradient. Click somewhere inside the 8-bit image to create a graduation of gray. Type the following in the Message window:

```
put member(1).image.setAlpha(member(2).image)
-- 1
```

Note that this has no effect on the sprite containing member 1, nor on the way member 1 appears in the Paint window or in the Cast window thumbnail. You need

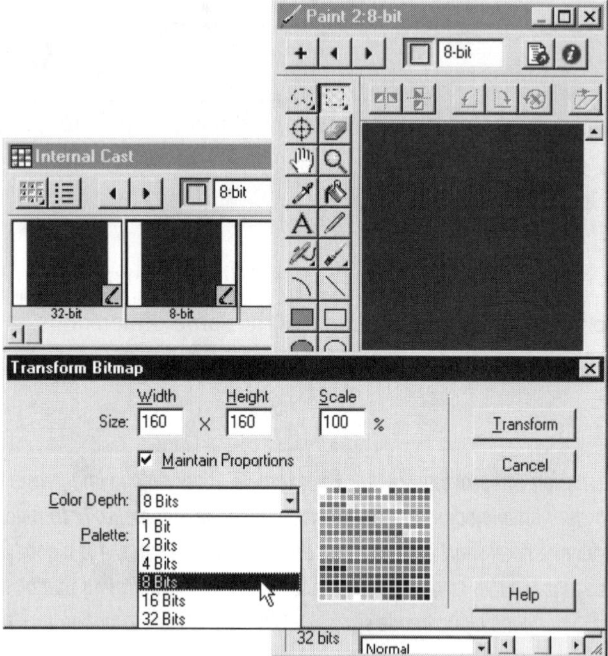

Figure 2-1 *Setting the bit depth of a member to 8 bits*

to tell Director explicitly to pay attention to the alpha channel data. Try this in the Message window:

```
member(1).useAlpha = TRUE
```

You also can use the Property Inspector to achieve the same ends.

On the Stage, the transparency of the sprite containing member 1 will change, despite the fact that the ink of the sprite is set to `#copy`.

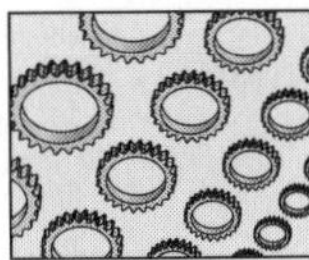

NOTE

The functions `extractAlpha()` and `setAlpha()` both act on an image; `useAlpha` is a property of a bitmap member.

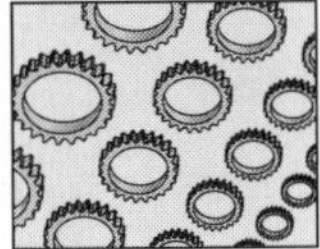

NOTE

The Paint window is not aware of any alpha information. You will not see any transparency effect in the Paint window. However, the thumbnail will update the next time you make a change to the image.

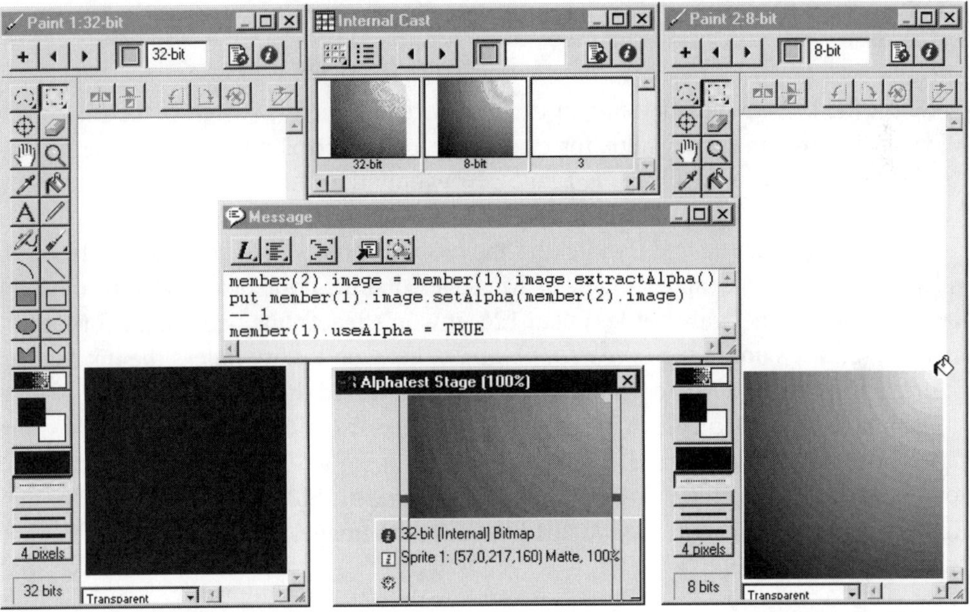

Figure 2-2 *Setting the alpha channel of a 32-bit member*

alphaThreshold

When you place an alpha channel bitmap member on the Stage, its edges might be somewhat fuzzy. If the sprite is interactive, you might wish to limit its hot zone to the more opaque parts. To do this, set `the alphaThreshold` of your bitmap member. By default this is 1; all pixels in the image will respond to a mouse click, except those that are completely transparent.

To test this, place the 32-bit member that you have just created on the Stage. Right-click it (CTRL-click if you are on a Mac) and choose Script from the contextual menu that appears. Type the following handler into the Script window:

```
property mySprite
property myAlphaChannel

on beginSprite(me)
  mySprite       = sprite(me.spriteNum)
  myAlphaChannel = mySprite.member.image.extractAlpha()
end beginSprite

on mouseUp(me)
  relativeLoc = mapStageToMember(mySprite, the mouseLoc)
  put myAlphaChannel.getPixel(relativeLoc) -- value of alpha channel under mouse
end mouseUp
```

Select the bitmap member and, in `the` Property Inspector, switch to the List View. You now can set the value for `the alphaThreshold` for the member; set it to 128. (You also can do this using Lingo). Now only the dark pixels will react to the mouse; lighter pixels will ignore mouse clicks, as shown in Figure 2-3.

Now run your movie and try clicking the bitmap sprite. You should see only values of 128 or greater appearing in the Message window. If the pixel under the mouse has an alpha channel value of less than 128, it won't react. Just one thing I forgot to mention (and it's not in the *Lingo Dictionary*): this won't work unless the ink for the bitmap sprite is set to Matte. But you could have guessed that, couldn't you?

An image object's `alphaThreshold` property also affects the result of the `createMatte()` command, which you will be using in Chapter 4 to make pieces for a puzzle. Altering the value of `the alphaThreshold` determines whether the lighter alpha channel areas are included in the matte image.

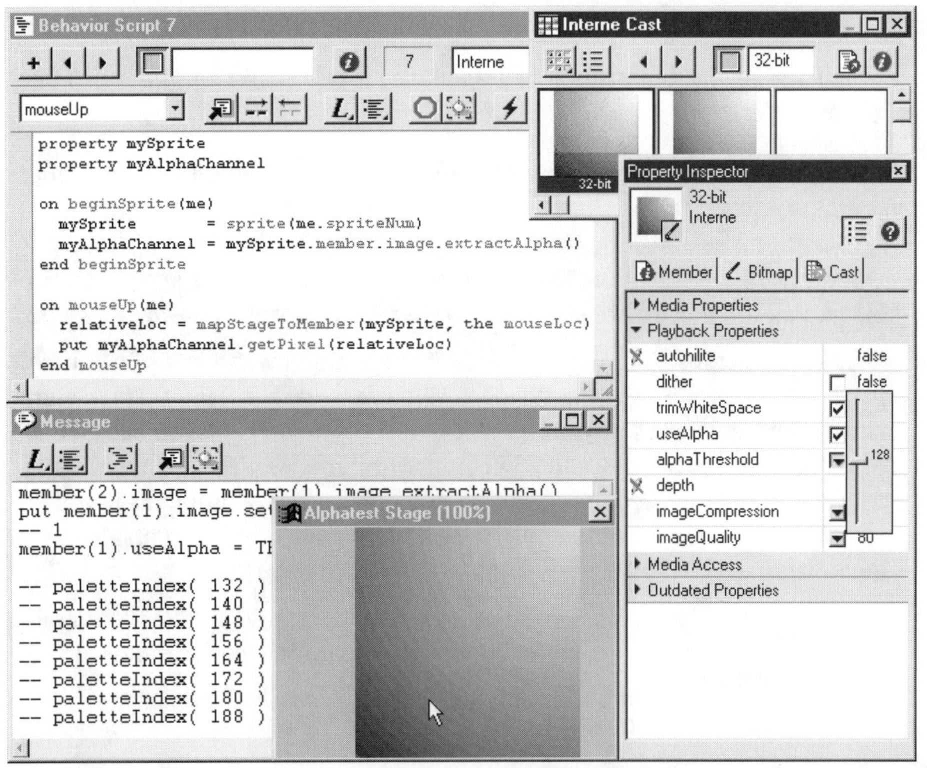

Figure 2-3 *Using the Property Inspector to set the alphaThreshold for a Bitmap member*

Palettes

Using 32 bits to define the color of each pixel is memory hungry. Until recently, the VRAM (Video Random Access Memory) required to display colors on the monitor was prohibitively expensive. To reduce the amount (and cost) of memory required, you can work with a limited palette of colors. When you use a palette, colors still are ultimately defined in terms of 32 bits, but the computer accesses these colors through a lookup table. The lookup table can provide for 4, 16, or 256 colors. These numbers correspond to powers of 2 that are in themselves powers of 2 (2^2, 2^4, and 2^8): the computer can handle tables of such dimensions particularly fast.

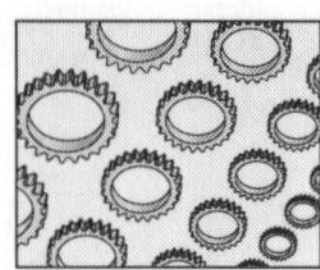

NOTE

Because they are the most useful, I'll just deal with 256-color palettes here. (The logic is the same for smaller palettes.)

Theoretically, you can choose any 256 colors for your palette. In practice, there are three constraints:

- Director will insist that the first color in your palette is white and the last color black. Palettes that do not conform to this rule will not be considered valid.
- Windows reserves a number of colors at the beginning and end of a 256-color palette. If you do not use the standard Windows colors for the first ten entries and the last ten entries in your palette, and your movie is played back on a machine running Windows in 256 colors (8-bit mode), the system windows will take on unexpected hues. This should not cause any problems if you create a projector to run your movie full screen, but it could be unacceptable in other circumstances.
- You cannot change the system palette from a Shockwave movie running in a browser. If your end users are likely to be using a 256-color monitor, it is best to use the Web 216 palette to ensure that the colors appear the same regardless of the platform or the browser.

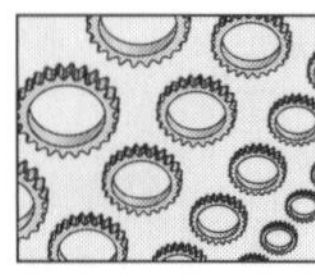

NOTE

At the time of writing, Director does not provide any way for you to define your own palettes through Lingo (you can create one using `new (#palette)`, but you cannot modify its color values). Instead, a palette will be created automatically for any image you import at 8-bit color depth, or any time you modify an existing palette. Look up "color palettes" in the index of the "Using Director" manual for information on how to modify palettes through the Palette window.

Simulating Director's Pop-Up Palette

Palette.dir

In the Imaging\Colors\ folder on the CD-ROM that accompanies this book, you'll find a movie entitled Palette.dir. Like the Chooser.dir movie you studied earlier, this movie is designed to run as a movie in a window (MIAW); you'll see it in use in the movie that demonstrates the full power of the `copyPixels()` command. The following is a simplified version of the handler that it uses to create a bitmap member that mimics a palette.

```
on createPalette(paletteSymbol)
  -- <paletteSymbol> should be a symbol for a built-in palette:
  -- #systemMac, #systemWin, #rainbow, #grayScale, #pastels, #vivid,
  -- #ntsc, #metallic, #web216#vga and #systemWinDir4.  Custom
  -- palette member references will also work
  -- (eg: member "Custom Palette")

  -- This handler returns a list of rgb values for the palette
  colorList  = []

  -- Create an image in RAM of the appropriate dimensions
  dimension    = 127
  bitDepth     = 32 -- Not 8-bit, as the Lingo Dictionary would suggest


  paletteImage = image(dimension, dimension, bitDepth, paletteSymbol)

  -- Prepare the color of the first color chip and its position
  colorIndex = 0
  vLoc       = 0
  repeat with row = 1 to 16
    hLoc     = 0

    repeat with column = 1 to 16
      -- Create a new color chip
      paletteColor = paletteIndex(colorIndex)
      paletteImage.fill(hLoc, vLoc, hLoc + 7, vLoc + 7, paletteColor)

      -- Determine the rgb value of the color
      paletteColor = paletteImage.getPixel(hLoc, vLoc)
      colorList.append(paletteColor)

      -- Prepare for the next color
      hLoc       = hLoc + 8
      colorIndex = colorIndex + 1
    end repeat
    vLoc = vLoc + 8
  end repeat

  -- Create a bitmap member to display the image
  bitmapMember           = new(#bitmap)
  bitmapMember.image     = paletteImage

  return colorList
end createPalette
```

The color for each chip in the palette image is defined using the `paletteIndex()` command. This returns a color object with the format `paletteIndex( 43 )`. It does not give you any information on what the red, green, and blue values are for that color. If you use the standard Macintosh or Windows palette, `paletteIndex( 43 )` is a pale gray: `rgb( 204, 204, 204 )`. If you use the Rainbow palette, `paletteIndex( 43 )` is purple: `rgb( 165, 0, 255 )`. Other palettes will give you different colors.

As you can see in Figure 2-4, the color returned by the `paletteIndex()` function depends on the current value of `the framePalette`. There is no direct way to determine the color of a particular color in an arbitrary palette. In the preceding handler I used one technique to get around this: I created a pixel of the appropriate color in a 32-bit image and then used `getPixel()` to determine the color of that pixel. If I use an 8-bit image, `getPixel()` will return the value in the `paletteIndex()` format. By using a 32-bit image, I can retrieve the `rgb()` value. (My thanks to Pim van Bochoven for pointing out this technique.)

NOTE

The entry for "image()" in the Lingo Dictionary *implies that only 2-, 4-, and 8-bit images can have a palette attributed to them. Experimentation proves that 32-bit images can also have a default patette.*

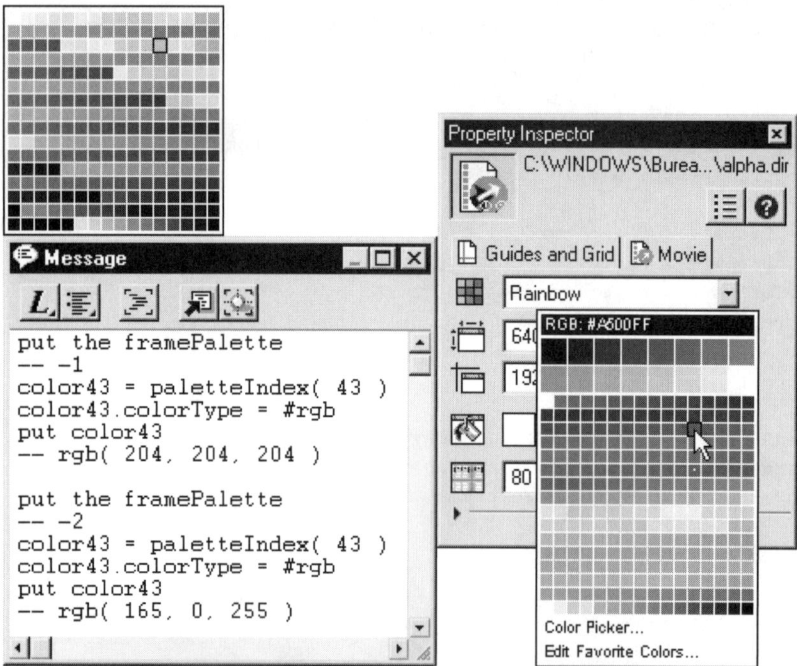

Figure 2-4 *The color returned by the paletteIndex() function depends on the framePalette.*

Another technique would be to change the current `framePalette`, using the `puppetPalette()` command before converting a given color from `#paletteIndex` to `#rgb`. Unfortunately, this could have unwanted consequences if the user's monitor was set to use 8-bit color.

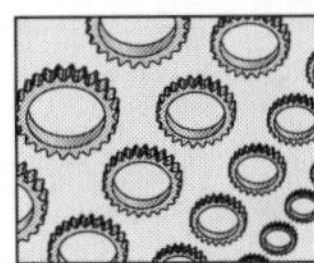

NOTE

The `image()` function will accept only palette symbols (such as `#web216`) or member references (such as `member "Custom Palette"`). The `puppetPalette()` command will accept only strings (such as `"Web 216"`) or palette member numbers (such as `123`). This inconsistent syntax can make working with palettes tricky. If Director cannot resolve a palette reference correctly, it uses `the framePalette` by default.

Palettes as Look-Up Tables

You can think of a palette as a two-column table. In one column, the entries correspond to the row number (or index number), starting at 0. In the other column, the entries correspond to 24-bit rgb colors. The following table is an example of what a lookup table for a 2-bit palette might look like.

0	rgb(255, 255, 255)
1	rgb(170, 170, 170)
2	rgb(85, 85, 85)
3	rgb(0, 0, 0)

When you use a color from a palette, you provide the index number to a function that returns the full 24-bit description of the color; thus, looking up a value in the table takes up a little CPU time, but you are unlikely to notice this.

If you need to create your own palette, you can use a list. Following is a list representing a palette of 16 colors, plus a function that lets you determine the color values. Note that an adjustment needs to be made because the first item in a color palette is `paletteIndex( 0 )` but the first item in a list is `theList[1]`. You can't use a list like this to set the puppetPalette or the framePalette, but you can use it in an Imaging Lingo routine to edit a bitmap member.

The following function should appear in a movie script:

```
on getPaletteColor(paletteList, colorIndex)
  if not listP(paletteList) then
    exit -- not a list
  else if integerP(colorIndex) then
    colorIndex = colorIndex + 1 -- palette colors start at 0, lists at 1
    if colorIndex < 1 or colorIndex > paletteList.count then
      exit -- index out of range
```

```
    end if
  else
    exit -- not an integer
  end if

  return paletteList[colorIndex]
end getPaletteColor
```

Type the following entry into the Message window:

```
mac4BitPalette = [ \
rgb( 255, 255, 255 ), rgb( 190, 190, 190 ), rgb( 255, 230,   0 ), \
rgb( 128, 128, 128 ), rgb( 159, 216, 255 ), rgb( 124,  96,  27 ), \
rgb(   0, 158,   0 ), rgb( 142, 210,   0 ), rgb( 222,   0, 191 ), \
rgb( 141,   0, 163 ), rgb( 250,   0,  57 ), rgb( 255, 140,  50 ), \
rgb(   0,   0, 234 ), rgb(   0, 240, 219 ), rgb( 100, 100, 100 ), \
rgb(   0,   0,   0 )]

put getPaletteColor(mac4BitPalette, 1)
-- rgb( 190, 190, 190 )
```

16-Bit Color

16-bit color (thousands of colors) is a halfway house. It allows you to display more colors at one time than 8-bit color (32,768 instead of 256) but does not give you such fine control over which colors are used. A picture with a predominant color tone, such as a sepia photograph, will look fine in 256 chosen colors but decidedly grainy when displayed in thousands of colors. Fine gradients might appear as broad bands of separate colors in 16-bit display; Figure 2-5 illustrates this. The colors in the three close-ups have been exaggerated to make the differences between the pictures clearer.

16-Bit Color Format

The reason for the graininess or the banding is that only five bits are used to code each level of red, green, and blue. The fifth power of 2 is 32; only 32 different levels of each primary color are available. A 16-bit color in binary notation might look something like this: a rrrrr ggggg bbbbb, where each letter indicates a value of either 0 or 1. The initial *a* can be used as a 1-bit alpha channel, but Director does not do this.

Figure 2-5 *Comparing color depths in a monochrome image*

The differences between two adjacent 16-bit colors are clearly visible to the human eye (for instance, snails would see no difference). A 32-bit image or a grayscale palette can give 256 levels of gray. 16-bit color can provide only 32 levels, from 0–31.

Approximations

The near-black colors in 16-bit images correspond to the following 32-bit colors:

```
rgb(0, 0, 0),  rgb(8, 8, 8), rgb(16, 16, 16), rgb(24, 24, 24), rgb(33, 33, 33)...
```

Note that there is not an exact match between 16-bit and 32-bit colors. Between black and white there are 31 steps in one case and 255 in the other. One step in 16-bit color corresponds to 8.2258 steps in 32-bit color; therefore, there will be a very subtle color shift when you convert a 16-bit image to 32 bits.

As mentioned earlier, computer processors work fast in powers of 2, such as 8. They are much slower when they have to deal with floating-point numbers such as 8.2258. Imaging Lingo is processor hungry, so shortcuts are used where possible. When the monitor is set to 16-bit color depth, the value returned by `getPixel()` appears just like a 32-bit color; this is an illusion. It is, in fact, a 16-bit color whose value has been multiplied by 8. This gives a good approximation to the equivalent 32-bit color, at least for the darker colors. For lighter colors, it can seem inaccurate.

Try this test. Set your monitor to 16-bit color. Create a new movie with a white stage. In 32-bit color, white is `rgb( 255, 255, 255 )`. In the Message window type the following:

```
put (the stage).image.getPixel(point (1, 1)) -- arbitrary point on stage
-- rgb( 248, 248, 248 )
```

In 16-bit color, the highest value for each primary color is 31. The value of 248 comes from 31 × 8. For 16-bit colors, `rgb( 248, 248, 248 )` means white. In 32-bit color depth it is a pale gray. Now that you know, this shouldn't throw you.

Dithering

To compensate for the obvious difference between adjacent colors, many 16-bit images are dithered. Dithering consists of using a mosaic of colors close together to give the impression of a single color that is the average of the separate colors. You can see how this softens the banding of the grayscale gradient in Figure 2-6. The technique is not limited to 16-bit color; it also is useful when you convert an image from a higher bit depth to 8-bit color.

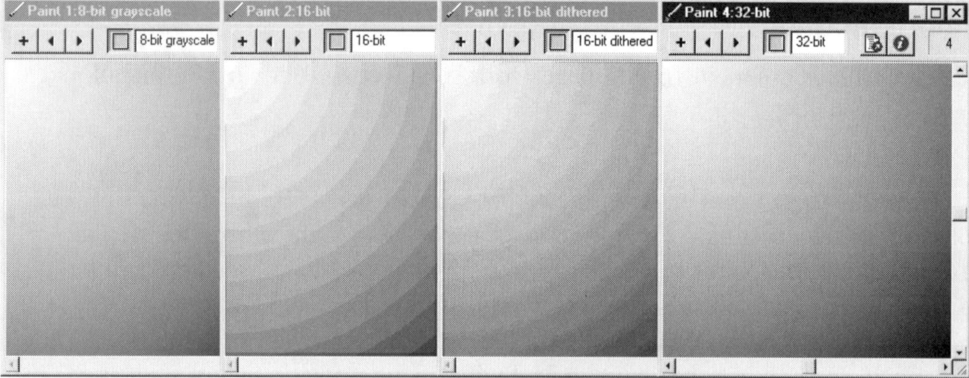

Figure 2-6 *How 8-bit, 16-bit, and 32-bit images deal with a grayscale gradient*

Alternative Dithering Algorithms

There are a number of different algorithms for dithering. Different software packages will give you different results. Even within Director, different algorithms are used. This explains why what you see in the Paint Window might not correspond with what you see when you place the same bitmap member on the stage. Here are details provided by Werner Sharp, the Macromedia engineer who conceived of Imaging Lingo:

> Transform bitmap in authoring uses a high-quality dithering and remapping algorithm, which is a lot slower than the one that copyPixels uses. You'll get slightly different results, especially for subtle variations of color. There's an undocumented feature in imaging lingo to get these same effects but you should be sure to check performance implications. If you pass in values for the dither parameter in copyPixels, you can get the same effects as transform bitmap.
>
> - **Use `[#dither:1215]`** This uses a remapping algorithm that searches the palette for the closest color instead of using 5 bits of R, G, and B to find a color. Good for very subtle palettes with lots of very similar colors.
> - **Use `[#dither:1969]`** This uses a high-quality dithering algorithm with better results than the regular dither, but a lot slower.
>
> These are undocumented, unsupported, etc. They worked when I put them in, but I haven't tried them out in a long time.

In a photograph, where there already is a great deal of detail, dithering can be very effective in fooling the eye; however, in a large area of flat color, it gives a dappled effect like daisies on a lawn. Dithering a large area of flat color also has the effect of making the image less conducive to compression; creating a mosaic of colors adds information that compression algorithms must take into account.

To clarify: Using `[#dither: 1215]` doesn't result in a dithered image; it results in better color remapping. You might find it worthwhile to experiment with a test image to see whether the differences between the fast `[#dither: 1]` method and the slower `[#dither: 1969]` are noticeable. If not, use the faster (supported) value.

Hands-on Experience with Bit Depth, Palettes, and Dithering

Dithered.dir

Let's try dithering. You could use the following handler to create a new bitmap member containing a dithered version of a 32-bit image:

```
on createDitheredImage()
  original       = member("32-bit Original").image
  imageRect      = original.rect
  imageWidth     = imageRect.width
  imageHeight    = imageRect.height

  bitDepth       = 8
  paletteSymbol = #systemMac -- or other palette of your choice

  copyImage = image(imageWidth, imageHeight, bitDepth, paletteSymbol)

  copyImage.copyPixels(original, imageRect, imageRect, [#dither: 1])
  new(#bitmap).image = copyImage
end createDitheredImage
```

You could try altering the values for `bitDepth`, `paletteSymbol` and `#dither`. In the Imaging\Colors\ folder on the CD-ROM, you'll find a movie entitled Dithered.dir, which allows you to do this without typing any code. It also displays the differences between the original image and the image that results from the `copyPixels()` command. This is done by superimposing sprites containing the original and the copy, and using Reverse ink on the higher-numbered sprite. Identical pixels appear as white. You can toggle to Not Reverse ink, in which case identical pixels will appear as black.

Optimizing Bitmap Display

You can use dithering when you transform a bitmap member. In this case, the result can be saved in a file on the hard disk and will appear as expected the next time you display your dithered image with the monitor set to the appropriate color depth.

The Director player also will dither on-the-fly if the color depth of the monitor is lower than the color depth of your bitmap member. You have no direct control over the dithering, so the resulting display might not be entirely satisfactory. If the quality of your images is important, you might want to create separate versions of your images for 8-, 16-, and 32-bit displays, and swap in the version that is appropriate for the current color depth of the monitor. This also will improve the rate at which the screen is refreshed because there will be no need to run dithering algorithms before displaying an image.

On a related point, when the monitor is set to 8-bit color depth (256 colors), only one palette is available at a time. If you want to show two 8-bit images that use different palettes, one of these will appear at less than optimal quality. You can use the movie property `the paletteMapping` to force the Director player to look for the colors in the current palette that are closest to the original colors. This will take a certain amount of processor time, and the results are never perfect.

A better solution is to use the same palette for all bitmap images that need to be shown together. You can use specialist tools such as Equilibrium's deBabelizer (http://www.equilibrium.com). Alternatively, you can create one big bitmap containing all the separate images, convert that image to 8-bit color depth so that all the separate images are automatically converted to the same palette, and then divide the big bitmap up into its separate component parts. If you do this in a graphics program such as Fireworks or Photoshop, a best-fit custom palette will be created, which Director then can import.

Pim van Bochoven has created a Mac-only ImageImport Xtra that you might like to discover: http://www.pimz.com/xtras/ImageImport.html.

Colors and Taste

This chapter has explained the issues and techniques you should be aware of when dealing with color. You have seen how colors are handled at the heart of the computer processor, and how variations on the theme provide greater color precision, greater speed, or better use of memory. You have also had practical experience with both building a color palette and experimenting with the effect of dithering.

There is no "best" way to deal with colors. You will have to work out for yourself, on a project-by-project basis, which bit depth to use; whether to use dithering; and, if you are using 8-bit color or lower, which palette provides the best compromise.

CHAPTER

3

Manipulating Pixels

IN THIS CHAPTER:

"And so these three little sisters—they were learning to draw, you know—"
"What did they draw?" said Alice, quite forgetting her promise.
"Treacle," said the Dormouse, without considering at all, this time.

—Lewis Carroll

Imaging Lingo proposes five commands that act directly on the pixels of an image:

- `copyPixels()`
- `draw()`
- `fill()`
- `floodFill()` (added in Director 8.5 but undocumented)
- `setPixel()`

Many newcomers to Imaging Lingo readily use `setPixel()` because it is the easiest to understand but, they tend to overlook others that are much faster. `draw()` and `fill()` have almost the same syntax, so we will discuss them together.

setPixel( )

setPixel.dir

`setPixel()` is a brute force command. It does one thing and it does it slowly: it sets the color of a given pixel in a given image object. The position of the pixel is defined by a point starting at 0, 0, which is in the upper-left corner of the image object. `setPixel()` is a function; it will return `1` if successful and `0` if the designated point falls outside the target image object. You can use either a point or two separate coordinates, and define the color using an rgb color object or a raw integer value, as in the following:

```
imageObject.setPixel(x, y, colorObject)
imageObject.setPixel(x, y, integerValue)
imageObject.setPixel(point(x, y), colorObject)
imageObject.setPixel(point(x, y), integerValue)
```

Why is it slow? If you want to set just one pixel in an image object, it is the perfect command. If you want to set a series of pixels, the Director Player needs to move back and forth repeatedly between your Lingo handler and the low-level pixel manipulation. If you can use one of the other pixel-manipulation commands and you issue just one Lingo instruction, the entire pixel manipulation is carried out in native C++ code. The slowness is not due to the `setPixel()` command itself, but to the negotiations between your Lingo and Director's own code.

How can you speed it up? If you must use `setPixel()`, you can't do much about the time taken for the round trip between Lingo and C++, but you can set the pixel itself just that little bit faster. You can use a raw integer value to define the color so the Director Player doesn't have to convert the color object or the hexadecimal string to a set of bits the processor can treat directly. (See the "Raw Integer Color Values" section of Chapter 2 for more information on this subject.)

As Figure 3-1 shows, the time saved by using the raw integer color value is minimal compared to the time saved by using one of the more intelligent pixel-manipulation commands. The example is based on the `setPixel()` entry in the *Lingo Dictionary*. You can find the original setPixel.dir test movie in the Imaging\Commands\ folder on the CD-ROM that accompanies the book.

DEBUGGING TIP

To complement the technique described in the "Raw Integer Color Values" section of Chapter 2, here are a couple of handlers that use a temporary image object and `setPixel()` to perform conversions between decimal and hexadecimal:

```
on hexToDecimal(hexadecimalString)
  x = image(1, 1, 32)
  -- alpha channel set to "FF"
  x.setPixel(0, 0, rgb(hexadecimalString))
  return x.getPixel(0, 0, #integer) + 16777216 -- adjust for alpha
end hexToDecimal


on DecimalToHex(decimal)
  x = image(1, 1, 32)
  x.setPixel(0, 0, decimal)
  return x.getPixel(0, 0).hexString()
end DecimalToHex
```

fill( ) and draw( )

You've already used the `fill()` command in the ColoRect.dir movie to create a filled rectangular or oval area. The `draw()` command enables you to create unfilled

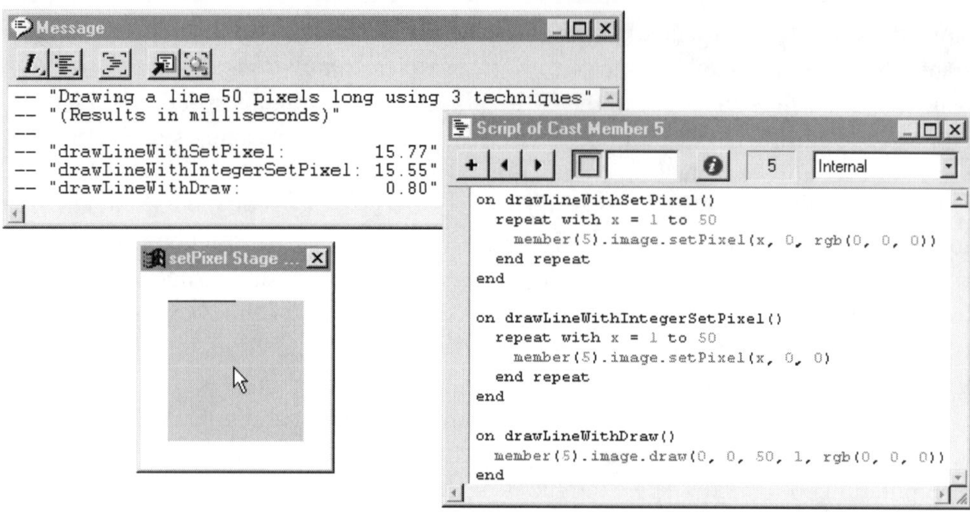

Figure 3-1 *Comparing two versions of setPixel( ) and draw( )*

shapes and draw straight lines. These commands accept a number of optional parameters: `#shapeType`; `#lineSize`; `#color`; and, in the case of `fill()`, `#bgColor`. To set these parameters you must use a property list, for example,

```
options = [#shapeType: #line, #lineSize: 4, #color: rgb(255, 0, 0)]
(the stage).image.draw(rect(5, 10, 150, 200), options)
```

The `#shapeType` parameter can take the values `#rect`, `#oval`, and `#roundRect` for both `draw()` and `fill()`. For `draw()`, the `#shapeType` parameter also can take the additional value of `#line`. (Despite what the *Lingo Dictionary* might say, this has no effect on the `fill()` command; the default value for the `fill()` command is `#rect`.)

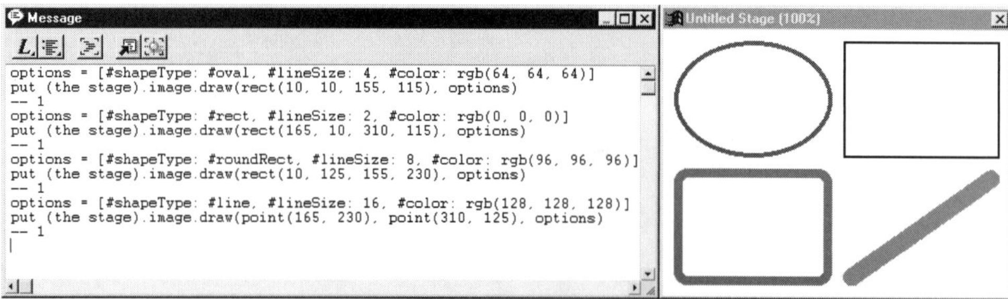

Although the other `#shapeType` parameters work happily with a `rect`, you probably will prefer to use two points to define a line to ensure that the line is sloping in the direction you expect. You also can define the dimensions of your shape by using four independent integers for `left`, `right`, `top`, and `bottom`. Here's how you could draw a cross using the default parameters:

```
(the stage).image.draw(point(20, 20), point(10, 10), rgb(128, 0, 0)) -- \
(the stage).image.draw(10, 20, 20, 10, rgb(128, 0, 0))               -- /
```

You also can use a `rect` with negative `width` or `height` to define an upward-sloping line:

```
(the stage).image.draw(rect(10, 20, 20, 10), rgb(128, 0, 0))         -- /
```

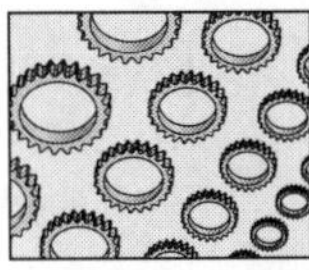

NOTE

In other circumstances, a `rect` with a negative `width` or `height` might be considered invalid. For instance, `copyPixels()` will fail gracefully with such a `rect` as either source or destination.

The draw( ) Command for Lines

Apart from lines, the shape you create will fit exactly inside the rect that you define for it. Lines are different; you will not get the same results on Macintosh and on Windows. The native drawing routines for lines for MacOS are different from those of Windows.

The Shape of a Line

On Macintosh, oblique lines will be drawn with a square point at each end; on Windows, oblique lines are rounded at each end. For lines with a `lineSize` greater than 1, this means a line drawn on Windows actually might not touch the points at the corners of the `rect`. Figure 3-2 shows a close-up of an oblique line drawn at various line sizes on both platforms. All the lines start from the same top-left point but finish in different positions. This lets you see how the end of lines are rounded on Windows: both the 24-pixel and the 1-pixel line have the same end point, but because of the rounding of the 24-pixel line, it doesn't actually reach that point.

Oblique lines appear thicker on Macintosh than those in Windows. Drawing a line on Windows is the equivalent of moving a circle of the appropriate diameter along the path of the line: the cross-section of the line always corresponds closely to the `lineSize`, regardless of the angle of the line. On Macintosh, drawing a line is the equivalent of moving a square of the appropriate side.

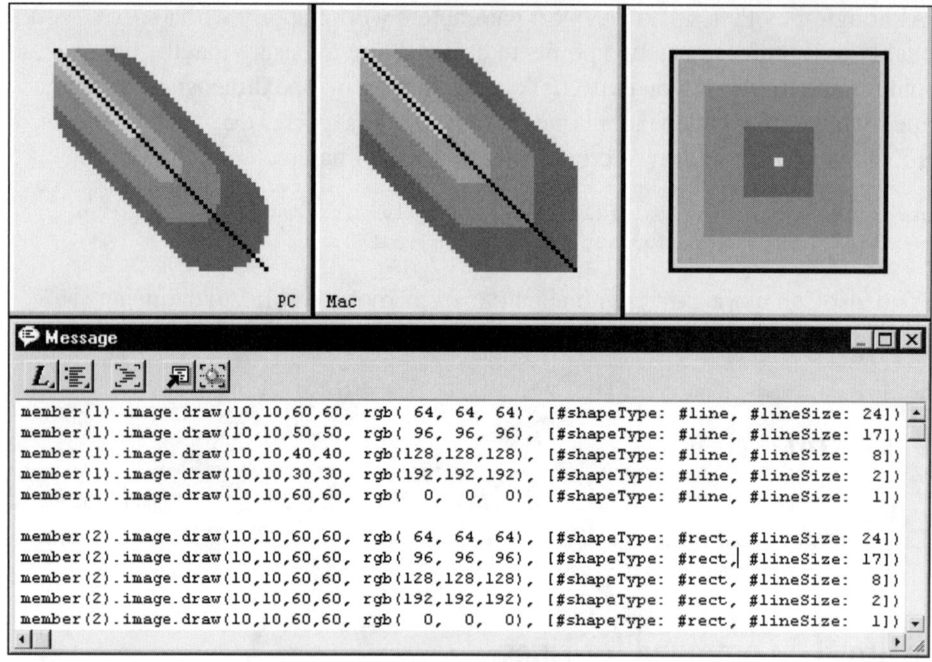

Figure 3-2 *Close-up of how lines and rects are drawn*

The thickness of a line on Macintosh will vary with its angle. If you want to draw a line with a particular cross-section, you have to resort to the Pythagorean Theorem, the similarity of triangles and the rule of three. Here is a function that returns values for `lineSize` that will give you similar results on both platforms.

```
on getLineSize(xSection, point1, point2)
  if the platform contains "Windows" then
    return xSection
  end if

  deltaH = abs(point1.locH - point2.locH)
  deltaV = abs(point1.locV - point2.locV)

  if deltaV = 0 then
    return xSection
  else if deltaH = 0 then
    return xSection
  end if
```

```
  hypotenuse = sqrt((deltaH * deltaH) + (float(deltaV) * deltaV))
  return (xSection * hypotenuse) / (deltaH + deltaV)
end getLineSize
```

Figure 3-3 shows the meaning of the variables in the preceding function. The calculation is based on the two black vertical lines being the same length. You might notice that this function uses an approximation to speed up calculations. The approximation is least accurate for very short, lightly angled lines, as shown in the box in Figure 3-3. Because the returned value will be rounded to an integer anyway by the `draw()` method, such minor inaccuracies are not significant.

Lines at Shallow Angles

Most of the time, Windows fits the line inside the bounding box `rect` you provide for it. If the line is at a slight angle, the width of the line will be clipped. Try this in the Message window on your PC:

```
options = [#color: rgb(0, 0, 0), #lineSize: 32]
(the stage).image.draw(10, 10, 230, 10, options)
(the stage).image.draw(10, 50, 230, 55, options)
(the stage).image.draw(10, 60, 230, 110, options)
updateStage
```

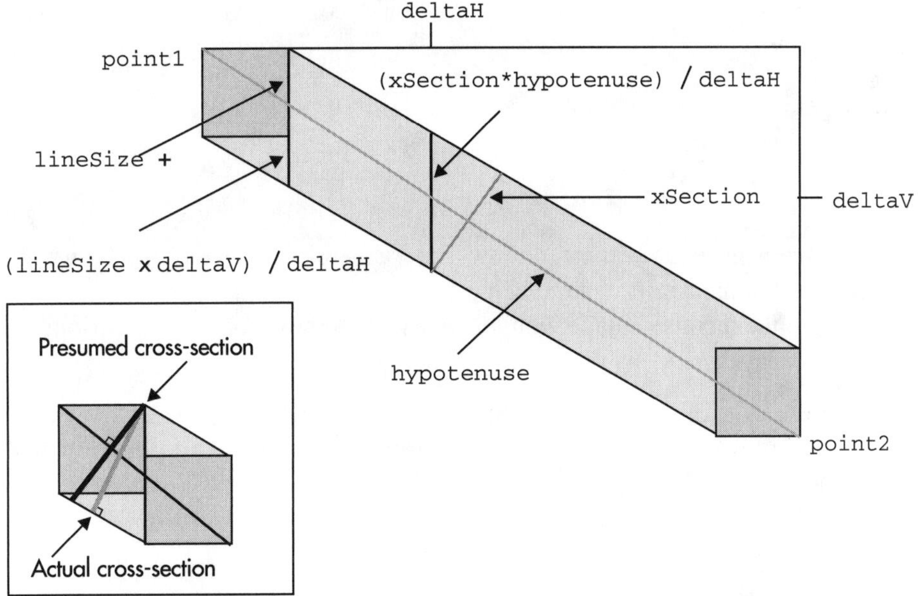

Figure 3-3 *The meaning of the variables in the getLineSize( ) function*

Although all the lines have a `lineSize` of 32, the second one appears only 5 pixels high.

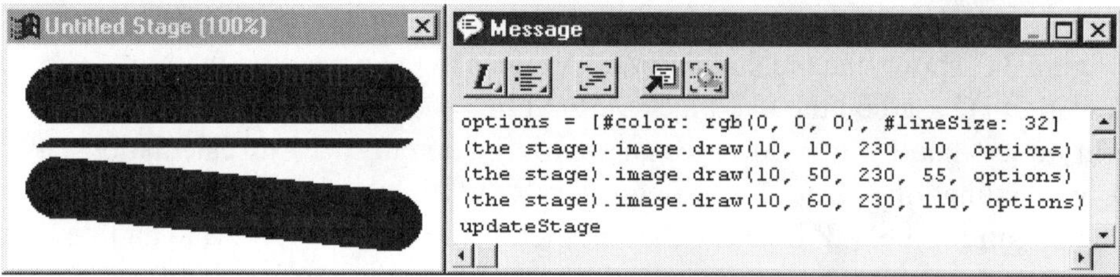

In Windows, a line that is perfectly horizontal or vertical will appear correctly; a line whose `lineSize` is wider than the narrowest dimension of its bounding box will not. One further quirk in Windows: A line that starts and ends at the same point and has a `lineSize` of 1 is drawn over two pixels. It appears as two dots: one at the start and end point, and the other 1 pixel up and to the left.

Macintosh has a completely different logic—or rather two. A line on Macintosh always appears at the expected `lineSize`, regardless of its angle; however, its length and orientation can be surprising. For some reason, what I have just said is not true if the line is drawn into `(the stage).image`. To test this on your Mac, create a Bitmap member in cast slot 1 and place it on the Stage so that its top left is at `point(0, 0)`. Now type the following into the Message window:

```
options = [#color: rgb (0, 0, 0), #lineSize: 32]
put (the stage).image.draw(40, 40, 40, 40, options) -- single point
-- 1
updateStage
put (member 1).image.draw(40, 40, 40, 40, options)
-- 1
```

Nothing happens when you try to draw into `(the stage).image`. However, the `draw()` command returned the value 1 to indicate that all had gone well. When you draw into the member image, you get an extended hexagon shape. Curious. Now try the following:

```
(member 1).image.draw(75, 75, 232, 80, options) -- slopes down \
options[#color] = rgb(255, 0, 0) -- change color so line is visible
(the stage).image.draw(75, 75, 232, 80, rgb(255, 0, 0), options)
updateStage
```

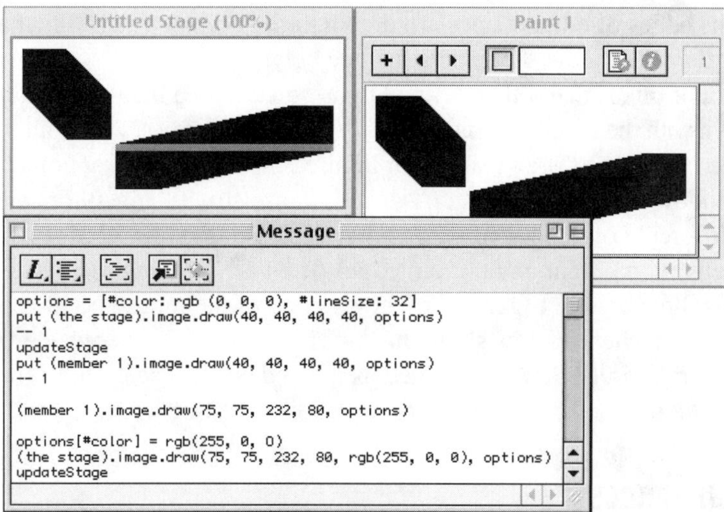

This time, when you try to draw a line that slopes *down* from `point(75, 75)` to `point(232, 80)`, the resulting line slopes *up*. The same command used on `(the stage).image` produces a horizontal line 5 pixels high. Curiouser! Now it is clear why the first `draw()` command used on `(the stage).image` had no visible effect: the line that was drawn had no width and no height.

Testing with the DrawFill Movie

DrawFill.dir

The DrawFill.dir movie, which you can find in the Imaging\Commands\ folder on the CD-ROM that accompanies the book, provides an easy way of visualizing how the `draw()` and `fill()` commands work. Set the `lineSize` to a fairly large number, select the Line tool, and then practice drawing lines. Be sure to test on both platforms.

As an aside, the DrawFill.dir movie uses better buffer management than the ColoRect.dir you first looked at in Chapter 1. Instead of making a copy of the entire canvas image, the `updateShape()` handler in the DrawFill Canvas behavior simply calculates the `rect` that is about to be changed, and makes a copy of that.

How Shapes Are Positioned

Except in the circumstances I have just described, lines are drawn to straddle the imaginary line between the two corners of the bounding `rect`, as Figure 3-2 shows.

However, the edges of other shapes are drawn to fall completely inside the bounding `rect`; they do not straddle the imaginary line between the corners.

One effect of this is that a line defined by a `rect` with a height or width of zero will be drawn with the specified `lineSize`. A `#rect shapeType` with a width or height of zero will not be drawn at all. In Figure 3-4, the last instruction in the Message window will have no effect. All the other instructions will draw the shape shown, in different colors. (`member(1)` has been enlarged for clarity.)

By convention, the right and bottom edges of a `rect` are not included in the rect itself. This is illustrated in Figure 3-4. The position of the mouse pointer and the readout in the Watcher window show that `point(60,10)` lies outside the line that is drawn with `point(60,10)`, defined as the end point. The color of the pixel of `member(1)` at that point is white; not colored like the line itself.

Soft-Edged Shapes

`draw()` and `fill()` both create hard-edged shapes; they provide no antialiasing. If you want soft edges, you will have to pass through a number of additional steps. This section explains those additional steps.

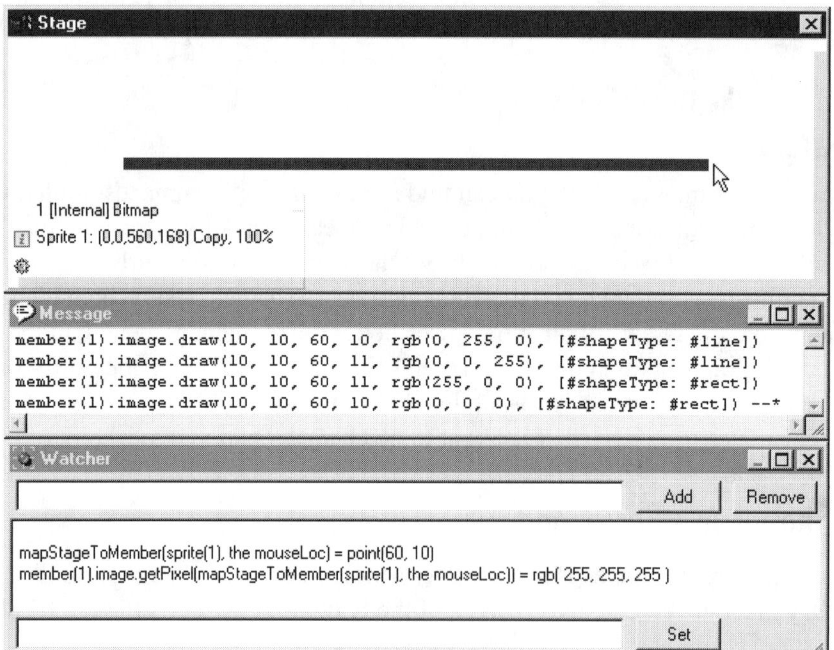

Figure 3-4 *Positioning of lines and rect shapes*

An Alpha Channel Approach to Antialiasing

Here's one approach. It is not the best, but I include it because it illustrates how the alpha channel works:

1. Create a temporary 32-bit image object with the appropriate bounding `rect`.
2. Fill it with the required color.
3. Create a double-sized 8-bit grayscale image object.
4. Draw or fill a double-sized shape in the 8-bit image object using black.
5. Create a real-sized, 8-bit grayscale image object.
6. Copy the double-sized. grayscale image into the real-sized image, thus downscaling it.
7. Use the real-sized grayscale image as the alpha channel for your 32-bit image.
8. Set the `useAlpha` of the 32-bit image to `TRUE`.
9. Use `copyPixels()` to add the antialiased shape to your target image object.

I chose to use a double-sized image as a compromise between quality and memory requirements. You might like to modify the handler so that the scaling factor can be passed as a parameter.

Here is a handler that does this to create antialiased filled shapes:

```
on antiAliasDraw(imageObject, shapeRect, options) --------------------
  -- Example syntax:
  -- options = [#shapeType: #oval, #color: rgb(255, 255, 0)]
  -- antiAliasDraw(member(1).image, rect(100, 100, 200, 300), options)
  --------------------------------------------------------------------

  -- Determine dimensions of the shape to be drawn
  rawWidth  = shapeRect.width
  rawHeight = shapeRect.height
  rawRect   = rect(0, 0, rawWidth, rawHeight)

  -- Create temporary image object at final size and fill with #color
  smoothImage = image(rawWidth, rawHeight, 32)
  smoothImage.fill(rawRect, options[#color])

  -- Scale up rect and lineSize
  scaledWidth  = rawWidth  * 2
  scaledHeight = rawHeight * 2
  scaledRect   = rect(0, 0, scaledWidth, scaledHeight)
```

```
  scaledLine = options[#lineSize]
  if voidP(scaledLine) then
    options[#lineSize] = 2 -- twice default value of 1
  else
    options[#lineSize] = scaledLine * 2
  end if

  -- Draw opaque line in double-sized alpha channel image
  options[#color] = rgb(0, 0, 0)
  scaledAlpha = image(scaledWidth, scaledHeight, 8, #grayScale)
  scaledAlpha.draw(scaledRect, options)

  -- Downscale alpha channel data and use it for the shape image
  smoothAlpha = image(rawWidth, rawHeight, 8, #grayScale)
  smoothAlpha.copyPixels(scaledAlpha, rawRect, scaledRect)
  smoothImage.setAlpha(smoothAlpha)
  smoothImage.useAlpha = TRUE

  -- Copy antialiased shape to the target image object
  return imageObject.copyPixels(smoothImage, shapeRect, rawRect)
end antiAliasDraw
```

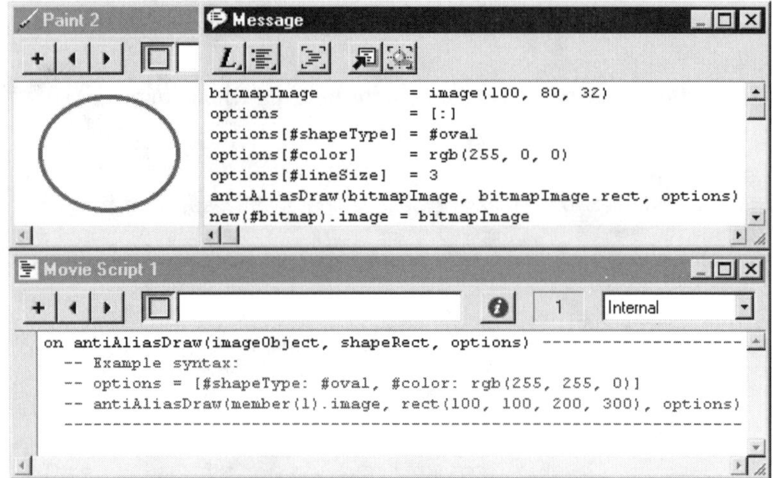

This handler perfectly illustrates how the alpha channel can be used to create antialiased edges. Unfortunately, it has other shortcomings. It works well with `#oval` shape types but does not treat the others as well as they deserve:

- `#rect` shapes do not benefit in any way from antialiasing because all their lines are straight.
- `#line` shapes can slope either up or down, but this handler makes them all slope down. For lines with very gentle slopes, the antialiasing might be unconvincing. Scaling up and down by a factor greater than `2` can help, although it will temporarily use more memory.
- `#roundRect` shapes will have smaller corners because the radius used is independent of the size.

The `smoothShapes()` handler in the DrawFill.dir movie deals with some of these issues. You also will find an electronic version of the `antialiasDraw()` handler in the preceding code, in the Unused scripts section of the cast. The following illustration shows shapes drawn in pairs, with the antialiased version on the right.

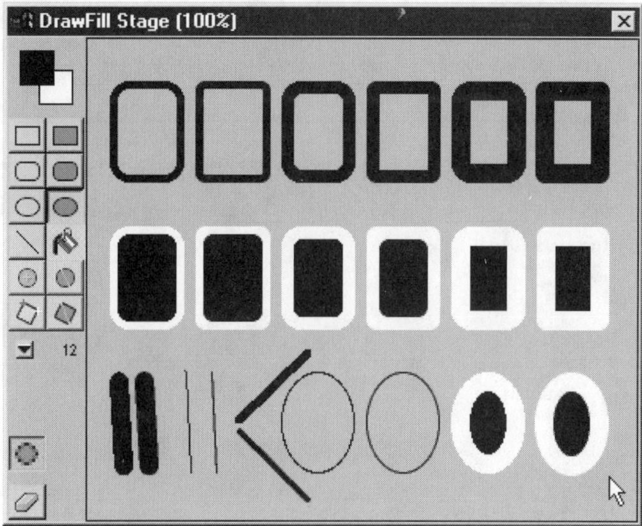

A Supersampling Approach to Antialiasing

The `antialiasDraw()` technique uses the alpha channel as a cookie cutter to make a hole in a rectangle of solid color. The line that is drawn is antialiased on both sides. In an `antialiasFill()` function, the border line should be antialiased against the central color on the inside and whatever background image there is on the outside. A few minor adaptations to the preceding handler (such as changing `draw` to `fill` everywhere) is enough to cope with the antialias on the outside, as you can see in the following illustration. However, antialiasing the border against the central color requires a different approach.

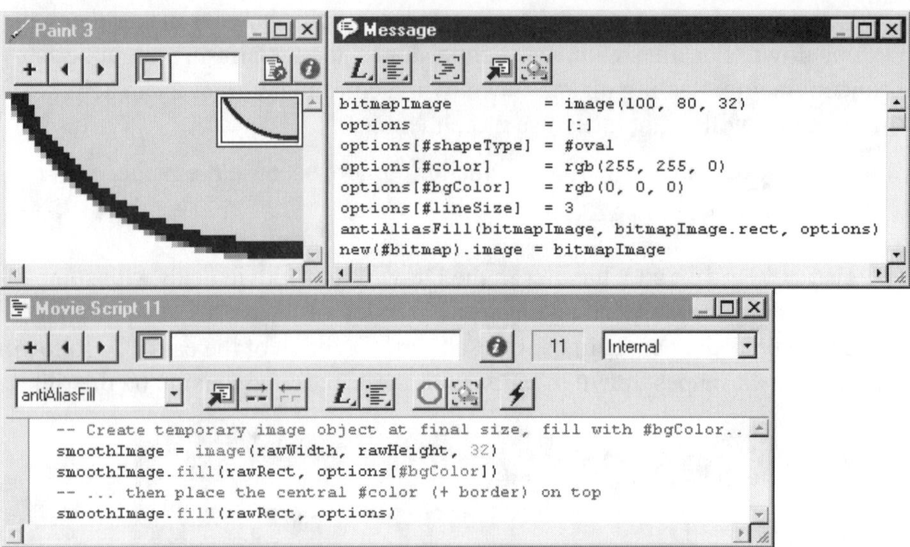

The `smoothShape()` handler in the DrawFill.dir movie provides an elegant single-pass solution, which also works for the `draw()` method. Here is a stripped-down version of the full handler:

```
on smoothShape(technique, imageObject, boundingRect, options)
  scaleFactor  = 2 -- Can be adjusted for greater smoothness
  scaledWidth  = boundingRect.width * scaleFactor
  scaledHeight = boundingRect.height * scaleFactor

 -- Create a double-sized copy of the appropriate rect of imageObject
  scaledImage = image(scaledWidth, scaledHeight, imageObject.depth)
  scaledRect  = rect(0, 0, scaledWidth, scaledHeight)
  scaledImage.copyPixels(imageObject, scaledRect, boundingRect)

  -- Scale up lineSize
  lineWidth = options[#lineSize]
  if voidP(lineWidth) then -- scale up default lineSize of 1
    options[#lineSize] = scaleFactor
  else
    options[#lineSize] = scaleFactor * lineWidth
  end if

  if technique = #draw then
```

```
    scaledImage.draw(scaledRect, options)
  else -- fill()
    scaledImage.fill(scaledRect, options)
  end if

  -- Copy antialiased shape to the target image object
  imageObject.copyPixels(scaledImage, boundingRect, scaledRect)
end smoothShape
```

The trick is to use an enlarged copy of the appropriate portion of the target image as a temporary patch image. The shape is drawn enlarged onto the appropriate background; then the whole patch is scaled back down and inserted into the target image. The unmodified sections of the patch simply will have been scaled up and down by the same factor; they will appear exactly as they did before. (My thanks to Sébastien Portebois for pointing out this technique.)

Rotated Shapes

Both the `draw()` and `fill()` commands produce shapes whose axes are parallel to the edges of the screen. If you want to draw a rectangle or an ellipse on a slant, you have to use a similar sequence of commands to that shown in the preceding; however, in this case, the destination area will be defined by a `quad` and not a `rect`.

When using a `quad` to define the destination area, the `copyPixels()` command provides no antialiasing, which means you can't use the `quad` to scale back down to the real size. If antialiasing is essential, you will need to create an intermediate double-sized image of the rotated shape; then downscale that when you copy it to the target image. The `diagonalSquare()` handler in the DrawFill.dir movie gives an example of how this can be done. A side effect of this two-step process is that you can use a `#blendLevel` property in your options list to blend the new shape with the background.

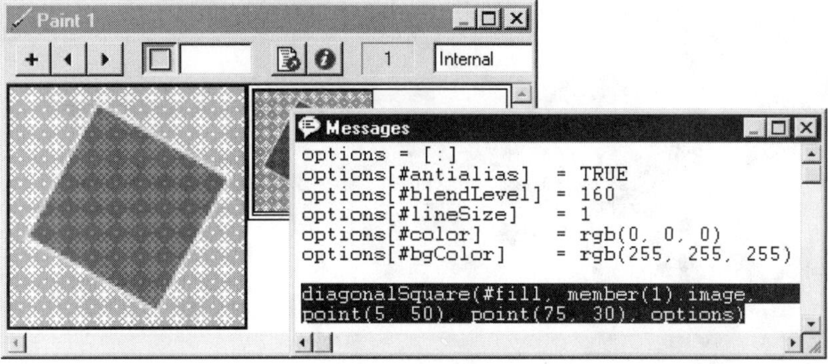

The `diagonalSquare()` handler uses the alpha channel approach. You might like to modify this so it uses the supersampling approach instead.

Alternatives to the Bounding Rect

As they stand, the `draw()` and `fill()` commands expect you to provide the bounding `rect` for a shape. This is not always intuitive. For instance, when drawing a circle, it can be more straightforward to indicate the center and the radius. If the user is to use the mouse to indicate this sort of information, you will need to indulge in some geometrical calculations to convert the points defined by the mouse into coordinates that the `draw()`, `fill()`, and `copyPixel()` commands can use.

In the DrawFill.dir movie, you'll find two such behaviors: Centered Circle, in which the user provides the center and a point on the circumference, and Diagonal Circle, where the user provides two diametrically opposed points on the circumference. In addition, the Diagonal Square behavior contains a `getThirdCorner()` handler, which allows you to define the square through two adjacent corners. These custom functions are illustrated by the blue-tinted buttons; the buttons for testing the built-in functions are gray. You can click the Antialias button near the bottom left to obtain antialiased shapes using all these methods.

In the following illustration all the shapes were created starting from the central point. The white shapes exploit the custom functions. The black circle is drawn using the standard oval tool. Antialiasing techniques were used for all shapes.

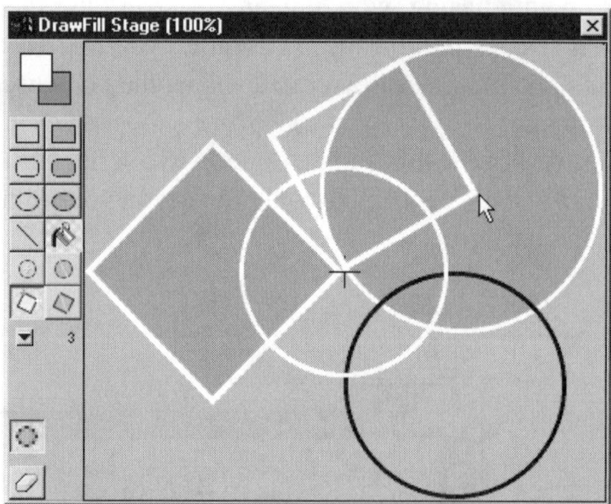

floodFill( )

Director 8.5 introduces a new Imaging Lingo command: `floodFill()`. The standard syntax,

```
imageObject.floodFill(<point>, <colorObject>)
```

acts like a bucket tool: all the contiguous pixels of the same color as the pixel at the chosen point will be changed to the new color. Testing which pixels should be filled with the target color requires an iterative algorithm, which is much more complex than simply defining a bounding `rect` and a line width, and calculating which pixels are affected. When filling a large area, be prepared to wait a fraction of a second before the command executes. However, it is considerably faster than attempting the same effect using `setPixel()`. The `floodFill()` command also is demonstrated in the DrawFill.dir movie. Run the DrawFill.dir movie in Director 8.5 to test the command using the bucket tool.

CopyPixels( )

Copyxel.dir

The entry for `copyPixels()` is one of the longest in the *Lingo Dictionary*. This in itself gives an inkling of the power of the command. In essence, it offers access to the native C++ code for manipulating bitmap data. Although it is possible to achieve the same effects through the `setPixel()` command, `copyPixels()` can be blindingly fast in comparison. The difficulty with `copyPixels()` is knowing just how to harness its speed and power.

If all its optional parameters were used, the `copyPixels()` command might look something like this:

```
  destinationImage.copyPixels( \
sourceImage, \
destinationRectOrQuad, \
sourceRect, \
[#color: rgb(128, 64, 32), #bgColor: rgb(53, 53, 53), #ink:
#backgroundTransparent, #blendLevel: 192, #dither: 1, #useFastQuads: FALSE,
#maskImage: member("Mask").image, #maskOffset: point(24, 48)] \
)
```

We will discuss all these parameters in detail in the pages that follow. The movie Copyxel.dir, which you will find in the Imaging\Commands\ folder on the CD-ROM that accompanies the book, will give you the chance to visualize the effect of each parameter.

Rects and Quads

QuadBox.dir

Although you probably are familiar with Lingo's `point` and `rect` data types, `quads` are less well known, so I will treat them in greater depth. Strictly speaking, `quads` are not a data type. There is no `#quad` ilk. The two most obvious uses of `quads` are to allow for the distortion of a flat image (as in the About Director… movie for Director 7) and to provide a two-dimensional representation of a 3-D plane. You can build a sense of perspective into a scene by placing rectangular images inside appropriately distorted quads.

Quads do not provide a true 3-D representation, in that distance into the screen (`locZ`) is not correctly handled. When you look down a long avenue of identical houses, the houses farthest away appear both shorter and narrower. Quad distortion of a flat facade of houses would make the houses farthest away appear shorter but the same width as the houses nearest to the viewer. Although there are ways of working around this, `quads` are better adapted for close-up interior views, where extreme perspective effects can be avoided.

Sprite Quads

Before exploring the use of quads in Imaging Lingo, it might help to review how quads work with sprites. The keyword `quad` was introduced in Director 7, as part of a mechanism for creating nonrectangular sprites.

The value of `sprite(spriteNum).quad` is calculated at runtime from the `rect`, `skew`, and `rotation` properties of the sprite; the `quad` of a sprite cannot be stored in the score. When the movie is halted, you can redimension, skew, and rotate a sprite, which effectively alters the quad; however, you cannot modify the lengths of its different sides separately. If you alter the `quad` of a sprite while the movie is running, modifying the sprite's `rect`, `skew`, and `rotation` properties will no longer have any effect. Indeed, even the `loc` of the sprite will behave strangely. Quads are not just for Christmas—once you quad a sprite, it's for life. (To be precise, you can remove the effect of quadding the sprite by using `puppetSprite` *`sprite-Number`*`, 0` to unpuppet the sprite even if it is not currently puppeted.)

You'll find a movie named QuadBox.dir in the Imaging\Commands\ folder of the CD-ROM that accompanies the book. The movie shows four square sprites, each of which you can drag. As you drag one of the square sprites, the `quad` of four other sprites is set to give the impression that you are dragging one face of a three-dimensional box. Each square sprite is controlled by a different behavior. Examining these behaviors will help you understand the issues involved in using quads for 3D simulation. Don't worry if the yellow box causes a variety of display problems. I include this behavior as a demonstration of the difficulties of mixing sprite movements and modifications to `(the stage).image`. We'll discuss this in the upcoming "Imaging Version" section.

The behavior on the red sprite at the top left is the simplest. As you can see in Figure 3-5, this Simple behavior does not draw the quads for the various extra faces in the best order; the faces at the bottom and the right should be hidden when the box appears in this position, but they are in fact drawn over the left and top faces. Here is the handler that determines the quad of each of the faces in the Simple behavior. It is called each time the user moves the square sprite to which the behavior is attached.

```
property mySprite    -- reference to this sprite (sprite spriteNum)
property myQuadList  -- list of 4 other sprites containing bitmap image
property myQuad      -- the original quad of the mySprite

on refreshQuads(me)
  currentQuad = mySprite.quad -- quad of mySprite in its new position

  repeat with i = 1 to 4
    secondSide = ((i + 2) mod 4) + 1 -- 1>4, 2>1, 3>2, 4>3
    faceQuad = []
    faceQuad[1] = myQuad[i]
    faceQuad[2] = currentQuad[i]
    faceQuad[3] = currentQuad[secondSide]
    faceQuad[4] = myQuad[secondSide]

    quadSprite = myQuadSprites[i]
    quadSprite.quad = faceQuad
  end repeat
end refreshQuads
```

Figure 3-6 shows how the points used to create `faceQuad` are obtained for the top face when `i = 2` and `secondSide = 1`.

Hidden Faces

The Hidden faces behavior on the green sprite at the top right decides which faces should be drawn. It does this by determining the orientation of the box to be drawn,

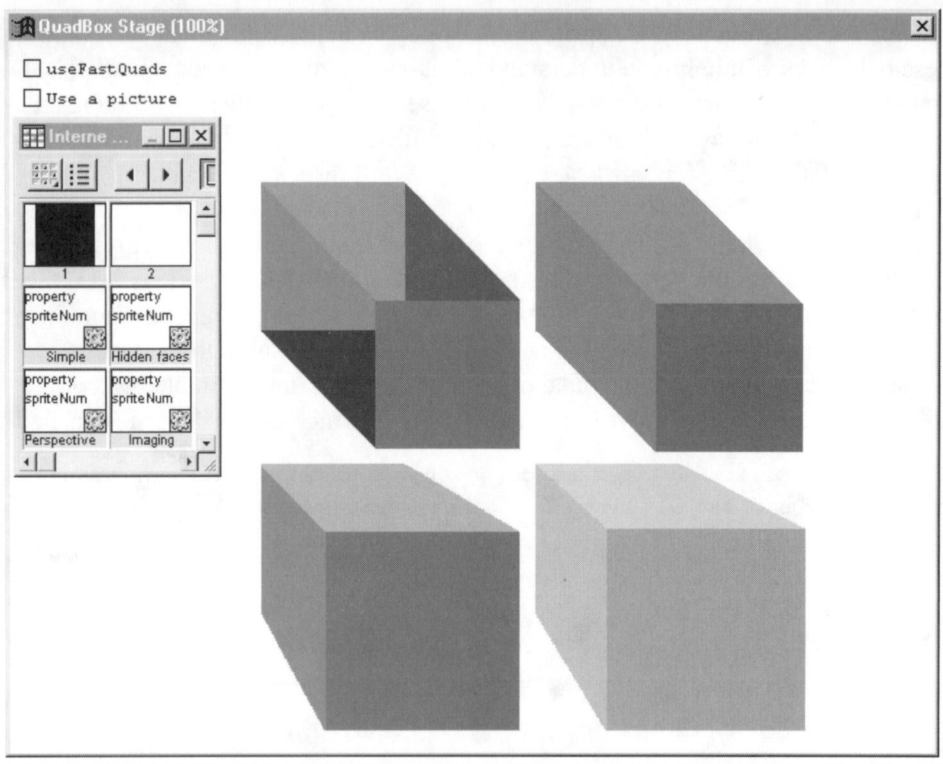

Figure 3-5 *Four behaviors that use quads to give a sense of perspective*

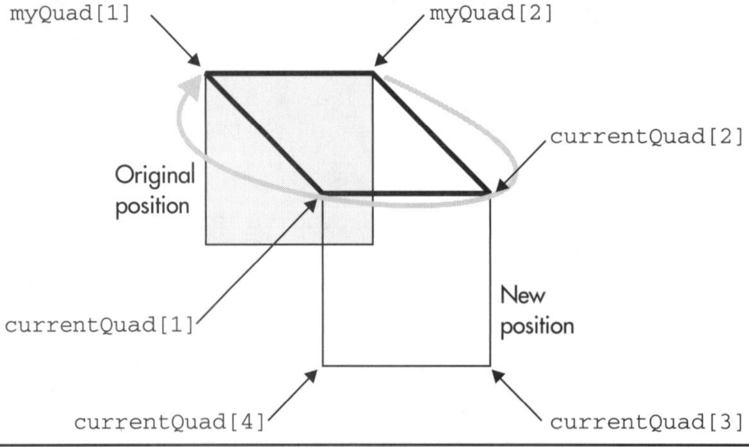

Figure 3-6 *Calculating the quad for the top face*

using a set of `if...then` statements that are added to the `refreshQuads()` handler. (I've trimmed the end of the handler, which is similar to the one shown previously. See the full handler in the movie.)

```
on refreshQuads(me)
  currentQuad = mySprite.quad

  delta = currentQuad[1] - myQuad[1] -- ilk(delta) = #point

  if delta.locH > 0 then
    if delta.locV > 0 then
      -- mySprite has been moved down to the right: show left and top
      faceList = [1, 1, 0, 0]
    else
      -- mySprite has been moved up to the right: show left and bottom
      faceList = [1, 0, 0, 1]
    end if
  else
    if delta.locV > 0 then
      -- mySprite has been moved down to the left: show top and right
      faceList = [0, 1, 1, 0]
    else
      -- mySprite has been moved up to the right: show right and bottom
      faceList = [0, 0, 1, 1]
    end if
  end if

  repeat with i = 1 to 4
    if faceList[i] then -- any non-zero integer = TRUE
      -- show the face (code as above)
      ...
    else
      -- cull the face (don't show it)
      faceQuad = [point(0, 0), point(0, 0), point(0, 0), point(0, 0)]
    end if

    quadSprite = myQuadSprites[i]
    quadSprite.quad = faceQuad
  end repeat
end refreshQuads
```

Perspective

The Perspective behavior on the blue sprite at the bottom left adds realism by increasing the size of the sprite as it moves toward the user. The new code in the `refreshQuads()` handler is shown in the following. Because the size of the sprite is changing, we can no longer use the top-left corner of it as a reference point; a new `getCenter()` handler is added to the behavior so that calculations can be made relative to the center of the sprite. The size of the sprite depends on its distance from its original position; the Pythagorean Theorem is used to calculate this. Note the use of the `inflate()`, `offset()`, and `union()` functions to determine new values for the sprite `rect`:

```
on getCenter(me, aRect)
  centerH = (aRect.left + aRect.right) / 2
  centerV = (aRect.top + aRect.bottom) / 2
  return point(centerH, centerV)
end getCenter


on refreshQuads(me)
  -- myOriginalRect is the original rect of mySprite
  -- myCenter is original center of mySprite

  spriteRect    = mySprite.rect
  spriteCenter  = me.getCenter(spriteRect)

  delta         = spriteCenter - myCenter
  deltaH        = delta.locH
  deltaV        = delta.locV
  hypotenuse    = sqrt((deltaH * deltaH) + (deltaV * deltaV))
  adjustment    = hypotenuse / 5 -- arbitrary value that gives good results

  inflatedRect  = myOriginalRect.inflate(adjustment, adjustment)
  mySprite.rect = inflatedRect.offset(deltaH, deltaV) -- correct position
  currentQuad   = mySprite.quad

  -- Test if the top or bottom of the original rect is visible
  unionRect     = myOriginalRect.union(spriteRect)
  showSidesOnly = (unionRect.height = spriteRect.height)

  if showSidesOnly then
    if delta.locH > 0 then
      -- mySprite has been moved right: show left only
      faceList = [1, 0, 0, 0]
    else
      -- mySprite has been moved left: show top only
      faceList = [0, 0, 3, 0]
    end if
  else if delta.locH > 0 then
    -- Handler continues as above
```

Note that the perspective effect requires more rigorous calculation of the hidden faces. Now that the surface that the user manipulates is larger than the original sprite, there are situations in which neither the top nor the bottom face is visible. This can be determined by calculating the height of the smallest `rect` that contains both the original and current `rect` of the sprite using the `union()` function. If the height of the resulting `unionRect` is the same as the current height of the sprite, no part of the original sprite `rect` protrudes above or below the current sprite `rect`; the top and bottom edges need not be shown.

In the QuadBox.dir movie, try changing this line

```
showSidesOnly = (unionRect.height = spriteRect.height)
```

to

```
showSidesOnly = 0
```

This will prevent the more rigorous hidden face detection from occurring. See the unwelcome effect this has when you drag the sprite horizontally:

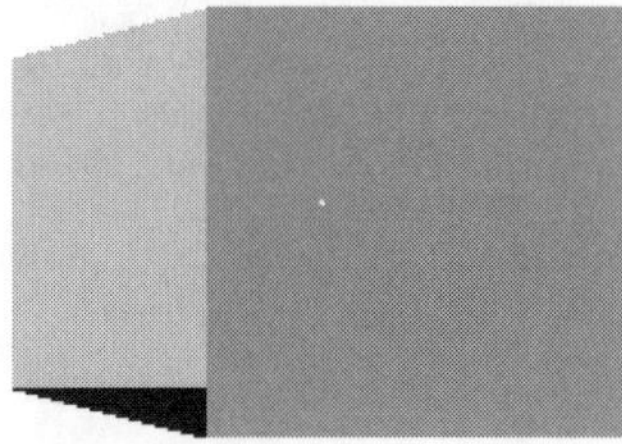

You might have noticed that the handler in the preceding code takes a shortcut: The left and right faces are not culled when you drag the sprite vertically from its starting position. The order in which the sprites are displayed means the left and right faces will be hidden automatically by the top or bottom sprites if necessary. The handler in the movie provides a fuller treatment.

Imaging Version

The yellow sprite at the bottom right uses only one sprite. The quads are drawn directly into the image of the Stage, as in the ColoRect.dir movie at the beginning of this part. The results are not perfect. The quadded faces appear as trails; the movement of the sprites will wipe them from the screen. You might notice that, in some circumstances, the movement of the yellow sprite itself wipes part of the quadded faces. I have included this version for two reasons:

- So you can compare Imaging Lingo quads with sprite quads.
- To demonstrate that using sprites while at the same time drawing into `(the stage).image` with Imaging Lingo is a complex process, not to be embarked upon lightly.

Here is the code, which draws the top face into the image of the Stage:

```
pixelImage     = mySprite.member.image
pixelRect      = pixelImage.rect -- rect(0, 0, 1, 1)


i = faceList.count
repeat while i
  case faceList[i] of
    #top:
      faceQuad    = []
      faceQuad[1] = myQuad[2]
      faceQuad[2] = currentQuad[2]
      faceQuad[3] = currentQuad[1]
      faceQuad[4] = myQuad[1]
      options     = [#color: rgb("#FFFF00")] -- yellow
      stageImage.copyPixels(pixelImage,faceQuad,pixelRect,options)
    -- etc
```

Compare this with the code for setting the `quad` of a sprite in the "Sprite Quads" section earlier in the chapter.

useFastQuads

Director has two algorithms for calculating the display of a quadded sprite. By default, the slower, more accurate algorithm is used. The faster algorithm treats the edges of the `quad` correctly but is less careful about how the distortion of the body of the image is handled when opposite edges are not parallel. In the QuadBox.dir movie, all quads are calculated from the image of a 1 × 1 pixel, 1-bit color depth Bitmap member, which means there is no image as such—only a flat area of color. Thus, there is no advantage to using the more accurate algorithm.

You can switch to the faster algorithm by setting the value of the global property: `the useFastQuads`.

```
the useFastQuads = TRUE
```

Selecting the check box in the top-left corner of the QuadBox.dir movie will do this for you automatically. You should see no differences in the display. You also can try using a larger bitmap with a pattern by clicking the Use A Picture button. You will see a difference on only the blue sprites because the opposite edges of the quads are not parallel. You'll have to move the blue box slightly so that the image is redrawn with the new value of `the usefastQuads`. (You won't see any difference on the yellow box because it uses Imaging Lingo, which is not directly affected by `the useFastQuads` global property. The `copyPixels()` command has its own independent `useFastQuads` parameter).

Concavities and Bowties

QuadKnot.dir

An arbitrary quadrilateral can have a concave shape (like a V), or a pair of opposing sides can be crossed to give it a bowtie shape. Neither of these shapes has any meaning in either 2D distortions or 3D effects. Neither the slow or fast algorithms treat such shapes with much compassion. The QuadKnot.dir movie in the Imaging\Commands\ folder enables you to test quads to destruction and includes a script that detects when a `quad` is concave or twisted. The movie uses the Drag Quad Point behavior written by Darrel Plant.

2D Distortion Effects

The `copyPixels()` command enables you to specify either a `rect` or a `quad` for the destination area. You've already seen a `quad` used for this twice:

- To create a triangle in the ColoRect.dir movie
- To draw the quadded faces for the box in the QuadBox.dir movie

To calculate the value of a `quad`, you've seen the Pythagorean Theorem, the use of sines and cosines, and a number of lesser-known `rect` functions. This should be a subtle hint: Effective use of quads requires a fair understanding of geometry and trigonometry. If either of these words breaks you out in a cold sweat, you might as well jump to the next section on inks now…but you'll be missing out on the Goo. You can find a refresher course on trigonometry in Chapter 6.

Goo

Goo.dir

In April 2000, Gary Rosenzweig published an article on Director Online Users Group entitled "Goo with Director 8." You can find this athttp://www. director-online.com/buildArticle.cfm?id=840.

Rather than echoing the same information here, I have decided to extend the idea by using more `quad` areas to give the impression of a powerful lens moving under the cursor (see Figure 3-7). You'll find both a simple and a complete version of the behavior in the Goo.dir movie in the Imaging\Commands\ folder on the CD-ROM that accompanies the book.

The Goo behavior works by mapping the intersections of a square grid onto the surface of a sphere, using polar coordinates. The flat grid is stretched like bubble gum from the point immediately below the cursor. The absolute distance between the intersection points is increased by the curvature of the bubble, but the ratio of the distances remains the same. The resulting points are used as the corners of a set of quads. You can see a graphical explanation of this in Figure 3-8.

The first diagram in the top row shows the initial grid. Two intersections, identified by a circle and a square, are shown. The circle intersection is one square to the left of the center—that is, one third of the distance from the center to point A.

In the second diagram in Figure 3-8, you see the same point in a cross-section view, as if your eye were flush with the screen, on the line A-B. You also see the cross-section of the sphere. The mapping of the circle intersection is shown on the surface of the sphere. This appears one-third of the distance between the top of the sphere and point A, measured along the curved surface of the sphere. Because the total angle between the top of the sphere to point A is 90°, the angle between the top of the sphere and the circle intersection points is 90° / 3 = 30°.

Figure 3-7 *Using quads with Imagining Lingo to simulate a concave lens*

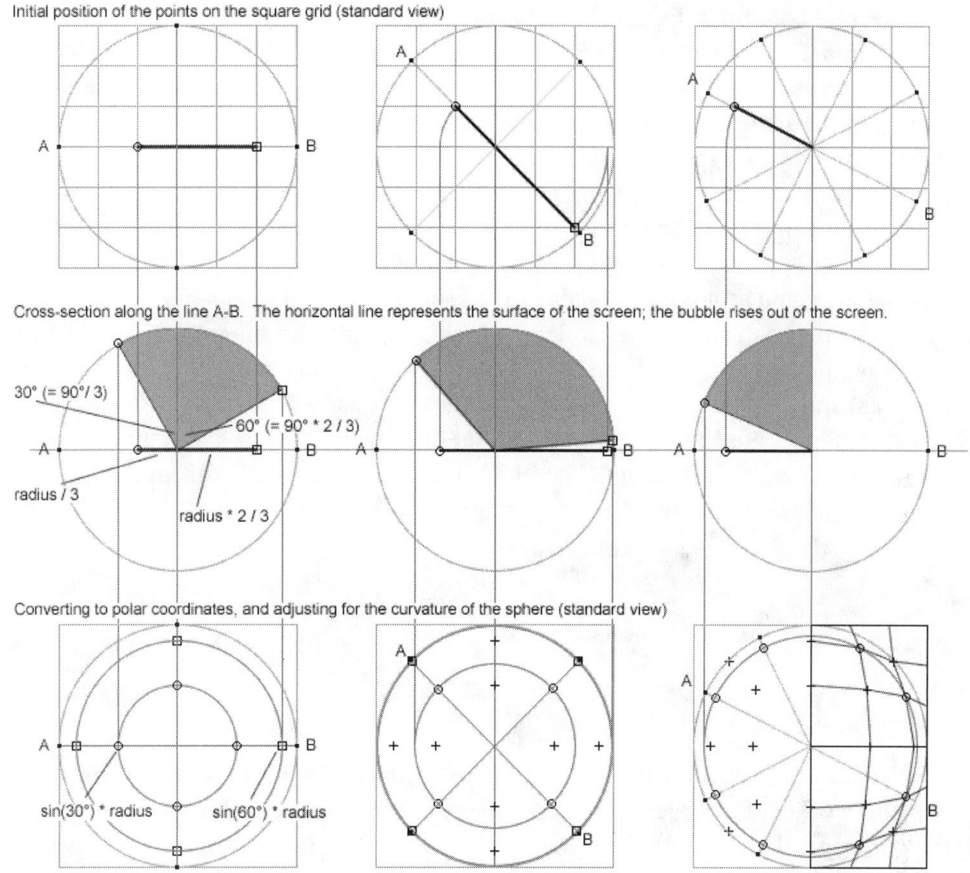

Figure 3-8 *Visualizing the calculations of the quad*

The bottom diagram in Figure 3-8 uses the same point of view as the top diagram, looking into the screen from above the bubble. This time, the circle intersection appears at the point `sin(30°) * the radius of the sphere` out from the center of the grid. Three other circle intersections are shown, obtained by applying the notion of symmetry to the grid.

The square intersection in the first column undergoes the same mapping process. Because originally it is two-thirds of the distance between the center of the grid and point B, it maps to a point on the sphere that is two-thirds of 90° = 60° down from the top. Its new position is `sin(60°) * the radius of the sphere` out from the center of the grid.

The second column in Figure 3-8 repeats the process for two new intersection points. Again, the ratio between the linear distance of the points from the center of the grid (at the top) and the angular rotation on the surface of the sphere (in the middle) are the same. In the bottom diagram, the points previously calculated are marked with crosses. Note that the middle diagram is a cross-section along a different line A-B, so the points in the top diagram need to be rotated around the center before being projected down onto the middle diagram.

The third column in Figure 3-8 shows the mapping of the remaining set of points, which are arranged around the center of the grid in eightfold symmetry. The left half of the lower diagram shows the circle to which the points are mapped; the right half shows how the mapped points are joined together to produce a network of quads. In the Goo.dir movie, you can see this exact pattern of quads. Click the Customizable Version button, choose the Stretch option, set the Facet factor to `3` and the Radius to `30`, and then click in the center of the black and white grid. (The Facet factor is the number of squares along the edge of each quadrant.)

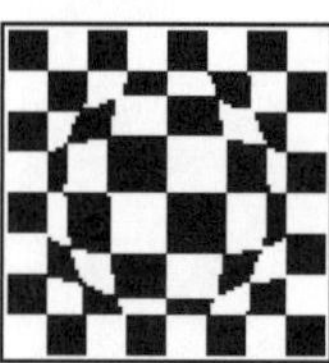

The edges of the quads will not be antialiased. If you want to soften the edges, you could work with a larger temporary image and scale down when you copy back into your original image, much as you saw previously with the antialiased shapes in the DrawFill.dir movie. However, this probably is not necessary, as the lack of antialiasing is not very noticeable when you use the behavior on a photo.

Here's the handler from the Goo behavior that maps each grid intersection to its position on the surface of the sphere.

```
property myRadius -- for this example, myRadius = 30

on getQuadPoint(me, hLoc, vLoc)
-------------------------------------
  -- PARAMETERS:
  -- <hLoc> and <vLoc> are integers defining a point on the flat grid
  --
  -- RETURNS: the equivalent point after mapping to the sphere
  --
  -- ACTION: calculates where the point(hLoc, vLoc) would appear when
```

```
  -- mapped onto the bubble.  If the point is outside the bubble, no
  -- alteration is made.

-------------------------------------------------------------------

  ratio = sqrt(float(hLoc*hLoc + vLoc*vLoc)) / myRadius

  if ratio > 0 and ratio < 1 then
    -- The point is on the surface of the sphere
    pointOnCircumference = point(hLoc, vLoc) / ratio
    arcRatio = sin(ratio * pi / 2)
    return pointOnCircumference * arcRatio

  else
    -- The point is under the mouse or outside the sphere
    return point(hLoc, vLoc)
  end if
end getQuadPoint
```

The various positions of the variable `pointOnCircumference` are shown as the black dots (such as A and B) on the edge of the circular area in Figure 3-8.

The Custom Goo behavior enables you to alter the radius and the number of facets used. You will notice that the quality of the effect does not increase greatly once you have a Facet factor of `4`. However, the time taken to calculate the image increases as the square of the Facet factor. A value of `4` creates 64 quads; a value of `10` creates 400. The number of `copyPixels()` operations thus is greatly increased, although this is slightly offset by the smaller size of the images that are copied.

The Custom Goo behavior also enables you to inverse this process of mapping a flat grid onto a sphere. Imagine that you etch a set of straight lines onto the surface of a bubblegum sphere; then deflate the sphere so it becomes a flat surface. Selecting the Shrink button makes the behavior do just this (see Figure 3-7). I'll leave you to study the `getQuadPoint()` handler in the Custom Goo behavior for yourself.

Inks

Inks are formulas used to determine how the colors of the pixels in one layer affect the colors of the layer below. Werner Sharp, the Macromedia engineer who wrote the Imaging Lingo code for Director, has compiled the following list of inks and their operations, as shown next.

```
d = destination, s = source, fg = foreColor, bg = bgColor

copy                  d = s
backgroundTransparent d = s if s <> bg
transparent           d = d AND s
reverse               d = d XOR s
ghost                 d = d OR (NOT s)
notCopy               d = NOT s
notTransparent        d = d AND (NOT s)
notReverse            d = d XOR (NOT s)
notGhost              d = d OR s
matte                 copy using a matte
mask                  copy using a mask
blend                 d = d * blend + s * (100% - blend)
add                   d = d + s (with wraparound)
addPin                d = d + s (max value 255)
subtract              d = d - s (with wraparound)
subtractPin           d = d - s (min value 0)
lightest              d = max(d, s)
darkest               d = min(d, s)
lighten               d = s * scaleFactor (bg) + addFactor (fg)
darken                d = s * scaleFactor (bg) + addFactor ((256 - bg) + fg)
```

You might have noticed that `d` is used both for the initial state and the state that results from the operation, which might seem curious at first. Elsewhere in Lingo, you can store the result separately from the inputs, as in `a = b + c`. You also can replace one of the inputs with the result, as in `x = x + 1`. However, ink effects are cumulative by nature, and image objects require a great deal of memory—up to 32 bits for each pixel. It makes sense to recycle the memory space used by one of the inputs for the result.

In the preceding table, you should consider that each operator acts separately on each of the red, green, and blue values of a color object. For example:

```
color1 = rgb( red, green, blue)
color2 = rgb(r, g, b)
color1 AND color2 = rgb(bitAnd(red, r), bitAnd(green, g),
bitAnd(blue, b))
```

However, rgb values must be in the range 0–255 so additions and subtractions must either wrap (by subtracting or adding 255 until the value falls inside the range) or be limited by maximum and minimum values. For similar reasons, the NOT operator has a special meaning:

```
NOT color1 =  rgb(255 - red, 255 - green, 255 - blue)
```

As a result, there is no neutral color: a value of 128 will map to 127 through the NOT operation, and vice versa. This can lead to situations in which the result of an ink effect is one degree (out of 255) darker or lighter than you might expect.

A Phantom Rectangle

Here's an example, using `#ghost` ink, to help you understand how to use the formulas in this table:

1. Create a new movie with a white stage and set the palette to System–Win.
2. In the Paint window, create a large rectangle using the dark red near the end of the last row of colors in the palette: `paletteIndex(254) = #800000 = rgb(128, 0, 0).`
3. Choose the dark cyan color near the middle of the last row of colors: `paletteIndex(249), #008080, rgb(0, 128, 128).`
4. Draw a smaller dark cyan rectangle inside the dark red rectangle.
5. Duplicate the Bitmap member.
6. Choose the dark yellow colored three chips to the right: `paletteIndex(252) = #808000 = rgb(128, 128, 0).`
7. In the second Bitmap member, fill the smaller rectangle with this dark yellow color.
8. Select both Bitmap members and drag them together onto the Stage, into sprite channels 1 and 2. The two sprites should cover each other exactly.
9. Set `the ink` of sprite 2 to `#ghost (sprite(2).ink = 3)`. Result: one pale cyan patch where the smaller rectangle appears with the rest of the Stage all white.
10. Now for the weird part. (Remember you are using ghost ink.) Click sprite 2 and drag it around. The cyan rectangle that belongs to sprite 1 appears to be *on top*

of sprite 2; the main dark red rectangle of sprite 2 appears underneath. The dark yellow rectangle in sprite 2 appears as pale magenta. (These colors will be converted to bright cyan and bright magenta, respectively, if your monitor is set to 256 colors.)

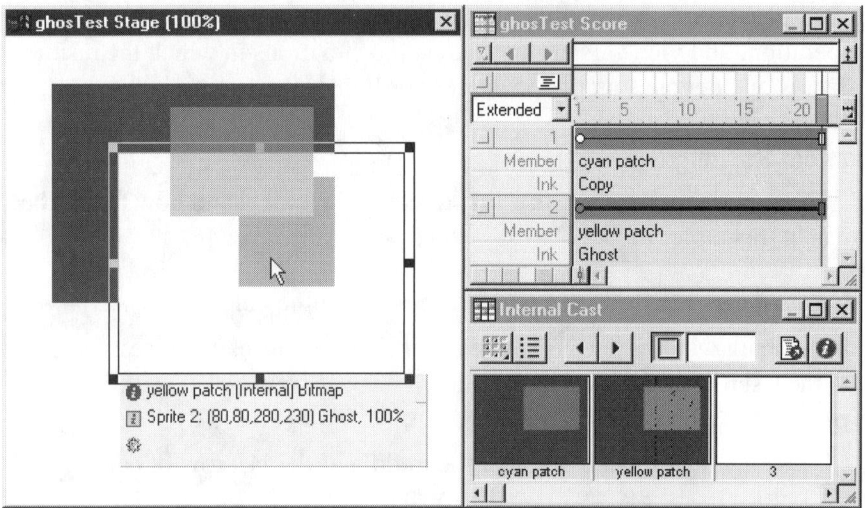

Here's what makes that dark cyan rectangle in sprite 1 lighter:

- Ghost ink means the final color is calculated by this formula: `d = d OR (NOT s)`.
- Where the dark cyan area in sprite 1 is below the dark yellow area in sprite 2, `d = rgb(0, 128, 128)` and `s = rgb(128, 128, 0)`.
- `NOT s = rgb(255 - 128, 255 - 128, 255 - 0) = rgb(127, 127, 255)`.
- `d OR (NOT s) = rgb(bitOr(0, 127), bitOr(128, 127), bitOr(128, 255)) = rgb(127, 255, 255)`, which gives a desaturated cyan.

Remember: in binary notation, 128 is written 10000000 and 127 is written 011111111, so `bitOr(128, 127)` = 11111111 (base 2) = 255 (base 10).

- Where the dark cyan rectangle in sprite 1 is below the dark red area in sprite 2, `d = rgb(0, 128, 128)` and `s = rgb(128, 0, 0)`.
- `NOT s = rgb(255 - 128, 255 - 0, 255 - 0) = rgb(127, 255, 255)`.

- `d OR (NOT s) = rgb(bitOr(0, 127), bitOr(128, 255), bitOr(128, 255)) = rgb(127, 255, 255)`, which gives a desaturated cyan.

In both cases, the ink effect on sprite 2 gives the dark cyan rectangle in sprite 1 the same color, which is why it appears to float above sprite 2.

Here's why the dark red areas cancel each other out to white:

- Both destination and source colors are the same: `d = s = rgb(128, 0, 0)`.
- `NOT s = rgb(255 - 128, 255 - 0, 255 - 0) = rgb(127, 255, 255)`.
- `d OR (NOT s) = rgb(bitOr(128, 127), bitOr(0, 255), bitOr(0, 255)) = rgb(255, 255, 255)`, which gives white.

Here's why the dark yellow patch on sprite 2 appears as pale magenta over the dark red area of sprite 1:

- `d = rgb(128, 0, 0) and s = rgb(128, 128, 0)`
- `NOT s = rgb(255 - 128, 255 - 128, 255 - 0) = rgb(127, 127, 255)`
- `d OR (NOT s) = rgb(bitOr(128, 127), bitOr(0, 127), bitOr(0, 255)) = rgb(255, 127, 255), which gives a desaturated magenta.`

Over a white background, ghost ink will convert all colors to white.

Names or Formulas?

InkTest.dir

The names of the different inks can give only an approximate description of their effect. Inks that use a Boolean operator, such as AND, OR, or XOR, act in cycles of 2, 4, 8, 16, 32, 64, and 128 degrees. Their names do not suggest any such set of cycles. For example, Transparent ink uses the AND operator. This can create dramatic differences when used on two adjacent colors; for example, `128 AND 128 = 128` but `128 AND 127 = 0`. The effect is clearly illustrated in the movie InkTest.dir, which uses Transparent ink to create a checkerboard pattern from two sprites with gradient images (see Figure 3-9). You can find the movie in the Imaging\Commands\ folder on the CD-ROM that accompanies the book.

This example shows that the effect of Transparent ink is more complex than its name would suggest. The names of the inks are more like mnemonic devices than

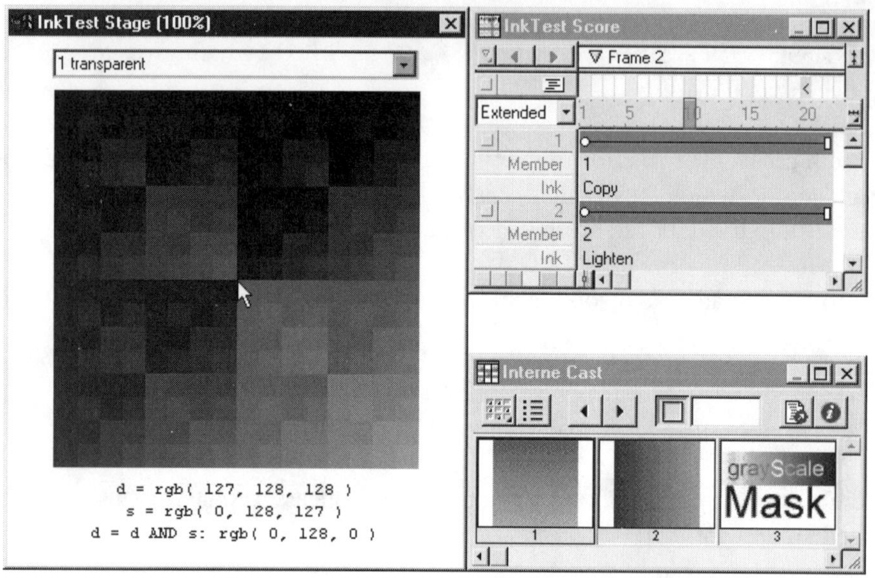

Figure 3-9 *An example of Transparent ink used in InkTest.dir*

accurate descriptions. On the other hand, the formulas are precise but cumbersome to remember. Trust the formulas.

color and bgColor

You can tint the image that you copy over by providing a `#color` property in your list of optional parameters. You also can define which color in the source image will be considered to be the background color by providing a `#bgColor` property. By default, the `#color` is black and the `#bgColor` is white. That means no colorization is added and white pixels will become transparent if you use `#backgroundTransparent` ink.

However, the situation becomes much more complicated when you start altering the values of these two parameters. The effect will depend on the ink you use. Not all inks pay any attention to the `#color` and `#bgColor` properties. The following inks do:

- Copy
- Matte
- Background Transparent

- Transparent
- Not Copy
- Not Transparent
- Darken
- Lighten

Here's how Werner Sharp explains the colorization effect for these inks:

> If the color tag is non black (its default), it will colorize all the copied over pixels. The formula for `#copy` or `#backgroundTransparent ink` colorization is
>
> ```
> dest = (s OR color) AND (NOT s OR bgColor)
> ```
>
> So it ORs in some color and subtracts out some bgColor in a way. It's certainly not tinting the color—it's more of a weird ink mode. But if you pass in equal colors for `#color` and `#bgColor`, your result will always be that exact color. In the highly useful `#backgroundTransparent` case, you can use it to isolate a single color.

To clarify, when using `#backgroundTransparent` ink, pixels of the color defined by `#bgColor` are not copied over to the destination image. The copied image becomes transparent for those pixels.

Isolating a Color

Imagine you want to replace all the pixels of a given color in an image, wherever they might be. If they were all grouped together, you could use the `floodFill()` command on any one of them; but in the case I imagine, they can be dispersed. Create a new movie and a new Bitmap member in cast slot 1. In the Paint window, create a work of art using many different colors. Use a brief burst of the Airbrush tool to spatter some bright red pixels on your work. Now try the following in the Message window:

```
sourceImage = member(1).image
iRect = sourceImage.rect
monochromeImage = image(iRect.width, iRect.height, 32) -- white
red = rgb(255, 0, 0)
options = [#ink: #backgroundTransparent, #color: red, #bgColor: red]
monochromeImage.copyPixels(sourceImage, iRect, iRect, options)
new(#bitmap).image = monochromeImage
```

In cast slot 2 you should now see a bright red rectangle. Assuming you did use `rgb(255, 0, 0)` for your bright red spatterings, there should be white holes in it where the red marks appear in the original. Using red as the `#bgColor` in the `copyPixels()` command means these pixels are not copied over into your monochrome image. Using red as the `#color` means all the other pixels are copied over as red.

Let's now use the same technique again to make a black and white mask:

```
colorMask = image(iRect.width, iRect.height, 1)
colorMask.fill(iRect, rgb(0, 0, 0)) -- fill with black
white = rgb(255, 255, 255)
options = [#ink: #backgroundTransparent, #color: white, #bgColor: white]
colorMask.copyPixels(monochromeImage, iRect, iRect, options)
new(#bitmap).image = colorMask
```

This time, the `#color` and `#bgColor` are white but the target image is black. All nonwhite pixels will be copied across as white; the white pixels (where the red was originally) will not be copied, leaving the `colorMask` black.

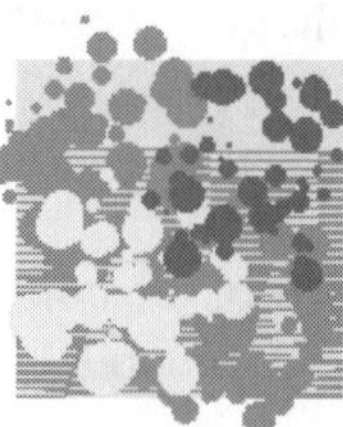 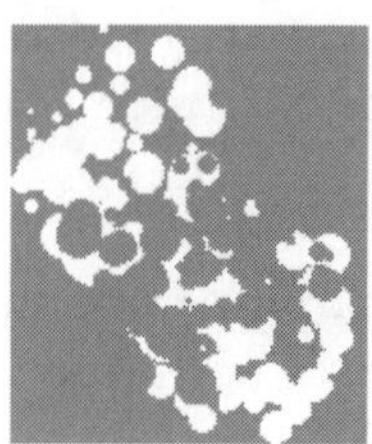 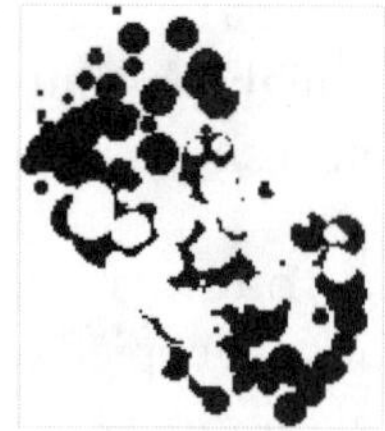 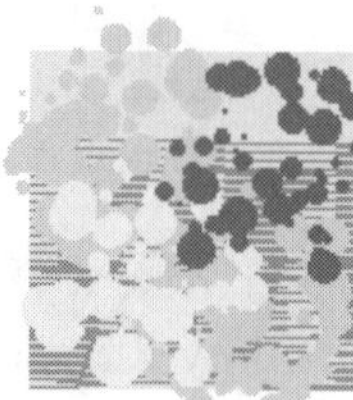

Let's now change the color of all the red pixels in the original image. To do this, create an image of the appropriate size and color, and copy it through the mask that you have just made:

```
colorImage = image(iRect.width, iRect.height, 32)
colorImage.fill(iRect, rgb(0, 0, 255)) -- blue
options = [#maskImage: colorMask]
sourceImage.copyPixels(colorImage, iRect, iRect, options)
```

We'll look at masks more closely in a moment.

Splitting an Image into Separate Color Channels

SplitRGB.dir

On a similar theme, here is a handler that will separate the red channel from the rest of the image. It creates a red rectangle the size of the original image and copies the original image onto this using `#transparent` ink. Transparent ink acts as a Boolean AND: this has the effect of setting all nonred color data to zero.

```
on getRedChannel(imageObject)
  imageRect   = imageObject.rect
  imageWidth  = imageRect.width
  imageHeight = imageRect.height

  colorLayer  = image(imageWidth, imageHeight, 32)
  options     = [#ink: #transparent] -- d = d AND s

  colorLayer.fill(imageRect, rgb(255, 0, 0))
  colorLayer.copyPixels(imageObject, imageRect, imageRect, options)
  return colorLayer
end getRedChannel
```

To test it, try this in the Message window:

```
new(#bitmap).image = getRedChannel(member(1).image)
```

You'll find a movie named SplitRGB.dir in the Imaging\Commands\ folder on the CD-ROM that accompanies the book. It contains a behavior that returns a list of three image objects, one for each color channel. If the original image is 32 bits, the list will contain a fourth image object for the alpha channel.

maskImage and maskOffset

The last optional parameters to cover are `#maskImage` and `#maskOffset`. The mask image can be any bit depth, except 16 bit. A 32-bit mask can be colored, giving a stained-glass effect. In Figure 3-10, a green source image is copied onto a white destination image using a colorful 32-bit mask. The result is a range of colors from cyan through green to yellow. Magenta pixels in the mask (in the first O, for instance) block the green source completely; the original white shows through. Other mask bit depths give a more or less limited alpha channel effect.

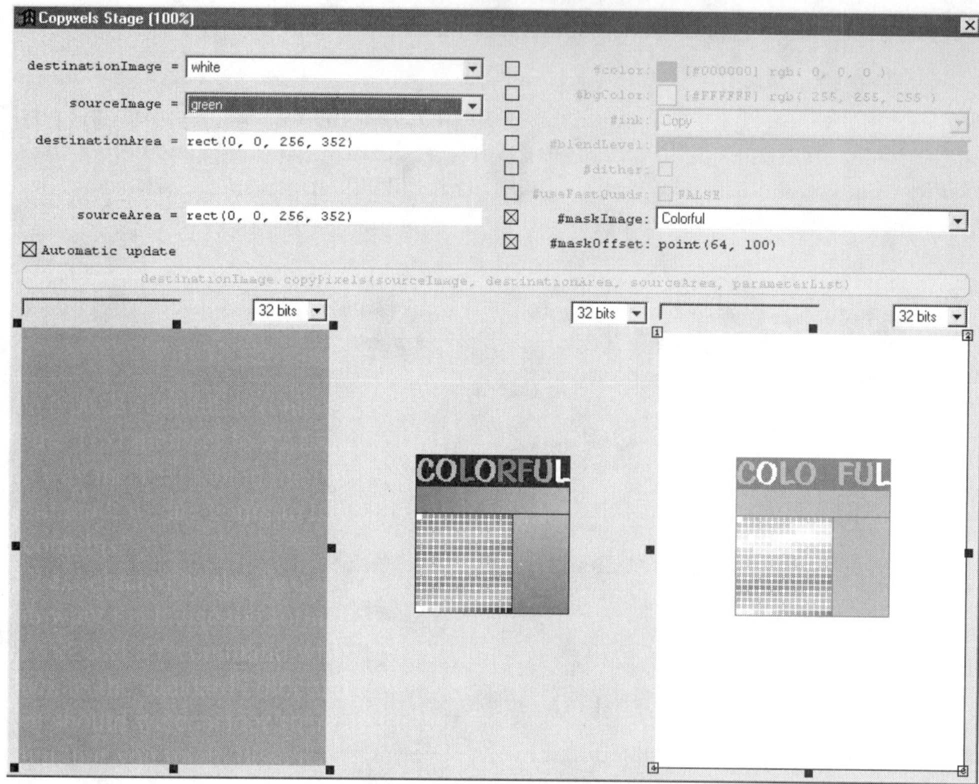

Figure 3-10 *Testing the copyPixels() command in the Copyxels.dir movie*

Without the `#maskOffset` parameter, the mask image will always be positioned with its top-left corner at the top left of the source rect. By specifying an offset for the mask, you can change its position. Varying the position over time can give a spotlight effect.

Copyxels.dir

The best way to get an idea of how the `#maskImage` and `#maskOffset` work—or indeed how any of the other parameters work—is to test using the Copyxels.dir movie. You'll find this in the Imaging\Commands\ folder. You'll find a description of its features in the following sections.

OSControls Xtra

Copyxels.dir uses the OSControls Xtra for the pop-up menus. Be sure that you have this installed. You will find a demonstration copy in the Xtras\ folder on the CD-ROM, and a projector named AddXtras.exe that can install it for you. You can download the latest version of the OSControls Xtra and purchase a license for it from http://www.peghole.com/xtras/osc_xtra/.

Exploring the Movie

You can add your own images to the Image and Mask castLibs if you wish. Your images will become available in the pop-up menus. Drag the black handles on the source and destination images to change the `rect` affected by the command. See what happens if you inverse the `rect` of the source area. Drag the numbered corners on the destination image to change the `quad`. Double-clicking the image will toggle between the last `quad` and the last `rect` that you set. Double-click any of the numbered corners to rotate the `quad`. Click the selected area and drag it to move it around.

A semitransparent vector shape lies over the areas of the source and destination image, which are outside the `rect` or `quad` affected by the `copyPixels()` command. You can modify the transparency by dragging the thermometer bars just above each image. You also can change the bit depth of each image, including the mask image, through the pop-up menus.

The parameters on the left are essential. Those on the right are added to the options list only if their check box is selected. Unused options are grayed out. By default, the `copyPixels()` command is executed once per frame, so that any changes you make to the parameters are immediately visible. Because this means refreshing a Bitmap member once per frame, it slows the movie down considerably. You can deselect the Automatic Update button and use the copyPixels(…) button instead if you wish. Notice how the frame rate improves when you do this.

While the `copyPixels()` command is in itself fast, you should try to control the rate at which onscreen and offscreen Bitmap members are modified. Poor control at this level can give rise to a sluggish user experience. You might like to read the comments at the beginning of the `paintStroke()` handler of the Canvas behavior in Director's Paintbox Library Palette. This describes a clever technique for providing immediate feedback to the user while limiting the operations on Bitmap members. In a word: The Bitmap member itself is updated only once at the end of a sequence of intermediate changes; the intermediate changes themselves are written directly to `(the stage).image`, where the user can see them immediately.

Conclusion

Now that you have read this chapter, you should have a clearer understanding of the power and precision of the five pixel manipulation commands. In particular, you should

- Beware the inefficiency of the `setPixel()` command for large images.
- Know that the draw line routine is treated differently on different platforms.
- Be able to create filled and unfilled shapes in a variety of ways.
- Be able to exploit the full range of possibilities of the `copyPixels()` command, including the use of quads, ink effects, masks, and color selection procedures.

You should be ready to explore the Paintbox and Animation | Transition behaviors in the built-in Library Palette. As you develop your own stunning visuals using Imaging Lingo, remember that you have Werner Sharp to thank for making it all possible; I am indebted to him for his patient explanations of all the concepts presented here.

CHAPTER

4

Using Images of Other Member Types

IN THIS CHAPTER:

Kennings are distinguished by three kinds of usage… It is a kenning to call battle "spear-clash," and it is a double kenning to call a sword "fire of the spear-clash," and it is extended if there are more elements.

—Snorri Sturluson, "Edda" (translated by Anthony Faulkes)

Until now in this part, we've been working with bitmap images. Bitmaps are not the only member type that has an `image` property: Text, Vector Shapes, Flash, and 3D members all have one, too. Custom member types might have an `image` property, too; Xtras written for Director 8.5 also can provide an `image` property for any members they create.

You can't set the `image` property of any members other than bitmap, but you can use it in a number of ways. The four standard member types store data in a coded form; the Director Player has to generate the actual image that is displayed on the screen on-the-fly. (Actually, text members can store the bitmap image, but the default does not. We will ignore this feature for the purposes of this discussion.)

The coding means the size of the member in bytes is much less than the size of the image it represents. This is important when you want to reduce the amount of data transmitted over the Internet.

Text Members

For Western alphabets, each character of raw text takes up one byte, or 8 bits. Other information needs to be provided to format the text: information on the type face, the font size, the style (**bold**, <u>underline</u>, *italic*, and so forth), alignment, color of the text, and so on. The less formatting there is, the less extra information needs to be provided. When the Director Player needs to display text, it sends this information to the system (MacOs or Windows), which then provides the image data that the Director Player puts up on the screen.

You can access this image data through Lingo by using a command such as this:

```
textImage = member("Text").image
```

Text member sprites are, by default, opaque; the image of a Text member is transparent. Create a text member called "Text", type something into it, and then try the following from the Message window:

```
bitmapText = new(#bitmap)
bitmapText.image = member("Text").image
```

Now drag the text member and the new bitmap member onto the stage. Set the stage color to something other than white; you will see that the bitmap version of the text is transparent. Open the bitmap version in the Paint window—you might be surprised at how it looks (Figure 4-1). Remember, the Paint window shows no alpha channel information; it contains only the rgb colors. Try the following line in the Message window, and then open the bitmap member that it creates. This will give you the image of the text itself (this might be in anti-aliased shades of gray).

```
new(#bitmap).image = bitmapText.extractAlpha()
```

To create an opaque image, you first need to create an empty image the same size as the text member and copy the text image onto this. The background of the empty image will be white by default; you can modify this background color by using the `fill()` command. The following lines will create an opaque bitmap image of the member "Text" with a pale yellow background:

```
textRect = member("Text").rect
textImage = image(textRect.width, textRect.height, 32)
textImage.fill(textRect, rgb(255, 255, 160))
textImage.copyPixels(member("Text").image, textRect , textRect )
new(#bitmap).image = textImage
```

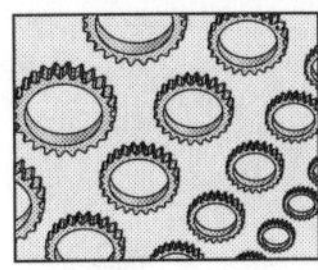

NOTE

The `image` of a Text member corresponds to that part of the Text member that would appear in a sprite on the Stage. If the `#boxType` of the member is set to `#fixed` or `#scroll`, the `scrollTop` and the `pageHeight` of the Text member will determine which part of the text appears in the Text member's `image` property. No scrollbars will be included in the image.

Creating the Missing drawText() Command

Conspicuous in its absence from the previous chapter is a `drawText()` command. In the Paint window, you can choose a Text tool and type text into your Bitmap members. To do this through Lingo, you have to create the text image separately using a Text member; then copy the image over to your target image object. There is a tool in the DrawFill.dir movie that acts like a Text tool. You'll see how it works later in this section.

Because Imaging Lingo doesn't provide it, let's create our own command to draw text into an image object. First, let's analyze what the command is going to do. The Text tool in the Paint window does not softwrap text. Unless you explicitly enter a `RETURN` character, the text will continue to extend to the right with each character

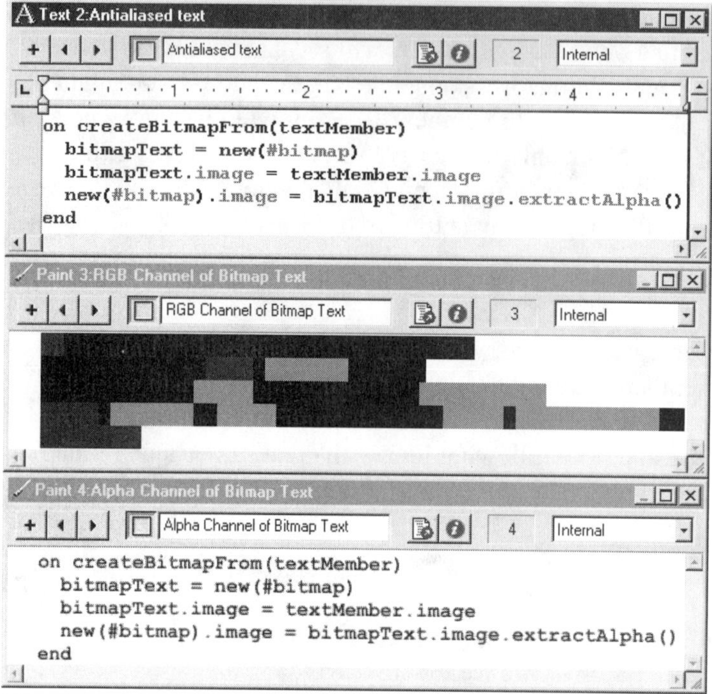

Figure 4-1 *A Text member and its transparent image (rgb and alpha channels)*

you type. By default, text members do softwrap text. If you set the `wordWrap` property of the Text member to `FALSE`, the end of a long line might not be visible. This is not the way the Text tool in the Paint window works either. To create our `drawText()` command, we are going to have to stretch a Text member horizontally to fit the text it contains.

Text created by the Text tool is uniform in color, size, font, and font style. If you want to change the format, you have to use the Text tool a second time. Our `drawText()` command will work the same way. It seems reasonable to define black as the standard color and plain as the standard fontStyle, but what size and font should we consider standard? In the DrawFill.dir movie, I choose Arial 12 point, but you might disagree; please feel free to modify the default settings.

What syntax should the command use? The ideal would be to imitate the `draw()` and `fill()` commands. This means that, if a future version of Director were to provide a native `drawText()` command, adapting your movies to exploit that new native method should be a simple matter. The following syntax is what I imagine a native `drawText()` command might use.

```
options = [:]
options[#font]       = "Times New Roman"
options[#fontSize]   = 18
options[#color]      = rgb(128, 0, 0)
options[#fontStyle]  = [#italic, #bold]
options[#alignment]  = #right
topLeft              = point(10, 30)
textToDraw           = "This text was drawn using"&RETURN&"the drawText() command"

imageObject.drawText(topLeft, textToDraw, options)
```

In practice, the syntax has to be slightly different: Because we have no means of changing the methods of an image object, we will have to use a more procedural approach. While we're at it, it might be worthwhile to make this a function, so it returns `TRUE` if the method succeeds:

```
put drawText(imageObject, topLeft, textToDraw, options)
-- 1
```

Here is a simplified version of the handler you can find in the DrawFill.dir movie. It assumes `optionsList` contains all the necessary properties and that all the values are of the correct ilk. The full version makes no such assumptions, and offers the option of setting an antiAlias property for the text.

```
on drawText(imageObject, topLeft, textToDraw, optionsList)
  -- Create a temporary text member
  tempMember           = new(#text)
  tempMember.font      = optionsList[#font]
  tempMember.fontSize  = optionsList[#fontSize]
  tempMember.fontStyle = optionsList[#fontStyle]
  tempMember.color     = optionsList[#color]

  -- Apply the text
  tempMember.text = textToDraw

  -- Determine the minimum width of the text member
  tempMember.wordWrap  = FALSE
  tempMember.alignment = #left
  maxWidth  = 0
  charCount = 0
  counter   = textToDraw.line.count
```

```
  repeat with i = 1 to counter
    charCount = charCount + textToDraw.line[i].char.count + 1
    lineWidth = tempMember.charPosToLoc(charCount).locH
    if maxWidth < lineWidth then
      maxWidth = lineWidth
    end if
  end repeat

  -- Modify the width of the member
  tempMember.width = maxWidth


  copyRect          = tempMember.rect
  boundingRect      = copyRect.offset(topLeft.locH, topLeft.locV)

  -- Copy its image into the target image object
  tempMember.alignment = optionsList[#alignment]
  imageObject.copyPixels(tempMember.image, boundingRect, copyRect)
  tempMember.erase()

  -- Return TRUE if at least part of the text was drawn
  return boundingRect.intersect(imageObject.rect) <> rect(0, 0, 0, 0)
end drawText
```

Printing Distorted Text

PrinText.dir

As far as I am aware, none of the third-party Print xtras you can buy for Director has a feature for printing rotated or quadded text members. For example, if you want to print the word "Specimen" diagonally across a page, you have two choices:

- Place a rotated Text member on the Stage and print the Stage. This will give you a pixelated image, printed at the same resolution as the screen (72 dots per inch).
- Create an image object of the page and copy a rotated version of your text onto it. You could make the dimensions of the page image five times those of the Stage, and then print at a fifth of the size. This would give you an effective 360 dots per inch, which is excellent quality for print.

While this second solution gives high-quality printing, it is an exceptionally memory-hungry process. If you are printing a 800 × 600–pixel screen full color and full size, you will need to create an image object that uses 800 × 600 × 4 × 25 bytes (45,8 Mb) for each page. You can reduce this to under 12 Mb per page by using an 8-bit grayscale or color palette for the image; but even so, many end users will not have that amount of free memory on their machines. Although you can check the freeBlock to see whether sufficient memory is available, it is best to reserve this sort of feature for kiosks and other situations where you can determine the memory specifications of the machine.

Alternatively, you could simply double the size of the image and then print at half size, which probably would be quite adequate for most uses.

In the Imaging\Members\ folder on the CD-ROM that accompanies the book, you will find a movie entitled PrinText.dir, which demonstrates the technique. It prints the word "Specimen" at an angle across an IOU note. The entire size of the movie, including all the text member data, is no more than 29 Kb. The screen buffer required to display the text is 300 Kb; the temporary bitmap member used to print the text at 360 dots per inch is more than 7 Mb. This gives you an idea of how effective the coding of text is.

When you print from many software programs, you don't have to prepare the data dot by printed dot in advance. Text often is sent to the printer in its coded form: one byte per character (for Western Languages). The printer knows (or knows how to ask) how each character should be represented. This information is stored in the form similar to that used by Vector Shapes: a set of formulas that creates the outline curves. The formulas are size independent; the same formula works for a small 9-point character as for a 255-point character. As it prints one line, the printer can thus work out for itself what dots it will need to use for the characters in the next line.

Director was not initially intended to be used for creating printed documents, and its native `printFrom()` command is far from powerful. It is not surprising that, even with third-party xtras, memory-expensive workarounds need to be found for any print job that is out of the ordinary.

Calculating the Quad

Here's an edited extract of the code that calculates the `quad` the `copyPixels()` command will use to rotate the text. (See the beginning of the "`copyPixels()`" section in Chapter 3 for more details on quads.) Figure 4-2 illustrates what the variables `a`, `b`, `c`, and `d` represent.

```
specimenSprite = sprite(2) -- sprite containing rotated "Specimen" text

angle   = specimenSprite.rotation -- angle in degrees
radians = angle * pi / 180        -- trig functions require radians

a = specimenSprite.height * sin(radians)
```

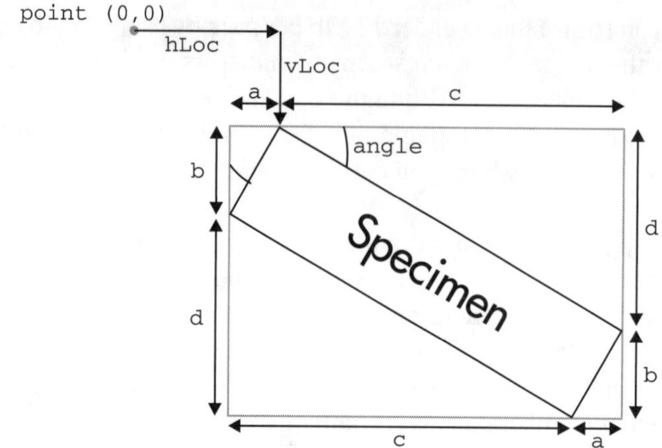

Figure 4-2 *Dimensions used to calculate the quad for the rotated text*

```
  b = specimenSprite.height * cos(radians)
  c = specimenSprite.width  * cos(radians)
  d = specimenSprite.width  * sin(radians)

  hLoc = specimenSprite.locH
  vLoc = specimenSprite.locV

  rotatedQuad = [ \
point(hLoc         , vLoc         ), \
point(hLoc     + c, vLoc      + d), \
point(hLoc - a + c, vLoc + b + d), \
point(hLoc - a    , vLoc + b     ) \
]
```

Vector Shapes

As with Text members, the `image` property of Vector Shapes is transparent. Unlike Text members, the color in the rgb channel of a Vector Shape's image is limited to the interior of the shape. The alpha channel data refines this shape at the edges, allowing the edges to be anti-aliased against any background. Figure 4-3 shows the image created from a standard Vector Shape circle, plus a close-up of the rgb channel, the alpha channel, and the anti-aliased image that results. Note that the anti-aliasing between the stroke color and the fill color is dealt with in the rgb layer itself because it does not need to be recalculated on-the-fly.

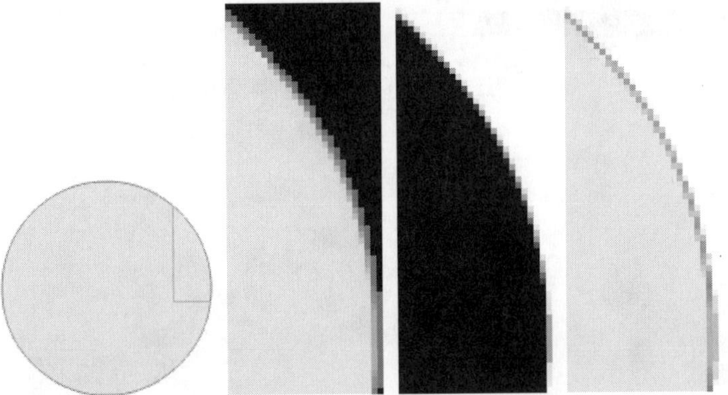

Figure 4-3 *Close-up of the rgb channel, alpha channel, and the resulting anti-aliasing*

Vector Shapes can be useful in Imaging Lingo in two ways: they can define irregular shapes and they can define gradients between two colors. We'll create a puzzle and a barber shop pole to demonstrate these.

Exploiting the Shape of a Vector Shape Member

Puzzle.dir

In the Imaging\Members\ folder on the CD-ROM that accompanies the book, you will find a movie entitled Puzzle.dir. This creates a set of interlocking puzzle pieces, each with a unique shape, out of any bitmap member. Each shape is defined by manipulating the `vertexList` of a temporary Vector Shape member and then applying the alpha channel of the Vector Shape's image to a bitmap member that is created specially for that particular puzzle piece.

Vector Shapes use Bézier curves to create smooth edges. As you alter the length and inclination of the handles of a vertex point, you also alter the curve. The Puzzle Piece parent script in the Puzzle.dir movie places a vertex point with no handles at each corner of a square, and then defines the interlocking shape for each edge of the square using three vertex points that do have handles. By altering the four variables over a limited range, you can create thousands of different interlocking shapes (see Figure 4-4).

Creating the Puzzle Pieces

The shape of the puzzle pieces is defined in the `createPuzzlePieces()` handler. This works in five steps, starting at the top-left corner of the shape. Shapes are created starting at the top-left corner of the puzzle, working along each row from left to right.

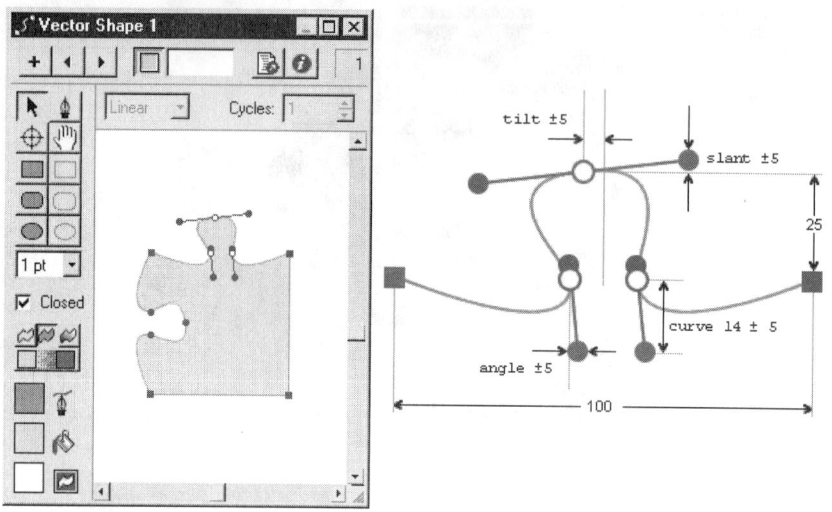

Figure 4-4 *Creating a range of puzzle shapes by modifying four variables*

Only two new edges are created for each piece: the bottom edge and the right edge. Formulas for each original edge are provided by the `randomEdge()` function. A list called `topsList` is used to remember the shape used for the bottom of each piece; this will be used again to create the top of the piece in the same column in the row below. The formula for the shape of the right edge of each piece is saved in a variable called `edge` so that it can be reused for the left edge of the next piece in the same row. The process is shown in Figure 4-5.

The sixth step shown in Figure 4-5 is carried out in the `createPuzzleBitmap()` handler. This will be explained shortly.

Manipulating the Vector Shape's vertexList

The `createPuzzlePieces()` handler is fairly long: it repeats the same steps with slight variations for each of the four edges. Following is the code that deals with the right edge of the puzzle shape (step 4 in Figure 4-5). Points in the Vector Shape are calculated from the center. Each piece starts a virtual square with a side of 100 pixels. The bottom-right corner will thus be at `point(50, 50)`, and the top-right corner at `point(50, -50)`. The tip of the lug that will fit into the next piece will be halfway between these two points, and somewhat to the right: `point (75, 0)`. The bulk of the following extract is concerned with placing the vertex points and handles for the two points either side of the "neck" of the lug, and for the point at its tip.

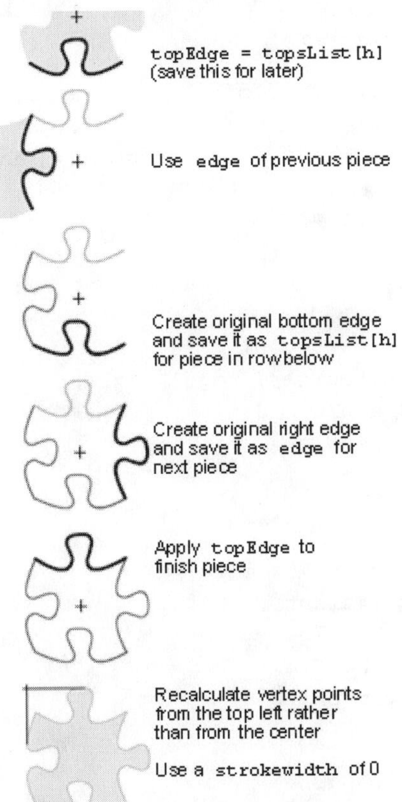

Figure 4-5 *Ensuring that each piece matches its neighbor*

Each vertex point is described in a list such as this:

```
[#vertex: point(50, 8), #handle1: point(4.0, 0.8), #handle2: point(-18.0, -3.6)]
```

The value of the `#vertex` property defines the position of the vertex point in relation to the center of the square. The values of the `#handle1` and `#handle2` properties are relative to the vertex point. In the preceding example, handle1 is to the right and slightly below the vertex point; handle2 is to the left and slightly above it. The second handle ensures that the curve is smooth at the vertex point. The points are placed in a counterclockwise order, starting (for the right edge) at the bottom right.

```
...
bezierList.append([#vertex: point(50, 50)])
```

```
if h = pHCount then
  -- The piece is at the edge of the puzzle, right edge is flat
else
  -- Create a unique curve for the right edge and remember it
  edge = randomEdge()
  -- Example: [#tilt: 0, #slant: -4, #angle: 2, #curve: 19]

  -- Calculate the vertexList for the right edge: first cheek
  cheek  = [:]
  cheek[#vertex] = point(50, 8)
  handle = point(edge[#curve], edge[#angle])
  cheek[#handle1] = handle / 5.0
  cheek[#handle2] = -handle
  bezierList.append(cheek)
  -- Midpoint
  vertex = [:]
  vertex[#vertex] = point(75, edge[#tilt])
  handle = point(edge[#slant], -25)
  vertex[#handle1] = handle
  vertex[#handle2] = -handle
  bezierList.append(vertex)
  -- Second cheek
  cheek = [:]
  cheek[#vertex] = point(50, -8)
  handle = point(edge[#curve], edge[#angle])
  cheek[#handle1] = -handle
  cheek[#handle2] = handle / 5.0
  bezierList.append(cheek)
end if
bezierList.append([#vertex: point(50, -50)])
...
```

Modifying the originMode

The `createPuzzlePieces()` handler builds the shape of a piece by adding lugs and hollows to a square. Positions are calculated with respect to the center of the square. However, once the lugs and hollows have been added, the center of the square is no longer necessarily at the center of the piece. How can you determine an absolute point on such an irregular shape? How do the curves created by the Bézier handles modify the bounding rectangle for the shape as a whole?

The answer is that Director can tell you, if you know how to ask. Vector Shapes have dozens of properties, all of which can prove useful, although some are not evident. Try this in the Message window:

```
showProps(new(#vectorShape))
```

You'll see a long list of properties and their default values, including this one:

```
originMode:           #center
```

(The same showProps command also works with any Flash or Shockwave 3D member).

If you check in the List View of the Property Inspector, you will see that `originMode` can take one of three values: `#center`, `#topLeft`, or `#point`.

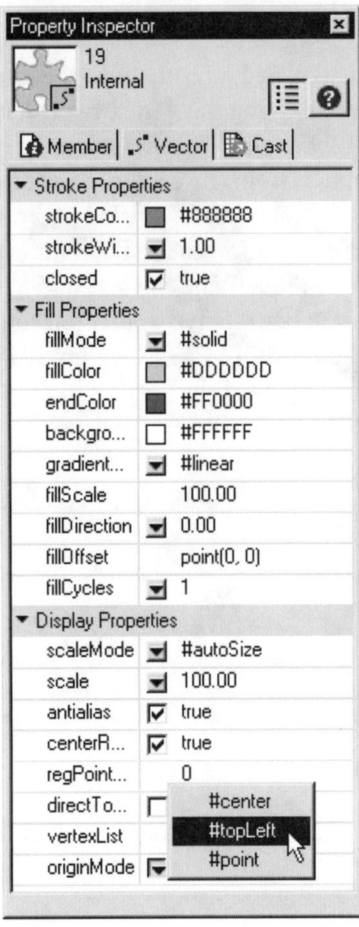

The `createPuzzleBitmap()` handler starts with the following lines (some lines have been removed for clarity):

```
property pVectorMember -- temporary Vector Shape member
property pPieceSize    -- size in pixels of the standard square shape

on createPuzzleBitmap(bezierList, h, v)
  -- Adjust the size and shape of the Vector Shape member
  pVectorMember.originMode = #center
  -- ...
  -- Determine offset of first vertex = regpoint of new bitmap
  pVectorMember.originMode = #topLeft
  adjustPoint = pVectorMember.vertexList[1][#vertex]
  -- More code
end createPuzzleBitmap
```

The first instruction resets the `originMode` of the temporary Vector Shape member to `#center` before applying the vertex list calculated for this piece by the `createPuzzlePieces()` handler. This corresponds with the fact that the points in the vertex list were calculated from the center of the square that the puzzle piece is based on. The second instruction sets the `originMode` of the temporary Vector Shape member to `#topLeft`. This forces the Director Player to calculate how much the curved lines bulge to the left and the top, and to reposition the vertex points in the Vector Shape member relative to that top-leftmost point.

A simplified version of the resulting `vertexList` for the Vector Shape in Figure 4-4 is shown here; the values of the various variables for the curve on the edge are as follows:

```
#curve:  20
#angle:  -4
#tilt:    0
#slant:  -5
[ \
[#vertex: point(11, 27)], \
[#vertex: point(11, 69), #handle1: point(4, -1), #handle2: point(-20, 4)], \
[#vertex: point(36, 77), #handle1: point(5, 25), #handle2: point(5, -25)], \
[#vertex: point(11, 85), #handle1: point(-20, 4), #handle2: point(4, -1)], \
[#vertex: point(11, 127)] \
]
```

Switching the `originMode` for the Vector Shape member to `#topLeft` moves the first vertex from `point(-50, -50)` relative to the center to `point(11, 27)` relative to the top-left point.

The position of the top-left vertex point relative to the top left of the member itself will be different for each puzzle shape. Knowing this value makes it much easier to align adjacent puzzle pieces. In my example, the `regPoint` of the resulting bitmap is set to the point corresponding to the first vertex; the variable `adjustPoint` holds this value.

Converting a Vector Shape to a Bitmap Member

Following is a simplified version of the handler that creates a Bitmap member with the shape defined by the `vectorMember`'s `vertexList` and the appropriate part of the source image. The `rect` of the `image` of `vectorMember` determines the dimensions of the area that will be copied. The position of the first vertex point is determined by `h` and `v`, the row and column of the piece. The precise area of the image to be copied, `puzzleRect`, is determined by offsetting the `rect` of `vectorMember` by the appropriate number of rows and columns, minus the position of its first vertex point.

```
on createPuzzleBitmap(bezierList, h, v, sourceImage) -----------------
  -- <bezierList>  is the list of vertex points for the shape
  -- <h and v>     integers indicating the column and row of the piece
  -- <sourceImage> image object containing image of the whole puzzle
  --
  -- This handler assumes that the distance between each corner of the
  -- puzzle piece is 100 pixels, and that the dimensions of vertexList
  -- already take this into account.
  ---------------------------------------------------------------------

    -- Create a temporary Vector Shape member
  vectorMember = new(#vectorShape)
  vectorMember.strokeWidth = 0

  vectorMember.closed      = TRUE
  vectorMember.fillMode    = #solid
  vectorMember.originMode  = #center

  -- Create the shape defined by bezierList
  vectorMember.vertexList = bezierList

  -- Determine offset of first vertex = regpoint of new bitmap
  vectorMember.originMode = #topLeft
  adjustPoint = vectorMember.vertexList[1][#vertex]
  adjustH     = -adjustPoint.locH
  adjustV     = -adjustPoint.locV

  -- Determine which part of source image appears on the piece
  rectOffset = (([h, v, h, v] - 1) * 100)-- 100 = size between corners
  puzzleRect = vectorMember.rect + rectOffset
  puzzleRect = puzzleRect.offset(adjustH, adjustV) -- force to integer

  -- Extract grayScale alpha image of shape of piece
  alphaImage = vectorMember.image.extractAlpha()

  -- The temporary Vector Shape member is no longer needed
  vectorMember.erase()

  -- Create 32-bit image of piece using alpha channel for shape
  puzzleImage = image(puzzleRect.width, puzzleRect.height, 32)
  puzzleImage.copyPixels(sourceImage, puzzleImage.rect, puzzleRect)
  puzzleImage.setAlpha(alphaImage)

  -- Create a bitmap member to store the piece
  puzzleMember          = new(#bitmap)
  puzzleMember.image    = puzzleImage
  puzzleMember.useAlpha = TRUE
```

```
  puzzleMember.regPoint = adjustPoint
  --puzzleMember.regPoint = puzzleMember.regPoint - ([h, v] - 1) * 100

  return puzzleMember
end createPuzzleBitmap
```

Using the Registration Point to Check for Matches

This handler sets the `regPoint` of the resulting member to match the first vertex point of the Vector Shape member. If you uncomment the second to last instruction, the `regPoint` of each Bitmap member will coincide with the same `loc` on the stage. You'll be able to select all the members created by the Puzzle Piece parent script in the Cast window, and drag them directly into the Score or onto the Stage; each piece will automatically be in its correct place.

When you work on the game play of the puzzle, you need only to check whether the puzzle piece that the user is moving has the same `loc` as the piece it is being connected to (within close limits); if so, the pieces should lock together.

Adding a 3D Light Effect

Your puzzle pieces would look better with a highlight on the top and left edges, and a shadow on the bottom and right edges. To do this, you would modify the `#strokeWidth`, `#strokeColor`, `#fillMode`, and `#closed` properties of your template Vector Shape member, to give you a single-pixel border line for the puzzle piece. You then would remove the vertex points that you don't require for the effect and create an image object of that. A `#strokeColor` of white for the highlight and black for the shadow, applied with a `#blendLevel` of 128 (50%) will produce a convincing 3D effect.

Simple code for creating the light effect images is given in the `on getShading()` handler in the Puzzle Pieces parent script in the Puzzle.dir movie. The effect is applied to the puzzle piece image near the end of the `on createPuzzleBitmap()` handler. In this demonstration, the top and left edges are lightened, and the bottom and right edges are darkened.

You can improve this in two ways:

- The outline shading is currently one pixel too high and too wide. This is because altering the `#strokeWidth` alters the dimensions of the Vector Shape member. You could add lines to the `on getShading()` handler, which moves the bottom vertex points up and the right-hand vertex points to the left.
- Shading is not realistic; for instance, the right-hand side of the lugs on the top edge is lightened, but, in fact, it should be in shadow. You could modify the

code in the on `getShading()` handler so that it creates a number of separate curves for the highlighting and a different set of curves for the shadows, so that light and shadow are applied in all the appropriate places.

The following section shows you how to provide more subtle 3D effects.

Using Vector Shapes to Add Gradients to Images

Barber.dir

You can use gradients to give an impression of relief to an image. Here's a handler that creates a Bitmap member in the shape of a barber shop pole. You could use such an image as a progress bar:

```
on createBarberPole()
  -- Set parameters
  stripeColor = rgb( 255, 0, 0 ) -- bright red
  shadowColor = rgb(  34, 0, 0 ) -- very dark red
  shadowBlend = 160 -- maximum 255

  -- Create an 256 x 16 pixel image object with diagonal stripes
  barberPole = image(256, 16, 32)
  parameters = [#color: stripeColor, #lineSize: 12]
  -- Use #lineSize: 8 on Macintosh.  See Chapter 3 for details.
  i = -16
  repeat while i < 256
    barberPole.draw(i, -9, i + 32, 23, parameters)
    i = i + 32
  end repeat

  -- Create a temporary Vector Shape member for the shading
  vectorMember               = new(#vectorShape)
  vectorMember.vertexList = [ \
[#vertex: point(0, 0)], \
[#vertex: point(256, 0)], \
[#vertex: point(256, 16)], \
[#vertex: point(0, 16)] \
]
  vectorMember.closed        = TRUE
  vectorMember.strokeWidth   = 0
  vectorMember.fillMode      = #gradient
  vectorMember.gradientType  = #linear
  vectorMember.fillColor     = shadowColor
  vectorMember.endColor      = rgb (255, 255, 255 ) -- white
```

```
  vectorMember.fillDirection = 90
  vectorMember.fillOffset    = point(0, -2)
  vectorMember.fillCycles    = 2

  -- Ensure that the white border at the top left of the Vector Shape
  -- is not included in the image extracted from it
  vectorImageRect = rect(1, 1, 257, 17)

  -- Add shading to the barberPole image
  barberPole.copyPixels( \
vectorMember.image, \
barberPole.rect, \
vectorImageRect, \
[#blendLevel: shadowBlend] \
)
  -- Destroy the Vector Shape member and create a Bitmap in its place
  vectorMember.erase()
  barberPoleMember = new(#bitmap)
  barberPoleMember.image = barberPole

  return barberPoleMember
end createBarberPole
```

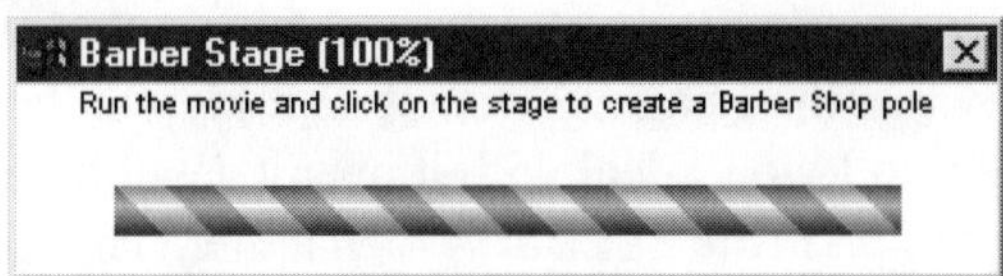

You can find a working example in the Barber.dir movie in the Imaging\Members\ folder on the CD-ROM that accompanies this book.

Border Changes in Director 8.5

In Director 7.0.2 and Director 8.0, Vector Shape members always have a single-pixel white border at the left and top, but not at the right or bottom. This was corrected for Vector Shapes created using Lingo in Director 8.5. Vector Shapes created in previous versions will continue to display the single-pixel border.

If you are using Vector Shape members from earlier versions of Director, it is important to take this border into consideration. A rectangular Vector Shape member with a `vertexList` of `[[#vertex: point(0, 0)], [#vertex: point(shapeWidth, 0)], [#vertex: point(shapeWidth,` shapeHeight)], [#vertex: point(0, shapeHeight)]] will have a rect of rect(0, 0, shapeWidth + 1, shapeHeight + 1). The image part of the Vector Shape appears in the area rect(1, 1, shapeWidth + 1, shapeHeight + 1). The regPoint of a Bitmap member created from the untrimmed image of a Vector Shape member might appear one pixel too high and to the left. The Barber.dir movie provides for both cases (see the vectorRect variable). Rather than cluttering your own code with such tests, you might find it easier to re-create your old Vector Shape members in Director 8.5. The following handler can help do this automatically in some cases (test on a copy of the member):

```
on trimBorder(vectorMember)
  vectorMember.defaultRect  = vectorMember.defaultRect - [0, 0, 1, 1]
  vectorMember.vertexList   = vectorMember.vertexList - 1
end
```

Page Layout

PageTurn.dir

You'll find a much more complex example of using Vector Shapes to create shading in the PageTurn.dir movie in the Imaging\Members\ folder on the CD-ROM. The code is fully commented, so I won't deal with it in any detail here. The Vector Shape manipulations occur in the getShadeImage() handler. This creates an image with two gradients: one to represent the way the page rises up at the center of the book and then curves down to the outside edge, and one to give the impression that the top corner of the page has a slight curl.

Rather than blending the gradient image with the main image (as I do for the barber pole) I use `#subtractPin` ink instead. This has the advantage of not dulling the main image, but it means the color of the shading image must be the opposite of the page color I wish to create. See the "Inks" section of Chapter 3 for more details.

This example shows another advantage of creating bitmap images out of Vector Shape members. Vector Shapes can have only one gradient; on the Stage they react to only copy, blend, or (background) transparent inks. Image objects created from Vector Shapes can be combined in ways the Vector Shapes themselves cannot.

Customizing the Pages

Figure 5-2 (in Chapter 5) shows the Behavior Parameters dialog box for the Page Turn behavior. You can set the page width and height, and the thickness of the border between the pictures or text and the edge of the page.

You also can change the page color: light colors are best. The color you choose will be inverted in the `on invertColor()` handler; the inverted color will be used with `#subtractPin` ink to create the curved effect on the pages. Subtracting a dark color has less effect than subtracting a light color, because the individual `red`, `green`, and `blue` values are smaller in a dark color.

The most interesting values as far as Vector Shapes and Imaging Lingo are concerned are the Shading and the Curvature parameters. Both these parameters have an effect on the `on getShadeImage()` handler.

The `#shading` parameter determines how dark the shadow on the page will be; thus, it determines whether the pages appear almost flat or very curved. It determines the contrast between the `fillColor` and `endColor` for the Vector Shapes.

The `#curvature` parameter determines how near the spine the pages begin to curve. In a thin book or magazine, the pages will curve evenly from the center to the edge. In a thick book, the pages will rise more vertically from the spine: The highest point of the page will be fairly near the spine, and the rest of the page will slope more gently. The value of the `#curvature` parameter affects the value of the `fillScale` property of the Vector Shapes. If this is 100, the gradient will be even from one side of the Vector Shape to the other (thin pages). If this is 50, half the page will be a flat color and the gradient will occur over the other half of the page.

Flash Members

Like Vector Shape members, Flash uses Bézier curves to define the shape of its elements. By definition, a Flash movie is a dynamic sequence of frames; an image object is one fixed view. When you ask Director for the `image` of a Flash member, what should it return? By default, it will return the first frame in the movie. To be precise, it will return the frame defined by the `posterFrame` property of the Flash member, and the `posterFrame` property for a Flash member is set to 1 by default.

Here's a handler that will convert a linear Flash movie into a series of bitmap images:

```
on flashToBitmap(flashMember)
  bitmapList = []

  savePosterFrame = flashMember.posterFrame

  frameCount = flashMember.frameCount
  repeat with i = 1 to frameCount
    flashMember.posterFrame = i
    flashBitmap = new(#bitmap)
    flashBitmap.image = flashMember.image
    bitmapList.append(flashBitmap)
  end repeat

  flashMember.posterFrame = savePosterFrame

  return bitmapList
end flashToBitmap
```

Changing the value of the `posterFrame` property changes the cast member's thumbnail image. This might take a moment when you are working in Director's authoring environment with the Cast window, the Property Inspector, or the Sprite toolbar on the Score window visible, because the entire thumbnail displays need to refresh.

Optimizing Both Bandwidth Use and Performance

But why would you want to do this? One reason is that a Flash member provides a very compact description of the images it represents, but displaying that image on screen requires a great deal of processor activity. In addition, each Flash sprite that you place on the stage requires a separate instance of the FlashAsset xtra, and this uses up precious RAM space. Flash members are small and bandwidth friendly, but exaggerated use of them can bring a computer to its knees.

If you are working on a Shockwave movie, you can optimize download times without sacrificing speed by storing your images as Flash members and expanding them to Bitmap members once the movie is loaded on the end user's machine. The down side is that this will create temporary Bitmap members that will remain in the end user's RAM until they are erased or the playback head jumps to a different movie. You would need to take handle memory usage with care.

Images from an Interactive Flash Movie

WhoAmI.dir

A Flash sprite is not only dynamic—it is interactive. You can manipulate it through Lingo so that it displays a custom arrangement of elements that do not correspond to any existing frame. The only way to obtain the image of such a custom arrangement is to place the Flash member in an on-stage sprite, capture the image of the Stage, and then crop this image to the `rect` of the sprite. Any part of the Flash sprite that does not appear on the Stage will not appear in the resulting image, and any other sprite that covers the Flash sprite will be added to the resulting image.

In the WhoAmI.dir movie, I have done something similar, which you will find in the Imaging\Members\ folder on the CD-ROM that accompanies this book. This uses a single Flash movie with a number of movable MovieClips to create a whole series of identikit faces. (Identikit photographs are used by the police to identify suspects.) Thirteen different faces need to be displayed simultaneously. The prototype version of the same movie (WhoAmI0.dir) uses 13 Flash members, which slows the Director movie down radically when the playback head jumps to a frame where the Flash sprites are displayed. The more polished version shows each Flash member only once, and then takes a bitmap snapshot of it that is used subsequently. This leads to a very slight increase in the time it takes for each face to be displayed the first time, and a dramatic increase in speed on subsequent occasions.

Here's the handler in the Flash Control behavior that takes the snapshot:

```
on createBitmap(me) ----------------------------------------------------
  -- Called once only by exitFrame() the first time this behavior is
  -- instanciated
  --
  -- ACTION: Sets the position of the Flash sprite's Movie Clips, then
  -- converts the resulting image to a bitmap for more rapid display.
  ----------------------------------------------------------------------

  mySprite.setFlashProperty("headGear", #posX, headGear * 100)
  mySprite.setFlashProperty("hair",     #posX, hair     * 100)
  mySprite.setFlashProperty("eyebrows", #posX, eyebrows * 100)
  mySprite.setFlashProperty("eyes",     #posX, eyes     * 100)
  mySprite.setFlashProperty("nose",     #posX, nose     * 100)
  mySprite.setFlashProperty("mouth",    #posX, mouth    * 100)
  mySprite.setFlashProperty("beard",    #posX, beard    * 100)
```

```
  mySprite.setFlashProperty("jewelry",   #posX, -100)

  mySprite.setVariable("name", name)

  -- Create a bitmap snapshot of the flash sprite
  new(#bitmap, bitmapMember)
  mySprite.locZ       = the lastChannel
  updateStage
  bitmapImage         = (the stage).image
  bitmapMember.image =  bitmapImage.crop(mySprite.rect)
  mySprite.locZ       = spriteNum
end createBitmap
```

The various properties #headgear, #hair, #eyebrows, and so on, define the distance that the MovieClip of the same name within the Flash movie needs to be

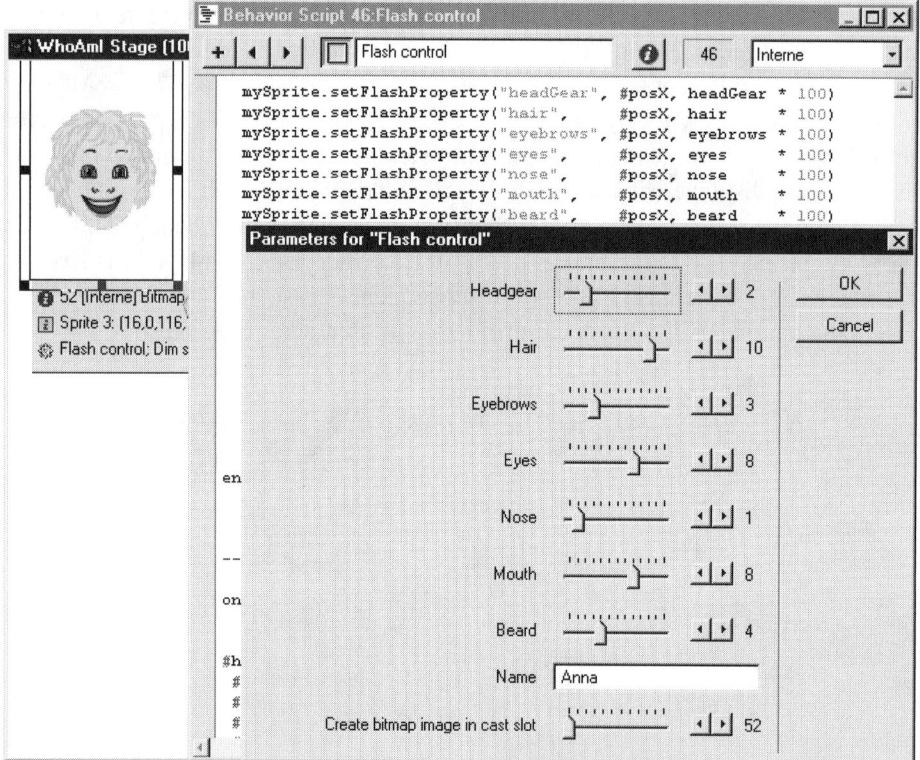

Figure 4-6 *Using the Behavior Parameters dialog box to create a particular face*

You might like to use the same principle to create a whole pack of cards as a single Flash movie and convert this to a set of 52 bitmaps as the cards are dealt. You could use different elements in the Flash movie for the pip shapes, numbers, and faces; and move the elements as appropriate to create each separate card.

Creating all the card images at once might take a while. You might like to arrange for each card image to be created when the card is first dealt. The end user probably will find a slight pause before the card is dealt preferable to a longer pause before the game starts.

Many thanks to Charlotte Thibault for her original artwork for this movie.

Creating an Enlarged Image of a Flash Member

What if you want to change the size of the Flash member's image? If you make a bitmap from the member's image and then scale the bitmap, the result will be pixelated. If you change the size of the Flash member before you create the image, the result will be smooth. To test this, import an *.swf Flash file into a Director movie and name the resulting Flash member "Flash." Now type the following in the Message window and compare the three Bitmap members that are created:

```
new(#bitmap).image = member("Flash").image -- original Size
revertRect = member("Flash").defaultRect
member("Flash").defaultRect = revertRect * 2 -- enlarged
new(#bitmap).image = member("Flash").image
member("Flash").defaultRect = revertRect -- restore original size
new(#bitmap).image = member("Flash").image
```

3D Members

3D members also have an `image` property; however, in Director 8.5 on some hardware configurations, only a rectangle with the 3D member's `bgColor` is returned. On all the machines I have tested on, the image property does work in software rendering mode, but the resulting `image` may be very different from what you see on the screen. Although I would encourage you to experiment with this property, I would not recommend it yet for commercial development in projects where you cannot be sure of the end user's configuration.

The Next Step

This chapter has demonstrated a number of techniques for exploiting the `image` property of Text, Vector Shape, and Flash members. I will have achieved my purpose if these examples inspire you to use a variety of sources from which to build up bitmap images.

In the next chapter, you will be building images from a variety of member types in order to create customized transitions.

CHAPTER 5

Transitions

IN THIS CHAPTER:

Change is not made without inconvenience, even from worse to better.

—Samuel Johnson

So far, most of the images you have created have been dealt with in a one-off operation; however, transitions require a series of imaging operations over time. Creating transitions is a great way to practice your Imaging Lingo skills. A generic transition behavior should not need to know in advance the size, type, or color depth of the graphic assets it might need to deal with. If you can write such a behavior, you will have proved to yourself that you understand the fundamental issues of Imaging Lingo.

The Sprite Transition behaviors written by Darrel Plant offer a variety of examples to study. Here, I provide six more examples, working up from a simple Dissolve behavior, which relies on sprite properties, to the complex Page Turn that you might have looked at in Chapter 4. On the way, you will see how to

- Grab the image of the previous screen
- Control interactions during a transition
- Provide parameters for your transitions

Working with Images Provided On-the-Fly

Theoretically, you could create a transition by working directly on `(the stage).image`. In practice, this will work only if none of the sprites on the stage change. Working with `(the stage).image` creates trails; moving sprites erases trails. Unfortunately, there is no opportunity to modify `(the stage).image` after the sprites have been moved and before the screen is refreshed, because these actions occur simultaneously.

Frame Events

Dissolve.dir

The order of events sent by the Director Player during the course of a frame is as follows. Events also sent to Movie Scripts are marked with an asterisk. Movie Scripts only receive these events if they are not intercepted by behavior, or if the behaviors explicitly pass the event. In either case, the Movie Script will receive the event last.

`new`	Sent to new sprites (Frame Script first)
`beginSprite`	Sent to new sprites immediately after `#new` (Frame Script first)
`stepFrame`	Sent to instances on the `actorList`
`prepareFrame`	Last chance to modify `(the stage).image` (Frame Script last)*

Sprite positions are updated and the screen is refreshed, overwriting changes to those parts of `(the stage).image` where sprites have moved.

`enterFrame`	Refreshed screen now visible (Frame Script last)*
`idle`	Sent only to Frame Scripts and Movie Scripts
`mouseWithin`	Sent to the frontmost sprite under the mouse that contains a `mouseEnter()`, `mouseLeave()`, or `mouseWithin()` handler
`exitFrame`	Sent to Frame Script last (Frame Script last)*
`endSprite`	Sent to sprites that will not appear in the new frame (Frame Script first)

Because you cannot modify `(the stage).image` after the sprites have been updated, even a full-screen transition has to be dealt with in a sprite if it is to display correctly. This implies that the sprite that deals with the transition must be full-screen and it should appear in the channel with the highest-numbered locZ.

So, to create your transition, you will be creating a behavior that you will attach to a sprite. A transition occurs when the display on the screen changes. Generally, this means you will stretch your transition sprite between the marker that indicates the beginning of a particular screen layout and the `go loop` frame script or the following marker, which indicates the end of the screen layout.

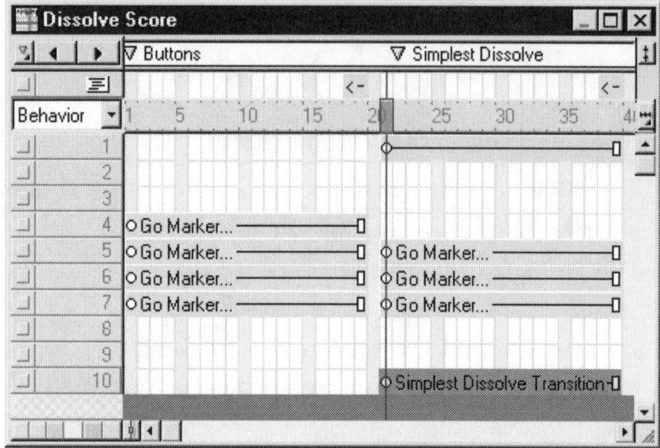

If the user can jump to this marker from any frame in the movie, how is the behavior to know what was on the previous screen? To find the answer, look at the preceding list of events. Which events occur before the screen is updated? What will `(the stage).image` contain before the screen is updated?

In the following simple behavior, I have chosen to capture `(the stage).image` in the `on beginSprite()` handler; however, `new()` or `prepareFrame()` could be used, too. The fade effect is achieved by reducing the sprite's `blendLevel` property in regular steps until the sprite becomes completely transparent.

```
-- SIMPLEST DISSOLVE TRANSITION --

property mySprite
property myFrame


on beginSprite(me)
  mySprite = sprite(me.spriteNum)

  -- Grab the image of the previous frame
  stageImage = (the stage).image

  -- Crop the image to the size of this sprite
  stageImage = stageImage.crop(mySprite.rect)

  -- Show image of previous frame in this sprite
  mySprite.member.image = stageImage

  -- Start countdown
```

```
  myFrame = 30
end beginSprite


on exitFrame(me)
  if myFrame then
    -- Reduce the opacity of this sprite
    myFrame = myFrame - 1
    mySprite.blendLevel = (255 / 30) * myFrame
  end if
end exitFrame
```

You can see this behavior in action in the Dissolve.dir movie, which you can find in the Imaging\Timing\ folder on the CD-ROM that accompanies this book; choose the Simplest Dissolve button.

Controlling Interactivity During the Transition

Director's built-in transitions and those provided by third-party xtras prevent all interaction while the transition is in progress. Transitions that are created using imaging Lingo maintain interactivity by default. Although this can be very useful, it also can prove awkward. For example, the user might double-click a button, and the second click might trigger a second button that is hidden beneath the transition sprite. As a result, the user might pass over an important section without realizing it. One of the transitions we will be looking at alters `the drawRect` property of the Stage. If this transition is interrupted, the rest of the movie can continue with essential controls out of reach. Therefore, it is essential to control interactivity intelligently during your transition.

The preceding behavior contains no mouse event handlers, which means the sprite used for the transition effect is transparent to the mouse; rollovers will be detected by the sprites in the lower-numbered sprites, and mouse clicks will be detected.

You can control such mouse activity in an intelligent way, by

- Including dummy mouse event handlers
- Using Matte ink
- Modifying the value of `the alphaThreshold` for the member of the sprite rather than the sprite's `blendLevel`.

Using the alpha channel means using a 32-bit image. Because `the colorDepth` of the screen might not be 32 bits, we will need to copy `(the stage).image` into a 32-bit image object.

```
-- DISSOLVE TRANSITION WITH CONTROLLED INTERACTIVITY --

property myMember
property myFrame


on beginSprite(me)
  thisSprite     = sprite(me.spriteNum)
  thisSprite.ink = 8 -- #matte
  myMember       = thisSprite.member

  -- Determine the dimensions of the stage
  stageWidth  = the stageRight - the stageLeft
  stageHeight = the stageBottom - the stageTop
  stageRect   = rect (0, 0, stageWidth, stageHeight)

  -- Create a 32-bit image of the previous frame
  stageImage  = image(stageWidth, stageHeight, 32)
  stageImage.copyPixels((the stage).image, stageRect, stageRect)

  -- Crop the image to the size of this sprite
  stageImage = stageImage.crop(thisSprite.rect)

  -- Ensure that the image is fully opaque
  stageImage.setAlpha(255)
  stageImage.useAlpha = TRUE

  -- Show image of previous frame in this sprite
  myMember.image          = stageImage
  myMember.alphaThreshold = 128

  -- Start countdown
  myFrame = 30
end beginSprite


on exitFrame(me)
  if myFrame then
    myFrame = myFrame - 1
```

```
    alphaLevel = integer((255 / 30.0) * myFrame)
    myMember.image.setAlpha(alphaLevel)
  end if
end exitFrame


on mouseUp  -- Makes parts of the sprite opaque to mouse clicks
end


on mouseEnter -- Makes parts of the sprite opaque to rollover events
end
```

Using an `alphaThreshold` value of `128` will prevent rollovers and mouse clicks from having any effect until the sprites in question are at least as visible as the image of the previous frame. You can see this in action in the Dissolve.dir movie. Click the Controlled Dissolve button; the buttons that take you to a different screen will not become active until the transition is half complete. An `alphaThreshold` of 1 also would be a good choice here; it would prevent all interaction until the transition is complete.

Frame-Based and Time-Based Transitions

On a slow machine or in a movie with a low `frameTempo`, the preceding transition behaviors might take an inordinate time to execute. One solution is to set a duration for the behavior rather than use a fixed number of frames.

Adjusting for Frame Duration

Following, you will find an extract from the Timed Dissolve Transition behavior in the Dissolve.dir movie: I've changed the name of the property from `myFrame` to `myTicks`, and modified the `exitFrame()` handler so that it calculates the alpha channel level from `the ticks` movie property rather than from `the frame`.

```
-- TIME-BASED TRANSITION --

property myMember
property myTicks


on beginSprite(me)
  -- The body of the handler is the same as the one shown above
```

```
  -- Start countdown
  myCounter = the ticks + 60
end beginSprite


on exitFrame(me)
  if myTicks then
    ticksLeft = myTicks - the ticks
    if ticksLeft > 0 then
      alphaLevel = integer((255 / 60.0) * ticksLeft)
      myMember.image.setAlpha(alphaLevel)

    else -- time has run out: jump to the end of the transition
      myMember.image.setAlpha(0)
      myTicks = 0
    end if
  end if
end exitFrame
```

Try altering `the frameTempo` of the movie via the Control Panel. The other transitions might take more or less time to execute, depending on the value of `the frameTempo`, but the Timed Dissolve Transition should always take around a second to complete. With a slower `frameTempo`, you will see fewer intermediate images. The time-based behavior might look somewhat disjointed at slow speeds, whereas the frame-based versions can still look fluid.

Using a timeOut Object

If your movie does not use animated Film Loops, you might prefer to use a timeOut object to artificially increase the frame rate during the transition. Here's a simple behavior written by Karina Steffens to get you started; attach it to a sprite that does not overlap the edges of the Stage.

```
property mySprite
property myFrame
property pTimeOut
```

```
on beginSprite me
  mySprite    = sprite(me.spriteNum)
  stageImage = (the stage).image
  stageImage = stageImage.crop(mySprite.rect)

  mySprite.member.image = stageImage
  myFrame     = 30
  mySeconds  = 2
  myTime      = (mySeconds * 1000 ) / myFrame

  pTimeOut=timeOut ("simple dissolve").new(myTime,#showTransition, me)
end beginSprite


on showTransition me
  if myFrame then
    myFrame = myFrame - 1
    mySprite.blendLevel = (255/30) * myFrame
    updateStage
  else
    pTimeOut = pTimeOut.forget()
  end if
end
```

If your movie does use animated Film Loop sprites during the transition, these will accelerate, because Film Loops advance one frame every time `updateStage` is called.

Artificially Slowing Your Movie

Another way to slow down your movie is to open the Transition member (member 22) in the Paint window. Although the image in the Paint window will not appear to change, the alpha channel will be modified during the transition. Having the Bitmap member visible in the open Paint window forces it to refresh each time the alpha channel is changed. Other images that might be refreshed are the thumbnails that show in the Cast window, the Property Inspector, and the toolbar in the Score window.

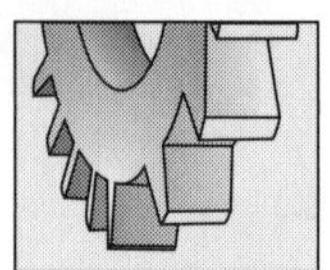

TIP

To see transitions at their best at authortime, take care that the windows that show the Bitmap member and all its various thumbnails are closed while you test the transition.

Customizing a Transition

All the preceding behaviors suffer from two defects: they use hard-coded values and modify an existing cast member. The fourth version of this behavior, Customizable Dissolve Transition, uses the `getPropertyDescriptionList()` handler to allow users to set custom values when they apply the behavior to a sprite, and creates a temporary Bitmap member that it destroys `on endSprite`.

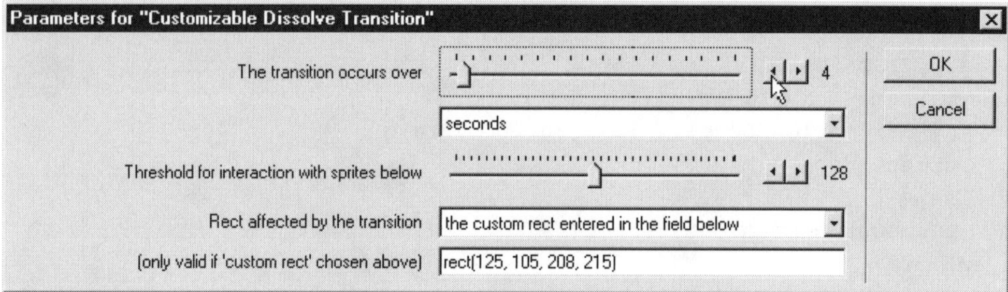

The `getPropertyDescriptionList()` handler asks the user to define a `#timeUnit` property that can be `#frame`, `#ticks`, or `#seconds`. If `#frame` is chosen, the transition will use frame-based animation; otherwise, the animation will be time based. The user also can decide how soon interaction will start: the greater the value of the temporary Bitmap member's `alphaThreshold`, the sooner the sprite will appear transparent to mouse clicks.

Whereas the previous versions of the behavior used the area of the sprite to determine the area affected by the transition, the Behavior Parameters dialog box of this version allows the user to choose from among the full Stage area, the area of the sprite, and a custom `rect`.

In the Dissolve.dir movie, three instances of the same behavior are attached to three different sprites. Each instance has its own time scale: 15 frames for the top one, 90 ticks for the one on the left, and 4 seconds for the one on the right.

More Complex Effects

Transits.dir

You can create any number of transition effects with a `beginSprite()` handler very similar to the one used in the preceding behavior. You'll see four more examples in the Transits.dir movie:

- Slide Rects Out
- Slide Rects In
- Draw Rect
- Fade to <color>

Revealing the New Screen

The Slide Rects Out transition modifies both the rgb channel and the alpha channel. The current image is divided into strips that move out from the center. The alpha channel is set to transparent in the areas that the strips in the rgb channel have left empty.

As before, the behavior creates an image object of the previous screen on `beginSprite` and then, in the `createStrips()` handler, divides that image up into the chosen number of rects. On each `exitFrame`, the current values of those rects are used to define the area of the image object that will be used as the source for a `copyPixels()` command. The `rect` is then offset a short distance, and the resulting `rect` is used as the destination area for the `copyPixels()` command. The new values of these rects are saved, the previous destination area is used as the next source area, and so on. In the following illustration, the lighter areas at the outside edges of the strips will not appear; they will be clipped at the edge of the image-object.

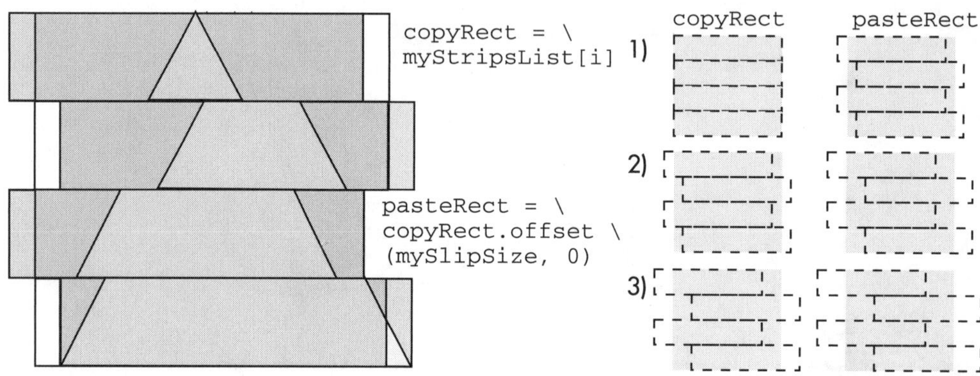

Here is a simplified version of the `createStrips()` handler:

```
property frameCount      -- Duration of the transition in frames
property stripCount      -- Number of strips used in transition
property transitionRect -- Area of the stage affected by the transition
property myStripsList    -- List of rects: one rect for each strip
property mySlipSize      -- Number of pixels the strips move each frame

on createStrips(me)
  myStripsList  = []

  stripRect    = rect(0, 0, transitionRect.width, transitionRect.height)
  fullSize     = transitionRect.width
  mySlipSize   = fullSize / frameCount
  stripHeight = transitionRect.height / float(stripCount)

  i = stripCount
  repeat while i
    i = i - 1
    -- Source rect of strip
    stripRect.top = integer(stripHeight * i)
    myStripsList.append(stripRect.duplicate())
    -- Prepare for next strip
    stripRect.bottom = stripRect.top
  end repeat
end createStrips
```

Using Duplicate Rects

Rects (like points, lists, image objects, and script instances) are pointers to a memory address where the data itself is stored. If two variables point to the same memory address, they will treat the same data. If the value of one of these variables is altered, the value reported by the other variable will alter, too.

Try this in the Message window:

```
x = rect(1, 2, 3, 4)
y = x
put y
-- rect(1, 2, 3, 4)

x[2] = 0
put y
-- rect(1, 0, 3, 4)
```

The value of `y` changes even though it is `x` that is manipulated. Try also using `x = list(1, 2, 3)` or `x = point(1, 2)`; the effect will be similar.

Pointers are a very powerful feature of Lingo; they also can lead to unexpected consequences if you are unaware of the way they work. The `createStrips()` handler modifies a `rect` named `stripRect`. A duplicate of this `rect` is appended to `myStripsList`; that is, a copy of the data is made to a different memory address and the new memory address is added to the list. Without the `duplicate()` function, the values added to `myStripsList` would change each time the `top` and `bottom` of `stripRect` is changed; `myStripsList` would be a list of identical `rects`.

The following illustration shows the meaning of the main variables that are used in the following extract of the `showTransition()` handler, which is called on each `exitFrame`.

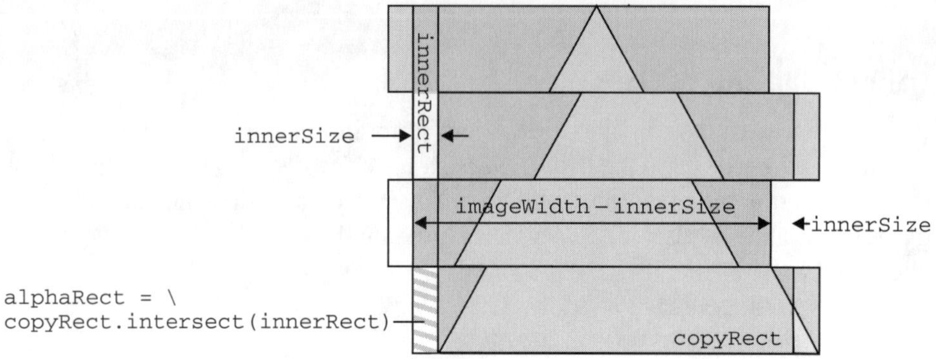

```
property memberImage -- Image of the member of this sprite
property imageWidth  -- Width of member image
property imageHeight -- Height of member image

on  showTransition()
  -- More code
  tempImage   = image(imageWidth, imageHeight, 32)

  innerSize   = mySlipSize * (frameCount - myFrame)

  repeat with i = 1 to stripCount
    copyRect  = myStripsList[i]

    -- Determine rect of vacated areas
    innerRect = rect(0, 0, innerSize, imageHeight)
    outerSize = imageWidth - innerSize
    outerRect = rect(outerSize, 0, imageWidth, imageHeight)

    if i mod 2 then
      -- Move strip right
      pasteRect = copyRect.offset(mySlipSize, 0)
      alphaRect = copyRect.intersect(innerRect)
    else
      -- Move strip left
      pasteRect = copyRect.offset(-mySlipSize, 0)
      alphaRect = copyRect.intersect(outerRect)
    end if

    -- Move strip and make space vacated by it transparent
    tempImage.copyPixels(memberImage, pasteRect, copyRect)
    alphaImage.fill(alphaRect, rgb(255, 255, 255)) -- transparent area
```

```
    -- Ensure that the present rect of strip is used next time
    myStripsList[i] = pasteRect
  end repeat
  -- More code
end showTransition
```

A Time-Based Version of the Transition

The Transits.dir movie also features a time-based version of the Slide Rects Out transition. This is more complex and it uses a little more RAM. In a time-based animation, the distance moved by the strips between two `exitFrame` events might vary. The solution I adopt is to use two lists: one for the `copyRect` data and one for the `pasteRect` data.

Hiding the Previous Screen

Making the new screen appear dynamically over the old screen is more difficult. The new screen appears behind the sprite that is making the transition, so it does not appear as such in `(the stage).image` until the old screen has become transparent. How can you capture an image of it before it appears? The Director Player builds up an image of the Stage, sprite by sprite, between the `prepareFrame` event and the `enterFrame` event. There is no way to interrupt this process just before the last sprite is added; in the case of a transition, this last sprite will cover the area of the transition. By the time the Director Player gives you any access to the image of the Stage through Lingo, it is too late.

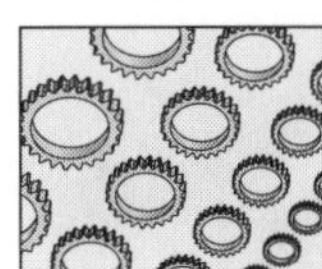

NOTE

Transitions that manipulate the upcoming image of the new screen should occur on a single frame, during which time no interaction is possible. During such a transition, the apparent position of interactive areas, such as buttons, does not coincide with the position of the sprites underneath. Maintaining interaction would mean mapping moving areas of an image object to the source sprites. This would lead to unnecessarily complex programming.

Building the Upcoming Screen in an Image Object

One technique is to build up the new image of the Stage, sprite by sprite, using the data for each sprite as it is stored in the score, in a separate image object. This has a major drawback: `#fields`, `#shape`, `#button` members, and many members created by third-party xtras, do not have an `image` property.

If you use any of these member types in your new screen, the process of creating the new screen image manually will be extremely complex. The Slide Rects In behavior provides an example that sidesteps such complexity by ignoring sprites whose members do not have an `image` property. This can be quite effective: the button sprites appear only when they can actually be used.

Here are highlights of the `getImageBehind()` handler used in the behavior, and the associated `getTextMemberImage()` and `getMaskedImage()` handlers.

```
property stageWidth, stageHeight -- dimensions of the Stage

property stageWidth, stageHeight

on getImageBehind(spriteNumber)
  -- Create a blank image the same size and color as the Stage
  imageData = image(stageWidth, stageHeight, the colordepth)
  imageData.fill(imageData.rect, (the stage).bgColor)

  previousSprite = spriteNumber - 1
  repeat with i = 1 to previousSprite
    if not (sprite i intersects spriteNumber) then
      next repeat
    end if

    -- Copy the appropriate part of the sprite into the blank image
    thatSprite = sprite(i)
    thatQuad   = thatSprite.quad

    -- Determine which options to use for the copyPixels command
    spriteInk = thatSprite.ink
    optionsList = [ \
#ink:        spriteInk, \
#blendLevel: thatSprite.blendLevel, \
#color:      thatSprite.color, \
#bgColor:    thatSprite.bgColor \
]
    -- Prepare the image of thatSprite
    if thatSprite.member.type = #text and spriteInk = 0 then
      -- Text members with #copy ink are opaque
      thatImage = getTextMemberImage(thatSprite.member)
    else if spriteInk = 9 then -- #mask
      thatImage = getMaskedImage(thatSprite.member)
      optionsList.deleteProp(#ink)
    else
```

```
      thatImage = thatSprite.member.image
    end if

    -- Copy the sprite's image onto imageData
    thatRect = thatImage.rect
   imageData.copyPixels(thatImage, thatQuad, thatRect, optionsList)
  end repeat

  return imageData
end getImageBehind


on getTextMemberImage(textMember) -- Opaque image for #copy ink
  imageWidth  = textMember.width
  imageHeight = textMember.pageHeight

  textImage   = image(imageWidth, imageHeight, 32)
  imageRect   = rect(0, 0, imageWidth, imageHeight)
  textImage.fill(imageRect, textMember.bgColor)
  textImage.copyPixels(textMember.image, imageRect, imageRect)

  return textImage
end getTextSpriteImage


on getMaskedImage(maskedMember)
  maskingMember = member(maskedMember.number + 1)
  maskedImage   = maskedMember.image
  memberWidth   = maskedImage.width
  memberHeight  = maskedImage.height
  maskAdjust   = maskedMember.regPoint - maskingMember.regPoint

  -- Use the grayscale data in the mask for the alpha channel:
  -- the masked image must therefore be at 32-bit depth...
  tempImage  = image(memberWidth, memberHeight, 32)
  memberRect = rect(0, 0, memberWidth, memberHeight)
  tempImage.copypixels(maskedImage, memberRect, memberRect)

  -- ... and the masking image must be the same size as maskedImage
  -- and at 8-bit color depth...
  maskingImage = image(memberWidth, memberHeight, 8, #grayscale)
  maskRect     = maskingMember.rect
```

```
  visibleRect  = maskRect.offset(maskAdjust.locH, maskAdjust.locV)
  maskingImage.copypixels(maskingMember.image, visibleRect, maskRect)
  tempImage.setAlpha(maskingImage)
  tempImage.useAlpha = TRUE

  return tempImage
end getMaskedImage
```

Capturing the Upcoming Stage Image in a MIAW

You can capture the full image of the Stage, including sprites whose members do not have an image property, but only if you are not working in a browser. You can use much less code (but more RAM) by using an off screen Movie In A Window to open a second instance of the current movie at the appropriate place, thus determining what the upcoming Stage image is to be. In Windows, you must ensure that your movie is set to read-only for this to work (no special setting is needed on Macintosh).

Here's a simplified version of the handler that does this:

```
on getImageBehind(spriteNumber, whichFrame)
  imageMiaw = window("MIAW "&the milliseconds) -- unique name
  imageMiaw.fileName = the moviePath & the movieName
  tell imageMiaw
    -- Hide sprites in higher numbered channels
    repeat with i = the lastChannel down to spriteNumber
      sprite(i).visible = FALSE
    end repeat

    go frame whichFrame
    updateStage -- otherwise image is not created
    imageBehind = imageMiaw.image.duplicate()

  end tell

  forget imageMiaw
  return imageBehind
end getImageBehind
```

To test this, follow these steps:

1. Copy the Transits.dir movie from the Imaging\Timing\ folder on the CD-ROM onto your hard disk.

2. Open the Slide Rects In behavior (member 4).
3. Change the name of the `on getImageBehind()` handler. A handler of the same name is provided in the following Movie Script, so this will be called instead if the behavior cannot find its own `on getImageBehind()` handler.
4. Save the movie.
5. If you are in Windows, you will need to set the read-only property of the movie (see Figure 5-1) by performing the following tasks:
   - Open a new movie in Director (so that you can modify the Transits.dir file).
   - Right-click the icon of the Transits.dir file.
   - Select Properties.
   - Select the Read-only check box.
   - Click OK.
   - In Director, reopen the Transits.dir movie, which will now be read only.

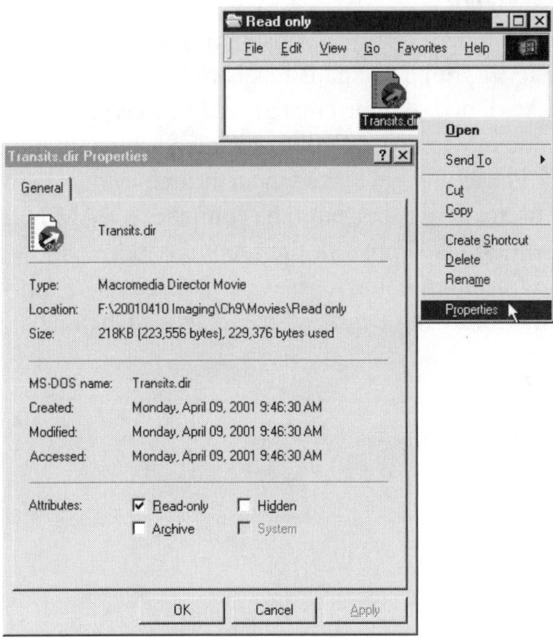

Figure 5-1 *Setting the read-only property of a movie in Windows*

6. Run the movie.
7. Click the Strips In button. This time, the image of the entire Stage should slide in, including the buttons, as shown here:

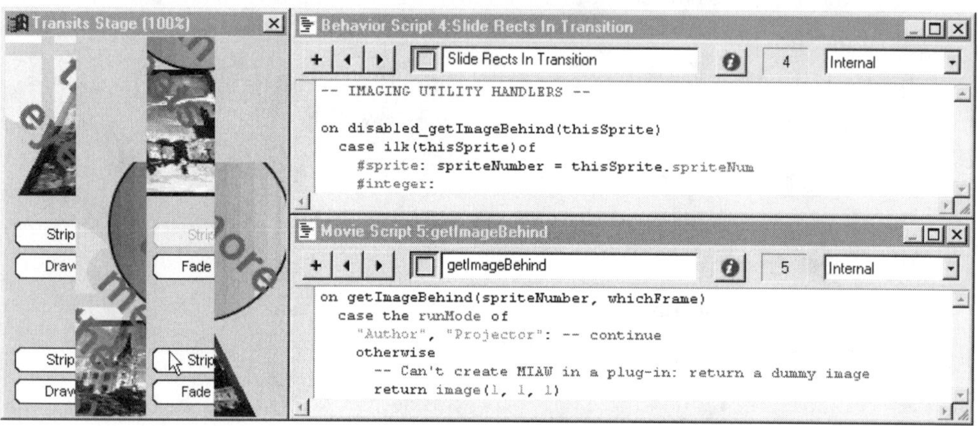

Avoiding Infinite Recursion

Does anything worry you here? Do you sense any danger? What will happen when the playback head enters a frame that calls this handler, using `the frame` as the value for `whichFrame`? A window will be created, and its playback head will jump to the same frame of the same movie that called the handler, which, in turn, will call the same handler. The Director Player will get locked in an infinite loop, creating more and more windows (which the user will not see), until the computer's RAM is saturated.

Fortunately, the solution is simple. In the second window, the `visible` property of the sprite with the transition behavior is set to `FALSE`. The transition behavior on that sprite includes the following `on beginSprite()` handler:

```
on beginSprite(me)
  mySprite = sprite(spriteNum)
  if mySprite.visible then
    me.initialize() -- Calls getImageBehind()
  end if
end beginSprite
```

This means that subsequent instances of the behavior will not get a chance to call the `getImageBehind()` handler themselves.

Manipulating the drawRect of the Stage

There is another way of manipulating the incoming screen dynamically without capturing an image of it beforehand. The native Cover. . . and Push. . . transitions move the new screen, but they treat the new screen as a single block. You can mimic this sort of transition by modifying `(the stage).drawRect`. The Draw Rect behavior does just this.

In authoring mode, you might see flashes of the background color during transitions that alter `(the stage).drawRect`. Fortunately, these disappear in a projector.

Push Transition

The technique consists of placing the transition sprite off the Stage to the left and setting the `drawRect` of the Stage so that only the transition sprite is visible; the Stage area itself is moved off to the right. The `drawRect` of the Stage then reverts gradually to its original value, thus pushing the transition sprite off to the left.

Cover Transition

The behavior has a variant where the position of the transition sprite is also adjusted, so that it continues to appear in the same position. At the same time, its alpha channel is modified; the sprite becomes transparent so that the image of the Stage underneath is visible through it. The result is similar to the built-in Cover Left transition.

The modifications need to be carried out `on prepareFrame` rather than `on exitFrame`; otherwise, there is a hiatus between the moment `(the stage).drawRect` is updated and the moment the position of the transition sprite is updated. Even so, the effect is much less fluid than the native version. Because a transition controlled by `(the stage).drawRect` is by its very nature a full-stage transition, using a Lingo version is justified only if you want to keep some other animation running at the same time. For instance, you could use the Lingo version to change the background while a Direct To Stage video is running.

Blocking Interactions

This transition must not be interrupted. If it were, the Stage would continue to remain only partially visible, which means if the user clicks another sprite, nothing should happen. Since the transition sprite might not cover the sprite the user clicks, how can it prevent any interaction with it?

The answer is to intercept the mouse event before the clicked sprite receives it. To do this, you must set the primary event properties, such as the `mouseDownScript`, to `stopEvent`. Primary event instructions are executed when Director receives a mouse or keyboard event, and before any behaviors or other scripts get a chance to react. It might be that certain primary event properties are not empty. The trick is to save the current value of each of the properties before the transition starts and to reset the original value as soon as the transition is finished. Here's how the Draw Rect Transition behavior does this:

```
-- Save primary event handlers while modal
property mySavedKeyDownScript
property mySavedKeyUpScript
property mySavedMouseDownScript
property mySavedMouseUpScript

on setModal(me, blockEvents)
 if blockEvents then
    -- Save the current primary event handlers
    mySavedKeyDownScript   = the keyDownScript
    mySavedKeyUpScript     = the keyUpScript
    mySavedMouseDownScript = the mouseDownScript
    mySavedMouseUpScript   = the mouseUpScript

    -- Prevent events from having any effect
    the keyDownScript   = "stopEvent"
    the keyUpScript     = "stopEvent"
    the mouseDownScript = "stopEvent"
    the mouseUpScript   = "stopEvent"

  else
    -- Reset the primary event handlers
    the keyDownScript   = mySavedKeyDownScript
    the keyUpScript     = mySavedKeyUpScript
    the mouseDownScript = mySavedMouseDownScript
    the mouseUpScript   = mySavedMouseUpScript
  end if
end setModal
```

Fade to Any Color

The last transition behavior that you will find in the Transits.dir movie is the Fade to <color> transition. This is a two-phase variant of the Dissolve transition. During the first phase, the previous image of the Stage is blended into an image object of the suitable color; blending increases with time until none of the previous image is copied at all—only the plain color remains. At this point, the second phase begins. Now, the transparency of the transition sprite is increased by modifying the value of the alpha channel, which makes the plain color dissolve into the new Stage image.

```
on showTransition(me)
  myFrame = myFrame - 1
  if myFrame then
    -- Continue with current phase of the transition
    if myPhase = #color then
      -- Blend previous stage image into a background color
      tempImage = image(myMemberRect.width, myMemberRect.height, 32)
      tempImage.fill(myMemberRect, fadeColor)
      options = [#blendLevel: (myBlendLevel * myFrame)]
      tempImage.copyPixels(myImage,myMemberRect,myMemberRect,options)
      myMember.image = tempImage
    else
      -- Dissolve the background color so that the Stage beneath is visible
      alphaLevel = integer((255.0 / myBlendLevel) * myFrame
      myMember.image.setAlpha(alphaLevel)
      myMember.useAlpha = TRUE
    end if

  else if myPhase = #color then
    -- End of #color phase: switch to #image phase
    myMember.image.fill(myMemberRect, fadeColor)
    myPhase      = #image
    myFrame      = frameCount / 2

  else
    -- Transition is over: make sprite transparent
    myMember.image.setAlpha(0)
    myMember.image.useAlpha = TRUE
    myFrame = 0
  end if
end showTransition
```

Turning the Page

PageTurn.dir

The Page Turn behavior you looked at in the "Vector Shapes" section of Chapter 4 doesn't just create an image that looks like a double-page spread. It also allows the user to turn the page by clicking in the sprite. You'll find this behavior in the separate PageTurn.dir movie in the Imaging\Members\ folder.

Like the Fade to <color> transition, the Page Turn transition also occurs in two phases. First, the image of the page the user clicks is squashed progressively toward the center to reveal the image of the page behind it. Second, when the page is upright, the image of the turning page is swapped with that of the other side; this image is progressively stretched from the center until the newly revealed page appears flat. The sequence is shown in the following illustration:

You'll find the code that prepares the transition in the `turnPage()` handler. The transition itself is executed on successive `exitFrame` events through the code in the `turnPageOver()` handler. The behavior is somewhat more complex than the ones I have described in the preceding. Rather than go into details here, I invite you to look at the scripts in the movie itself.

If you are feeling inspired, you might like to replace the linear progression by a sinusoidal one to give a clearer impression that the page is rotating through space. If you are feeling really inspired, you could divide the page into vertical strips and modify the quad of each strip independently, giving an impression of 3D perspective as the page is turning. Both of these improvements require a solid understanding of mathematics.

Note that the Page Turn behavior requires a second behavior on the same sprite to provide details of the images to show on each page. The Page Data behavior provides a number of handlers that the Page Turn behavior can call, each of which provides a different effect. By choosing the `readFromExternalFolder()` handler, for instance, you can get the behavior to read in images stored in the same folder as the movie.

Press the SHIFT key while opening the Behavior Parameters dialog box for the Page Turn behavior; this will provide a drop-down list of handlers in the Page Data behavior to choose from. This is shown in Figure 5-2.

Apart from its interest from an Imaging Lingo point of view, this behavior contains a number of handlers that make it more user friendly during authoring. Among other things, it includes code that simplifies adding it to a sprite on-the-fly. If you need to

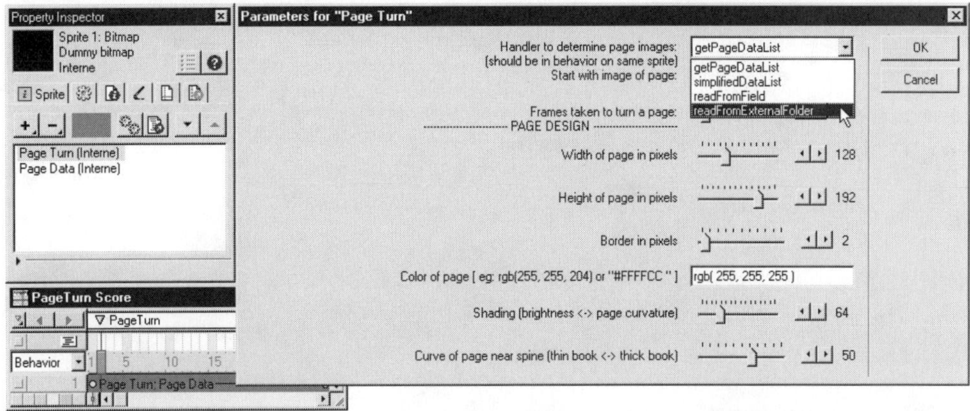

Figure 5-2 *Press SHIFT when opening the Parameters dialog for the Page Turn behavior*

create behaviors for other users—both artists and programmers—you might find it useful to study these aspects of the behavior.

Further Inspiration

The five chapters in Part I are intended to give you a solid foundation in the possible uses of Imaging Lingo. They do not pretend, however, to cover the whole range of possibilities. You might be interested in seeing how others have put Imaging Lingo to good use. Here are a few sites where you may find material to inspire you:

- http://www.simtek.dircon.co.uk/deight/
- http://www.setpixel.com/content/democomp/
- http://www.noodlebox.com/bitsandpieces/

PART

II

Shockwave 3D

OBJECTIVES

- Discovering how 3D space is modeled
- Revising your knowledge of the physics of motion
- Manipulating 3D models with the mouse
- Creating and animating a mesh primitive
- Exploring the properties of shaders and textures
- Designing your own textures and shaders
- Understanding the possibilities and limitations of a virtual camera
- Understanding how virtual lights differ from real lights
- Coping with collisions
- Working out how Director works

CHAPTER

6

Understanding the 3D Coordinate System

IN THIS CHAPTER:

Australia, they say, is on the other side of the world. Phoowee! This is a flat slab of asteroid and they know it. I thought, I'll call their bluff, and purchased a ticket to go to Australia… They had to keep me locked up in a plane for twenty four hours, on the pretence of flying there, to give them time to transform Brighton into Bondi Beach and Luton into Adelaide.

—Jasper Carrott

This part of the book provides an introduction to the Shockwave 3D members introduced in Director 8.5. Simulating a three-dimensional world is far from simple. Using only a flat computer screen, you must explicitly control many features that, in the real world, you tend to take for granted: gravity, friction, solidity, light, atmospheric effects, and so on.

In this and the following chapters, I assume that you know nothing about 3D, either from an artist's point of view or from a programmer's. You will be discovering the six essential ingredients of a virtual 3D world:

- How space is simulated in a virtual world
- How to create 3D models from basic shapes
- How to give your models textures, such as wood and glass
- How to use camera objects to view your 3D scenes
- How to light your 3D scenes
- How to detect when two models touch each other or collide

One of the most useful sources of information is Ullala's 3D Property Inspector. You will find an unregistered version of 3DPI.dcr in the Xtras\ folder of the CD-ROM that accompanies the book. You can download the latest version and register it through http://www.ullala.at/3DPI/. Drag the protected 3DPI.dcr movie into the Xtras folder alongside the Director application; the next time you launch Director you will be able to open it through the Xtras menu. Although a registered copy of 3D Property Inspector is not essential to understanding the content of this book, I thoroughly recommend it as an investment.

Reinventing the Wheel

Wheel.dir

Let's start with something fairly simple: the wheel. Let's make a 3D wheel that we can roll and steer in an otherwise empty world. The sample Wheel.dir movie in the

3D\Space\ folder on the CD-ROM that accompanies this book will give you an idea of what you should be able to accomplish by the end of this chapter.

This example will acquaint you with the concepts of

- Model resources
- Models
- Primitives
- The 3D coordinate system
- Position and rotation in space
- Frames of reference

Create a new movie and use the menu Insert | Media Element | Shockwave 3D to create a new 3D member. Name the member (so that it will not be deleted when you save the movie) and drag it onto the Stage. It will appear black, flat, and uninteresting. In the Shockwave 3D editing window, the member will appear square; on the stage it will appear by default as a 320 × 240 pixel rectangle.

Model Resources and Models

A 3D member contains its own version of cast members, stage, score, and sprites. In Director 8.5 you can see only the emerged part of the iceberg: the Stage is visible, but the assets are only accessible through Lingo. Ensure that your 3-D member is in the first Cast Member slot; then type the following in the Message window.

```
put member(1).modelResource.count
-- 1
```

Model resources are the equivalent of cast members. An empty 3D member contains a default resource: a plane. You cannot delete this default resource, but you can modify it. We won't be using it in this example.

This default plane is available but not visible, just like a Cast Member is not visible until it is placed in a sprite on the Stage. The 3D equivalent of a sprite is a model. Many models can share the same model resource. If you modify the resource, all the models that use it will change. You can swap the model resource used by a given model, just as you can swap the member of a sprite. Try the following in the Message window:

```
put member(1).model.count
-- 0
```

Now let's create a new model resource and make it visible by creating a model from it:

```
cylinderResource = member(1).newModelResource("Resource 1", #cylinder)
wheelModel = member(1).newModel("Wheel model")
wheelModel.resource = cylinderResource
```

You might have to click the Stage to give it focus before the cylinder model appears.

The first line creates a model resource named "Resource 1." Because there is no Resource window for you to visualize the resource in, you'll just have to take this on trust. The second line creates a new model in the 3D member. The model does not yet have anything in it to show; you could consider it to be the 3D equivalent of an empty sprite channel. By default, the model will be placed at the center of the 3D world. The third line tells this new model to display an instance of the model resource created in the first line. You can see the result in Figure 6-1.

Names and Numbers

Each model and each model resource must have a unique name. If you try to create a second model with the same name, you will see a script error alert complaining that the name you propose for the model already exists (see Figure 6-1).

Models and model resources also have a number:

```
put member(1).modelResource(1)
-- plane("DefaultModel")
put member(1).modelResource[2]
-- cylinder("Resource 1")

put member(1).model(1)
-- model("Wheel model")
```

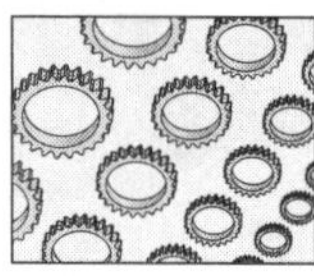

NOTE

You can use either parentheses or square brackets to access a model or a resource by its number. Using parentheses is about 15 percent faster. If you use the name of a model or resource, you must use parentheses—using square brackets will cause a script error.

```
put member(1).model("Wheel model")
-- model("Wheel model").
```

Primitives

When you create a new model resource you must define the `type` of primitive that you wish to create; in this case, `#cylinder`. A primitive is a simple 3D shape, a

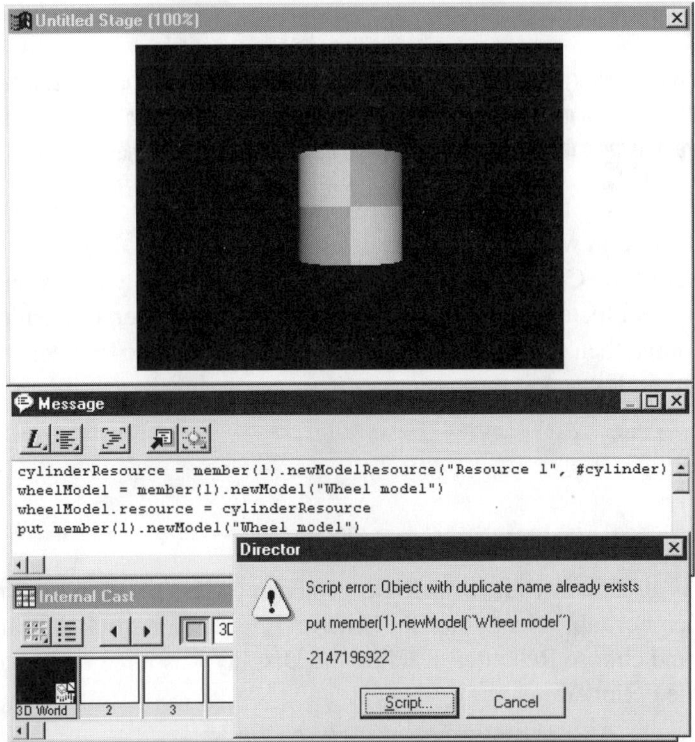

Figure 6-1 *Resources and models must each have a unique name.*

building block from which you can create more complex models. Director 8.5 offers six types of primitive for the `newModelResource()` command: `#sphere`, `#cylinder`, `#box`, `#plane`, `#mesh`, and `#particle`. Third-party Director Xtra developers may provide other primitive types.

Two other `types` are available, but they are created in a different way: `#extruder`, generated from a text member, and `#fromFile`, generated when you import a model resource created in a third-party 3D design program.

Modifying the Model Resource

When you first create a resource, it has a default size and shape. The cylinder primitive that you have created has a height of 50 units and a radius of 25 units at both top and bottom. The top and bottom of the cylinder are closed, and the curved wall forms a complete circle.

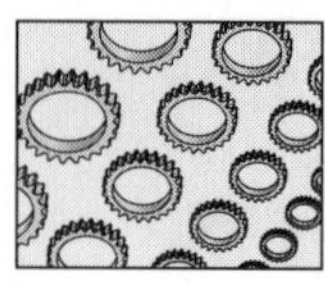

NOTE

A unit is an arbitrary measure. In a 3D world, a model can appear at any scale. If you are creating a landscape for an aerial view, you might find it useful to consider that a unit represents a mile. If you are creating a watch mechanism, it might be more helpful to think of it as a millimeter.

You will find it easier to visualize your resource using the 3D Property Inspector created by Ullala. You will find an unregistered version of 3DPI.dcr in the 3D\Space\ folder of the CD-ROM that accompanies the book. If you have not already done so, drag the protected 3DPI.dcr movie into the Xtras folder alongside the Director application; then open it in a window by typing one of the following commands in the Message window:

```
open window (the applicationPath&"Xtras\3DPI.dcr") -- if you are using Windows
```

or

```
open window (the applicationPath&"Xtras:3DPI.dcr") -- if you are using Macintosh
```

If 3DPI.dcr is already in your Xtras folder, you can open it through the Xtras menu.

Click the Member tab, select your Shockwave 3D member, click the Model Resource tab, and choose Resource 1. Click the Display Resource button to show a thumbnail of the cylinder.

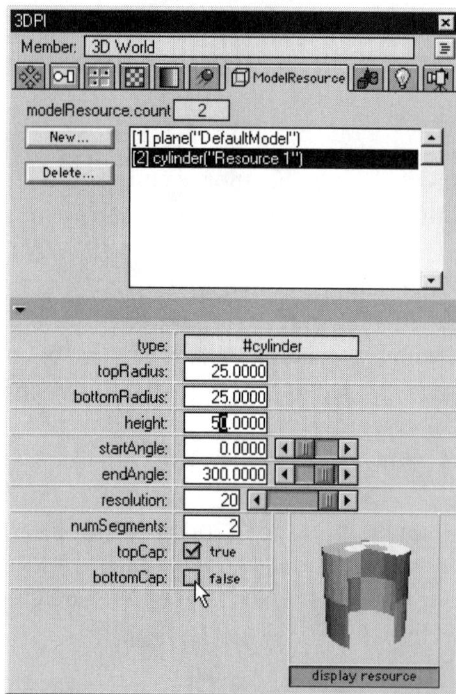

You can now visualize and modify the properties of the model resource. In the preceding illustration, I have set the `#endAngle` of the cylinder resource to 300° so that the cylinder does not wrap in a complete circle; I also have removed the bottom cap. These modifications are for illustrative purposes only; you should restore the default values before you continue.

There are many ways to make the cylinder look more like a wheel. You could increase the `topRadius` and `bottomRadius` of the resource or modify the scale of the model itself along the vertical axis, so that the model that appears in the 3D sprite is a squashed version of the default resource. The most obvious way is to reduce the height of the resource. Try this in the Message window:

```
member(1).modelResource(2).height = 10
```

The cylinder will now appear more like a tire lying on its side.

Manipulating the Model

How can you stand the wheel on its edge? A cylinder resource always appears as a column. To turn it on its side; you need to work on the model, not on the resource. Try this in the Message window:

```
wheelModel.transform.rotation = vector(-90.0, 60.0, 0.0)
```

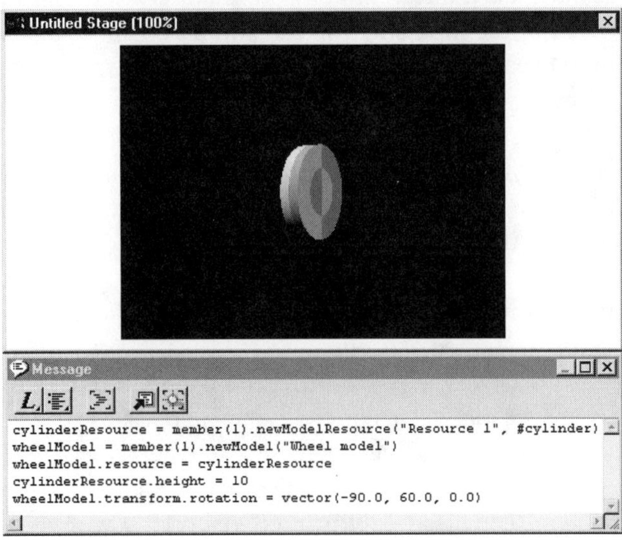

This last line of Lingo gives rise to three questions:

- How is 3D space modeled?
- What is a vector?
- What is a transform?

If you want to get on with creating your wheel, you can skip the answers to these questions for now and go directly to the "Back to the Grindstone" section later in this chapter. (Do not pass Go; do not collect $200.) You can always come back and look at the details later.

The 3D Coordinate System

2DTo3D.dir

The Stage uses a two-dimensional coordinate system: `point(0, 0)` is at the top left of the stage. The horizontal value increases as you move to the right and the vertical value increases as you move down.

3D members use a three-dimensional coordinate system, which uses a different convention. Since the keyword `point` is already used for a two-dimensional system, a 3D point must use a different keyword that allows for a third value: `vector(x, y, z)`. For the moment, you can simply consider that `vector(x, y, z)` is a point in 3D space. In fact, vectors can have several other meanings, as you will see in a moment.

The point defined by `vector(0, 0, 0)` is in the center of the 3D world. Whether it is in the center of what you see in the 3D sprite is another matter. What you see in your sprite depends on the position of the sprite's active camera (we'll deal with cameras in more detail in Chapter 12). As with the 2D Stage coordinates, the value of x increases to the right. However, in a 3D world the y coordinate increases upward. You might find this more familiar, as this is the convention for the Cartesian system that you learned at school.

What about the z axis? This is perpendicular to both the x and the y axes. Different conventions exist: one says that values on the z axis increase as they go deeper into the screen; the other says that the values increase as they come out of the screen toward the viewer. If you have worked with 3D modeling software, you might be used to one or the other. (You also might be used to working with the y and z axes being interchanged.) For its Shockwave 3D members, Macromedia has adopted the second convention. By default, you—the viewer—sit at a positive z value; what you see inside the screen is at a negative z value.

The 3D coordinate system adopted in Director 8.5 is known as a *direct* or *right-handed* system. Hold your right hand in front of your eyes, palm toward you and your thumb out to the right. Point your index finger straight upward and point your middle finger toward your eyes. Curl your other two fingers up out of the way. The thumb, index, and middle fingers of your right hand should now all be at right angles to each other. Your thumb points along the x axis, your index finger along the y axis, and your middle finger along the z axis. You hold the 3D world in the palm of your hand and look at it down the z axis.

As you will discover, all this is relative and depends on the position of the camera. The default camera position is `vector(0, 0, 250)`, looking down the z axis to the center of the world at `vector(0, 0, 0)`. To help you come to terms with this, I have provided a movie that allows you to move models and other elements through 3D space by manipulating them in 2D space: "2Dto3D.dir". You'll find this in the 3D\Space\ folder on the CD-ROM that accompanies this book.

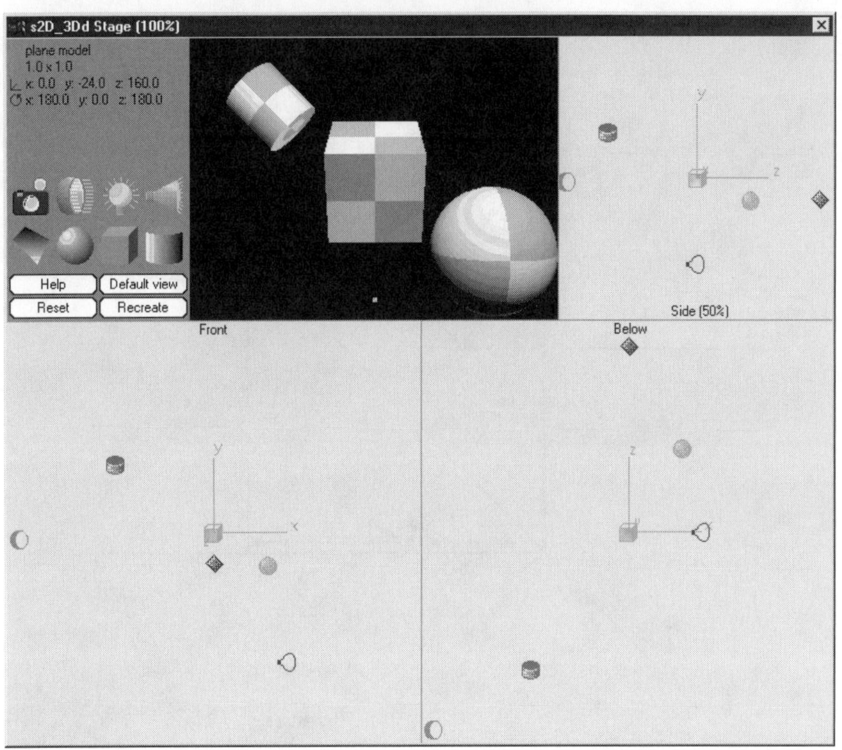

Vectors

In Director, a vector is a way of providing information in three dimensions. The information can be of several types: position in 3D space, displacement in 3D space (line, movement, or direction), 3D scaling, rotation in 3D space, and others that we will look at later. There is no information in the vector itself to determine which type of information it contains: everything depends on the context. In Chapters 10 and 11, that deal with Shaders and Textures, and in Chapter 13, which deals with lights, you will find other types of information provided in vector form. The four just mentioned are those described in this chapter.

Position in 3D Space

A point in space is given in absolute terms, starting from the intersection of the x, y, and z axes. This point is defined by `vector(0, 0, 0)`. A vector used to define a point in 3D space would look like this:

```
vector (xPosition, yPosition, zPosition)
```

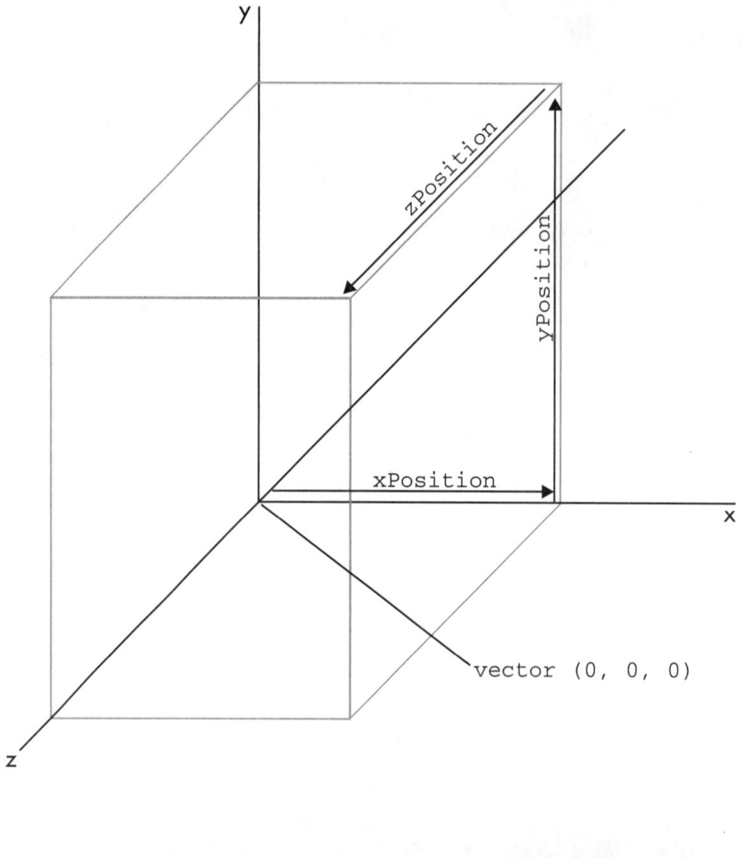

Both for points and displacements, the order of the movements is of little importance: you would get to the same point in space if you moved zPosition units along the z axis, then xPosition units along the x axis, and finally yPosition units along the y axis. The thin gray lines that represent a rectangular box illustrate this: there are six possible paths from the near-bottom-left corner to the far-top-right corner.

Displacement in 3D Space

A vector used to define a displacement in 3D space would look very similar to one used to define a point in space. The difference is that a point is defined in absolute terms starting from the origin at `vector(0, 0, 0)`, whereas a displacement in space is given in relative terms:

```
vector (xLength, yLength, zLength)
```

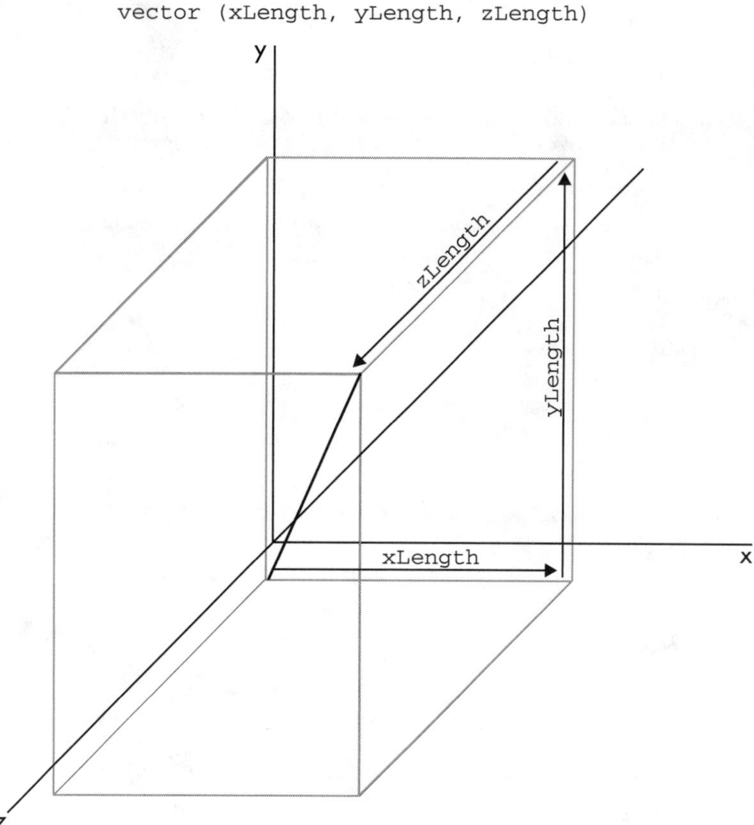

The starting point can be anywhere in space. A displacement actually can represent many different things, for instance:

- A straight line
- An axis (think of the world spinning around the line between the North and South Poles)
- A movement (think of a knight's move in chess)
- A velocity (think of a torpedo)
- A force (think of a taut rope between a tug and an ocean liner)
- A direction (think of pointing with your finger)

Using Vectors to Indicate a Direction

If used to define a direction, the length of the line is unimportant. Directions usually are defined by a vector that is one unit long, which means the direction vector can be used in mathematical calculations without changing the dimensions of the result. You can use the Pythagorean Theorem (twice) to calculate the length of the vector itself; then divide the x, y, and z components by that value so that the resulting vector is one unit long.

```
x = vector(3, 4, 12)
xLength = sqrt(3*3 + 4*4 + 12*12) -- 13
put x / float(xLength)
-- vector( 0.2308, 0.3077, 0.9231 )
```

However, it is simpler to use the built-in `normalize()` vector method, which does this for you:

```
x.normalize()
put x
-- vector( 0.2308, 0.3077, 0.9231 )
```

The `normalize()` method acts directly on the vector itself. You might prefer to create a copy of the vector, leaving the original vector unchanged. You can use the `getNormalized()` function to do this:

```
put x.getNormalized()
-- vector( 0.2308, 0.3077, 0.9231 )
```

3D Scaling

You can stretch sprites on the 2D stage. The original cast member maintains its dimensions, but the size and proportions of the sprite might change. In a Shockwave 3D member, you can stretch models in three dimensions; the original model resource is unchanged.

To create a wheel shape, I altered the height of `modelResource("Resource 1")`. I could have achieved the same effect by altering the vertical scale of the model based on that resource. By default, a model has a scale of `vector(1.0, 1.0, 1.0)`, which means the model has the same size and dimensions as the resource it is based on.

Try the following in the Message window:

```
newCylinder = member(1).newModelResource("Resource 2", #cylinder)
newWheel = member(1).newModel("New wheel")
newWheel.resource = newCylinder
newWheel.transform.scale = vector(1.0, 0.2, 1.0) -- Change vertical scale
newWheel.transform.rotation = vector(-90, 60, 0)
newWheel.transform.position = vector(20, 0, 0)
```

This will create a new `#cylinder` model resource with default dimensions, create a new wheel-shaped model out of it, and place it to the right of the first wheel you created. The cylinder is flattened by scaling the model rather than reducing the height of the resource.

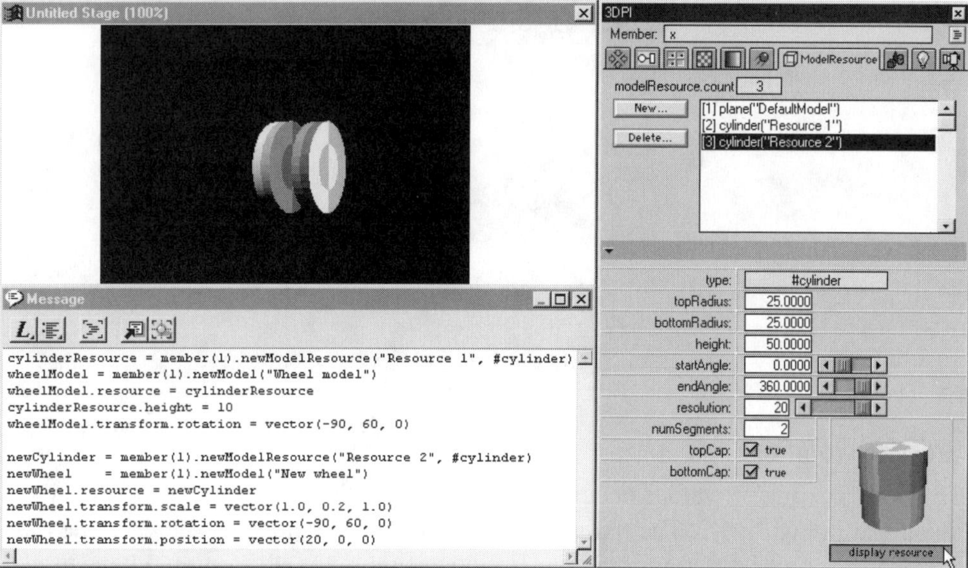

Rotation in 3D Space

Rotation.dir, RotateXY.dir, SelfRef.dir

Rotation in 3D space is complex. It is worthwhile taking time to understand it well. The rotation `vector(-90.0, 60.0, 0.0)` indicates a rotation of –90° around the x axis, a rotation of 60° around the y axis, and no rotation around the z axis.

Positive and Negative Rotation

When you look at a Shockwave 3D sprite using the default camera view, you are looking down the z axis; your eye is at a positive value (+250), and you are looking toward the origin—`vector(0, 0, 0)`—and the negative z values beyond. Looking in this direction, a positive rotation occurs in a counterclockwise direction. If you studied polar coordinates at school, you might remember that this is the mathematical convention. You can use this image to help you remember: when you open a faucet, you turn it counterclockwise to increase the flow of water, and the water flows from a positive height toward the center of the world. Alternatively, you can imagine that you grasp the axis of rotation (as if it were a broomstick) with your right hand, so that your thumb is pointing up the axis toward increasing positive values. Your fingers curl counterclockwise around the axis, in the direction of positive rotation. You will find a movie named Rotation.dir in the 3D\Space\ folder on the CD-ROM, which you can use to visualize which way rotation takes place around each axis.

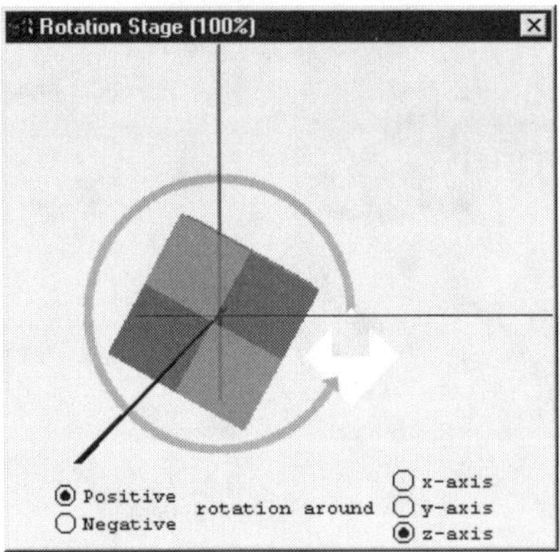

Ordering Rotations

The order in which rotations occur is important, as is the frame of reference, as is illustrated in Figure 6-2. The initial position of the wheel model is shown at the top. Following are four different rotations. For concision in the illustration, I have used the `rotate()` method rather than a vector, but the principles are similar.

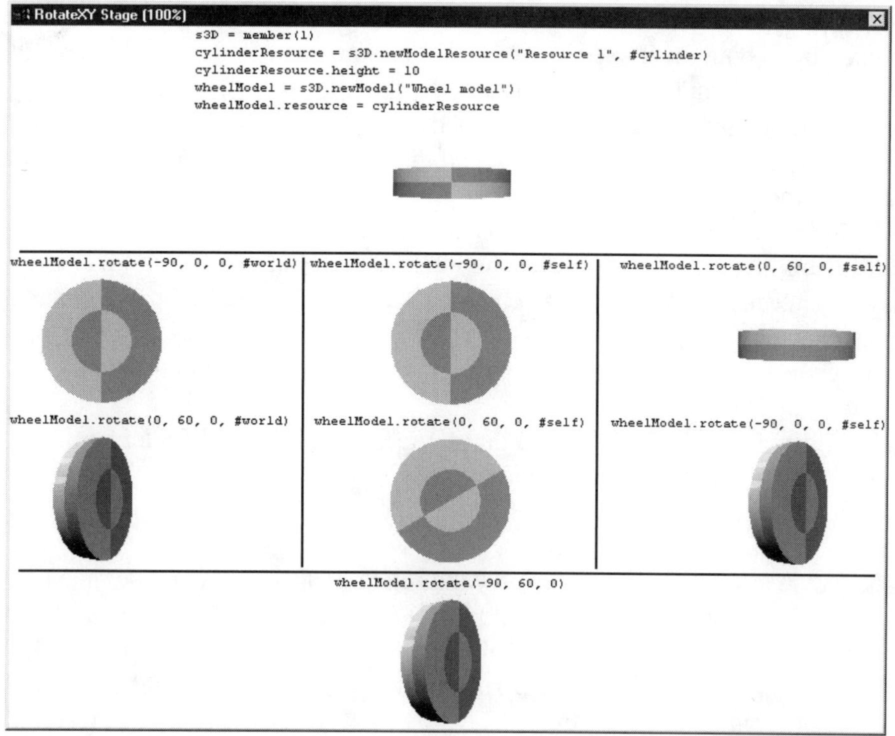

Figure 6-2 *Rotation depends on a frame of reference (#self, #parent, #world, node, or axis)*

The first column shows a 90° counterclockwise rotation around the x axis of the world, followed by a 60° clockwise rotation around the y axis of the world. Because the axes of the 3D world are fixed, this second rotation pivots the wheel model around a vertical axis, just like a car's front wheel is pivoted by the steering system.

The second column shows the same rotations, but this time the model itself is used as the frame of reference. Initially, the model's y axis is vertical. After the 90° counterclockwise rotation around the x axis, the model's y axis continues to point out of the top surface. Because this top surface is now parallel with the screen, the model's y axis now points out of the screen toward the viewer. When the 60° clockwise rotation is made around the model's y axis in its new position, the effect is to turn the wheel as if it were rolling.

The third column shows that the order of the two rotations must be inverted if you use the model's frame of reference. Rotating the model around the y axis makes its x axis point into the screen at an angle of 60 degrees. The model is then rotated counterclockwise around its x axis in this new orientation, which brings it into the intended position.

The fourth rotation is shown at the bottom of Figure 6-2. This applies a compound rotation around both the x and the y axes at the same time. In this case, the result is identical whether you use the 3D world or the model (`#self`) as the frame of reference, because a compound rotation is made with respect to the initial orientation of the x, y, and z axes in the order x, y, and then z. Because the model and the world share the same axes before the compound rotation begins, the effect is the same.

Of course the effect would be different if axes of the model and the world were not identical. Figure 6-3 shows the same rotation vector applied to a tilted model that is not at the center of the world. When `#world` is used as the frame of reference, the model is moved through space as it turns. When `#self` is used as the frame of reference, the center of the model does not move. The final orientation of the two rotations is different.

You will find the original SelfRef.dir movie in the 3D\Space\ folder on the CD-ROM. You will discover that you can display the x, y, and z axes for any given model in a 3D world by setting its `debug` property to `TRUE`. This is illustrated for the model at the top of Figure 6-3.

The movie also allows you to display the rotation of the wheel model in each 3D world. For the wheel rotated around `#self` at the bottom left in Figure 6-3, this is `vector(0.0, 5.0, 0.0)`; the cumulative result of the various rotations is that the wheel is rotated 5° around the y axis. For the wheel rotated around the `#world` at the bottom right, this is `vector(0.0, 0.0, 5.0)`; the cumulative result is that the wheel is rotated 5° around the z axis.

Rotating Real Objects in Real Space

You might find it helpful to simulate these rotations in real space using, say, a CD-ROM instead of the virtual model of a wheel. Find a chubby pen that you can slip through the hole in the CD-ROM, which can act as the CD-ROM's y axis. Make a fist with your right hand (even if your are left-handed) and hold the pen upright in your fist in the curl of your index finger. Balance the CD-ROM flat on the plateau made by your index finger and thumb, making sure that the label is uppermost and is turned so that you can read it. The CD-ROM's z axis points toward you. This is the initial position at the top of Figure 6-3.

First, rotate the CD-ROM –90° around the x axis; the end of the pen that you are not holding should now be pointing horizontally away from you, the CD-ROM should be vertical, the engraved bottom side facing you, and the lettering upside down on the far side. The CD-ROM's z axis is currently pointing vertically upward. Now rotate it +60° around the world's y axis; the CD-ROM should still be vertical with the lettering upside down, and your pen should be pointing horizontally to your left

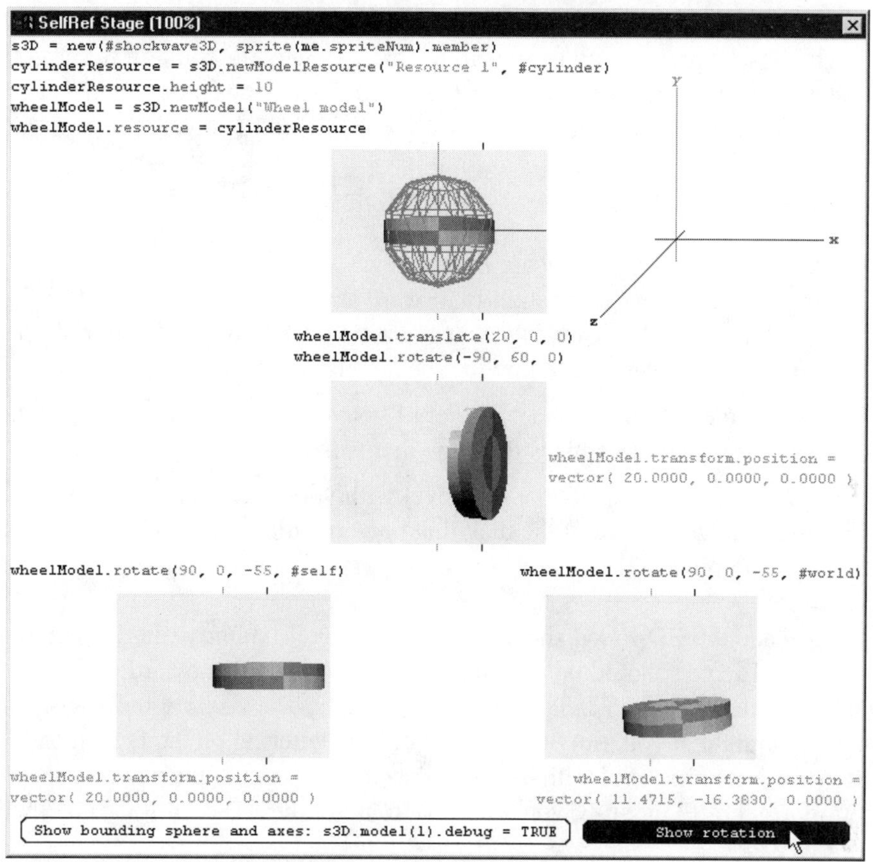

Figure 6-3 *Rotation around #self maintains position; rotation around #world can change it.*

and slightly forward. The z axis is still vertically upward. (this is important). The CD-ROM should now appear in the same position as the wheel model in the center of Figure 6-3.

Now try rotating the CD-ROM +90° around its own x axis. The x axis runs across the face of the disk: your pen should now be facing straight up again, the printed face of the CD-ROM should be on top, but the lettering should be slanting away from you and a little to the right. To end up in the position shown at the bottom right of Figure 6-3, you will have to turn the CD-ROM –55° around the pen. Now think about this carefully: Your pen is now vertical, so it is parallel with the world's y axis. However, the rotation illustrated at the bottom right of Figure 6-3 is a compound rotation, done in one movement. Before the rotation started, which axis of the CD-ROM was pointing vertically upward? Before the rotation started, it was the CD-ROM's z axis, which was parallel with the world's y axis. Hence, the rotation is correctly described as `vector(90, 0, -55, #self)`. Because the compound rotation is performed in one movement, the z axis is still considered to be vertical until the movement is finished.

Visualizing the rotation illustrated at the bottom right is slightly more complex:

1. Start from the position you were in at the end of the last paragraph, but with your pen horizontal and pointing slightly forward and to your left, and the CD-ROM upside down with the printed face away from you. (If you hold your right hand at the level of your chest, the following movement will appear easier.)
2. With your the thumb and index finger of your left hand, pinch the left-hand edge of the CD-ROM (this is the edge that is nearest to your chest).
3. Lift your right hand up so that it is level with your eyes and let your left hand follow, so that the edge of the disk that you are holding in your left hand is now the lowest point.

Your pen and the CD-ROM should now appear like a slightly tilted X in front of your eyes: The pen should be pointing to your left and 30° upward; the disk should be perpendicular to this, tilted 60° up to the right. The z axis of the disk should be pointing straight at you, out of the bottom of the lettering on the face of the CD-ROM. It is now parallel with the world's z axis. To get to the position shown at the bottom right of Figure 6-3, you will have to pivot the CD-ROM 55° clockwise around this z axis.

These manipulations might appear fastidious, but I thoroughly recommend that you try them. The more you move real objects through real space—considering its movement in terms of the world frame of reference and the object's own frame of reference—the easier you will find it to understand how to simulate these movements in virtual 3D space.

Inverting a Rotation

Figure 6-3 also illustrates another point. To obtain the inverse of a rotation, you cannot simply inverse the sign of each component of the rotation; you also have to take into account the order in which the rotations are made around each axis. Rotation is always made first around the x axis, both when making the initial rotation and when you perform the reverse rotation. As you saw when simulating the rotation `vector(90, 0, -55, #world)` with your pen and CD-ROM, this means the return path that the model follows is likely to be different from the path it followed for the initial rotation. Whereas the original rotation of `vector(-90, 60, 0)` occurred around the x and y axes, the inverse rotation of `vector(90, 0 -60)` is effected around the x and z axes.

You don't need to worry about working out how to undo a rotation. *Transform objects,* which we will look at shortly, possess an `inverse()` method that can do the work for you.

Other Frames of Reference

In the simplified example in this chapter, you will be concerned only with the two frames of reference we have already discussed: `#world` and `#self`. However, in most projects, you also will need to use the other three frames of reference: `#parent`, node, or an arbitrary point and axis.

All models have a *parent*. The parent of the wheel that you have been working with is the 3D world itself. This concept of parent makes complex mechanisms easy to construct. Imagine that you need to build a truck that you can steer. You might join two wheels together around an axle. As the axle rotates around its y axis, so the wheels move with it. Simply setting the parent of both the wheels to the axle will ensure that they rotate around it.

Models can have many children (the axle just described has two), but each child can have only one parent. A simple truck would need two such axle groups: A back axle attached to a chassis and a front axle attached to a steering mechanism, which would, in turn, be attached to the chassis. The chassis's parent could be the 3D world itself. In this hypothetical example, the front wheels rotate around the front axle and the front axle rotates around the steering mechanism; each structure will use its parent as the frame of reference.

However, as it rolls forward, the whole truck will turn around an arbitrary point in space defined by the intersection of the lines extended from each axle. There will be nothing in particular in the 3D world at that point; the frame of reference would be defined simply as a point vector and an axis pointing vertically upward from that point.

The state of the front wheels would thus depend on the result of four separate rotations:

- The rotation of the chassis around an arbitrary axis in space
- The rotation of the steering mechanism around a point in the chassis
- The rotation of the axle within the steering mechanism
- The differential rotation of the left wheel compared to the right as the truck turns

The `getWorldTransform()` command allows you to resolve the rotations of all the intermediate parents, and gives you information on the model's state in the 3D world itself. You'll find more information on transforms in the next section of this chapter.

You also can use a *node* as a frame of reference. A node is any kind of physical entity in the 3D world: a model, light, camera, or a group of such entities. If you were creating a virtual solar system to show the phases of the moon, your `camera("Earth")` might use the `light("Sun")` as its frame of reference for rotation. Your `model("Moon")` could rotate around `camera("Earth")`.

The default frame of reference for the `rotate()` command is `#self`. If you want to use a different frame of reference, this must be made explicit, either by including a keyword such as `#world` or `#parent`, or by defining which node (model, light, camera, or group) is to be used.

Making Your Head Spin

Even though we haven't yet explored all the possibilities, it should by now be apparent that controlling rotations in 3D space is a complex process. The choice of frame of reference is crucial. I strongly recommend that you create your own movies to explore the concept, and that you try to predict how a given rotation will affect the model you apply it to. If you predict wrong, you should revise your understanding of the process.

Transforms

A transform object is a summary of the current position, scale, and orientation of a model. To be more accurate, a transform is a shorthand recipe for moving a node (model, light, camera, or group) from its default position at the center of its parent to its given situation in 3D space. It might help you to think of the word "transform" as a process rather than as a result—as a verb rather than as a noun. If a node is the child of another node, two transforms are applied to it: the first is applied to the node's parent with respect to the 3D world; the second is applied to the child node with respect to its parent.

Internally, a transform is a 4 × 4 matrix. Because Director does not have a `#matrix` data type, the information is presented as if it were a special type of list, with 16 items. You don't need to know anything about matrix math in order to use transforms, because 3D Lingo provides you with a set of methods and properties that allow you to manipulate the transform without having to get your hands dirty.

However, it might help to take a quick look inside, just to understand what sort of beast a transform is.

If you are not interested in the details, you can jump to the "Transform Properties and Methods" section later in the chapter. If you do want the details, but you don't need a refresher course in trigonometry, you can skip the next section and go straight on to explore the Identity Matrix.

A Brief Look at Trig

Trig.dir

Trigonometry means "the measurement of trigons." You won't find "trigon" in your dictionary, though you might find "polygon." A polygon is a geometrical figure with many angles. A trigon is a figure with three angles—more commonly known as a triangle. Trig is all about triangles.

Trig's favorite triangle is the right-angled triangle. The godfather of the right-angled triangle is Pythagoras, so we'll start with him. If you don't remember what the Pythagorean Theorem was all about, go and check out the Trig.dir movie in the 3D\Space\ folder on the CD-ROM that accompanies the book. This demonstrates in non-mathematical terms that the area of the square drawn on the hypotenuse of a right-angled triangle is equal to the sum of the areas drawn on the other two sides. If you know the length of two sides of a right-angled triangle, you can use the Pythagorean Theorem to calculate the length of the third side.

Circles and Triangles

Believe it or not, triangles have a lot in common with circles. You can draw a circle through the three summits of any triangle: defining the triangle also defines the circle. Circles + math = pi. Pi (or π, as it is known to its friends) is a weird number; nobody knows exactly what its value is. If you ask Director, you'll get a close enough approximation. Type this in the Message window:

```
set the floatPrecision to 14
put pi()
-- 3.14159265358979
```

Where does this number come from? It's simply the ratio between the circumference of a circle and its diameter. There's a demonstration of this in the Trig.dir movie.

So what does pi have to do with triangles?

Pi and Angles

Imagine that each angle of a triangle is at the center of a circle. You can define the angle as being a certain proportion of the whole circle. But how do you measure that proportion? You can't use a straight ruler, because the edge of a circle is round. So you have to divide the edge of the circle up into equal parts.

The Babylonians divided the circle into 360 degrees for two reasons:

- They reckoned the year to have 360 days, plus five extra days, one for each of the known planets; 360 was thus a number that described the full circle of the year.
- They did their arithmetic in base 60. This is an extraordinarily handy base when it comes to calculating fractions. 360 is conveniently 6 times 60.

Radians

Director uses degrees to rotate both sprites on the Stage and objects in a Shockwave 3D member. However, for basic trigonometrical calculations, Director uses radians. There are `2*pi` radians in one complete rotation. Although you might be more familiar with measuring angles in degrees, you'll find that the radian is a very powerful unit. Let's try to understand why.

When you draw a circle with a pair of compasses, you need to know only one thing: its radius. A curved section of the circumference of a circle is called an *arc*. To imagine a radian, simply imagine an arc exactly one radius long. If you draw two lines, one from each end of the arc to the center of the circle, the angle between the two lines is a radian. There's a demonstration of this in the Trig.dir movie.

By definition, the circumference of a circle is `pi` times its diameter. The diameter is twice the radius, so you could express the circumference as `2*pi` times the radius, or $2\pi r$. You need `2*pi` radians to rotate once in a complete circle, and you need `2*pi` radius lengths to draw the complete circumference. In other words, each time you turn a line through an angle of one radian, each point on the line will move along an arc whose curved length is equal to its distance from the center of rotation. Obvious, isn't it?

Sines and Angles

There's another way of determining angles, a way that deals only with straight lines. Imagine that you have a ladder that is exactly one ladder length long. (That's a mathematician's way of saying that we will say that its length is 1 unit, so that we can conveniently simplify things.) If you lean the ladder against a wall, it will make a certain angle with the ground. You could measure that angle in degrees or radians, or any other unit of circular measurement. Conversely, you could simply measure how high the top of the ladder is from the ground.

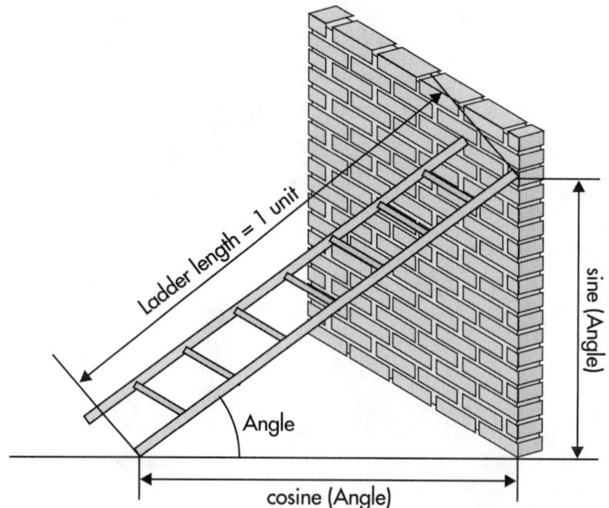

If you change the angle, you change the height of the ladder. If you change the height, you change the angle. So why can't we use the height of the ladder as a measure of the angle? You can—if you use *sines.* A sine is a proportion: the height of a right-angled triangle compared to the length of the hypotenuse. In our example, the ladder makes a certain angle with the ground. The sine of that angle is equal to the height of the ladder divided by its length.

Converting from Angles to Sines

You can measure straight lines in feet or meters. Maybe you still have a school ruler with inches on one side and centimeters on the other, or a table that allows you to convert from one unit of measurement to the other. You could create a similar sort of conversion table with angles on one side and sine values on the other. The only difference will be that the values will not change in a linear fashion because we're dealing with circles and not with straight lines. Director has access to just such a table. It is stored in special logic circuits in the heart of the microprocessor. You can access this table by using the `sin()` function. The value inside the brackets must be expressed in radians.

Cosines

Is there any other straight line we could measure in order to determine the angle? What about the horizontal distance between the foot of the ladder and the foot of the wall? That would give us a result that is complementary to the sine; it's called the *cosine*.

An angle of zero corresponds to a ladder lying flat on the ground. The height of the ladder (the sine) is zero, and the distance between the foot of the ladder and the wall (the cosine) is one. When the ladder is standing vertically against the wall, it will be at an angle of 90° or `pi/2` radians from the ground. In Lingo terms, `sin(pi/2) = 1`, and `cos(pi /2) = 0`. When the ladder is at 45° (or `pi/4` radians), the sine and the cosine are equal. From the Pythagorean Theorem, you can calculate that they will both be $\sqrt{2}$ (or `sqrt (2.0)`, for those who prefer their math in Lingo).

Identity Matrix

When a model is first created, it is placed at the center of the world (its default parent), with a scale of 1.0 in all dimensions and with no translation in any direction. Its transform property just after creation is equivalent to an identity matrix:

```
testModel = new(#shockwave3D).newModel("Test")
put testModel.transform
-- transform(1.00000,0.00000,0.00000,0.00000, 0.00000,1.00000,0.00000,0.00000,
0.00000,0.00000,1.00000,0.00000, 0.00000,0.00000,0.00000,1.00000)
```

It takes a little editing of the data to make this look like a 4 × 4 identity matrix. If you look closely, you'll notice that the figures are bunched in groups of four, each group separated by a space. In the following layout, I have trimmed some of the trailing zeros and arranged the transform data on four separate lines:

```
-- transform( \
1.0, 0.0, 0.0, 0.0, \
0.0, 1.0, 0.0, 0.0, \
0.0, 0.0, 1.0, 0.0, \
0.0, 0.0, 0.0, 1.0)
```

This should make it clear that all the entries are zero, except those that appear on the diagonal of the 4 × 4 matrix; these diagonal values are equal to 1.0. In the following code snippets, I will continue to apply this layout so that the information in the transform is easier to read.

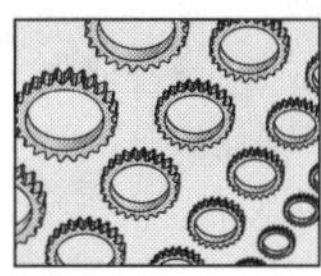

NOTE

Director always displays transforms with 5 figures after the decimal point, regardless of the value of the global `floatPrecision` property. For speed reasons, transforms are calculated using single-precision, floating-point numbers (32 bit). Such numbers are accurate only to 5 decimal places, hence the five figures after the decimal point.

What the Transform Data Means

It can help you to think of a transform as being a table like the one shown in Table 6-1.

The first three columns of the first three lines specify the scale and orientation of each axis of the transform. The data is written in a shorthand form; once a transform has been rotated, what you see in the table might need a bit of number crunching before it yields human-usable information (you'll see how to avoid this in the "Transform Properties" section later in this chapter). The first three columns of the fourth line indicate the position of the transform in 3D space (no number crunching is required).

The fourth column is a neat mathematical trick to simplify matrix manipulations. This is described in the following note. If you fill in Table 6-1 using the data from the default transform that is applied to a new model, you will see that a new model is placed so that

- The model's x axis lies along the world's x axis.
- The model's y axis lies along the world's y axis.
- The model's z axis lies along the world's z axis.
- The center of the model is in the center of the world.

In the following pages, you will see how displacing, scaling, and rotating the model affects the values in the transform matrix.

	World x axis	World y axis	World z axis	Data is a point?
Model x axis				0
Model y axis				0
Model z axis				0
Model position				1

Table 6-1 *The Meaning of a Transform*

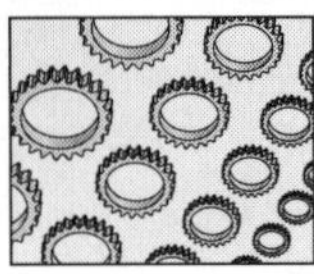

NOTE

If you are used to working with affine transformations, you will notice that the columns and rows are transposed in Table 6-1. I will continue to use this layout as it is simple to generate from the Lingo output. The values used for the fourth column are significant. Using four 4×1 matrices makes it easy to distinguish points from vectors. A vector has no position; a point has no length. A `0` in the fourth place is used to indicate a vector; a `1` is used to indicate a point. Adding or subtracting two vectors produces another vector (the fourth value is still `0`). Adding a vector to a point produces a point (the fourth value is `1`). Adding a point to a point has no meaning: it would give rise to a fourth value of `2`, which is invalid for affine transformations. Subtracting a point from a point produces a vector (the fourth value becomes `0`).

Translation to a New Position in the World

You can move a model to a different point in space without scaling it or rotating it, using the `translate()` command. Notice how the position information is stored in the first three items of the last line of the 4 × 4 matrix:

```
testModel.translate(10, 20, 30)
put testModel.transform
-- transform( \
 1.0,  0.0,  0.0, 0.0, \
 0.0,  1.0,  0.0, 0.0, \
 0.0,  0.0,  1.0, 0.0, \
10.0, 20.0, 30.0, 1.0)
```

Scaling the Model

Let's now change the scale of our test model to see how that affects the transform. The scaling information appears in the first three items on the diagonal of the 4 × 4 matrix:

```
testModel.scale(4, 5, 6)
put testModel.transform
-- transform( \
 4.0,  0.0,  0.0, 0.0, \
 0.0,  5.0,  0.0, 0.0, \
 0.0,  0.0,  6.0, 0.0, \
10.0, 20.0, 30.0, 1.0)
```

Rotating the Model

As you saw earlier, rotations are more complex. Let's rotate around one axis at a time and check how the transform is affected after each rotation. Figure 6-4 shows the effect of a series of rotations that I will apply to the test model. Compare the values in the transform matrices that appear in the following sections with those in the appropriate image in the figure. Can you see how the transform stores the model's dimensions in terms of the world's frame of reference?

90° Rotations

When you rotate the model 90° around the x axis, the model maintains its scale along the x axis, but its scale along the other axes changes. The model's dimension along its own y axis now appears parallel to the world's z axis. The model's z axis is now pointing the wrong way down the world's y axis, which gives it a negative value:

```
testModel.rotate(90, 0, 0)
put testModel.transform
-- transform( \
 4.0,  0.0,  0.0, 0.0, \
 0.0, -0.0,  5.0, 0.0, \
 0.0, -6.0, -0.0, 0.0, \
10.0, 20.0, 30.0, 1.0)
```

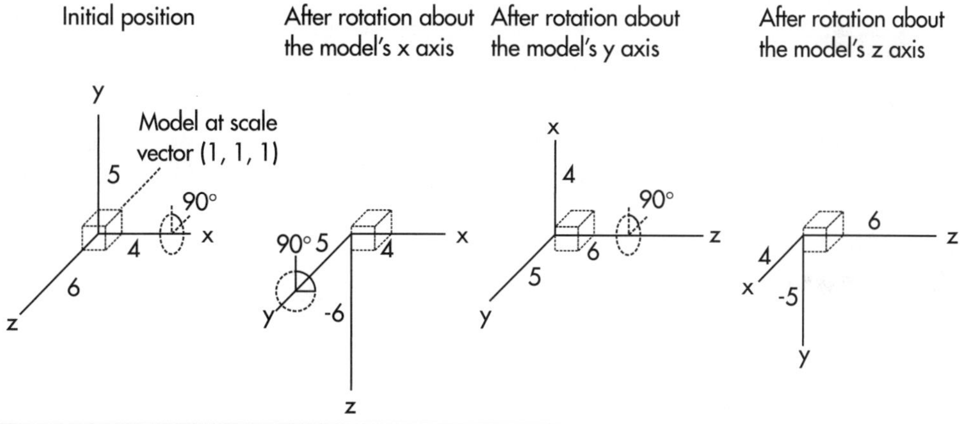

Figure 6-4 *Graphic representation of rotations around each axis of the model*

A subsequent 90° rotation around the model's y axis (the world's z axis) will bring the model's x axis parallel to the world's y axis and the model's z axis parallel with the world's x axis:

```
testModel.rotate(0, 90, 0)
put testModel.transform
-- transform( \
-0.0,  4.0,  0.0, 0.0, \
 0.0, -0.0,  5.0, 0.0, \
 6.0,  0.0,  0.0, 0.0, \
10.0, 20.0, 30.0, 1.0)
```

A third rotation of 90° around the model's z axis (the world's x axis) will again result in a negative value—this time for the y component:

```
testModel.rotate(0, 0, 90)
put testModel.transform
-- transform( \
 0.0, -0.0,  4.0, 0.0, \
 0.0, -5.0, -0.0, 0.0, \
 6.0,  0.0,  0.0, 0.0, \
10.0, 20.0, 30.0, 1.0)
```

Rotations Other Than 90°

Let's now see what happens if we rotate a model through an angle of less than 90°. We'll use a new model with no translation and the default scale of `vector(1.0, 1.0, 1.0)`. We will rotate it 30° around the z axis because this leads to the simplest illustration (Figure 6-5). You might remember that cos(30°) = `sqrt(3/4.0)` = 0.866, and sin(30°) = 0.5.

```
testModel = new(#shockwave3D).newModel("Test")
testModel.rotate(30, 0, 0)
put testModel.transform
-- transform( \
 0.866, 0.5,   0.0, 0.0, \
-0.5,   0.866, 0.0, 0.0, \
 0.0,   0.0,   1.0, 0.0, \
 0.0,   0.0,   0.0, 1.0)
```

As Figure 6-5 shows, the x dimension of the model is drawn at an angle: the 1.0 unit line can be described as starting at the point vector(0, 0, 0) and ending at

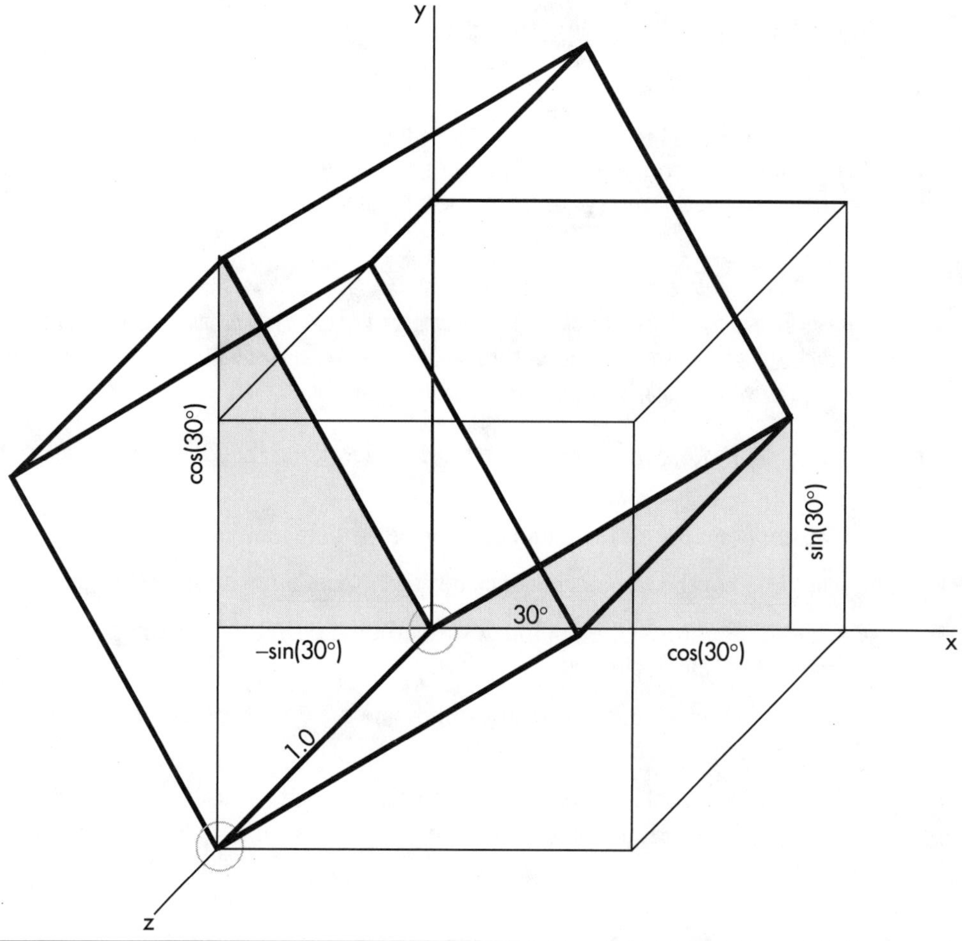

Figure 6-5 *A rotation of 30° around the z axis*

the point `vector(cos(30°), sin(30°), 0)`, or `vector(0.866, 0.5, 0)`. Do you see how this end point corresponds to the first line of the transform? Can you see how the second line of the transform corresponds to the y axis of the model described according to the world's frame of reference? The third line of the transform simply states that the z axis of the model continues to lie along the z axis of the world.

If you feel confident with 3D geometry, you could create further examples for yourself using rotations around two or three axes.

Transform Properties and Methods

Trnsform.dir

Once a transform has been rotated, it becomes more complex to decipher the shorthand it contains. Fortunately, 3D Lingo provides you with ways to do this without resorting to trigonometry, in the guise of transform properties.

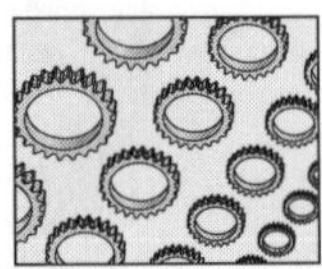

NOTE

If you want to take a deeper look at the mathematics, you can find a demonstration of the basic techniques in the Trnsform.dir movie in the 3D\Space\ folder on the CD-ROM that accompanies this book. You will lose no Brownie points if you do not do so.

The main points to remember are these:

- A transform contains all the data necessary to situate a model in 3D space.
- The last "line" of the transform describes the model's position in 3D space.
- The scale of an unrotated model is described by the first three items on the diagonal of the transform matrix.
- The first three "lines" of the transform indicate the how each of the three axes of the model appears in 3D space.
- A transform knits scale and rotation together: you need to use the Pythagorean Theorem and basic trigonometry to retrieve the individual scale and rotation vectors.

Transform Properties

Fortunately, 3D Lingo provides you with properties that return this information automatically:

```
put aTransform.scale
-- vector(1.0, 0.2, 1.0)
put aTransform.rotation
-- vector(-90.0, 60.0, 0.0)
put aTransform.position
-- vector(0.0, 0.0, 0.0)
```

You can set these properties directly, as I did earlier when rotating the wheel model into its starting position:

```
wheelModel.transform.rotation = vector(-90.0, 60.0, 0.0)
```

When you set a property directly, you manipulate the transform in terms of the node's parent. In the preceding example, the wheel's parent is (by default) the world, so the rotation is made with respect to the world's frame of reference. If you want to manipulate the transform relative to its current values, you probably will find it easier to use one of the many transform methods detailed here.

Following is a full list of transform properties, each with a brief description of its purpose. You will find more information on all of these in the *3D Lingo Dictionary*, and specific examples on most of them in the pages that follow (the first three have already been dealt with):

- **`position`**
- **`rotation`**
- **`scale`**
- **`worldPosition`** Position of the model with respect to the 3D world. The translations, rotations, and scalings of the model's parents are resolved within the `#world` frame of reference.
- **`pointAtOrientation`** Allows you to determine which part of the model is considered to be its front. This is used in association with the `pointAt()` method (see the following), so that you can turn a node (model, light, camera, or group) to point toward another or toward a particular point.
- **`xAxis`** Gives you the current orientation of the node's x axis, with respect to the world. This is a vector that uses the first three values in the transform.
- **`yAxis`** Gives you the current orientation of the node's y axis, with respect to the world. This is a vector that uses values 5, 6, and 7 in the transform, or the first three values in the second line of the 4 × 4 matrix. We will be using this shortly to determine which way the wheel is facing. Because we will be rotating the wheel around its y axis, the wheel's x and z axes will be turning continuously. The y axis will remain fixed; the wheel will roll along a horizontal line perpendicular to its y axis.
- **`zAxis`** Gives you the current orientation of the node's z axis with respect to the world. This is a vector that uses values 9, 10, and 11 in the transform, or the first three values in the third line of the 4 × 4 matrix.

You also can get and set the individual items in a transform object as if it were a list:

```
put transform()[1]
-- 1.0000
x = transform()
x[2] = 2
put x
-- transform(
1.00000,2.00000,0.00000,0.00000,
0.00000,1.00000,0.00000,0.00000,
0.00000,0.00000,1.00000,0.00000,
0.00000,0.00000,0.00000,1.00000)
```

The preceding example will produce a shear; that is, its axes of the transform will no longer be *orthogonal* (at right angles to each other). Imagine that your model is a vertically stacked deck of cards. Shearing the deck would slide each card a fixed distance compared to the card below it. The result is a distortion of the original deck.

CAUTION

If you manipulate the items of a transform directly, you can create an invalid transform. The transform will be invalid if any two axes are parallel. It also will be invalid if you modify the numbers in the last column. An invalid transform could crash certain 3D hardware.

Transform Methods

What can you do with a transform? All you can do can be broken down in terms of translation, scaling, and rotation, which we have already examined. Fortunately, for the most common movements, you don't have to work out for yourself what the new value of the transform needs to be; you'll find a list of transform methods in the *3D Lingo Dictionary*. Rather than repeat here what each method does, I present the information from the opposite perspective: you won't be using any of these methods in this chapter, but knowledge of their existence will help you understand what a transform is. It would be a good idea to look up the appropriate entries in the 3D Lingo Dictionary to familiarize yourself with the various possibilities for each method.

- **Tweening** You can convert one transform progressively into another in a linear fashion. Imagine a space shuttle turning up to 180° around itself along one or more of its axes as it moves in a straight line toward a target position. The `interpolate()` function and the `interpolateTo()` method will give you the means to do this. You can repeat the process many times to create several intermediate positions. The transform object that you use as the final state of the interpolation can itself change between each iteration, thus allowing you to home in on a moving target.

- **Extending** You can apply more than one transform at a time to a node (the result will always be a single transform). Imagine that a passerby asks you for directions to get to a nearby landmark. You probably can give the person several routes to get to the same place. Your directions will probably include several instructions: go straight on until you come to the four-way stop; then turn left. The instructions have to be carried out in the correct order; if not, the passerby will get lost. In a virtual 3D world, a transform is one instruction. You can use the `multiply()` method to string a set of transform instructions together. The first transform might place your `model("passer-by")` at the four-way stop, the second might make it turn to face the left.

  You also could use `multiply()` to apply the same transform a number of times in succession to the same node. This would make the node tumble in a regular loop.

  The `multiply()` method applies a complete transform (translation, rotation, and scale) to the current transform. You can apply each of these movements separately using the `translate()`, `rotate()`, and `scale()` methods.

- **Following** Imagine an aerial display team flying in formation. Whenever the team leader maneuvers his or her plane, the other team members maneuver to remain in exactly the same relative position, as if their planes were glued to the leader's. You can achieve this effect by setting the `parent` of each of the other team member's planes to the leader's plane. You also can achieve it by using the `multiply()` method described in the preceding. For each of the other team member's planes you could store a transform that describes its position relative to the leader's plane. On each `exitFrame`, you would multiply a duplicate of this transform with the leader's transform and apply the resulting transform to the appropriate team member's plane.

- **Ordering** Transforms contain rotational information, and the order in which rotations are applied is important. As a result, the order in which transforms are applied is important, too. A rotation followed by a translation has different effect than a translation followed by a rotation. Try it: Stand up facing the nearest door, walk forward two paces; and then turn left. Assuming that you have space to do this, you now should be nearer the door, which should be on your right. Go back to your starting position, turn left, and then walk forward two paces. If you didn't walk into any walls on the way, the door should be diagonally behind you on your right. You can determine which order transforms are applied by using the `multiply()`, `rotate()`, `scale()`, and `translate()` methods described in the preceding, or their preemptive versions: `preMultiply()`, `preRotate()`, `preScale()`, and `preTranslate()`. The sequence `walkTwoPaces.multiply(turnLeft)` will take you forward before you turn; `walkTwoPaces.preMultiply(turnLeft)` will make you turn first and then move you forward.

- **Facing** You can instruct a node (model, light, camera, or group) to turn to face a particular point or another node. Imagine a golf ball being driven off the tee; following it with a camera is one of the most difficult jobs for a TV cameraman. You can achieve the same result very simply by applying the `pointAt()` method so that your virtual camera follows your virtual golf ball automatically.
- **Undoing** A transform is a process that you can undo. Imagine a film of someone dropping an open box of matches being played backward: the transform applied to each individual match as it falls can be inverted so that the matches appear to return to their initial position in the box. The `inverse()` function and the `invert()` method can help you do this. If you want to retrace the exact steps taken by a match on its way from the box to the floor, you would need to store the `inverse()` of each transform applied to the match and apply these inverse transforms in the reverse order.
- **Reverting** A transform never forgets its parent. The `identity()` method sets the transform to its default value, indicating no translation, no scaling, and no rotation. Using the `identity()` method on a transform is the equivalent of returning the node to the center of its parent, with the same orientation and scaling as the parent. (Wouldn't it be nice to be able to apply the `identity()` method to your car keys?)

There is one other method that is not restricted to transforms:

- **`duplicate()`** Like points, rects, vectors, and lists, transforms are pointers. They do not contain data directly: they contain the address in the computer's RAM space where the data is stored. If two variables contain the same transform (RAM address), modifications made to one variable will automatically be reflected in the other. If you want to modify a transform without affecting the node (model, light, camera, or group) it is attached to, you should first use the `duplicate()` command to copy the same information to a different memory address. Subsequent modifications to data at that memory address will not affect the original transform.

Back to the Grindstone

We've taken a long detour from the original project of creating a wheel that the user can roll and steer, but now you have some insight into how to proceed. In this section, you will see how to control the movement of the wheel in 3D space.

3D Behaviors

Up to now, you've typed all the 3D Lingo into the Message window. Now we'll make a behavior to attach to the 3D sprite so that we can use the `#exitFrame` event to animate the wheel. Before we start, it might help to note a couple of particularities in the way Director 8.5 handles 3D elements.

You Can't Save Changes

The first particularity is that you cannot save changes made to a Shockwave 3D member. Changes to the 3D member persist as long as you keep the movie open; when you halt the movie, the various nodes freeze in their current position, ready to move on again when the movie is relaunched. Do not let this lull you into a false sense of security: As soon as your movie leaves the stage, your 3D members revert.

You can create a 3D world using a third-party 3D design program and import this into Director 8.5. The 3D world will appear as a new Shockwave 3D member. Each time you open the movie, you will find the 3D world in exactly the same state as when you first imported it. This seems fair enough: Flash members, for instance, work the same way.

The current example does not use an imported 3D world. The cylinder model resource and the wheel model are created from primitives at run time. The 3D world we are using starts out empty. When the movie closes and the 3D member reverts, all elements created at run time are destroyed. This means that you have to re-create the 3D world from scratch each time you open the movie. Re-creating the world requires four steps:

1. Creating or importing any resources that you will need.
2. Creating any nodes (models, cameras, lights, or groups) that you will need.
3. Setting the parent of each node as appropriate.
4. Setting the transforms of each node to its initial position.

You Can't Control a Node Directly

The second particularity is that you cannot attach a behavior directly to a node; you have to attach it to the sprite. Because this is true of all types of sprites in Director, you might not find this surprising. However, one 3D sprite can contain more data and interactivity than the rest of the sprites put together. Controlling the 3D world from outside the sprite can seem akin to wallpapering a room through a keyhole. For a complex world, you might require a whole bunch of behaviors attached to your sprite, each controlling a different node and each referring to that node by name or number. A behavior is to a 3D sprite what a Movie Script is to the rest of the movie: effective but unfocused.

Creating the World Anew

Our behavior needs to start by running through the instructions you have already typed in the Message window. The following `createWorld()` handler performs the four steps described in the preceding during the `beginSprite` event. The `initialize()` handler takes us into new territory, so I will discuss it in more detail further on. The handlers that appear here are slightly simplified versions of those you will find in the Wheel.dir movie on the CD-ROM.

```
property myWheel       -- Model of a tire-shaped cylinder


on beginSprite(me)
  me.createWorld()
  me.initialize()
end


on createWorld(me)
  s3D = sprite(me.spriteNum).member
  -- Destroy the world so that it can be rebuilt from scratch
  s3D.resetWorld()

  -- Create a new cylinder resource
  tire         = s3D.newModelResource("Cylinder", #cylinder)
  -- Make it roughly tire shaped
  tire.height = 10

  -- Create a model from it that will be visible in the world
  myWheel          = s3D.newModel("wheel")
  myWheel.resource = tire

  -- Place the wheel in its initial orientation
  myWheel.rotate(-90.0, 60.0, 0.0)
end createWorld
```

Rolling the Wheel

Wheel0.dir

To make the virtual wheel appear to roll, we are going to have to do two things on each `#exitFrame`:

1. Rotate the wheel model around its y axis, which is currently lying horizontally.
2. Move the wheel by the appropriate distance and in the appropriate direction.

Steering the wheel means we need to know the orientation of the wheel's axle. The `initialize()` handler serves to initialize the properties that allow us to control these interactions

Properties of the Wheel

The distance the wheel moves forward will depend on the wheel's speed of rotation, which is measured in degrees. We will start by setting `mySpeed` to zero. The user will be able to alter this value via the Up and Down arrow keys.

The distance rolled also will depend on the circumference of the wheel. The `myTread` property is a constant that represents 1/360th of the circumference of the wheel. Multiplying this length by the wheel's angular rotation will give the distance the wheel moves forward.

Because the wheel rotates around its y axis, the direction it rolls will be perpendicular to the wheel's y axis and will lie in the world's horizontal plane (note the different frames of reference used here). The current orientation of the wheel's y axis, in terms of the wheel's parent (the 3D world), is given by `myWheel.transform.yAxis`. The user will be able to alter this value through the Left and Right arrow keys.

```
property mySpeed       -- Number of degrees the wheel rotates per frame
property myTread       -- Circumference of cylinder
property myAxleVector -- Orientation of the wheel's axle (yAxis)


on initialize(me)
  -- Wait for the user to presses the up or down arrow before moving
  mySpeed      = 0

  -- Determine the circumference of the wheel and its orientation
  myTread      = myWheel.resource.topRadius * pi / 180
  myAxleVector = myWheel.transform.yAxis
end initialize
```

Methods of the Wheel

You now have all the elements that you need to roll and steer the wheel. Let's now work out how to make the wheel roll. Let's start with a simple hard-coded simulation:

```
on exitFrame(me)
  me.rollWheel()
end exitFrame

on rollWheel()
  myWheel.rotate(0, 10, 0) -- rotate 10° about the model's y axis
end rollWheel
```

You'll find an unfinished movie entitled Wheel0.dir in the 3D\Space\ folder of the CD-ROM that accompanies this book. This movie contains a Wheel behavior with all the handlers shown so far. When you run the movie, the wheel rotates on the spot.

Run the movie; then type the following in the Message window:

```
member("Wheel").model("wheel").debug = TRUE
```

You'll see the bounding sphere of the model appear as a gray wire frame; the model's axes appear as colored lines. The red x axis and the blue y axis will be turning clockwise as the wheel turns. The green y axis will appear fixed.

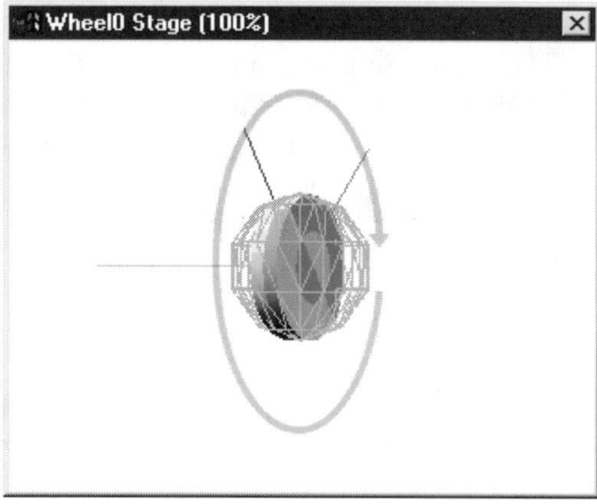

Let's look at the y axis more closely. Type this in the Message window:

```
put member("Wheel").model("wheel").transform.yAxis
-- vector( -0.8660, 0.0000, -0.5000 )
```

This means the y axis runs –0.866 units along the world's x axis and –0.5 units along the world's z axis. As mentioned earlier, lines that are used to indicate a direction are 1 unit long (0.866 × 0.866 + 0.5 × 0.5 = 1.0).

In which direction should the wheel roll? It should go into the screen, so its position on the world's z axis should decrease; and it should go to the left, so its position on the world's x axis should increase. Its movement into the screen should be greater than its movement left. This illustration shows the view looking down on the wheel from above.

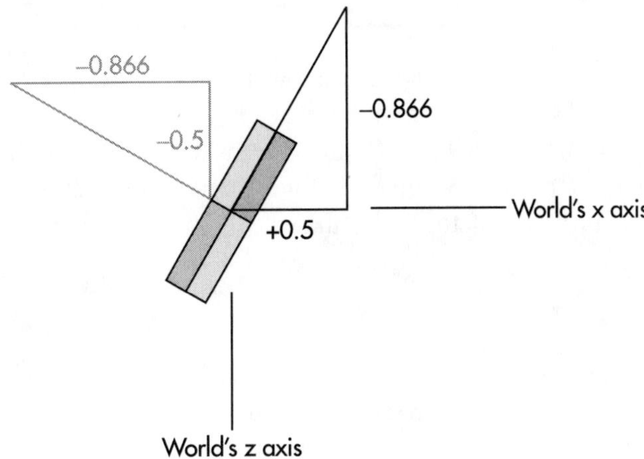

From this you can see that the wheel should roll along the `vector(0.5, 0, -0.866)`. You can generalize this by using the following formula:

```
axleVector    = myWheel.transform.yAxis
xTranslation = -axleVector.z
zTranslation =  axleVector.x
```

You can make the wheel move in the correct direction by using the `translate()` method on the wheel's transform:

```
myWheel.transform.translate(xTranslation, 0, zTranslation)
```

Try adding this to the `rollWheel()` handler, then run the movie. The wheel seems to slip as it turns. Place a debug breakpoint in your `rollWheel()` handler to see why:

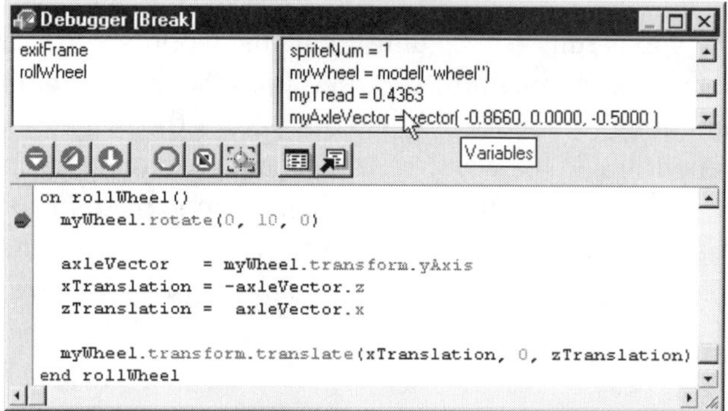

In the Variables pane of the Debugger window, the `myTread` property shows that the wheel should move 0.4363 units forward for every 1° it turns. You have hard-coded the wheel to turn 10° on each `exitFrame`, which means it should move forward 4.363 units. The direction vector that you are using for the translation is only 1 unit long. Let's multiply it by the appropriate factor so that the wheel moves forward correctly:

```
on rollWheel()
  mySpeed = 10
  myWheel.rotate(0, mySpeed , 0)

  axleVector   = myWheel.transform.yAxis
  xTranslation = -axleVector.z * mySpeed * myTread
  zTranslation =  axleVector.x * mySpeed * myTread

  myWheel.transform.translate(xTranslation, 0, zTranslation)
end rollWheel
```

Run your movie again to see if this looks better.

Steering the Wheel

We haven't finished with the `rollWheel()` handler yet, but it's now time to see how to steer the wheel so that it doesn't quickly run out of the sprite image. Previously, you used the simplest form of the rotate() method. If you look it up in the 3D Lingo Dictionary, you will see that the syntax can take a variety of forms, including

```
node(whichNode).rotate(position, axis, angle {, relativeTo})
```

This is the form of syntax that we shall use here.

Rotating Relative to the World

What axis should we rotate the wheel round to steer it? It should turn around an axis that is parallel to the world's y axis and that passes through the center of the wheel. Because we have rotated the wheel model around the z axis, its own y axis is now lying horizontally, so we cannot use that. We'll have to find a different way of defining the vertical axis around which the wheel should be steered. Look back to the "Transform Properties" section to see which property will tell us where the center of the wheel is in relation to the world: `.worldPosition`. To define an axis parallel to the world's y axis, you can create a unit vector that points directly upward: `vector(0, 1, 0)`. Now that you have a point and an axis, you can use the `rotate()` method to steer the wheel. (Be sure to indicate that the rotation is relative to the world—or test what happens if you don't.)

Add the following handler to your behavior:

```
on turn(me, turnAngle)
  wheelCenter = wheel.worldPosition
  axis        = vector(0, 1, 0) -- yAxis
  relativeTo  = #world
  myWheel.rotate(wheelCenter, axis, turnAngle, relativeTo)
end turn
```

Now type the following instruction in the Message window, but don't press RETURN until you have started your movie:

```
sendSprite(1, #turn, 45)
```

Execute the line a number of times by pressing RETURN and then BACKSPACE repeatedly. Can you keep the wheel in view?

Providing User Control

Your end user is not going to be able to type into the Message window, so you need to provide a neater way to turn. I propose that you use the Left and Right arrow keys, whose key codes are `123` and `124`, respectively. While you are at it, why not use the Down and Up arrow keys (`keycode 125` and `126`) to change the value of `mySpeed`. I've limited the forward and reverse speeds so that the rotation remains realistic:

```
on keyDown(me)
  case the keyCode of
```

```
    123: me.turn(5)                         -- turn left
    124: me.turn(-5)                        -- turn right
    125: mySpeed = max(-5, mySpeed -1)  -- slow down / increase reverse
    126: mySpeed = min(20, mySpeed + 1)-- speed up / decrease reverse
  end case
end keyDown
```

The Up and Down keys won't have any effect until you make a change to the `rollWheel()` handler. (I'll let you work out what that is—or you can cheat and look at the finished movie.)

Tidying Up

The code you have added to the Wheel0.dir movie is not exactly the same as that in the finished Wheel.dir movie; the finished behavior is better optimized. For instance, the orientation of the y axis of the wheel is stored in the `myAxleVector` property, which is updated each time the user steers the wheel. In the movie you have been working on, the `rollWheel()` handler reads the `myWheel.transform.yAxis` property on every exitFrame, which is less efficient. Now that you understand the purpose of each line of code, see if you can find other ways of making the behavior neater and more CPU friendly.

Conclusion

This chapter barely scratches the surface of what Shockwave 3D can do; however, it should give you an idea of how 3D space is modeled, and how much trigonometry and geometry you are going to have to use to make a realistic 3D world.

It also should have reassured you about how intuitively 3D Lingo allows you to control your world. Although a fair understanding of mathematics is helpful, all the complex work (such as dealing with matrices) is taken care of for you. As long as you can create a mental image of what each keyword represents, you should be able to exploit the mathematical powerhouse on which 3D Lingo is built.

I have used diagrams to illustrate certain transforms, and proposed exercises in which you manipulated a real object (such as yourself) in real space. You also may find it helpful to sketch a movement, either on paper or in the air, to break the movement down into its component parts: translation, rotation, and scale.

In the next chapter, we will look at two new 3D primitives and see how to use vectors to describe the force of gravity.

CHAPTER

7

Rays and the Physics of Motion

IN THIS CHAPTER:

an assassin's crosshair on his victim's temple
a ladder raised up towards the moon
the distance between the bee and the hive
a crow flies
the tug on your arms as you swing your child

This chapter extends the study of vector mathematics begun in the last chapter. It shows you how to model the movement of a ball on a sloping plane using vectors. You also will discover how to use invisible rays to "see" through 3D space. This chapter introduces two new primitives: the plane and the sphere.

Setting the Ball Rolling

Teeter.dir

Open the Teeter.dir movie, which you will find in the 3D\Physics\ folder on the CD-ROM, and run it; you should see a ball sitting motionless on a flat plane. Now press one of the arrow keys. The plane will tilt downward in the direction you chose and the ball will start rolling down the slope. If you leave the plane tilted, the ball will accelerate. If you tilt the plane in the opposite direction, the ball will come slowly to a halt, and then it will start rolling in the opposite direction.

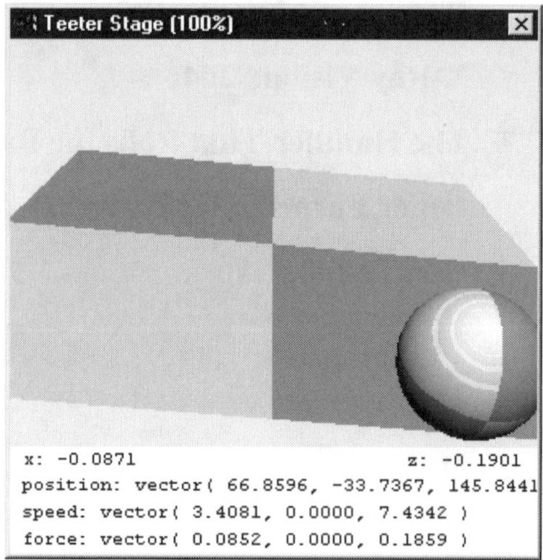

It looks very much as if the ball is affected by the force of gravity. Gravity is not preprogrammed into a 3D world; you have to create it. Later in this chapter, you will see that the Havok Xtra member can be used in association with a Shockwave 3D member to simulate gravity. However, in this exercise you will create a gravitational effect unaided, which will enable you to see how vectors can be used to represent forces. You will learn how to add two vectors, how to find the angle between them, and how to calculate a third vector that is at right angles to both. You'll use this last technique to make sure the ball rolls realistically and in the right direction. You'll also get the chance to revise the equations of motion that you might have last seen in your high school science class.

In the previous chapter, you manipulated the wheel directly; in this exercise, you move the plane and the plane moves the ball. This means you will need to know where the ball is in relation to the plane. To do this, you will use the `modelsUnderRay()` function. This is like a cross between a laser and radar: It allows you to send out a thin, invisible ray in a given direction and learn about the models that it meets as it travels.

To see the scene clearly, you'll also move the camera that looks into the sprite to a better viewpoint than its default position. You won't win an Oscar for your camera work (you'll have to wait for Chapter 12 for that), but you will get an inkling of the importance of the camera.

Creating a Flat Earth

Create a new movie, and create a Shockwave 3D member in cast slot 1. Give your member a name so that it does not get deleted automatically when you save your movie. Place the Shockwave 3D member on the Stage. Add a "go loop" Frame Script to your movie or ensure that the Loop Playback button is checked so that the movie keeps running.

Right-click (Windows) or CTRL-click (Macintosh) on the 3D sprite, and choose Script in the contextual menu that appears. The Script window will open to allow you to create a new behavior. Delete the default handler and enter the following:

```
property myPlane

on beginSprite(me)
  thisSprite = sprite(me.spriteNum)
  s3D = thisSprite.member
  s3D.resetWorld()

  flatArea = s3D.newModelResource("Plane", #plane)
  myPlane  = s3D.newModel("plane")
  myPlane.resource = flatArea
end
```

Now, run your movie. If you look closely, you might make out a tiny red-and-white square in the center of the 3D sprite. Other primitives have a basic size of 50 units along each axis; planes are different. Try this in the Message window:

```
put member(1).modelResource("Plane").width
-- 1.0000
put member(1).modelResource("Plane").length
-- 1.0000
```

Length and Width Properties

To make the plane more obvious you can make it larger. While the movie is running, type this in the Message window:

```
member(1).modelResource("Plane").length = 100
member(1).modelResource("Plane").width = 100
```

When you change the `#length` of the plane, it grows taller. The default orientation of a plane is upright. This means it is visible from the default camera position. The `#length` of a plane is defined along the y axis. This can be a little confusing. As you will discover in the next chapter, changing the `#length` of a box is defined along the z axis. A box's `#height` corresponds to a plane's `#length`.

Vertices Properties

A plane is a very simple, rectangular shape. You might be surprised to learn that it actually is made up of triangles. While the movie is running, type this in the Message window:

```
member(1).shader(1).renderStyle = #wire
```

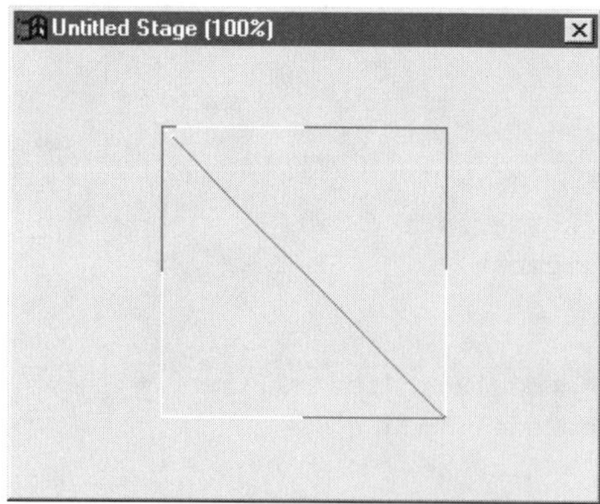

You should now see a *mesh*, made up of two triangular *faces*. All 3D models are made up of such faces; each face has three vertex points: one at each corner. A mesh is simply a group of triangular faces linked up to form a given 3D shape. You will see in Chapter 9 how to create a freeform mesh, where you define each of the vertices, and how they to join the dots to create triangles. The plane model resource is just the simplest form of mesh.

You can get and set the number of vertices that will be used along each side to make up the plane. The number and shape of the faces will adapt to suit.

```
put member(1).modelResource("Plane").lengthVertices
-- 2
member(1).modelResource("Plane").lengthVertices = 3
member(1).modelResource("Plane").widthVertices = 6
```

We won't be manipulating vertices or faces in this chapter, but the `modelsUnderRay()` function that you will see later does return information concerning them. However, the concepts are important and we will come back to them in later chapters. Let's now switch back to the regular display mode:

```
member(1).shader(1).renderStyle = #fill
```

Laying the Plane Flat

If the plane were shown lying flat, it would appear end on, and you wouldn't see it. Execute the following line a few times in the Message window and watch the plane progressively tilt and disappear:

```
member(1).Body Text Indent 3 0, 0)
```

Stop! Once you have done this three times, the plane will have become very dim, but you'll need to execute the line nine times to rotate the plane through 90°. The default light in a 3D world shines down at 45° from above your head; you will hardly catch on the plane at all. You can make the plane more visible by rotating the default directional light to a more appropriate angle:

```
member(1).directionalPreset = #middleCenter
```

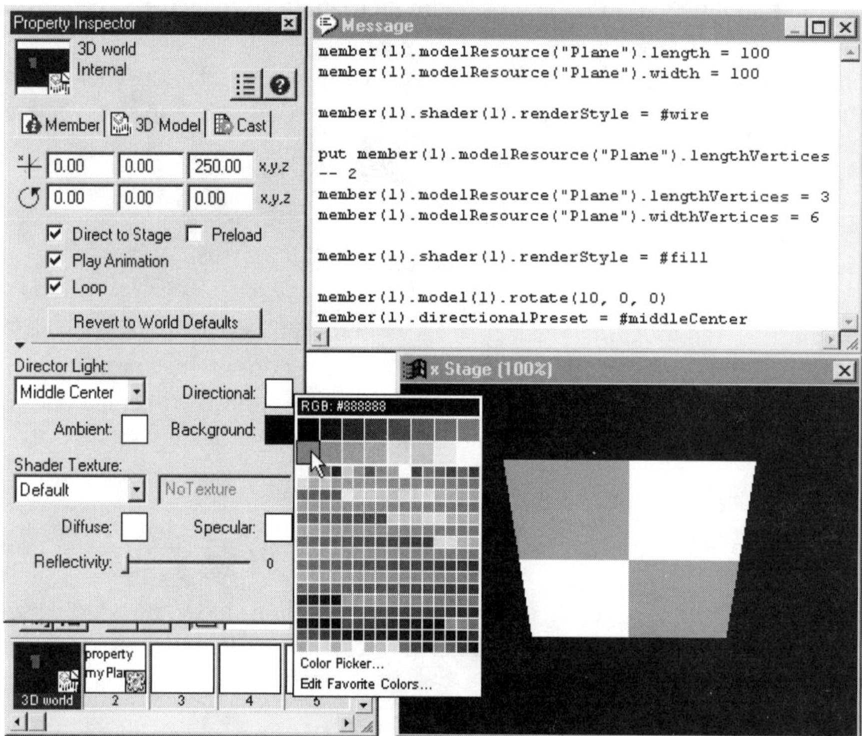

Altering the color of the Ambient, Directional, and Background lights also can help to show the plane more clearly. We'll be looking at lights and cameras in more detail in Chapter 13. Continue rotating the plane until it is lying at 90° to its original position.

Getting a Better View

Now that the plane is lying flat, you'll have to set the `directionalPreset` light back to `#topCenter` so that some light falls on it. You'll also need to dolly the camera up along the y axis to see it, and out along the z axis so that it is not quite so close. Let's leave the Message window and go back to the behavior. Actually, we'll want the plane to be quite a bit larger than the one we've been testing: 300 × 300 units. Add the following lines to your behavior, recompile it, and run your movie:

```
flatArea.length = 300
flatArea.width  = 300
myPlane.rotate(90, 0, 0)
thisSprite.camera.translate(0, 100, 100) -- moves camera up and back
```

You also can tilt the camera so that it is looking directly at the center of the plane:

```
thisSprite.camera.pointAt(0, 0, 0)
```

Run your movie again and observe how the plane appears now.

Tilting the Plane

Now you are ready to create the interaction with the plane using the arrow keys. Add the following code to your behavior

```
on keyDown(me)
  case the keyCode of
    123: me.tilt(#z,  1) -- / tilt
    124: me.tilt(#z, -1) -- \ tilt
    125: me.tilt(#x,  1) -- drop front
    126: me.tilt(#x, -1) -- drop back
  end case
end keyDown

on tilt(me, whichAxis, whichDirection)
  case whichAxis of
    #x:
      xRotation = myPlane.transform.rotation.x - 90
      if (xRotation * whichDirection) < 10 then
        myPlane.rotate(whichDirection, 0, 0)
      end if
    #z:
      zRotation = myPlane.transform.rotation.z
      if zRotation * whichDirection < 10 then
        myPlane.rotate(0, whichDirection, 0) -- model's y-axis
      end if
  end case
end tilt
```

The `tilt()` handler uses `myPlane.rotate()` to change the angle of the plane after it has ensured that the current angle of the plane lies within certain limits using `myPlane.transform.rotation`. You have already rotated the plane

90° around the x axis. The `tilt()` handler will allow you to alter the angle between 80° and 100°. You also will be able to tilt around the world's z axis from –10° to +10°. The plane's y axis is now lying along the world's z axis. Rotating the plane around its own y axis alters the plane's rotation around the world's z axis.

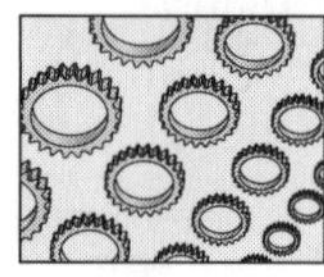

NOTE

When working in Director's authoring environment, key events are sent to the active window. You'll need to click the Stage window to make it active before pressing the arrow keys will have the expected effect.

Having a Ball

It's time to add a sphere to your movie. Add the following lines to your `beginSprite()` handler; then run your movie:

```
ball = s3D.newModelResource("Sphere", #sphere)
myBall = s3D.newModel("Sphere")
myBall.resource = ball
```

Sharing Space

The sphere will appear embedded in the plane. Virtual objects have no density, so they can pass through each other with no problems. You can tilt your plane around the sphere as if there were a circular hole in the plane.

To make the ball appear to sit on the plane, you can move it upward by its radius. By default, a sphere model resource has a radius of 25. Add the following line to your `beginSprite()` handler and run your movie again:

```
myBall.transform.position = vector(0, 25, 0)
```

The Properties of a Sphere

Like a plane, a sphere has only four properties: `#radius`, `#resolution`, `#startAngle`, and `#endAngle`. You can use Ullala's 3D Property Inspector to help you visualize these properties.

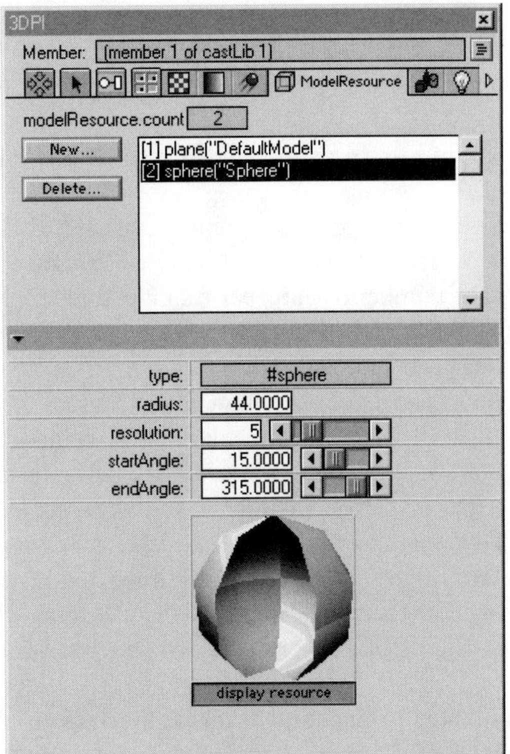

The `#resolution` property determines how many different vertices are used to calculate the curve of the sphere. Spheres are made up of triangles in the same way planes are. A high-resolution sphere looks prettier, but takes longer to render, which could slow the movie down unacceptably on some machines. With some 3D graphics cards, very high resolutions might result in screen artifacts.

Properties to Declare

You are going to refer to the ball model in other handlers, so you should declare `myBall` as a property. While you are at it, you should declare all the other properties that you are going to be using:

```
property s3D            -- sprite(me.spriteNum).member
property myPlane        -- Model of 300x300 unit plane
```

```
property myBall          -- Model of a 25 unit radius sphere
property myVelocity      -- Vector speed of ball
property myAnglePerUnit -- 1 / radius (angle in radians)
```

To complete your `beginSprite()` handler, you should initialize these last two properties.

We will be using a vector to store the current speed of the ball. To be exact, speed is the number of units per frame the ball is moving at. What we will be measuring is the ball's velocity, or the number of units per frame in a given direction. I'll come back to this in a moment. For now, the ball is stationary, so it is not moving in any direction. Its velocity can thus be described as `vector(0, 0, 0)`.

In the previous chapter, you determined how many degrees the wheel would turn in each frame, and from that, you calculated the distance it would travel. In this section, we shall do the opposite: we will work out how far the ball rolls and calculate the angle that makes it turn through. To help us do this, we can work out a constant, based on the ball's radius. The ball's circumference is `(ballRadius * 2 * pi)`. If the ball rolls forward that distance, it will turn through 360°. So if we divide 360° by the ball's circumference, we will get the number of degrees the ball turns when it moves forward 1 unit: `360 / (myBall.resource.radius * 2 *pi)`. We can simplify this by dividing both the top and bottom line of the fraction by 2.

You can find an animated explanation of this in the Trig.dir movie in the 3D\Space\ folder on the CD-ROM that accompanies the book.

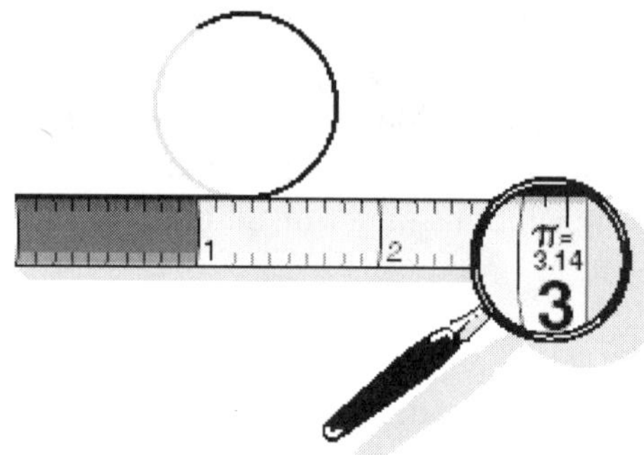

Here are the two lines you should add to complete your `beginSprite()` handler:

```
myVelocity       = vector(0, 0, 0)
myAnglePerUnit  = 180 / (myBall.resource.radius * pi)
```

Save your work and test again.

More About Vectors

Before we can go any further, you will have to be prepared to delve deeper into vector mathematics. (Don't worry—it won't hurt). We'll be using vector mathematics to determine in which direction the ball will roll and how it will accelerate under the force of gravity. We'll also use it to determine around which axis the ball is currently rolling.

In the previous chapter, you used vectors mostly for rotation: standing the wheel on its edge and determining which axis it should turn around. This is just one of the many ways of using a vector, and a rather unorthodox one at that. Mathematically speaking, a vector is a line in space; it has a direction and a magnitude.

For convenience, 3D Lingo also uses the vector format to store information on a transform's position in space, a transform's rotation in space, a transform's scale along each of its axes, and other data that has three elements. This extended usage can obscure the real meaning of a vector. In the discussion that follows, vectors are lines. I've given a number of poetic descriptions of a vector at the beginning of this chapter. Try to find a line (that is, a distance and direction) in each of the images I propose.

The Components of a Vector

A vector has three components: x, y, and z. Any arbitrary line in 3D space can be described in terms of how far it extends along each of the three axes of 3D space. Think of a broomstick propped up at an angle against a wall. You can measure

- The height of the top of the broomstick where it touches the wall
- The distance of the bottom of the broomstick from the wall
- The distance along the foot of the wall from the point nearest the bottom of the broomstick to the point nearest to its top

Suppose a spider starts at the top of the broomstick and lets itself down on a thread, vertically down the wall. The spider's movement could be represented as `vector(0, broomstickHeight, 0)`. The spider now turns 90° and moves along the foot of the wall until it is at the point nearest the foot of the broomstick. This movement could be represented as `vector(broomstickWidth, 0, 0)`. The spider now turns 90° in a different plane and makes off across the floor to the foot of the broomstick. This movement could be represented as `vector(0, 0, broomstickDepth)`.

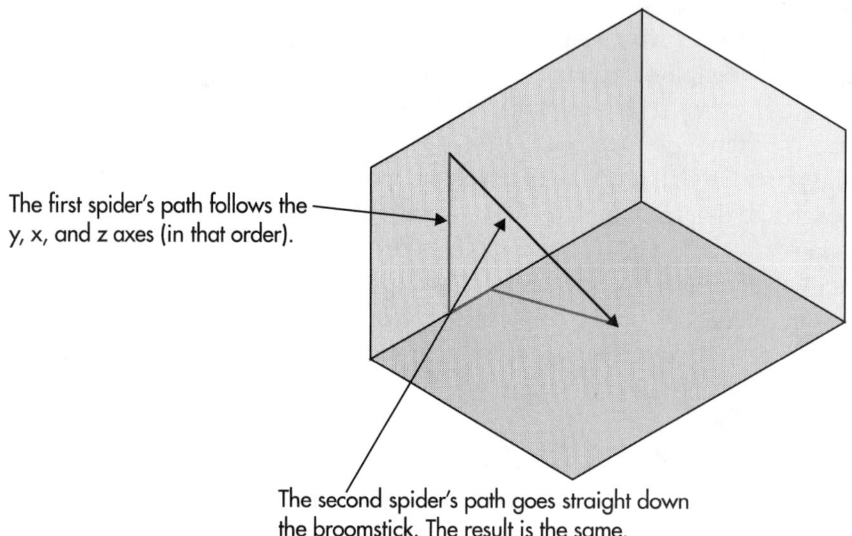

The spider's thread now represents the sum of the three vectors: `vector (broomstickWidth, broomstickHeight, broomstickDepth)`. A second spider running down the broomstick would come to exactly the same point. Separating the vector represented by the broomstick into three discrete movements (as the first spider did) yields the same result as treating it as one compound movement (as the second spider did).

Adding and Subtracting Vectors

Now suppose you place a second broomstick so that it touches the foot of the first broomstick and leans in a different direction against a different wall. Our first spider now climbs up the second broomstick to the top and reels its silk thread in taut.

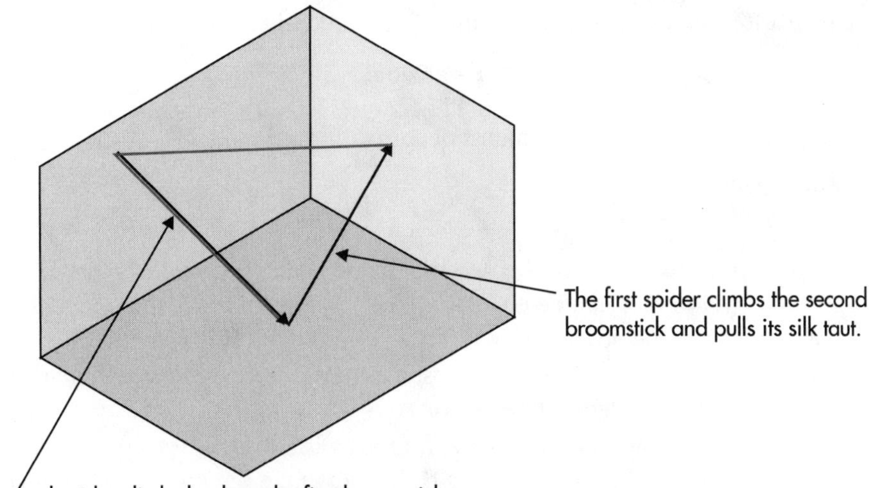

If each broomstick is a vector, the spider's thread now represents the sum of the vectors: `spidersThreadVector` = `broomstick1Vector` + `broomstick2Vector`. To perform that addition, you would simply add the appropriate components together:

```
broomstick1Vector   = vector(width1, height1, depth1)
broomstick2Vector   = vector(width2, height2, depth2)
spidersThreadVector = vector(width1+width2, height1+height2, depth1+depth2)
```

Our second spider, which is now at the foot of the broomsticks, climbs back up the first broomstick and along the first spider's thread. In doing so, it performs a subtraction:

```
secondSpidersPath = -broomstick1Vector + spidersThreadVector
```

The result is as if it had simply climbed the second broomstick:

```
broomstick2Vector = spidersThreadVector - broomstick1Vector
```

The order in which the movements occur is unimportant.

Triangles of Vectors

Let's now turn the example of the two broomsticks and the spider's thread on its head. If any two vectors can be added together to make a third, the opposite also is true: any vector can be described in terms of two others. If I have a vector A and you give me a vector B, which you have chosen at random, I now can find a vector C such that vector B plus vector C = vector A.

Let's try this with ordinary numbers. Suppose I choose 42 for my number A, and you choose 1 000 009 for your number B. If I now take the number –999 967 and add it to your number, I end up with 42. There's nothing mysterious about this at all.

Adding vectors follows the same rules as adding numbers, except the result is in three dimensions rather than one. The three vectors A, B, and C will form a triangle in space. For convenience, we usually will choose vectors B and C so that they form a right-angled triangle, with A as the hypotenuse. You can use the principles of trigonometry that you saw in the previous chapter to calculate the length of the various sides and the angles between them.

In the current example, we'll use a triangle of vectors to break the force of gravity up into two components: one perpendicular to the plane; the other parallel to the slope of the plane. The component parallel to the plane will accelerate the ball. The steeper the slope of the plane, the stronger this component will be and the faster the ball will accelerate.

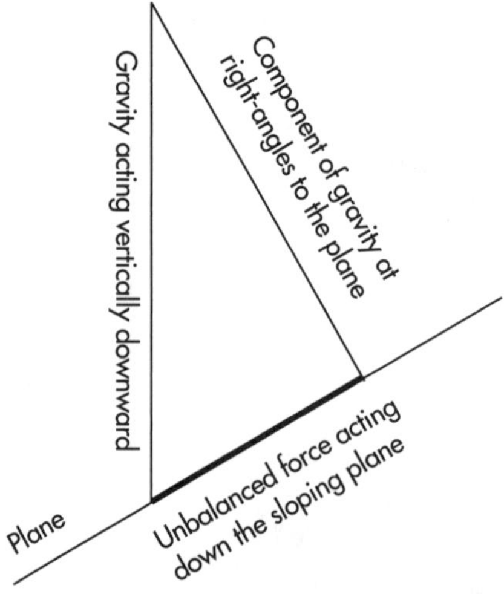

Multiplying Vectors

You can't meaningfully divide one vector by another. To make up for this, you can multiply two vectors in two different ways. In vector mathematics (but not in Lingo), the two operations are identified by different symbols, the dot and the cross:

```
dotProduct = vector1 . vector2
crossProduct = vector1 x vector2
```

Fortunately, you don't have to worry about how these operations are carried out. Director 8.5 will do both of them for you, using the `dot()` and `cross()` functions. But just in case you are curious:

```
vector(x1, y1, z1).dot(vector(x2, y2, z2)) = x1*x2 + y1*y2 + z1*z2
vector(x1, y1, z1).cross(vector(x2, y2, z2)) = \
  vector((y1*z2 - z1*y2), (z1*x2 - x1*z2), (x1*y2 - x2*y1))
```

So what do these operations mean? Why, among all the possible combinations of multiplication, addition, and subtraction that can be performed on the components of vectors, did mathematicians decide to consecrate these two?

Perpendicular Vectors

The cross product returns a vector. This vector turns out to be perpendicular to the two vectors that were used in the operation. To help you remember this, 3D Lingo provides three synonyms:

```
cross()
crossProduct()
perpendicularTo()
```

These all give exactly the same result. If you want to shave a fraction of a nanosecond off your calculations, you should use `crossProduct()`, as that seems to be infinitesimally faster than the other two. The quickest to type is `cross()`, so you are more likely to save your own time by using that. If you think of the "cross" as being a three-dimensional affair, like the intersection of the x, y, and z axes, you should have no difficulty in remembering that it produces a perpendicular vector.

DEBUGGING TIP

`vector1.cross(vector2)` is not the same as `vector2.cross(vector1)`. The two vectors will be parallel, but they run in opposite directions:

```
put vector(1.0, 0.0, 0.0).cross(vector(0.0, 1.0, 0.0))
-- vector( 0.0, 0.0, 1.0 )
put vector(0.0, 1.0, 0.0).cross(vector(1.0, 0.0, 0.0))
-- vector( 0.0, 0.0, -1.0 )
```

You can use a "right-hand rule" to remember which way the resulting vector will point. Use your right thumb to indicate the direction of the first vector and point your right index finger to indicate the direction of the second vector (the one in brackets). Hold the middle finger of your right hand at right angles to the other two; that is the direction the result of the cross product is pointing. You can use the same technique to indicate the x, y, and z axes.

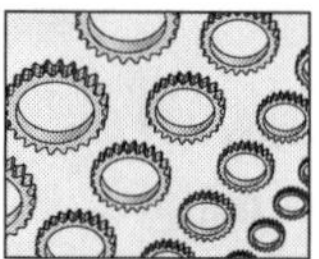

NOTE

If the two vectors are exactly parallel, their cross product is `vector(0, 0, 0)`; there would be an infinite number of possible perpendicular vectors from which to choose.

Normals

There is a special word used to refer to a vector that is perpendicular to a surface: `normal`. Think of a plane as being the flat surface of a mirror. Imagine you are standing in front of the mirror with one eye closed, and that you are looking yourself straight in the eye. The line from the mirror image of your eye to your own eye is exactly perpendicular to the surface of the mirror at that point.

The surface that a normal is perpendicular to need not be flat, however. Imagine a distorting mirror in a fairground. Regardless of how crazily the mirror is curved, the line between your mirror image eye and your own always forms a normal to the mirror's surface. A *normal* is a vector at a right angle to the surface of a plane. For a sphere, the normal to any point on the surface will start at the surface of the sphere and point outward. A sphere with all its normals showing would look like a sea urchin. From whatever angle you look at yourself in a spherical mirror, your eye will always appear in the center of the sphere.

Police interrogation rooms often have one-way mirrors along one wall. From inside the interrogation room, the wall appears as a mirror; from the outside it appears as transparent glass. Suspects in the room see their own reflection in the mirror, whereas police officers outside observe the suspects' behavior through the glass, as if the mirror wasn't there. Virtual 3D surfaces are the same: The normal points out of one side only: the mirrored side, if you like. That side is described as "front facing." As you will discover shortly, the virtual light rays in a 3D world can see only front-facing surfaces. The same surface seen from the other side is invisible.

Figure 7-1 shows a sphere rendered as a wire frame. The normals of each triangular face point outward (normals are not shown). The camera has been adjusted so that your point of view starts partly inside the sphere. Only the front-facing triangles on the outside of the sphere will appear in the standard `#fill` render style. The faces seen from behind are transparent; you can see through the sphere when you look through the hole.

The normal of the plane will help us determine which way the ball is rolling. We will use the cross product of the ball's velocity vector and the normal of the plane to determine the orientation of the axis around which the ball is revolving.

The Angle Between Two Vectors

The dot product happens to provide information on the angle between the two vectors. To be precise, if you multiply the lengths of the vectors together and divide the dot product of the vectors by the result, you get the cosine of the angle between the two vectors.

There are three ways to express the dot operation in Lingo:

```
floatingPointResult = vector1 * vector2
floatingPointResult = vector1.dot(vector2)
floatingPointResult = vector1.dotProduct(vector2)
```

I shall explicitly use `dot()` to make the nature of the operation clear. To test the operation, create a Movie Script and type the following handler into it:

```
on testAngle
  savePrecision = the floatPrecision
  the floatPrecision = 9

  x1 = random(99) - 50
  y1 = random(99) - 50
  z1 = random(99) - 50
  vector1 = vector(x1, y1, z1)

  x2 = random(99) - 50
  y2 = random(99) - 50
  z2 = random(99) - 50
  vector2 = vector(x2, y2, z2)

  squareArea = vector1.magnitude * vector2.magnitude
```

```
  cosine1 = vector1.dot(vector2) / squareArea
  cosine2 = cos(vector1.angleBetween(vector2) * pi / 180)

  put cosine1
  put cosine2
  the floatPrecision = savePrecision
end
```

Test this in the Message window. You should see something similar to this:

```
testAngle()
-- -0.783797186
-- -0.783797202
```

"Aha!" you might say. "The results are different. The dot product doesn't give the exact answer value of the cosine but only a close approximation." Don't say it—you'd be wrong. The mathematics are exact. What gives the approximation is the way your computer does the calculations. Since 3D requires a monumental amount of calculations, developers who program those calculations take as many reasonable shortcuts as they can. In this case, it helps to use only 32 bits to represent a floating-point number, rather than 64, which means each calculation takes about half the time. The down side is that the accuracy is reduced. Calculations are still accurate to better than one part in a million, so you are unlikely to notice any differences.

Besides, you might have noticed that the handler in the preceding code cheats—it compares `dot()` with `angleBetween()`, whereas `angleBetween()` depends on the same principle as `dot()`. It's almost like comparing an apple to itself, only to find that it's different.

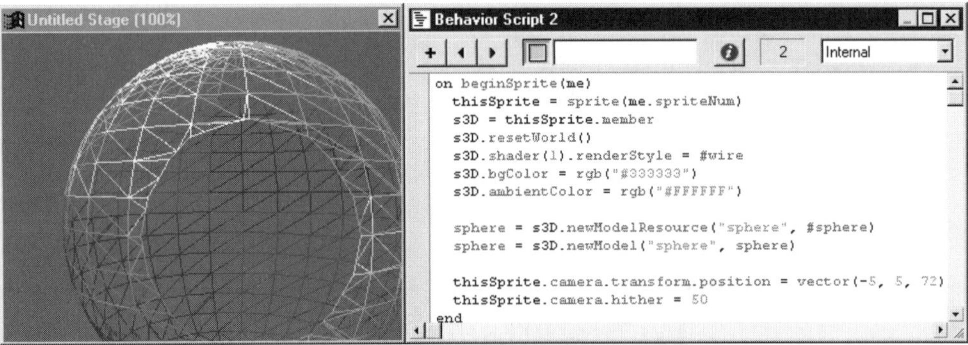

Figure 7-1 *Faces viewed from behind through the hole will be ignored*

The dot product is useful in a variety of ways, as you will see. If you know the position of a point in space, a point on a plane and the normal to the plane, you can use the dot product to determine how far the point in space is from the nearest point on the plane. Dividing the dot product by the magnitudes of the vectors gives you the cosine of the angle between the vectors. Resolving this cosine to the angle itself gives you yet more information. Indeed, 3D Lingo provides the angle directly through one simple function: `angleBetween()`.

An Example of Vector Mathematics

Let's put all this into practice. Suppose you have two vectors called `v1` and `v2` that start from the same point:

```
v1 = randomVector() * random(100) / 10.0
v2 = randomVector() * random(100) / 10.0

put v1
-- vector( -6.7763, 1.5312, 1.8913 )
put v2
-- vector( 3.6594, 3.8685, -1.7330 )
```

The two vectors have different lengths and point in different directions. How could you transform one vector into the other? If you rotate the first vector by a certain angle around a certain axis and then scale it just right, it will be identical to the second vector. The certain angle and the certain axis are easily determined using the vector methods we have just seen.

```
tAngle = angleBetween(v1, v2)
tAxis  = perpendicularTo(v1, v2)
```

Calculating the vectors' relative scale is even easier:

```
tScale = v2.magnitude / v1.magnitude
```

The question now is this: how do you rotate a vector? Well, you can't rotate a vector as such, but you can rotate a transform object and then use that to transform your vector. You can rotate a transform object using this syntax:

```
transform.rotate(position, axis, angle)
```

This means you must define a `position` for the `axis` to pass through. The obvious point is the center of the transform itself.

```
position = vector() -- short for vector( 0, 0, 0 )
t = transform()
t.rotate(position, tAxis, tAngle)
```

Now for the magic: To apply the rotation contained in the transform to the vector, you simply multiply transform and vector. The order of the operands is important—the transform must come first. To calculate `v2` in terms of `v1`, you simply multiply `t` by `v1` and then scale it to the right size:

```
put t * v1 * tScale
-- vector( 3.6594, 3.8685, -1.7330 )

put t * v1 * tScale = v2
-- 1
```

To calculate `v1` in terms of `v2`, the mathematics are only a little bit more complex:

```
put t.inverse() * v2 / tScale
-- vector( -6.7763, 1.5312, 1.8913 )

put t.inverse() * v2 / tScale = v1
-- 1
```

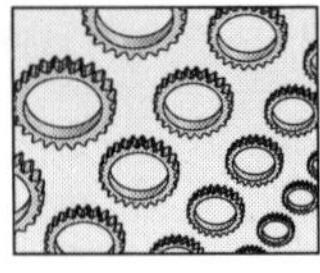

NOTE

You can multiply a transform by a vector to get a transformed vector; you also can multiply a vector by an integer to get a scaled vector. You cannot multiply a transform by an integer. To scale a transform, you have to use the `scale()` method.

You can include the scale information in the transform itself by using the `scale()` method. In the preceding, we applied the scale after the rotation; you need to respect this order also when using `scale()`:

```
on getTransform(v1, v2)
  tScale    = v2.magnitude / v1.magnitude
  tAngle    = angleBetween(v1, v2)
  tAxis     = perpendicularTo(v1, v2)
  position = vector()
  t         = transform()
```

```
  t.rotate(position, tAxis, tAngle)
  t.scale(tScale, tScale, tScale)

  return t
end
```

Test this handler in the Message window:

```
v1 = randomVector() * random(100) / 10.0
v2 = randomVector() * random(100) / 10.0
t = getTransform(v1, v2)
put t * v1 = v2
-- 1

put t.inverse() * v2 = v1
-- 1
```

Physics of Motion

3D space looks like a great place to test the physics of motion. Unless you explicitly change things, 3D space is a friction-free vacuum with no gravity. In 3D space, time is granular.

Because you might not have done any science since high school, this section provides a crib sheet so that you can fully appreciate the potential and the drawbacks described in the preceding paragraph. Feel free to skip this section if you are already familiar with this and want to get on with the new 3D Lingo.

Newton's Laws of Motion

Let's start with Newton's Laws of Motion. Isaac Newton wrote in Latin, so the translation you know might not use the exact words here.

1. "An object at rest tends to stay at rest and an object in motion tends to stay in motion with the same speed and in the same direction unless acted upon by an unbalanced force." In a 3D world, models tend to stay at rest. Period. To get them to move takes a conscious effort. However, to make the 3D world seem realistic, you must give the impression that your models continue to move once they are pushed.

2. "The acceleration of an object is dependent upon two variables: the net unbalanced force acting upon the object and the mass of the object." This gives rise to the formula F = ma. In Lingo that would be: `force = mass * acceleration`.

3. "For every action, there is an equal and opposite reaction." In other words, the sum of all forces in a closed system = zero. We'll also be looking at the conservation of momentum and the conservation of energy.

Distance, Mass, and Time

You can get a great deal of mileage out of three concepts: distance, time, and mass. In the real world, distance is measured in meters, mass in grams, and time in seconds. In a 3D world, we are free to invent our own units. The radius of our sphere is 25. But 25 what? And what mass does it have, measured in what units? For the sake of this discussion I will use the same terms, in quotation marks, to indicate that the units are not real: "meters," "grams," and "seconds." If I'm not referring explicitly to the 3D world, I'll drop the quotes.

Time is the only concept that seems to use the same units as in the real world, but that also is deceptive. In the real world, at the scale at which humans live, time can be subdivided into infinitely small units. (Okay, so if you get into quantum physics, things can look different.) In a 3D world, you cannot see time in units smaller than a millisecond. Most repetitive actions in Director occur once per frame; frames divide time into even larger chunks. Time is like silk in the real world, and like sandpaper in a 3D world. Sometimes we will be forced to fill in the gaps or pretend they don't exist.

Speed and Velocity

There are major questions that Newton leaves unanswered. What is space and why does it have three dimensions? Why can we go forward and backward in space but not in time? I'll follow his example and leave these questions unanswered, too. However, our study of physics must take the three dimensions of space into consideration.

Speed is a change of distance over time. You measure it in meters per second. Velocity is a more precise term. Velocity also has a direction. Whereas speed can be written as a single integer or floating-point number, velocity needs to be written as a vector. The vector says this: distance is changing by this much along the x axis, that much along the y axis, and the other much along the z axis in a given time span.

Lingo doesn't let you use units. A velocity vector of `vector(2.1, 3.4, 5.9)` should be accompanied by a unit: "meters/second"—but this would cause a Script error.

The speed of a given velocity vector is equivalent to the vector's magnitude:

```
velocity = vector(2.1, 3.4, 5.9)
speed = velocity.magnitude
put speed
-- 7.1260
```

Here's how you can calculate the magnitude of a vector for yourself:

```
put sqrt(velocity.x*velocity.x + velocity.y*velocity.y + velocity.z*velocity.z)
-- 7.1260
```

You might notice that this is a 3D application of the Pythagorean Theorem.

Distance, Displacement, and a Wagging Finger

Just as a velocity is a speed with a direction, so a displacement is a distance with a direction. After one "second" traveling at `velocity`, an object would be displaced by `vector(2.1, 3.4, 5.9)` "meters." Because the velocity and displacement vectors have the same value, it is tempting to think that they are identical; they are not. The units are different, even if Lingo doesn't encourage us to show them. The Hitchhiker's Guide to 3D Space recommends that you should always know what your units are.

Acceleration and Gravity

Acceleration is a change of velocity over time. Again, it has a directional element, which means we will use vectors to describe acceleration. According to Einstein, what we call gravity is due to a curvature of space-time that results in an acceleration toward the center of the Earth. In the real world, using real units, the velocity of an unsupported object in a vacuum will increase by roughly 9.81 meters per second every second. (This might be true at sea level on the equator, but gravity varies depending on where you are.) In our 3D world, our units can be elastic: we can stretch them to fit our needs and simplify our calculations—as long as we are consistent. We could define gravity in our 3D world such that unsupported objects will fall 10 "meters" per "second" faster every "second." (We could indeed use any arbitrary value, as you will see.)

The Position of an Accelerating Object

It's easy to calculate the distance traveled by an object at a constant velocity. In a given time *t*, the object will move *v* * *t* meters, where *v* is measured in meters per second and *t* in seconds. But what about an object that is accelerating?

The standard formula (written in Lingo) is

```
displacement = (initialVelocity * time) + (acceleration * time * time / 2)
```

To illustrate this, imagine a car driving at 10 meters per second (about 20 mph) along the x axis and over the edge of a cliff. In a 3D world, at the moment the car goes over the edge, its velocity is `vector(10, 0, 0)`. It is now unsupported and starts accelerating downward. At the end of one second, its speed along the y axis is –10 "meters" per second. Because its speed along the y axis was zero at the beginning of the first second, its average speed during that second is half its final speed: –5 "meters" per second. If it had traveled at its average speed during the whole second, it would have traveled –5 "meters." The minus sign indicates that the car is moving downward while the y axis points up. If we use `vector(0, -10, 0)` for `acceleration` and `1` for `time`, our equation becomes

```
displacement = (vector(10, 0, 0) * 1) + (vector(0, -10, 0) * 1 * 1 / 2)
put displacement
-- vector( 10.0000, -5.0000, 0.0000 )
```

The car will follow a parabola until it splashes into the sea. You can calculate its trajectory every tenth of "second" for the first "second":

```
on getTrajectory()
  repeat with tenths = 1 to 10
    t = tenths / 10.0
    put getPositionAtTime(t)
  end repeat
end

on getPositionAtTime(t)
  initialVelocity = vector(10, 0, 0)
  acceleration = vector(0, -10, 0)
  displacement = (initialVelocity * t) + (acceleration * t * t / 2)
  return displacement
end
```

In the Message window:

```
getTrajectory()
-- vector( 1.0000, -0.0500, 0.0000 )
-- vector( 2.0000, -0.2000, 0.0000 )
-- vector( 3.0000, -0.4500, 0.0000 )
-- vector( 4.0000, -0.8000, 0.0000 )
-- vector( 5.0000, -1.2500, 0.0000 )
-- vector( 6.0000, -1.8000, 0.0000 )
-- vector( 7.0000, -2.4500, 0.0000 )
-- vector( 8.0000, -3.2000, 0.0000 )
-- vector( 9.0000, -4.0500, 0.0000 )
-- vector( 10.0000, -5.0000, 0.0000 )
```

Every tenth of a "second," the car's vertical speed is increasing by –0.1 "meters/second." Let's illustrate this in a graph.

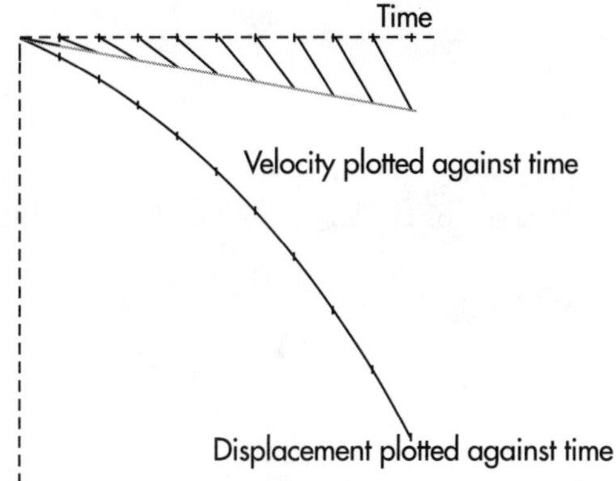

Slipping into a Time Warp

CanCliff.dir

The `getPositionAtTime(t)` handler in the preceding assumes we know exactly when the acceleration began and have been tracking it ever since. This might be a fair assumption for a car falling over a cliff; but in an action game, you might be accelerating in all sorts of random ways at random times. Suppose we know only the car's instantaneous velocity and acceleration at a given point in time, such as the moment when an `#exitFrame` event is issued. Here's a behavior that you can attach to an empty Shockwave 3D sprite. The `on exitFrame()` handler calculates the average speed in meters per frame and uses this to calculate the new position of `myCarModel`. You can find the original behavior in the CarCliff.dir movie in the 3D\Physics\ folder on the CD-ROM that accompanies this book.

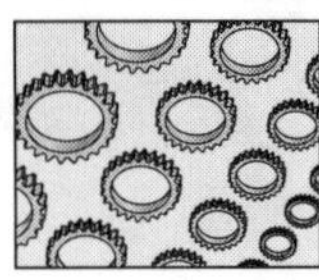

NOTE

In this behavior, the value of `myAcceleration` *is* `-0.1`*, not* `-10`*, because I consider that 10 frames make up one "second." Acceleration is measured in meters per second, per second, or m/s². If I divide my time frame of reference by 10, I must divide my frame of reference for acceleration by 10².*

```
property myCarModel      -- default plane model
property myVelocity      -- velocity at (the last) exitFrame
property myAcceleration -- 0.1 "meters" per frame per frame downwards

on beginSprite(me)
  myCarModel     = me.createCar()
  myVelocity     = vector(1, 0, 0) -- "meters" per frame
  myAcceleration = vector(0, -0.1, 0) -- "meters" per frame per frame
end beginSprite


on createCar(me)
  s3D = sprite(me.spriteNum).member
  s3D.resetWorld()
  -- Move camera up close to get a good view
  s3D.camera(1).transform.position = vector(9, -9, 35)
  -- Show trails
  s3D.camera(1).colorBuffer.clearAtRender = FALSE

  carResource = s3D.newModelResource("Box", #plane)
  return s3D.newModel("Car", carResource)
end createCar


on exitFrame(me)
  averageVelocity = myVelocity.duplicate()
  myVelocity = myVelocity + myAcceleration
  averageVelocity = (averageVelocity + myVelocity) / 2

  myCarModel.translate(averageVelocity)
  put myCarModel.worldPosition -- Output into message window
end exitFrame
```

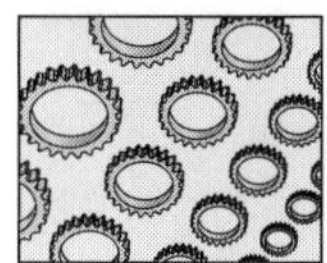

NOTE

You can create trails in a Shockwave 3D sprite by setting the `clearAtRender` *property of the* `colorBuffer` *of the current camera to* `FALSE`*.*

The `exitFrame()` handler uses an accurate technique for calculating the position of `myCarModel`. You can verify this by comparing the output in the Message window with that of the `getTrajectory()` handler you saw earlier. But accuracy has its price; you can get almost the same results with a much faster technique. To test this, launch the CarCliff.dir movie; then, while it's running, alter the `exitFrame()` handler so that it no longer calculates the `averageVelocity` but uses the new value of `myVelocity` directly instead. You'll see the amended handler in Figure 7-1 and also in the Approximation behavior in the movie. Now recompile the script without halting the movie. Director will issue a new `#beginSprite` event to the behavior, and you will see the trails for the new handler appear alongside those for the previous version. In Figure 7-2, I've inverted the colors so that it is more visible on the printed page and shown the accurate positions in a paler shade of gray.

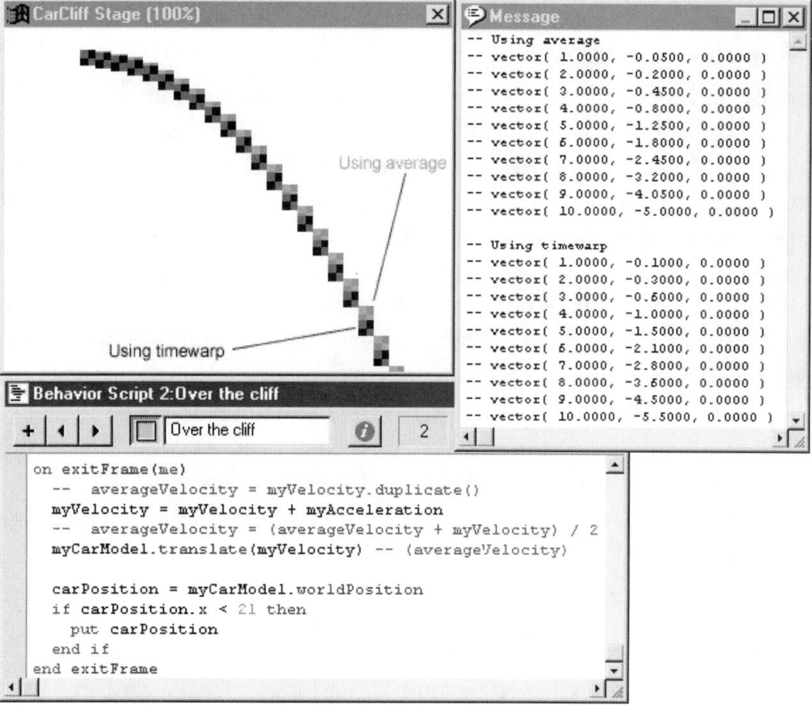

Figure 7-2 *Comparing textbook and approximate physics*

The simplified version is much faster. Because 3D sprites are CPU-hungry beasts, every little time-saving shortcut helps. With the CarCliff.dir movie open, try typing `test` into the Message window (your results might vary):

```
test
-- "0.0116 ms for accurate calculation" vector( 0.0000, -0.5000, 0.0000 )
-- "0.0007 ms for timewarp calculation" vector( 0.0000, -1.0000, 0.0000 )
-- "speed ratio = 1:16"
```

Why do I describe the simplified version as a "timewarp"? By using the final velocity rather than the average velocity, the effects of the acceleration are felt half a frame before the acceleration is applied. Isaac Asimov would have found this amusing; Isaac Newton was not noted for his sense of humor.

As you can see, the result is as if the acceleration due to gravity were slightly greater than expected. However, because we are free to define the units of time and distance in our 3D world, this is easy to resolve. The important point to note is that both techniques give realistic results. I prefer to be a pragmatist rather than a purist in my projects. In your projects, you're the boss.

Force and Mass

Like velocity and acceleration, force has both magnitude and direction; you'll use vectors to describe forces as well. An object accelerates because an unbalanced force is applied to it. The key word here is "unbalanced." When an object (such as your computer monitor) is placed on a level surface (such as your desk), the force upward from the surface is equal and opposite to the force of gravity. If you now lift one end of your desk, the desk top is no longer able to balance the force of gravity. The force applied by the desktop is perpendicular to its surface (along its normal), whereas the force of gravity bears straight down. The result will be a net unbalanced force down the slope of your desk (and an untidy situation to explain to your insurance company).

The unit of force is the *newton*. A force of one newton is required to make one kilogram of mass accelerate at one meter per second every second. Force is thus defined in terms of distance, mass, and time; 1 newton = 1 kgm/s^2.

Conservation of Momentum

It's easier to stop a runaway hors d'oeuvres trolley than a runaway horse—the horse has greater mass. If both are traveling at the same speed, the horse has greater momentum. The same force has to be applied for longer or a larger force has to be applied for the same length of time to slow it to a stop. In Lingo,

```
momentum = mass * velocity
momentum = force * time
```

Momentum has direction; thus it is written as a vector. Its units are kgm/s.

When two objects collide, the total momentum is conserved. Suppose you are in friction-free weightless space and are struck from behind by a hors d'œuvres trolley that is less massive than you are. You will gain momentum from the collision and float away from the trolley. It will lose momentum and might even bounce back the way it came. The sum of your momentum and the trolley's momentum after the collision will be the same as it was before the collision. The only difference will be in the way that momentum is distributed between you and the trolley.

Conservation of Energy

Energy has no direction, but it can be stored in many forms. The computer monitor sitting on your desk has potential energy because of its height from the floor. If you topple it off your desk, it gains kinetic energy because of its downward acceleration and loses potential energy as it nears the floor. When it hits the floor, the kinetic energy is converted to heat. In Lingo,

```
energy = (mass * speed * speed) / 2
```

Mass is expressed in kilograms and speed in meters per second, so the units of energy are kgm^2/s^2. This is true even if the object has no speed. The potential energy of your computer monitor is identical to its kinetic energy when it hits the floor. You also can think of the potential energy of your computer as its weight in newtons (kgm/s^2) times its height from the ground (m):

```
energy = force * distance
```

Like momentum, energy is always conserved. In a frictionless world, your monitor would be traveling at the same speed when it hit the floor whether you drop it vertically, slide it down a mile-long chute, or swing it to the floor on the end of a long rope. Its initial potential energy would be converted entirely to kinetic energy as it slides or swings. Because it descends the same height in all three cases, it must be going at the same speed; however, the direction of its motion will be different.

In the real world, much of the energy will be converted into heat through friction as the monitor rubs against the chute and the surrounding air.

X-Ray Vision

That's almost the end of the theory for this exercise. There's just one more Lingo keyword to assimilate: `modelsUnderRay()`. Reopen the movie you saved earlier, run it, and type the following in the Message window:

```
pointInSpace = vector(0, 50, 0)
rayDirection = vector(0, -1, 0)
put member(1).modelsUnderRay(pointInSpace, rayDirection)
-- [model("Sphere"), model("plane")]
```

What does this sequence of instructions do? The first line chooses a point in space from which to look (on the top surface of the ball model); the second chooses a direction in which to look (vertically downward). The third line asks the Shockwave 3D member to tell us what it sees when it looks with its X-ray eye in the way we've defined. The member returns a list of the models that the X-ray encounters, the closest model appearing first.

What the Ray Can't See

Let's now move a fraction downward. We'll start the ray from just inside the sphere:

```
pointInSpace = vector(0, 49.9999, 0)
put member(1).modelsUnderRay(pointInSpace, rayDirection)
-- [model("plane")]
```

The sphere is now missing from the list—yet the ray traverses it. Why can't the ray see the sphere?

Front-Facing Sides

As mentioned earlier, the surface of a 3D object has two sides. The ray used by `modelsUnderRay()` can see only the front-facing side. This is the side from which the normal points out, or what I described as the mirror side in the preceding discussion about normals. If the ray starts from inside the 3D object, it cannot see the object at all (see Figure 7-1, earlier in the chapter).

However, this explanation is not complete. You'll see in the next chapter that the `#mesh` primitive can be used to create a model that folds back on itself. Even if the ray passes through multiple folds, it will report seeing it only once the first time it encounters a front-facing surface.

However, a ray will always see a default plane. Planes have no thickness, so the ray can't ever start inside it. You can think of a default plane as a double-sided mirror. Planes can't be folded, so the ray can traverse it only once.

Creating Double-Sided Resources

You can in fact create all primitives so that they are double sided. To do this, you need to provide a third parameter when you use the `newModelResource()` function. The full syntax for this command is

```
member(whichCastMember).newModelResource(<name>, <type>, <faces>)
```

As you have seen, the `name` parameter should be a unique string and `type` should be one of the following symbols:

- `#plane`
- `#box`
- `#sphere`
- `#cylinder`
- `#particle`

The faces parameter can be one of the following symbols:

- `#front`
- `#back`
- `#both`

If you choose `#both`, a double-sided primitive will be created, which the `modelsUnderRay()` function can detect from either side. By default, a plane is created with `#both` faces, whereas all other primitives are created by default with only `#front` faces. In the case of the particle primitive, there is little point in changing the default value; particles are always turned to face the camera and cannot be detected by `modelsUnderRay()`.

We'll be using box primitives created with `#both` faces in Chapter 8.

Detailed Data

If seeing models was all `modelsUnderRay()` could do, then it wouldn't be very helpful. You can use a third parameter to obtain much more information about the models it sees. I've arranged and simplified the output in the following extract so that it is easier to read:

```
put member(1).modelsUnderRay(pointInSpace, rayDirection, #detailed)
-- [
[#model:          model("plane"),
 #distance:       50.0,
 #isectPosition: vector( 0.0, 0.0, 0.0 ),
 #isectNormal:   vector( 0.0, 1.0, 0.0 ),
 #meshID:         1,
 #faceID:         1,
 #vertices:      [vector( -150.0, 0.0, 150.0 ),
                  vector( 150.0, 0.0, -150.0 ),
                  vector( -150.0, 0.0, -150.0 )],
 #uvCoord:       [#u: 0.5, #v: 0.0]
]
]
```

The details on each model encountered will appear as a separate property list inside the main linear list. In the current example, the ray only encounters one model: the plane. We're not going to need all the information here now. Only two of these properties interest us for the moment: `#isectPosition` and `#isectNormal`. "Isect" is short for "intersection": `#isectPosition` tells us where in world space the ray passed through the plane, and `#isectNormal` tells us which way the plane is facing at that point.

Detecting the Tilt of the Plane

Right now, the plane is facing straight upward. Launch the movie then use the arrow keys to tilt the plane, and try again. This time, the `#isectNormal` data might look like this (I'm ignoring the rest of the data):

```
#isectNormal: vector( 0.1045, 0.9762, 0.1898 )
```

This shows that the plane is tilted down at the near right corner. Under the effect of gravity, the ball should now start to roll toward us and to the right.

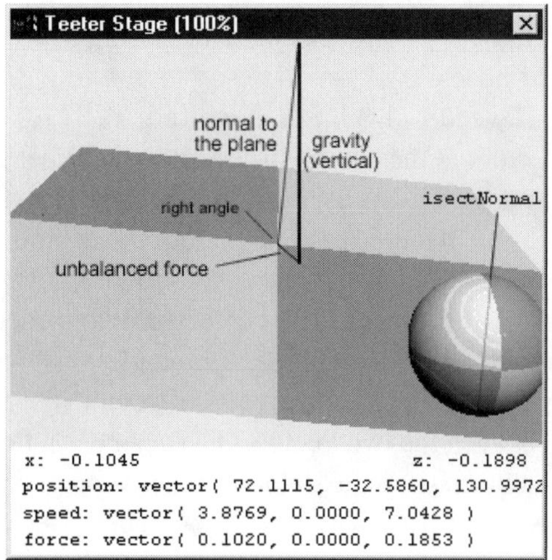

Reality check: what are the units of the `#isectNormal` vector? The vector is indicating a direction. It tells you how far to travel along each of the axes in order to move one "meter" in the chosen direction. But this is a trick question: a direction vector in itself has no units. You can think of it as a set of ratios.

Actually, there's an easier way of getting the tilt of the plane that doesn't require you to use `modelsUnderRay()`. Remember that the default position of the plane is vertical? That is, its `#width` is measured along the x axis and its `#length` along the y axis. This means that the plane's z axis acts as a normal to the plane.

```
put member(1).model("plane").transform.zAxis
-- vector( -0.1045, -0.9762, -0.1898 )
```

The vector is pointing in the opposite direction. It's an "anti-normal," if you like. This is because we rotated the plane +90° to make it lie flat, with its z axis pointing down. As it happens, this direction is more useful to us, since it points from the ball into the plane. We can thus use it to define the `rayDirection` for the `modelsUnderRay()` method. We'll then use the `#isectPosition` value returned by `modelsUnderRay()` to determine where the ball touches the plane.

Gravity

The force of gravity pulls us straight downward. You can use a vector to describe it. Since we are in a virtual world, we are free to choose our units of time and distance so that we don't have to worry about the magnitude of the force. For the time being, let's just use a directional vector with a magnitude of 1: `vector(0, -1, 0)`. This will allow us to concentrate on the process without getting lost in the figures. We can adjust the figures later if necessary.

The `#isectNormal` vector also has a magnitude of 1. As a result, the dot product of these two vectors is the cosine of the angle between them (we don't have to divide by the magnitudes). This is extraordinarily handy: it allows us to create a right-angled triangle that breaks the force of gravity down into two vectors—one along the normal and one parallel to the slope, as shown in Figure 7-3.

For simplicity, Figure 7-3 illustrates the vectors in two dimensions and the angle of the slope is exaggerated. The normal to the plane (`isectNormal`) is exactly one unit long. Dot multiplying the normal by a vertical vector (`gravityVector`) gives the cosine of the angle between the two vectors. The cosine is a floating-point number, not a vector. Scaling the normal by the value of the cosine gives a vector that points in the same direction as the normal, but with a `magnitude` (length) equivalent to the cosine. You can now create a right-angled triangle whose hypotenuse is one unit long using the scaled normal as one of the other sides. The third side will be parallel to the slope of the plane. To calculate the vector representing this third side, you can simply add the vectors that define the two known sides. Starting at the foot of the normal, moving up to the summit of the triangle and down the vertical gravity vector will have the same end result as sliding down the slope.

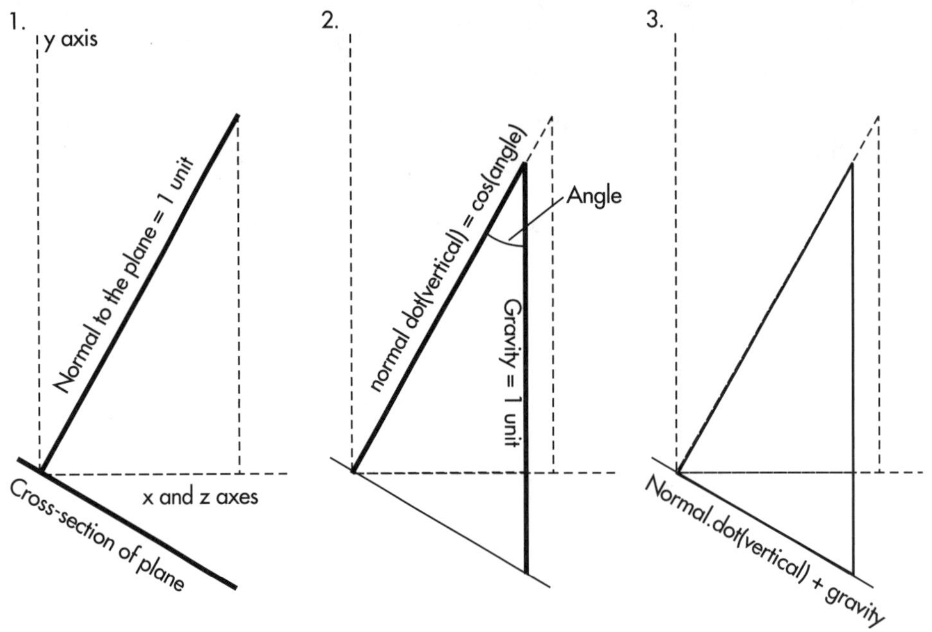

Figure 7-3 *Calculating the unbalanced force down the slope*

In Lingo:

```
resistanceToGravityUpNormal = isectNormal * isectNormal.dot(gravityVector)
gravityComponentDownSlope   = resistanceToGravityUpNormal + gravityVector
```

To put this particular example into figures:

```
gravityVector = vector(0, -1, 0)
isectNormal   = vector(0.1045, 0.9762, 0.1898)
resistanceToGravityUpNormal = isectNormal * isectNormal.dot(gravityVector)
put resistanceToGravityUpNormal
-- vector( 0.1020, 0.9530, 0.1853 )

gravityComponentDownSlope = resistanceToGravityUpNormal + gravityVector
put gravityComponentDownSlope
-- vector( 0.1020, -0.0470, 0.1853 )
```

This means that the force acting on the ball is `0.1020` units to the left and `0.1853` units toward us. The force of `-0.470` in the `y` direction ensures that the ball remains in contact with the slope. As we will see, it would be better to ignore it. Let's leave it for now so you can see later why we should remove it.

This `gravityComponentDownSlope` force will increase the velocity of the ball during every frame in which it is applied. At the beginning of the last frame, the ball was at rest; its velocity was `vector(0, 0, 0)`. Because we are in a virtual world, we can define the mass of our sphere as 1 kilogram, which means we don't need to modify the values of our force vector when we calculate the acceleration vector. The acceleration vector also will be `vector(0.1045, 0.9762, 0.1898); in` other words, by the end of the current frame, the ball will be traveling at a velocity of `vector(0, 0, 0)` + `vector(0.1020, -0.0470, 0.1853)`.

Although the values are the same, the vectors are not identical. The units of the force vector are newtons or kgm/s^2. The units for the acceleration are m/s^2. The units for the velocity vector are m/s.

Bending the Laws of Physics

So far, my calculations obey the laws of Newtonian physics. When it comes to calculating the displacement of the ball, I am going to cheat in the way I described in the earlier section called "Slipping into a Time Warp." I'm going to consider that the effects of the acceleration occur half a frame before they are applied, which means I am going to use the same vector again to determine the distance the ball will move during the frame. Your CPU will thank you for it and your end users won't notice.

The Handler That Rolls the Ball

To summarize: I started by calculating a force vector parallel to the slope of the plane. By choosing the appropriate units, I can use the same vector unchanged (except for the units) to express the acceleration of the sphere. I add this acceleration vector to the current velocity vector once per frame to obtain the "average" velocity during that frame. (I write "average" in quotation marks to indicate that this is where I cheat.) I add the velocity vector to the current position vector (where the units are "meters" from the origin point), and so obtain the new position of the ball.

Moving to Almost the Right Position

Here's a handler that applies much of what you've just seen. It slides the ball down the slope when you tilt the plane. Don't be surprised if the ball won't roll yet, disappears into the distance, or sinks into the plane—we'll deal with these problems later. For the moment, just watch how the ball accelerates as it slides down the slope:

```
on exitFrame(me)
  gravity        = vector(0, -1, 0)
  -- Determine the anti-normal into the plane
  rayDirection   = myPlane.transform.zAxis
  -- Get cosine of angle of normal with respect to the world's y-axis
  cosineOfAngle  = rayDirection.dotProduct(vector(0, 1, 0))
  -- Get resistance to the force of gravity orthogonal to the plane
  resistance     = rayDirection * cosineOfAngle
  -- Get the sum of forces acting on the ball
  appliedForce   = gravity + resistance

  -- We have chosen our units so that the sphere has a mass of 1.
  -- The acceleration of the sphere thus uses the same values as
  -- appliedForce.  (We could omit the following name change).
  acceleration   = appliedForce

  -- Ignore vertical motion
  --acceleration.y = 0
  -- Update the instantaneous velocity of the ball
  myVelocity     = myVelocity + acceleration
  -- Move the ball to its new horizontal position (via timewarp)
  myBall.transform.translate(myVelocity)
end
```

Stopping the Ball from Sinking

The worst flaw in this handler is that the ball might sink into the plane when you tilt it first one way and then the other. To solve this, we'll use `modelsUnderRay()` to determine where the ball should touch the plane; then we'll move the ball up the normal to the plane so that it only just touches the plane. If `modelsUnderRay()` returns an empty list, it means the ball has fallen off the edge; if it does, we'll just place it back in the center of the plane, ready to roll again.

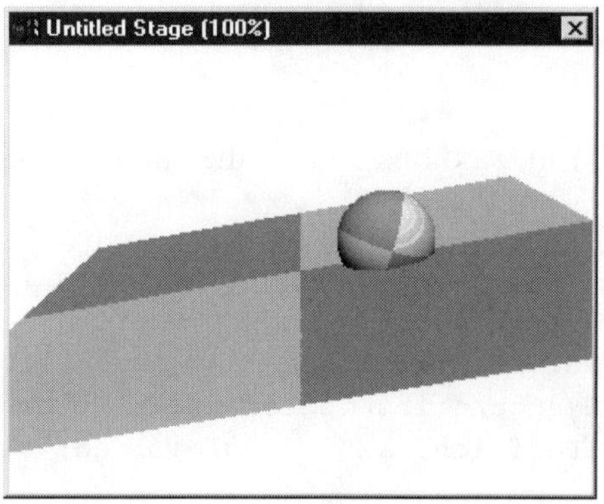

Add this to the end of the `exitFrame()` handler:

```
  ballPosition   = myBall.worldPosition
  data = s3D.modelsUnderRay(ballPosition, rayDirection, #detailed)

  if data.count then
    -- The ball is still on the plane
    intersection = data[1].isectPosition
    -- Place center of ball at intersection with the plane...
    myBall.transform.position = intersection
    -- then move the ball the length of its radius away from the plane
    myBall.transform.translate(-rayDirection * 25)
  else
    -- The ball has fallen off the edge: replace it center of plane
    myBall.transform.position = vector(0, 25, 0)
    myVelocity = vector()
  end if
end
```

Test the new code by see-sawing the plane to the right and left. With a little skill, you should be able to keep the ball on the plane.

Place a debug breakpoint at the beginning of the new code and follow it through step by step. Watch how the line

```
myBall.transform.position = intersection
```

makes the ball sink halfway into the plane, so that its center is at the intersection point. The following line moves it out again along the normal to its correct position. When you are not using the Debugger, the screen is not refreshed between the two actions, so the ball appears to remain on the plane at all times.

Rolling the Ball

Let's now make the ball roll. Add this code at the end of the `exitFrame()` handler:

```
   -- Make the ball roll as it moves: find the axis of rotation
  axis          = myVelocity.crossProduct(vector(0, -1, 0))
  angleTurned   = myVelocity.magnitude * myAnglePerUnit
  -- Rotate the ball around its center relative to the world
  myBall.rotate(ballPosition, axis, angleTurned, #world)
end
```

Relaunch your movie and test it.

Tidying Up

There are still a couple of bugs to eliminate. You also might want to adjust this time scale of the animation.

Rotating Around the Right Axis

To be strictly accurate, this last piece of code should be placed immediately after this line:

```
ballPosition = myBall.worldPosition
```

Why do you think this should be? The idea is to rotate the ball around its center. The way we have programmed it, the ball first slides to a new position, then is moved out of the plane to its correct position, and then we rotate it. Its center is not in quite the same place after it slid as it is after it moved out of the plane. Rotating the ball before we move it out of the plane corrects this.

Calculating the Correct Displacement

You can see the other bug if you roll the ball gently back and forth, to the left and right, and then try to bring it to a halt. The ball seems to roll on the spot. The farther you roll it before you bring it to a halt, the faster it rolls on the spot. Why?

The line `myVelocity = myVelocity + acceleration` is executed on each `exitFrame()`. The acceleration vector has three components: along the x axis, along the z axis, and straight down. When we correct the position of the ball so that it remains on the plane, we are effectively ignoring the down component; however, this doesn't stop it from growing. Try watching this expression in the Watcher window:

```
sprite(1).myVelocity.y
```

The longer you keep the ball rolling, the greater the value becomes, negatively speaking. The value has no impact on the position of the ball, but it does have an effect on the magnitude of the `myVelocity` vector. That magnitude is used to determine how far the ball has rolled since the last frame:

```
angleTurned = myVelocity.magnitude * myAnglePerUnit
```

The solution is easy. Uncomment the line:

```
--acceleration.y = 0
```

This means that not only is movement in the y direction ignored but it no longer interferes with the calculation of the rotation. Ironic, isn't it? To get a realistic movement, we have had to neutralize the downward motion that makes the movement occur.

Scaling the Acceleration

In the earlier section called "Moving to Almost the Right Position," the vector used to express the unbalanced force of gravity was applied without any coefficient. You might want the ball to be more sensitive to the tilt of the plane. Try replacing the line

```
-- Update the instantaneous velocity of the ball
myVelocity = myVelocity + acceleration
```

with

```
myVelocity = myVelocity + (acceleration * 3.0)
```

To make the ball easier to control, try dividing by `3.0` instead. Test scaling the acceleration up or down with a variety of values, until you get the appropriate sensitivity. You could even provide a means for the user to control the effect.

Commenting Your Code

The Teeter.dir movie discussed at the start of this chapter uses the same techniques, but the code has been spruced up and commented. I've used different names for the variables in some places, which might help you to see them in another light. I've also added feedback on the tilt of the plane and on the movement of the ball, through a separate Show Data behavior. You might like to try to perform a similar cleanup on the movie you have created.

Other Forms of Gravity

HvkDash.dir, HvkTilt.dir, TiltDrop.dir

Now that you have come this far, you might be inclined to think that there must be an easier way of achieving the same results. In the 3D\Physics\ folder on the CD-ROM that accompanies this book, you'll find two movies named HvkTilt.dir and HvkDash.dir. Both of these use the Havok Xtra to create solid body physics in your Shockwave 3D member. To create a Havok member, you choose menu Insert | Media Element | Havok Physics Scene. You'll find a manual in Acrobat format and a set of behavior libraries in the Havok folder on the Director CD-ROM to get you going. We'll be looking at the Havok Xtra again in Chapter 14.

A Brief Glimpse of the Havok Xtra

If you want to work effectively with the Havok Xtra, you'll need to understand all the concepts, such as mass, force, momentum, and so on, which we discussed in this chapter. You can rely on the xtra to do the calculations for you, but there's no shortcut to understanding the physics concepts. For example, the ball will slide and not roll if you set its friction to zero. As you will see, even a simple movie such as this requires a little ingenuity.

Using a Skyhook to Hold the Plane

Why have I created two movies to demonstrate the same idea? Both the plane and the ball are movable. In a Havok Physics Scene, movable bodies are by definition affected by gravity. However, the plane should stay at a fixed position in space. There are two ways to cope with this. One is to attach the plane to a fixed point in space using a *dashpot,* which is a strong, damped spring. An undamped spring will be bouncy; a damped spring acts like a shock absorber.

To tilt the plane, I alter the angular momentum of the plane while one or more arrow keys are held down. Thanks to Brian Robbins of Clevermedia for the original movie that I adapted.

Tilting the World

The drawback of a dashpot is that, however powerful you make it, it is still flexible. The plane sags a little when the movie starts. An alternative technique consists of making the plane fixed and unmovable in space. Because the plane cannot be moved, I tilt the camera instead. This appears to make the plane tilt, but, in fact, it tilts the whole world. At the same time as I tilt the camera, I tilt the force of gravity, so that it is still acting straight down, as far as the camera is concerned. Thanks to Dr. Steven Collins of Havok for suggesting this technique.

The disadvantage of this is that gravity depends on the tilt of the camera. When the ball falls off the edge, you can change the direction of its fall by tilting the camera. I minimize this effect by placing the plane low in the sprite.

Falling with Lingo

The advantage of the Havok approach is that it takes care of the trickiest aspects of physics. The Teeter.dir movie doesn't let the ball fall off the plane—and for good reason: falling is easy to simulate and rolling is not hard. However, the transition between the two is not easy to manage at all. The Havok Xtra does this for you. If you were to do it in Lingo, one of the most difficult questions is how does the ball know where the edge of the plane is?

I provide a third movie: TiltDrop.dir. This goes a long way to solving the problem of rolling over the edge of the plane. The Lingo required is no more complex than what you've already seen, but there is just so much more of it. You might like to analyze the `getClosestPointTo()` handler to see if you can apply your understanding of vector mathematics to it. The handler calculates which point on a line (defined by its two end points) is closest to a third point.

This example helps you see how complex the mathematics can get even in a relatively simple situation. In complex situations, the Havok Xtra can be a great time saver.

Conclusion

This chapter has explored the concepts expressed by vector mathematics and shown you how to use these concepts to create realistic interaction between two models. Once again, mental images will prove helpful in understanding the abstract notions. You will be able to unleash the power of the 3D Lingo vector commands only if you can visualize their effects.

You have seen how vectors can be used to express force, acceleration, velocity, displacement, position in space, and ratios. A vector with the same values can be used in each case, but the units associated with the vector will be different. Noting the right units in your Lingo script can help you build your mental image, and thus help you determine what operations to use.

You've used your understanding of vectors to build a movie where you simulate the effect of gravity acting on a ball. You've also seen how the same effect can be achieved in a different way using the Havok Xtra.

CHAPTER

8

Playing with Fire

IN THIS CHAPTER:

The toe bone's connected to the foot bone, the foot bone's connected to the ankle bone, the ankle bone's connected to the shin bone. . .
Dem bones, dem bones

In this chapter you'll be working with the box and particle primitives. The box primitive has a few simple properties that you can set. The particle primitive is inherently animated, which provides for endless possibilities, and demands a number of properties that interact in complex ways. This chapter cannot hope to explore all of these, so we shall limit ourselves to creating a flame. We'll use the box primitive to create a matchbox and a match, and the particle primitive to make the match burn.

You'll also be using the mouse to manipulate the models in the 3D world. On a 2D Stage, the mouse position is easy to define. You can select a sprite by clicking it; the sprite appears to be immediately under the mouse. When you drag the mouse, you expect the sprite to follow. In a 3D world, you use the mouse to act on models at a distance, rather like a lion tamer with his whip.

Clicking a model and dragging the mouse can be interpreted in a number of ways. Designing a 3D interface that responds appropriately to the mouse requires patience and training. (Be sure to reward your models with a tasty tidbit when they perform as expected.) In this chapter, you'll be pushing models, rotating them about various axes, picking them up, and moving them in more or less complex ways. Indeed, you'll be simulating all the movements you normally make to light a match.

The third concept you'll be discovering is that of parent-child relations. The matchbox will consist of two parts, a sleeve and a tray, which you will combine to create a group. Similarly you will create a match from a stick and a head. The separate models will be the children of a group. Modifying the transform of the parent match will automatically modify the position and orientation of its children; the match stick and head will move as one.

In the example movies for this chapter, I use a number of hard-coded values. This is not recommended practice; I can justify it only by explaining that it makes the code simpler to read. The example is usable but not polished. There are a number of suggestions on how to improve it at the end of the chapter.

The Particle Primitive

MakeFire.dir

The particle primitive produces multiple planes, which always face the camera. These planes can be animated in an infinite variety of ways, to produce effects such as stars, water, smoke, explosions, grit thrown up from the tires of a car, and so on. Working with particles is more of an art than a science. With experience, you will be able to judge how to set the parameters to produce a given effect, to a near approximation; but as often as not, you'll discover that you find the best settings only by trial and error.

On the Director 8.5 CD-ROM, you'll find a folder named Intel 3D Examples\ParticleTool\. Inside, you'll find a movie entitled ParticleTool.dir. You can use this to give you an idea of the range of possibilities (see Figure 8-2). However, it does not let you set all the possible properties, nor does it tell you the names of the properties you are modifying. An alternative is to use Ullala's 3DPI, in which you can consult the names and values of the properties of a particle primitive that is displayed on the Stage.

The particle primitive can create upward of 50,000 planes, each of which has to be tracked and displayed in 3D space. This can reduce your movie to a standstill.

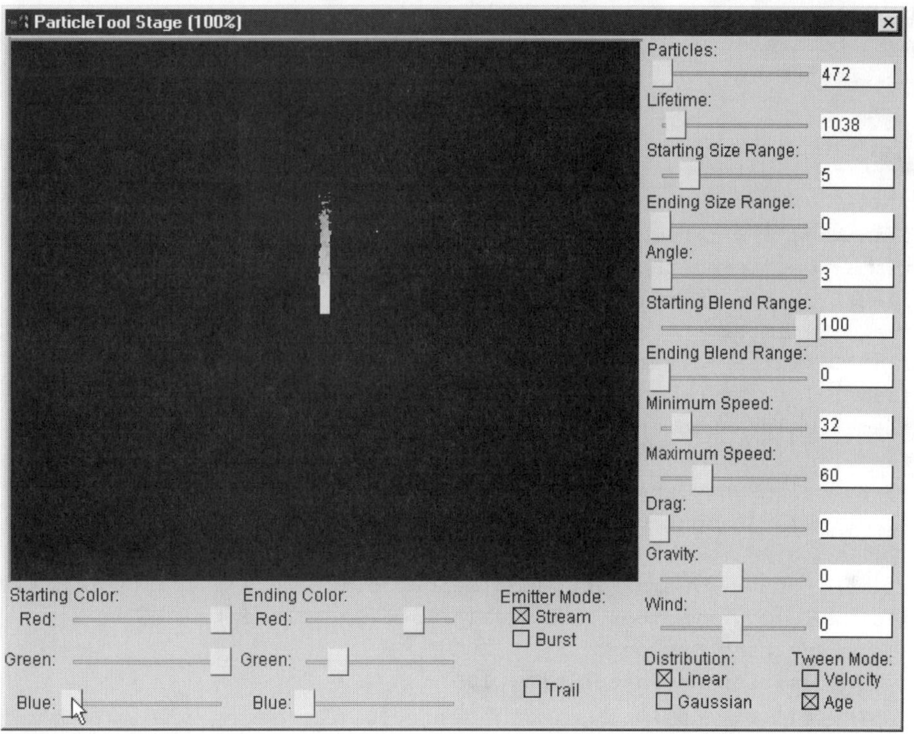

Figure 8-1 *Setting parameters for a match flame in the ParticleTool.dir movie*

You should try to reach a happy medium between the number of particles you use and the frame rate you want to achieve on your slowest target machine.

In the example movie, I'll be using a low frame rate of 15 frames per second, and no more than 350 particles to animate the flame. You'll find that a higher frame rate gives a smoother looking flame as does a higher number of particles, but the values I have chosen give an acceptable result without overloading the CPU.

Creating a Flame

You'll find a movie named MakeFire.dir in the 3D\Dragging\ folder on the CD-ROM that accompanies this book. This contains a behavior with a `createFrame()` handler, which we will use later to provide the flame for the match. Here's the behavior:

```
property myMember

on beginSprite(me)
  myMember = sprite(me.spriteNum).member
  myMember.resetWorld()
  me.createFlame()
end

on createFlame(me)
  flame1      = myMember.newModelResource("Flame 1", #particle)
  flameModel1 = myMember.newModel("Flame 1", flame1)
  flame1.emitter.maxSpeed     = 60
  flame1.emitter.numParticles = 250
  flame1.emitter.angle        = 2
  flame1.emitter.direction    = vector( 0.0000, 1.0000, 0.0000 )
  flame1.lifeTime             = 1000
  flame1.colorRange.start     = rgb(255, 255, 128)
  flame1.colorRange.end       = rgb(192, 96, 0)
  flame1.sizeRange.start      = 3
  flame1.blendRange.end       = 0

  flame2      = myMember.newModelResource("Flame 2", #particle)
  flameModel2 = myMember.newModel("Flame 2", flame2)
  flame2.emitter.maxSpeed     = 100
  flame2.emitter.numParticles = 100
  flame2.emitter.angle        = 2
  flame2.emitter.direction    = vector(0, 1.0, 0.0 )
  flame2.lifeTime             = 600
  flame2.colorRange.start     = rgb(255, 255, 0)
  flame2.colorRange.end       = rgb(192, 128, 0)
```

```
  flame2.sizeRange.start        = 5
  flame2.blendRange.end         = 0

  flame1.emitter.region         = [vector(0, -2, 0)]
end createFlame
```

In the movie, most of the lines in the handler have been commented out. This means that, when you first run the movie, you will see the default settings for the particle primitive. Open the behavior in the script window and, while the movie is running, uncomment the lines one at a time. Click the Recompile All Modified Scripts button while the movie is running. This will provoke a new `#beSprite` event, and thus create a new particle primitive with the modified parameters.

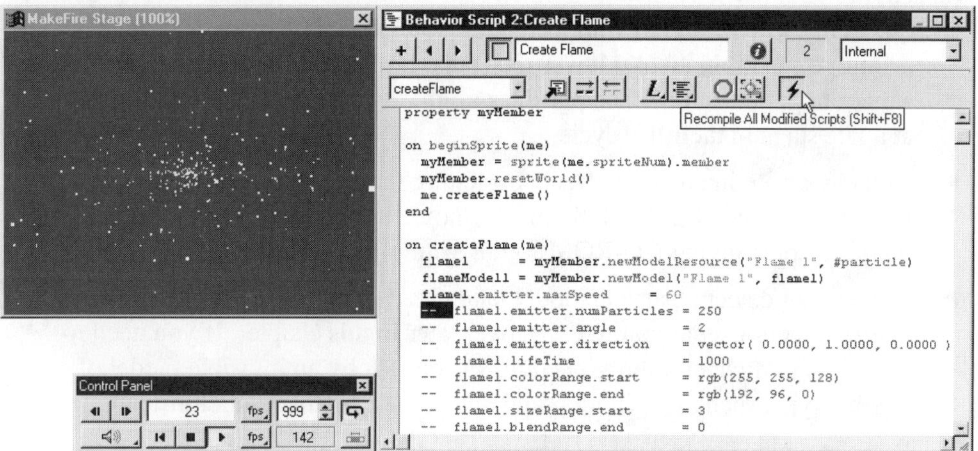

You will see the initial starburst gradually reorganizing itself into a fair imitation of a match flame. Notice that I have used two primitives to create a flame with a more realistic tapering volume: one is short and stout; the other is taller and thinner. I use slightly different color schemes and particle speeds for the two primitives to give a better flickering effect.

Creating Other Particle Effects

Balloons.dir

Although I could provide recipes for other effects, I believe that you will learn more by experimenting for yourself. With either the ParticleTool.dir movie or the 3DPI, try adjusting the parameters for a particle primitive to create variations on the theme. The match flame could be modified to become a burst from a flame thrower, a burst of sparks from a cigarette lighter, or a Roman candle firework. Alternatively, you could change its color to white and experiment with gravity to produce a fountain.

Here are some points to note:

- Although you can set the size of the particles directly as a parameter, the total size of the particle model is a function of many factors, including `emitter.maxSpeed`, `lifeTime`, `drag`, `gravity`, `wind`, and so on.
- The particles remain "attached" to their source. If you move the `transform.position` of the primitive, the particles that have already been emitted will move by the same amount. We'll see in a moment how to make the particles appear to behave more independently.
- Giving your particles a short `lifetime` can lead to unexpected consequences, especially when coupled with low frame rates. Because using a particle primitive can dramatically lower the frame rate, you should check this on your slower target machines. The particles might fail to appear at all or appear only at a late stage in their life cycle.
- You can create interesting effects by setting the `texture` property of the particle resource. See the Balloons.dir movie in the 3D\Dragging\ folder on the accompanying CD-ROM for an example.
- You cannot detect a particle model using `modelsUnderRay()` or the two similar functions that you will discover later in this chapter. If you need to identify a particle emitter, you could surround it by an invisible model of another type, such as #cylinder, and detect the invisible model instead.
- Particles emitted from a particle model will pass through other models. If you need to have them bounce or land on a surface, you might need to build your own particle system using plane primitives, which you can detect and control independently.

Moving a Particle Primitive

MoveFire.dir

As noted earlier, the position of each particle emitted by a particle primitive is calculated with reference to the particle's source. In our animation, we'll be moving a lighted match. Unless you deliberately intervene, the flame will remain unrealistically steady and vertical, regardless of the speed with which you move the match around.

You can see this in the MoveFire.dir movie, which you'll find in the 3D\Dragging\ folder on the CD-ROM that accompanies this book. Ensure that the Modify transform .position button is selected; then click the Shockwave 3D sprite, hold the mouse down, and move it around. The flame stays rigid as it moves. (For the moment, don't worry that the flame doesn't stay under your mouse; we'll look at ways of doing this properly later.)

Modifying the emitter.region

Click the Modify emitter.region button and try again. This time, particles that have already been emitted continue upward from the point they were emitted from. The effect is more realistic, but it's still not pretty.

Press the COMMAND key down before you click. This will force the movie into a tight `repeat while the mouseDown` loop, so that it updates the Stage as rapidly as possible, regardless of `the frameTempo`. The result is better, but the flame seems to have two tails. The disadvantage is that it blocks the playback head.

This time press both the COMMAND key and the SHIFT key before you click. This activates code that ensures that both particle primitives create a flame of the same height. The result is much cleaner.

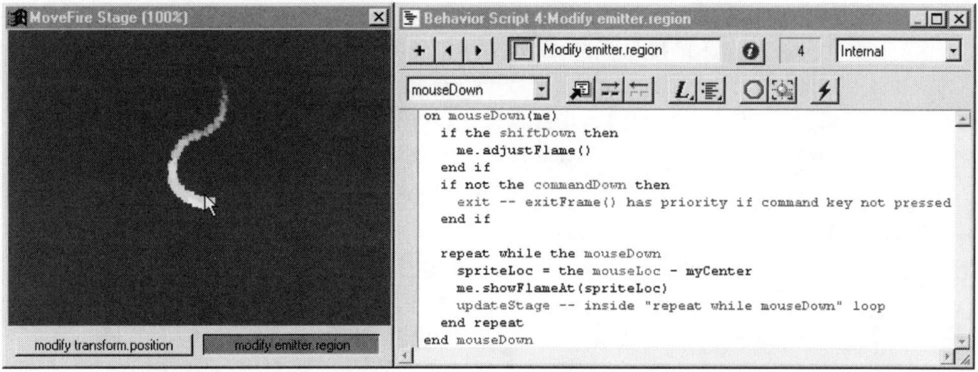

So what is the `emitter.region`? In literal terms, it is a list of points in space, defined as a displacement from the particle model's `transform.position`. By default, a Model Resource's `emitter.region` contains a single 3D point, `vector(0.0, 0.0, 0.0)`, which coincides with the particle model's position in space. However, you can set it to

- Any other point
- Two points that define the ends of a line
- Four points that define the corners of an area in space

You will provoke a script error if you use any number of 3D points other than 1, 2, or 4. The particles will be generated at random over the whole of the region that you define.

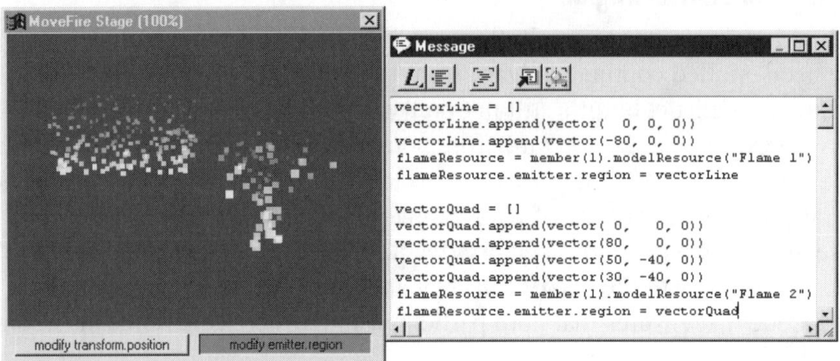

Throughout its `lifetime`, a particle's position is calculated in terms of the point from which it was emitted. This point is defined in terms of a displacement from the particle model's `transform.position`. If you move the particle model's `transform.position`, all the particles move together. If you move the `emitter.region` of the Model Resource, each particle will evolve independently.

Modifying the Model Resource

When you modify the `emitter.region`, you modify the Model Resource itself, not the model instance of the resource. As you will see in the following, this makes it somewhat cumbersome to move our lighted match realistically. We will be able to create a single group of the match head and the match stick, and move them as one. However, we will have to move the match group separately from the `emitter.region` of the two particle primitive resources we use for the flame.

The Box Primitive

Now that you have an idea of how to create the flame, let's look at how to build the match and the matchbox. For the match head, we'll use a sphere primitive. For the two parts of the matchbox and the matchstick, we'll use a box primitive. Later, we will see how to add the flame to the match so that both move together.

A box could be described as a group of six planes, all at right angles to each other. A plane has width and length (length being determined along the y axis); a box also has a height. Logically, the height of a box is measured along the y axis, which means its length is measured along the z axis, just to confuse you. As you can see in Figure 8-2, not all the walls of a box need be used. You can set the value of the properties `#top`, `#bottom`, `#left`, `#right`, `#back`, and `#front` to `FALSE` to hide the appropriate wall.

Which wall do you expect to be the `#front`? Use Ullala's 3D Property Inspector to check. The `#front` wall is the one farthest away from you. The box is traveling in the same direction that you are, not looking back at you.

The other main difference between a box and a set of six planes is that a plane automatically has two visible faces. A box, by default, has sides that are visible only from the outside. There's a test to illustrate this in the following section.

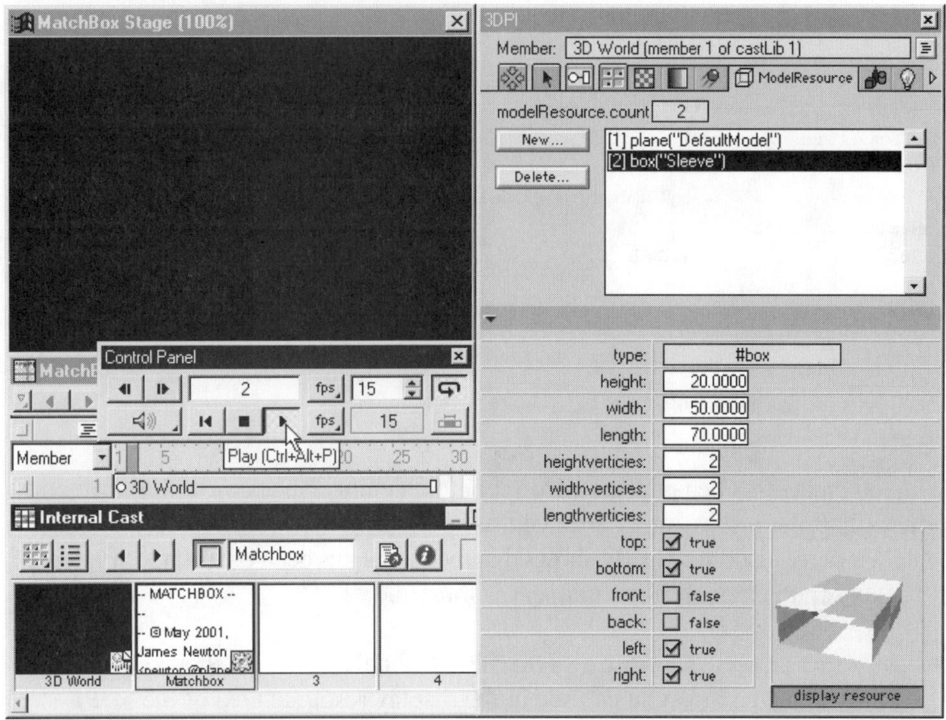

Figure 8-2 *The inside faces of a box are invisible by default.*

The Outer Sleeve

Matches0.dir

Here's the beginning of the behavior you'll be creating.

```
property mySprite
property myMember
property mySleeve    -- box model: outer sleeve of matchbox (no ends)
property myTray      -- box model: inner tray of matchbox (no top)


on beginSprite(me)
  mySprite = sprite(me.spriteNum)
  myMember = mySprite.member

  me.createWorld()
end beginSprite


on createWorld(me)
  myMember.resetWorld()

  aResource          = myMember.newModelResource("Sleeve", #box, #both)
  aResource.front    = FALSE
  aResource.back     = FALSE
  aResource.length   = 70
  aResource.height   = 20
  aResource.width    = 50

  mySleeve = myMember.newModel("Sleeve", aResource)
end createWorld
```

If you create this behavior and drop it onto an empty Shockwave 3D sprite, the sprite will appear just as empty after you run your movie as it did before. Nonetheless, the 3D Property Inspector clearly shows that the model has been created (see Figure 8-2).

The reason the model doesn't appear is threefold:

- **`visibility`** The `createWorld()` handler removes the front and back walls of the box (as you can see in the display resource area of the 3DPI window). Because the model is placed at the center of the world, it is the inside surface of the remaining walls that faces the camera. To make the walls visible, you will need to change the `visibility` property of the model to `#both`. The visibility property of a model has four possible values: `#front` (the default value), #back, #both, or #none. The value #back will display only the inside walls (useful if you are creating rooms from primitives), whereas #none will hide the model altogether and make it invisible to detection using rays.

- **Lighting** As you saw in the previous chapter, the visibility of a plane depends on the angle from which light falls on it. Adding more lights, increasing their brightness, or changing their angle may help.
- **Camera position** The default camera view looks at the model from end on. Changing to a more cavalier angle can help make the walls more obvious.

Add the following lines to your createWorld() handler, run your movie, and uncomment the lines one at a time. Recompile the behavior each time you uncomment a line and see how the line affects the way the model appears.

```
  -- mySleeve.visibility = #both

  -- myMember.ambientColor = rgb(255, 255, 255)

  -- mySprite.camera.transform.position = vector(100, 40, 100)
  -- mySprite.camera.pointAt(vector(0, 0, 0))
end createWorld
```

You can find a movie where this is all already typed out for you in the 3D\Dragging\ folder on the CD-ROM that accompanies the book. It's called Matches0.dir.

The Inner Tray

Let's create the other part of the matchbox: the inner tray. This will have five walls; only the top will be missing. We'll make it just slightly smaller than the outer sleeve, so that it slides comfortably inside.

Add this to your createWorld() handler:

```
  aResource          = myMember.newModelResource("Tray", #box, #both)
  aResource.top      = FALSE
  aResource.length   = 70
  aResource.height   = 19
  aResource.width    = 49

  myTray = myMember.newModel("Tray", aResource)
  myTray.visibility = #both
```

Now, of course, the question is how do you open the box?

Manipulating Models with the Mouse

When you hold the mouse over a Shockwave 3D sprite, what part of space are you pointing at? There are two and a half ways to answer this question:

- `modelUnderLoc()` can tell you which model (if any) is immediately under a given `loc`.
- Like its cousin `modelsUnderRay()`, which you saw in the previous chapter, `modelsUnderLoc()` can give you a list of models. If necessary, it also can give you a `#detailed` report on them. (Note that `models` is plural in this case.) Both these functions only detect front-facing surfaces, which is the reason I have ensured that the Sleeve and Tray resources are created so that both inside and outside surfaces are front facing.
- `spriteSpaceToWorldSpace()` gives you a different outlook on the matter. Imagine a curtain, woven from transparent pixel units some distance from the camera; `spriteSpaceToWorldSpace()` gives you the coordinates of the "pixel unit" on the curtain immediately under the loc in question. The expression pixel units is significant. Because of the effect of perspective, close to the camera, a movement of one 3D unit (one "meter," as I called it in the previous chapter) covers several pixels. Far away from the camera, a single pixel corresponds to a movement of several 3D units. The transparent curtain you are imagining is at exactly that distance where one pixel on the Stage corresponds to one 3D unit in the world. The distance will depend on the focal length of the camera: For a wide-angle lens, the curtain will appear nearer; with a telephoto lens you will be able to distinguish pixel unit details farther away.

Try these functions in the Watcher window:

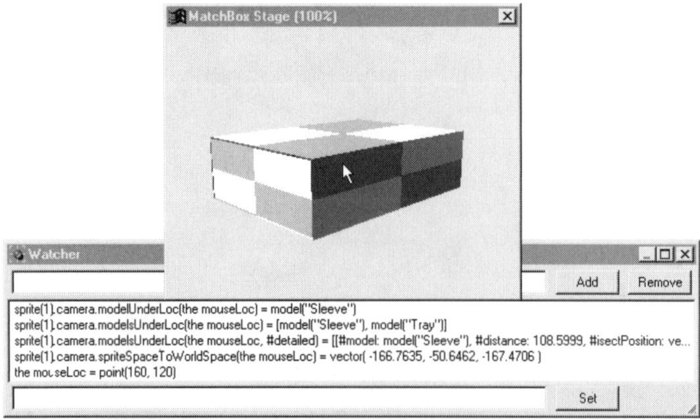

It's easier to map from a point in the 3D world to a point on the surface of the sprite. A fourth function, `worldSpaceToSpriteSpace()`, does this for you.

Camera Functions

All these functions are dependent on the camera. As you will see in Chapter 12, the same Shockwave 3D member may have a number of cameras, each giving different views of the same world. At an important sporting event, there are TV cameras at strategic points around the stadium, but you, and the TV viewer at home, see only one view at a time. If you touch the screen to point out a particular player, the TV editor cuts to a different camera, suddenly your finger is pointing at something quite different.

The Shockwave 3D member might have many cameras, but the sprite in which it appears generally shows only one view at a time. This is why I use `sprite(1).camera...`, rather than `member(1).camera(1)...`; although these two expressions might refer to the same camera, `the mouseLoc` is more meaningful when you think in terms of the sprite than in terms of the member.

Triggering an Action with the Mouse

Matches1.dir

We now want to give the user the impression that he or she is pushing the tray out of the sleeve to get at the matches inside. The simplest `modelUnderLoc()` function is all we need to know when the mouse is over the tray. The only part of the tray that is visible at the moment is the back. When the user clicks the back, we'll move the tray along the negative z axis as if it were being pushed.

We don't want the tray to pop out suddenly. We want a steady movement, over a number of frames. To do this, we'll execute the animation on `exitFrame`. But first, we must decide how far to move the tray per frame, and for how many frames.

Launch your movie, and in the Message window, type a command to move the tray out of the sleeve. By now, you should be able to do this without my help, so don't read any further until you've done it. You'll need to find, by trial and error (or by thinking about it for a moment) how far down the z axis to make the tray travel before it will be possible to remove a match from it. Here's the `transform.position` that suits me:

```
member(1).model("Tray").transform.position = vector(0, 0, -48)
```

How many frames are we going to animate this over? Say `the frameTempo` is set to 15 and we take a little over a second to open the box: 16 frames × 3 units per frame should do just fine.

The movement is simple, so we could just use `model("Tray").translate(0, 0, -3)` on every `exitFrame`, until the box is open:

```
on exitFrame(me)
  if the mouseUp then
    exit
  else if mySprite.camera.modelUnderLoc(the mouseLoc) <> myTray then
    exit
  end if

  if myTray.transform.position.z > -48 then
    myTray.translate(0, 0, -3) -- Use the simple translate command
  end if
end exitFrame
```

The Matches1.dir movie that you'll find in the 3D\Dragging\ folder on the CD-ROM illustrates all the code up to this point.

Although this simple solution is adequate here, there will be many cases where we want to animate a movement that is not so simple: a combination of translation and rotation, for instance. So let's try out a more powerful method that produces the same result. In this case, it will be like using a sledge hammer to crack a nut, but it helps to know that the sledge hammer exists.

NOTE

Like the `modelsUnderRay()` function, `modelUnderLoc()` cannot "see" the inside surfaces of models.

Moving with a Transform

Interpol.dir

Instead of using a translation, we'll create a transform that embodies the movement that we want to give to the matchbox tray. We'll take the difference between the initial transform of the tray and its final transform, and we'll divide that difference by the number of steps that the tray should take to move between the two positions.

You can subtract one 3D point from another to obtain a vector, and you can divide a vector by a *scalar* (a unidimensional number) to obtain a portion of the movement between the two points. However, you can't subtract and divide transforms. Or rather, if you do so, you must do it under another name.

Dividing a Transform

To divide a transform, you can use the `interpolate()` function or the `interpolateTo()` method. The `interpolate()` function returns a new transform, and the `interpolateTo()` method modifies an existing transform, but otherwise the principle is the same.

To divide a transform, you take an identity transform (unrotated, unscaled, and sitting in the center of the world) in one hand and the transform you want to divide in the other, and you think of the `interpolate()` function as a sort of rigid Slinky™ spring between the two. You choose how far along the spring you want to be, as a percentage, and the `interpolate()` function tells you the position and rotation of the spiral of the Slinky™ at that distance along. The trick in this division technique is to start with an identity transform at the center of the world.

Subtracting One Transform from Another

To subtract one transform from another, you need to untranslate and unrotate one of the transforms so that it is sitting in the center of the world. You can use the `inverse()` function or the `invert()` method to do this. You then translate and rotate the other transform by exactly the same amount. The two transforms will now be in the same relative position, but one will be an identity transform.

Actually, you probably are more likely to want to work with copies of the transform than with the originals. You'll find an example of these subtraction and division techniques in the Interpol.dir movie in the 3D\Dragging\ folder on the CD-ROM that accompanies the book. The Curved Multiply behavior uses the principles I describe in the `startAnimation()` handler.

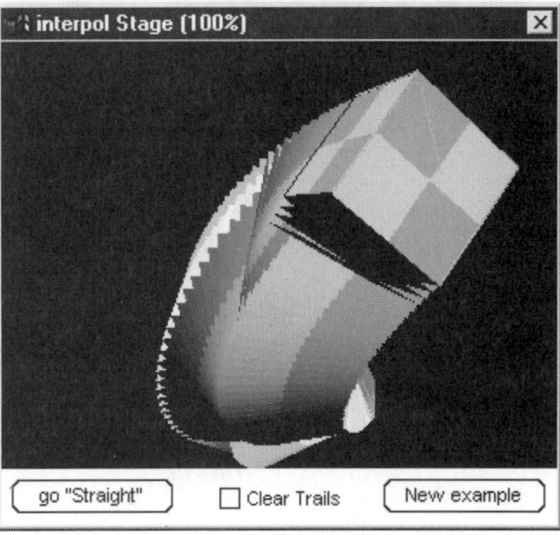

Interpolation

Matches2.dir

For the time being, we are lucky: the initial position of the matchbox tray is already at the center of the world, its transform is already the identity transform. In the following `mouseDown()` handler, I build the `targetTransform` by taking an identity transform and setting the intended final position. I then take a second identity transform and ask it to `interpolateTo()` a point part of the way to the target. I ensure that the animation will take about a second by dividing the target transform by a percentage based on `the frameTempo`:

```
property myAction    -- #open | #rotate | ...
property myTransform -- transform used for the current movement

on mouseDown(me)
  spriteLoc = the mouseLoc - [mySprite.left, mySprite.top]
   case mySprite.camera.modelUnderLoc(spriteLoc) of
    myTray:
      myAction   = #open
      targetTransform = transform()
      targetTransform.position = vector(0, 0, -48)

      myTransform = transform()
      percentage  = 100.0 / the frameTempo
      myTransform.interpolateTo(targetTransform, percentage)

      put #myTransform
      put #position, myTransform.position
      put #rotation, myTransform.rotation
      put #scale,    myTransform.scale
  end case
end mouseDown
```

This is what you would see in the Message window if `the frameTempo` is set to 16:

```
-- #myTransform
-- #position vector( 0.0000, 0.0000, -3.0000 )
-- #rotation vector( 0.0000, 0.0000, 0.0000 )
-- #scale vector( 1.0000, 1.0000, 1.0000 )
```

The values of `myTransform.position` are the same as those we used previously with the simple `translate()` method. The rotation and scale values are, understandably, neutral.

So, how do we apply a `transform` to `model("Tray")` to make it move?

Multiplying Transforms

On `exitFrame`, instead of translating `myTray`'s transform by a vector, I `multiply()` it by the transform I have calculated. This has the same effect; test it for yourself and see:

```
on exitFrame(me)
  if the mouseUp then
    exit
  end if

  case myAction of
    #open:
      spriteLoc = the mouseLoc - [mySprite.left, mySprite.top]
      if myTray.transform.position.z > -48 then
        myTray.transform.multiply(myTransform)
      end if
  end case
end exitFrame
```

"Multiply" might seem a strange term in this context. The name of the method indicates the matrix mathematics it involves. Director controls the matrix side of things, so all you really need to be concerned with is the result; multiplying one transform by another has the effect of concatenating the movements implicit in the transforms. Here, the same translation transform is multiplied by itself repeatedly, moving the matchbox tray along steadily in the same direction.

You'll find all the code so far in the movie Matches2.dir. This also includes a text member named Multiplying Matrices where the multiplication of transforms is explained in more detail.

Rotating a Model with the Mouse

Matches3.dir

The matchbox is now open, but you can't see the matches in it. (Okay, so there aren't any yet, but we'll deal with that in a moment.) First, we have to provide a way for the user to rotate the box so that the tray is facing the front.

The question is what is the best way to translate the horizontal and vertical movements of the mouse into a rotation around an arbitrary axis in three dimensions? There is not one right answer to this question that can be applied to all situations. In this case, the axis of rotation is known (we want to rotate around the world's y axis), and there is an obvious point in the sprite (the center of the top face of the matchbox sleeve) around which the rotation takes place. Other cases you might deal with in your own projects will need different solutions.

Here it makes sense to start the rotation when the user clicks the matchbox sleeve, and to stop turning when the user releases the mouse. We can determine where the center of the top face of the sleeve is by using the `worldSpaceToSpriteSpace()` camera method we saw earlier. We can draw an imaginary line between the point on the sprite where the user clicked and this center point, and calculate its angle. Each time the user moves the mouse, we can calculate a new angle, and turn the matchbox by the difference between the old and new angles. Here is a handler that can give us this angle:

```
on getMouseAngle(me)
  -- spriteLoc is the position of the mouse relative to the top left
  -- corner of the sprite

  topCenter = vector(0, 10, 0)
  centerLoc = mySprite.camera.worldSpaceToSpriteSpace(topCenter)
  -- Find the position of the mouse relative to centerLoc
 spriteLoc = the mouseLoc - [mySprite.left, mySprite.top]
  delta   = centerLoc - spriteLoc
  deltaH = delta.locH
  deltaV = delta.locV

  if deltaH <> 0 then
    slope = float(deltaV) / -deltaH
    angle = atan(slope)
    if deltaH < 0 then
      angle = angle + pi
    else if deltaV < 0 then
      angle = angle + (pi * 2)
    end if
  else if deltaV < 0 then
    angle = pi / 2
  else if deltaV > 0 then
    angle = (3 * pi) / 2
```

```
  else -- deltaH = 0, deltaV = 0
    angle = 0
  end if

  -- Convert to degrees
  return (angle * 180) / pi
end getMouseAngle
```

We'll save the previously calculated value of the `mouseAngle` in a `myAngle` property, so you'd better declare that at the top of your script:

```
property myAngle     -- previous angle for rotation
```

You'll need to add a new case statement to each of your `mouseDown()` and `exitFrame()` handlers. Add this to the beginning of the case statement of the `mouseDown()` handler:

```
mySleeve:
 myAction = #rotate
 myAngle  = me.getMouseAngle()
```

Add this to the case statement of the `exitFrame()` handler:

```
#rotate:
  mouseAngle = me.getMouseAngle()
  turnedAngle = mouseAngle - myAngle
  myAngle     = mouseAngle
  origin      = vector(0, 0, 0)
  vertical    = vector(0, 1, 0) -- parallel to the world's y-axis
  myTray.rotate(origin, vertical, turnedAngle)
  mySleeve.rotate(origin, vertical, turnedAngle)
```

Grouping Models

This works fine—until you slide the tray out of the sleeve. If you first slide the tray out of the sleeve, and then turn the matchbox, the tray rotates separately from the sleeve, and in the wrong place. If you turn the matchbox first, and then slide the tray out of the sleeve, it heads off in the wrong direction (the only one it knows), and destroys the fragile illusion that this pixel image represents a matchbox.

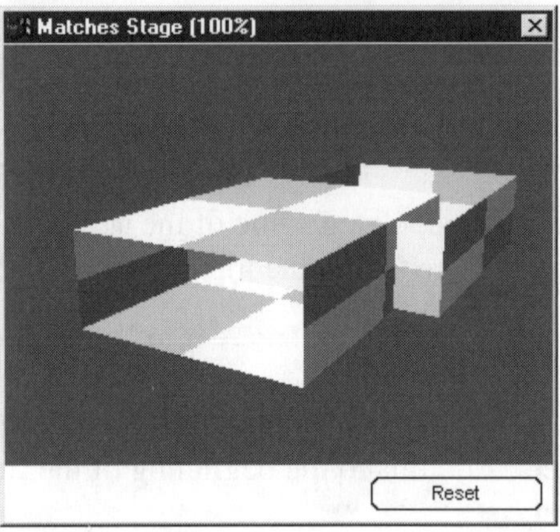

Fortunately, this is easy to fix. 3D Director allows you to create groups of nodes (a node being a model, camera, light, or another group). The elements in a group are known as its *children.* The children of a parent node are other nodes that move relative to the parent node, in terms of position, rotation, and scale. A child with an identity transform is located in the center of its parent; its axes are oriented in the same direction as the parent's axes and it shares the same scale as the parent. All nodes can have children; *groups* are nodes with nothing but children.

A node can have any number of children, but each child can only have one parent. By default, the parent of all nodes is the default group known as "World":

```
put member(1).group.count
-- 1
put member(1).group(1)
-- group("World")
```

How many children are there in the world already? There may be more than you think:

```
put member(1).group(1).child.count
-- 5
put member(1).group(1).child(1)
-- camera("DefaultView")
put member(1).group(1).child[2]
-- light("UIAmbient")
put member(1).group[1].child(3)
```

```
-- light("UIDirectional")
put member(1).group[1].child[4]
-- model("Sleeve")
put member(1).group(1).child(5)
-- model("Tray")
put member(1).group(1).child[6]
-- <Void>
```

DEBUGGING TIP

As with the other nodes, you can use either parentheses () or square brackets [] with the group and child properties, as long as you use integers. If you use names you must use parentheses:

```
put member(1).group("World").child("Tray")
-- model("Tray")
```

If we put the sleeve and tray in the same group, and then rotate the group, the tray will act as expected. (See Figure 8-3.)

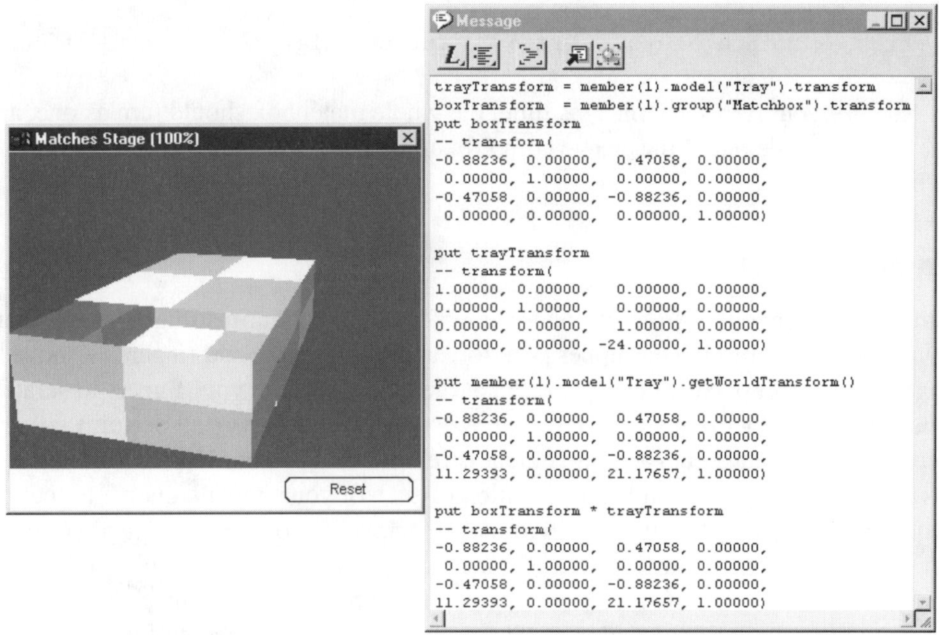

Figure 8-3 *getWorldTransform() gives the same result as multiplying child transforms with their parents.*

Modify your behavior as follows:

Add a property declaration at the top:

```
property myMatchbox -- group consisting of mySleeve and myTray
```

Create the myMatchbox group in the createWorld() handler after you create the individual models that belong to it:

```
-- Groups
myMatchbox = myMember.newGroup("Matchbox")
myMatchbox.addChild(mySleeve)
myMatchbox.addChild(myTray)
```

In the exitFrame() handler, replace the lines

```
myTray.rotate(origin, vertical, turnedAngle)
mySleeve.rotate(origin, vertical, turnedAngle)
```

with

```
myMatchbox.rotate(origin, vertical, turnedAngle)
```

Now try your movie again. This time, the whole matchbox should turn as one, and the tray will slide out of the sleeve correctly, regardless of which way it is facing. Why? Read on.

Parents

Stretch your arm out in front of you and then, keeping your arm straight, move your hand above your head. Your upper arm, forearm, wrist, hand, and fingers all move together as a group. Now bend your arm at the elbow and use your fingers to scratch your shoulder. Your upper arm, forearm, wrist, hand, and fingers all perform separate movements, but each movement is relative to a "parent" bone. You don't have to control the position and orientation of each of your fingers relative to the world; instead you get your forearm to move backward and downward, and your wrist to pivot so that your fingers are in the right position. Then you can concentrate on the scratching movement of your fingers. If you try to imagine the path that your fingers are going to follow and concentrate on getting your fingers to follow that path, it slows your movement down considerably.

This demonstration shows that you already think implicitly in terms of parent and child groups when you make an action in real space. It doesn't take much effort to think of your shoulder as the parent of your upper arm, your elbow as the parent of your forearm, your wrist as the parent of your hand, and your hand as the parent of your fingers. When you move the parent, the children maintain their position and orientation with respect to their parent; the children's position and orientation in the world as a whole might change quite dramatically, but you don't have to think about that explicitly.

However, suppose you want to know where a given child is in the world. How do you find out?

getWorldTransform()

In a Shockwave 3D member, the great-granddaddy of all nodes is `group ("World")` itself. All nodes that have `group("World")` as their parent are independent of each other. You can move them around the world by altering their transforms. When you alter the transform of a child of such a node, you move the child's relative position to its parent. To obtain the child's position relative to the world, you need to multiply the two transforms together. The shortcut is to use `getWorldTransform()`.

In your movie, rotate the matchbox group and slide the tray part way out of the sleeve. Now try the commands shown in the Figure 8-3. (Your values might be different, and I have arranged the transforms to make them more readable.)

The order in which you multiply the transforms is important. If you use the * operator, as I do in Figure 8-3, the parents should appear in descending order starting from the left. You also can start with the child's transform and work back up the hierarchy using `multiply()`:

```
trayWorldTransform = member(1).model("Tray").transform.duplicate()
trayWorldTransform.multiply(boxTransform)
put trayWorldTransform
-- transform(
-0.88236, 0.00000,  0.47058, 0.00000,
 0.00000, 1.00000,  0.00000, 0.00000,
-0.47058, 0.00000, -0.88236, 0.00000,
11.29393, 0.00000, 21.17657, 1.00000)
```

DEBUGGING TIP

The `multiply()` method modifies the transform it is applied to. If you don't use the `duplicate()` function, you will find that the transform of `model("Tray")` changes after the `multiply()` function is applied to it. The tray will now adopt a position relative to its parent that corresponds to its previous position relative to the world. Try it and see.

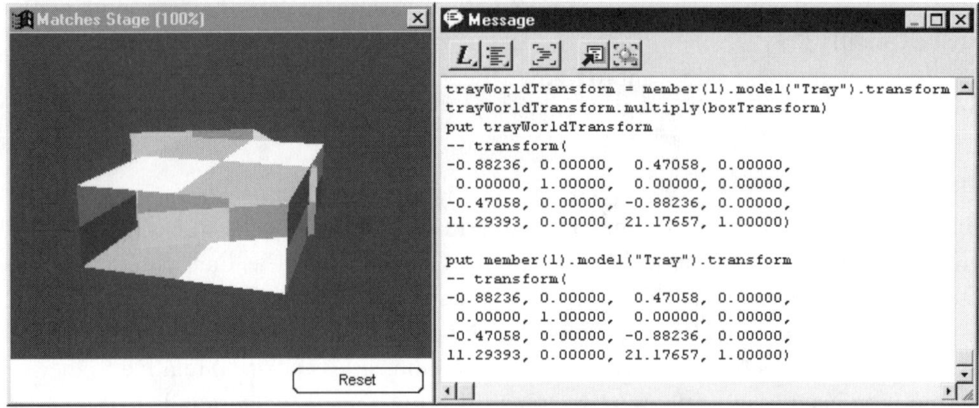

Adopting Suitable Parents

Custody.dir

You can change the parent of any node at any time. For example, if you are simulating a football game, you can change the parent of the ball depending on which player is in control of it. Because a node can have only one parent, when you adopt a new parent for a given node, you automatically divorce it from its previous parent. The transfer of custody of the child must be undertaken with care. You can see an example of this in the Custody.dir movie, which you will find in the 3D\Dragging\ folder on the CD-ROM that accompanies the book.

This movie makes a ball model pass back and forth between two box models. Here is the handler that changes the parent of the ball model from one box model to the other:

```
property myBall          -- sphere model
property myBoxList       -- list of 2 box models
property myBox           -- 1 or 2 depending on which item in
--                          myBoxList is currently parent of myBall
property myTarget        -- transform of the box model which is not
--                          currently the parent of myBall
property myTotalFrames   -- number of frames in animation
property myFrameCounter  -- varies between 1 and myTotalFrames
```

```
on exitFrame(me) -- move ball between boxes
  percentage = 100.0 / myTotalFrames * myFrameCounter
  myBall.transform = transform().interpolate(myTarget, percentage)
  myFrameCounter = myFrameCounter + 1

  if myFrameCounter > myTotalFrames then
    me.catchBall()
  end if
end exitFrame


on catchBall(me)
  -- Invert parent and target boxes
  newTarget     = myBall.parent.transform -- current parent
  myBox         = (myBox mod 2) + 1       -- 2 -> 1 -> 2 -> 1 ...
  myBall.parent = myBoxList[myBox]        -- change parent
  myTarget      = newTarget * myBall.parent.transform.inverse()

  --myBall.transform.identity() -- uncomment to eliminate flash
  myFrameCounter = 1
end catchBall
```

As you run the movie, you will see that the ball disappears for a frame, just as it is caught. Why is this? The ball moves from the center of its parent to the center of the target box. When the ball is caught by the target box, its transform places it at some distance from its parent. Changing its parent means the ball is now that same distance from its new parent; in other words, it is off Stage. Uncommenting the third-to-last line in the preceding extract cancels the translation stored in `myBall.transform`, and places `myBall` at the center of its new parent, which is its correct world position.

Respecting the New Child's Position

There is another way of achieving the same ends. You could replace the line

```
myBall.parent = myBoxList[myBox]        -- change parent
```

with

```
myBoxList[myBox].addChild(myBall, #preserveWorld)
```

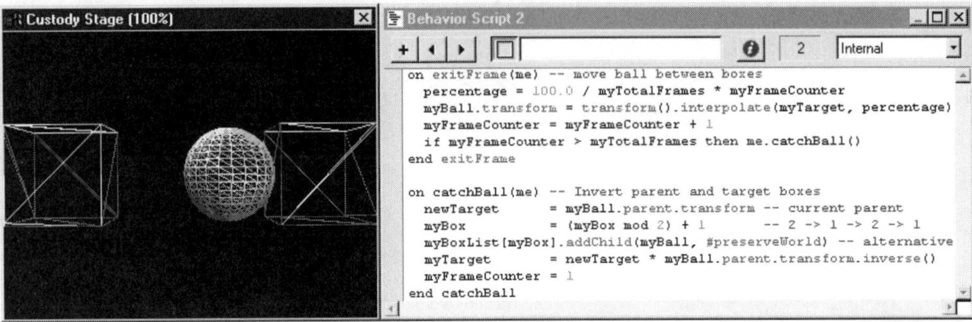

This forces Director to recalculate the transform of `myBall` such that its position in 3D space is preserved. The default alternative for the `addChild()` command is `#preserveParent`, which maintains the current transform for the model, and thus changes the model's position in the world. This makes the `addChild()` command more powerful than simply changing a model's parent; Director can do all the work of calculating the new transform for you.

Matchmaking with Parents

It's time we made a match to put in the matchbox. We'll make it in two parts: a match head and a matchstick. We could make the head the parent of the stick, so that both move together and all movements are calculated in terms of the head of the match. Alternatively, we could create a "Match" group to act as the parent of both parts. In this case, there is little difference between the two approaches. I choose to create a group, because I then can think of the group as the "Match".

We'll need to detect when the user clicks the match. The `modelUnderLoc()` function works only with models, not with groups. This means we will need to store a `myStick` property so we can detect when it is clicked. Add this declaration at the top of your script:

```
property myStick -- box model used for the matchstick
```

To begin with, the match will be inside the matchbox. Here, it makes sense to make the match a child of the tray. As long as the match is in the tray, it will move as the tray moves. When the user takes the match out of the box, we will change its parent. We'll use a `myHand` group as its parent when we actually strike the match, and finally make the lighted match a child of the `group("World")` so it can be moved freely.

Later, we will add a flame to the match, using a couple of particle primitives. We might be tempted to make these children of the match head, but we won't. You saw earlier that to move the flame realistically, you must move the `emitter.region` of the resource—not the model itself. Making the flame a child of the match head would make the particle model move with the match head and lead to a rigidly upright animation of the flame.

The Matchstick

The sleeve and the tray use different Model Resources because each of them is made from a box that has one or more of its faces missing. The resources need to be different because the missing faces are different. Because the resources were different, it made sense to make them exactly the right size for the job, so that the model did not need to be scaled.

The matchstick can be made of a complete box with none of its sides missing, so we'll need to make a third box Model Resource for this. This time, instead of resizing the resource to suit the match, we're going to use a standard box resource and scale the match model instead. This is simply a demonstration of an alternative technique.

Add this to your `createWorld()` handler:

```
aResource  = myMember.newModelResource("Box", #box)
myStick = myMember.newModel("Stick", aResource)
myStick.scale(0.04, 0.04, 1.2) -- 2 x 2 x 60 units
myStick.translate(0, 0, -30)
```

The last line moves the front edge of the stick back to the center of the world. When we make the stick a child of the `group ("Match")`, the `position` of the group will coincide with this front edge.

The Head of the Match

A match head is an ellipsoid—it looks like an elongated sphere. We can't create an ellipsoid resource; the nearest we can get is a regular sphere. This means we're going to have to scale the head model as well.

Add this to your `createWorld()` handler:

```
aResource = myMember.newModelResource("Sphere", #sphere)
myHead = myMember.newModel("Head", aResource)
myHead.scale(0.08 , 0.08, 0.12) -- 4 x 4 x 6 units
```

This makes the head twice as thick as the matchstick and slightly longer than it is thick. We won't move the head from where it is at the center of the world; when we make the head a child of `group ("Match")`, the `position` of the group will coincide with the center of the head.

Making the Match

Although the stick and head are now in the correct relative position, they are still two distinct objects. We'll now group them so we can manipulate them as one match. Add this to your `createWorld()` handler:

```
myMatch = myMember.newGroup("Match")
myMatch.addChild(myStick)
myMatch.addChild(myHead)
```

You'll need to make a `property myMatch` declaration at the top of the script, so other handlers can manipulate the group. The variables `myStick` and `myHead` will be used again to detect whether the user clicks the match. You can't detect a group with the `modelsUnderLoc()` group of functions. You should declare these two variables as properties at the top of your script.

The two models retain their relative positions when they are added to `group("Match")`. There is no need to use either `#preserveParent` or `#preserveWorld` as the additional parameter to the `addChild()` command; the world is the current parent and the group is at the center of the world, so both modes would have the same effect.

Placing the Match in the Box

The match group is currently floating in midair with its head at the center of the matchbox. Let's move it forward so it is fully inside the matchbox and place it explicitly on the floor of the tray before making the tray its (temporary) parent. Add this to your `createWorld()` handler:

```
myMatch.translate(0, -8, 30)
myTray.addChild(myMatch)
```

Actually, only the head of the match is touching the floor of the tray. The matchstick itself is floating a couple of units above the floor, but this is not obvious. It would be obvious if the matchstick lay on the floor and the head of the match passed through the floor. If you want to be a purist, you could rotate the match slightly around the y axis so that both ends touch.

Again, there is no distinction here between `#preserveWorld` and `#preserveParent`, so you can safely ignore the second parameter of the `addChild()` method.

Now that you have a match in the matchbox, try opening the box and rotating it so you can see the match. In the 3D\Dragging\ folder on the CD-ROM, you'll find a movie named Matches4.dir that includes all the code you have looked at so far.

Handling the Match

We now come to the trickiest set of mouse manipulations: picking up the match and striking it. Why are these manipulations tricky? For three reasons:

- The user will be moving an object more or less freely in 3D space, but a mouse can indicate only two dimensions.
- The movement needs to pass through a given point. When the match is picked up, it must pass through the gap between the tray and the sleeve. It should not seem to pass through either of these solid objects. When the match is struck, its head should touch the edge of the box.
- The orientation of the matchbox is unknown because the user might have rotated it to any angle.

In the real world, when you take a match out of a box, you can subsequently use it for any purpose. In a virtual 3D world, your use of a match is cruelly limited by the developer's imagination. In this case, the cruelly unimaginative developer (played by me) has decided that you must strike the match and light it. You may not use it to build a model of the Eiffel Tower or to pick your teeth.

Breaking Down a Complex Movement

Matchbox.dir

Having determined the aim, I can also determine the movements the user may make in advance. Indeed, I could go so far as to reduce the user to clicking on the match, and controlling the rest of the animation myself. However, my purpose in this exercise is to study how to make the use of the mouse appear natural, and how to map a two-dimensional movement into a 3D world.

In the Matchbox.dir movie, I have tidied up the existing code and provided a separate handler for each movement that is required. Here is how I break the movement down into its component parts:

- **`takeMatch()`** The match must move along a curved path so that it can pass diagonally through the gap between the tray and the sleeve. This is achieved by using interpolation.
- **`prepareToStrike()`** To strike the match, we will rotate it around a point a short distance from the match itself. In the real world, this point would be defined by the position of your wrist. In this handler, I calculate the center of rotation to ensure that, as the match turns, it will pass through the center of the nearest striking edge on the matchbox sleeve. The calculation is both sophisticated and simple: it relies on the dot product of two perpendicular vectors being 0.
- **`closeBox()`** A matchbox should be closed before a match is struck. In the real world, you can use two hands: one to hold the match and the other to close the box. In a 3D world, there is only one mouse. I have therefore decided to use an automatic animation to close the box, so that the mouse can continue to manipulate the match.
- **`strikeMatch()`** Striking the match must be a swift movement. The user must be able to control when it occurs. Because we can't rely on the user to move the mouse swiftly and in the right direction, I wait until the mouse moves at all, in any direction, and then execute the striking movement automatically. This automatic movement allows for no user interaction. Any mouse movements between now and the moment the `waveMatch()` handler is executed will have no effect.
- **`lightMatch()`** At this point, two particle models are added to the world to simulate the flame. The models are located at the center of the world, but the `emitter.region` of the Model Resources is altered so the particles appear to come out of the head of the match.
- **`bringMatchToCamera()`** The match is currently located with its head near the center of one of the striking edges of the sleeve. Before the user can move it around freely, it must be brought forward so that it will not pass through the matchbox. This handler moves the match toward the camera along a line parallel to the striking edge of the sleeve. Although the particle primitives are already active, the first particles appear only during this movement. This adds to the impression that the flame is due to friction along the edge of the matchbox.

- **`waveMatch()`** Finally, I'll let the user move the match freely in the two dimensions, using a technique that places the match exactly under the mouse.

At each step I am effectively limiting the movement of the match to one or two dimensions. Switching between steps occurs when the match moves past a position of no return, either because of the user's interaction with the mouse or as part of an automatic sequence. Each time this happens, I'll change the value of the property `myAction`. The `exitFrame()` handler will check the value of `myAction` to know what movement to apply to the match.

The Matchbox5.dir movie also contains a number of complete handlers: `getOutOfBoxTransform()`, `determineCenterAndAxis()`, plus slightly revised versions of the flame handlers you've already looked at in the MoveFire.dir movie. We'll look at the two new handlers in detail shortly.

Taking the Match Out of the Box

The new `prepareAction()` handler, which is called on `mouseDown`, contains a new element in the case statement; if any part of the match is under the mouse when the mouse is clicked, `myAction` is set to `#take` the match out of the box.

The `takeMatch()` handler interpolates the position of the match between its current position on the bottom of the tray and a new transform, stored in the property `myTransform`, which represents the position and orientation of the match outside the box. The principle is similar to that used in the Interpol.dir movie, except the percentage used for the interpolation is determined by the position of the mouse.

```
on takeMatch(me)
  -- (Snipped: code to calculate <delta>, depending on the position of
  -- the mouse: <delta> varies between 0 and 50)

  trayBottom = transform()
  trayBottom.position = vector(0, -8, 30)
  percentage = (100.0 / 50) * delta
  myMatch.transform = trayBottom.interpolate(myTransform, percentage)
end takeMatch
```

Because the match is still a child of the tray at this point, the target transform is relative to the tray. The matchbox can be rotated to any angle. For clarity, I make sure the match is moved to the side of the matchbox nearest to the center of the sprite. The same transform, or its mirror image, is used in all cases.

The realism of the movement depends on the choice of the target transform. This is defined in the `getOutOfBoxTransform()` function, which is called when the match is first clicked. Here's a simplified version (for right handers):

```
on getOutOfBoxTransform(me)
  targetTransform.position = vector(-28, 15, 5.5)
  targetTransform.rotation = vector(35, 50, 0)
  return targetTransform
end getOutOfBoxTransform
```

I worked this transform out largely by trial and error. The `x` and `y` elements in the position vector were chosen so that the head of the match would be slightly above and to the left of the matchbox tray. The edge of the matchbox is 25 units to the left and right of its center, and the top of the edge is 10 units above its center. The values of `-28` and `15` place the head of the match 3 units to the left of the edge and 5 units above it. I arrived at the values of the rotation angles and the `z` element in the position vector after numerous tests. The tests failed if the `takeMatch()` handler moved either end of the match through any part of the matchbox sleeve or tray. The following illustration shows how an inappropriate value for targetTransform can spoil the realism of the movement. You might like to alter the values of the position and rotation of the transform returned by `getOutOfBoxTransform()` to test this for yourself.

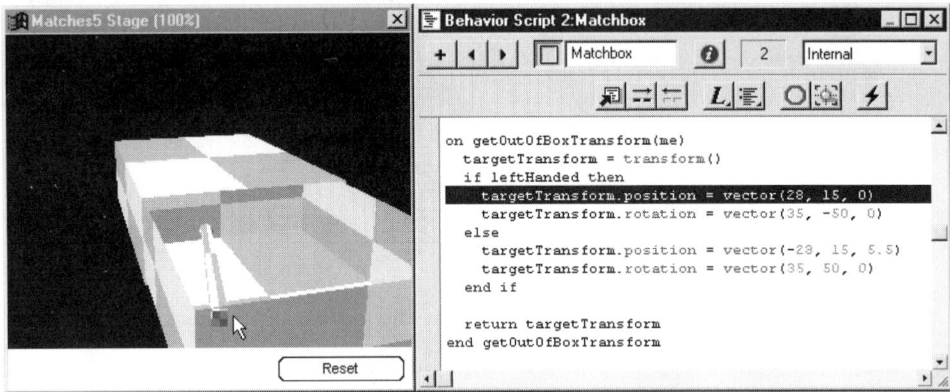

Calculating a Center of 3D Rotation

Once the user has moved the mouse more than 50 pixels either horizontally or vertically, the match will appear in the position defined by the `getOutOfBoxTransform()` handler. Here it is, seen from a right hander's perspective:

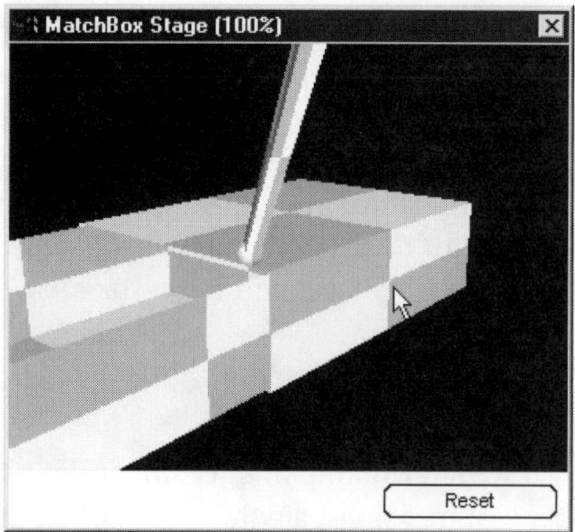

The match should now sweep down in an arc so that the head passes from its current position through the center of the side of the matchbox sleeve (where the mouse arrow appears in the preceding illustration). We know the position of the center of the side of the sleeve; because the matchbox is 50 units wide and its `transform.position` indicates the center of its volume, the center of its right side will be `vector(25, 0, 0)`, and of its left side, `vector(-25, 0, 0)`. How do we calculate the position of the head of the match, relative to the transform of the matchbox sleeve? (I gave you the answer near the beginning of the earlier "Parents" section.

Finding the Position of a Child in Terms of Its Great-Grand-Parent

The match head is a child of the match, the match is a child of the tray, and the tray is a child of the `group("Matchbox")`. The sleeve is sitting at the center of `group("Matchbox")`, so its transform is the same as its parent. Multiplying these transforms in the correct order will give the transform of the match head in terms of the `group("Matchbox")`.

```
  t = myHead.transform
  u = myMatch.transform -- parent of head
  v = myTray.transform  -- parent of match
  headPosition = (v * u * t).position -- in terms of
group("Matchbox")
```

Choosing a Radius

We now need to find a point that is the same distance from the head of the match and from the center of the edge of the sleeve. In fact, there are an infinite number of such points. Imagine you hold a child's hoop in both hands, with your hands fairly close together. Without moving your hands in space, you can rotate the hoop in a full circle (you would have to step through it as it turns). The center of the hoop will always be the same distance from both of your hands, but its position depends on the rotation of the hoop.

So we need to choose a third datum in order to specify a unique circle. For simplicity, let's say the center of rotation must lie on a line perpendicular to the center of the edge of the sleeve (the normal to the surface). We now have two points and a line to define our circle.

Tricks with the Dot Product

For a moment, let's forget we are working in three dimensions. Because vectors work in space with any number of dimensions, anything that works in two dimensions also should work in three. This is what the matchbox looks like from above:

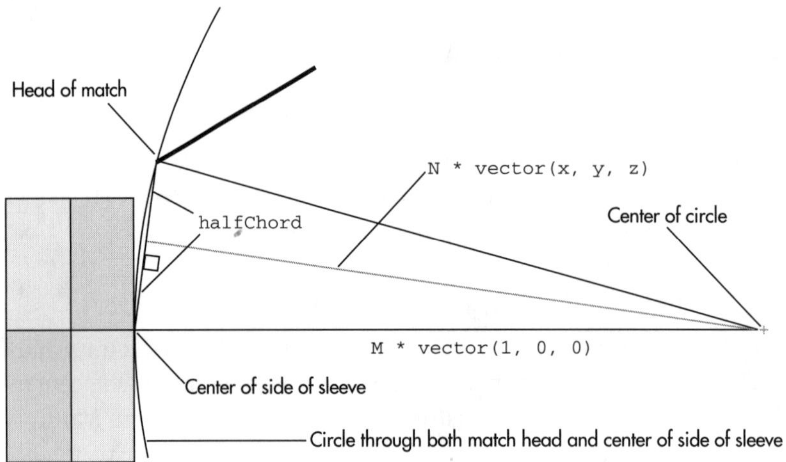

We can calculate the value of the `halfChord` vector from the two points we know. We know the direction of the horizontal `vector(1, 0, 0)`, because we chose it ourselves. We need to work out the value of `M`, the magnitude of the vector between the side of the sleeve and the center of the circle. To do this we invent a `vector(x, y, z)` that is perpendicular to `halfChord`. Adding `halfChord` and `vector(x, y, z)` will give us the vector whose magnitude we are looking for. As it turns out, we actually don't need to know the values of `x`, `y`, and `z`.

In the previous chapter, I mentioned that the dot product of two vectors was the product of the magnitudes of the vectors times the cosine of the angle between them. The cosine of 90° is zero. So, `halfChord.dotProduct(vector(x, y, z))` is zero.

If we add the vectors, we get this equation:

```
M * vector(1, 0, 0) = halfChord + vector(x, y, z)
```

Using halfChord to create a dot product of both sides of the equation gives us

```
M * vector(1, 0, 0).dot(halfChord) = halfChord.dot(halfChord) + 0
```

The unknown vector(x, y, z) disappears because vector(x, y, z) and halfChord are at right angles to each other. So we can now calculate M:

```
M = halfChord.dot(halfChord) / vector(1, 0, 0).dot(halfChord)
```

Because we know M, we can calculate the position of the center of the circle. While we are at it, we can take a crossProduct of vector(1, 0, 0) and halfChord to determine the axis of rotation, and we can use angleBetween() to determine how far the match will need to rotate before it touches the center of the sleeve. (What vectors do you need to use with the angleBetween() function?)

You'll find the code for this in the determineCenterAndAxis() handler. We'll use a variant on this technique in the waveMatch() handler to find the nearest point on the ray under the mouse to a given point.

Moving Relative to a Camera

The closeBox(), strikeMatch(), and lightMatch() handlers all use techniques you have already seen. The bringMatchToCamera() handler uses a simple translate() command to move the match parallel to the z axis of the matchbox, and the magnitude property of a vector to determine when the match will be clear of the matchbox.

The only technique that remains to be explained is that used in the waveMatch() handler. The purpose of the handler is to place the head of the match immediately beneath the mouse and move it on a plane parallel to the sprite view.

Creating a Ray Under the Mouse

The modelUnderLoc() and modelsUnderLoc() functions implicitly use a ray that starts at the surface of the sprite and disappears into the distance. If we want the match to appear directly under the mouse, it must be situated somewhere along such a ray.

To move the match from its current position to a point on the ray, we will have to calculate the direction of the ray explicitly. Fortunately, we know its two end points: one is the worldPosition of the current camera of the sprite; the other is given by the `spriteSpaceToWorldSpace()` function I mentioned in the preceding. Both of these points are expressed in world coordinates.

If we want the match to remain the same distance from the camera, we can move it along a line that is at right angles to the z axis of the camera. We also can calculate the vector from the camera to the match itself. Looking down on the scene from a point vertically above the screen, the situation appears as in Figure 8-4. The variables are those used in the `waveFlame()` handler following.

Variation on the Dot Product Theme

We can use the same dot product trick that we used in the preceding. The new position of the match is `distanceDownRay * ray` from the camera (`ray` is a unit-length directional vector). The vector from the current position of the match to its new position is at right angles to `zVector`, the unit-length vector representing the z axis of the camera. Let's call this perpendicular vector `xVector` (although it doesn't necessary lie parallel to the camera's x axis). `A`, `B`, and `C` are the magnitudes of lines shown in Figure 8-4.

Here is one equation:

```
A * zVector = cameraToFlame + B * xVector
```

Applying `zVector.dotProduct()` to both sides

```
A * zVector.dotProduct(zVector) = zVector.dotProduct(cameraToFlame) + 0
```

gives us the value for A:

```
A = zVector.dotProduct(cameraToFlame) / zVector.dotProduct(zVector)
```

Here is a second equation:

```
distanceDownRay * ray = A * zVector + C * xVector
```

Let's apply `zVector.dotProduct()` to both sides:

```
distanceDownRay * zVector.dotProduct(ray) = A * zVector.dotProduct(zVector) + 0
```

This gives us

```
distanceDownRay = A * zVector.dotProduct(zVector) / zVector.dotProduct(ray)
```

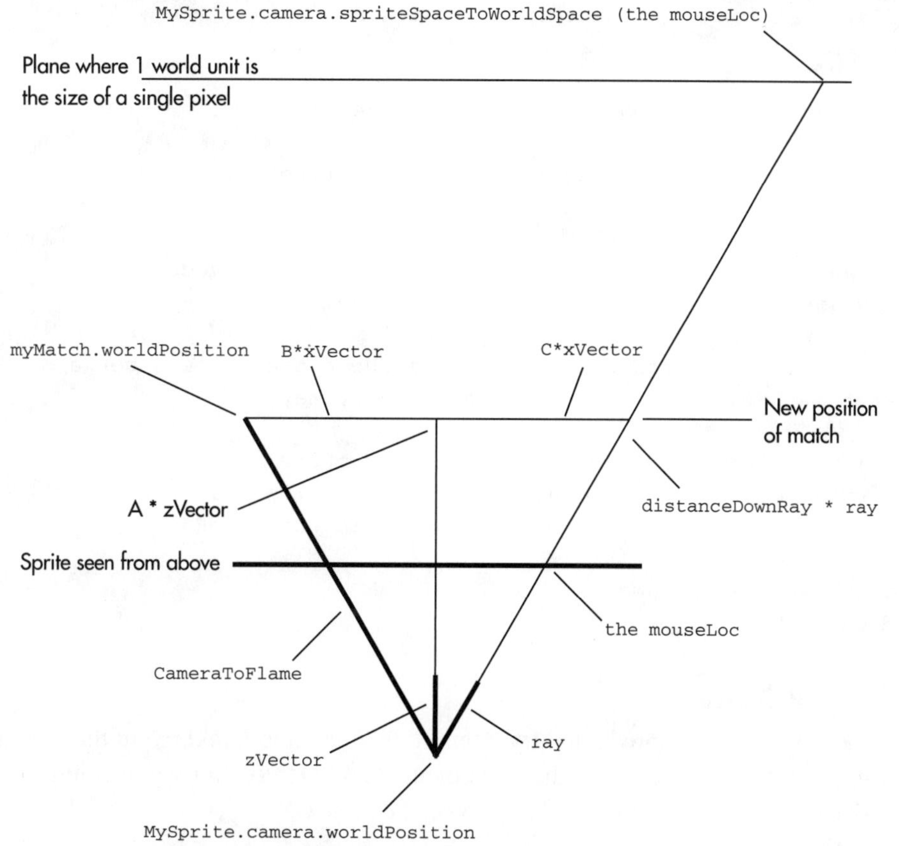

Figure 8-4 *Plan view of the* spriteSpaceToWorldSpace() function

We know the value of `A` from the first equation in the preceding, so we can replace it. We'll find `zVector.dotProduct(zVector)` in both the numerator and the denominator, so it cancels itself out:

```
distanceDownRay = zVector.dotProduct(cameraToFlame) / zVector.dotProduct(ray)
```

I've used the `*` operator in the following for concision, but its effect is the same as `dotProduct()` when used on vectors.

```
on waveMatch(me, spriteLoc)
  -- <spriteLoc> is the position of the mouse relative to the top
  -- left corner of the sprite
```

```
  flamePosition    = myMatch.worldPosition
  cameraLoc        = mySprite.camera.worldPosition

  -- Find a distant point under the mouse
  worldLoc         =
mySprite.camera.spriteSpaceToWorldSpace(spriteLoc)
  -- Draw a ray between that point and the "user's eye"
  ray              = worldLoc - cameraLoc
  -- We want to work with a unit-length direction vector
  ray.normalize()

  -- Use the dot product to determine the closest point between
  -- flamePosition and the line defined by ray.

  cameraToFlame    = flamePosition - cameraLoc
  distanceDownRay = (cameraToFlame * zVector) / (ray * zVector)
  flameLoc         = cameraLoc + (ray * distanceDownRay)

  me.showFlameAt(flameLoc)
end waveMatch
```

Lighting the Match

Run the Matchbox.dir movie and try opening the matchbox, taking out the match, and striking it. How natural do the movements feel? Do you think you could improve on the handling of the objects with the mouse?

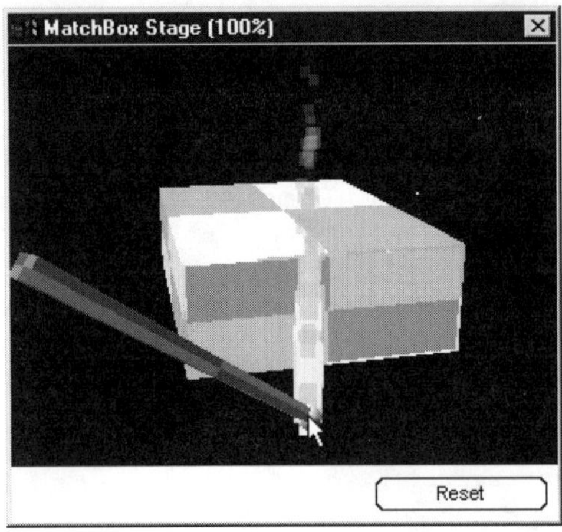

Suggested Improvements

The Matchbox.dir movie is not polished. It could be improved in a number of ways, in particular,

- When a real match burns, it produces light. In Chapters 10 and 11 you'll see how to make the head of the match glow, and in Chapter 13 you'll see how you can add a light source to the head of the match.
- Adding a sound when the box is opened and when the match is struck would make the experience more lively; or you could simply try adding a second match to the existing matchbox.
- Textures also would be useful to make the visible primitives look more convincing.
- It is currently possible to take the match before the box is fully open, in which case, the match may pass through the "solid" walls of the match box. In Chapter 14 we will look at the collision modifier, which gives feedback on when such intersections occur and provides ways to prevent it.
- Currently, if you start taking the match out of the matchbox and then let go, the match remains in midair. Clicking it again returns it to the box. You might find other similar dysfunctions. In general, the code I provide assumes that the user is not going to release the mouse in the middle of an action. You could see if you can fix this.
- There is another malfunction that you might not be aware of. After you have completely taken the match out of the matchbox (after `prepareToStrike`) and before you light the match, the user may release the mouse. In this case, all the animation stops. If you then click the match, it is pushed farther from the matchbox (and hardly visible in the world). You also can still click the tray to move it out again. If you turn the matchbox to find the little match on the left side, and click again on the few pixels representing the match, you could come to a script error where you want to animate with a number of frames of 0 and a division by 0 error. Check this out and either correct it or suggest it as an improvement. Other modifications are possible without an additional knowledge of 3D Director.
- Oh, and perhaps you'd like to make the flame gradually move up the match as the stick burns into a black and twisted shape. The mesh primitive we'll be looking at in the next chapter will provide you with the techniques you need.

Conclusion

This chapter has dealt with three different themes: the particle primitive, parent-child relationships between models, and techniques for manipulating models with the mouse.

Many more chapters could be written to explore the use of the particle primitive in greater detail. Here I chose to concentrate on a technique for making the particles appear to belong to the world rather than the particle model. This technique could be transferred to many other situations: exhaust from a motor, dust thrown up by tires, or water poured from a jug are but three examples.

Up until now, all the models you have created have had `group ("World")` as their default parent. In this chapter, you explicitly added models to custom-built groups and changed parents on-the-fly. You saw how using parent-child relationships allows you to simplify the calculations of the transform of any given model, and how a child's transform can be viewed from the perspective of nodes higher up the hierarchy.

This chapter has shown that using the mouse to manipulate 3D models is much more complex than when working in two dimensions. The key to creating a usable mouse interface is to break a complex movement down into its component parts, each of which can be fully determined by mapping from a two-dimensional movement of the mouse.

I presented a number of mathematical techniques for controlling 3D animations; including interpolation; the multiplication of transforms; calculation of angles, axes, and centers of rotation; and mapping points onto a line. These techniques build on the vector mathematics you have seen in the earlier chapters.

CHAPTER

9

Creating and Animating a Mesh Primitive

IN THIS CHAPTER:

Give me a lever long enough and a place to stand, and I will move the earth.
—Attributed to Archimedes

The mesh primitive is extremely powerful; it allows you to make all the 3D shapes that the other primitives can't cope with. However, power comes with a price: complexity. You need to define every vertex point on the shape you make and say which points are linked together to create your shape. It's like three-dimensional string art: first, you hammer your nails into an empty 3D space and then you join them together with string.

To get the most out of the mesh primitive, you must approach it with method. We'll start by creating a simple plane mesh, deforming it, and changing its colors in real time. To introduce a little discipline, I'll then get you to treat the same plane mesh as if it were a sheet of paper that you can fold but cannot stretch. This will involve using vectors, transforms, rotations, and groups, all of which you have already seen in the previous three chapters. The final result will be the hard-coded animation of a basic origami figure.

Once you've come to terms with the possibilities of the mesh primitive, we'll embark on a much more ambitious project: the creation of a lathe tool. The finished version of this, Lathe.dir, is in the 3D\Meshes\ folder of the CD-ROM that accompanies the book. You might like to take it for a test run before you go any further, so that you can see what sort of things you could use the mesh primitive for.

Making a Mesh

Origami0.dir

Start by creating a new movie and a new Shockwave 3D member. Give the member a name so that Director won't destroy it automatically at the first opportunity. Drop the new member on the stage. Right-click (Windows) or CTRL-click (Macintosh) the new 3D sprite and choose Script in the contextual menu that appears. You're now ready to make a mesh-making behavior. Delete the default handler and type

```
on beginSprite(me)
  myMember = sprite(me.spriteNum).member
  myMember.resetWorld()
```

The rest of the behavior is detailed in the following sections.

Triangles in Space

The principle of a mesh is very simple: you start by defining a set of points. Here is a set of nine points arranged to create four squares around the center of the world. All the points have a y value of 0, so the points all lie flat on the floor, as it were.

```
  tVertexList   = [ \
vector(  0, 0,   0), \
vector(  0, 0,  50), \
vector( 50, 0,  50), \
vector( 50, 0,   0), \
vector( 50, 0, -50), \
vector(  0, 0, -50), \
vector(-50, 0, -50), \
vector(-50, 0,   0), \
vector(-50, 0, 50) \
]
```

Here's a view of these points as seen from above:

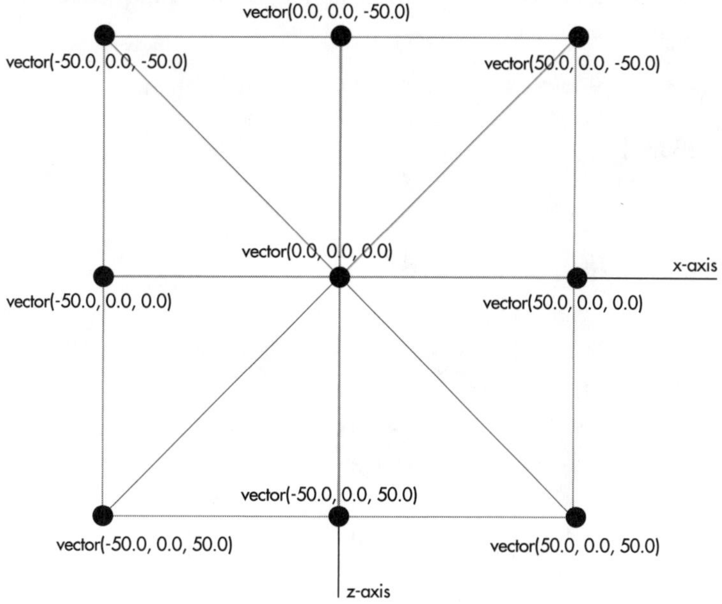

To create a solid shape from these points, you need to group them together in sets of three. Each set defines a triangle:

```
  tFaceList  = [ \
[1, 2, 3], \
[1, 3, 4], \
[1, 4, 5], \
[1, 5, 6], \
[1, 6, 7], \
[1, 7, 8], \
[1, 9, 8], \
[1, 9, 2] \
]
```

The result is shown in Figure 9-1.

I have chosen to start my mesh in the center and to start each triangle from the central point. I have deliberately included an error: All the triangles are defined in a counterclockwise order except for the second-to-last one. When you come to test it, you will see that the order in which the vertices are included in the lists is important.

As with other model resources, your mesh must have a unique name. I'll be unimaginative and use "Test":

```
  myMeshResource = myMember.newMesh( \
"Test", \
tFaceList.count, \
tVertexList.count \
)
```

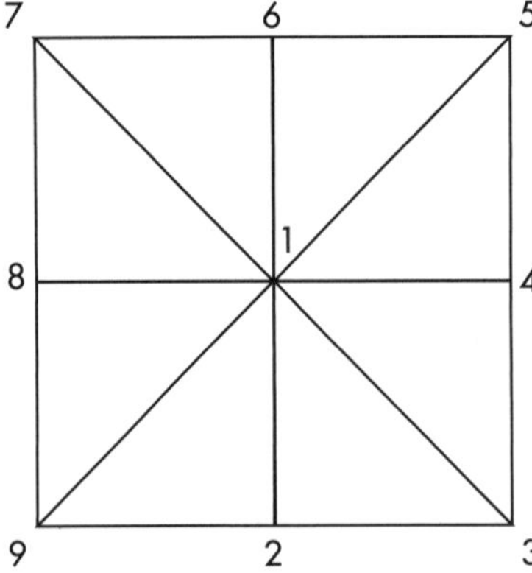

Figure 9-1 *The faces defined by tFaceList*

Your mesh now exists inside the Shockwave 3D member, but you won't be able to use it for anything yet. First, you have to tell it what vertices you have prepared for it and how to link them together:

```
myMeshResource.vertexList = tVertexList
repeat with i = 1 to 8
  myMeshResource.face[i].vertices = tFaceList[i]
end repeat
```

Faces Need Normals

You're still not done. Although you have told the mesh where its faces are, you haven't defined a front-facing direction for them. The front face is defined by normal vectors. You can enter these by hand if you want to create a shape that bulges in a particular way, or you can ask Director to do it for you. For simplicity, we'll use the automatic `generateNormals()` command.

```
myMeshResource.generateNormals(#flat)
```

You can ask for `#flat` normals or `#smooth` normals. For flat faces, each face has only one normal; or rather, each of the vertices in a given triangle has the same normal. This means each vertex will have as many normals as it has faces touching it. The vertex as `vector(0, 0, 0)` will find itself with a bunch of eight normals; all but one looking straight up.

If you choose `#smooth`, each vertex has only one normal. On a three-dimensional surface, this would mean each triangle appears to be bent around a 3D curve. We'll use this possibility shortly.

Finishing the Job

The Shockwave 3D member now has a complete set of blueprints with which to make a meaningful mesh. You just have to give it the signal:

```
myMeshResource.build()
```

All you need to complete your behavior and enjoy the fruits of your labor is to create a model from the new resource, and to place a camera where it can see the model.

Because we created the mesh lying flat, end on to the default camera position, we'll move the camera up to look down on your model from above.

```
  myMember.newModel("Model 1", myMeshResource)
  myMember.camera(1).transform.position = vector(0, 170, 1)
  myMember.camera(1).pointAt(0, 0, 0)
end
```

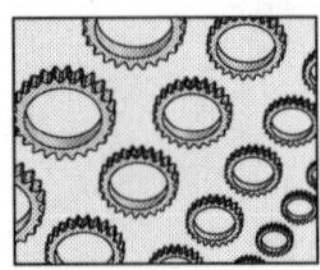

NOTE

If you set the camera to look directly down the y axis, it doesn't know which way is up. By placing it slightly in front of the y axis and making it look slightly backward, you can force it to show the x axis pointing to the right, as usual, and the z axis pointing down out of the bottom of the screen. You'll see a more sophisticated technique for handling this in Chapter 12.

Save your movie and run it. You should see something like this:

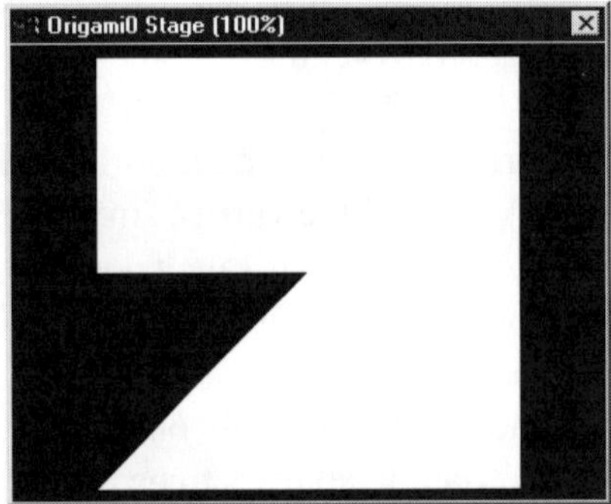

There's a piece missing. Remember I told you I'd made a deliberate mistake in the order of the vertices for the second-to-last face? Well, this is the result. If you open the Origami0.dir movie, which you'll find in the 3D\Meshes\ folder on the CD-ROM that accompanies the book, you'll find all the code you've already typed (and more commented out). You'll also find that if you click the Shockwave 3D sprite, and drag the mouse left or right, you can get the mesh model to rotate. You'll see that the seventh face is facing backward; it appears only when you look at the model from behind. If you correct the order in which the vertices are declared for the seventh face and then recompile you script and run the movie again, you should see a complete square.

What Meshes Can Do

So what makes a mesh different from the other primitives? Why do you need so much code just to make one appear? There are two major differences: architecture and appearance. You can place the vertices of the mesh at any position in space with respect to the model resource's origin and define the normals for each face individually. For other primitives, the origin point is always at the center of the model, the vertices are always arranged in a regular pattern around the origin, and the normals are always predefined. You can color the individual faces of a mesh model, as you shall see in this chapter, or you can apply textures individually, as you will see Chapter 11.

Position and Orientation

First of all, let's compare the simple mesh you have just created with the plane primitive. By giving details of the vertex positions, you can determine where the origin point of your mesh is; in this model, I have placed it at the center. When you position a model or rotate it around itself, such movements are always made relative to the point `vector(0, 0, 0)` of the model resource. This point could be at any of the vertices of a mesh, or even outside it altogether.

Try adding the following lines of code immediately after you create `tVertexList`:

```
tTransform = transform()
tTransform.position = vector(0, 20, 0)
-- tTransform.rotation = vector(30, 30, 30) -- see next section
repeat with i = 1 to 9
  tVertexList[i] = tTransform * tVertexList[i]
end repeat
put tVertexList
```

This moves the vertices 20 3D units along the y axis, so the mesh now is floating above its origin point. (Remember, you are looking at it from above.) The shape of the plane that is created is identical; only its position has changed. Launch your movie and rotate the model with the mouse to see the difference that this makes.

DEBUGGING TIP

Click near the edge of the sprite and drag toward the center, so you can use the position of the mouse to give you an idea of where the axis of rotation appears. Alternatively, use

```
tModel.visibility = #both
tModel.debug = TRUE
```

in your behavior to show the axes of the model and the bounding sphere.

If you uncomment the third line in the additional preceding code, you can apply a rotation to `tVertexList` before it is applied to the mesh resource. As we will see shortly, you can modify the `vertexList` of a mesh resource on-the-fly. Imagine that you have a scene of a whole field of solar panels, each of which is a model based on the same mesh resource. As your virtual sun moves, you could change the position of the vertices within the mesh resource, and all the solar panel models in your scene will instantly reflect the change.

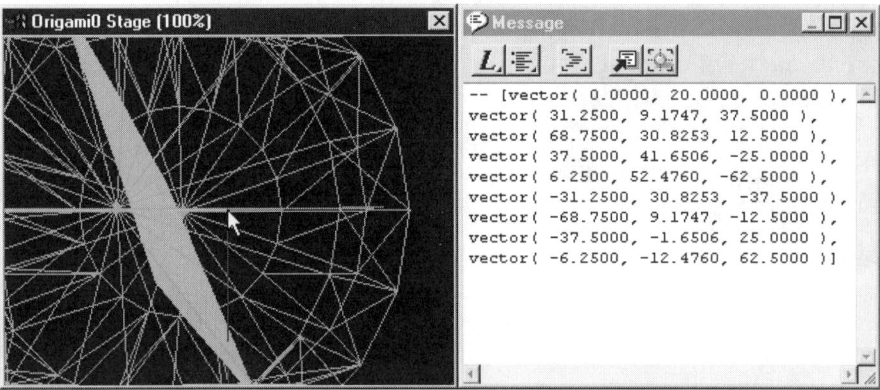

You can use any type of transformation (translation, rotation, or scale) to modify the `vertexList`. You also can move each vertex independently, as we shall do in the "Animating the Mesh" section later in the chapter. Now that you have seen its effect, delete or comment out the code that modifies `tVertexList` so that, in the following exercises, you will be using the unmodified list of vertexes.

Curved Surfaces?

The second advantage over the other geometric primitives is that you can define the normals for each face of a mesh. This allows you to shade the various faces of a mesh as if they were curved. To start with, let's see what difference it makes to use the `#smooth` option for the `generateNormals()` command. You'll need to make the change in your `beginSprite` handler. If you previously corrected the order of the vertices for the seventh face, restore the original (incorrect) order now, if only temporarily.

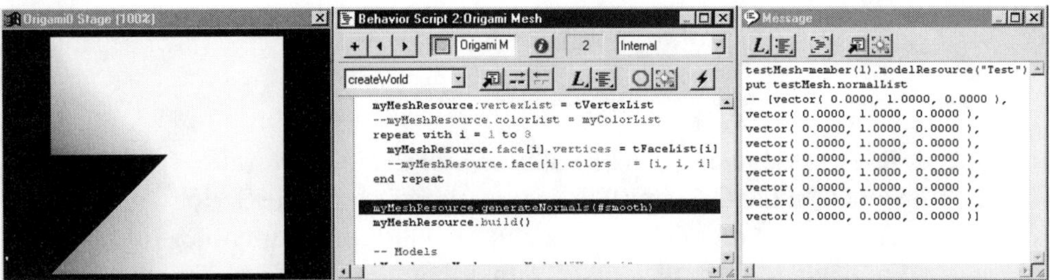

Relaunch your movie, and in the Message window, type

```
put member(1).modelResource("Test").normalList
```

You should see a list of nine direction vectors. Note that the last two are directionless: `vector( 0.0000, 0.0000, 0.0000 )`. This is because the seventh face, which uses vertices `[1, 9, 8]` in the vertex list, is facing in the opposite direction to the others. When you use `#smooth` value for the `generateNormals()` command, each vertex has only one normal, shared with all the faces that surround the point. Entries 8 and 9 in the `normalList` are canceled out by the fact that the adjacent triangles are facing opposite ways.

Normals and Light

This leads to the color at these vertices being a neutral gray. The way directional light reacts to a surface at a given point depends on the orientation of the surface at that point. This direction is defined by the normal at that point. At vertices 8 and 9, the normal is undefined, so the face reacts only to ambient light and not to directional light, leading to its dimmed appearance. You can see this effect more clearly if you set the ambient and directional colors of the default lights to complimentary values and change the `directionalPreset`:

```
member(1).ambientColor = rgb(0, 255, 255)    -- cyan
member(1).directionalColor = rgb(255, 0, 0) -- red
member(1).directionalPreset = #middleCenter
```

You also can set these values using the Property Inspector. Remember to set them back to their original values when you've finished; otherwise, the colors in the following exercises will not look right. One way to do this is to destroy the Shockwave 3D member and re-create it in the same cast member slot.

Handmade Normals

You can change the values of the normals for these rogue vertices, either separately,

```
member(1).modelResource(2).normalList[8] = vector( 0.0000, 1.0000, 0.0000 )
```

or by changing the value of the `normalList` of the mesh resource as a whole. Let's do just that. In the Origami0.dir movie, there is a Movie Script with a `createBulge()` handler. This sets the normals for the four corners of the plane to point outward from the center, rather than upward. Open the movie if you haven't done so already, launch it, and type the following command in the Message window:

```
createBulge()
```

The directional light will now react as if the quarters of the plane were curved. If you drag the model to turn it endways on, you will see that it is just as flat as ever. The effect created by altering the normals at the corners is purely an optical illusion.

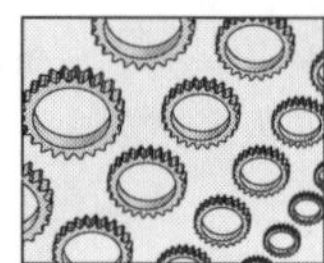

NOTE

Do not confuse the normals for the vertices of a mesh, which are used for lighting calculations, with the normals of the surface of the mesh as returned by the `modelsUnderLoc()` and `modelsUnderPoint()` functions. As you can see in Figure 9-2, the normal detected by the `modelsUnderLoc()` function refers to the orientation of the mesh triangle under the mouse, in terms of world space. The same value will be returned over the whole surface of the triangular face. The values of `myMeshResource.normalList` are expressed in terms of resource space.

Building Normals into the Mesh

Figure 9-2 also demonstrates another point: you can modify the vertices of a given face of a model resource on-the-fly. This has to be done with caution, however. The change will not take effect unless you issue a new `modelResource(n).build()` instruction. Even so, the result might be unexpected. If you restart the movie and then try the code shown in the Message window, you will see that the seventh face does not have the same appearance as the others. This can be fixed by issuing a `generateNormals()` command after changing the vertices of face 7, and before applying your own normals. In the code shown, this means uncommenting the second line of code and executing all four lines in order.

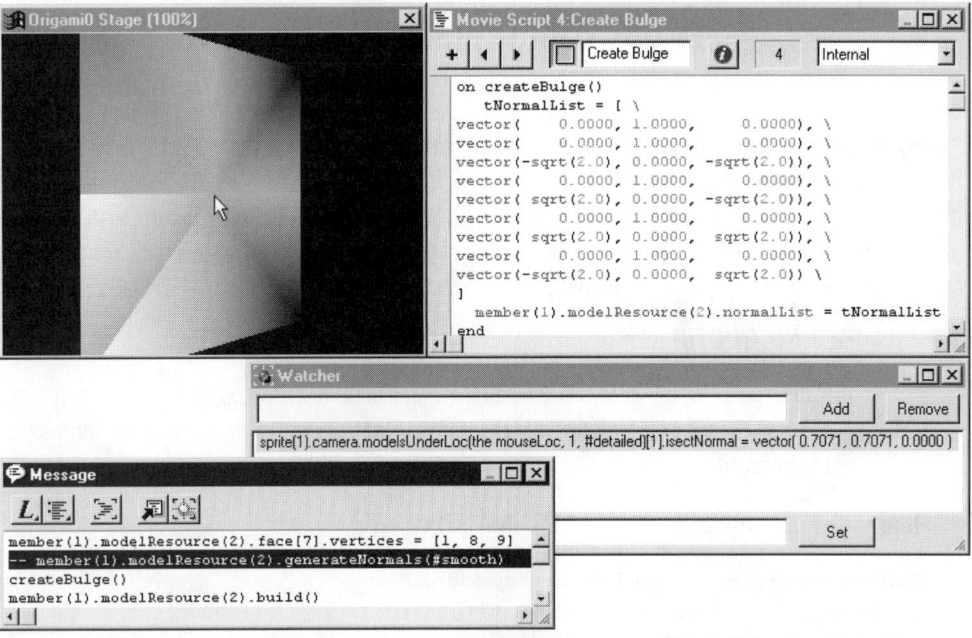

Figure 9-2 *A model resource's normalList data affects only the shading of the faces.*

If you want to apply shading information to your mesh, you would tend to do this at the moment you initially create the mesh. If you are still working on your own movie, try replacing the simple `newMesh()` command with the following lines of code:

```
  tNormalList = [ \
vector(    0.0000, 1.0000,     0.0000), \
vector(    0.0000, 1.0000,     0.0000), \
vector(-sqrt(2.0), 0.0000, -sqrt(2.0)), \
vector(    0.0000, 1.0000,     0.0000), \
vector( sqrt(2.0), 0.0000, -sqrt(2.0)), \
vector(    0.0000, 1.0000,     0.0000), \
vector( sqrt(2.0), 0.0000,  sqrt(2.0)), \
vector(    0.0000, 1.0000,     0.0000), \
vector(-sqrt(2.0), 0.0000,  sqrt(2.0)) \
]

  myMeshResource = myMember.newMesh( \
"Test", \
tFaceList.count, \
```

```
tVertexList.count, \
tNormalList.count \
)
```

If you are working on Origami0.dir, you can simply uncomment the appropriate lines. According to the 3D Lingo Dictionary, if you are going to be using your own normals, you should inform the `newMesh()` command as to how many you will be using. If you don't, in practice, nothing dramatic happens. Indeed, nothing will happen at all unless you issue a `generateNormals(#smooth)` instruction.

DEBUGGING TIP

The 3D Lingo Dictionary does not make it clear that a mesh resource cannot apply a custom `normalList` unless at least one `generateNormals(#smooth)` instruction has been issued.

Here is the sequence of instructions that I find works best:

```
myMeshResource.generateNormals(#smooth)
myMeshResource.normalList = tNormalList
myMeshResource.build()
```

The `build()` command is necessary for the data in the new `normalList` to take effect. Normally, you would issue this command at the end of the sequence of creation of your mesh resource. However, as we shall see, you can alter both the `vertexList` and the `colorList` after the `build()` command has been issued.

Colors

Instead of shading, or in addition to it, you can set the color of each vertex of each face. If the three vertices of a given face are the same color, the face will be a flat area of color. If one or all the vertex colors are different, the result will be a gradient between the chosen colors.

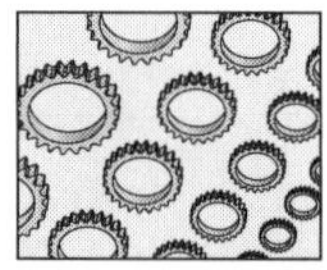

NOTE

You now can correct the face data for the seventh vertex definitively. The illustrations for the examples that follow assume that the second-to-last entry in `tFaceList` is `[1, 8, 9]`.

Flat Colors

Let's start by giving each face a flat color. To do this, you need to define a list of colors in much the same way that you defined a list of vertices. There can be any number of colors in the list. You can think of it as a specific palette of colors from which you can choose for this particular mesh resource. You don't have to use all the colors that you define in the list, but you cannot use any colors that are not defined in it. This last limitation can be overcome, as you can change the values in the list on-the-fly, and thus change the palette. What you can't do is change the number of colors in your list. In other words, when you define your `colorList` for your mesh resource, you are, in fact, defining something akin to its color depth.

Here's a list of bright colors:

```
   myColorList    = [ \
rgb(255, 255, 255), \
rgb(255, 255,   0), \
rgb(255,   0,   0), \
rgb(255,   0, 255), \
rgb(  0,   0, 255), \
rgb(  0,   0,   0), \
rgb(  0, 255,   0),\
rgb(  0, 255, 255) \
]
```

To apply this `colorList` to the mesh resource, you need to use a more complete version of the `newMesh()` command, as shown here:

```
   myMeshResource = myMember.newMesh( \
"Test", \
tFaceList.count, \
tVertexList.count, \
0, \
myColorList.count \
)
```

The zero passed as the fourth parameter tells the mesh resource that we are not defining any normals, because we will use the `generateNormals()` command to do this automatically. If you are defining your own normals, you should use the appropriate number here instead, as mentioned in the earlier section "Building Normals into the Mesh."

What is important is that the fifth parameter refers to the number of colors you will use. Director is less forgiving about an error concerning the number of elements in the `colorList` than it is about the number of elements in the `normalList`. An insufficient value will provoke a rather misleading Script Error alert:

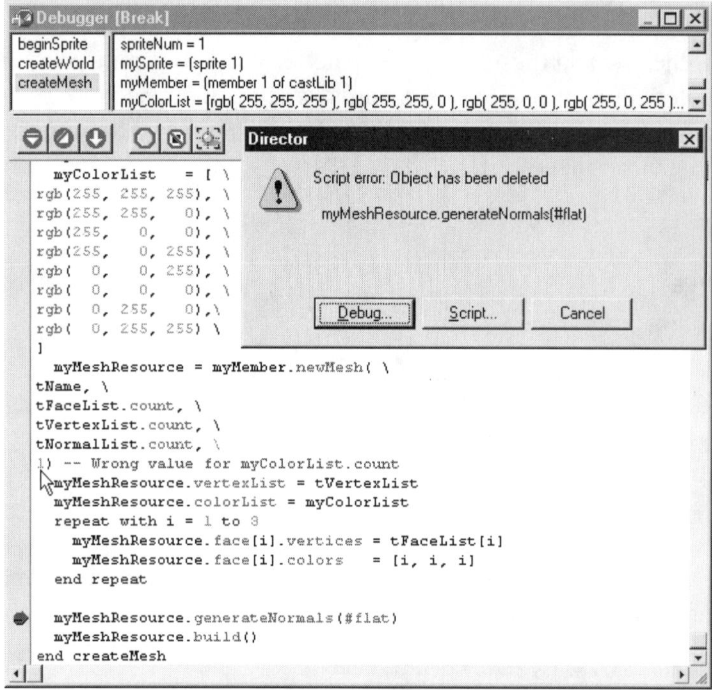

If the value you give is larger than the number of elements in the list you provide for the colorList, the extra spaces are filled with black: rgb(0, 0, 0). Conversely, you can include black as many times as you like in the list you provide; then you can get away with not counting any of them. Try entering a value of **7** in the place of `myColorList.count` in the preceding command; you'll find that no error is provoked, but the last color (cyan) is not available. This probably is not intended and might be corrected in future versions of Director. The point to note is that you can specify fewer colors than the number you declare, and thus give yourself space for changing the values of the additional colors later.

As you have already seen, if you specify no colors at all, white is used by default for all your faces. As with the `vertexList` data, the `colorList` must be applied separately to the mesh after it has been created. Indeed, you also must declare which colors to use with each vertex of each face. The easiest way to do this is to set the color data at the same time as you create the faces. Modify the lines after the `newMesh()` instruction so that they read as follows:

```
myMeshResource.vertexList = tVertexList
myMeshResource.colorList = myColorList
repeat with i = 1 to 8
  myMeshResource.face[i].vertices = tFaceList[i]
  myMeshResource.face[i].colors   = [i, i, i]
end repeat
```

When you run your movie again, the mesh will have on its party dress.

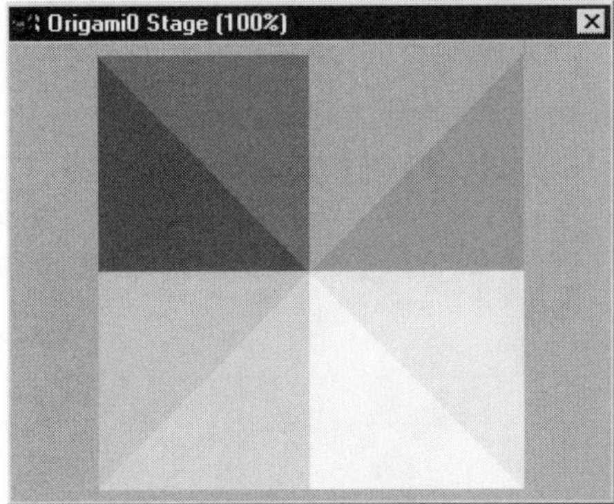

Gradient Colors

In the preceding repeat loop, you set the three vertices of each face to the same color. Let's now try using a different color for each vertex. Replace the last line inside the preceding repeat loop with the following:

```
myMeshResource.face[i].colors   = [1, i, (i mod 8 + 1)]
```

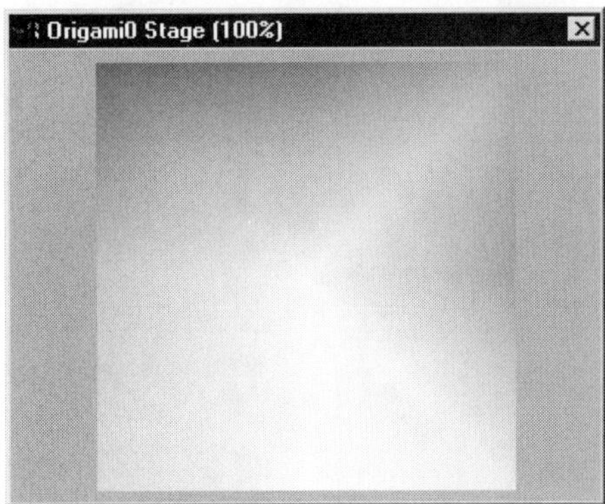

Each triangle now starts out white at the center point, and follows a gradient toward each of two other colors on the outside edge. You can combine this effect with the use of a nonstandard `normalList`, but the results might be unsatisfactory. If strong shading created as a result of the `normalList` is coupled with dark colors, the color of a given face might be clipped to black. This also is true if you use flat colors with custom normals.

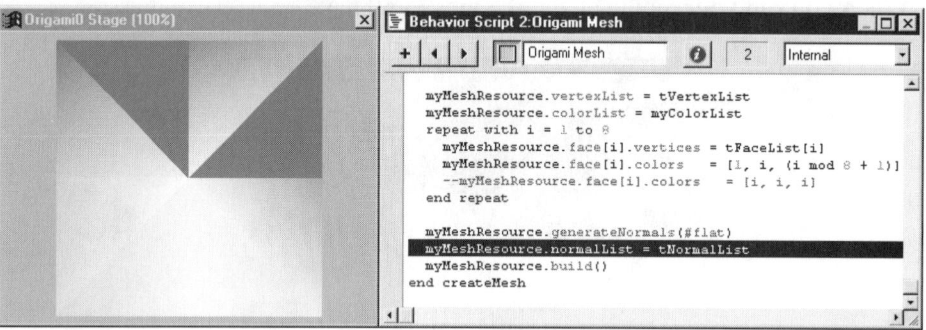

Animating Colors

You can modify the `colorList` of a mesh resource on-the-fly. Depending on how you do it, you may or may not need to rebuild the mesh. Here is one technique you can add to your behavior. It will cycle the colors one step each time you click the Shockwave 3D sprite by changing the index numbers of the color to apply to each face:

```
on mouseDown
  tColors = myMeshResource.face[1].colors -- Ex: [1, 1, 1]
  repeat with i = 1 to 8
    tColors = (tColors mod 8) + 1 -- the mod operator works on a list
    myMeshResource.face[i].colors = tColors
  end repeat

  myMeshResource.build()
end mouseDown
```

If you comment out the last line, nothing will happen.

DEBUGGING TIP

You do not seem to be able to access a given color in a `colors` *list for a face directly. The following expression will return the* `colors` *list as a whole, not its first item:*

```
put myMeshResource.face[1].colors[1]
-- [1, 1, 1]
```

To get the index number of a color for a given vertex of a given face, you need to pass through a temporary variable:

```
tColor = myMeshResource.face[1].colors
put tColor[1]
-- 1
```

You also can work around this by using parentheses around the expression:

```
put (myMeshResource.face[1].colors)[1]
-- 1
```

Here's another technique that will dim the colors progressively and does not need you to rebuild the mesh.

```
on mouseDown(me)
  myColorList = myColorList - [17, 17, 17, 17, 17, 17, 17, 17]
  myMeshResource.colorList = myColorList
end
```

It would appear that, as long as the new colors are sufficiently close to the old ones, no rebuild is necessary.

DEBUGGING TIP

You can perform mathematical operations on color objects. The resulting red, green, and blue values will be constrained to the range 0–255:

```
put rgb(0, 0, 0) + 300
-- rgb( 255, 255, 255 )
```

You can alter individual values by using a second color object as the operand. Note that non-integer values are converted to integers before the operation:

```
put rgb(255, 255, 255) / rgb(2, 2.5, 3)
-- rgb( 127, 85, 85 )
```

Here is a third technique, which is unsure of whether it works without a rebuild; this moves a random color to the end of the list and moves the others up:

```
on mouseDown(me)
  tRandom = random(8)
  myColorList.append(myColorList[tRandom])
  myColorList.deleteAt(tRandom)
  myMeshResource.colorList = myColorList
  --myMeshResource.build()
end
```

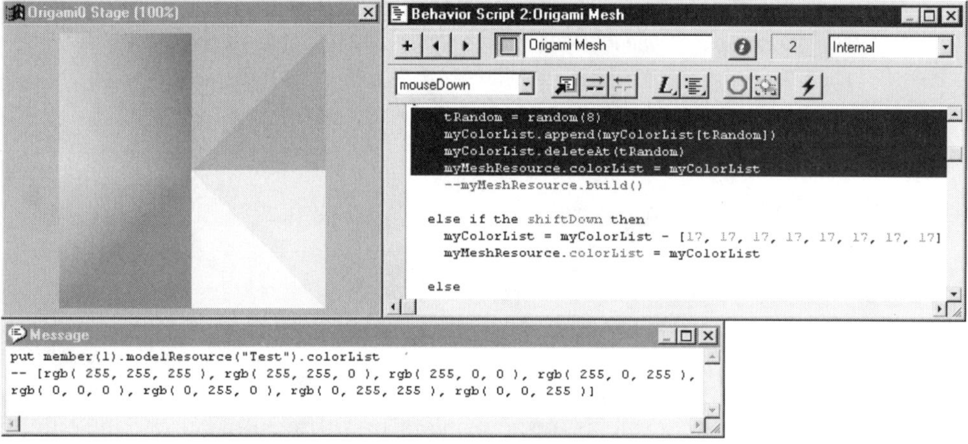

If you uncomment the last line so that the mesh is rebuilt, the colors swap places and remain pure. On some machines, if you don't rebuild the mesh, the effect on the colors that have changed is complex, and probably not intended.

In both this and the previous techniques, the values in the mesh resource's `colorList` are changed. Here, the colors are changed radically, and Director sometimes finds it hard to follow. The moral of the story is that you ought to rebuild a mesh after modifying its `colorList`.

Textures

You don't need to limit yourself to colors; you also can apply textures to your mesh, just as you can to the other primitives. However, this is a subject in itself, so I'll deal with it separately in Chapter 11.

Animating the Mesh

You can use meshes to create models with an infinite variety of shapes. Many of these shapes will be static; however, one of the most powerful features of the mesh primitive is that you can manipulate the position of the vertices in real time without rebuilding the resource. I will continue with the simple plane shape that you have been working with so far, but now I'll show you how to fold it.

The challenge that faces us here is how to move the vertex points in a realistic fashion without distorting the faces. I'll deal with this in four parts, each illustrated by a separate movie: First, I'll show you how you can modify the `vertexList` of a mesh resource. Second, I'll create an animated version that uses simple, easy-to-program movements. Then I'll make a brief aside on how to solve a lighting problem that mesh resources can suffer from. In the fourth movie, I'll create a much more natural movement, which characteristically is more complex to program.

Normally, I like to create generic behaviors and handlers that can be reused in other circumstances. Animated meshes open up an ocean of possibilities, and we will have time here only to paddle at the edge. Rather than generalizing and introducing you to topology, the branch of mathematics that deals with the manipulation of surfaces, I have opted for the opposite course: I will write the movies for this section in a hard-coded manner. I do not recommend this as a habit, and encourage you to be on the lookout for all the bad practices in which I indulge. The advantage for you is that all the code for a given step is provided in one place. Oh, and if you're just about to order a pizza or finish off that packet of breakfast cereal, keep the cardboard packaging handy: you'll be doing some real-world cut and paste.

Manipulating the vertexList

Origami1.dir

By now, I imagine you will have altered Origami0.dir beyond all recognition. If you open Origami1.dir, you'll find the code has been stripped down to the basics, and three new handlers have been added. These are triggered by the three buttons beneath the Shockwave 3D sprite.

OSControls Xtra

The buttons require that you have the OSControls Xtra installed. You can find a demo version of this in the Xtras\ folder on the CD-ROM that accompanies the book.

Also on the CD-ROM, you'll find a projector called AddXtras that will propose to install this and other useful xtras for you. You can download the latest version of OSControls Xtra and acquire a license for it from http://www.peghole.com/xtras/osc_xtra/. You'll also need the xtra for the Lathe.dir movie later on in this chapter.

Point of View

In Origami0.dir, I placed the camera to look down at the mesh model, so that you could see the effect of the shading and color changes. In Origami1.dir, I've placed the camera differently, out along the z axis and just above the center of the world:

```
mySprite.camera.transform.position = vector(0, 25, 170)
```

By default, the camera looks along a line at right angles to the y axis. In this case, it is important to leave it facing straight ahead. If I were to pan the camera up or down, the vertical edges of the folded mesh would appear skewed. Try it and see: run the movie, click the Fold In Half button, and then type the following in the Message window:

```
sprite(1).camera.pointAt(0, 0, 0)
```

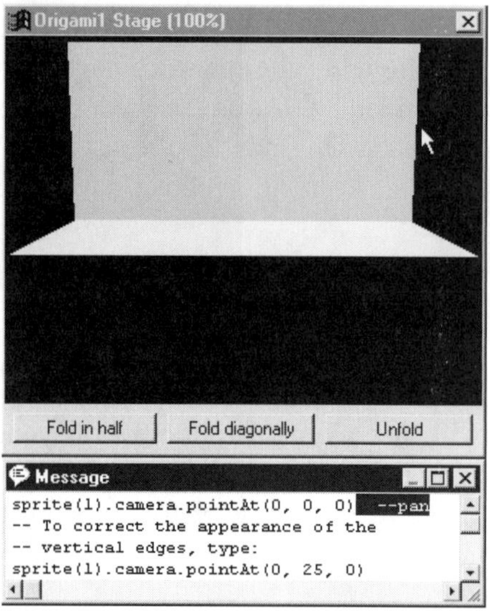

The camera is 25 units above the z axis. This command you've just typed makes it point downward so that the center of the mesh model appears in the center of the sprite. Notice how the vertical edges are adversely affected by the vertical pan of the camera, because the plane of the camera is no longer parallel to the plane of the mesh. You can restore the original view by typing

```
sprite(1).camera.pointAt(0, 25, 0)
```

See Figure 9-3.

A Simple Technique

The Origami1.dir movie illustrates the simplest version of the technique we're going to explore. It simply replaces the current version of the mesh resource's `vertexList` with a new list of values. Clicking on the Fold in Half button calls this handler:

```
on foldInHalf(me)
  myMeshResource.vertexList = [ \
vector(  0,   0,   0), \
vector(  0,   0,  50), \
vector( 50,   0,  50), \
vector( 50,   0,   0), \
vector( 50,  50,   0), \
vector(  0,  50,   0), \
vector(-50,  50,   0), \
vector(-50,   0,   0), \
vector(-50,   0,  50) \
]
  myMeshResource.colorList = myColorList - [0,0,64,64,64,64,0,0]
end foldInHalf
```

Figure 9-3 shows the shape of the mesh immediately after these two lines of code have been executed.

This places the three vertex points that are farthest from the camera (vertices 5, 6, and 7) on a line 50 units above the x axis. Notice that the change is immediate: if you place a debug breakpoint in the handler, you will notice that the shape of the mesh changes even before the end of the handler is reached.

For a heightened effect, I slightly darken the color of the four farthest faces of the mesh. This is necessary because, in Director 8.5, the lighting applied to a mesh appears to be determined by its initial geometry. Changing the shape of the mesh does not change the way light falls on it. You'll see a more striking example of this shortly. The technique I use to change the colors is the one that proved to be simplest in the previous section. I use a similar technique in the `foldDiagonally()` and `unfold()` handlers.

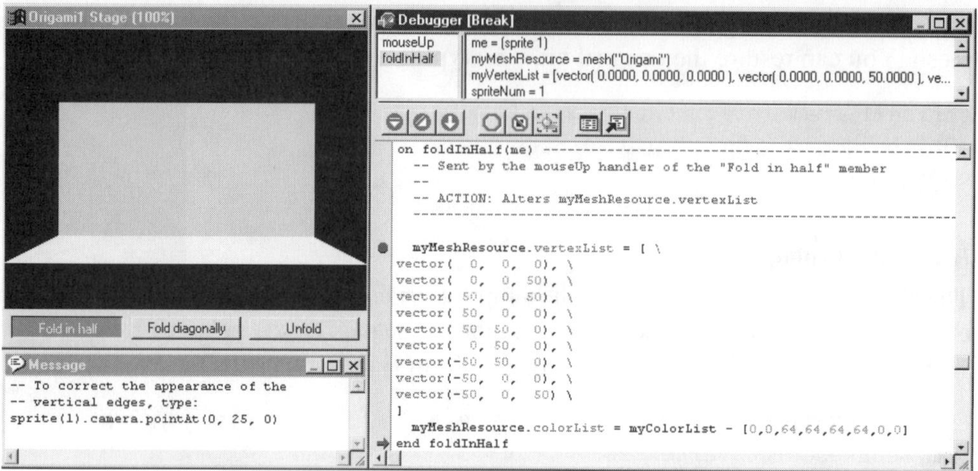

Figure 9-3 *Modifying the vertexList has an immediate effect.*

Trying It for Yourself

The new positions I chose for the vertex points maintain the size and shape of the faces. There is absolutely no obligation to do this; on the contrary, it is much easier to move a vertex point without respecting its shape. Try modifying the position of different vertices or the color of different faces by typing commands in the Message window:

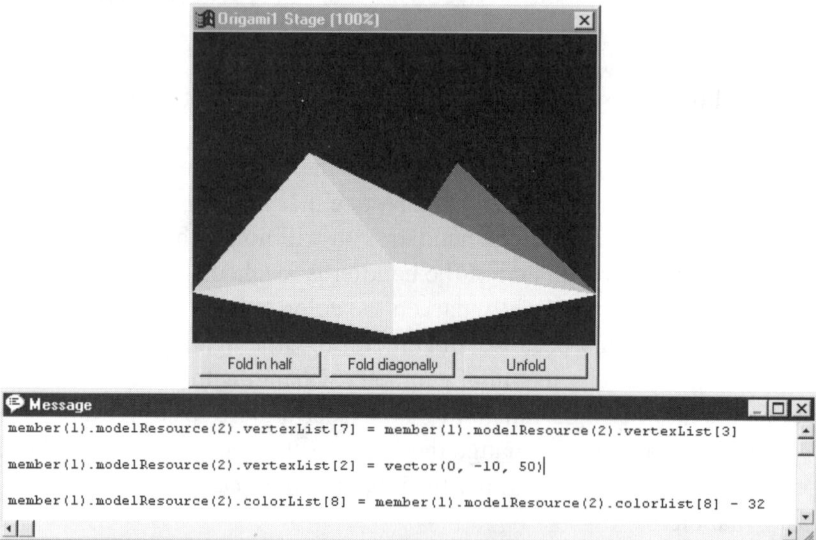

Cardboard-Assisted Design

If you've ever done origami before, you'll be surprised by what I'm going to ask you to do now. (If you have never done any origami, it might help to know that normally it is done with fine paper.) I'd like you to find yourself a fairly large piece of fairly stiff cardboard; a ruler; a pencil; a pair of scissors; and, just for good measure, a roll of sticky tape. For the cardboard, the box that your corn flakes come in is just the right size and thickness.

Build Your Own 3D Hardware

Cut yourself a square piece of cardboard about the size of a dinner plate, and place it with the printed side uppermost (if there is a printed side). With the back of the scissors, score the square diagonally, from corner to corner, so that it is easy to fold. You might want to reinforce the card on the side you didn't score with sticky tape, because you're going to be flexing the card quite a bit. With the sticky-taped side uppermost, find the midpoint on each edge and score two lines, one vertically and one horizontally, across the card. Your diagonal scores should be on the opposite side. All the score lines should cross at the center of the card. Once again, you might like to reinforce the reverse of the card with sticky tape.

Make sure you can fold the card easily along the score lines. The folds need to work only one way. When you fold your square along the diagonals, you bring one face in contact with itself; when you fold along the horizontal or vertical score, you bring the other face in contact with itself. You now have a hardware version of the mesh that you've been working with (or should that be cardware?).

With the diagonal score marks uppermost, use the pencil to mark the index numbers of the vertices on the card: 1 in the center, 2 in the middle of an edge, 3 in the near right-hand corner, and the numbers from 4 to 9 in rotation counterclockwise around the other edge centers and corners. Your numbering system should be the same as that in Figure 9-1 at the beginning of the chapter. Because you will be folding the card, you might like to write the index number for each vertex several times: once on each triangular face in which it appears.

Turn the card over and number the vertices on the other side. Make sure each vertex has the same number on both sides of the card.

Simulation

Place your card on a table with the diagonal folds uppermost and vertices 9, 2, and 3 toward you. You should be able to fold the far side of the card toward you, so you have the same shape as that shown in Figure 9-3. Continue folding the card so it is folded double. With your right hand, press down on the face [1, 4, 5] so it remains where it is. With your left hand, take hold of the two triangles [1, 7, 8] and [1, 8, 9] so they remain in contact. Now, lift your left hand and fold the square defined by vertices 1, 2, 9, and 8 over as if you were closing a book. If you have scored the card correctly, vertex 6 should rise toward you; then fold over so that, when the figure is closed, vertices 8, 6, and 4 all coincide.

If you are more comfortable with a demonstration, take a sneak peak at the movie Origami3.dir. Click the Fold 1 and Fold 2 buttons; your movements should be the same. You can rotate the model in the movie by dragging it with the mouse if you prefer to have the same perspective you have with your cardboard model. You can now lift vertex 8 and rotate the two triangles to which it belongs so it lies finally on top of vertex 2. This is fold 3 in the Origami3.dir movie.

The movements you have just made are fairly easy to program. However, they are not the movements that an experienced origamist would use. A more realistic movement is shown in Origami4.dir (but we'll cross that bridge when we come to it).

Visualizing the Movements

Why have I made you go to the lengths of creating a cardboard mock-up of a computer simulation? I think it is much easier to work out how to program a movement if you can practice it physically beforehand. You can move your cardboard model backward and forward slowly between two positions, watching how a particular vertex moves. Once you can describe that movement clearly in your own mind, it is much easier to describe it in Lingo.

Fold 1

Origami2.dir

The first movement is fairly straightforward; it consists of rotating vertices 5, 6, and 7 around an axis defined by the line 4-1-8. The question is, how do you rotate a point? There are two possible answers. Here, I'll get the point to hitch a lift inside a transform and then rotate the transform. In the Lathe.dir movie I examine in the following, I use a transform to represent the rotation and multiply this transform by the point.

When you click the Fold 1 button, the `startFirstFold()` handler is called in the Origami Mesh behavior. This creates a separate transform for each of the vertex points we want to move, and sets the position of the transform to the position of the vertex. It also determines how many frames to make the animation last, and what handler to call to make it happen.

```
property myAction        -- handler executed on exitFrame()
property myFrames        -- number of frames to the end of the
--                          current animation
property myAngle         -- number of degrees to rotate on each frame
property myTransformList -- list of transforms containing the
--                          position of points being rotated

on startFirstFold(me)
  -- Create transforms for each of the vertices 5, 6 and 7
  myTransformList = []

  tTransform = transform()
  tTransform.position = myVertexList[5]
  myTransformList.append(tTransform)

  tTransform = transform()
  tTransform.position = myVertexList[6]
  myTransformList.append(tTransform)

  tTransform = transform()
  tTransform.position = myVertexList[7]
  myTransformList.append(tTransform)

  -- Prepare an animation which will last about 2 seconds
  myFrames = the frameTempo * 2
  myAngle  = 180.0 / myFrames -- counter-clockwise

  -- Tell the exitFrame() handler which action to execute
  myAction = #firstFold
end startFirstFold
```

Once `myAction` has been set to `#firstFold`, the `on firstFold()` handler will be called on every exitFrame:

```
on exitFrame(me)
  if myFrames then
    call(myAction, me) -- #firstFold, #secondFold, #thirdFold
  end if
end exitFrame


on firstFold()
  myFrames = myFrames - 1
```

```
  -- Rotate around the axis that passes through vertices 1 and 4
  centerPoint = vector(0, 0, 0)
  axis = myVertexList[4] - myVertexList[1]

  repeat with i = 1 to 3 -- + 4 for vertices 5 to 7
    tTransform = myTransformList[i]
    -- Rotate the transform
    tTransform.rotate(centerPoint, axis, myAngle)
    -- Apply the transform's new position to the appropriate vertex
    myMeshResource.vertexList[i + 4] = tTransform.position
  end repeat

  if not myFrames then
    -- The animation is over: get ready for the next one.
    myVertexList = myMeshResource.vertexList
  end if
end firstFold
```

Transforms and Frames of Reference

Let's take a moment to review what a transform is and how you can use it. A transform is a record describing a position, a rotation, and a scale. A transform on its own is pretty meaningless, just like the number 4 is meaningless until you apply it to leap years, grandparents, your bank balance, or some other concrete entity (remember my insistence on the use of the appropriate units in Chapter 7?). A transform becomes meaningful when it refers to some object or a point in some reference framework.

What a Transform Tells You

A transform is like a written clue in a treasure hunt. Suppose you find a transform that has the following properties:

```
tTransform.position = vector(Tx, Ty, Tz)
tTransform.rotation = vector(Rx, Ry, Rz)
tTransform.scale    = vector(Sx, Sy, Sz)
```

This tells you

- Take Tx steps along your x axis, Ty steps along your y axis, and Tz steps along your z axis.
- Now rotate Rx degrees around your x axis, Ry degrees along around y axis, and Rz degrees around your z axis.

- Now grow to Sx times your current size along your new x axis, Sy times your current size along your y axis, and Sz times your current size along your y axis.

Notice that you move first, so your subsequent rotation and scaling occur around your new position. Then you rotate so that the scaling occurs when you are facing in the new direction. Finally, you scale.

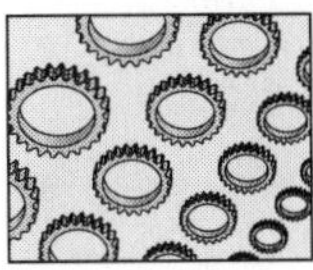

NOTE

A transform applies all these operations at once, maintaining the original position and axes until all the operations are finished. If you apply the operations one at a time using `translate()`, `rotate()`, and `scale()`, the position and orientation of the transform will change between each operation, giving a different result.

What a Transform Knows

As I imply in the preceding, a transform knows only about its own frame of reference. Its translations, rotations, and scalings all are done according to its own x, y, and z axes. A transform is a flat Earther—it cannot begin to imagine its position in the cosmic scheme of things.

When you act on a transform, you act on it from a point of reference in your virtual cosmos. Imagine a node whose parent is the `group("World")`. This node's transform describes the position, rotation, and scale of that node, with respect to the center of the world and the orientation of the world's axes. If you want to move the node, you must do so in relation to the world or in relation to another node that is itself in the world.

In the example we are working on, we are not concerned about world space but about space within the model resource itself. As our model is sitting unrotated and unscaled in the center of the world, world space and model resource space happen to coincide. If you click the Shockwave 3D sprite and drag the mouse, the model will rotate and the world frame of reference will no longer correspond to that of the model. The two frames of reference are independent.

When we create a transform for three of the vertex points inside the model resource, the transform itself is independent of either of these frames of reference. Its significance is based on us treating it in relation to the model resource's frame of reference. In the same way, the number 4 takes on a different significance depending on whether you treat it in relation to the number of your grandparents (typical value) or your bank balance (alarming).

What You Can Do to a Transform

Because a transform describes a position, a rotation, and a scale, it seems obvious that you should be able to position, rotate, and scale it. Scaling is always done relative to the axes of the transform itself.

The position of a transform is always relative to some other transform. Because all nodes in a 3D world have the `group("World")` at the top of their hierarchy of parents, the position of all nodes can be expressed as a displacement relative to the center of the world. In the mesh resource you are currently working with, all vertex positions are expressed in relation to the point `vector(0, 0, 0)` of the model resource. In this case, I made the center of the mesh coincide with this point to simplify the subsequent calculations.

The `rotate()` command takes three forms of syntax (see the "Corrections to the Lingo Dictionary" sidebar). Two of these make the transform rotate about its current position and with respect to the current orientation of its axes, in the same way that you can rotate your hand about your wrist or swivel a canon in a gun turret. The position of the transform does not change.

The third form of syntax allows you to rotate the transform about a point in an external frame of reference:

```
transform.rotate(position, axis, angle)
```

This is the form of syntax that I used in the `firstFold()` handler earlier in the chapter. For the `position` parameter, I use the center of the mesh resource; for the `axis` parameter, I use the vector that describes the movement from vertex 4 to the center; and for the `angle` parameter, I use the incremental value previously calculated in the `startFirstFold()` handler.

This form of syntax moves the transform through space, and thus changes its position. You can think of this as the way your hand moves around your shoulder or how the moon moves around the earth. The orientation of the transform will change as it turns; its orientation with respect to the center of rotation will be the same, but its orientation in space will have changed. The moon, for example, does not change its orientation with respect to the earth; the same face is always visible. The phases of the moon are because its orientation with respect to the sun (the point that corresponds to vector (0, 0, 0) for our solar system) changes as it turns around the earth.

As we rotate the transform we created for each of the vertices, so its position will update to reflect its new position inside the model resource. (The transform's rotation around its z axis will increase as it turns, but we are not interested in that.) By tracking the transforms `position` property, we can determine how it is moving through the model resource's frame of reference.

Corrections to the Lingo Dictionary

The entries for `translate` and `rotate` in the 3D Lingo Dictionary section of "What's New in Director Shockwave Studio" contain errors. On page 381, the entry for `rotate` proposes three examples of using `rotate` with a transform. These suggest that you can use a fourth parameter, `relativeTo`, when working directly with a transform. As I said earlier, the transform is aware only of its own frame of reference. Using a fourth parameter will provoke a script error. The fourth parameter is valid only if you are dealing with a node. Nodes belong to the world and can be moved in relation to each other or to any point in the world.

The transform-only syntax examples should read as shown here. The use of italics in this code and the next is consistent with the entry in "What's New in Direcor Shockwave Studio."

```
transform.rotate(xAngle, yAngle, zAngle)
transform.rotate(rotationVector)
transform.rotate(position, axis, angle)
```

Similarly, on page 424 of "What's New in Director Shockwave Studio," you should remove the reference to the fourth `relativeTo` parameter for the two examples that refer to transforms rather than to nodes:

```
transform.translate(xIncrement, yIncrement, zIncrement)
transform.translate(translateVector)
```

The example on the following page also should be corrected:

```
t = transform()
t.rotate(0, 90, 0)
t.translate(100, 0, 0)
gbModel = member("scene").model("mars")
gbModel.transform = t
put gbModel.transform.position
-- vector( 100.0000, 0.0000, 0.0000 )
```

Fold 2

The second fold is only marginally more complex, because we will be moving four vertex points around two different axes. By manipulating your cardboard model as described in the earlier "Simulation" section, observe which points and which axes these will be. Try to answer the following questions (you'll find the answers in the following handlers):

- Which three points will rotate around the axis defined by the line between vertex 2 and the center (vertex 1)?
- Around what axis will vertex 6 rotate?
- What total angle will each vertex move through?
- We will be moving four vertices, but will we need one transform for each?

Here is an extract of the `startSecondFold()` handler, which prepares the transforms for the second movement.

```
on startSecondFold(me)
  myTransformList     = []
  tTransform          = transform()

  tTransform.position = myVertexList[6]
  myTransformList.append(tTransform.duplicate())

  tTransform.position = myVertexList[7] -- same as myVertexList[9]
  myTransformList.append(tTransform.duplicate())

  tTransform.position = myVertexList[8]
  myTransformList.append(tTransform)
  -- as before...
end startSecondFold
```

In this handler, I recycle the same transform object, resetting its position for each vertex. I use the `duplicate()` function to clone a copy of the transform, which I then add to `myTransformList`. If I didn't add a copy to the list, all the transforms on the list would be identical. This is because transforms are pointers. As I mention elsewhere, a pointer indicates the memory address where the relevant information is stored. Changing that information means all pointers to that memory address see the new information. Creating a duplicate of the transform places a copy of the information in a different memory address, so its value is secure even if the data at the original address is overwritten. This saves me a few lines of code, but the two techniques are equivalent.

The handler called on exitFrame is a little longer than that for the first fold, as there is one more point and one more axis to deal with.

```
on secondFold(me)
  myFrames = myFrames - 1

  centerPoint = vector(0, 0, 0)

  -- Rotate vertex 6 around the axis defined by points 5->1
  axis       = myMeshResource.vertexList[5]
  tTransform = myTransformList[1]
  tTransform.rotate(centerPoint, axis, myAngle)
  myMeshResource.vertexList[6] = tTransform.position

  -- Rotate vertices 7 and 9 around the axis 2->1
  axis       = myMeshResource.vertexList[2]
  tTransform = myTransformList[2]
  tTransform.rotate(centerPoint, axis, myAngle)
  myMeshResource.vertexList[7] = tTransform.position
  myMeshResource.vertexList[9] = tTransform.position

  -- Rotate vertex 8 around the same axis (2->1)
  tTransform = myTransformList[3]
  tTransform.rotate(centerPoint, axis, myAngle)
  myMeshResource.vertexList[8] = tTransform.position

  if not myFrames then
    -- The animation is over: get ready for the next one.
    myVertexList = myMeshResource.vertexList
  end if
end secondFold
```

If you watch your animation very closely, you will see that there is one question I didn't ask: do both the rotations occur at the same relative rate? The answer is no. Vertex 6 turns through 90 degrees before the others do. Maintaining the same rate of rotation squashes the face [1, 6, 7] somewhat. We will resolve this problem in the final version of the movie.

Fold 3

The third fold is simplicity itself. You need to rotate only one vertex around one axis. I'll leave you to work out which vertex and which axis by manipulating your cardboard model.

Lighting the Back of the Mesh

The movement looks fine, but the back of the mesh appears black—at least in the version of Director 8.5 available at the time of writing. If, by the time you read this book, the Origami2.dir behaves as expected, you can skip to the next section.

Let's see if we can do something about this lighting problem. In the `createWorld()` handler, I explicitly set the `#visibility` of the mesh model to `#both`. In Origami0.dir, only the front face of the model is visible, at least initially. When you rotated the model to view it from the back, the front-facing faces disappeared altogether. Here, the back-facing faces are visible; they simply are not lit—yet the default directional light is shining down from above.

You can alter the direction of the default directional light in the Property Inspector, or by changing the value of the Shockwave 3D member's `directionalPreset` property. Try different values and see whether you can get the back of the mesh to appear in color. You might be surprised to discover that the best value for the `directionalPreset` is `#bottomLeft`. In other words, to light the back of the mesh, even when it is on the top, you need to light the mesh from below.

Reporting Bugs to Macromedia

The Director Player is not correctly informed that the geometry of the mesh model has changed. When the resource is modified, the model's geometry changes automatically and the updated shape is displayed. Unfortunately, the lighting routines don't seem to be made aware of this change. (The lightening routines require a `build()` command.)

When you encounter an anomaly such as this, it helps the whole of the Director community if you report it to Macromedia. Send a message to wish-director@macromedia.com describing the issue and detailing the minimal steps to reproduce it. It helps the Director engineers greatly if you can provide a movie that exhibits the problem. This means they don't have to spend precious time building such a movie themselves. Ideally, the movie should be entirely focused on the issue you are raising. Strip it of all unnecessary media and code. Although you'll receive only an automated acknowledgment, you can be sure your message will be acted upon.

Working Around the Bug

Origami3.dir

Because a Shockwave 3D member has only one default directional light, you need to create a second one to shine up from below. We'll look at cameras and lights in more detail in Chapters 12 and 13, so I'll just give you a few simple lines of code here.

As it happens, we can turn this bug into a feature—at least in the current version of Director. When the bug is fixed, the feature will be fixed, too. Currently, the front and back of our mesh are simply mirror images of each other. Typically, the two sides of a sheet of origami paper are different. By applying a different light source from below, we can change the apparent color of the underside of the mesh. I've used a spotlight placed close to the back of the mesh resource so there is a color gradient from the center to the edges.

Here's how I fixed the issue in Origami3.dir:

```
on createWorld()
   -- ...
   -- Add a light from below... to shine on the "back" of the mesh
  tLight = myMember.newLight("Spot", #spot)
  tLight.transform.position = vector(0, -50, 0)
  tLight.pointAt(0, 0, 0)
  --...
end
```

Once you've read up on cameras and lights, you might want to come back and try altering the color of the light or some other technique.

Animating the Mesh More Realistically

Origami4.dir

The movements you looked at in the "Animating the Mesh" section are simple to program, but your origamist client would not be convinced. In this section, I'll use a parent-child group and a helping of trigonometry to create a much more natural movement.

Visualizing the Realistic Movements

As before, place your cardboard model in front of you with the diagonal score marks uppermost and vertex 2 facing you. The first fold will be the same as before: fold vertices 5, 6, and 7 up and forward around the line between vertices 4 and 8.

Fold 2 Revisited

The second fold is different: With your right hand, hold the face [1, 4, 5] so that it cannot move (as before). Now take hold of vertex 6 by itself, and rotate it around the line between vertex 5 and the center until vertex 6 is on top of vertex 4. As you do this, vertex 7 should move upward and backward until it is standing directly above vertices 4 and 6. Your model should now be shaped like three faces of a cube. You might want to watch the simulation in Origami4.dir.

Repeat this fold forward and backward a number of times. Ask yourself the following questions:

- How do vertices 8 and 9 move? Around what axis do they rotate? Through what angle do they move?
- Around what axis is vertex 7 rotating? Will the techniques you used earlier in the chapter suffice to create this rotation?
- Is vertex 6 turning through the same angle as the other vertices?
- Which vertices are moving clockwise and which counterclockwise around its axes? (Think particularly about the rotation around the axis; not the movement through space.)

The Definitive Fold 3

For the third fold, use your left hand to press vertex 9 rightward and downward, as if you were catching it behind the knee. The vertical square formed by vertices 1, 6, 7, and 8 should close like the top of a treasure chest, trapping vertex 9 underneath it.

The movement of vertices 7 and 8 is fairly simple: a counterclockwise rotation around 90°. But what about the movement of vertex 9? It remains vertically above the line between vertices 2 and 3 at all times. But how high up is it? How far to the right? How does its movement correlate to the angle of rotation of vertices 7 and 8? Is it easier to determine the angle that it turns through or its position?

Now go and make yourself a cup of something stimulating. Here's a cheering thought: Origami4.dir reproduces this particular movement faithfully, so there must be a solution to all these questions.

Out of the World Parent and Child Groups

In the `createWorld()` handler of Origami Mesh behavior in Origami4.dir, I've added four new lines:

```
-- Groups
myParentGroup = myMember.newGroup("Parent")
myChildGroup  = myMember.newGroup("Child")
myParentGroup.addChild(myChildGroup)
```

I've declared these new properties at the top of the behavior:

```
-- Used to rotate one vertex around another that is moving
property myParentGroup    -- group for vertex 6
property myChildGroup     -- group for vertex 7
```

Does this help you to see how we are going to deal with fold 2?

Virtual Reality

In Chapter 8, you saw how a child node could be made to move in relation to its parent group. If the parent group moved, the child moved with it. I presented a group as being a node that has nothing but children. I should have qualified that: nothing but children and a transform.

When you create a group, the group becomes a child of the world. It moves in world space. We are currently working in the space defined by the model resource; you cannot create a group inside a model resource. So how are groups going to help us?

As I explained in the section "Transforms and Frames of Reference," the significance of a transform depends on its context. What we are going to do is to manipulate a parent-child group in world space and apply the resulting transform to a vertex in the model resource space. This will be like a hi-tech doctor in a virtual reality suit whose ample gestures control the precision movements of a microtool inside a patient's heart (except that the equipment doesn't cost so much).

Although it is important to understand which frame of reference you are currently working in, you can, with care, work in more than one frame of reference simultaneously.

Using the Parent-Child Group Explicitly

Let me start by answering the questions on the second fold that I asked in the earlier section "Fold 2 Revisited." Vertices 8 and 9 rotate through 90 degrees clockwise around the axis defined by the line from vertex 2 to the center. This is very similar to the movement they made in Origami1.dir, so I will omit the code that deals with it in the extracts that follow.

Vertex 6 rotates 180° clockwise around the axis defined by the line between vertex 5 and the center. Vertex 7 rotates 90° counterclockwise around a moving axis: the line between vertex 6 and the center. We will make `myParentGroup` follow the same trajectory as vertex 6 while its child, `myChildGroup`, will rotate around it; thus, describe the same movement as vertex 7. These groups do not contain any models; we are interested only in how the child group's transform moves relative to its parent and, as a consequence, to the world.

Here is the code that prepares this. Note how I subtract the position of vertex 7 from vertex 6 to obtain the position of vertex 7 relative to vertex 6.

```
on startSecondFold(me)
  -- ...
  tTransform = transform()
  tTransform.position = myVertexList[6]
  myTransformList.append(tTransform)
  -- For vertex 7, we will use a parent-child set of groups
  myParentGroup.transform = tTransform  -- vertex 6

  -- Create a new transform for the child group
  tTransform = transform()
  tTransform.position = myVertexList[7] - myVertexList[6]
  myChildGroup.transform = tTransform -- vertex 7 relative to 6
  -- ...
  myAngle  = -180.0 / myFrames -- clockwise
end startSecondFold
```

Here is how the animation of vertices 6 and 7 are treated. Remember that vertex 6 is rotating clockwise through 180°, and vertex 7 counterclockwise through 90°, so we'll use `myAngle` for the rotation of vertex 6 and `-myAngle/2` for the rotation of vertex 7.

```
on secondFold(me)
  myFrames = myFrames - 1

  centerPoint = vector(0, 0, 0)

  -- Rotate vertex 6 around the axis defined by points 5->1
  axis       = myMeshResource.vertexList[5]
  tTransform = myTransformList[3]
  tTransform.rotate(centerPoint, axis, myAngle)
  myMeshResource.vertexList[6] = tTransform.position

  -- Move myParentGroup with vertex 6, rotate myChildGroup around
  -- it, and apply the world position of myChildGroup to vertex 7
  myParentGroup.transform = tTransform
  myChildGroup.rotate(0, 0, -myAngle / 2, #parent)
  myMeshResource.vertexList[7] = myChildGroup.worldPosition
  -- ...
end secondFold
```

multiply() or How to Be a Parent Implicitly

Now that you have seen how the parent-child relationship can be used to rotate one vertex around a moving axis, I'll show you how to achieve the same effect without using parent and child groups. Here's the entry in the 3D Lingo Dictionary for `multiply()`:

> `multiply()`
>
> **Syntax**
>
> `transform.multiply(transform2)`
>
> **Description**
>
> 3D command; applies the positional, rotational, and scaling effects of transform2 after the original transform.
>
> **Example**
>
> This statement applies the positional, rotational, and scaling effects of the model Mars' transform to the transform of the model Pluto. This has a similar effect as making Mars be Pluto's parent for a frame.
>
> ```
> member("scene").model("Pluto").transform.multiply(member("scene")\
> .model("Mars").transform)
> ```

Did you notice that line: "This has a similar effect as making Mars be Pluto's parent...."?

So how could you use `multiply()` to make vertex 6 the parent of vertex 7 and not use any explicit parenting at all? When you prepare the transforms for the animation, in the `startSecondFold()` handler, the transform you create for vertex 7 would not use its absolute position on the mesh, but its position relative to vertex 6. In other words, the position defined by `myVertexList[7] - myVertexList[6]`. While animating vertex 7 in the `secondFold()` handler, you would start by rotating this relative position around its center and then multiply the resulting transform by the transform of vertex 6. This could give you code such as

```
-- Prepare for rotation
tTransform6          = transform()
tTransform6.position = myVertexList[6]
tTransform7          = transform()
tTransform7.position = myVertexList[7] - myVertexList[6]

-- Rotate
```

```
centerPoint = vector(0, 0, 0)
axis        = myMeshResource.vertexList[5]
tTransform6.rotate(centerPoint, axis, myAngle)
myMeshResource.vertexList[6] = tTransform.position

tTransform7.rotate(0, 0, -myAngle / 2)
tTransform7.multiply(tTransform6)
myMeshResource.vertexList[7] = tTransform7.position
```

Unfortunately, because vectors are pointers and `multiply()` modifies the original transform, this solution is a little cumbersome. You can make it more elegant if you use the `*` operator for transforms. This returns a new transform rather than modifying an existing one. See the text member in the movie Matches2.dir for details on how transforms are multiplied.

This is the solution I adopted. Here are the appropriate lines of code from the final Origami.dir movie:

```
on startSecondFold(me)
  myTransformList      = []
  tTransform           = transform()

  tTransform.position = myVertexList[6]
  myTransformList.append(tTransform.duplicate())

  -- Determine the position of vertex 7 relative to vertex 6
  tTransform.position = myVertexList[7] - myVertexList[6]
  myTransformList.append(tTransform.duplicate())
  -- ...
end startSecondFold


on secondFold(me)
  centerPoint = vector(0, 0, 0)

  -- Rotate vertex 6 around the axis defined by points 5->1
  axis       = myMeshResource.vertexList[5]
  tTransform = myTransformList[1]
  tTransform.rotate(centerPoint, axis, myAngle)
  myMeshResource.vertexList[6] = tTransform.position

  tTransform7 = myTransformList[2]
  tTransform7.rotate(0, 0, -myAngle / 2) -- modify transform in list
  tTransform7 = tTransform * tTransform7 -- create new transform
```

```
  myMeshResource.vertexList[7] = tTransform7.position
  -- ...
end secondFold
```

The Third Fold

The difficulty with the third fold is the movement of vertex 9. If you consider that vertices 7 and 8 rotate at a steady rate, vertex 9 starts off moving faster and ends up moving slower. I deal with this through trigonometry. I rotate the vertices 7 and 8 at `myAngle` degrees per frame around the axis defined by vertex 6 and the center (or vertex 4 and the center, because this now is the same axis). I calculate the position of vertex 9 from the current angle of rotation of vertices 7 and 8.

```
 on thirdFold(me)
  -- ...
  tAngleLeft = myFrames * myAngle * pi / 180
  t9y        = tan(tAngleLeft / 2)
  t9x        = sqrt(1 - (t9y * t9y)
  myMeshResource.vertexList[9] = vector(t9x, t9y, 1) * 50
  -- ...
end thirdFold
```

The graphical explanation of the variables I use in the preceding is shown in Figure 9-4.

A Final Tweak for Fold 2

Earlier, we noted that the face [1, 6, 7] was squashed during fold 2. Let's check whether this has been corrected by adopting a different folding technique. In the Origami4.dir movie, I include a `checkVertices()` handler, which is called `on exitFrame`. If you press the SHIFT key while executing a fold, this prints out in the Message window an indication of the distances between each vertex and its neighbors.

If you press the SHIFT key during fold 2, you will see that this time the distance between vertices 7 and 8 is being squashed. Here is the output in the Message window when the distortion is greatest:

```
-- 50.0000 2 3
-- 50.0000
-- 50.0000 3 4
-- 50.0000
-- 50.0000 4 5
-- 50.0000
-- 50.0000 5 6
```

```
-- 50.0000
-- 50.0000 6 7
-- 50.0001
-- 43.4074 7 8
-- 50.0000
-- 50.0000 8 9
-- 50.0000
-- 50.0000 9 2
-- 50.0000
```

Dealing with this requires solving a quadratic equation. Either you like doing this sort of thing or you don't. If you don't, you can be forgiven for leaving the movie as it stands. Even a keen-eyed origamist is unlikely to notice the slight error.

If you do like solving quadratics, you can study the fully commented `startSecondFold()` and `secondFold()` handlers in the final Origami.dir movie. You'll also find a scan of a page of algebraic notes in the movie, so you can follow the logic that leads to the lines of code.

Taking Mesh Manipulation Further

In this example, I have deliberately used a simple mesh so that we can concentrate on the process of animating it. You can, of course, use the same techniques on more complex meshes. Here are some possible examples:

- A 3D Goo program
- A program for creating landscapes

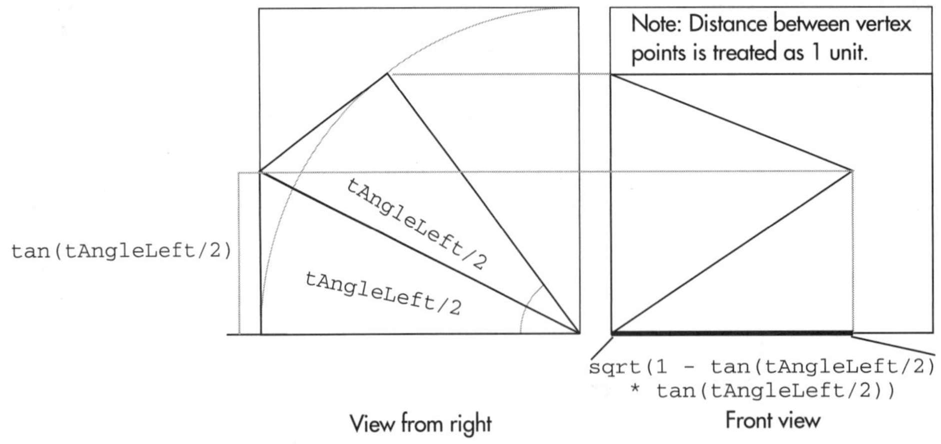

Figure 9-4 *Calculating the position of vertex 9 for fold 3*

- Blowing up a balloon
- Deforming a car when it crashes
- Simulating the movement of a heartbeat

The Lathe Tool

Lathe.dir

So far in this chapter, the mesh you have been working with has been simple enough for you to determine its vertices by hand. Now we'll look at a technique for building vertices automatically from a template. I have created a lathe tool, but you could use the same principles to create an extruder.

The lathe tool consists of four parts:

- A 2D interface in which you can edit a Vector Shape member to create a line made of a series of straight segments
- A set of three slider controls that allow you to determine the angle and resolution of the mesh resource that will be created
- A script that performs the operation of sweeping the 2D line through the chosen angle and builds a mesh resource from the result
- A Shockwave 3D sprite that shows the model produced of the lathe operation

I will deal only with the third part here.

An Open-Source Project

The editing interface is functional but not perfect. It could be improved by a marquee selection for the vertex point handles by adding more keyboard shortcuts and tidying up a number of bugs. The scripts that control the interface are fully commented. I provide the movie as an open-source project. You are welcome to improve the interface in any way that suits you. Please keep me informed of any changes that you make, so that I can update a central version of the movie to share with the rest of the Director community. You can contact me through jjames.newton@openspark.com or the address given in the scripts themselves.

Exploring the Possibilities of the Lathe Tool

Open the Lathe.dir movie and run it. If you click the Auto Build button, you will see the changes you make in the 2D editing panel appear in real time in the Shockwave 3D sprite. Press A to select all the vertex point handles, and use the arrow keys to move them around. Press the SHIFT key at the same time to jump 10 pixels at each keypress. You can select multiple handles by SHIFT-clicking. You can delete handles by pressing the BACKSPACE key. (If you delete all the handles, you'll discover the most major bug; you can fix this by restarting the movie.)

When you are happy with your work, click the Export button. You will get a chance to create and save a Linked Script file. This script contains all the code you need to re-create the same mesh resource in another movie. This is the code we will be looking at. You also can import scripts that you have already saved for re-editing.

The code included in the exported Linked Script file has been stripped of most of its comments to reduce the file size. Apart from a couple of handlers that are best looked at in a Linked Script file, it's best to consult the fully commented newLatheResource Parent Script (member 5) in the movie itself for the rest of the handlers.

Building a Mesh Automatically

The main issue in creating a complex mesh is in being systematic. As you saw at the beginning of the chapter, inverting two values in the list of vertices used for one of the faces can result in a hole appearing in the mesh.

The two essential steps are creating the vertices for the mesh resource's `vertexList` and setting the vertices list for each individual face. In the simple example above, I created a separate `tFaceList` and applied its contents item by item to the faces of the newly created mesh resource. Here, this technique is doubly useful: it allows me to be methodical and it allows me to calculate how many faces there will be, which is a detail that the `newMesh()` command requires.

Converting 2D to 3D

The 2D template editor modifies the vertex points of a Vector Shape member. This member's `vertexList` is the raw material from which the lathed mesh is built. In the exported Linked Script file, the `vertexList` is hard-coded into the `template()` handler. Here is an example of a `template()` handler that will produce a shape like a drum. I've arranged the `vertexList` data to make it easier to read:

```
on template(me)
  tDataList = [:]

  -- Lathe data

  tDataList[#startAngle] = 0
  tDataList[#endAngle]   = 360
  tDataList[#resolution] = 16

  -- Template data
  tDataList[#vertexList] = [ \
[#vertex: point(159, -160)], \
[#vertex: point(159, 160)], \
[#vertex: point(-160, 160)], \
[#newCurve], \
[#vertex: point(0, -50)], \
[#vertex: point(50, -50)], \
[#vertex: point(50, 50)], \
[#vertex: point(0, 50)] \
]

  return tDataList
end template
```

The first four vertices in `vertexList` are ignored; they are used simply to create a separate line that ensures a minimum size for the Vector Shape sprite.

Conversion from the 2D coordinates in `vertexList` to 3D vector point coordinates is simple enough. The `mConvertTemplate()` handler that you will find in the exported Linked Script takes care of this; here's an edited version:

```
on mConvertTemplate(me)
  tLatheData    = me.template()
  tVertexList   = tLatheData.vertexList

  tVectorPoints = []
  tVertexCount  = tVertexList.count

  i = tVertexList.getPos([#newCurve]) + 1
  repeat with i = i to tVertexCount
    tVertexPoint = tVertexList[i].vertex
    -- Invert locH to correspond to y, which is positive upwards
    tVectorPoint = vector(tVertexPoint.locH, -tVertexPoint.locV, 0)
```

```
    tVectorPoints.append(tVectorPoint)
  end repeat
  tLatheData[#points] = tVectorPoints

  return tLatheData
end mConvertTemplate
```

Creating the vertexList

The variable tLatheData now contains a list of 3D points that lie on a plane, plus information concerning the startAngle, the endAngle, and the resolution of the mesh to be created. Resolution here means the number of faces that will be created as the 2D line is swept around a vertical axis. A solid shape must have at least three faces. For the built-in cylinder and sphere primitives, the resolution property starts at 1. This doesn't mean you can have a single-faced sphere; it means the number of faces around a sphere or a cylinder is always two more than the value of its resolution. I have been lazy and simply ensured that the value for resolution cannot fall below 3. For me, resolution is exactly equal to the number of faces around any row in the mesh.

In creating a lathed mesh, there are two issues to consider:

- Will the mesh form a complete circle? If so, we will have as many vertex points in any given row as there are faces, as the last face will connect back around to the first vertex. If not, we will need an extra vertex point at the end of each row to ensure that there is the correct number of faces.
- Do the first and last points on the 2D template coincide? If so, the last row of faces will connect back around to the first row of vertex points. We won't need to include the last point in the 2D template in our list of 3D vertices since it is the same as the first. If the first and last points on the 2D template do not coincide, there will be one less row of faces than there are points on the 2D template line.

These points are considered in a handler we'll look at shortly. In the following mLathe() handler, the parameters aCircleFlag and aClosedFlag will be TRUE if the answer to the preceding questions is yes.

The mLathe() handler takes each point on the 2D template and sweeps it around the model resource's y axis. In doing so, it creates a number of new points in 3D space; this number is determined by the variable resolution. In the preceding origami example, we inserted the point in a transform and rotated the transform. Here I use a different technique: I create a transform that represents a rotation (`tAngleTransform`) and multiply this transform by the point vector. This gives me a new vector that is the correct number of degrees farther round the circle.

```
on mLathe(me, aLatheDataList, aCircleFlag, aClosedFlag)
  tVertexList = []

  tResolution = aLatheDataList.resolution
  tStartAngle = aLatheDataList.startAngle
  tEndAngle   = aLatheDataList.endAngle

  -- Create a transform for the startAngle
  tStartTransform = transform()
  tStartTransform.rotation = vector(0, tStartAngle, 0)

  -- Create a transform for the incremental angle
  tFacetAngle     = float(tEndAngle - tStartAngle) / tResolution
  tAngleTransform = transform()
  tAngleTransform.rotation = vector(0, tFacetAngle, 0)

  tPoints = aLatheDataList.points
  i = tPoints.count - aClosedFlag -- *
  -- * Ignore final point in 2D template if it identical to the first

  repeat while i
    tVertex = tPoints[i]

    -- Create a circle of vertices around the y-axis starting
    -- at startAngle
    tVertex = tStartTransform * tPoints[i]

    repeat with j = 1 to tResolution
      -- Add the current point to tVertexList...
      tVertexList.append(tVertex)
      -- ...then rotate it around the y-axis for the next iteration
      tVertex = tAngleTransform * tVertex
    end repeat

    if not aCircleFlag then
      -- Add the final vertex since the lathe does not turn 360°
      tVertexList.append(tVertex)
    end if

    i = i - 1
```

```
  end repeat -- move to the next point along the 2D template line

  return tVertexList
end mLathe
```

You might notice that I start with the last item in the tPoints list and work back down to the beginning of the list. There is a good reason for this: it means the vertices in the list for each face of the mesh will be created in the correct order. I'll explain this in more detail shortly, in the "Ensuring the Faces Face the Front" section.

Room for Improvement

If we use the example provided in the preceding template() handler, I will now have 64 vertices: 4 rows of 16 points each. As it happens, almost half these points are unnecessary: 16 vertices coincide at the center of the top surface and 16 points coincide at the bottom. It would be more logical to use only one point, and have all the faces meet at that point. This would mean you could animate the "skin" of the drum by moving a single point up and down.

However, the code required to deal with such singularities is a little complex. For didactic reasons, I have preferred to keep the code simple, at least for this first version. I intend to publish a more intelligent version in due course.

Making the Faces

My vertexList now contains a continuous string of vertex points so I know how many points it will have. The number of faces this represents depends on whether the circle is closed and whether the 3D template is closed. I have this data available so I could calculate the number of faces now, call the newMesh() command, and then stitch the vertices together to make faces. However, I believe it is neater to create a list of lists, each of which will contain the vertices for a given face. This means, if necessary, I can put the list into the Message window and examine it for debugging purposes.

DEBUGGING TIP

If you use `put` to display a list in the Message window, the result is pretty much unreadable. I have developed a `reportProps()` handler that will create a neat layout. It can be used for both lists and instances, and will run through the entire hierarchy of objects. In the case of a linear list, the index number of each entry is shown in the place of the property name. Here's an example that shows the scriptInstanceList of the Export button sprite, plus the properties of the instance:

```
put reportProps(sprite(23))
-- "
[1]: <offspring "Export" 4 4879e8>
     #scriptField: (member 25 of castLib 1)
     #spriteNum:   23
```

You can find this in the Object Utilities script in member 33. You'll also find `findValue()` and `findIlk()` handlers for tracking down that hidden variable deep in a hierarchy of lists and instances. See the comments in each handler for details.

Here is a simplified version of the `mMakeFaces()` handler, which returns a list of faces. This version assumes the lathed shape is not a complete circle and that the 2D template has two distinct ends. You'll find the complete version, fully commented, in the newLatheResource script in member 5:

```
on mMakeFaces(me, aResolution, aVertexList)
  tFacesList = []

  tFaceCount   = aResolution -- number of faces in a row
  tRowVertices = tFaceCount + 1 -- number of vertices in a row
  tStripCount  = (aVertexList.count / (tRowVertices)) - 1 -- # of rows
  -- It helps to count the strips starting from 0
  tStripCount  = tStripCount - 1

  repeat with i = 0 to tStripCount
    -- Create a row of faces along one arc
    repeat with j = 1 to tFaceCount
```

```
      -- Create a rectangular set of two triangular faces at each pass
      tVertex1  = (i * tRowVertices) + j
      tVertex3  = tVertex1 + tRowVertices
      tFacesList.append([tVertex1, tVertex1 + 1, tVertex3])
      tFacesList.append([tVertex1 + 1, tVertex3 + 1, tVertex3])
    end repeat
  end repeat

  return tFacesList
end mMakeFaces
```

The double repeat loop works along each circular row of vertices, creating two triangular faces at iteration of the inner loop, using the next vertex in the same row and the two corresponding vertices from the next row.

Let's look at an example. Figure 9-5 shows the `vertexList` for a simple mesh resource. This has three faces and four vertices in each row: `tRowVertices` = 4. When the `mMakeFaces()` handler is executing and i = 1 and j = 2, the values inside the inner loop will be as follows:

```
tVertex1 = (i * tRowVertices) + j) --> 6 (See cursor arrow in Figure 9-5.)
tVertex1 + 1                       --> 7
tVertex3 = tVertex1 + tRowVertices --> 10
tVertex3 + 1                       --> 11
```

The two faces that are created during this iteration are thus `[6, 7, 10]` (the dark gray triangle in Figure 9-5) and `[7, 11, 10]` (the light gray triangle). Both these faces are correctly defined with the vertices in a counterclockwise order.

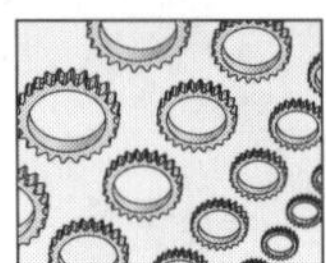

NOTE

You can obtain a wire frame or a point view of the model through a contextual menu. Right-click (Windows) or CTRL-click (Macintosh) on the Shockwave 3D sprite to bring up the contextual menu. There is no option to show the vertex numbers; these were added to Figure 9-5 by hand.

Ensuring the Faces Face the Front

As you saw at the beginning of the chapter, the order in which the vertices are added to the list for each face is important. If the vertices are placed in a clockwise order, the face is created back to front. I reversed the order of the vertices in the `mLathe()` handler by starting at the end of the list of 2D points and working back to the beginning. This allows me to use the logical order for the vertices in the `mMakeFaces()` handler. However, a little experiment shows that all is relative.

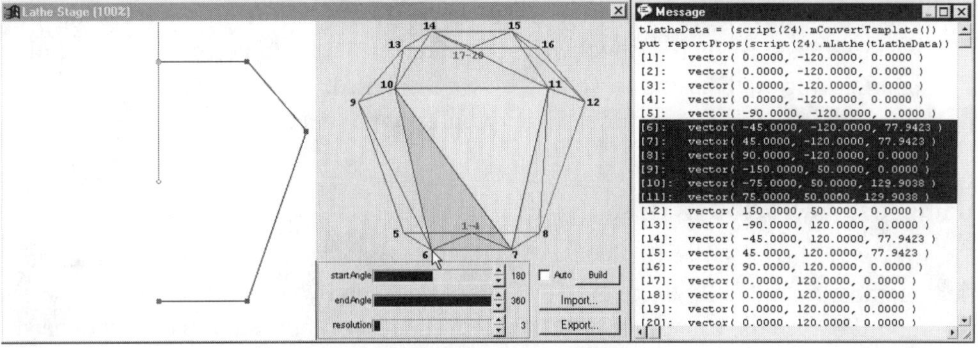

Figure 9-5 *One iteration of the repeat loop in mMakeFaces()*

The default template creates a *torus,* or donut shape, when you first run the movie. The points in the template run clockwise because on the 2D stage, angles increase in a clockwise direction. Try this:

1. Run the movie.
2. In the Message window type
   `member(1, 2).model(1).visibility = #front`
   (By default, the movie creates models with `visibility` = `#both`.)
3. Click the Stage and press A to select all the points.
4. Drag the circle to the left of the axis line.
5. Click the Build button.

The vertex points now have been created in the opposite order. You will see through the outside of the torus, because all the faces look inward. You will see only the inward-facing surface on the inside of the model.

To avoid this issue, by default, all models created by the Lathe.dir movie have their `visibility` property set to `#both`. However, when you use an exported Script in a different movie, the default value for `visibility` is `#front`. If you get strange results, try switching it to `#back` or to `#both`.

Putting the Resource Together

The handler that orchestrates the whole process is the `newLatheResource()` handler. I have deliberately styled both the name and the syntax of the handler on that of the native `newModelResource()` function. Because Lingo does not let me make the handler a method of the Shockwave 3D member itself, I have done the next best thing and made the Shockwave 3D member the first parameter of the call. The handler follows the same logic as the `createMesh()` handler you've been working with in the Origami movies, so I won't go into details here.

Using the Exported Scripts

The exported Linked Script file is based on the text in the "Model for exported script" field member (member 25). The only difference between two exported scripts is the hard-coded data in the `template()` handler. The rest of the code provides the means of converting the data returned by the `template()` handler into a mesh resource.

This means that, if you use several lathe models in a project, you need only one complete script. You can cut the different `template()` handlers from your different exported scripts, rename them, and place them all together in a single Movie Script cast member.

Importing a Lathe Model Into Another Movie

Using the Lathe.dir movie, create a new mesh resource and export the script. Now follow these steps to re-create the resource in a new movie:

1. Create a new movie.
2. Create a new Shockwave 3D member in cast slot 1.
3. Name your member and drag it onto the stage.
4. Click File | Import to open the Import dialog box.
5. Find the script you have just exported and import it into the new movie.
6. Open the script. You will find a commented-out section of notes at the beginning of the script, including a number of lines of code labeled "Example usage." Uncomment these lines, copy them, and then comment them out again.
7. Paste the lines into the Message window.
8. You'll need to provide the number of the script member and the number of the Shockwave 3D member in the place of the text in tags: `script(<number of this script>)` and `member(<3D member of your choice>)`.
9. Execute the lines one after the other.
10. Run your movie. The exported model should appear in your new movie. You might want to adjust the camera position to see the new model completely. You

also can use the Shockwave 3D member window to manipulate the scene; thus, you can look at your model from all sides.

11. This process is resumed in this illustration.

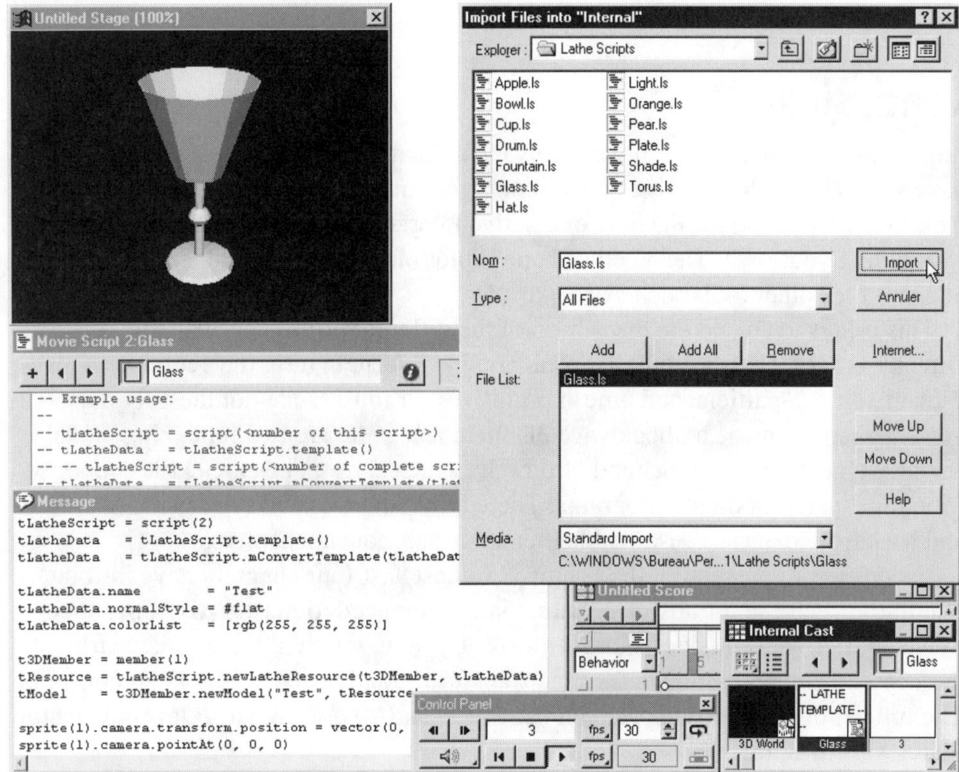

Overriding the Default Values

The newLatheResource() handler requires information concerning the name, normal style (#flat or #smooth), and a colorList for the resource you are about to make. For simplicity, the mConvertTemplate() handler provides default values for these. You might want to override these default values.

For this reason, I have divided the process of creating the resource into three:

- Retrieving the template data from the template() handler or some renamed version of this.
- Converting the template to a form usable by the newLatheResource() handler through the convertTemplate() handler. This includes adopting default values for the name, normal style, and colorList.

- Creating the new mesh resource by calling the `newLatheResource()` handler.

As in the example in the illustration, you can intervene between these last two calls in order to produce a mesh resource with the parameters of your choice.

Conclusion

This chapter has dealt with the creation and animation of a mesh resource. As you have seen, the mesh primitive enables you, via Lingo, to create any shape of model. You can compensate for the lack of a native interface for designing a mesh resource by building your own. The Vector Shape Editor included in the Lathe.dir movie can be reused for other tools such as an extruder.

This brings to an end the discussion of the different primitives available in Director 8.5. In these last four chapters you have seen, in turn, the #cylinder, #plane, #sphere, #box, #particle, and #mesh primitives. Primitives are not the only objects you can display inside a Shockwave 3D member. There are two remaining model resource types: text #extruder and #fromFile, which corresponds to 3D files imported from third-party modeling programs. There also is the possibility of using overlay and backdrop images. These will be treated in subsequent chapters.

In addition to presenting the primitives, these last four chapters have introduced you to the vector and transform mathematics you need to master to control the movement of nodes inside your 3D world. By now, you will have used nearly all the keywords concerning vectors and transforms, and tested all the main concepts. The full list of keywords appears on pages 190 and 191 of "What's New in Director Shockwave Studio."

Now that you know how to make things move in 3D, the next few chapters will deal with how things look.

CHAPTER

10

Introduction to Shaders and Textures

IN THIS CHAPTER:

All art is at once surface and symbol. Those who go beneath the surface do so at their peril.

— Oscar Wilde

By default, the sphere, plane, box, and cylinder primitives all have a default red-and-white checkerboard appearance. In this chapter and the next, you will see how to make your models look much more attractive by exploring the complex hierarchy of shaders, shader layers, and textures that can be applied to each surface of your models. Figure 10-1 shows a scene created entirely within Director. You will be creating this scene in Chapter 11.

A *texture* is an image. A *shader* defines the way a texture appears on the surface of a model. A shader is like a magical paint roller that paints a texture onto a surface. Depending on how your roller is configured, it can color the texture, give a matte or a shiny finish, make the texture appear to shine, and so on.

The shader produces some features that depend on using more than one layer of texture. The shader is the end result of your decoration process; the textures are the individual coats of paint. Individual coats can be applied in different ways: one coat can provide the basic image; another can define which parts of the image are glossy; and a third can define what is reflected in those glossy parts.

Textures are not just simple images; the image you provide can be treated before it is displayed. Treatment requires processing power. Achieving similar effects without treatment requires larger textures—thus, more RAM. Creating good-looking models on a wide range of target machines is a question of balancing requirements for power, memory, and appearance.

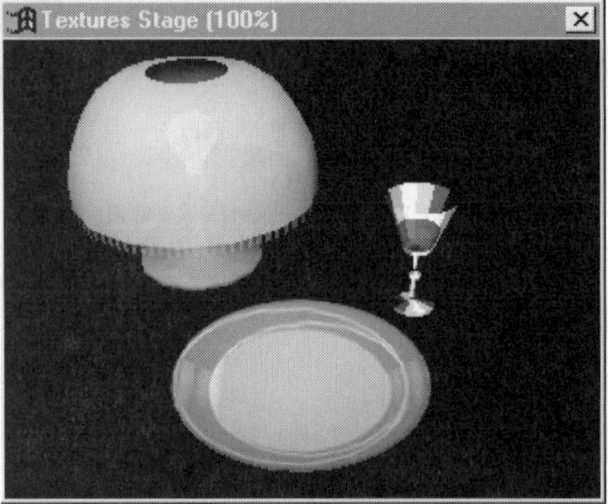

Figure 10-1 *Using shaders and textures on 3D models*

You can use a shader without any textures to create a flat area of color. In certain circumstances, you can use a texture without a shader: as a texture for a particle primitive, as you saw in Chapter 8, and as a backdrop or overlay for a camera, as you will see in Chapter 12. As you read this chapter, I encourage you to try out each example.

To simplify your task, I have created an MIAW utility movie called Shaders.dir. You'll find this in the 3D\Surface1\ folder on the CD-ROM. The Shaders.dir movie uses two other files: the -picker.dir movie and the -texture.cst cast. These three files are intended to be placed in your Xtras folder. (The "-" character means the filename won't show up in Director's Xtras menu.)

In this chapter, you'll be using the Shaders.dir movie to explore the various properties of textures and shaders, and how the values of these properties interact. In the next chapter, you'll study how shaders and textures are applied in *.w3d files created by third-party 3D design programs, and how to create and optimize the shaders and textures you need to build a scene of your own.

The Lingo you will be meeting is straightforward. Indeed, the Shaders.dir movie can export the necessary code automatically. Coming to terms with shaders and textures is a matter of understanding what each property does and how each property affects others.

An Interface for Exploring Shaders and Textures

Shaders are rather complex objects, as they need to be flexible enough to work in a variety of ways. Every shader has

- Eleven general properties you can set for a shader as a whole
- Eight properties you can set for each of the eight layers of the shader
- Six properties you can set for each texture used by various shaders
- Nine special properties you can set for the three specialist shaders: `painter`, `newsprint`, and `engraver`

It is possible (but unnecessary) to set more than a hundred values for a single shader. The relationship between the properties is not always simple: the effect of certain properties is canceled by the value of others.

Overview of the Shaders.dir Movie

Shaders.dir

Shaders are intrinsically visual. Director 8.5 offers no visual interface for dealing with them, so I have built one for you. You can install the Shaders.dir movie in your Xtras folder by launching the AddXtras.exe projector on the CD-ROM. This also will install a demo version of the OSControls Xtra and the two helper movies that the Shader.dir movie uses. Once you have done this, you can choose the menu Xtras | Shaders to open the movie in a window.

The Shaders.dir movie provides you with a drag-and-drop interface for

- Creating new shaders and textures
- Setting the shader for a given mesh on a given model
- Setting the texture for a given layer of a given shader
- Setting all of the properties of the current shader, current shader layer, and current texture
- Inspecting the properties of existing shaders
- Duplicating existing shaders and textures
- Exporting scripts that recreate the shaders and textures that you build using the Shader Inspector
- Importing such scripts for editing

Although it would be nice to be able to drag and drop a bitmap image from the Cast window onto the Texture preview or a shader layer button, this is not currently supported. However, because you have the source code, you might like to tackle this yourself. The Shaders.dir movie is shown in Figure 10-2.

The 3D Scene

At the top left of the screen in Figure 10-2, you will see a Shockwave 3D containing the scene. This is where you will see the effect of the shaders and textures you use. You can use the mouse and keyboards to view the scene from any angle.

When you click a model in this 3D sprite, two things happen:

- The property display updates to show the data for the mesh you clicked. The Model and Mesh pop-up menus beneath the sprite will indicate where you clicked.
- The point you clicked becomes the anchor point for the camera. All rotations and zooms are subsequently made relative to that anchor point. If there is no

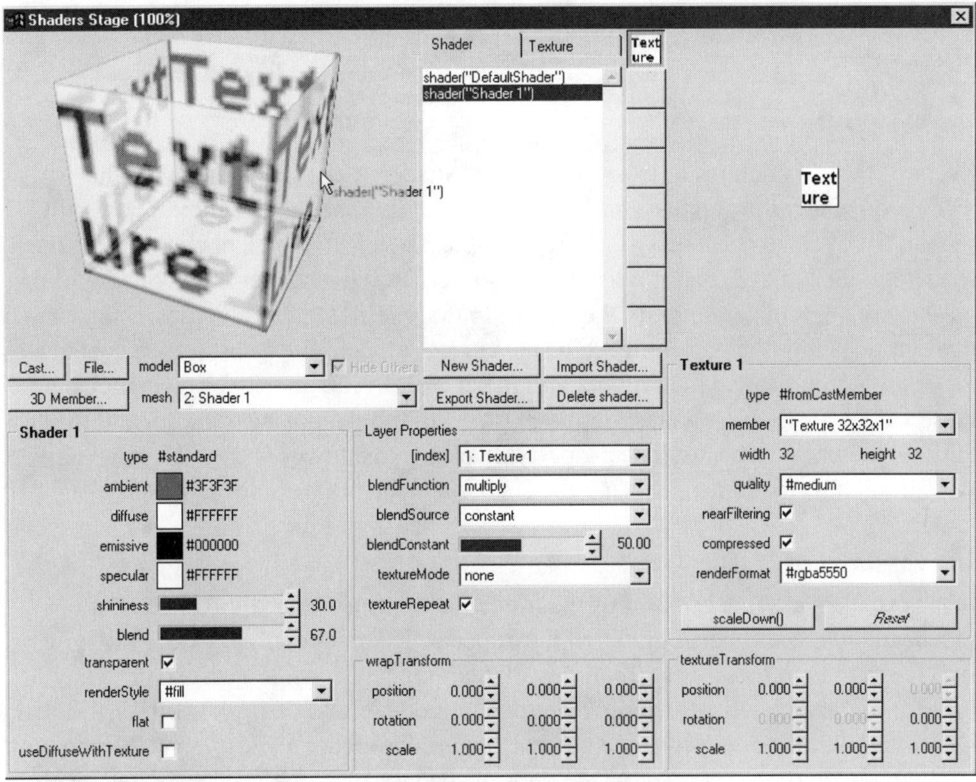

Figure 10-2 *Dragging a custom shader onto a model using the Shaders.dir movie*

model where you click, the scene moves so that the current anchor point appears beneath the mouse.

You can move the scene by dragging any model with the mouse. The following keys allow you to manipulate the camera:

- **X, Y,** and **Z** Preset views along the corresponding axes
- **C** Preset cavalier view
- **Arrow keys** Rotate the camera around the current anchor point
- **I** Zoom in toward the current anchor point
- **O** Zoom out
- **R** Revert to the initial camera position

You can use the SHIFT key to accelerate any zoom or rotation, or to invert the preset views.

The Shader List

Every 3D world contains at least one shader. Shaders exist independent of the models on which they appear. In the top center of the Shaders.dir movie, you will see the list of shaders currently available in the 3D world. You can click one of the shaders in the list and drag it over the 3D sprite. Drop the shader name on one of the meshes of a 3D model to apply the shader to that mesh. Double-clicking a shader name applies it to the current mesh of the current model. The pop-up menus beneath the 3D world indicate which model and mesh are currently active. You can change these values by clicking a mesh in the 3D world, or by choosing a model and mesh through the pop-up menus. The property display in the lower half of the movie gives you all the information concerning the shader attached to the current mesh.

The Texture List

Just as shaders are independent of the models they appear on, so textures exist independent of the shaders in which they appear. If you click the Texture tab, you will see the list of textures currently available in the 3D world. You can drag any of these textures onto any of the eight buttons immediately to the right of the list. Each button represents one layer in the current shader. Dropping a texture on a button will apply that texture to that layer of the current shader. The name of the current shader appears in bold on the right.

If you click any of the eight buttons, the display on the left will update to show the image and the properties of the texture for the chosen layer. You also can choose a layer through the [index] pop-up menu just below the center of the movie. The Shockwave 3D sprite on the right displays the image of the current texture in its raw form and at full size. If the texture image is larger than 256 × 256 pixels, only the center of the image will be shown. You can drag such large images around inside the sprite to see the areas that go beyond the visible zone.

A shader does not have to have a texture. You can drag the `<Void>` item from the list of textures onto one of the buttons to remove the texture for any given layer. If you remove all the textures from a shader, only the properties in the leftmost column will have any effect. As you will see when we study the way shaders and textures are used in the *.w3d files provided on the Director 8.5 CD-ROM, shaders can be used on their own to create areas of solid color.

If you right-click (Windows) or CTRL-click (Macintosh) any of the layer buttons, you will have the option of switching the creation of thumbnails on or off. Creating thumbnails is a slow process, especially when working with textures of the type

`#importedFromFile`. (This is because the Director Player must switch to `#software` rendering mode in order to capture the image of the Shockwave 3D sprite.) If you find that the 3D world to the left reacts slowly to the mouse, switch off the creation of thumbnails. It is off by default; but for clarity, all screen shots are shown with it on.

General Shader Properties

The lower half of the movie displays the names and values of the different properties of the current shader. As shown in Figure 10-3, the left-hand column shows the properties of the shader as a whole. If the shader uses no textures, only these properties will have any effect.

Properties for One Layer of the Shader

The central column and the foot of the right-hand column display the properties for one layer of the shader at a time. Remember, there are eight layers in a shader, and each layer has a separate value for each of the properties shown. Considerations of both space and clarity make it impractical to show the details of more than one layer at a time.

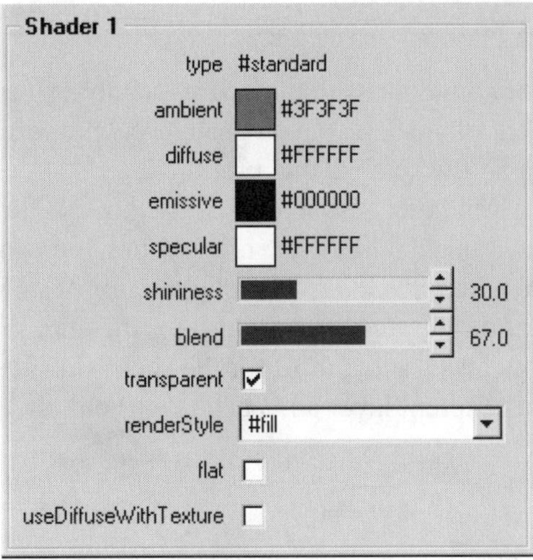

Figure 10-3 *General properties for a standard shader*

The layer number and the name of the texture in that layer (if there is one) are shown in the [index] pop-up menu. The index number is not, strictly speaking, a property of the shader, so it is shown in square brackets. The texture used by the layer is indeed a property of the layer, but its details are shown separately in the column on the right.

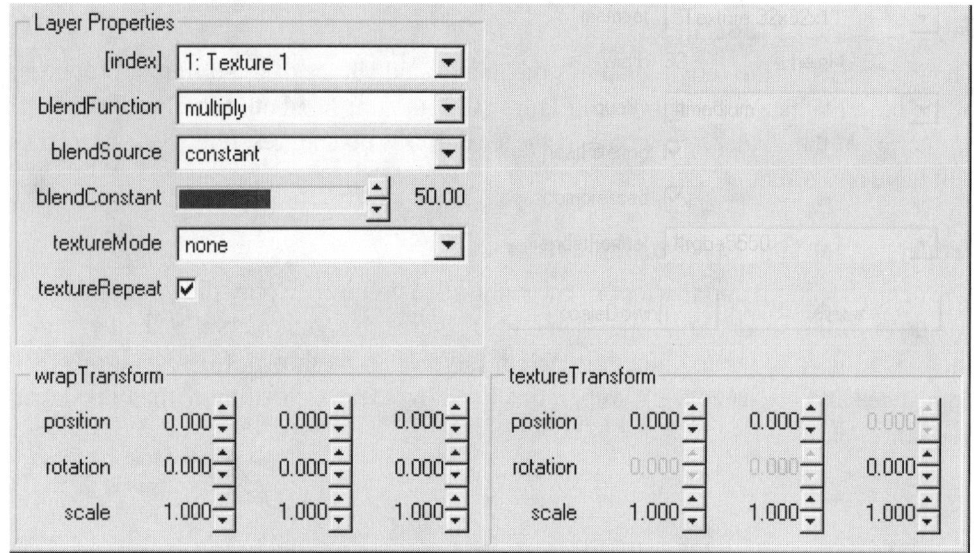

The main property of a layer is its texture. If it has no texture, a layer is ignored. Textures are independent of shaders. If you change the properties of a texture, the effect will be visible in all the shaders that use it.

The properties of a given layer of a shader define how the texture is used by the shader. Most shaders will use only a single texture, but you can create compound effects by using different textures in different layers; for example, a window with a lace curtain in front of it might use one texture for the curtain, a second for the reflection in the window glass, and a third for the scene outside the window. Each texture will appear in a different layer and each layer is likely to have different values for its properties.

Shader Tips

- You can use the SHIFT key as an accelerator when clicking the arrow buttons; the value will change by ten units at a time. Additionally, you can use the OPTION key (Macintosh) or the ALT key (Windows) when clicking an arrow to step by tenths of a unit. Use both OPTION/ALT and the SHIFT key to step by hundredths of a unit. You also can click the text display and enter a valid number manually.
- The scale values of a transform should not be set to zero or less. It is possible to do so, but it creates a *singular transform,* a transform that cannot be undone. In this movie, the minimum value for the scale inputs is 0.01.
- The `textureTransform` displayed at the foot of the right-hand column is a property of the shader, not a property of the texture. It appears beneath the texture properties display for reasons of space.

The Texture Property Display

The properties of the texture itself are shown in (most of) the right-hand column. This is shown in Figure 10-4.

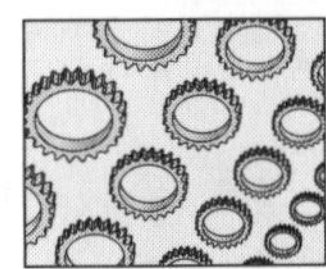

NOTE

In the Shaders.dir movie, you cannot select a texture directly to modify its properties. The layout of the movie means you must select a shader that uses the texture, and then select the layer that contains the texture. Working this way simplifies the interface, but don't let this design choice deceive you. Texture properties are totally independent of shaders.

The Buttons

Beneath the main 3D scene and the Shader and Texture lists, you will see a set of buttons. The Cast… button allows you to link any external castLib to the Shaders.dir movie. Any Bitmap members in the castLib will become available as images for textures.

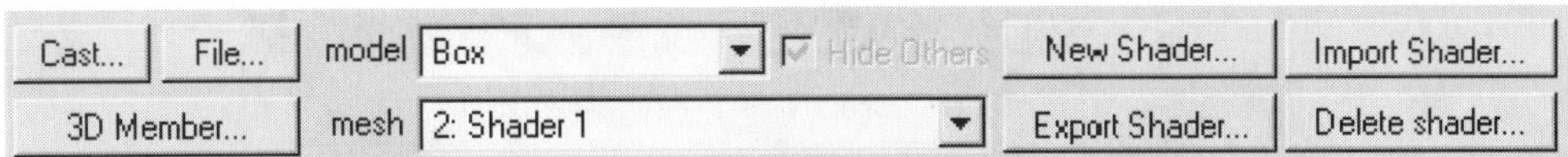

Figure 10-4 *Texture properties are independent of the shader*

The 3D Member… button allows you to choose any Shockwave 3D members in the chosen external castLib as a source of models. This means you can use the Shaders.dir movie in a window to experiment with shaders and textures for a different movie. The only constraint is that the Shockwave 3D member in the other movie must be in an external castLib. This is dealt with in more detail in the next chapter. If no external Shockwave 3D members are available, you can always experiment using the set of default primitive models that appear when the movie is first launched.

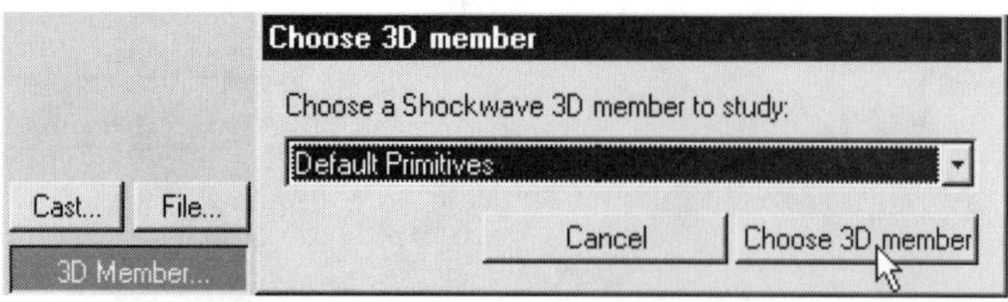

The File… button allows you to load a *.w3d file created by a third-party 3D design program. You will find a number of such files in the 3D Models folder on the Director 8.5 CD-ROM. We'll be looking at a few of them later.

If the 3D world you are studying contains many models, you might find it useful to hide all models but the one you are interested in. You don't need to click the model to select it; you also can use the model pop-up menu. If you click the Hide Others button, all the other models will be temporarily hidden. If the world goes blank, try zooming in with the I key to bring the chosen model into view.

The four buttons below the list display have a double function. Click the Shader or Texture tab above the list to change the action of these buttons. You can drag an item from the list onto any of the buttons (except the Import… button) to apply the button's action to the item. The New… button has an additional function if you use it in this way; it allows you to create a copy of an existing shader or texture with a different name.

Shader and Texture Names

As with models, model resources, groups, lights, and cameras, each shader and texture in a Shockwave 3D member must have a unique name. The Shaders.dir movie uses a simple script to ensure that a different name is proposed each time you create a shader or a texture. It also ensures that the name you have chosen is unique.

Using the Interface

Already, just by looking at how the Shader.dir movie is laid out, you should have gleaned some idea of how shaders and textures are organized. Now it's time to take the movie for a test drive. To start with, launch the Shaders.dir movie on the Stage. Later, once you are used to working with it, you can open it in a window through the Xtras menu while another movie is open on the Stage.

A box model named "Cube" should appear in the Shockwave 3D sprite at the top left. If you click different sides of the box, you will see that the value in the Mesh pop-up menu beneath it updates to show which mesh you clicked, and what shader it is currently using. For the moment, there is only one shader, which all meshes use, so only the mesh number will change.

Creating a Shader

Click the New Shader… button. A dialog box will appear that allows you to name the new shader and choose which type of shader it should be. Accept the default values ("Shader 1", `#standard`), and click Create New Shader. The name of the new shader will now appear in the list of shaders. Click this name and drag the mouse toward the cube model. When you are over one of the front faces of the box model, drop the shader name onto it. You might not notice much difference because the new shader, by default, uses the default texture. In fact, a couple of things have changed:

- The mesh you chose now uses a different shader from the other sides of the box. The mesh number and the new shader name will appear in the Mesh pop-up menu.
- The `shininess` property of the new shader is 30.0. The default shader has a value of zero. To see the effect of this, press the Z key to view the model along the world's z axis; then press the Down arrow to rotate the camera down a little. Now that the camera is pointing slightly upward, the overhead directional light will reflect in the new shader. Rotate the camera to view other faces: they appear matte. We'll look at `shininess` in more detail in a moment.

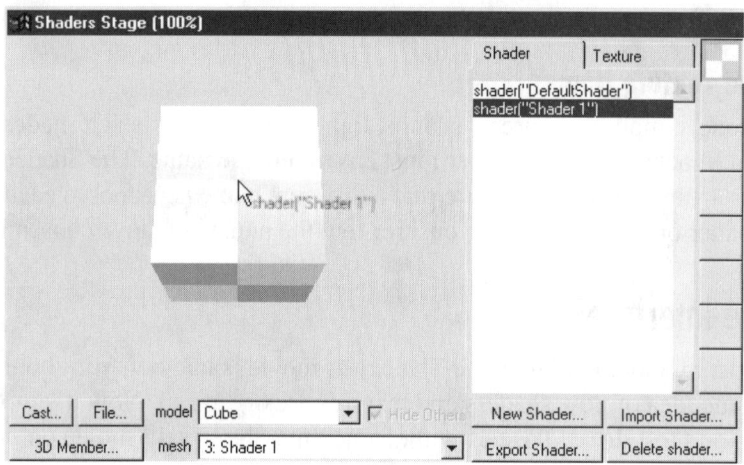

Creating a Texture

Now, click the Texture tab in the center at the top. You should see a list of textures; in fact, currently there is only one. Click the New Texture… button, which appears in place of the New Shader… button, and accept the default name ("Texture 1") proposed by the dialog box. Drag the name of this new texture onto the top button to the right of the list of textures. This sets the first texture of the new shader to your new texture.

The surface of the box with the new shader suddenly goes white. In fact, by default, the new texture has no image, not even the default red-and-white image. Check in the Texture display to the right: both the `width` and `height` of the texture are zero.

Just above the width and height display is a pop-up menu where you can choose a bitmap member whose image will be used for the texture. Choose the first one in the menu: “Texture 32×32×1”. The word “Texture” should appear on the box on the surface with the new shader. If you press the R key, the view should be identical to that in the following illustration.

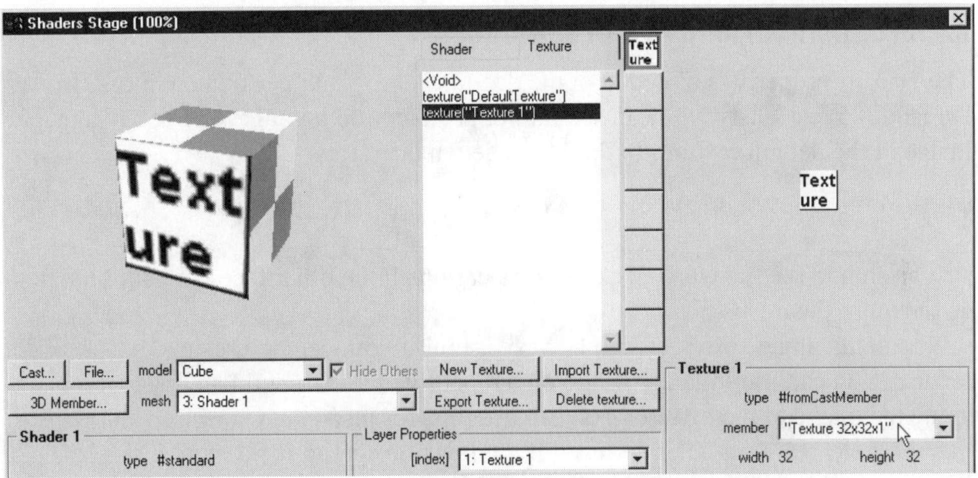

Texture Properties

Textures are more straightforward than shaders. A texture has eight and a half properties:

- `type`
- `width`
- `height`
- `member/image`
- `quality`
- `renderFormat`
- `nearFiltering`
- `compressed`

The first three in my list are read-only; you cannot set them directly. Changing the Member or the image of the texture will modify the value of these properties indirectly. You've already set the `member` property when you selected a Bitmap member from the Member pop-up menu. Before you continue, note the value of the `type` property of the default texture: `#importedFromFile`.

texture.member and texture.image

The `image` property is hinted at in the documentation, but not treated in full. In Director 8.5, curiously, you can set but not get a texture's image. Try it: Change the image of the default texture. In the Message window, type

```
member("3D World").texture(1).image = member(1, "Textures").image
```

You should see the word "Texture" appear on all the other faces of your model, as shown in Figure 10-5.

Setting the image property can be very useful if you want to create a dynamic texture. You can use Imaging Lingo on a repetitive basis to build an image; then apply the image to the texture. You can use this, for instance, with Flash and Real members to create, say, the texture for a television screen inside the 3D world. We'll be looking at this at the end of the next chapter.

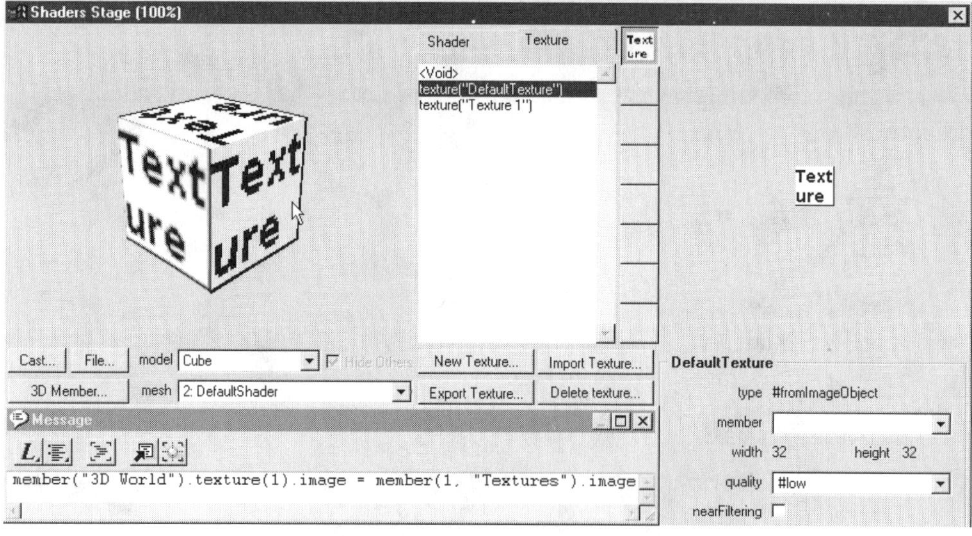

Figure 10-5 *Setting the image of a texture*

width and height

The image used internally by a texture will always be stretched or squeezed so that its dimensions correspond to the nearest power of 2 (1, 2, 4, 8, 16, 32, 64, and so forth). Try setting the member of texture ("Texture 1") to "Stretch 13×12×1"; the resulting texture will be 16×8. Try setting it to "Stretch 13×24×1." This time, the resulting texture will be 16×16.

You can find the original Bitmap members in the Textures castLib. Compare the shape and pattern of the original with the texture that is created from it. In the following illustration, the `nearFiltering` property is set to `FALSE` for the texture for clarity. (See the next section for an explanation of `nearFiltering`.)

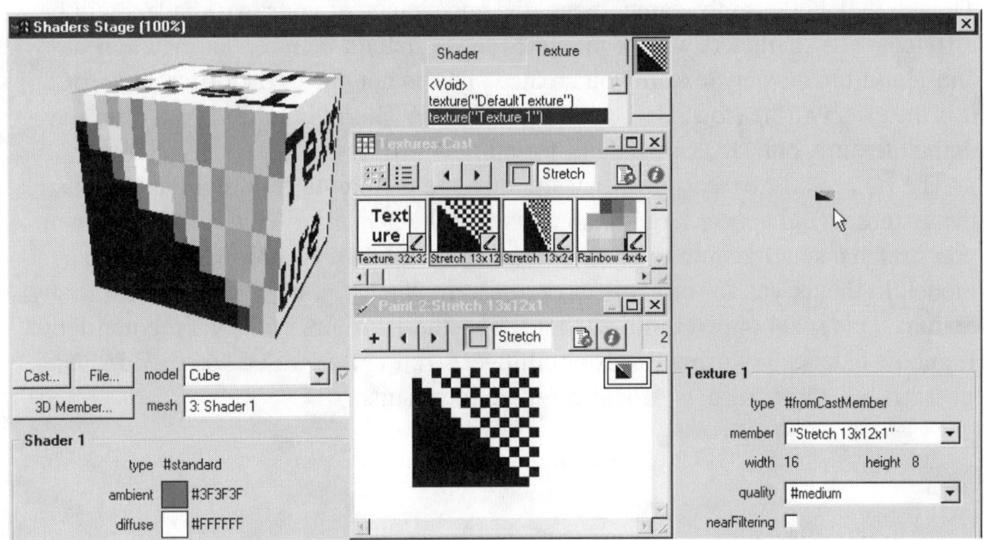

Using internal images whose dimensions correspond to a power of 2 improves processing speed. Converting a nonstandard image size distorts the image. It is thus advisable to create any images that you intend to exploit as textures using the appropriate dimensions. As you will see, you can then use the `textureTransform` shader layer property to scale the texture manually to fit the shader for which it is intended, if necessary.

type

Click one of the faces of the box model that displays the default shader; then look at the value of the `type` property for the default texture that it uses: `#fromImageObject`. The `type` of Texture 1 is `#fromCastMember`. As you might have noted, the `type` of the default red-and-white texture is #importedFromFile. (Now that you've overwritten it, the only way to restore it would be to restart your movie. . . but don't do that yet.)

Textures used in *.w3d files also will be #importedFromFile. The Shader.dir movie can create textures from Bitmap cast members. You can work on the Bitmap member, and then reapply the texture to see the result immediately. The scripts exported by the movie create textures of the type #fromImageObject. Because you cannot get the image of a texture of the type #fromImageObject, you might need to keep a copy of the image itself if you intend to modify it dynamically.

nearFiltering

Though they both use the same image, the appearance of your two shaders will be different. The characters will be pixelated in the default texture, but they appear anti-aliased in the new texture you created. This is not due to the different type; it is the effect of the nearFiltering property. This is initially FALSE for the default texture, but TRUE by default for all new textures.

The nearFiltering property smooths the texture when individual pixels in the texture would appear larger than a pixel in the 3D sprite. This can occur when you stretch a small texture to cover a large area, or when you zoom in close to a model. In the movie, the effect is most apparent when you use the "Rainbow 4×4×4" texture. This is a 4×4 pixel bitmap that shows the 16 colors of the 4-bit color depth Rainbow palette. Try using this for both texture("DefaultTexture") and texture("Texture 1"), and compare the results.

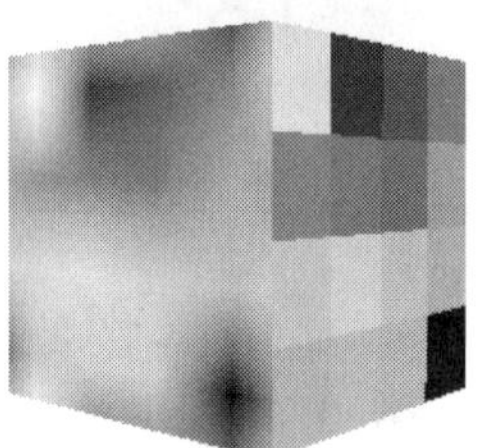

There are several versions of the "Italian" image available, in varying Bitmap member sizes from 16×16×16 up to 128×128×16. Try setting the nearFiltering property to TRUE, and use each of the "Italian …" members in turn. You'll notice that the effect diminishes as the size of the original image increases. Now try zooming in very close to the texture that uses the largest version of the image, and toggle nearFiltering on and off. The more pixelated the texture appears, the greater the effect of the property.

The scaleDown() Command

The `nearFiltering` technique means you can save download time and memory usage by using smaller textures, and compensate by using more processor time. The `scaleDown()` method for textures can be used to free memory manually on-the-fly, if necessary. You can start using a high-quality image for your texture; then scale it down dynamically if the end user is likely to run out of memory. To test this, set the member for your texture to "Italian 128×128×16" and then click the `scaleDown()` button; your initially high-quality image is downgraded so it uses less memory.

Because the data is removed from the computer's memory, the only way to restore the initial quality is to rebuild the texture. The Reset button I provide uses custom Lingo—it is not a built-in command, which explains why the button name appears in italic. The `scaleDown()` method has no effect on textures of the type `#importedFromFile`.

compressed

The `compressed` property of a texture is another way to save memory space, but only when the texture is not currently being used. When you change the `member` or `image` property of a texture, the `compressed` property will automatically be reset to `TRUE`. When a texture is required for rendering, an uncompressed version is copied into the computer's RAM.

quality

When you first applied the same "Texture 32×32×1" image to your new texture and the `texture("DefaultTexture")`, you might have noticed another difference between the two: The value for `quality`. Like the `nearFiltering` property, this can also be used to smooth pixels, but in different circumstances. When you look at a surface from an acute angle, the texture on the surface is foreshortened. If you set the quality of the texture to `#medium` or `#high`, a process known as *mipmapping* is applied. This smooths the foreshortened pixels.

An illustration is less convincing than a test. Press the `R` key to reset the camera in its original position. The top and right side of the cube appear foreshortened. Choose the "Abstract 128×128×32" cast member for the default texture. Watch how the display changes as you set the value of `quality` to `#low`, `#medium`, and `#high`.

In the following illustration, I've used a slightly different setup: the `#quality` on the top surface is set to `#medium`; the value for the other two surfaces is `#low`.

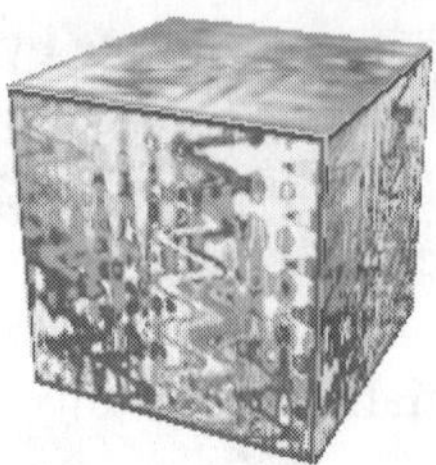

The `#quality` setting for a texture has most effect when the image is large and detailed, and when it is shown at an angle. You might see no difference at all with small images and with images viewed directly from the front. The `#quality` setting is thus not responsible for the differences between the two textures shown earlier in Figure 10-5.

renderFormat

3D implies up-to-date end user machines, with plenty of RAM, a fast processor, and hardware acceleration. Rendering is thus done either in 16-bit or 32-bit mode (although there are ways of forcing the renderer to use fewer colors). 16-bit mode is faster and less memory hungry. The question is, how do you divide the 16 bits between the red, green, blue, and alpha channels? Or, if you want a high-quality 32-bit texture, do you want to use the alpha channel or not? The `renderFormat` property allows you to use the most appropriate setting for each texture.

The Complete Range of Values

Director 8.5 supports four settings for 16-bit rendering: two with alpha channels and two without:

- `#rgba4444` gives you 16 levels of transparency and 16 levels for each primary color, giving you 4,096 colors in all: 4 bits for the alpha channel, and 4 bits each for red, green, and blue.
- `#rgba5551` gives you a greater range of 32,768 colors but transparency is all or nothing.
- `#rgba5550` gives you the same range of colors, with no possibility of transparency.
- `#rgba5650` gives you greater subtlety for opaque images as far as green is concerned, green being the color the eye is most sensitive to.

The 32-bit values follow a similar logic: `#rgba8888` gives you the most flexibility because it includes 256 levels for the alpha channel. A value of `#rgba8880` creates only fully opaque textures. However, an opaque texture can be used to create a transparent shader, as you will see. I've provided three Bitmap members for you to use to test the `renderFormat` property.

The following illustration uses three shaders, each with a different texture and the same "Grayscale 256×256×8" Bitmap cast member. The left surface uses a `renderFormat` setting of `#rgba4444`, so it can show only 16 levels of gray. The top surface uses `#rgba8880`, and can thus display up to 256 levels of gray. The memory requirement is twice as great. The right surface of the cube uses the best 16-bit setting for an opaque image: `#rgba5650`.

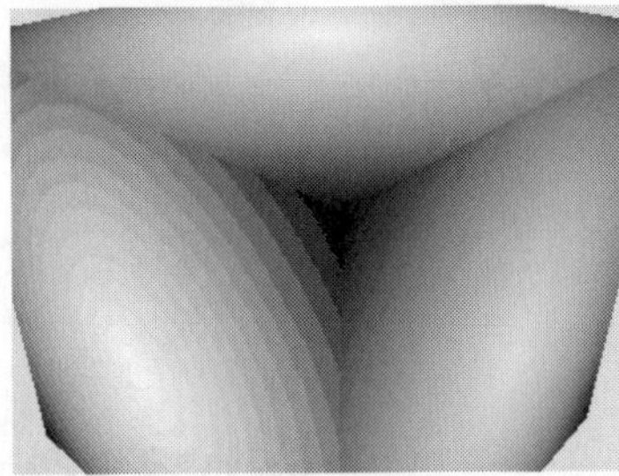

The following image was created by restarting the movie and selecting the Box model in the Model pop-up list. The member of the default texture then was set to "Bear 64×64+alpha1," which has a solid black alpha channel. The `nearFiltering` property was set to `TRUE` and the quality set to `#medium`. The default renderFormat of `#rgba5551` was used. If you set use a `renderFormat` with a value of `0` for the alpha channel, all transparency is lost. The use of nearFiltering makes the differences between `#rgba8888`, `#rgba5551`, and `#rgba4444` less noticeable.

The following image was created using the "Bear 64×64+alpha8" Bitmap member. The grayscale image of the bear is placed in the alpha channel; the color is provided by the rgb channel. The texture at the bottom left uses a `renderFormat`

of #rgba4444, whereas the texture at the top uses #rgba8888. The barely distinguishable image at the bottom right is due to a renderFormat of #rgba5551: only the darkest parts of the bear are visible. I set the bgColor of the Shockwave 3D member to white for clarity.

These examples should make it clear that the correct choice of renderFormat is dictated by the image content.

The Limited Range Available to a Given Machine

Not all video cards support all these renderFormats. You can test the values supported by the video card on a given machine through Lingo:

```
hardwareInfo = getRendererServices().getHardwareInfo()
put hardwareInfo.supportedTextureRenderFormats
-- [#rgba8888, #rgba8880, #rgba5650, #rgba5551, #rgba4444]
```

In the preceding example, the value #rgba5550 is missing. The Director Player will do its best to provide the most appropriate replacement for the missing value (in this case, the higher-quality format of #rgba5650), but you can test this manually in your 3D movies and make the most intelligent adjustments.

One technique for getting the best quality format is to set the renderFormat several times, with your preferred format in the final place. For instance, you could use the following lines of code to get the best format for the transparent texture stored in the variable aTexture, regardless of the computer's hardware:

```
aTexture.renderFormat = #rgba5551
aTexture.renderFormat = #rgba4444
aTexture.renderFormat = #rgba8888
```

The renderFormat pop-up menu in the Shader.dir movie will display only the formats your machine's video card supports.

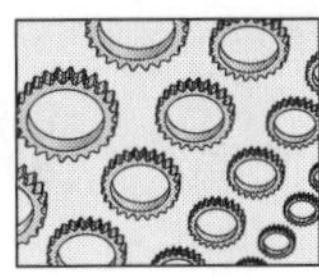

NOTE

There is enormous variety in the 3D capabilities of different machines. If you are aiming at providing the most acceptable performance to a wide audience, you will find yourself writing specific code to handle specific hardware configurations.

Shaders, Lights, and Cameras

In the real world, the way your eye sees an object depends on lights shining on the object and the way the surface of the object reacts to light. In a virtual Shockwave 3D world, you simulate the surface of the object by setting the properties of a shader, and simulate the lights by creating light objects and positioning them in 3D space. You simulate the user's eye by manipulating a camera object (I'll deal with cameras in detail in Chapter 12 and lights in Chapter 13). For now, I'll just explain briefly about the lights and camera in the Shockwave 3D member that you'll be using to study shaders in the Shaders.dir movie.

There are three directional lights in the main 3D World member. The brightest one shines down from directly over your head, at an angle of 45°. This illuminates the front and top surfaces of any model. The second brightest shines from the far-right corner onto the back and right surfaces of any model. A third, dim light, shines up from the left. If you launch the movie and then rotate the default cube model, you should see how the position and brightness of these lights affect the shading of the different faces of the cube.

Specular Light

Only the main overhead light is *specular*, which means it reflects off shiny shaders. In the real world, all light is specular. In a virtual 3D world, calculating how light reflects off an object is a costly business in terms of processing time. As a result, 3D programmers have invented the lights that do not reflect off shiny objects. In Director 8.5, lights are specular by default. You might be able to increase performance by switching off the `specular` property of all but the most crucial lights.

shininess

As you saw when you created your first shader earlier in the section "Using the Interface," shaders have a `shininess` property, which is set to `30.0` (per cent) by default. Specular lights will reflect from shaders whose `shininess` is not `0`. Non-specular lights will not reflect. Since the two secondary lights are non-specular, the models you are working with will appear to be shiny only when seen from the front.

I have set these lights up like this on purpose so that you can see what happens when shininess and specularity combine, and what happens when they don't. Understanding shaders is all about understanding how different properties combine. Shininess and specularity is just the first of many similar compound situations you will encounter.

Camera Manipulation

As you work through this section, you will often be manipulating the camera. The scene you are observing never moves; you move the camera around it. When you are working with symmetrical models, it is easy to become disoriented, so that you are not sure which way you are facing, whether you are upright or upside down, and how you stand in relation to the lights. I recommend that you make frequent use of the keys X, Y, and Z to realign your point of view along a known axis, the R key to revert to the initial position, and the C key to obtain a cavalier view. You can use the SHIFT key with X, Y, and Z to look up the chosen axis rather than down, and with the C to obtain a cavalier view from below.

It also can help to swap models for a moment. The cylinder, mesh, and hemisphere models are asymmetrical. Switching briefly to one of these models and then back again can give you a clue to which way you are facing.

General Shader Properties

As noted earlier, every shader has a large number of properties, though these properties may not all be used. Shader properties can be divided into three groups:

- Properties that apply to the shader as a whole, which I show in the left-hand column of the Shader.dir movie
- Properties that may be applied differently to different layers in the shader, which I show in the central column and at the foot of the right-hand column
- Special properties that apply to shaders of the types `#painter`, `#newsprint`, and `#engraver`.

I'll deal with each of these groups of properties separately, starting with the general properties.

ambient

The `ambient` property of a shader defines the way it reacts to the 3D member's Ambient light. By default, the value of this property is `rgb( 63, 63, 63 )`. This is a fairly dark gray. It means that the shader will take on the color of the Ambient light at about a quarter of its intensity. I've set the `ambientColor` of the member (3D World) to white: `rgb( 255, 255, 255 )`. Let's modify the `ambient` property of the default shader and the member's `ambientColor`, and study how these interact.

Relaunch the Shaders.dir movie, so that you start over from scratch. Press the SHIFT key and C simultaneously. This will place the camera beneath the model, where it can see three faces of the cube, one lit by each of the directional lights. Now click the `ambient` color chip. The -picker.dir movie will open in a window and allow you to select a new color. If you hold the SHIFT key down while you drag one of the sliders, all three sliders will move together to give you a choice of grays.

If you reduce the brightness of the `ambient` color, the cube model will react less to the Ambient light. If you increase it beyond `rgb( 192, 192, 192 )`, all faces of the cube model will appear without any shading at all: the shader's reaction to the Ambient light is sufficient to fill in any shading due to the dimness of the directional lights.

Now try using a color rather than a shade of gray. Set the shader's `ambient` property to yellow: `rgb( 255, 255, 0 )`. The model will appear yellow because the shader is reacting to all the red and green light in the member's Ambient light. What happens if the member's Ambient light is not white? Open castLib 2 (Media) and click member 2 (3D World). Now open the Property Inspector at the 3D Model display and change the color of the Ambient light, as shown in Figure 10-6.

If you make the Ambient light blue, the model will appear gray. If you set it to cyan or green, the model will be colored green. If you set it to magenta or red, the model will be colored red. Why is this? Why do different values of Ambient light give the same result?

There is no blue component in the color yellow. You have set your shader to react fully to only red and green light. The shader ignores the blue component in cyan and magenta light; it only reacts to the green or red component. Blue light is invisible to your shader. The `ambient` property of the shader serves as a filter, similar to `#transparent` ink for sprites and in Imaging Lingo. The shader compares its ambient color property with the color of the ambient light falling on it, and it responds to the lower value for each of the red, green, and blue components.

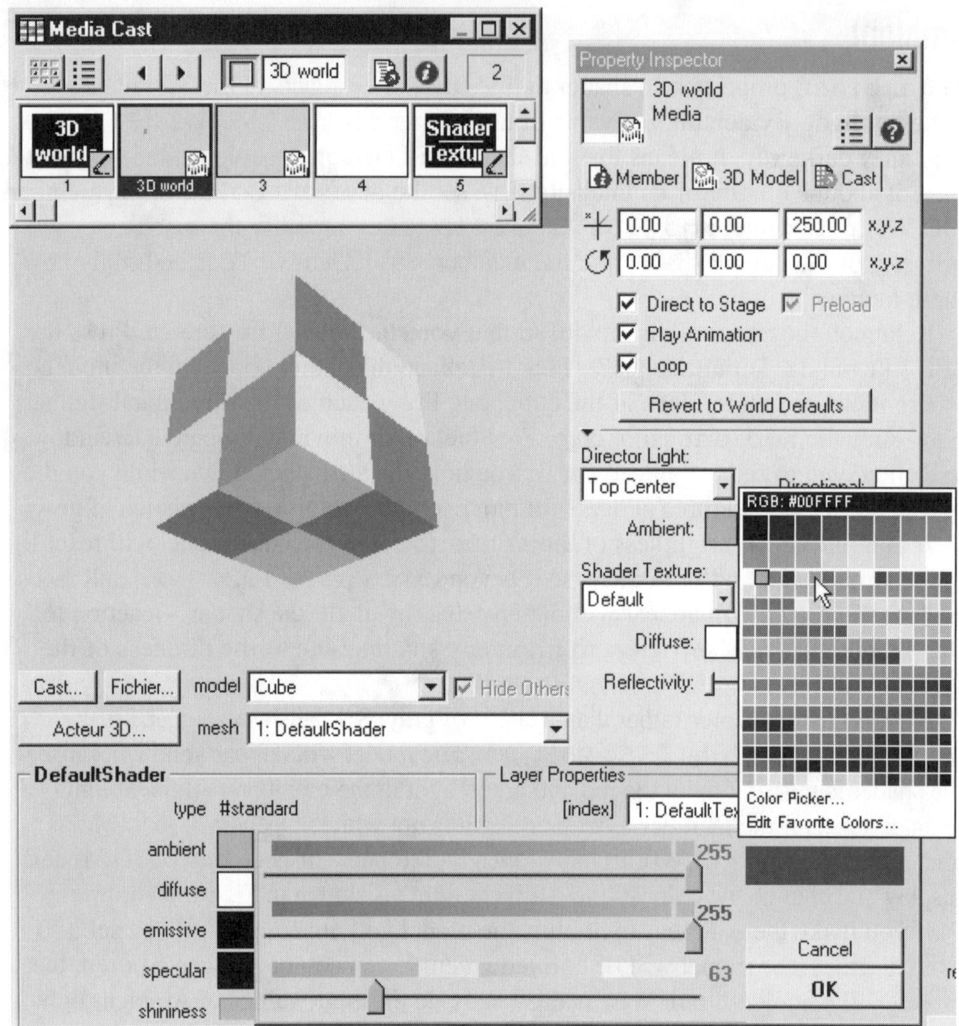

Figure 10-6 *Using the Property Inspector to change the color of the Ambient light*

Experiment with the light and shader ambient colors until the relationship between the two becomes clear. When you're done, reset the `ambient` property to `rgb( 63, 63, 63 )`, or simply restart the movie.

diffuse

Now try altering the value of the `diffuse` color for the shader. If nothing seems to happen, don't be alarmed. There's a second property that deals with diffuse color:

useDiffuseWithTexture. By default, this second property is FALSE. There are two ways to make the diffuse color property have an effect. One is to remove the texture. (Click the Texture tab and drag the <Void> item onto the first layer button. Drag the texture("DefaultTexture") back onto the button before you continue.) If you want to use a texture with your shader, the other method is to set useDiffuseWithTexture to TRUE. You'll find a check box that does this at the bottom left.

A shader's diffuse color is independent of the Ambient light. To verify this, set the shader's diffuse color to any color you like, and the ambient property to black. Now alter the color of the member's Ambient light. The color of the model will not change at all.

You can, however, combine the diffuse color with the ambient color. The two will be added together. The value for ambient is more heavily weighted: red ambient and green diffuse, for example, will give you orange, not a pure yellow. When you subsequently alter the color of the member's Ambient light, the change in the color of the model is due entirely to the shader's ambient color.

emissive

Indeed, you can even combine a third color, the emissive color. Try the following test. Press SHIFT-C to view the cube model from a position where each visible face is lit by a light with a different brightness. Set the shader's ambient color to red and the diffuse color to green. The result, as I have said, will be orange. Now click the emissive color chip and gradually add blue. Do you see how the color of the darker faces of the model reacts to the blue emissive color sooner than the lighter faces?

The emissive property makes a shader appear to glow in the dark. Where light is strong, it has little effect. It does not produce any light that would affect other models. You can, however, place a light inside a model, and thus combine the emissive appearance of the model and the properties of the light object.

specular

The specular color of a shader does not affect the whole surface of the shader as the other color properties do. It determines the color that light reflected from the shader will take on. It thus will have no effect at all unless the shader is shiny. Try altering the value for specular; you will see no change unless you set the shininess property to some value other than zero. Even then, only light from a light object whose specular property is TRUE will affect the shader.

Press R to reset the camera to a position where you can observe reflections from the specular light at the top center of the world. Set the shininess of the default shader to 4.0; then alter the color of the `specular` property as you see fit. Notice how only the front face appears to be affected. The top face receives specular light, too, but the angle is such that no specular light is reflected toward the camera. Press the Up arrow to rotate the camera over the top of the model. You should see the effect of the specular light diminish on the front face and increase on the top face. Changing the angle of the camera changes the amount of specular light reflected toward it. Now rotate the camera around the model using the left or right arrows. However you turn, the faces that receive no specular light do not change color at all.

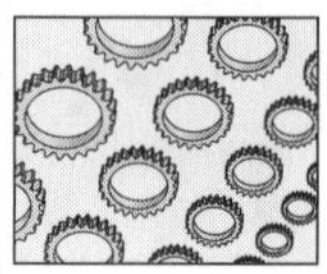

NOTE

*Experimenting with the color picker and the 3D member's Ambient light is useful for understanding the concepts involved. The arrangements of colors you create need not be realistic at this stage. You'll get a chance to look at realistic color arrangements when we use the Shaders.dir movie to study the *.w3d files on the Director 8.5 CD-ROM.*

DEBUGGING TIP

None of the color properties addressed in the preceding has any effect if the `blendFunction` *of any layer in the shader is set to* `#replace`*. The* `#replace blendFunction` *has a similar function to Copy ink for sprites: It covers any image or color information present in lower layers.*

shininess

You've already seen how specular lights will not reflect in a shader unless the shader's `shininess` property is set to a value other than zero. Did you notice that the shader is shiniest when its `shininess` is set to 1? The shader is matte if its `shininess` is set to zero and brilliant if it is set to 1. Increasing the value decreases the effect of specular lights: A value of 100 is only slightly more shiny than zero.

blend and transparent

Like `specular` and `shininess` or `diffuse` and `useDiffuseWithTexture`, `blend` and `transparent` are two properties that work together but don't work separately. Actually, the situation is even more complex: When using Director 8.5 with certain renderers on certain machines, certain `blendFunction` values for the texture layer of the shader might override transparency—and, as if that isn't enough, you might need to use a secret handshake to set the value for `blendFunction` in a way that the 3D Xtra can handle. I call this a quirk, but you might have another name for it. If, by the time you read this, a newer version of Director is available, the situation might be simpler than that I describe in the following.

Making a Semitransparent Shader

Let's start with the simplest situation: restart the Shaders.dir movie so that the values for the default shader are reset to their original values. The initial values for the properties that interest us here are as follows:

- `blend`: `100.0`
- `transparent`: `TRUE`
- `blendFunction` (for the first texture layer): `#multiply`

Choose the Box model in the Model pop-up menu. This is a box model with no top, and created with both front and back faces. It gives you the best visual feedback on the transparency of the shaders.

A Rendering Quirk

Try changing the value of the `blend` property. If you are using the DirectX 5.2 renderer, nothing happens. Set the `blend` to, say, `50.0`; then set the `blendFunction` of the first texture layer to `#add`. Now set the `blendFunction` back to `#multiply`, as shown in Figure 10-7. The shader retains its capacity for transparency.

Now, set the `blendFunction` to `#blend`, and back to `#multiply`. The shader has once again lost its capacity for transparency with a `blendFunction` setting of `#multiply`. It appears as certain properties of the shader are not set or reset correctly when you change the value of `blendFunction`. You can force the recalcitrant renderer to respect the blend value by setting the `renderFormat` of the texture to a value with no alpha channel, such as `#rgba5650`.

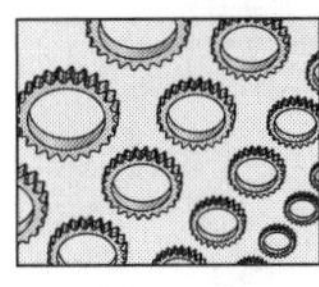

NOTE

You might not experience this on your machine, but you need to take it into account when you are writing for machines that have different configurations. Try setting the renderer to DirectX 5.2 by hand to see if you can reproduce the situation; try setting the renderer to Software to make it disappear (see Figure 10-8).

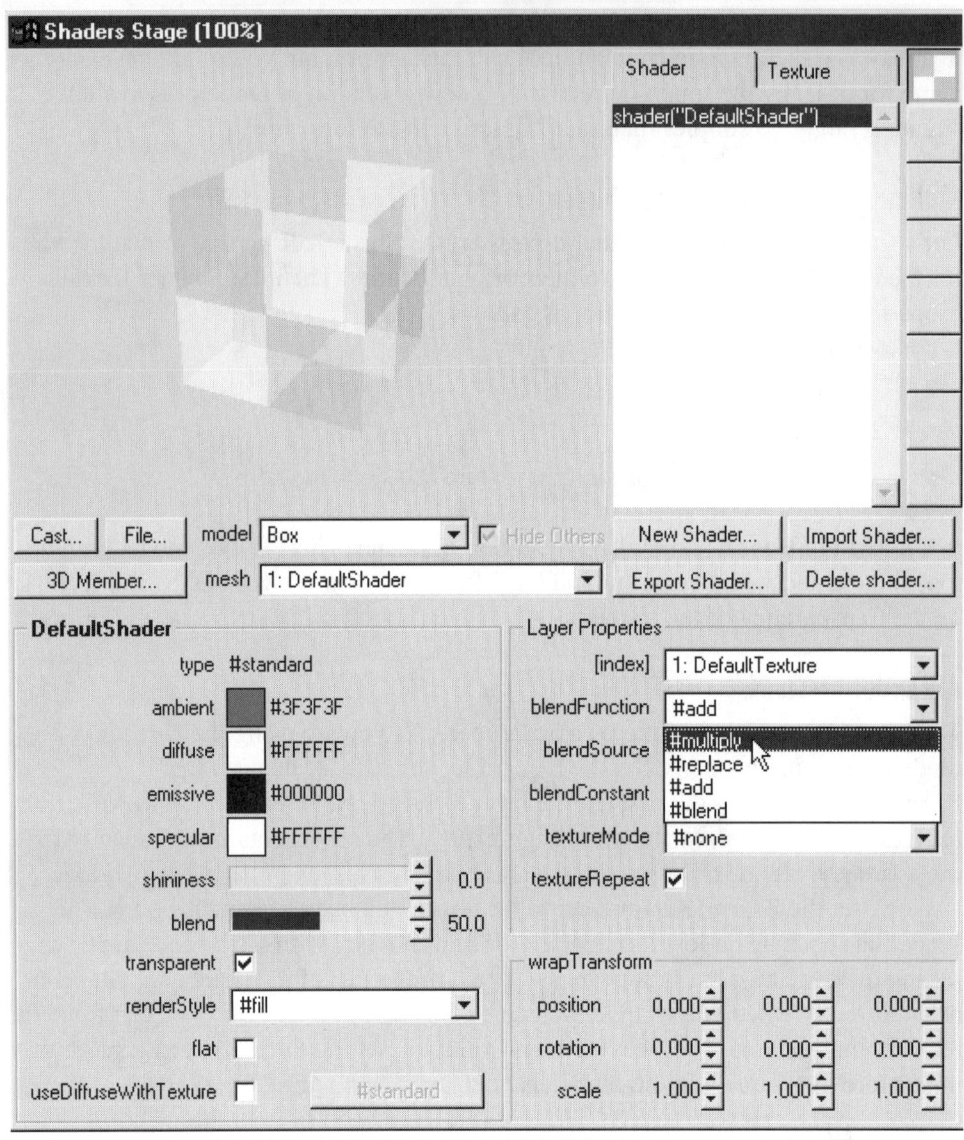

Figure 10-7 *Testing how different blendFunctions affect transparency*

It seems safe to assume that if a feature is available in Software rendering mode, it is intended to be available in other modes, too. (The reverse is not true: Software rendering mode is much slower, so certain processor-intensive features have been omitted from this mode.) In Software rendering mode, the `blend` value for the shader has an effect, regardless of the value for `blendFunction` of any texture layer. With certain DirectX 5.2 drivers, a value of `#replace` for `blendFunction`

Figure 10-8 *Choosing a renderer for your movie*

can cancel out transparency, whereas a value of `#blend` can interfere with the rendering of the texture. If you need to create shaders that use these features and can't wait for Macromedia or the driver manufacturers to provide a point upgrade, you might be forced to use Software rendering for your project. The alternative is to juggle with the order in which you set and reset the value for `blendFunction` and textures that have a non-alpha-channel `renderFormat`.

Another blendFunction Quirk

While we are on the subject, let's jump ahead to look at how you can blend a texture layer onto the layers beneath it, which brings to light another manifestation of the quirk you have just seen. Choose Software rendering and restart your movie to reinitialize all properties. Choose the Box model in the Model pop-up. Set the `diffuse` value for the texture to yellow, `rgb( 255, 255, 0 )`, and click the `useDiffuseWithTexture` button. Now choose `#blend` in the `blend Function` pop-up menu for the first texture layer of the shader, and modify the value for `blendConstant`. You should be able to vary the color of the shader smoothly from solid yellow through to the red-and-white checker pattern. Choose a value somewhere between the two extremes.

Now switch the renderer to DirectX 5.2; the red-and-white texture disappears. Choose `#replace` in the `blendFunction` pop-up menu; then switch back to `#blend`. The red-and-white texture reappears. Now set the `blend` value of the shader to something other than `100.0`. The red-and-white texture disappears again. Switch back to Software rendering mode—here at least you can have a blended texture on a semitransparent shader.

The moral of the story is clear: test your shaders on all your target machines, using all the renderers that your end users are likely to own. You can also help Macromedia to fix these problems by reporting them to wish-director@macromedia.com. Be sure that your report includes all the relevant information concerning the computer manufacturer and model, operating system, hardware, renderer, and so on. This information will allow the Director Engineering Team to reproduce the symptoms you observe.

Simulating Glass

Transparent shaders can, of course, be used to simulate glass. The simplest way to do this is to remove the texture from the shader altogether. Click the Texture tab and drag the `<Void>` item onto the button for the first shader layer, as shown in Figure 10-9. You'll need to add a certain amount of `shininess` and turn the camera to a position where it catches the reflected light. This works well with all renderers.

You can heighten the effect by using a `specularLightMap`, rather than a simple specular color. The `specularLightMap` command applies a given texture to the fifth layer and automatically sets certain values for both that layer and the first texture layer. We'll look at this and the other shortcut commands for setting the `textureMode` shortly. The following illustration is just to whet your appetite. In the Shaders.dir movie, you can right-click (Windows) or CTRL-click (Macintosh) a texture to display a contextual menu that allows you to apply these commands. We'll look at this in more detail shortly. Unfortunately, the `specularLightMap` and the other multitexture features need to be tweaked before they work acceptably in Software rendering mode.

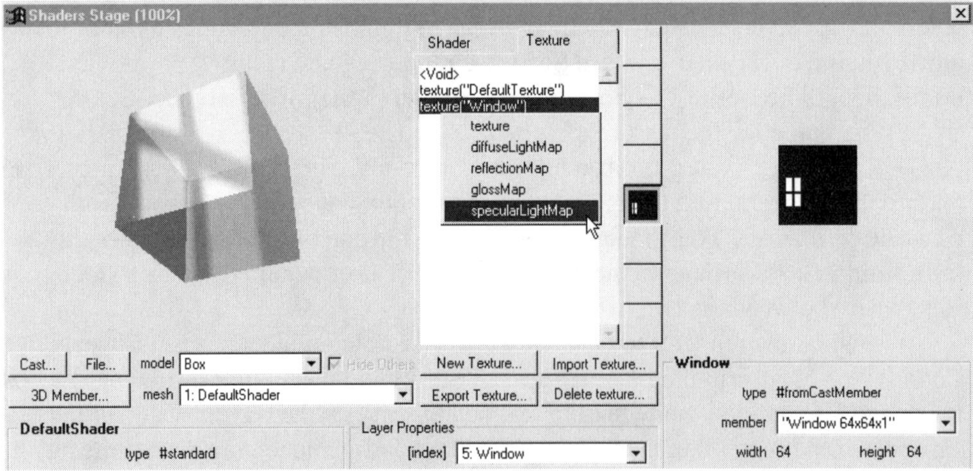

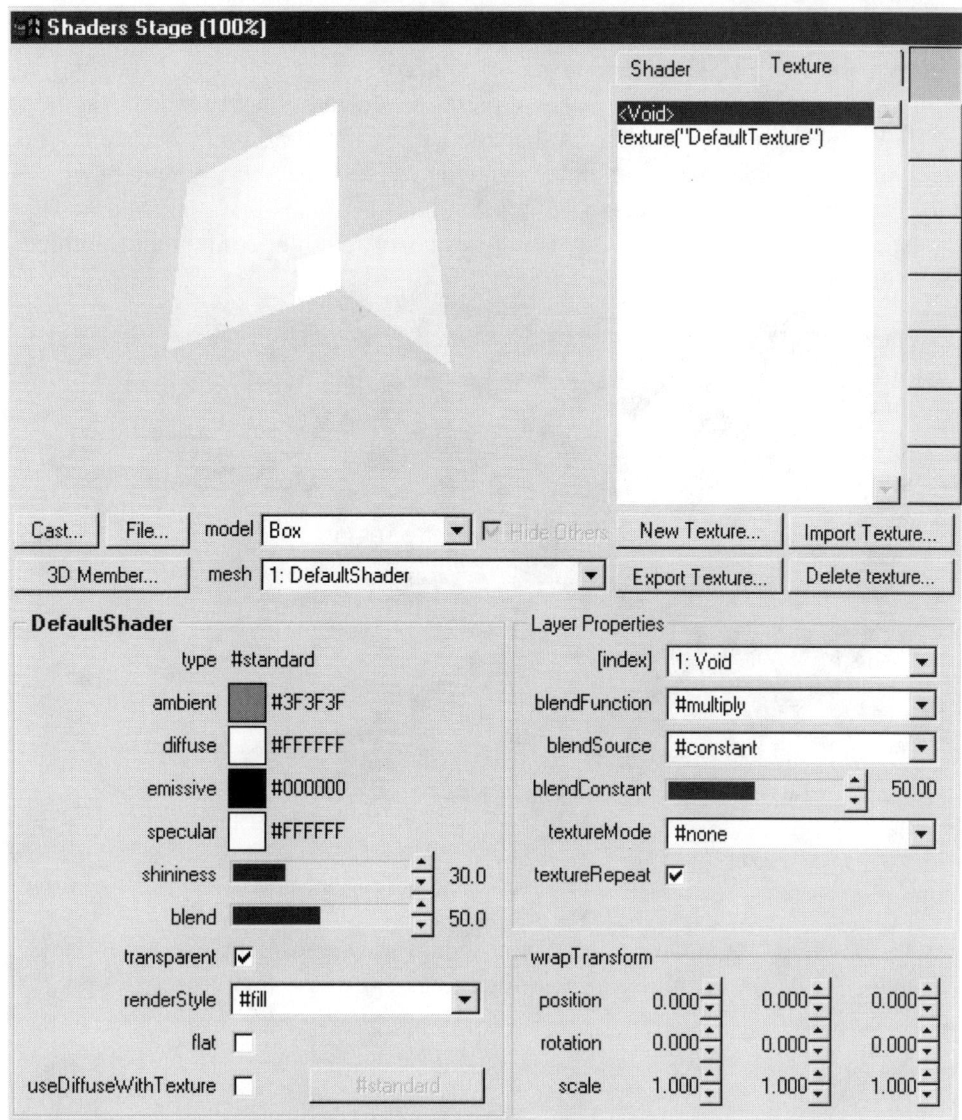

Figure 10-9 *Setting a shader to simulate glass*

renderStyle

The `renderStyle` property allows you to display a shader so that only the vertex points of mesh are visible (`#point`), or so that just the outlines of the faces of the mesh are visible (#wire). These values are mainly useful while authoring. They can help you visualize the faces and vertex points of a given model for debugging purposes. For playback, you are likely to prefer the default #fill render style mode.

The following illustration shows shaders that use the #wire and #point render style modes, applied to the Box model. As you can see, the #wire render style might break faces up in an unexpected fashion if one of the vertex points used for the faces is outside the sprite's display area. In Software rendering mode, all three renderStyle values act as #fill.

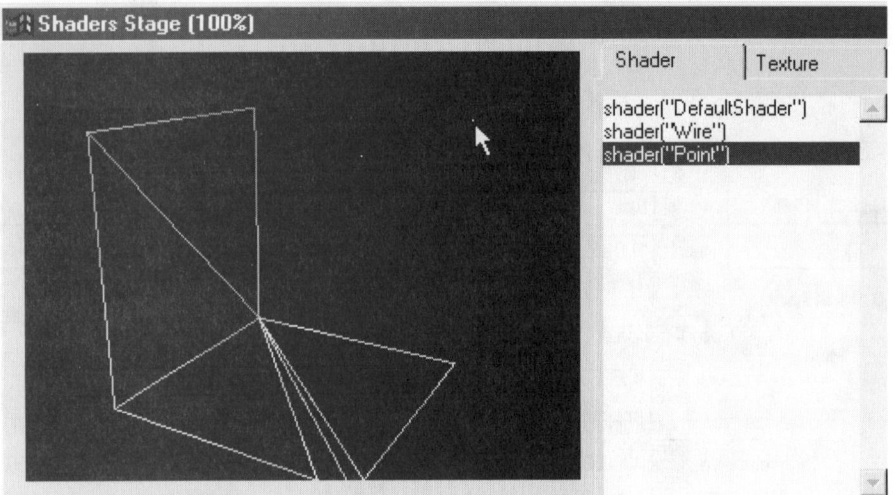

flat

To see the effect of the flat property, you should use the Model pop-up menu under the main 3D sprite to choose a model with curved sides, such as the cylinder or the cone.

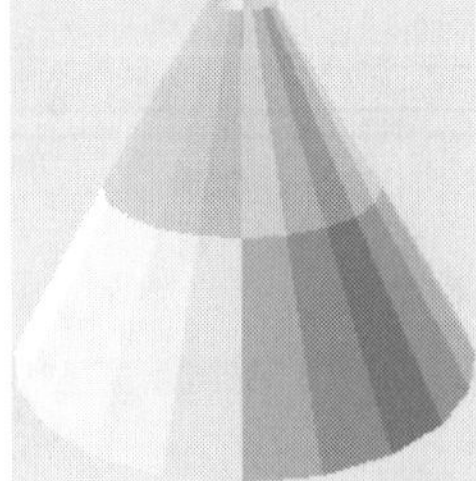

Flat shading is easier to render because it creates a solid area of color for each face in the mesh. When a shader's `flat` value is set to `FALSE` (which it is by default), a more processor-intensive technique called *Gouraud shading* is used.

Gouraud shading treats each pixel in each face separately. Each vertex of the face has a *normal,* an imaginary line that points directly out of the surface at that point. Faces are triangular; a face thus has three normals: one at each of the three vertices. If the face is flat, all three vertices point in the same direction. If the vertices point in different directions, the face can be rendered to appear curved. If you use `flat` shading on such a face, the average of the three vertices is used for the whole face, making it appear flat anyway. If you use Gouraud shading, an adjusted normal is calculated for each pixel on the face. The value of this adjusted color depends on the pixel's relative distance from each of the three vertex points.

When you are using directional and specular lights, the normal at a given point determines how much light is reflected from that point toward the camera. In other words, the color of a pixel depends on the value used for its normal.

In short, if you choose to use flat shading, the processor has less work to do. If you choose to use Gouraud shading, faces are rendered to look as if they are curved.

useDiffuseWithTexture

As you saw in the earlier "diffuse" section, setting `useDiffuseWithTexture` to `FALSE` prevents the diffuse color from having any effect when you apply a texture to the shader. If all the texture layers in the shader are `VOID`, `useDiffuseWithTexture` has no effect—the `diffuse` color is used in any case.

Shader Layer Properties

So far, you have seen how a shader appears when used with a basic texture or with no texture at all. Now we are going to look at the ways in which the shader can modify the texture's appearance and how you can create a shader from multiple texture layers. You had a brief foretaste of this in the illustration of the window reflected in a transparent shader.

Layer Properties and Layer Property Lists

You can use up to eight layers of texture in a shader. Eight is chosen as a suitable power of two; in practice, you probably will never set more than five at a time. The more texture layers you use, the longer the shader takes to render. Simple shaders give better performance than multitextured ones.

There are eight properties that you can set for each layer. We'll study these in this order:

```
texture
blendFunction
blendSource
blendConstant
textureMode
wrapTransform
textureTransform
textureRepeat
```

There are two Lingo keywords associated with each of these properties. For the `texture` property, for instance, the keywords are `texture` and `textureList`. The list property associated with `blendSource` is `blendSourceList`, and so on. The `...List` keyword gives you access to an eight-item list, where each item refers to a specific layer. Try this in the Message window:

```
put member("3D World").shader("DefaultShader").textureModeList
-- [#none, #none, #none, #none, #none, #none, #none, #none]
```

For example, `textureModeList[2]` allows you to get and set the texture mode used in the second layer.

Setting Layer Properties

The simple version of the keyword gives you a shortcut to the first item in the list. The expression `aShader.textureRepeat` provides the same result as the expression `aShader.textureRepeatList[1]`.

Setting the `...List` as a whole to a given value has a somewhat unexpected result: Instead of changing the value of the `...List` property, it changes the values of all the items in the list. In Director 8.5, you will provoke a script error (see Figure 10-10) if you try to set any of the `...List` properties to a list. As a result, you must set the items in each list individually. You can, however, get the whole list as usual.

Shortcuts to Setting a Particular Layer

Because each property for a given layer is stored in a different list, setting the properties for a given layer can require several lines of code. To simplify your task, there are four shortcut commands for standard shader map features that set all the necessary values of a given layer in one go. These are

- `diffuseLightMap` (layer 2)
- `reflectionMap` (layer 3)
- `glossMap` (layer 4)
- `specularMap` (layer 5)

The basic texture goes in layer 1.

In the Shader.dir movie, you can apply one of these commands to a given texture by using a right-click (Windows) or a CTRL-click (Macintosh) on a texture in the list of textures, and choosing the command from the contextual menu that appears. A tick in the contextual menu indicates where the texture in question has been applied as a map. This is illustrated in Figure 10-11 and treated in depth in the "textureMode"

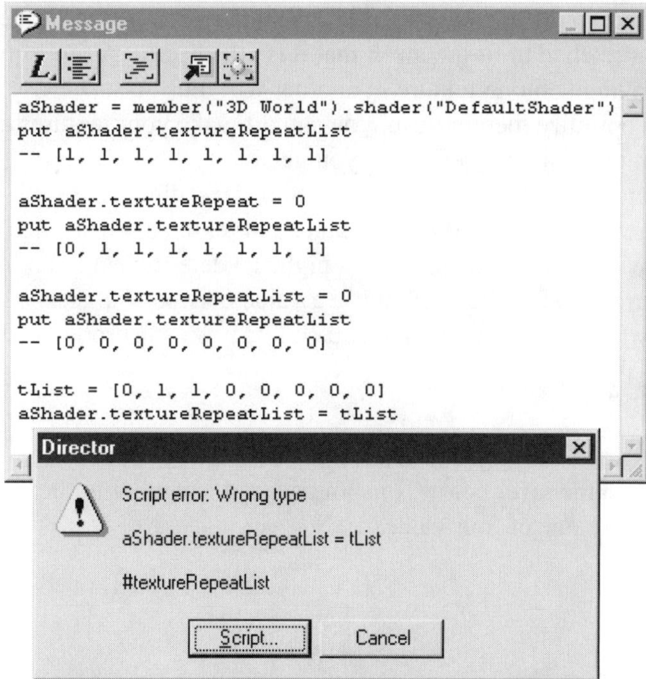

Figure 10-10 *The script error provoked by setting a textureRepeatList to a list*

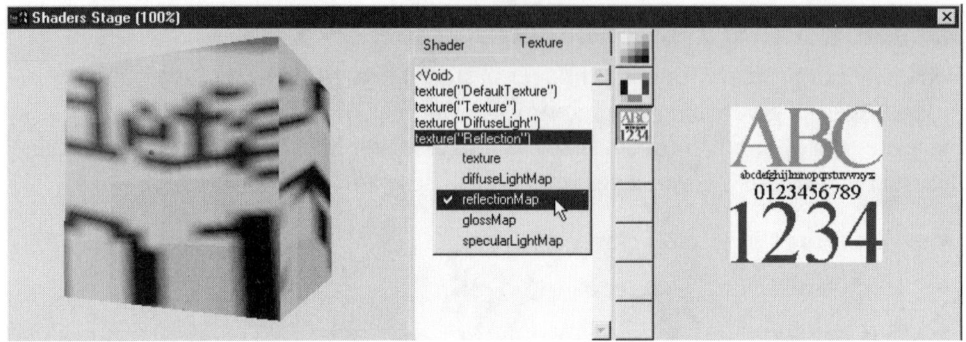

Figure 10-11 *Applying one of the standard shader map features*

section later in this chapter. You are, of course, not limited to using these built-in settings, but studying how they work can help you understand how to create your own custom settings.

texture

You have already seen the effect of setting the texture for a shader. You can apply a different texture to different layers. The layers are stretched to fit the shader. The shader then is stretched to fit the mesh that it is attached to. A tiny square texture in one layer and a huge oblong texture in another will thus be superposed exactly inside the shader. To optimize memory use, you should make your textures as small as you reasonably can to obtain the definition you need.

Because textures can be different shapes and sizes, dimensions inside the shader are not measured in pixels or 3D world units. All textures are deemed to be 1.0 shader-width wide and 1.0 shader-height high. To determine a point in a texture inside a shader, you therefore need to use a value between 0.0 and 1.0. You'll see this in action when we look at the `textureTransform` property.

blendFunction

The `blendFunction` property determines how the texture in one layer is blended into the texture in the layer below. In some ways it is similar to the `ink` property of a sprite. It can take one of four values:

```
#multiply
#replace
#add
#blend
```

The default value is `#multiply`.

#replace

The #replace value is like Copy ink. A shader layer that uses #replace will be opaque. Lower numbered layers will be completely hidden. As a result, #replace is really justified only in the lowest numbered layer, although you might want to use it temporarily in other layers while authoring as a debugging techniques.

#multiply

The #multiply value acts as follows for each pixel in the shader layer:

```
-- lowerColor is the color created from the lower shader layers
-- layerColor is the color provided by the texture in this layer
resultingColor = rgb( 0, 0, 0 )
resultingColor.red   = (lowerColor.red   * layerColor.red)   / 255.0
resultingColor.green = (lowerColor.green * layerColor.green) / 255.0
resultingColor.blue = (lowerColor.blue * layerColor.blue) / 255.0
```

This algorithm filters colors and makes them darker. Some examples are shown in this table.

Lower Color	Layer Color	Resulting Color
Black rgb(0, 0, 0)	Any color	Black rgb(0, 0, 0)
Any color	Black rgb(0, 0, 0)	Black rgb(0, 0, 0)
White rgb(255, 255, 255)	Any color	Layer color
Any color	White rgb(255, 255, 255)	Lower color
Red rgb(255, 0, 0)	Yellow rgb(255, 255, 0)	Red rgb(255, 0, 0)
Yellow rgb(255, 255, 0)	Cyan rgb(0, 255, 255)	Green rgb(0, 255, 0)
Gray blue rgb(64, 64, 128)	Yellow green rgb(128, 255, 0)	Dark green rgb(32, 64, 0)

You can test this for yourself by following these steps with the Shaders.dir movie:

1. Restart the movie to clear all changes.
2. Click the Texture tab.
3. Create two new textures; name them Vertical and Horizontal.
4. Drag texture("Vertical") onto the first shader layer button.
5. Choose the texture "Vertical 16×16×8" for this first layer.
6. Set the nearFiltering of the texture to FALSE.
7. Set the blendFunction to #replace for the first layer.
8. Drag texture("Horizontal") onto the second layer button.

9. Choose the texture "Horizontal 16×16×8" for this second layer.
10. Set the `nearFiltering` of the texture to `FALSE`.
11. Set blendFunction to `#multiply` for the second layer.
12. Press Z key and then I to zoom in on one face of the cube model.

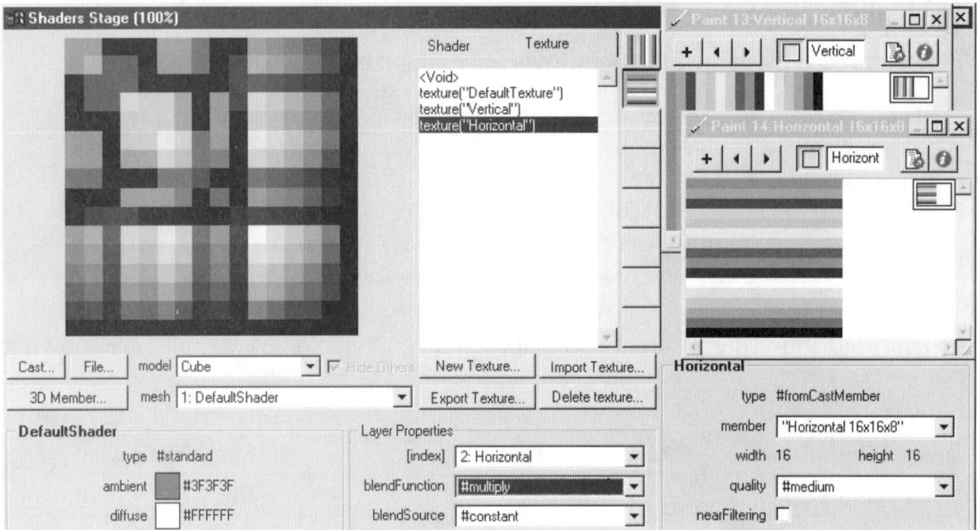

You'll see the original colors along the diagonal from the top left to the bottom right.

#add

The `#add` value for `blendFunction` is similar to the Add Pin ink for sprites. Here is how it works:

```
-- lowerColor is the color created from the lower shader layers
-- layerColor is the color provided by the texture in this layer
resultingColor = rgb( 0, 0, 0 )
resultingColor.red   = min (lowerColor.red   + layerColor.red,   255)
resultingColor.green = min (lowerColor.green + layerColor.green, 255)
resultingColor.blue = min (lowerColor.blue + layerColor.blue, 255)
```

This makes colors brighter, and might bleach them to white. To test this, simply change the `blendFunction` for the second layer of the shader in the Shaders.dir movie to `#add`.

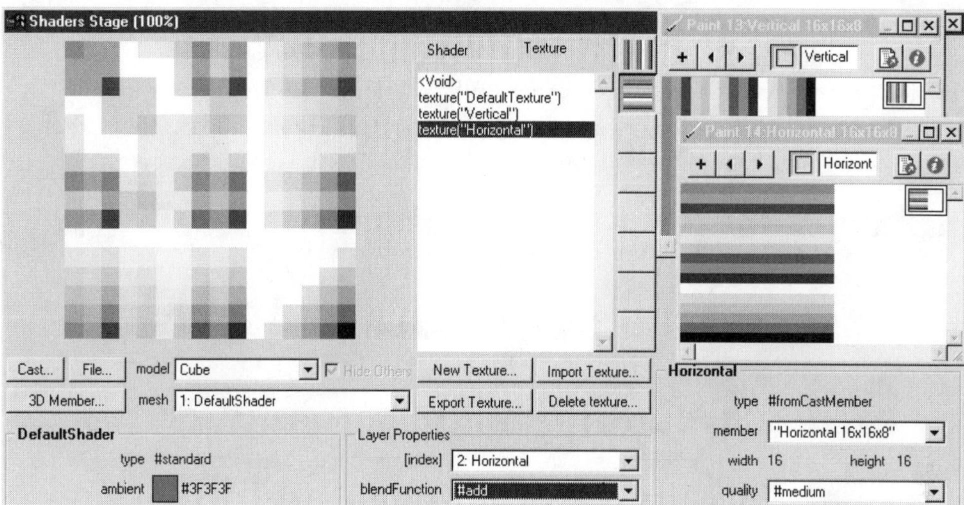

#blend

When you use the value #blend for the blendFunction of a shader layer, two additional properties might take effect: blendSource and blendConstant. If the blendFunction is not set to #blend, the values of these two additional properties are ignored.

If blendSource is set to #alpha, the blendConstant property is ignored. In this case, the value used for blending depends on the information in the texture image's alpha channel. This might be different for each pixel of the texture's image.

If blendSource is set to #constant, then the color applied by the shader layer depends on the value of blendConstant for the layer, and is calculated as follows:

```
-- lowerColor is the color created from the lower shader layers
-- layerColor is the color provided by the texture in this layer
-- blendRatio = blendConstant / 100.0 -- varies from 0.0 to 1.0
resultingColor.red   = lowerColor.red * (1 - blendRatio) \
                     + layerColor.red * blendRatio
resultingColor.green = lowerColor.green * (1 - blendRatio) \
                     + layerColor.green * blendRatio
resultingColor.blue  = lowerColor.blue * (1 - blendRatio) \
                     + layerColor.blue * blendRatio
```

When blendConstant is set to 100.0, the result is equivalent to using #replace for the blendFunction. You can test this by setting the blendFunction for the second layer of the shader in the Shaders.dir movie to #blend. If the blendSource is set to constant, you will be able to alter the effect of the shader layer by modifying the value for blendConstant.

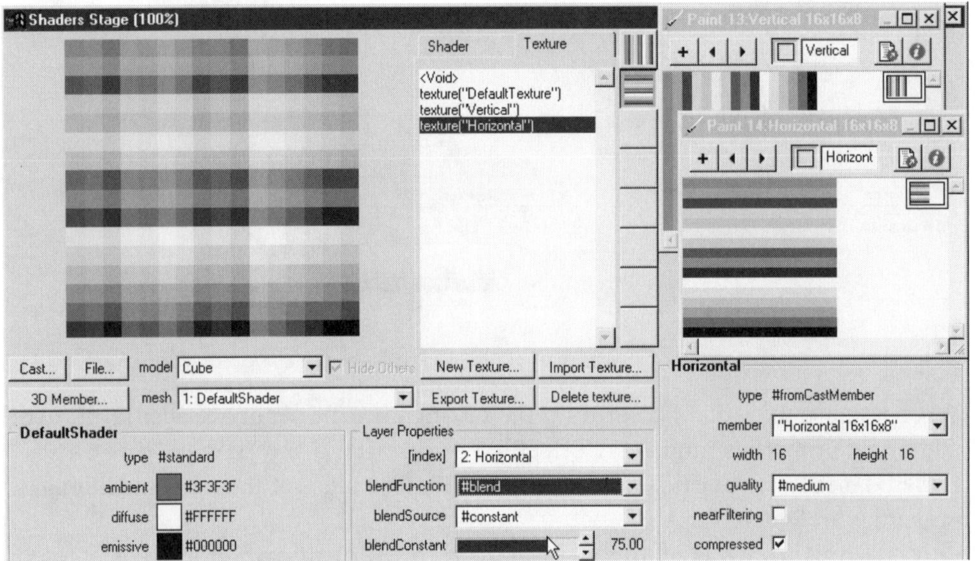

blendSource

The blendSource property can take one of two values: #alpha or #constant. The value of blendSource is ignored unless the blendFunction property for the shader layer is set to #blend. The effect of the value #constant is illustrated in the preceding. Using a value #alpha means the blend is determined by the alpha channel of the texture image. You can test this by using the "Bear 64×64+alpha1" and "Bear 64×64+alpha8" images for texture for the second layer of the shader. Remember to set the renderFormat of the texture to #rgba8888 to see the "Bear 64×64+alpha8" image correctly.

Don't be alarmed if you see nothing appear; the transparent property for the shader as a whole might need to be set to FALSE before the alpha channel texture is rendered. You also can switch to Software rendering to see the effect with a transparent shader. This might be due to the same causes as the quirk discussed in the earlier section called "General Shader Properties: blend and transparent."

blendConstant

The value for `blendConstant` is ignored unless `blendFunction` is set to `#blend` and `blendSource` is set to `#constant`. The use of the property is illustrated in the earlier section called "blendFunction: #blend."

textureMode

The `textureMode` property defines how the pixels in the texture map onto the pixels of the model. Possible values are as follows:

```
#none
#wrapPlanar
#wrapCylindrical
#wrapSpherical
#diffuseLight
#reflection
#specularLight
```

The default value is `#none`.

The three wrap... values and #none are used to define the material aspect of the model under the shader. They provide the skin for the model, as it were. The last three values are used to define how the surface of the model under the shader reacts to the environment. Textures applied using these modes act at a distance.

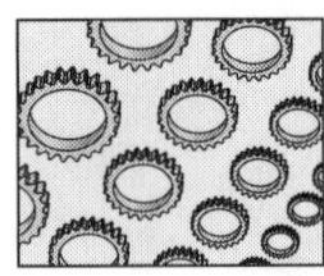

NOTE

Software rendering might not cope properly with multilayer shaders. Because the #diffuseLight, #reflection, and #specularLight settings are intended primarily for multilayer shaders, you might need to use a different rendering mode to see all the effects described in the following.

Wrapping a Texture

The way you wrap a texture onto a model depends on the shape of the model. If you want to apply the same material characteristics to several models with radically different shapes, you might need to create a number of shaders where only the `textureMode` is different. I've provided two Bitmap members to help you visualize how each wrap mode works: "WrapTest 8×4×4" and "WrapTest 64×64×8". The first image is rectangular and twice as wide as it is tall. You'll see the reason for this when you test the `#wrapCylindrical` and `#wrapSpherical` modes in conjunction with the `textureTransform` property.

Restart the Shaders.dir movie to clear the properties; then click the Texture tab and create a new texture that you can call simply "Texture." Drag this texture onto the first layer button for the default shader, and set the `member` of the texture to "WrapTest 8×4×4". Deselect the `nearFiltering` check box for the texture. Now use the Model pop-up menu to select each of the models in turn. Use the arrow keys to move the camera around the model so that you can examine it from all sides.

#none

The `#none` texture mode applies the shader indiscriminately to the whole of the mesh to which the shader is attached. For a model like Box, the shader will appear ten times: once for each face. The sphere has only one mesh, which covers the whole of its outer surface, so the shader is stretched around it once. The hemisphere has two meshes: one on each surface. Figure 10-12 shows how the rectangular image is squeezed to a point at the top and bottom, and stretched around the circumference of the hemisphere in the middle.

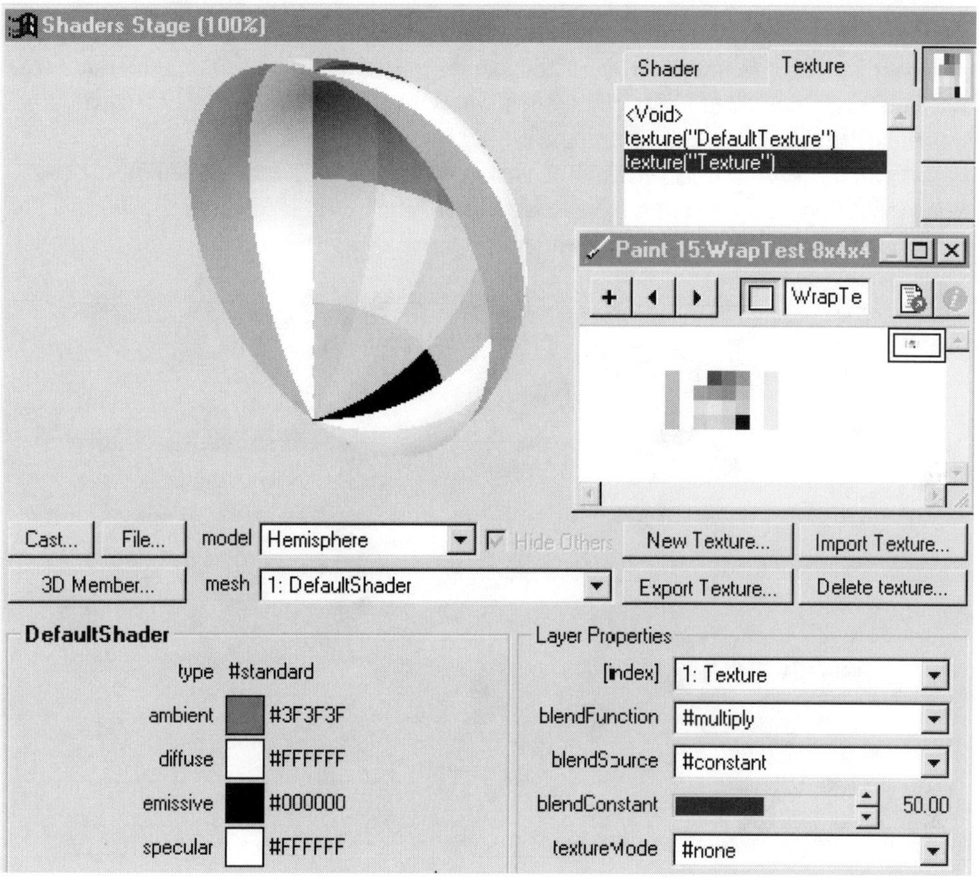

Figure 10-12 *Using the #none textureMode on a hemisphere*

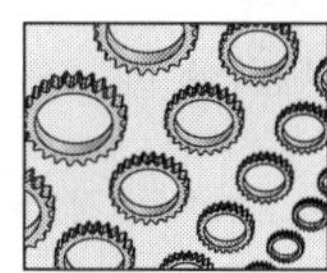

NOTE

The `#none` texture mode does not work with meshes unless the texture coordinates of the mesh resource are defined. This is dealt with in detail in Chapter 11. Without such a texture mapping, the whole of a mesh will take on the color of the bottom-left pixel of the texture image.

#wrapPlanar

The `#wrapPlanar` mode projects the shader onto the model as a whole, once from the front and once from the back, as if the model were a flat plane. For Box models, this means the top, bottom, and sides are left somewhat undefined.

Choose the #wrapPlanar mode in the textureMode pop-up menu; then press the Z key to view each model along the z axis. The differences you see in the appearance of the shader are minimal, and due to either perspective or to the silhouette of the model.

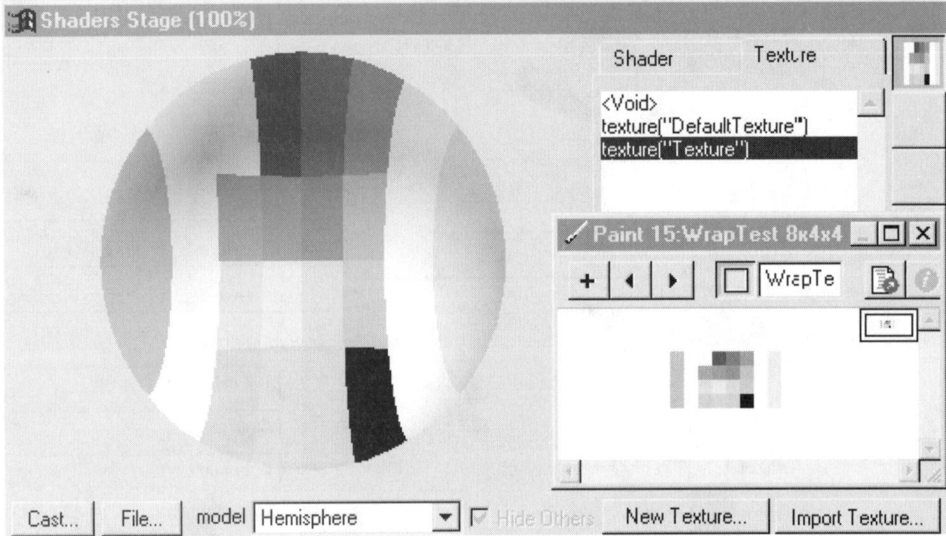

#wrapCylindrical

Using `#wrapCylindrical` with the texture "WrapTest 8×4×4" will produce an almost meaningless mapping, even on a cylinder. You'll see how to deal with this in the section on `textureTransform` later in the chapter. Changing the texture member to "WrapTest 64×64×8" produces a more comprehensible mapping. This can be used successfully both with cylinder and sphere models. On box models, you'll find that half of the model receives a mirror image of the shader. On a cylinder without end caps, such as the Cone model, you might find a `#wrapPlanar` mode is more appropriate.

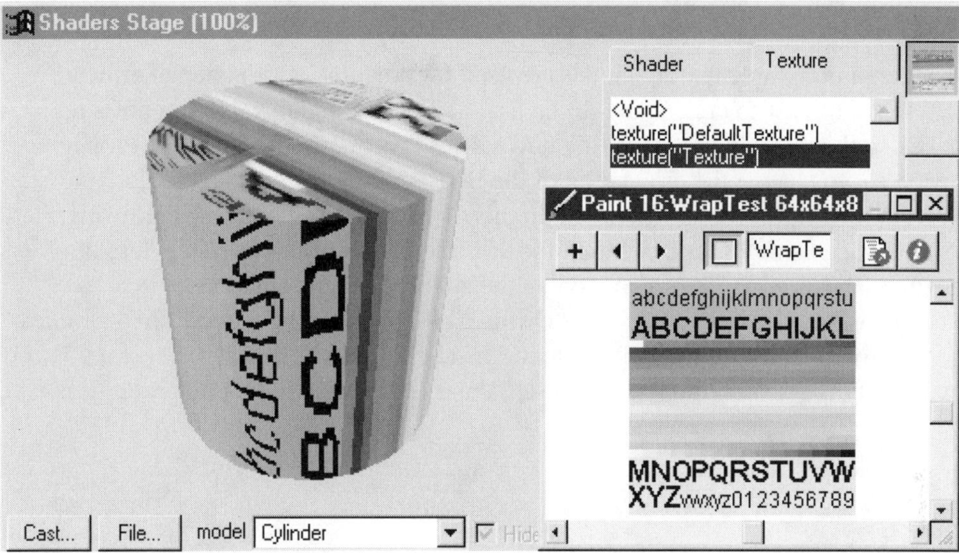

#wrapSpherical

Using the same "WrapTest 64×64×8" texture on a sphere with the `#wrapSpherical` texture mode has the effect of trimming the top and bottom quarter of the texture image. Only the central band is used.

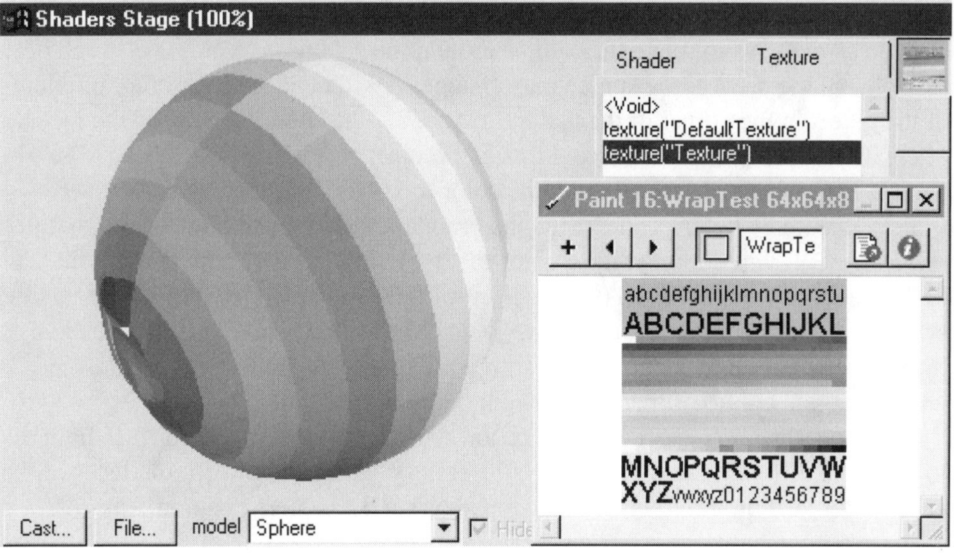

#diffuseLight

The remaining three texture modes are used for creating environmental effects. These are easiest to understand if you use the Sphere model and if you press the Z key so that the camera is looking down the z axis. You'll be using the Property Inspector to change the orientation of the Director Light. If you are not looking directly down the z axis when you do this, the display can become confusing. You also can simplify the situation for the time being by setting the texture of texture("Texture") to <Void>, so that the sphere appears a neutral white.

Create a new texture and call it "Diffuse." Right-click (Windows) or CTRL-click (Macintosh) on the new "Diffuse" texture and choose `diffuseLightMap`. This will apply the texture to layer 2 and set it, and also set the following properties:

```
<shader>.textureModeList[2]   = #diffuseLight
<shader>.blendFunctionList[2] = #multiply
<shader>.blendFunctionList[1] = #replace
```

The texture in layer 2 has no image yet: click the member pop-up menu and choose "Diffuse 4×4×4". To make the effect easier to see, deselect the `nearFiltering` check box for the "Diffuse" texture. Now open castLib 2 (Media) and click member 2 (3D World). This is the member where the sphere appears. In the Property Inspector, test each of the orientations of the Director Light, as shown in Figure 10-13.

You should see colors projected onto the sphere from the Director Light. As you change the orientation of the light, so the positions of the colors on the sphere change. Use the arrow keys to rotate the camera around the sphere. As you pass behind it, the color of the back of the sphere may change. It will always be the color of one of the pixels in the corner of the texture image, but the color depends on the precise orientation of the camera. To avoid this in a project, you should ensure that the corners of your texture are all the same color.

Press the Z key before you change the orientation of the Director Light. Do not select None. If you do, the diffuse color that was projected onto the sphere will stick to it. Changing the orientation of the Director Light subsequently will have no further effect on the diffuse light map. (Okay, so do choose None, so that you can see this for yourself. You'll then need to restart the movie and re-create your textures in order to regain control of the diffuse light map.)

Try using the Cube model instead of the sphere. You can use the diffuse light map to color the different faces of the cube differently. The back and bottom faces of the cube might take on different colors, depending on the camera position.

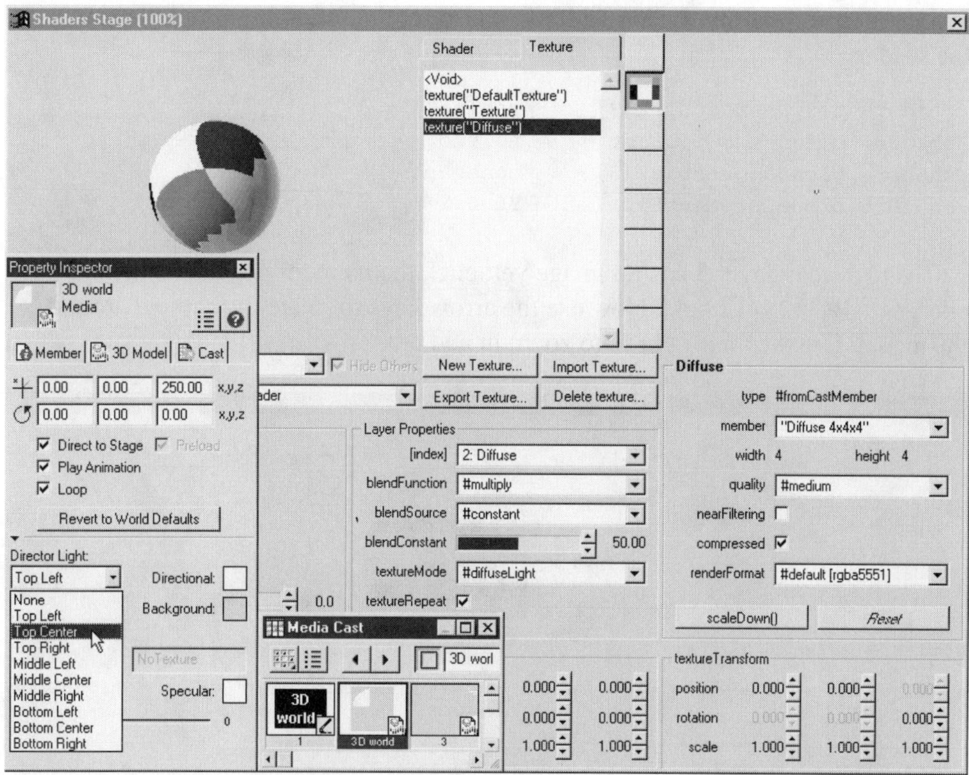

Figure 10-13 *Testing the #diffuseLight textureMode with light coming from different angles*

Try also using `nearFiltering`, now that you have seen how the mapping works. You will probably not see any difference on any of the flat-faced models. On curved-faced models, the gradients between colors will be more subtle.

#reflection

The `reflectionMap` feature we will test does not work consistently if layer 1 of the shader is empty. (You can get this to work, but it can require tweaking.) Let's choose a very simple texture, so that the reflection remains the main attraction: drag texture("DefaultTexture") onto the layer 1 button. Drag `<Void>` onto the layer 2 button, so that the diffuse light map doesn't interfere with the reflection.

Now create a new texture named "Reflection." Right-click or CTRL-click the name of your new texture and choose `reflectionMap`. This will apply your new texture to layer 3 of the shader, and it will also set the following properties of the shader:

```
<shader>.textureModeList[3]    = #reflection
<shader>.blendFunctionList[3]  = #blend
<shader>.blendSourceList[3]    = #constant
<shader>.blendConstantList[3]  = 50.0
```

The texture in layer 3 has no image yet: click the member pop-up menu and choose "ABC 128×128×4." Now use the arrow keys to rotate the camera around the model. Use the I and O keys to zoom in and out.

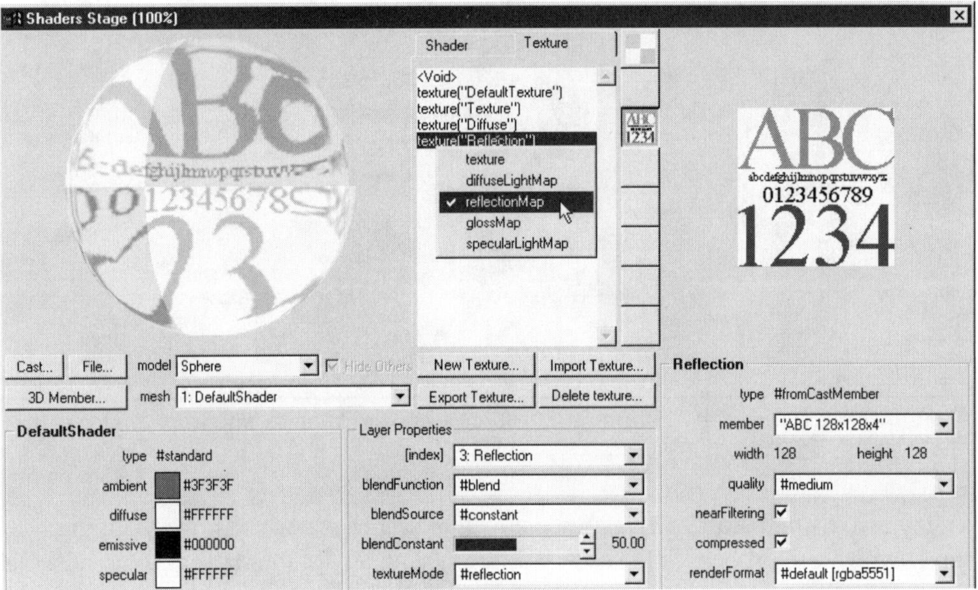

The reflection remains static as you turn around the model. To be exact, the faces of the sphere mesh make the reflection ripple slightly, but the position of the reflection remains the same. That is, the position of the reflection map depends on the position of the camera itself.

DEBUGGING TIP

The reflection map works only if the `blendFunction` of the first layer is set to `#replace`. This was done for you automatically when you used the `diffuseLightMap` command on the "Diffuse" texture. If you now select layer 1 in the [index] pop-up menu and set its `blendFunction` to something other than `#replace`, the sphere will stop reflecting. When you set the value back to `#replace`, the sphere starts reflecting again.

The key settings here are a `textureMode` of `#reflection` and a `blendFunction` of `#blend`. You can vary the value of `blendConstant` to make the surface more or less shiny; and you can use alpha channel images for the texture, and so use the `#alpha` setting for `blendSource`. (If you see no reflection, try setting the `transparent` property of the shader as a whole to `FALSE`.)

Using the Sphere model shows you the entire image reflected at once. The reflected image is, in fact, mapped onto a hemisphere whose central axis is the same as that of the camera. The Sphere model reflects the whole of this hemisphere. Use the Model pop-up menu to choose the Box model. With its flat faces, the box reflects discrete parts of the hemisphere. The reflected image changes as you turn the camera around the box.

Switch to the Hemisphere model, and press the Z key to view it directly from in front; the reflection will appear inverted. This underlines the fact that, in ordinary circumstances, the reflected image is the same way round as the initial texture image. When you look in a mirror, the image you see is inverted. If you want to simulate a mirror that reflects part of your virtual 3D world, you'll have to ensure that the texture image you provide is correctly oriented.

glossMap()

The keyword `glossMap` is a command and not a value for the `textureMode` property of a shader. I'll treat it here, though, so that it fits in the logical succession of ideas. Setting a gloss map, either by the built-in command or by using the same principles, produces a different kind of reflection: brightness on the surface of the model.

Create a new texture and name it "Gloss." Right-click or CTRL-click the new texture name, and choose `glossMap` in the contextual menu. This will apply your new texture to layer 4 of the shader, and it will also set the following properties of the shader:

```
<shader>.textureModeList[4]   = #none
<shader>.blendFunctionList[4] = #multiply
```

The value of #none for the texture mode is somewhat arbitrary. You might want to modify this depending on the shape of the model. If you do, you might as well simply use the #multiply blendFunction on its own. Through the member pop-up menu, set the member of "Gloss" texture to "Graydient 4×4×4." Use the arrow keys to rotate the camera around the model.

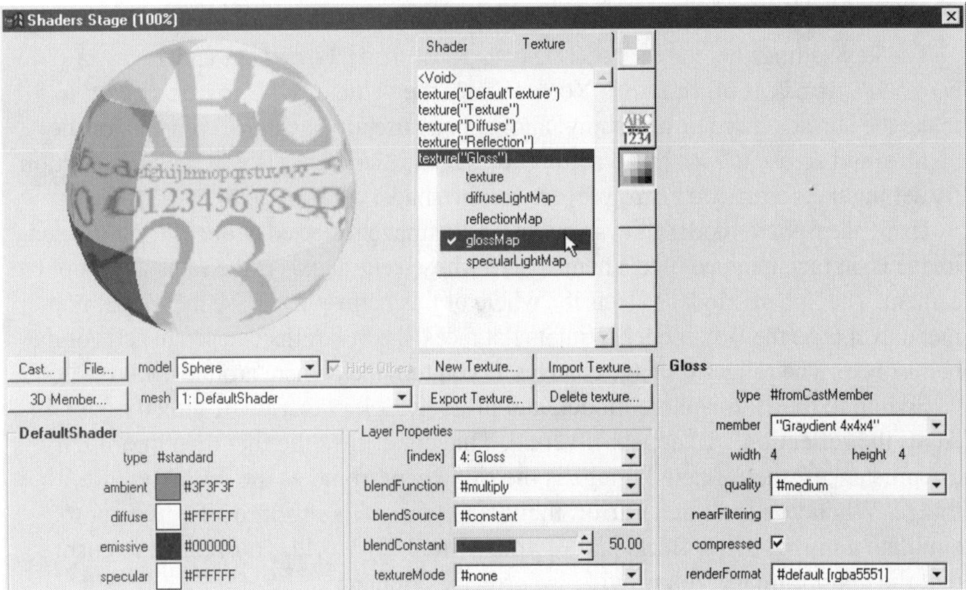

Using the #multiply blend function means the reflection is duller where the "Gloss" texture is darker; the pure black area is completely matte. Of course you don't have to use a grayscale image—you could test using "Rainbow 4×4×4" for the "Gloss" texture. This gives the effect of a colored varnish.

Test what happens if you remove the texture: use <Void> instead of texture("Reflection") for the third layer. Without the reflection, the gloss layer loses much of its significance. It simply provides coloration, but no sense of shininess. Leave the shader layers as they are, with the rainbow gloss and no reflection. We'll now look at a different way to achieve a shiny finish.

#specular

Create a new texture and name it "Specular." Right-click or CTRL-click the new texture name and choose specularLightMap. Set the member of the texture to "Window 64×64×1". You might for an instant see the new layer appear, and then it will vanish again. Why? Think back to the discussion on the specular color property and how you simulated a glass box with a void texture. Specular means shiny. You have to set the shininess of the shader to something other than zero for it to have any effect.

Use the arrow keys to rotate the camera around the model. Can you tell which fixed point the specular mapping is applied from?

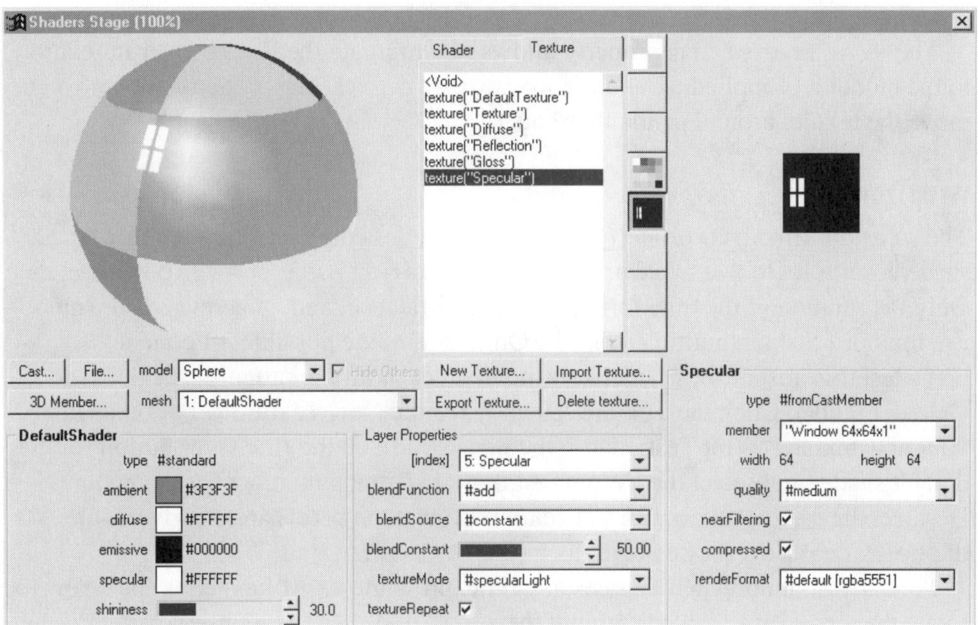

Like the `diffuseLightMap`, the `specularLightMap` is oriented to coincide with the light source. I have placed the window to the left of the texture image, so that it does not appear at exactly the same place as the specular halo. If they coincided, the halo would overwhelm the image of the window, unless you use a `shininess` value of nearly `100.0`. Try editing the Bitmap image to center the window; then reapply the member to the texture.

Try using other models with the same shader, to see how the shape of the specular image depends on the shape of the model. If you want to save your work, drag the name of each texture in turn to the Export Texture button, and save a script that will re-create the texture onto your hard disk. Then click the Shader tab so that you can export the shader as a whole. You won't be able to save the shader with the name "DefaultShader." First, drag the default shader to the New Shader… button to create a copy of it with a different name; then export the new shader. You'll see in the next chapter how to use the scripts you create.

wrapTransform, textureTransform, and textureRepeat

Earlier, when the `#wrapCylinder` texture mode was applied to it, the "WrapTest 8×4×4" texture looked very strange. I indicated that there was a way to deal with this. When I presented the `texture` and `textureList` properties, I explained that the dimensions of a texture were measured in terms of 1.0 shader-width and 1.0 shader-height.

The `wrapTransform` property allows you to rotate the shader layer in relation to the model it is applied to, and the `textureTransform` property allows you to move the texture around inside the shader.

wrapTransform

The `wrapTransform` property has no effect unless the `textureMode` of the shader layer is set to `#wrapPlanar`, `#wrapCylindrical`, or `#wrapSpherical`. Only the rotation of the transform has any significance, and, generally, you would use rotations that are multiples of 90°. Other angles are possible, of course.

To test this, restart the Shaders.dir movie to clear all the properties. Choose the Cylinder model. Click the Texture tab and then the New Texture… button. Name your new texture "WrapTest." Drop the new texture on the first layer button for the default shader and select the "WrapTest 8×4×4" Bitmap member for the texture. Deselect the `nearFiltering` check box so that the pixels are clearly visible. Set the `textureMode` for this layer to `#wrapCylindrical`.

So that you jump by ten degrees at a time, press the SHIFT key, click the arrow to rotate the `wrapTransform` around the x axis, and hold the mouse down until the shader has turned through 90°. Alternatively, you could enter the value of 90 directly in the input field. Does that look better? Try this with other angles, other axes, other models, and other textureModes. When you are satisfied that you see the purpose of the `wrapTransform` property, reset all the rotations to zero.

textureTransform and textureRepeat

Choose the Cylinder model and the `#wrapCylindrical` texture mode as before. This time, hold the SHIFT key down and click the arrow to rotate the textureTransform 90° around its z axis (not the x axis this time). The effect is different, but just as neat. Now deselect the `textureRepeat` button. The effect is neater still.

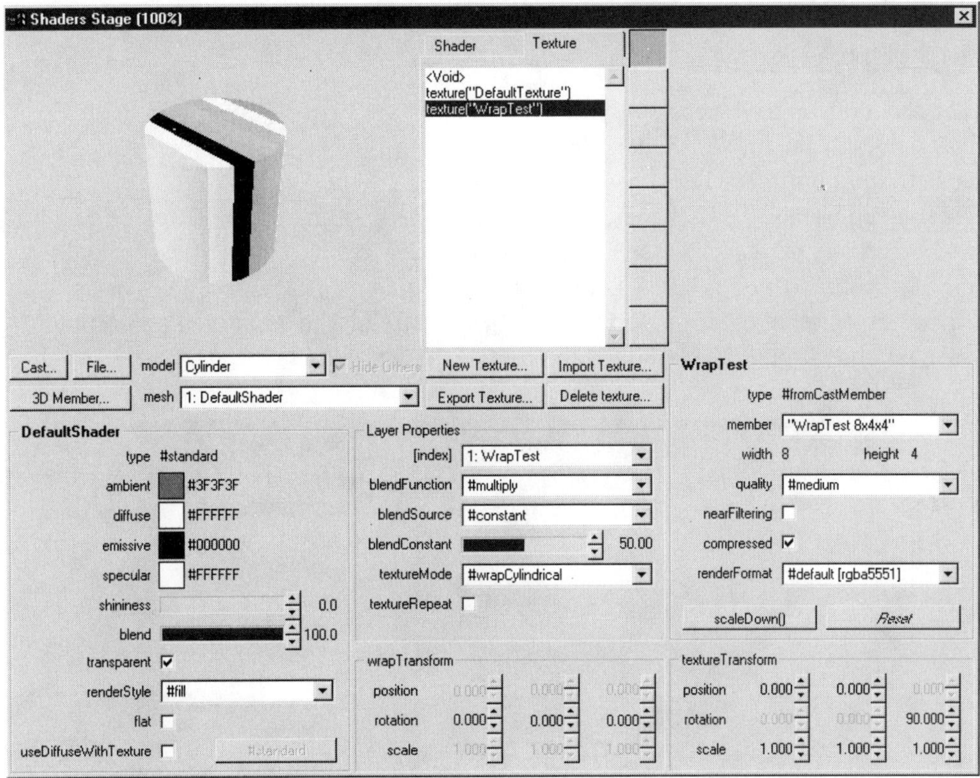

You can also scale the texture up or down inside the shader. If you scale it down and `textureRepeat` is `FALSE`, the colors at the edges of the texture are extended to the edges of the shader. If textureRepeat is `TRUE`, the same pattern appears repetitively.

Try also altering the position of the `textureTransform`. There is no point in moving more than 1.0 unit along the x or y axes, because that would take the texture out of one side and put it back in the other. Nor is there any point in moving the `textureTransform` at all along the z axis, because by nature a texture is flat. In any case, the values in the two . . . `Transform` properties that cannot meaningfully be modified are disabled in the Shader.dir movie.

Experiment. Observe the results you can achieve. Try to predict what effect each manipulation is likely to have before you act. Once you have come to terms with these two properties, you have come to the end of the surprises that shaders and textures have in store for you—almost.

Special Shaders

The shaders you have been studying have been of the type #standard. You also can create much simpler shaders that ignore most of the properties you've looked at so far, but introduce new ones.

You can use the New Shader… button to create #painter, #newsprint, and #engraver shaders (see Figure 10-14). These react to the ambient and diffuse colors you might set, and can be rendered as #fill, #wire, or #point. Altering other property values has no effect. The additional properties are available through the button at the foot of the left column.

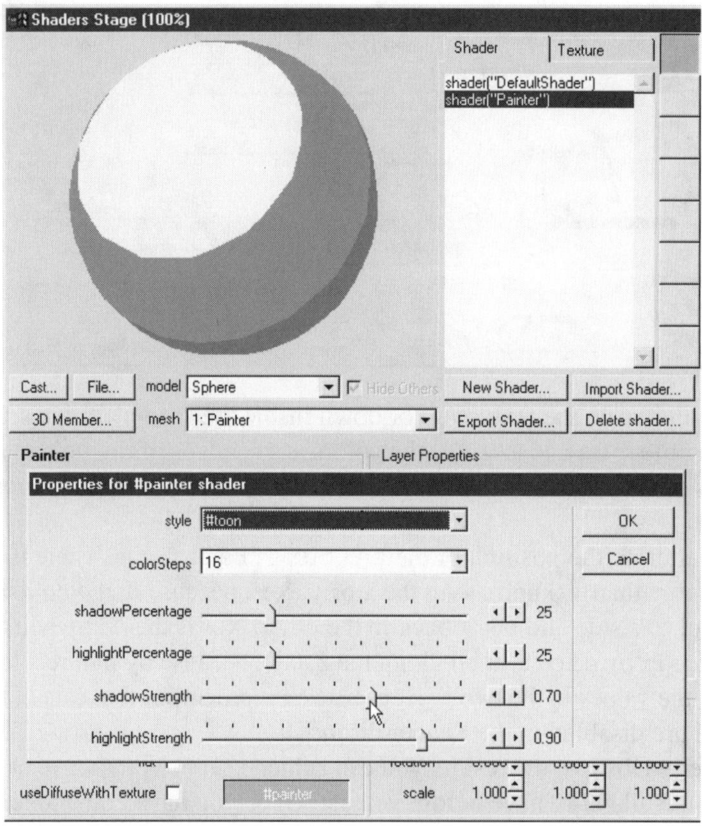

Figure 10-14 *Testing the #toon style of the #painter shader on a sphere*

I leave you to test these for yourself. Here are a few suggestions that might help you:

- Set the ambient and diffuse colors to contrasting values. The shader can add black and white to these colors, in varying proportions, and may ignore the diffuse value.
- You get more clues about how the shaders work if you experiment using a model with a curved surface, such as the sphere.
- The `#painter` shader has three styles: `#gradient`, `#toon`, and `#blackAndWhite`. There are five other properties you can set, but only the `#toon` style reacts to them all. The `#gradient` style ignores the `...Percentage` properties and the `#blackAndWhite` style ignores the `...Strength` properties.
- You will see the effect of the properties set by the sliders more clearly if you set the `colorSteps` value to 16 and test the `#gradient` style first.
- The value of `shadowStrength` refers to the diffuse color; not to black. The effect of the `highlightStrength` property depends on whether the value is above or below 50.
- For the `#toon` and `#blackAndWhite` styles, the values of `shadowPercentage` and `highlightPercentage` are linked: the sum of these cannot be more than 100.
- The sensitivity of the `...Percentage` properties depends on the number of `colorSteps`. With 2 `colorSteps`, all values of more than 50 have one effect and all values less than 50 have another. With 16 `colorSteps`, a difference of 6 or 7 is enough to change the effect.
- For the `#newsprint` and `#engraver` shaders, the `density` property is set at `45.0` by default. You will see a change if you reduce this value, but all greater values have more or less the same effect.

Exploring on Your Own

This chapter has used the Shaders.dir movie to demonstrate the effects of all the properties of textures and shaders. Each time the value of one property affects the effect of another, the interaction was illustrated by an example.

The examples have been chosen for their clarity; not for their realism. In the next chapter, you will look at how others developers create realistic shaders and textures and use the Shaders.dir movie to build your own.

The text of the chapter has focused on the standard use of the various properties. The Shaders.dir movie is designed to allow you to explore more offbeat uses of these properties on your own. Even if you count only the eight default primitive models and the twenty Bitmap images I provide for textures, there are still quantities of combinations that you have not yet tested. The more you experiment, the clearer the concepts will become. In the next chapter I take the understanding of the concepts as read.

CHAPTER

11

Using Shaders and Textures

IN THIS CHAPTER:

I am a simple man, I use simple textures.

—L. S. Lowry

In the last chapter you saw the significance of each property of textures and shaders, but you saw only the strict minimum of Lingo. In this chapter you will first see how other developers use these properties to good effect, then I'll show you how to achieve these effects for yourself. I'll be completing the discussion of building a mesh that I started in Chapter 9 by showing you how to apply specific parts of a texture to specific parts of a mesh model, using texture coordinates. Once you've done this, you will have encountered all the theory and should be ready to build a scene using textures and shaders that you will create yourself. The models used for this scene were created in the Lathe.dir movie you saw in Chapter 9.

Apart from the foray into texture coordinates, you won't see much Lingo until the end of the chapter. The Shaders.dir movie you encountered in Chapter 10 will continue to help you explore textures and shaders visually. You will be able to design textures and shaders using drag-and-drop techniques and export scripts that re-create your work automatically in other movies. These scripts are designed so that they can be reused as behaviors. Each script thus includes all the code it requires to work. You can use these exported scripts with a minimum of fuss to build materials for a prototype of your project.

For the shipping version of your project, however, you will be keen to save disk space, download time, and processor usage. In the last part of this chapter you will learn how to strip out all the code that simplifies your prototyping work, but would be redundant in streamlined movie. In doing so, I will finally bring you face to face with the Lingo for shaders and texture. Fortunately, this is more laborious than it is complicated.

Studying Shaders in 3D Files

Before you start creating your own shaders and textures, it can help to study how others have gone about this. With the Shaders.dir movie, you can load any *.w3d file and examine how the models, shaders, and textures interact.

You will find a number of such files on the CD-ROM that Director 8.5 is delivered on. Insert the CD-ROM into the appropriate drive, launch the Shaders.dir movie, and click the File… button; a dialog will appear. Navigate to the 3D Models folder on the Director 8.5 CD-ROM; then open any of the files in any of the subfolders.

Following I have singled out three files that illustrate points of interest:

- Shaders without any textures
- High-resolution images for textures
- A single texture to provide multiple images

Textureless Shaders

A shader need not use any texture at all. You saw an example in the previous chapter where a shader was used to simulate glass, and where all the texture layers of the shader were Void. A shader with no texture produces an area of uniform color. The color can be uniform without appearing flat; the incidence of the lighting on the contours of the model will create areas of light and shade. One example of this is the Knight.w3D file, which you will find in the 3D Models\Cache Force\Knight\ folder. This uses ten shaders, which differ only by their color.

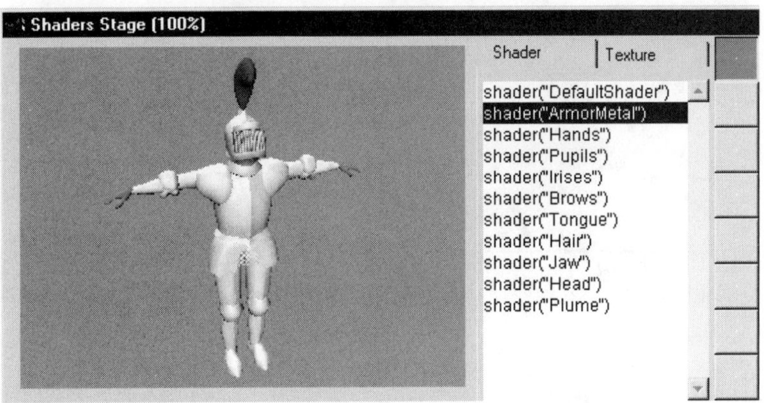

Even the knight's face is constructed from uniform color shaders. In the Model pop-up menu, choose Head; then check the Hide Others box (see Figure 11-1). All the other models will be temporarily hidden. Click the knight's nose; then press the I key to zoom in on it. Click in succession the hair, pupils, irises, and eyebrows. You'll see the `diffuse` color change, but all other properties will remain the same.

The Knight.w3d file relies on sophisticated geometry to achieve its effect. The other Cache Force files use a similar technique. When the model is simple, as in the Bazooka or the Waraxe1 files, the file size can be kept very small.

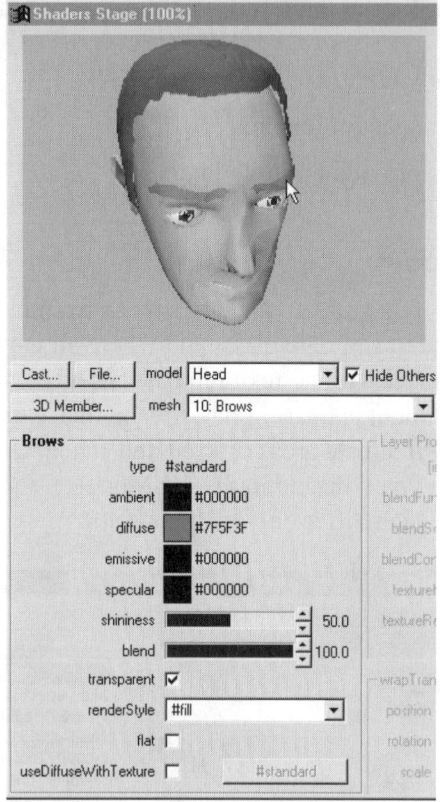

Figure 11-1 *Using shaders without textures to color features*

Using High-Resolution Images

You'll find another human figure named jos_srti.w3D in the 3D Models\Iw43d\ jos_srti\ folder on the Director 8.5 CD-ROM. This uses a number of fairly large texture images, plus a number of shaders with a Void texture for the white shirt, teeth, gums, belt, buckle, and shoe soles. Because these materials can be defined using a uniform color, only the `ambient`, `diffuse`, `specular`, and `shininess` properties of their shaders need be set.

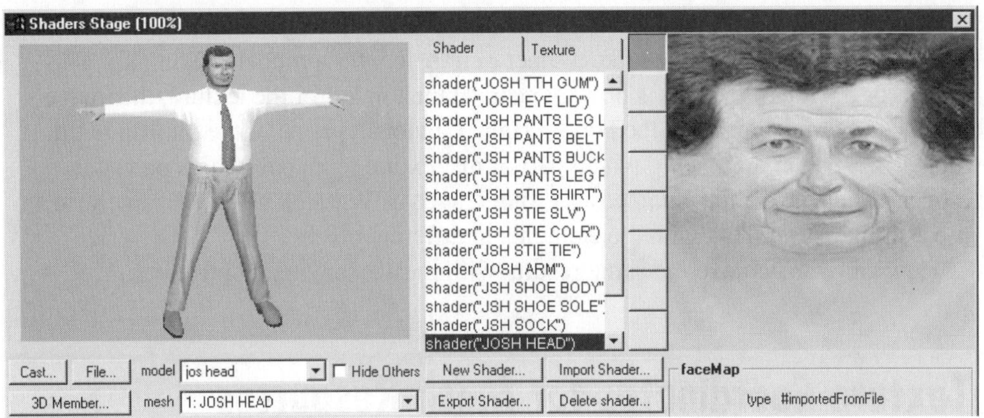

The geometry in the file is less complex than in the Knight.w3d example. The expressive textures take up a fair amount of disk space, but the overall file size is smaller. Moral: if used intelligently, large textures can be more appropriate than sophisticated geometrical modeling.

One Texture; Multiple Images

A single texture can, on its own, provide all the visual data required for a model. When you create a mesh resource, you can define a number of key points in the texture through the `textureCoordinateList` for the model resource, and then determine which of these key points is used by each face in the mesh through the `textureCoordinates` property. First, we'll look at a *.w3d file that uses the technique; then, in the next section, you'll use the same technique to create a playing card for a Happy Families game. In the Shaders.dir movie, click the File. . . button and select the file \3D Models\Geo-metricks\warrior\warrior.W3D on the Director 8.5 CD-ROM.

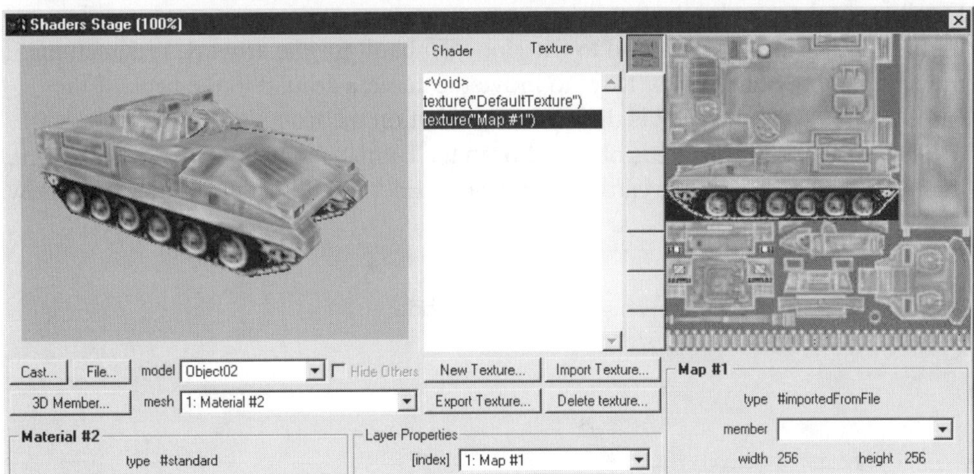

This file uses a single shader named Material #2 and a single texture named Map #1. The texture image is arranged like a sheet of transfers for a model-making kit. The image for the top of the tank's body appears at the top left of the texture; the image for the gun turret appears at the bottom right. Obviously, none of the built-in texture modes is capable of knowing which part of the texture to map to which part of the model. Other files in the Geometricks folder, such as Warlock.w3d or Hearse.w3d, use a similar system but with the elements in different places.

How can you achieve the same results with meshes created using Lingo?

Texture Coordinates for Mesh Resources

TexCoord.dir

In Chapter 9, I mentioned the texture coordinate properties of a mesh resource only in passing. When working in Chapter 10 you might have noticed that the texture mode `#none` does not have the intended effect on model resources of the type `#mesh`—at least, not automatically.

Now that you have a clear idea of how textures work, it's time to deal with this feature in detail. The discussion that follows is more closely related to the construction of a mesh resource than it is to the design of shaders and textures. Once you have built the mesh resource correctly, all textures will be mapped to the mesh model according to the same logic.

Using Texture Coordinates to Create a Playing Card

In the 3D\Surface2\ folder on the CD-ROM that accompanies the book, you'll find a movie named TexCoord.dir that illustrates a playing card for a game of Happy Families: in the Amphibian family, the tree frog *Rana temporaria*, as shown in Figure 11-2. (I am very grateful to Charlotte Thibault for the artwork.) Launch the movie; then press the Arrow Keys to move the camera around to the back of the card; the image on the back is different from that on the front.

The image for the texture is obtained from the Bitmap member Card. In this image, the front and the back of the card appear side by side. Try this in the Message window:

```
put member(1).model(1).resource.type
-- #mesh
put member(1).model(1).shader.textureMode
-- #none
```

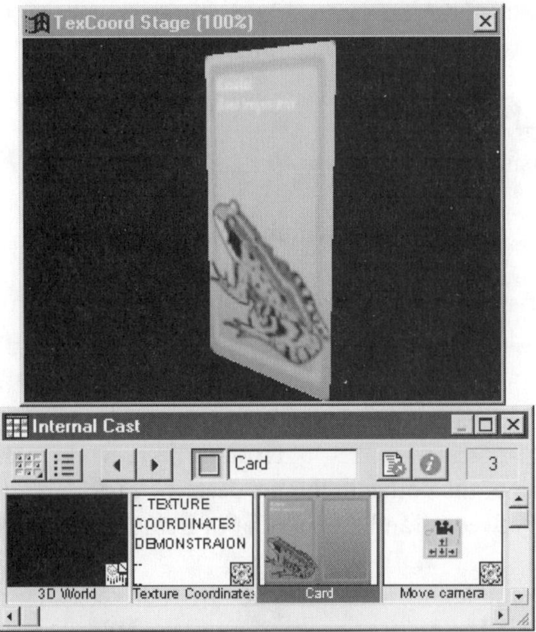

Figure 11-2 *Mapping a texture around a flat card*

This demonstrates that the texture mode `#none` can be made to work on a `#mesh` model. Not only that, but it can provide more flexibility than the other texture modes. Try this in the Message window:

```
member(1).shader(2).textureMode = #wrapPlanar
```

Now rotate the camera around the card model with the arrow keys. The whole texture image appears on both sides of the card; the back is identical to the front. You can test with the other texture modes: `#wrapCylindrical`, `#wrapSpherical`, and so on. None of these will give the desired recto-verso effect. Before you go on, set the `textureMode` back to `#none`.

Creating a Texture Map

To create your own texture map for a mesh model, you need to work on the mesh resource itself. The coordinates used for each face need to be validated by the `aResource.build()` method. If used on a complex resource, animation in the movie can be suspended during the build() process. As you will see, this means certain manipulations of the texture map might prove impractical to execute on-the-fly.

The Components of a Texture Map

A texture map consists of two parts:

- A list defining specific points within the texture. This has the following structure:
  [[<float between 0.0 and 1.0>, <float between 0.0 and 1.0>], ...]
- A three-item list for each face of the mesh indicating which of the specific points should appear at each vertex of the face. This has the structure [<integer>, <integer>, <integer>], where each item is the index number of one of the points in the list described in the preceding, thus the range varies between 1 and the number of items in the preceding list.

In this simple example the mesh is defined by four vertex points, one at each corner of a rectangle. The mesh consists of four triangular faces: two front faces and two back faces. The texture also is divided up into four triangles: one for each face. The vertex points, faces, and texture triangles all are defined by a four-item list. The information in these lists is used to create the mesh resource. You'll find the full code for this in the createMesh() handler of the TexCoord.dir movie. Following, I quote only the essential highlights of this handler.

Defining the Faces of the Mesh

If the vertex points for a face are arranged in a counterclockwise order, the face is visible from the front; a clockwise arrangement makes the face visible from the back. This is illustrated in Figure 11-3.

Defining the Texture Coordinates

The textureCoordinateList for the mesh resource is a list of points inside the texture. Because a texture can be any size, its dimensions are considered to be 1.0 texture-height by 1.0 texture-width. Coordinates are defined from the point [0.0, 0.0] in the bottom-left corner; thus, the point at the top center will be at [0.5, 1.0]—half the width texture and the whole height. This is illustrated in Figure 11-4.

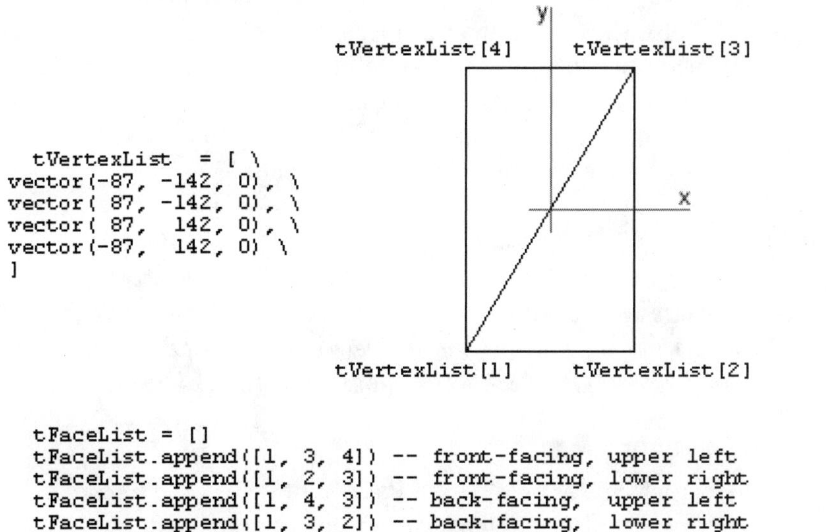

Figure 11-3 *Creating the vertexList and faces for the card*

```
tTextureCoordinateList = [ \
[0.0, 0.0], \
[0.5, 0.0], \
[1.0, 0.0], \
[0.0, 1.0], \
[0.5, 1.0], \
[1.0, 1.0]\
]
```

4: [0.0, 1.0]   5: [0.5, 1.0]   6: [1.0, 1.0]

1: [0.0, 0.0]   2: [0.5, 0.0]   3: [1.0, 0.0]

```
tCoordinates = []
tCoordinates.append([1, 5, 4]) -- upper left of left half
tCoordinates.append([1, 2, 5]) -- lower right of left half
tCoordinates.append([3, 6, 5]) -- upper right of right half
tCoordinates.append([3, 5, 2]) -- lower left of right half
```

Figure 11-4 *Creating the texture coordinates for each face of the card*

Figure 11-2 also shows how the `textureCoordinates` for each face of the mesh are defined. Like the `tFaceList` in Figure 11-4, the `tCoordinates` list contains four items: one for each of the faces of the mesh. Note that the triangular faces at the back of the card appear as a mirror image of those on the front. The coordinates used for the texture take this into account.

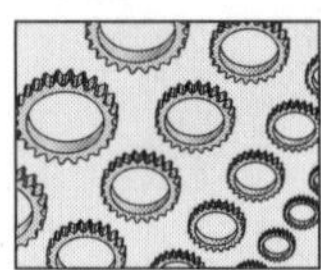

NOTE

The dimensions of the Bitmap member used here for the texture are not exact powers of 2; therefore, the texture will be resized to 128 × 128 rather than 174 × 142 pixels. This will reduce the resolution of the resulting image. However, because the texture coordinates are defined in the range 0.0 to 1.0, the altered shape and size of the texture will have no impact on the relative position of the coordinate points.

Applying the Texture Map

I now have four lists: `tVertexList`, `tFaceList`, `tTextureCoordinateList`, and `tCoordinates`. Here is an edited version of the end of the `createMesh()` handler from the TexCoord.dir movie. This code is incomplete; for clarity, I've removed lines concerning the `colorList`, which I treated in Chapter 9. Please refer to the movie itself for a working version of the code.

```
  on createMesh()
  tMeshResource = myMember.newMesh( \
"Card", \
tFaceList.count, \
tVertexList.count, \
0, \
1, \
tTextureCoordinateList.count \
)
  -- Apply the vertex, face and texture data
  tMeshResource.textureCoordinateList = tTextureCoordinateList
  tMeshResource.vertexList = tVertexList

  repeat with i = 1 to 4
    tMeshResource.face[i].vertices            = tFaceList[i]
    tMeshResource.face[i].textureCoordinates  = tCoordinates[i]
  end repeat

  -- Create a flat mesh
  tMeshResource.generateNormals(#flat)
  tMeshResource.build()

  return tMeshResource
end createMesh
```

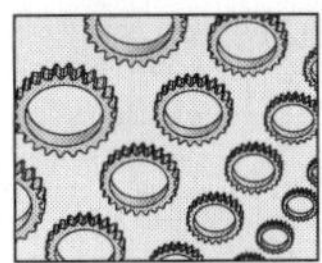

NOTE

Texture coordinates are respected only when the texture mode is `#none`.

Two Ways of Altering the Texture Map On-the-Fly

To change the way a texture maps to a mesh model you can, in theory, modify either the `textureCoordinateList` for the mesh resource or the `textureCoordinates` for each face. However, in practice, only the first approach is recommended.

Setting the textureCoordinateList

Run the TexCoord.dir movie; then type this into the Message window:

```
tList = [[0.0,1.0],[0.5,1.0],[1.0,1.0],[0.0,0.0],[0.5,0.0],[1.0, 0.0]]
member(1).model(1).resource.textureCoordinateList = tList
```

Immediately, the texture on the card model flips vertically. This is because you have swapped the first three entries in `textureCoordinateList` with the last three entries—the points defining the top of the texture replace those defining the bottom, and vice versa. This example shows that it is quite feasible to change the `textureCoordinateList` of a resource on-the-fly.

A More Cumbersome Approach

On the other hand, changing the way the texture is mapped to each face requires the mesh to be rebuilt. Try the following two lines of code in the Message window after you've consulted Figure 11-4 to see what effect the new `textureCoordinates` for each face should have:

```
member(1).model(1).resource.face[1].textureCoordinates = [5, 1, 2]
member(1).model(1).resource.face[2].textureCoordinates = [5, 4, 1]
```

Nothing happens. Continue with

```
member(1).model(1).resource.build()
```

For a complex model resource, this step can be time consuming. An additional drawback is that the image of the tree frog is abruptly replaced with that of the default shader. So now you have to reapply the tree frog shader manually as an extra step:

```
member(1).model(1).shader = member(1).shader(2)
```

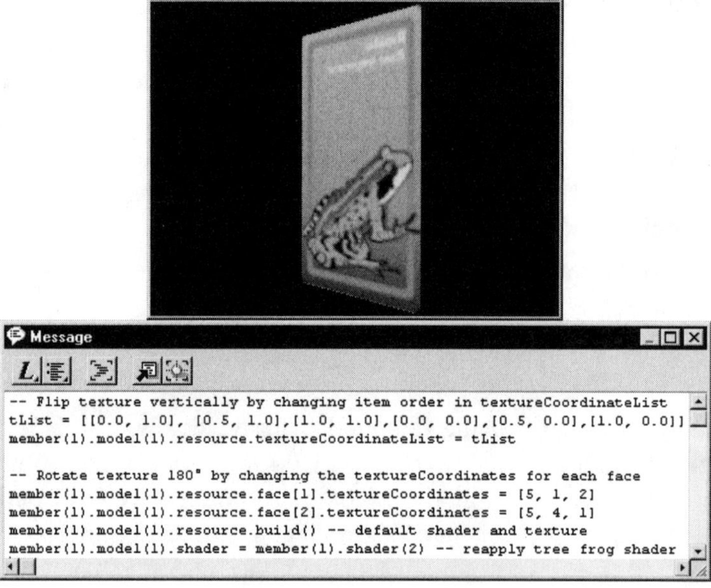

Duplicating Values to Get the Best of Both Worlds

If you do need to alter the texture mapping on-the-fly, it is more efficient to change the values in the `textureCoordinateList` than to alter the way each face uses those coordinates. Depending on how you need to manipulate your textures, this can prove more or less tricky. You can simplify your task by using unique values for the `textureCoordinates` for each face and duplicating entries in the mesh resource's `textureCoordinatesList` wherever two points need to coincide. For example, face 1 might use the `textureCoordinates [1, 2, 3]` and face 2 might use `[4, 5, 6]`. If the `textureCoordinateList` is

```
[[0.0, 0.0], [1.0, 0.0], [1.0, 1.0], [0.0, 0.0], [1.0, 1.0], [0.0, 1.0]]
```

points 1 and 4 coincide, as do points 3 and 5. Changing the `textureCoordinateList` to

```
[[1.0, 0.0], [1.0, 1.0], [0.0, 1.0], [1.0, 0.0], [0.0, 1.0], [0.0, 0.0]]
```

would rotate the texture 90° counterclockwise more efficiently than the cumbersome approach, as follows:

```
aShader = aMeshModel.shader
aMeshResource.face[1].textureCoordinates = [2, 3, 6]
aMeshResource.face[2].textureCoordinates = [2, 6, 1]
aMeshResource.build()
aMeshModel.shader = aShader
```

You can test this using the movie FlyCoord.dir, as shown in Figure 11-5. On my test machine, the duplicate `textureCoordinateList` technique is more than three times as fast.

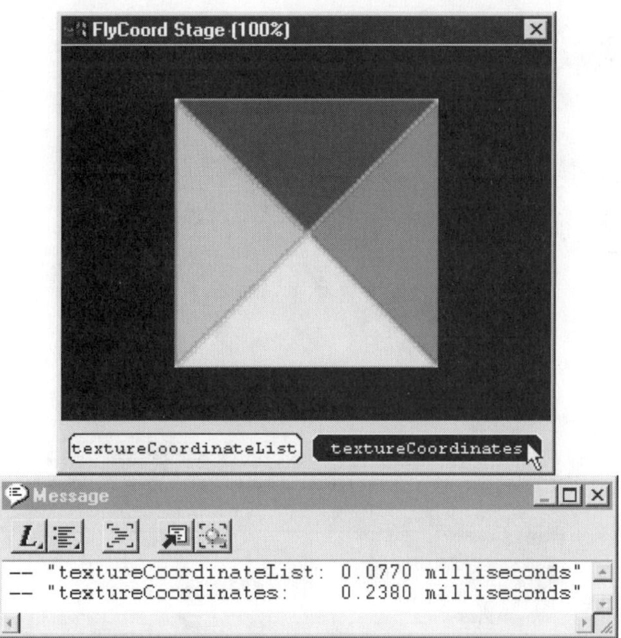

Figure 11-5 *Comparing two techniques for changing a mapping on-the-fly*

Texture Coordinates on Your Own

Die0.dir, Die1.dir, Die.dir

A two-faced playing card is the simplest possible example of the use of texture coordinates. The next level of difficulty would be to create a gaming die from a mesh in the shape of a cube. This would require 8 vertex points, 12 triangular faces organized into 6 squares, and a texture divided into 6 square sections. Because both the width and height of your texture should be exact powers of 2, the texture will have room for 8 square sections; two of these will not be mapped to any face.

You'll find three movies in the 3D\Surface2\ folder on the CD-ROM, in different stages of completion. Die.dir contains the finished example (don't look at the code unless you really have to). You can see the result in Figure 11-6. Die1.dir creates the cubic mesh, but the code that deals with the shader is missing. Die0.dir does not even create the mesh; you need to flesh out the skeleton code. A mesh model will be created, but it will contain no vertices so it will not appear in the Shockwave 3D sprite.

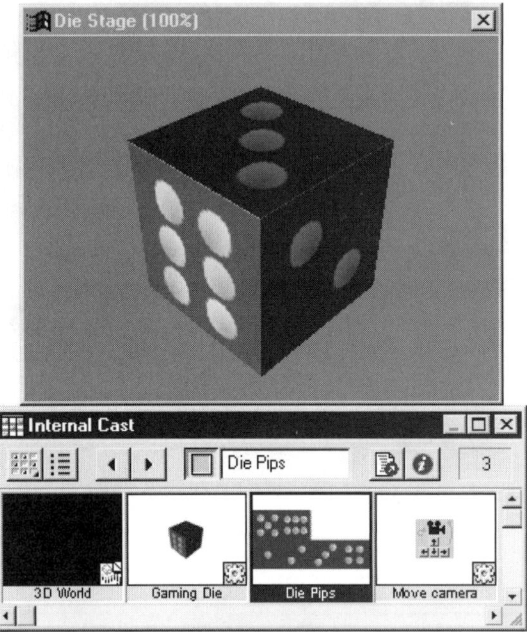

Figure 11-6 *Mapping a texture to a cube built from a mesh*

Here are some points to note:

- The triangular faces on the mesh and the triangle groups of `textureCoordinates` should start at the same relative point and turn in the same counterclockwise direction
- The order in which the faces of the cube are defined should match the order in which the texture sections are defined. The following illustration shows one suggestion for defining the texture coordinates:

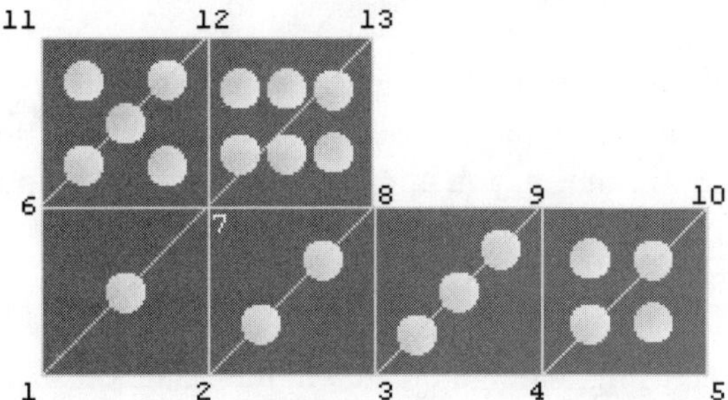

- The order you use might be different from mine and yet yield the same results, as long as the texture data and face data match.
- In this particular case, you don't need to worry about which way up each texture section appears.
- The total number of pips on opposite faces of a die is always 7.

TIP

A cube created from a mesh is much more efficient than a cube created from a box primitive. A mesh is assigned a single shader, whereas a box primitive is assigned one shader per surface. The technique used in Die.dir allows you to use a different image on each face of the cube without using extra shaders. Thanks to NoiseCrime for bringing this to the attention of Director users.

Designing Textures and Shaders

In the `createWorld()` handlers of both the TexCoord.dir movie and the Die.dir movies, you'll find code that creates first a texture and then a shader that uses it; and which then applies the shader to the model. Here are the seven lines of code used in the TexCoord.dir movie:

```
tTexture               = myMember.newTexture("Card")
tTexture.member        = member("Card")
tTexture.renderFormat  = #rgba8880
tShader                = myMember.newShader("Card", #standard)
tShader.shininess      = 0
tShader.texture        = tTexture
tModel.shader          = tShader
```

As you can see, the code is very straightforward. You start by creating a default texture or shader; then you customize the values of any properties that should differ from the default values. Finally, you apply the shader to the model. The difficulty lies not in writing the Lingo but in choosing the custom values, which is where the Shaders.dir movie comes into its own. It can help you design textures and shaders for models in your own movies.

Let's build a scene using a model created in the Lathe.dir movie (see Chapter 9), and look at how you can use the Shaders.dir movie to customize a shader and texture for it.

Working Around a Limitation in Director 8.5

In Director 8.5 Shockwave, 3D members created using the Insert menu or by using a keyboard shortcut have a `media` property with a value of 0. This means that you cannot copy the media of one Shockwave 3D member and paste it into another. Generally speaking, this is unlikely to bother you in your own projects; however, the Shaders.dir movie is slightly handicapped by this.

Ideally, you should be able to use the Shaders.dir movie in a window as a MIAW, to experiment with textures and shaders in a copy of the movie that appears on the Stage. In practice, you can work this way, but only if you place your Shockwave 3D member in an external cast. This allows the Shaders.dir movie to link to the same cast, and thus gain access to the same models as the movie on the Stage.

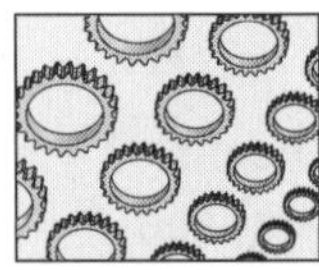

NOTE

In Director 8.5, if you use `new(#shockwave3D)` to create your member, or if you import an external file using the Standard Import option, the value of the `media` property of the member will be valid.

Working with an External Cast

KeyViews.cst

In the 3D\Surface2\ folder on the CD-ROM that accompanies this book, you'll find an external cast named KeyViews.cst. This contains a behavior named Move Camera that allows you to rotate the camera around a scene using the arrow keys, and to jump to preset views using the X, Y, Z, C, and R keys. This gives you the same control of the camera in your own movies as you are used to in the Shaders.dir movie and the other movies studied in this chapter.

Create a new movie and use the menu Modify | Movie | Casts… to link the KeyViews.cst to your movie. Now use the menu File | Save As… to save the linked cast under the name External.cst on your hard disk. This means now you will be able to save all changes you make to this cast.

From within your movie, the castLib will still be called KeyViews, regardless of the name of the external file. To avoid confusion, open the Cast window and use the Choose Cast button in the top-left corner to display the KeyViews cast. Open the Property Inspector at the Cast tab and change the movie's name for the castLib to External, as shown in Figure 11-7.

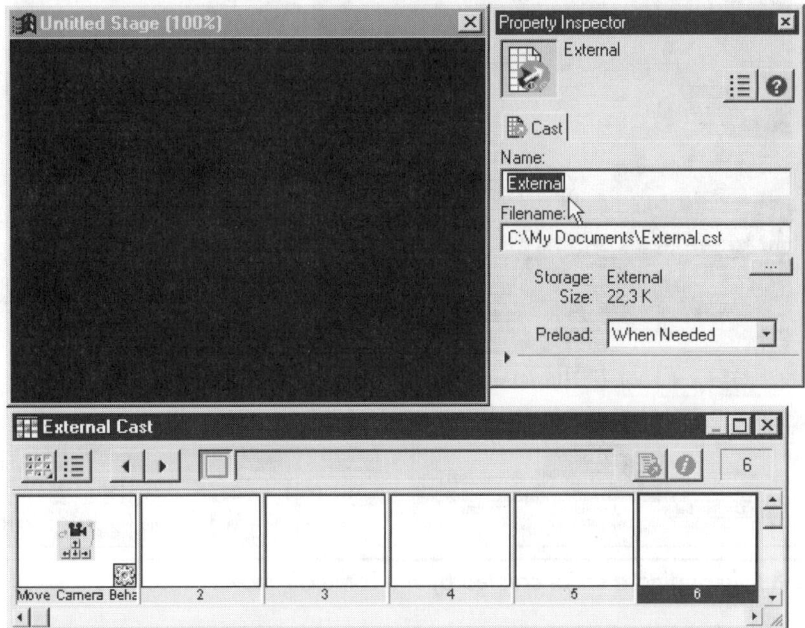

Figure 11-7 *The KeyViews.cst after it has been imported and renamed*

In the second cast slot, create a new Shockwave 3D member. Name this member 3D World so that it is not deleted when you save your movie, and drag the new member onto the Stage.

You are now ready to import a script that will create a model for you in your empty 3D world. Use the menu File | Import… to choose the script file mPlate.ls, which you'll find in the 3D\Surface2\Scene\ folder on the CD-ROM (the "m" stands for "mesh"). The script will be imported as a Movie Script. Click the Script member in the Cast window; then open the Properties Inspector. Click the Script tab, and set the member's type to Behavior. You now can drag the imported script and drop it on the Shockwave 3D sprite. Now drop the Move Camera behavior onto the Shockwave 3D sprite. This behavior was already in cast slot 1 when you linked the cast to your new movie.

Launch your movie; an opaque white plate should appear, as in Figure 11-8. You can use the keys mentioned at the beginning of this subsection to move the camera to view the plate from different angles.

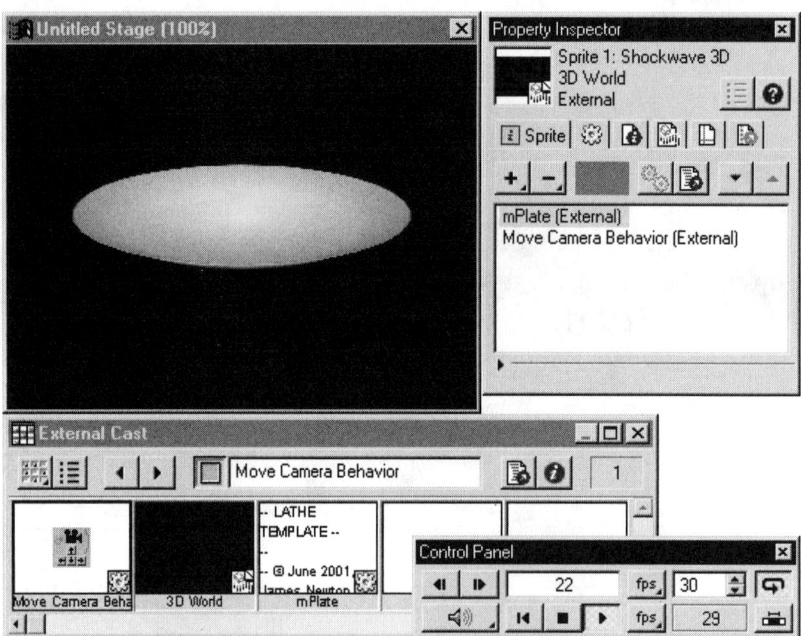

Figure 11-8 *Importing a script created by the Lathe.dir movie*

Linking the Shaders.dir Movie to the Same External Cast

Save your movie as Plate.dir; then create a new movie. If you don't do this, you won't be able to load the Shockwave 3D member in the Shaders window. As far as Shockwave 3D members are concerned, Director 8.5 is somewhat particular about the order in which you link two different movies to the same external cast. You'll need to link the cast to the Shaders MIAW first, and then reopen your Plate.dir movie. If you do things in the wrong order, an alert and a set of instructions in the Message window will put you on the right track, as Figure 11-9 shows.

If you have copied the Shaders.dir movie and its helper -picker.dir movie to your Xtras folder, you should be able to use the menu Xtras | Shaders to open the Shaders.dir movie in a window. If not, run the AddXtras.exe projector on the CD-ROM and restart Director before you continue.

Now that you have the Shaders.dir movie open in a window, click the Cast… button and use the dialog to locate the new External.cst file you created in the

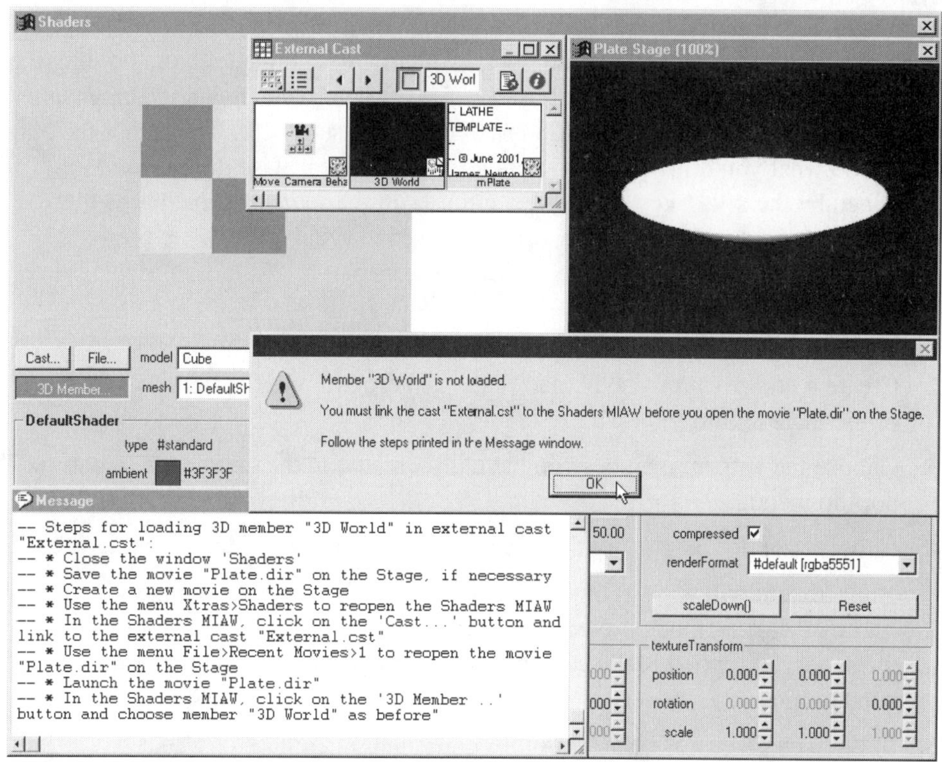

Figure 11-9 *Linking the Shaders MIAW to an external cast on the Stage requires a workaround.*

preceding section. Reopen the Plate.dir movie and run it so the plate model appears in the Shockwave 3D sprite. In the Shaders MIAW, use the 3D Member… button in the Shaders MIAW to select the 3D World member where the plate model appears. The plate now should also appear in the Shaders MIAW. Granted, the steps you have just followed are somewhat tortuous, but from here on you are free to be creative.

Designing a Shader

You are now ready to design a texture for the plate model. You might notice that the initial view of the plate corresponds to the current view in the movie on the Stage. The Shockwave 3D member in the Shaders MIAW contains a clone of the model in the member on the Stage. Changes you make in the MIAW will not affect the movie on the Stage directly. To change the movie on the Stage, you will need to export scripts from the Shaders MIAW and import these into the movie on the Stage.

Both the movie on the Stage and the Shaders MIAW share the same External cast file, which means any Bitmap members you create in the External cast are immediately available to both movies. Use the menu Window | Cast to open the External cast window and create a new Bitmap member. Using the Rectangle tool and holding the SHIFT key down, create a square. Adjust the size of the square so that its dimensions are a power of 2: 64 × 64 or 128 × 128 is a good size to start with. Remember the plate is round, so what you draw in the corners might not appear. Use the Ellipse tool, constrained by the SHIFT key, to create a circle with the same dimensions as the rectangular frame. Inside this circle, draw a design for your plate.

To apply your design to the plate, follow these steps:

1. Create a new shader, name it Plate, and drag it onto the plate model.
2. Create a new texture, also named Plate, and drag it onto the first layer button of the Plate texture.
3. Choose the Bitmap member you have just created in the `texture member` pop-up menu.
4. Choose `#wrapPlanar` in the `textureMode` pop-up menu.

   Your texture will appear, but it will be distorted because, by default, the `#wrapPlanar` mode projects the shader layer along the z axis. In this case, the shader is applied to the edge of the plate rather than to the top. You will need to rotate the shader:
5. In the `wrapTransform` section, set the rotation around the x axis to –90°.

The result of these steps is shown in Figure 11-10.

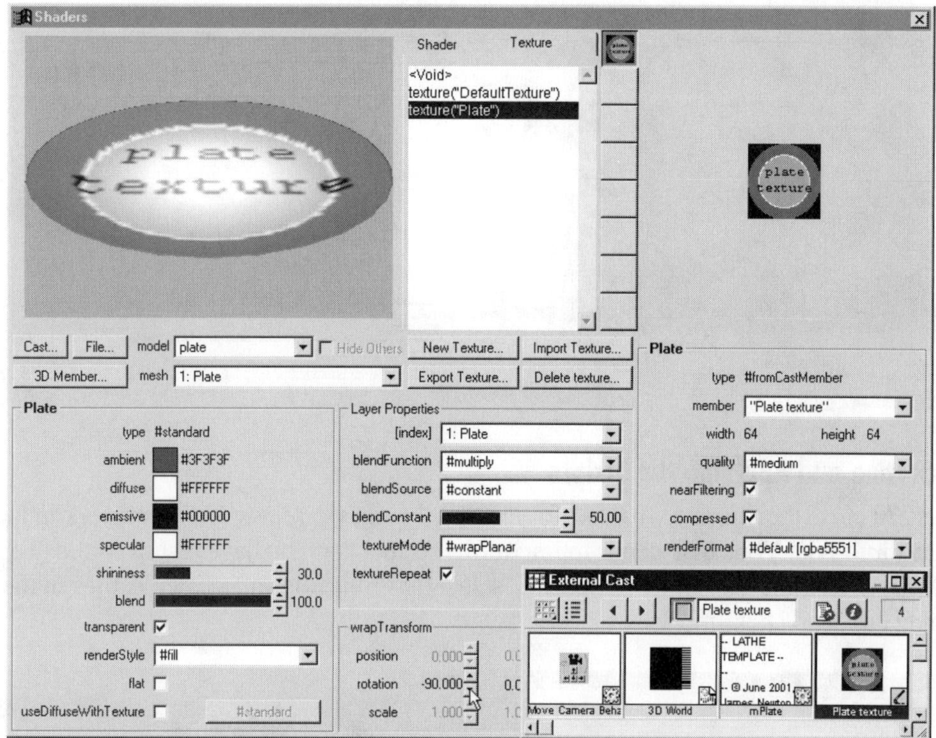

Figure 11-10 *Applying a shader and texture using the Shaders.dir movie*

If you wish, you can alter any of the other properties in order to make your design appear to its best effect.

Importing Shader and Texture Scripts into Your Movie

Your work in the Shaders window has no effect on the Shockwave 3D member in your original Plate.dir movie. To use the shader and texture that you have just designed, you need to export linked scripts from the Shaders window, and re-import them into the Plate.dir movie.

Exporting the Scripts

Click the Export Texture… button and save the texture as txPlate.ls (the "tx" is for "texture"). Now click the Shader tab to show the Export Shader button, and save the shader as shPlate.ls.

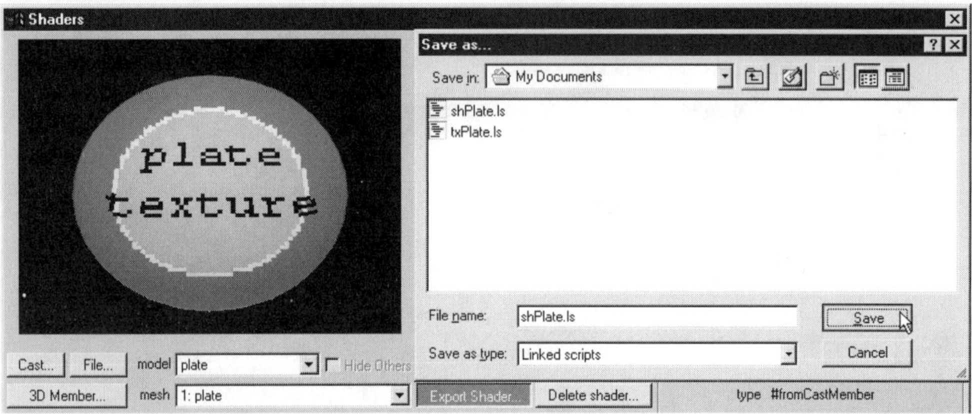

Importing and Applying the Scripts

You can close the Shaders window, for the time being; we're now going to work in the Plate.dir movie. Your first step is to import the scripts that you have just exported. To do this, choose the menu File | Import…, select the shPlate.ls and txPlate.ls files in the dialog box, and click Import.

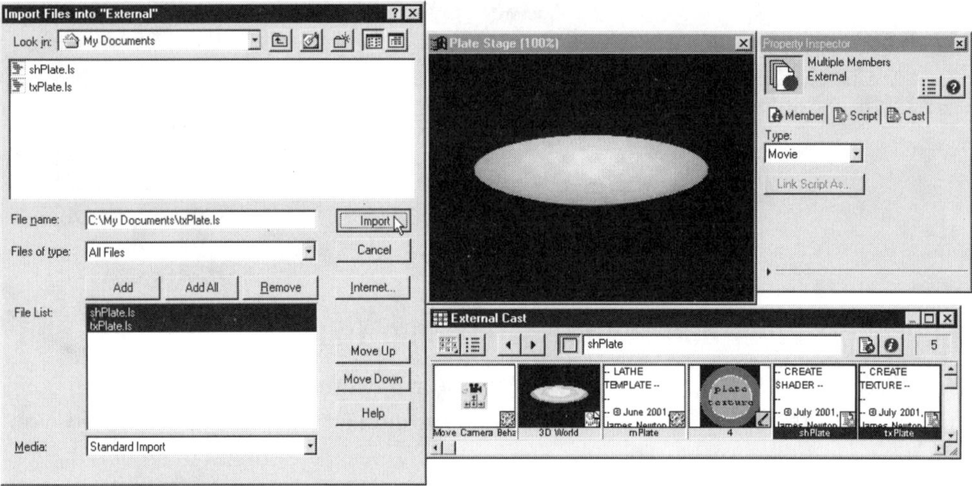

Both files will be imported as Movie Scripts. Select both imported scripts and use the Script tab in the Property Inspector to convert them to behaviors. Drop both behaviors on the Shockwave 3D sprite.

The order in which the behaviors appear on the sprite is important: the model needs a shader and the shader needs a texture. So the texture behavior should be instantiated first, followed by the shader behavior. The model behavior should be instantiated last. Use the Shuffle arrow buttons on the Behaviors tab of the Property Inspector to place the behaviors in the right order. See Figure 11-11.

Now run your movie. The plate model should appear just as it did in the Shaders window when you exported the scripts.

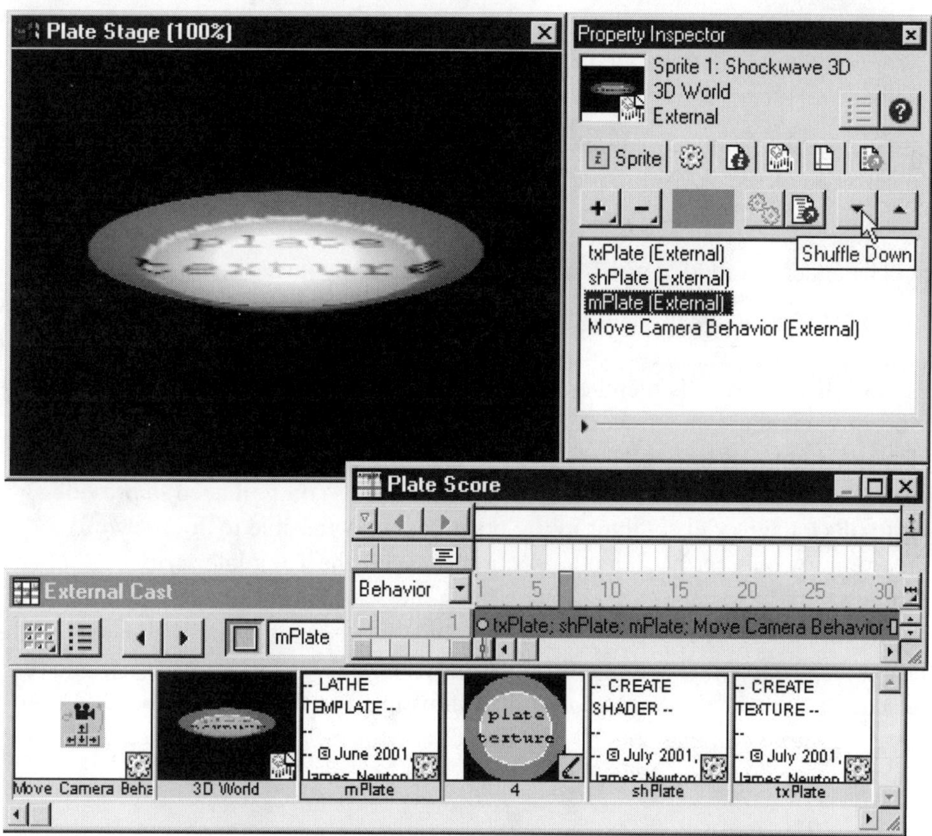

Figure 11-11 *Arranging texture, shader, and model behaviors in the right order on the sprite*

Using Imported Scripts as Behaviors and as Movie Scripts

All the imported scripts, whether they come from the Lathe.dir movie or the Shaders.dir movie, can be used as behaviors. This is intended simply to allow you to visualize your models and materials quickly while creating a prototype, as you have just done. We'll look at a better technique, designed for industrial-strength applications, in the next section.

The behavior part of the script appears at the very end. These scripts only work together successfully when the following conditions are met:

- Any texture behaviors are instantiated before any shader behaviors that use those textures.
- Any shader behaviors are instantiated before any model behaviors that use those shaders.
- All models require only one shader.
- The shader used by a given model has the same name as the model itself.
- As a consequence of the last point, every model must use a different shader.

If your Shockwave 3D member needs to display many models and materials, it can become cumbersome to work with multiple behaviors on the same sprite.

The most obvious difficulty in a multimodel world is that all the models will be created at the center, at the point `vector(0, 0, 0)`. You will need to provide code to place the models in their initial positions. It is possible to do this while prototyping by editing the Behavior section of the Lathe Template scripts. A better solution would be to centralize the code in one script.

In a moment we will look at two movies: one that uses numerous behaviors on the same sprite (Scene0.dir) and one that uses only two behaviors (Scene2.dir): one for the scene itself and the other to control the movement of the camera. In the second movie, the imported behaviors have been left as Movie Scripts and edited to remove all unnecessary duplicate code.

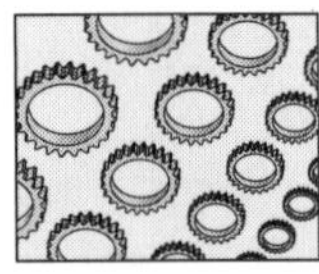

NOTE

Scripts that have been edited manually might no longer function correctly if you re-import them into the Shader window, as described in the next section. Since they are uneditable, the scripts and media for Scene1.dir and Scene2.dir have been placed in the internal cast.

Editing Exported Scripts

You can re-import scripts into the Shaders.dir movie to edit them. Such scripts are imported into the external cast. If you have the Shaders window open to work with a movie on the Stage, this means re-imported scripts are added to the external cast of the movie on the Stage. These imported scripts will not be saved unless you save the movie that you are working with on the Stage.

If you already have a script with a given name, you will be given the option of replacing the existing script. The current texture or shader will be replaced at the same time. If you import the script without overwriting the original, the original texture or shader will be maintained.

After you have made your modifications you can re-export the scripts. The changes you make are saved to an external file. The imported scripts are not updated automatically, which means any changes you make will not take effect in your final movie unless you do one of the following:

- You import the scripts into your final movie as Linked Scripts, in which case the movie will load the latest version of the script each time it is run. This assumes that you overwrite the initial script when you re-export.
- Or you re-import the edited script into your final movie, using the Standard Import option. This approach allows you to make a number of different versions of your script simultaneously. You can thus revert to a previous version by erasing the Script member and importing the previous Linked Script in its place.
- Or (and this is the simplest solution) you link the Shaders window to the external cast of the final movie before you make your changes. You then can export the modified script onto the hard disk and immediately re-import it. The imported script will be added to the external cast and you will be given the option of overwriting the previous version. The next time you save the movie on the Stage, the changes will become permanent.

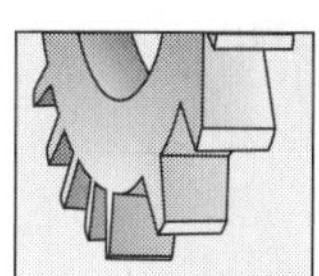

TIP

Always import textures first. An imported shader will not be able to use a texture unless the texture is already present at the time the shader is imported. If you forget, first import the required textures; then re-import the shader. A dialog will ask you to confirm that you want to overwrite the existing script. If you do so, the faulty shader will be deleted and a new one created in its place.

A Multimodel Example

Scene0.dir, Scene0.cst

The Plate.dir movie uses a single model, shader, and texture. The Shaders.dir movie can cope with multiple models, shaders, and textures. You will find an example of this in the 3D\Surface2\Scene\Multiple\ folder. The movie Scene0.dir portrays a scene made of six models:

- The plate is a single model.
- The wine glass and the wine it contains are two separate models, each with a transparent shader. The techniques used to create the shaders are different.
- The lamp is a superposition of a base, a bulb, and a lampshade—each with a different shader.

The shaders are designed for download over the Internet. The textures images are as compact as possible; none is larger than 64 × 64 pixels. The compressed version of the movie and its cast together weigh just more than 15K. Less than 6K of this is due to the texture Bitmaps.

Examining the Shaders and Textures

All the media and scripts for this scene are stored in the external Scene0.cst. Copy the 3D\Surface2\Scene\Multiple\ folder to your hard disk. If you are working in Windows, open the Properties dialog for each file and uncheck the Read-only box. With an empty movie open on the Stage, open the Shaders.dir movie in a window and use the Cast… button to link to your copy of Scene0.cst. Now, open your copy of the Scene0.dir movie on the Stage and launch it. Use the 3D Member button in the Shaders window to open the Scene Shockwave 3D member. You now should be able to view and edit all the shaders and textures in the movie. The Scene0.dir movie uses Linked Scripts, so any changes you make to the shaders and textures and re-export will take effect the next time you reopen the Scene0.dir movie.

Shaders Recipes

Three of the shaders used are transparent to some extent: the wine glass, the wine in the glass, and the lampshade—the lamp base, the bulb, and the plate are opaque. You have already seen in detail how the plate shader is created. Here I will simply draw your attention to the key features of the other shaders.

The Wine Glass Shader, or Using a Bug to Find a Feature

The crystal effect of the wine glass is rather tricky to produce. I discovered it through a bug in Director 8.5. The models seen in the Shaders window are cloned from the Shockwave 3D member in the external cast. In Director 8.5, the `colorList` property of a mesh is not copied when you use `cloneModelFromCastMember()`. As a result, all the mesh models in the Shaders window have an empty `colorList`.

This bug can be corrected by a couple of lines of Lingo. Here is an extract from the 3D World Object script in the Shader.dir movie (`pmWorld` is the main Shockwave 3D member, `a3DMember` is the member in the external cast, and `tName` is the name of the model to clone):

```
tModel = pmWorld.cloneModelFromCastmember(tName,tName,a3DMember)
-- -- Director 8.5 bug workaround: however the bug can be useful
-- if tModel.resource.type = #mesh then
--  tModel.resource.colorList = tModel.resource.colorList
-- end if
```

As you can see, I have chosen not to correct the bug in this instance. If you drop the Glass shader on any of the models in the Shaders window, you will obtain a faceted glass effect.

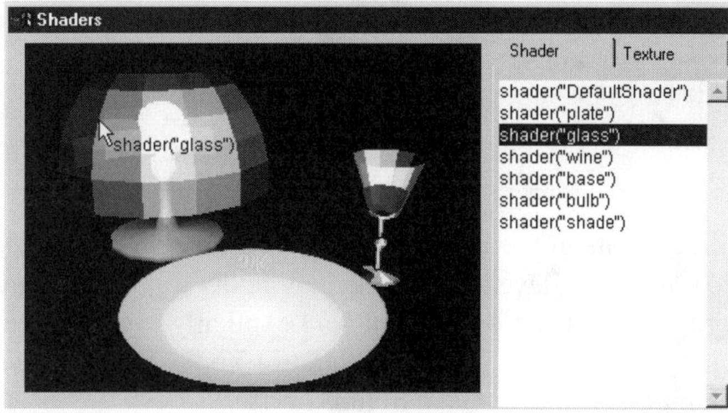

However, in the Scene0.dir movie, this effect will only work on the wine glass mesh.

Try the following steps:

1. Open the `shGlass` shader behavior in the Scene cast of the Scene0.dir movie.
2. At the beginning of the `mCreateShader()` handler you will find the following line:

   ```
   tName = "Glass"
   ```

3. Modify this so that it now reads

```
tName = "Shade"
```

This means there will be no shader named Glass, and the shader defined by the `shGlass` shader behavior will be used by the lamp `Shade` model instead.

4. In the Message window, type

```
member("Scene").resetWorld()
```

5. Restart the Scene0.dir movie. The glass will no longer be visible and the lampshade will be opaque; not transparent. To restore your movie, reopen it without saving the changes or choose File | Revert.

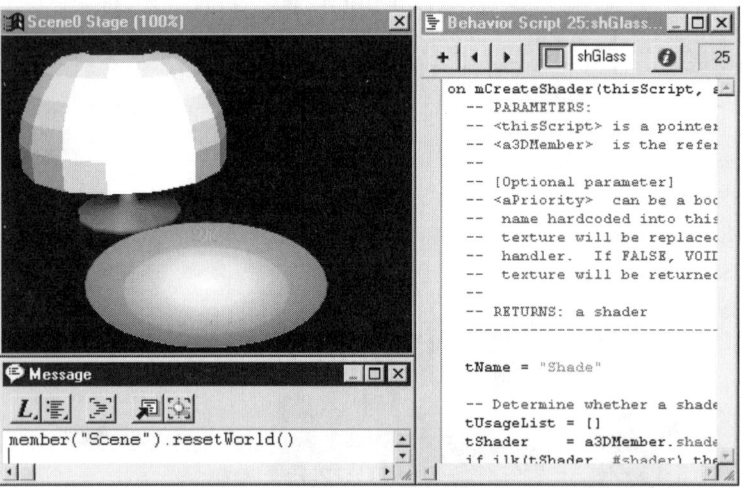

So what is different about the wine glass model resource? After I discovered that the crystal effect I could achieve in the Shaders window was due to a missing `colorList` property for the cloned resource, I explicitly avoided setting the property during my construction of the Glass mesh. You can see the two extracts of the mGlass.ls script that achieve this in Figure 11-12.

If you do not set the `colorList` property for a mesh resource, a default value of `[rgb( 0, 0, 0 )]` is used instead. However, setting the `colorList` to this value does not yield the same results.

I now must sound a note of warning. The technique I use for the Glass shader seems to rely on unexpected—and perhaps unwanted—side effects of the current 3D

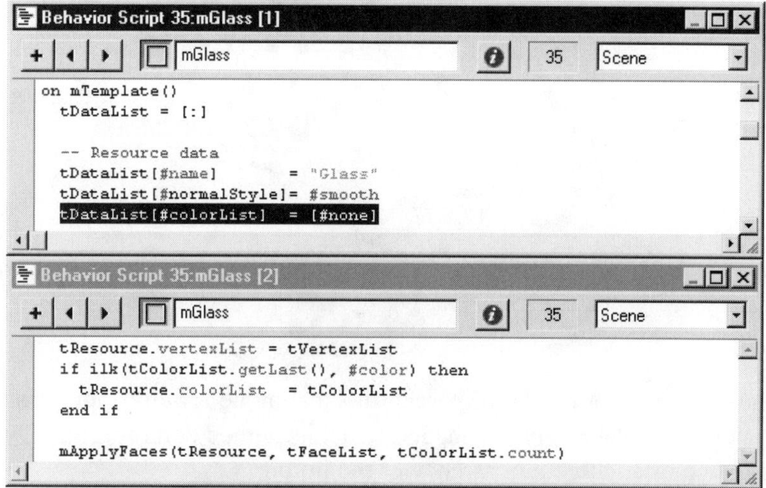

Figure 11-12 *Failing to apply a colorList to a mesh resource can result in a transparent shader.*

codebase. It is possible—even likely—that future versions of Director will render this shader differently. Perhaps Macromedia will decide to officialize the effect; perhaps a bug fix or enhancement to the codebase will stop the effect from working. I hope for the former, but I cannot guarantee it.

Another caveat: The `#software` renderer does not cope with this technique. When using the `#software` renderer, the glass becomes invisible.

The Wine Shader

The Wine shader uses a much more orthodox technique. It uses a single-pixel, 32-bit Bitmap member. The rgb channel of the member's image defines the wine color; the alpha channel defines its transparence. The texture is set to use the `renderFormat` most suitable for semitransparent images: `#rgba8888`. The `ambient` and `specular` values of the shader also are set to a wine color.

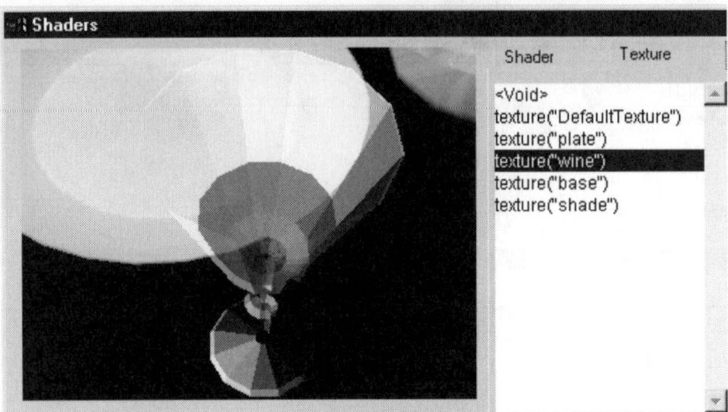

For wine, which is not fully transparent, this technique is quite appropriate. The alpha channel value of 119 gives a shader, which is a good compromise between the density of the color and the transparency of the liquid.

However, for glass you would need to set a much lower value. The result is not so convincing: a very low value makes the glass almost invisible; a moderately low value makes the glass look frosted. Try creating a texture and shader for the glass using a white single-pixel Bitmap member, and the same approach as the Wine shader. Assuming you call it "White pixel," you can set the alpha channel for your single-pixel 32-bit member by typing the following into the Message window:

```
member("White pixel").image.setAlpha(10) -- or any value from 0 to 255
```

Can you find a setting that gives as good an effect as the Glass shader I describe in the preceding? No? The `flat` property of the Wine shader is set to `TRUE`. This has no effect on its transparence. Rather, it ensures that the shape of the wine corresponds to the shape of the glass, which also uses the value `TRUE` for its `flat` property to give a faceted appearance.

The Shade Shader

For the lampshade, I wanted to give the effect of a woven material, which would be just sufficiently transparent for the bulb to be visible. I achieved this by creating a 32-bit Bitmap member whose rgb channel is the color of the lampshade, and by creating a very dark checkerboard-style pattern for the alpha channel. None of the pixels in the alpha channel is black, so the texture is slightly transparent everywhere, but not uniformly so.

I also wanted the shade to have tassels. To create tassels directly in the mesh resource would be complex and memory intensive. Instead, I made the texture transparent between the tassels.

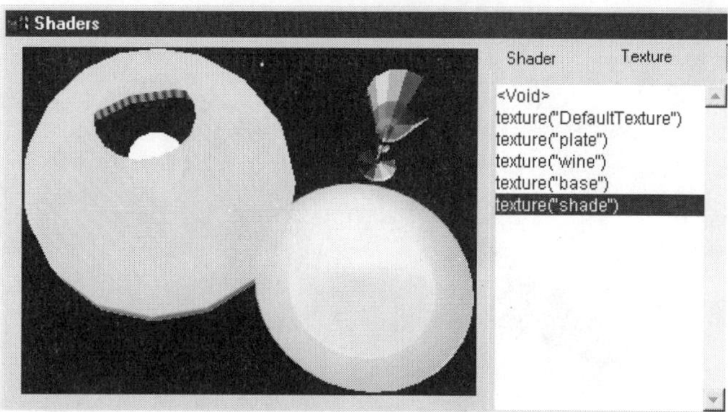

I've included the alpha channel image in a separate Bitmap member. If you decide to edit it, you'll need to reset the alpha channel of the member used for the texture using the following code:

```
put member("Shade rgb").image.setAlpha(member("Shade alpha").image)-- 1
```

As you saw in Chapter 2, there are many reasons setting the alpha channel might fail, so it is always good to `put` the result of the operation, just to be sure it has succeeded.

The Bulb Shader

The Bulb shader itself uses no texture. Its main feature is the bright `emissive` color used to give the impression that the bulb is glowing. Of course, the mesh model does not produce light. You need to use a light object to do that. As shown in Figure 11-13, the `emissive` color is slightly yellow, so it looks like a 40W incandescent bulb.

The Base Shader

To give an effect of polished wood, I've used a texture with vertical lines of slightly different colors of brown. By twisting the shader through 45° around both the y and the z axes, I've managed to create a wood-knot pattern at the base of the stand.

A Bunch of Behaviors

To get the textures and shaders to appear in the Shockwave 3D sprite, a behavior is attached for each one. A separate Lathe Script behavior also is attached for each model. An additional one-off behavior named Model Positions is required to set the shader for each model, and to place each in its appropriate group and position. Counting the Move Camera behavior, that makes 18 behaviors in all.

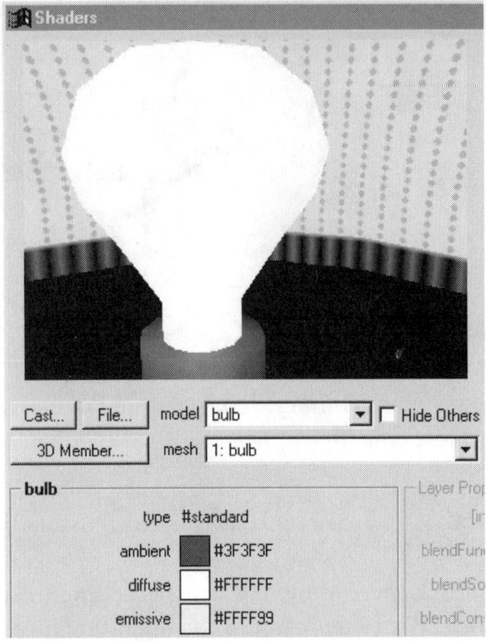

Figure 11-13 *Setting the parameters for the bulb shader*

The advantage of working this way is that it requires the minimum of coding. The disadvantage is that the sprite becomes overloaded with behaviors. The Behavior tab of the Property Inspector can show you only seven behaviors at one time. In a more complex world, this multibehavioral approach would become unmanageable. In the next section, we'll look at another way of organizing your code so that it is both accessible and comprehensible.

Looking at the Lingo

Scene1.dir, Scene2.dir, Scene.dir

After all the fun of experimenting with the texture and shader properties, let's come back down to earth and look at the Lingo that makes them materialize. There are four versions of the Scene movie. The version you've been working with, Scene0.dir, contains the scripts exported by the Shaders window. These scripts are long and complex because they are designed to work in a wide variety of situations. The simplest version, Scene.dir, is stripped down to the bare minimum. Take a look at this movie first, as this is where the code is clearest.

Later, we'll look at the Scene2.dir movie, as this illustrates an interesting technique for initializing your 3D world. The Scene1.dir movie contains exactly the same scripts and media as Scene0.dir. The only difference is that they all are integrated into the internal script, which allows you to make a direct comparison of the sizes of the resulting compressed *.dcr files:

- 15.1K for Scene1.dcr, with the scripts exactly as exported from the Shaders window
- 16.2K for Scene2.dcr, because it includes additional scripts and label members for clarity
- 13.0K for Scene.dcr, where the code and media are stripped to a minimum

In other words, despite their sophistication, the scripts exported by the Shaders window are not gluttons.

Code Stripped to Its Essentials

Compared to the complexity of the concepts involved, the code required to create a texture or a shader is straightforward.

Code for a Texture

Texture.ls

Here is a handler that contains all the necessary ingredients for creating a texture. You'll find an electronic version in the 3D\Surface2\ folder on the CD-ROM, under the name Texture.ls. The scripts in the Scene.dir movie all follow this schema.

```
on mCreateTexture(a3DMember)
  tName = "<texture name>"

  -- Determine whether a texture with the given name already exists
  tTexture = a3DMember.texture(tName)
  if ilk(tTexture, #texture) then
    return tTexture
  end if

  -- Create a new texture
  tTexture = a3DMember.newTexture(tName)
  tTexture.member = member("<Bitmap member name>")
```

```
  -- Customize properties whose values differ from default
  tTexture.quality       = #medium -- #low | #high
  tTexture.nearFiltering = TRUE -- FALSE
  tTexture.compressed    = TRUE -- FALSE
  tTexture.renderFormat  = #default  -- #rgba5550 | #rgba5650 |
  --                       #rgba 8880 | #rgba4444 | #rgba5551 |
  --                       #rgba8888

  return tTexture
end mCreateTexture
```

Because each texture must have a unique name, the handler first tests to see whether a texture with the given name already exists. If so, it returns that texture and goes no further. A texture with no member or image is of little value; so, once you've created a new texture, you should provide it with an image source. The `newTexture()` method actually allows you to do this all in one go:

```
tTexture = a3DMember.newTexture(<string name>, <symbol type>, <image source>)
```

It is even possible to include an undocumented property list to define inks and other `copyPixel`-like information. For example, if you want to use Mask ink on a Bitmap member, place the Bitmap member that provides the mask in the following cast member slot; then use Lingo such as this:

```
tBitmap  = member("Masked image")
tTexture = scene.newTexture("Name", #fromCastMember, tBitmap, [#ink: 9])
```

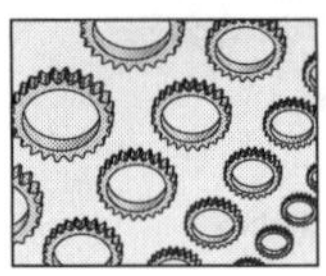

NOTE

Tom Higgins, one of the Macromedia engineers who developed the 3D features, has an unofficial site where such undocumented features are described: http://www.shockwavemovies.com/. In particular, you'll find a note concerning the ink property list parameter at http://www.shockwavemovies.com/undocd/3D/textures/inksMasks_newTexture.html.

Once you have defined the image source, you might wish to set other property values that differ from the defaults. In the preceding handler, the default values are all given first, followed by the alternative values.

Code for a Shader

Shader.ls

A shader has many more properties that you might want to set than a texture does, so I won't provide the full list here. You'll find a Linked Script named Shader.ls in the 3D\Surface2\ folder on the CD-ROM, which provides a template for creating a shader.

Here, as an example, is the Base shader from Scene.dir:

```
on mCreateShader(thisScript, a3DMember)
  tName = "Base"

  -- Determine whether a shader with the given name already exists
  tShader = a3DMember.shader(tName)
  if ilk(tShader, #shader) then
    -- Return the existing shader
    return tShader
  end if

  -- Create a new shader
  tShader = a3DMember.newShader(tName, #standard)

  -- Customize properties whose values differ from default
  -- Colors
  tShader.ambient = rgb( 0, 0, 0 )
  tShader.specular = rgb( 119, 68, 0 )

  -- General properties
  tShader.shininess = 50.00000

  -- Textures
  tShader.textureList[1] = a3DMember.texture("base")

  -- Layer list properties
  tShader.textureModeList[1] = #wrapCylindrical

  -- Wrap transform list
  tTransform          = transform()
  tTransform.position = vector( 0.00000, 0.00000, 0.00000 )
  tTransform.rotation = vector( 0.00000, 45.00000, 45.00000 )
  tTransform.scale    = vector( 1.00000, 1.00000, 1.00000 )
  tShader.wrapTransformList[1] = tTransform

  return tShader
end mCreateShader
```

Here are some points to note:

- You can't set any of the ...`List` properties (such as `textureList`) to a Lingo list. If you want to set values in the list, you must use the appropriate index number. To set the value of the first item in the list, you can use the listless shortcut. For example, to set `tShader.textureList[1]`, you can use the shortcut `tShader.texture`.

- To manipulate a transform, it is easiest to set its position, rotation, and scale properties. You can't save a transform to disk and then restore it later, but you can do this with a vector.
- All shader properties except `ambient`, `diffuse`, and `renderStyle` are ignored by the special shaders: `#painter`, `#engraver`, and `#newsprint`.
- For `#standard` shaders, certain properties are ignored, depending on the value of other properties. For example: the `wrapTransform` property is ignored if the corresponding `textureMode` is not set to one of the `#wrap...` symbols.

For both shaders and textures, you can, of course, modify the property values at any time.

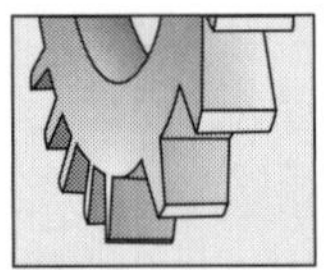

TIP

You can export such stripped-down scripts from the Shaders window if you press the OPTION key at the same time as you click the Export... button. These slim scripts cannot be used as behaviors. For textures exported in this way, you might need to modify the member name and reference by hand.

Organizing Texture and Shader Scripts

When you create your 3D world, you need to create the texture and shader required by each model, and apply them appropriately. You also need to position the various models, lights, and cameras, and arrange them in groups. As you saw in the Scene0.dir movie, using multiple behaviors for this quickly becomes cumbersome.

In the Scene2.dir movie, I have opted for a different approach. There are only two behaviors attached to the Shockwave 3D sprite: Create World in cast slot 52 and Move Camera in cast slot 53. The rest of the scripts are all movie scripts. If you set the Cast window to show rows of 10 thumbnails, you'll see that the scripts are arranged logically. Each row deals with a certain object type; each column deals with all the aspects of a particular model (see Figure 11-14).

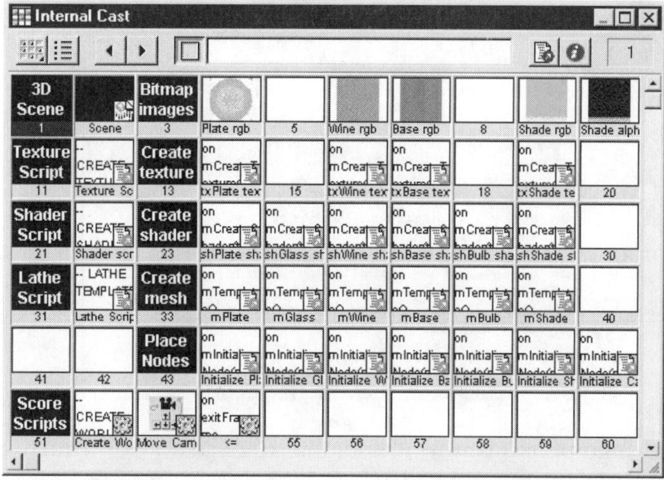

Figure 11-14 *The organization of the scripts in Scene2.dir*

Each texture and shader is created by a separate Script member. I've used stripped-down versions of the scripts, exported from the Shaders window by pressing the OPTION key and clicking the Export… button at the same time. Members 12 and 22 contain the complementary part of the scripts—all the handlers that are not included in the slim version. I obtained these scripts by exporting full texture and shader scripts, and removing the hard-coded `mCreateTexture()` and `mCreateShader()` handlers. We will look at the usefulness of these scripts during authoring in a moment.

Calling Movie Scripts

Each texture script contains the same handler:

```
on mCreateTexture(thisScript, a3DMember, aSourceList, aPriority)
```

If you were to call the handler like a global Movie Script handler, only the first script member with that handler would respond. So how do you create the textures defined by the other scripts? The answer is to call the Movie Script object directly:

```
Message
put mCreateTexture(#dummyParameter, member(2))
-- texture("Plate")

put mCreateTexture(script 16, member(2))
-- texture("Wine")
put mCreateTexture(script 17, member(2))
-- texture("Base")
put mCreateTexture(script 19, member(2))
-- texture("Shade")
```

If you are a Lingo purist, you would set the `scriptType` of each script to `#parent` before doing this, but this step is, in practice, unnecessary. (It would become necessary if your handler used the `new()` function: Movie Scripts handle the `new()` function in a different way than Behaviors and Parent scripts.)

Instead of attaching each script to the Shockwave 3D sprite as a behavior, I use one behavior to call each of the Movie Scripts in turn. I use the function `aScriptObject.handlers()` to determine which scripts can respond to the `mCreateTexture()` call. Here is a simplified version of the Create World behavior:

```
on beginSprite(me)
  tTextureScripts  = []

  -- Iterate through the cast, looking for script members that
  -- create textures
  tMemberCount = the number of members of castLib(1)
  repeat with tMemberNumber = 1 to tMemberCount
    tMember = member(tMemberNumber)

    if tMember.type = #script then
      tScript = script(tMember)
      tHandlers = tScript.handlers()
      if tHandlers.getPos(#mCreateTexture) then
        tTextureScripts.append(tScript)
      end if
    end if
  end repeat

  -- Use the listed scripts to create the required textures
```

```
  me.mCreateTextures(tTextureScripts)
end beginSprite


on mCreateTextures(me, aScriptList)
  t3DMember = sprite(me.spriteNum).member
  tCount = aScriptList.count
  repeat with i = 1 to tCount
    aScriptList[i].mCreateTexture(t3DMember)
  end repeat
end mCreateTextures
```

This approach requires certain discipline: it assumes that all scripts use the `mCreateTexture()` handler name function in the same way. The same technique works just as well with shaders, mesh resources, or initializing the position and group for each node. In the full script in the Scene2.dir movie, I create separate lists for each key handler name—and iterate through the cast members only once—placing pointers to the various scripts in the appropriate lists. Once all the scripts have been found, I call the key handler in each script in each group.

Advantages and Disadvantages

This technique is slightly slower than using behaviors attached to the sprite, since the Create World behavior has to check each cast member in turn before acting, whereas the sprite already knows what behaviors are attached to it. The more casts and the more cast members you have, the longer this script census is going to take.

The main advantage is that the scripts simply have to be available in the cast in order to be activated. You don't have to drop each one individually on the sprite, and you thus avoid having to order the behaviors correctly. You also can test different versions of the same script, with a minimum of fuss. For example, if you have two script members that define (differently) a shader with a given name, you simply move the version you want to test to a lower-numbered cast slot. When the second script is called, it will realize that a shader with the given name already exists and will leave things as they are. The Create World behavior is generic; you can use it in different movies to create completely different worlds. The result depends on the Movie Scripts you feed it on.

Help While Authoring

The full version of the exported texture scripts include authortime code to help you locate the Bitmap members you want to use for textures. If you unlink the external cast containing a needed Bitmap member, the scripts are smart enough to find the member for you, or to ask for your help if they can't manage on their own. As a bonus, the full scripts even allow you to use Flash, Text, Vector Shape, and other Shockwave 3D members as sources for your texture images.

The main reason for this sophistication is that the Shader window and the movie you are working on are likely to have different file paths; the code is required by the Shader.dir movie itself. I have left the code in the exported scripts so that, while you are still at an early stage in your development, you can rely on the scripts to do much of the fastidious fetching and carrying that otherwise you would have to do for yourself.

Another feature required by the Shader.dir movie is the capability to overwrite an existing texture or shader with a given name, so it can provide a different version with the same name. In your projects, you are more likely to want to reset the property values of the existing texture or shader. However, there might be cases in which the user's interaction modifies a texture or shader, and you might wish to re-initialize it. I have left the `mRemove...()` and `mReplace...()` handlers in the full version of the code for that purpose.

In the Scene2.dir movie, both these features are dealt with by separate scripts (members 12 and 22).

Animated Textures

Textures need not be static. Here's a simple behavior that uses the `image` of an animated Flash member for the texture. The `image` of the texture is changed on every `exitFrame` by changing the `posterFrame` property of the Flash member. You'll find this code in the movie Aquarium.dir in the 3D\Surface2\ folder on the CD-ROM. There are a couple of lines you can uncomment; you can use the same image to produce more than one fish:

```
property myTexture
property myFlashMember
property myFrameCount
property myFrame
```

```
on beginSprite(me)
  myFlashMember = member("Fish")
  myFrameCount  = myFlashMember.frameCount

  tMember = sprite(me.spriteNum).member
  tMember.resetWorld()

  -- Texture
  myTexture              = tMember.newTexture("Fish")
  -- Shader
  tShader                = tMember.newShader("Fish", #standard)
  tShader.texture        = myTexture
  --tShader.textureList[2]= myTexture
  --tShader.textureTransform.translate(0.5, 0, 0)
  -- Resource
  tResource              = tMember.newModelResource("Aquarium", #plane)
  tResource.length       = 64
  tResource.width        = 256
  -- Model
  tModel                 = tMember.newModel("Aquarium", tResource)
  tModel.shaderList      = tShader

  -- Camera
  tMember.camera(1).transform.position = vector(0, 0, 150)
end beginSprite


on exitFrame(me)
  myFrame = (myFrame mod myFrameCount) + 1
  myFlashMember.posterFrame = myFrame
  myTexture.image = myFlashMember.image
end exitFrame
```

By using Imaging Lingo in association with textures, you can create very spectacular effects.

Conclusion

There are endless variations on the theme of shaders and textures. Instead of describing a handful of recipes in the space available, I provided you with a powerful and flexible MIAW tool—the Shaders.dir movie—that you can use to develop and share your own recipes, and showed you how to exploit it. You are welcome to adapt the Shaders.dir movie to suit your own needs and share your modifications with other developers.

I have also discussed a number of techniques for creating and positioning models and for applying shaders and textures to them. These range from a no-code, drag-and-drop technique suitable for prototyping to a minimalist technical approach. The movies in the following chapters all adopt the technical approach, since this leads to the clearest code.

Now that you have learned to deal with both architecture and appearance, it's time to look at cameras and lights.

CHAPTER

12

Ways of Seeing

IN THIS CHAPTER:

The great Japanese artists changed their names and their status ten or even twenty times in their ceaseless effort to renew themselves. . . it is not right that the originality of that first vision should become a trick of the trade, a formula a thousand times repeated.

—Brassaï

Without a camera, a Shockwave 3D member would be a blank rectangle. In previous chapters, you have had the chance to see certain camera techniques. In this chapter, the process of handling a camera is made explicit.

Using a camera successfully is an art. The secret lies not in the Lingo keywords but in the choice of viewpoints and angles. You will learn more about the art of handling a camera by studying the sequences of a classic film such as Robert Flaherty's *Nanook of the North*, Serguey Eisenstein's *Battleship Potemkin*, or Orson Welles's *Citizen Kane* than you will by poring over the entries for camera properties in the online help files.

Once you have chosen a film to study, don't let yourself get carried away by the story line: Watch the film on video; stop it at the end of each camera sequence; and analyze where the camera was placed, how it was oriented, and how it was moved. Ask yourself how the camera work contributes to the atmosphere of the film and what it says about the relations between characters. Note the simplicity and restraint of each camera movement. Note how, in general, a new scene is shown in full before the camera closes in on a point of detail.

To take the other extreme, first-time video camera users tend to film everything from shoulder height; they constantly move around, turn the camera, and zoom in and out. The result is hard to follow; often there are too few wide-angle views to give an idea of the space in which the action occurs and the incessant movement of the camera nauseates the viewer. When working in a virtual 3D world, with an invisible, weightless virtual camera, an arbitrary upward direction, and no physical presence in the scene, the risk of producing a suboptimal sequence of images is even greater.

In this chapter, I shall try to show you how to use camera objects with restraint. I will demonstrate only a few basic techniques. To illustrate these techniques I have created a simple race game (see Figure 12-1), which you can find in the 3D\Cameras\ folder on the CD-ROM that accompanies the book, under the name gForce.dir. This movie provides the essential ingredients: a space filled with a simple decor and a means for moving around that space.

You might find that the game is interesting in itself, or wish to extend and improve on it for your own ends. So much the better. However, for my purposes here, it is simply a means to an end: a way to illustrate the various Lingo features of the camera object and the basic camera techniques.

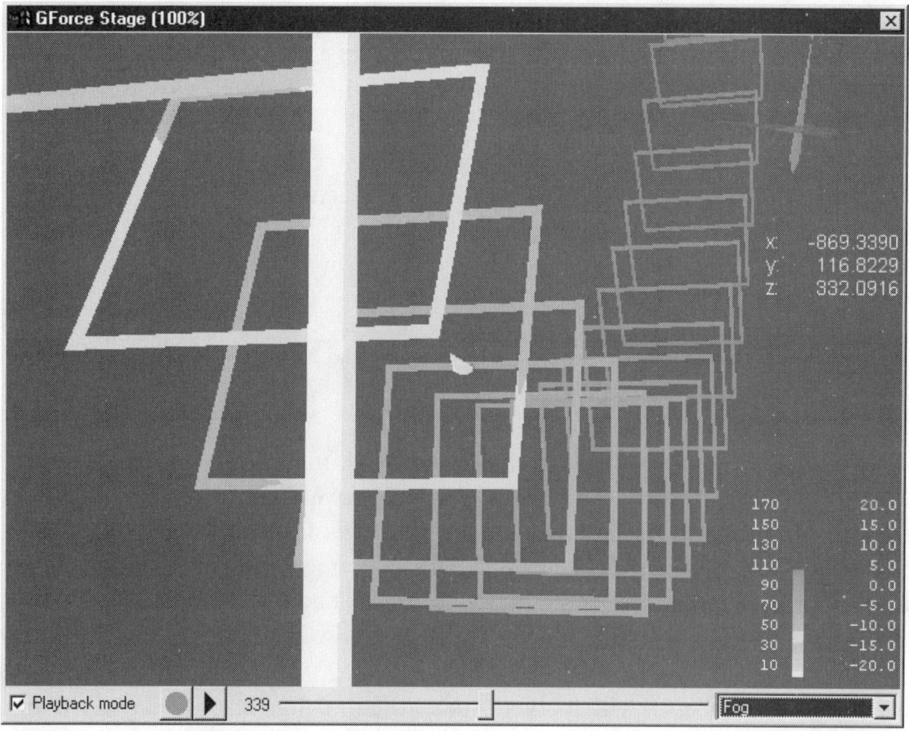

Figure 12-1 *Using the Fog camera in the gForce.dir*

Through the View Finder

If you have normal vision, your eyes allow you to see roughly half of a given space: everything in front of you and a little extra on the sides. You are used to the way your eyes deal with objects on the periphery of your vision, so you don't have the impression that there is any distortion there. A camera that has the same field of view as your eyes produces what appears to be a highly distorted image because the camera image is projected onto a flat plane, which you then look at from a respectful distance using the center of your vision. Distortions you ignore when they occur at the edges of your vision are thus exaggerated in the flat camera image.

The Frustrum

To counterbalance this effect, images taken with a camera tend to use a very narrow angle of vision. The shape you see out of your eyes is roughly oval. For simplicity, cameras tend to produce rectangular images. Combining a narrow angle of vision with a rectangular image produces a field of view in the shape of a rectangular pyramid, where the tip of the pyramid has been cut off. This shape is technically known as a *frustrum.* The light issuing from a film projector has this shape: The rectangular image being projected sits at the truncated tip of the pyramid and the rectangular screen sits at its base. In a smoky cinema, the volume occupied by the light beams is visible.

The Frustrum.dir movie shows four views of the frustrum of a camera (see Figure 12-2). This is made visible by creating a second camera for the Shockwave 3D member, and then creating a mesh model with the same dimensions and position as the camera's frustrum. The tip of the small red pyramid indicates the `worldPosition` of the camera, which also is the position of the user's eye when the camera is being used.

hither and yon

Your eyes can see anything from your hair dangling in front of them to galaxies millions of light years away. A Shockwave 3D camera has a more limited range: it will not see objects nearer than a certain point (`hither`) or further than a certain distance (`yon`). By default, an object becomes invisible to a camera if it is less than 1 world unit away, or further than 3.40×10^{38} world units. That appears to be a quite sufficient range. You would be most unlikely to create objects so big that they would appear even a pixel high when seen from a distance of 3.40×10^{38} world units. In my tests, there are circumstances in which objects that are more than 32,768 (2^{15})world units from the camera may fail to be fully rendered, regardless of the `yon` setting.

The real interest of the `hither` and `yon` settings is that you can set them yourself. If there is a wall between the camera and the character you want to see, you can set

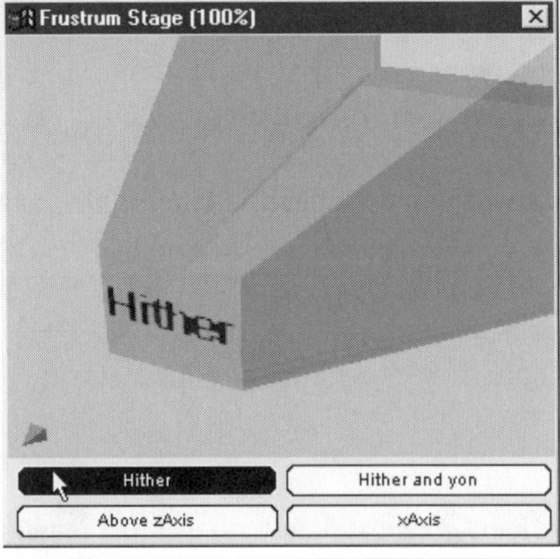

Figure 12-2 *The frustrum of a camera*

the camera's `hither` property so that it ignores the wall and only sees the character. You can prepare separate scenes in different places in your 3D world, and set the `yon` property to ensure that a camera placed in scene A will not see any of the models in the distant scene B.

fieldOfView, projectionAngle, Zoom, or Focal Length

Another difference between your eyes and a camera is that, without moving the camera, you can zoom in or out. In Shockwave 3D, this is done by modifying the camera's `projectionAngle` property (see Figure 12-3). This property actually has two names—the `fieldOfView` property has exactly the same effect. I prefer the term *projection angle* because, in my opinion, this describes the property more accurately.

The easiest way to test this property is through Ullala's 3D Property inspector. You will find a demonstration copy of this on the CD-ROM that accompanies the book; you can install it automatically by running the AddXtras.exe projector. Ullala prefers to use the `fieldOfView` property name. Figure 12-4 shows the xyzCone.dir movie, which we will be looking at in more detail in a moment. The `projectionAngle` of the cameras are set respectively to 10, 20, 40, and 80, starting at the bottom left and rotating clockwise. All the cameras are the same distance (250 units) from the center of the cone.

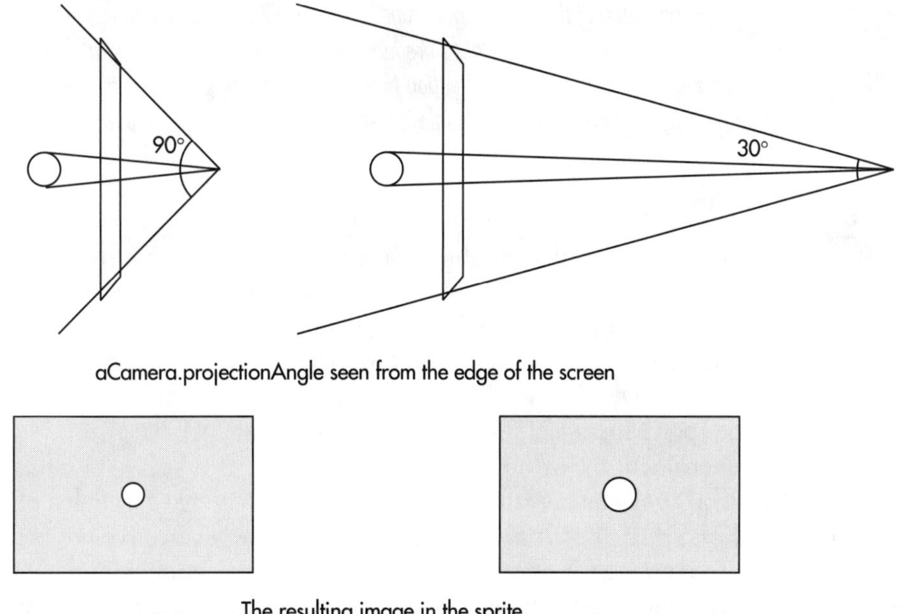

Figure 12-3 *Decreasing the projectionAngle increases the zoom.*

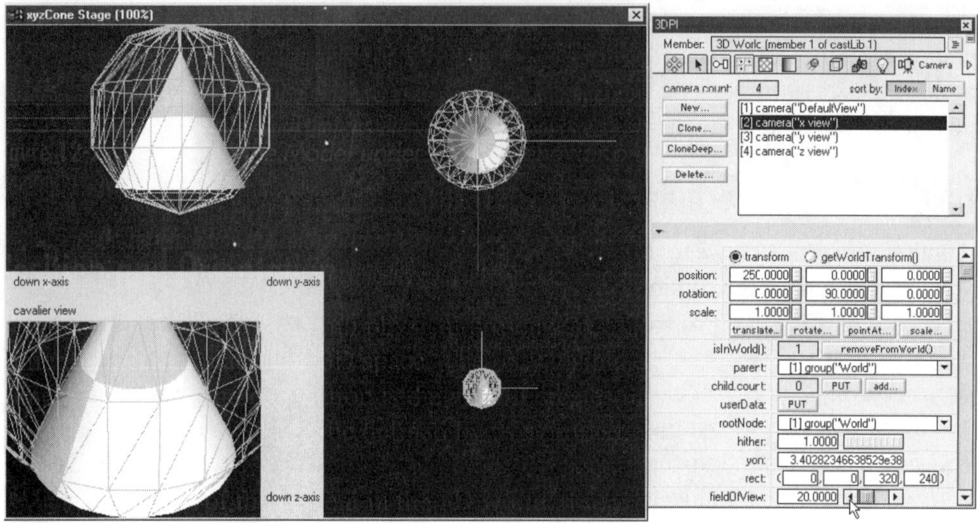

Figure 12-4 *Modifying the projectionAngle of a camera*

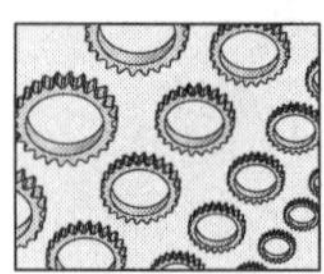

NOTE

If you have experience with a still or movie camera, you will be used to adjusting the focus of the camera in two ways: altering the focal length (zooming) and adjusting the aperture to change the range that appears in focus. You might have produced interesting effects by deliberately making part of the image out of focus, to draw attention to the rest of the image. In Shockwave 3D, everything is always in focus, from zero to infinity. There is no way to adjust the focal range.

Orthogaphic Projection

The effect of perspective makes distant objects appear smaller. Using a small `projectionAngle` counteracts this, to some extent. The opening scene of David Lean's *Lawrence of Arabia* shows Peter O'Toole on horseback, galloping toward the camera across the desert. An extremely long lens with a tiny `projectionAngle` was used to take this shot. Despite their breakneck speed, the horse and its rider appear to be running on the spot. Movement toward the camera is flattened; the effect emphasizes the immensity of the desert.

With Shockwave 3D you can take this idea to its extreme. You have a choice of two projection types: `#perspective` or `#orthographic`. A perspective projection provides the sort of views we are used to. An orthographic projection will make all objects appear at the same scale, regardless of their distance from the camera. Seen through an orthographic projection, Peter O'Toole would never get any larger until his horse knocked the camera over.

To alter the fixed scale at which objects are seen using an orthographic projection, you can alter the orthoHeight property of the camera. Run the Frustrum.dir movie, select the "Hither" view, and then type the following in the Message window:

```
sprite(1).camera.projection = #orthographic
```

The camera will not move, but suddenly the frustrum model will appear to be much farther away because the value for orthoHeight is 200.0 by default; the height of the sprite will correspond to 200 world units. The hither plane is only 0.54 units high, so it becomes insignificant. Try typing the following line:

```
sprite(1).camera.orthoHeight = 2
```

The view now will resemble the original perspective view more closely, as you can see in Figure 12-5. However, the "Hither and yon" and "xAxis" views both show the yon plane, which is much larger.

To see a meaningful version of these views, you need to reduce the scale considerably:

```
sprite(1).camera.orthoHeight = 30000
```

You might notice that the height of the yon plane is the same in all views, regardless of its distance from the camera.

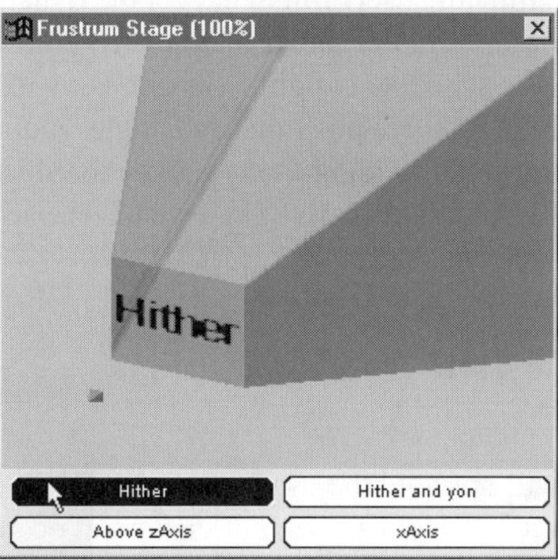

Figure 12-5 *An orthographic view from the same position shown in Figure 12-2*

You could think of the #orthogonal projection as providing a view through an infinitely powerful telescope from the infinite confines of space. In most cases, you will find that the #perspective projection gives you morc natural results. You can see a useful example of orthographic projection in the Collide.dir movie you'll be studying in Chapter 14. The rest of this chapter deals only with the #perspective projection.

Using a Fixed Viewpoint

The very first moving picture sequences were shot from a fixed viewpoint. There are both technical and aesthetic reasons for this: early film cameras were cumbersome, and early audiences had no experience of interpreting moving images. In 1895, the public showing of a short moving picture by Louis Lumière provoked a stampede. The film was of a train pulling into the station of La Ciotat in the south of France. The audience believed that the train was real and that they were in its path.

Using a fixed camera has three advantages:

- You maintain full control of what the user sees.
- You provide an image that can be easily interpreted.
- You minimize the Lingo required to deal with the camera.

Although modern multimedia users might expect the dynamic camera control found in games such as Tomb Raider, other interactive games such as Myst use fixed views to great effect. If the schedule is tight, your project will be less exposed to criticism if you choose your camera positions and angles judiciously than if you spend the same amount of time building a custom keyboard-mouse-and-joystick interface for a subjective camera. So let's start with techniques for placing a fixed camera.

Many Cameras; One View

xyzCone.dir

A single fixed camera will not hold the user's attention for long. In most feature films, a new camera sequence from a different viewpoint occurs on average once every 20 seconds or so. A rapid succession of shorter sequences can be difficult to assimilate; longer sequences can slow the rhythm. Alternating between two viewpoints can be enough to add interest to a lengthy scene.

Single Cameras in Multiple Sprites

You needn't limit each Shockwave 3D member to a single camera. You'll find a simple example of a Shockwave 3D member with multiple cameras in the xyzCone.dir movie in the 3D\Cameras\ folder on the CD-ROM. This movie uses four cameras and four sprites (see Figure 12-6). Each sprite uses a different camera to look at the same cone model from a different angle. A behavior attached to all four sprites allows you to move the model with the mouse in the same plane as the sprite's camera. Run the movie; then drag the cone model in one of the sprites to see its position updated in all the other sprites. (The behavior uses a variant of the `waveMatch()` handler, which you saw in the Matchbox.dir movie in Chapter 8.)

In most projects, you will use only one Shockwave 3D sprite, and therefore only one camera view at a time. Although you could use a single camera object that you would reposition for each view, you probably will find it easier to organize your project if you create a number of different camera objects, each with a position and

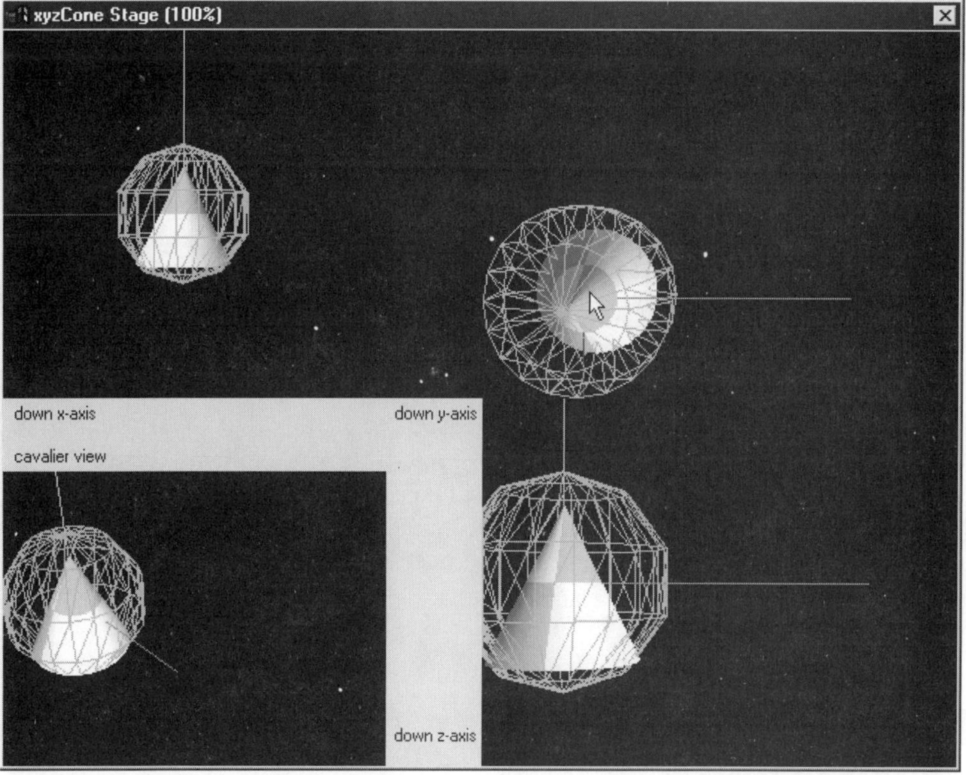

Figure 12-6 *Four camera views of the same model*

orientation and a self-explanatory name. Changing views then becomes a question of changing the active camera for the sprite. To do this, use this command:

```
sprite(whichSprite).camera = whichCamera
```

Multiple Views in a Single Sprite

RearView.dir

Director 8.5 also allows you to show multiple camera views in a single sprite. This allows you to provide inserts, rear-view mirrors, mosaic views, and the like. The first camera you use fills the sprite. You define the insert area for the second and subsequent cameras by using the `sprite(whichSprite).camera(whichCamera).rect` property. The additional camera images are rendered on top of those following, which means the same area of the sprite can be overwritten several times. The `camera.rect` property will not have the intended effect unless you have previously used

```
sprite(whichSprite).addCamera(whichCamera, index)
```

to place the extra camera on the list of cameras for the sprite.

You can see an example of this in the movie RearView.dir. Note that the scale of the image in the additional camera `rect` depends on the height of the insert `rect`. As you saw earlier, you can modify the camera's `projectionAngle` to counteract this effect.

Creating a New Camera Object

As with other nodes (models, groups, and lights), each camera object you use must have a unique name. Each Shockwave 3D member already possesses a camera named "DefaultView." When you first create a new member, this is placed at the position vector(0, 0, 250) and looks down the z axis. If you use an imported *.w3D file, the camera("DefaultView") can be in any position. Until you explicitly change it, camera("DefaultView") is the camera that will be used to create the view for the sprite.

Here is the `beginSprite()` handler from the xyzCone.dir movie that creates three new camera objects and places them to look down the x, y, and z axes. It then repurposes the `camera("DefaultView")` to create a cavalier view of the cone model.

```
on beginSprite(me)
  tMember = sprite(me.spriteNum).member
  tMember.resetWorld()

  -- Create a cone model
  coneResource = tMember.newModelResource("Cone", #cylinder)
```

```
  coneResource.topRadius = 0
  myCone         = tMember.newModel("Cone", coneResource)
  myCone.debug = TRUE

  -- Create three new cameras, looking along different axes
  tCamera = tMember.newCamera("x view")
  tCamera.worldPosition = vector(250, 0, 0)
  tCamera.pointAt(0, 0, 0)

  tCamera = tMember.newCamera("y view")
  tCamera.worldPosition = vector(0, 250, 0)
  tCamera.pointAt(vector(0, 0, 0), vector(0, 0, -1))
   -- see the "Which Way is Up?" section below

  tCamera = tMember.newCamera("z view")
  tCamera.worldPosition = vector(0, 0, 250)
  tCamera.pointAt(0, 0, 0)

  -- Use the default camera for a cavalier view
  tCamera = tMember.camera(1)
  tCamera.worldPosition = vector(144, 144, 144)
  tCamera.pointAt(0, 0, 0)
end beginSprite
```

The xyzCone0.dir movie is an unfinished version of the same movie. Only the behavior listed in the preceding is active. It is attached only to sprite 1. Because it modifies the Shockwave 3D member itself, its effect is seen in all four sprites.

If you run the xyzCone0.dir movie, all the sprites will show the same image, viewed from the default camera. If you select all the Shockwave 3D sprites and drop the Model under mouse behavior onto one of them, each sprite will adopt a different camera. In this case, the choice of camera is determined by the sprite's channel number:

```
property spriteNum

on beginSprite(me)
  mySprite = sprite(spriteNum)
  tMember  = mySprite.member
  myCamera = tMember.camera(spriteNum)
  mySprite.camera = myCamera
end
```

Figure 12-7 shows the situation just before the behavior is dropped on the four Shockwave 3D sprites.

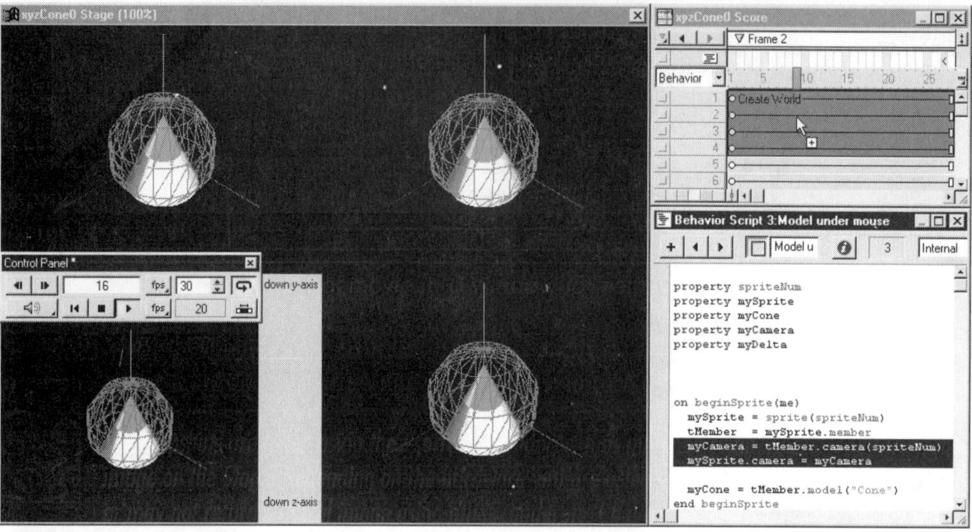

Figure 12-7 *Dropping the Model under mouse behavior onto the four sprites*

Position and Orientation

In Director 8.5, a camera has no physical presence. Unlike a model, you cannot see a camera when you place it in 3D space. The only visible evidence you have of the camera's position and orientation is the view it creates in the sprite. In the simplest possible terms, this view can be defined by two properties:

- The position of the camera in the 3D world
- The direction in which the camera is pointing

Position

Both the position and orientation of a camera are fully defined by the camera's transform. You also can use the `worldPosition` property to set the position of the camera. This will not affect the direction in which it is pointing.

Rotation and pointAt()

Until now, I have tended to use `aNode.transform.rotation` to set the orientation of a model or a group. Although this also works with cameras, it is more practical to use a different approach because we are used to looking at the world from an upright position. We therefore need to ensure that the camera is not tilted in some arbitrary direction. Besides, it helps to be able to determine the rotation of the camera by defining a target point or node.

The `pointAt()` command fits the bill. In the `beginSprite()` handler quoted in the preceding, all the cameras are turned to `pointAt` the origin point `(0, 0, 0)`. The syntax for the `pointAt()` command is more flexible than the official documentation implies. Officially, the syntax is as follows:

```
aNode.pointAt(vectorPosition{, vectorUp})
```

Here are two examples of this syntax:

```
member("3D World").camera(1).pointAt(vector(12, 34, 56))
member("3D World").camera(1).pointAt(vector(12, 34, 56), vector(0, 0, 1))
```

In practice, you also can replace the `vectorPosition` parameter by a node reference or by a series of three coordinates. Here are examples of this undocumented syntax for you to test with xyzCone.dir:

```
tCamera    = member("3D World").camera(1)
tModel     = member("3D World").model(1)
tUpVector = vector(0, 0, 1) -- z-axis

tCamera.pointAt(tModel)
tCamera.pointAt(tModel, tUpVector)
tCamera.pointAt(12, 34, 56)
```

Note that if you use three coordinates, as in the last example, you cannot also provide an up vector, as doing so will cause a script error.

Which Way Is Up?

The `pointAt()` command rotates the camera so that it is facing the world position defined by the vector, coordinates, or node. In doing so, it aligns the up axis of the camera with the up direction of the 3D world as best it can. In other words, cameras, like all other nodes, have a front and a top, and the world itself has an upward direction. Let's look at these ideas more closely.

By default, a node faces down its negative z axis. Viewed from the default camera position, the "front" of a node in its default position faces into the screen. This makes sense: a camera is itself a node and, by definition, the active camera faces into the screen.

By default, the y axis of the world points upward. If you provide a vector as the second parameter of the `pointAt()` command, you can modify, on a one-off basis, the direction that the node considers to be up. Suppose you are fixing a lock onto a cupboard door. If the door is attached to the cupboard, the lock, door, and world all share the same up direction. If you have temporarily taken the door off the cupboard so that you can place it flat on your workbench, up for the lock and the door would be a horizontal direction.

Changing the up direction for a node is not the same as changing the top of the node. Suppose you have two cupboard doors, side by side; and suppose the doors open outward from the center. Suppose you wish to fix the same lock model on both doors. To do this, you would need to turn one of the locks upside down. For this lock, you would still consider the top of the door to be the up direction. Mentally, you would redefine the side of the lock you consider as its top. The front of the lock (the side you attach to the inside of the door) would still be the same side.

The code in the earlier "Creating a New Camera Object" section contains an example of using a second parameter in the `pointAt()` command:

```
tCamera = tMember.newCamera("y view")
tCamera.worldPosition = vector(0, 250, 0)
tCamera.pointAt(vector(0, 0, 0), vector(0, 0, -1))
```

The camera("y view") is looking directly down the y axis. By default, the y axis is considered to be the up direction for the world. It is impossible for the camera to align its own negative z axis with the world's y axis, and at the same time align its own y axis with the world's y axis. In a situation like this, Director uses the world's x axis as a fall-back up direction for the world; however, in this case, this does not suit us. Here's an experiment to see why:

Remove the second parameter in this last line as follows:

```
tCamera.pointAt(vector(0, 0, 0)) --, vector(0, 0, -1))
```

Then relaunch the movie. The cone in sprite 3 (at the top right) will appear rotated through 90°. Dragging it to the left will make the cone in the sprite below move into the screen. Reinstate the second parameter and try again: the same movement will move both the right-hand cones to the left. The second parameter indicates that we want to consider the world's negative z axis as the up direction for the camera. This gives us the standard view from above we want.

pointAtOrientation

gForce.dir

To modify the top and front of a node in Lingo, you need to modify the node's `pointAtOrientation` property. This has a permanent effect on the way the `pointAt()` command aligns the node.

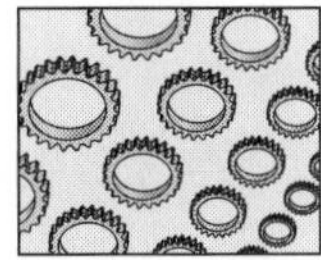

NOTE

Because the `pointAtOrientation` property is related to the `pointAt()` command, I treat it here. However, the `pointAtOrientation` property is more useful with models than with cameras. Changing the `pointAtOrientation` of a camera will simply point the camera in the wrong direction the next time you use the `pointAt()` command.

The body of the spacecraft in the gForce.dir movie is made from a cylinder model. The `topRadius` of the resource is set to zero to create a cone shape. The tip of the cone points upward, along the model's y axis. To make the tip of the cone into the front of the spacecraft, I modify the cone model's `pointAtOrientation`. Here is a simplified version of the handler that creates the spacecraft:

```
on mCreateCraft(a3DMember)
  tResource = a3DMember.newModelResource("Cone", #cylinder)
  tResource.topRadius = 0

  tCraft = a3DMember.newModel("Cone", tResource)
  tCraft.scale(1, 1, 0.5)

  -- Determine forward and up axes
  tCraft.rotate(-90, 0, 0) -- model's y-axis = world's z-axis
  tCraft.pointAtOrientation = [vector(0, 1, 0), vector(0, 0, 1)]
end mCreateCraft
```

In the preceding I use unit direction vectors to set the `pointAtOrientation`, but any nonzero vectors will do. Director will convert them automatically to unit direction vectors. From now on, using `tCraft.pointAt()` will point the nose of the spacecraft in the desired direction.

Aligning with the World's Up Direction

The `pointAt()` command includes a self-righting mechanism: the top of the node is aligned as near as possible with the world's up axis (the y axis); see Figure 12-8.

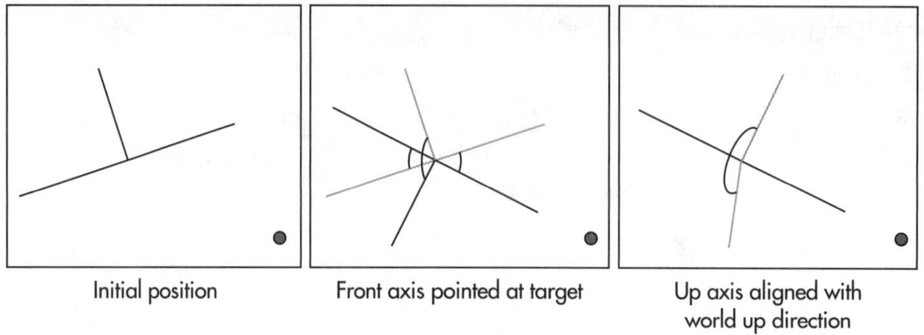

Figure 12-8 *Using the pointAt( ) command*

The command is executed in two steps: first, the node's front axis (the negative z axis by default) is pointed at the appropriate world position; then the node is rotated around the front axis so that the y value of its up axis is as large as possible.

If the node is facing exactly along the world's y axis, the y value of the node's up axis will be zero for all possible rotations. In this case, the world's x axis will be used as the "up" direction instead. This means that, as the node becomes vertical, it is likely to spin abruptly to a new orientation.

Pointing a Camera at Itself

There is no logical way to point a camera—or indeed any node—at its own world position. Attempting to do so will provoke a script error, as shown here:

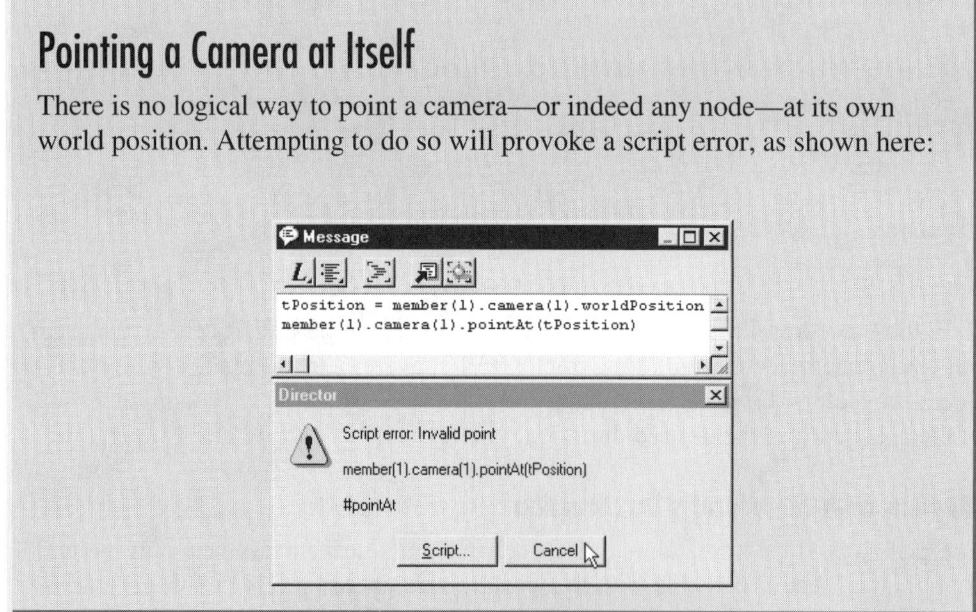

In the Camera parent script of the gForce.dir movie, I work around this by testing that the camera position and the pointAt target are distinct:

```
property pCamera -- pointer to the camera used by this instance
property pTarget -- pointAt target (vector or node) for camera

on stepFrame(me)
 case ilk(pTarget) of
 #camera, #group, #light, #model:
  tPosition = pTarget.worldPosition
 #vector:
  tPosition = pTarget
 end case

 -- Track pointAt node or vector
 if tPosition <> pCamera.worldPosition then
 pCamera.pointAt(tPosition)
 end if
end stepFrame
```

Scale

A camera's transform has three properties: `position`, `rotation`, and `scale`. Altering the scale of a camera has no direct effect on the view. However, it does have an effect on any children the camera might have: the scale of the parent camera is used to calculate the world transform—thus the position and size—of its children. Generally speaking, it is best to leave the scale of a camera at its default value of `vector( 1.0, 1.0, 1.0 )`. The following pages assume this is the case.

Finding the Best Vantage Point

Finding the best `worldPosition`, `pointAt` target, and `projectionAngle` for your camera can require some trial and error. To simplify the task, I have built a Snapshot.dir movie, which you can use in a window to grab still images of a given Shockwave 3D sprite on the Stage (see Figure 12-9). Snapshots are saved to the internal cast of your movie as Bitmap members; the script of the Bitmap member contains a handler, which will set the parameters of a chosen camera to those used for taking the snapshot.

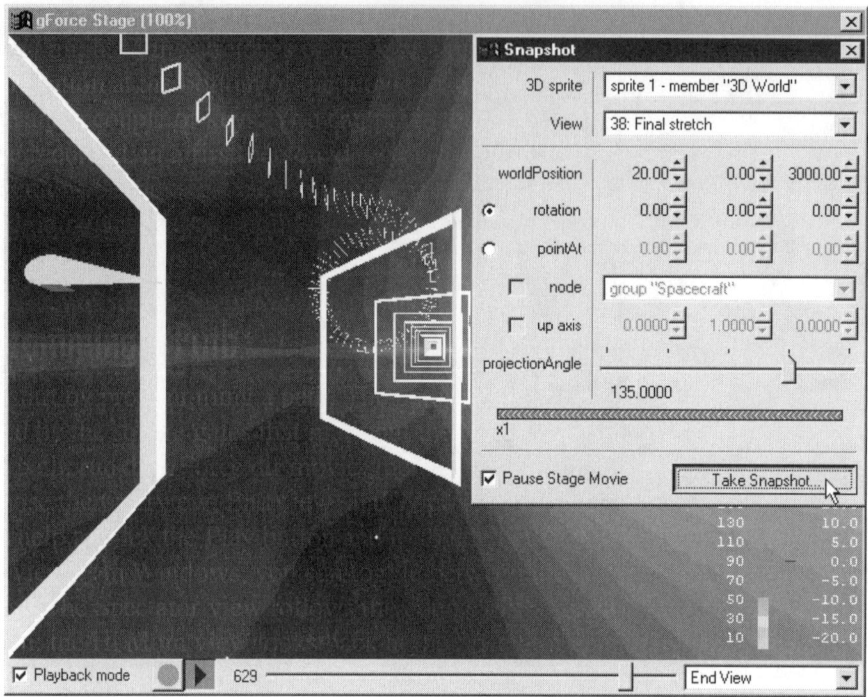

Figure 12-9 *Using the Snapshot movie in a window to memorize a camera position*

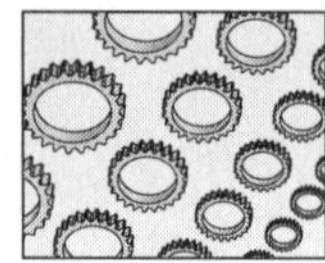

NOTE

The snapshots are taken using the #software renderer; thus might be somewhat different from the image on the Stage. Depending on the hardware you are using, `a3DMember.image` *may or may not return a useful image using other renderers. I have chosen to use the lowest common denominator to be sure that the Bitmap image is not blank, whatever your setup.*

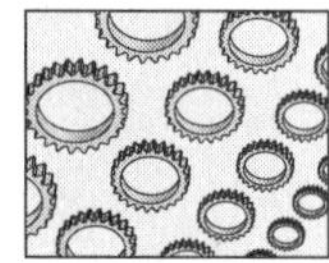

NOTE

On certain hardware configurations, only camera("DefaultView") can be used to take an image of the member. To ensure compatibility with all machines, the Snapshot movie sets the position of camera("DefaultView") to that of the current camera of the sprite, grabs the member image, and then resets camera("DefaultView") to its initial position.

Using the Snapshot Window

Place the Snapshot.dir movie in the Xtras folder beside your Director 8.5 application; then restart Director. If you run the AddXtras.exe projector, which you will find on the CD-ROM, this should be done automatically for you. To open the Snapshot window, simply choose the menu Xtras | Snapshot.

While the Snapshot window is open, you can move the Shockwave 3D sprite's current camera on the stage by dragging the sprite with the mouse. You also can use the controls in the Snapshot window. If necessary, select the Pause Stage Movie check box to halt any animation or camera movements on the Stage. The Snapshot window provides two modes: rotation and pointAt. In the #rotation mode

- The camera is turned to face in a given direction across 3D space.
- The camera can dolly forward and backward freely (the default movement is 1 unit vector). To dolly the camera, click the dolly strip (see the following illustration) and drag the mouse horizontally. To dolly forward, move the mouse to the left; to dolly back, move it to the right.

- By pressing different combinations of the SHIFT, OPTION, and COMMAND keys as you drag along the dolly strip, you can vary the rate of movement between 1/100 and 1000 units.
- Dragging the mouse across the Shockwave 3D sprite on the stage will move the camera in its x-y plane.
- The pointAt, node, and upAxis controls are disabled and ignored.

In the pointAt mode, you can specify a `worldPosition` for the camera to point at. You can either enter a point vector using the vector input controls or choose a node from the Node pop-up menu. Alternatively, you can press the CTRL key (Windows) / COMMAND key (Macintosh) and click the surface of a model to choose that point of the model as the pointAt position. If you click empty space rather than a model, the `spriteSpaceToWorldSpace()` method will be used to determine which point in space you clicked. When you CTRL-click/COMMAND-click, the scene will jump; the point you clicked will now appear in the center of the sprite.

Examples of Camera Manipulations

Here are six example manipulations to get you accustomed to controlling the camera using the snapshot movie. I recommend that you restart the movie between each manipulation, simply so that you are starting from a known position each time. You can, of course, perform a whole sequence of manipulations.

- **Rotating horizontally about a point** Run the gForce.dir movie on the Stage and open the Snapshot movie in a window. If necessary, select pointAt mode, select the Node check box, and choose group("Spacecraft"). Now click one side of the Stage and drag the mouse across to the other side. The camera will move around the spacecraft but remain pointing at it at all times. The camera will perform a 360° turn as you drag from one side of the sprite to the other.
- **Rotating vertically about a point** Restart the gForce.dir movie. Ensure that pointAt mode is selected in the Snapshot window and that the node group("spacecraft") is chosen as the pointAt target. Now click the Stage above the spacecraft and drag the mouse down. The camera will move downward, rotating around the spacecraft and pointing at it at all times. The rotation will stop when you reach the bottom of the sprite; at this point, you will be looking straight up from below. You cannot rotate the camera beyond the lowest point; however, you can rotate horizontally at the same time as you rotate vertically.
- **Dragging toward a chosen point** Restart the gForce.dir movie. Ensure that pointAt mode is selected in the Snapshot window and that the node group("spacecraft") is chosen as the pointAt target. In the Snapshot window, click the horizontal dolly bar with the grayscale gradient, a few pixels from the right-hand end. If you drag to the right, you will move swiftly away from the spacecraft. The distance from the center of the spacecraft will be indicated under the dolly bar, as will the relative distance compared to your starting point. If you drag left, you will move progressively closer to the center of the spacecraft. You might even pass through the rear of the spacecraft and find yourself inside it, in which case the external walls of the spacecraft will become invisible. However far you drag left and however many times you release the mouse and repeat the drag, you will never get the camera to reach the target point. You can reduce the distance only between the camera and the target point. This is illustrated in Figure 12-10.

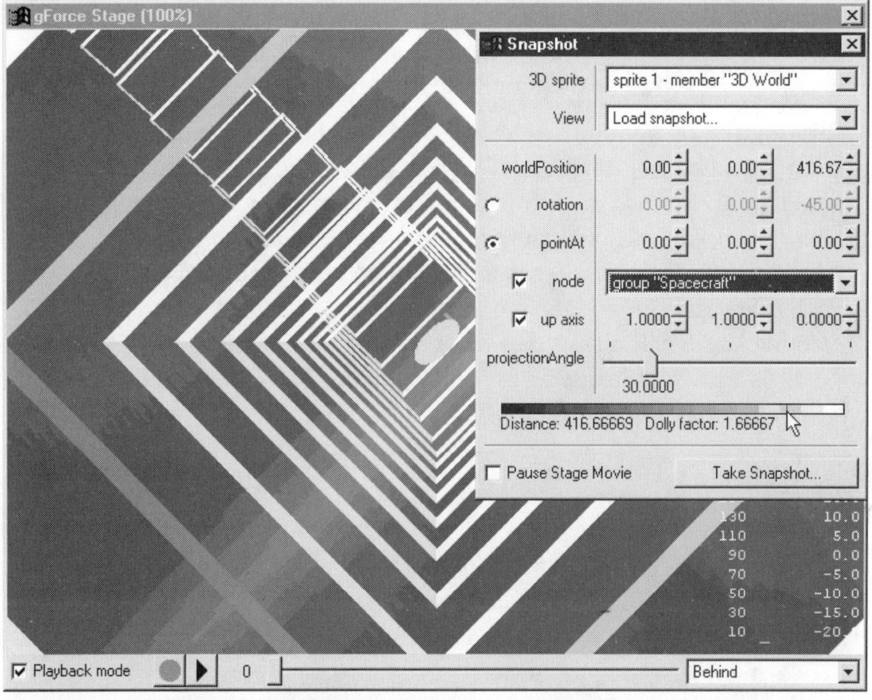

Figure 12-10 *Dragging toward a given point in pointAt mode*

- **Dragging the camera without rotating it** Restart the gForce.dir movie and select rotation mode. Click the spacecraft model and drag the mouse. The camera will move so that the spacecraft remains under the mouse. It will continue to look in the same direction (the camera's rotation will not change). When you click any model, the point on the model that you click will remain under the mouse as you drag. If you click empty space, an arbitrary point will be chosen to remain under the mouse.
- **Dragging the camera in a given direction** Restart the gForce.dir movie and select rotation mode. The dolly bar will appear in a solid gray with little arrows pointing to the left. Click anywhere on the bar and drag left or right. The camera will move one world unit along its z axis for every pixel you move the mouse horizontally. Hold down the SHIFT key; the camera will move 10 times as fast. With the COMMAND/CTRL key held down, it will move 100 world units per pixel dragged. With both SHIFT and COMMAND/CTRL, you move 1000 units per pixel. You can hold the OPTION key down for fine tuning: the OPTION key

alone moves the camera 1 unit for every 10 pixels dragged; the OPTION and SHIFT keys together move the camera 1 unit for every 100 pixels dragged. You can change scale like this without releasing the mouse.

- **Changing the projectionAngle** Restart the gForce.dir movie. In the Camera pop-up menu, choose Monitor. Note that the spacecraft is sitting in the center of a red gate. Now use the Camera pop-up menu to switch back to Behind. In the Snapshot window, click the projectionAngle slider and drag it to the right. It might look as if the camera is moving backward, but this is not the case. Only the first gate behind the red gate becomes visible. An extremely wide projectionAngle will distort the whole view. At an angle of 179°, the spacecraft appears as a tiny dot inside a very small square. The camera is still only 250 world units away.

In pointAt mode:

- The camera turns automatically to face the chosen node or worldPosition.
- The camera can dolly forward, in ever decreasing steps, but can never reach the pointAt anchor point. (See Figure 12-10.)
- As the camera dollies out from the anchor point, so its rate of movement increases.
- Dragging the mouse across the Shockwave 3D sprite on the stage will rotate the camera about the anchor point.
- A horizontal movement from one side of the sprite to the other will make a rotation of 360° around the world's y axis.
- A full vertical movement will turn the camera so that it almost looks down the world's y axis. Rotation is around an axis through the anchor point parallel to the camera's own x axis.
- The rotation control is disabled, but updated automatically.

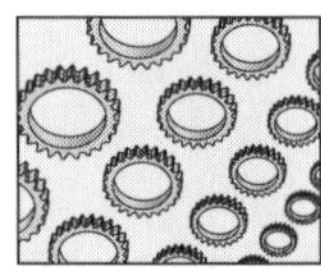

NOTE

The Snapshot window and the movie on the Stage both might try to control the current sprite camera at the same time. The Snapshot window updates its display automatically once per second, which might make the animation on the Stage appear to stutter. If the movie on the stage controls the camera in any way, the pointAt data you enter can be overridden without warning. Conversely, changes made through the Snapshot window will alter the position and orientation of the current sprite camera relative to its parent. Selecting the Pause Stage Movie check box will give the Snapshot window full control; deselecting Intercept Mouse will give the Stage full control.

Snapshot Scripts

Once you have taken your snapshots, you can compare them and choose the best view. While you have the Snapshot window open, you can select a snapshot in the View menu. To re-create the viewpoint at runtime, simply call the `mSetCameraView()` handler of the appropriate script. To save space, you can copy the handler and the thumbnail to a script member and erase the original Bitmap member. Here is an example:

```
tCamera = sprite(1).camera
tScript = script("Final stretch")
tScript.mSetCameraView(tCamera)
```

The `scriptText` of the "Final stretch" snapshot member might look something like this:

```
on mSetCameraView(me, aCamera)
  tTransform                  = transform()
  tTransform.position         = vector( 0.0000, 0.0000, 3.00000e3 )
  tTransform.rotation         = vector( 0.0000, 0.0000, 0.0000 )

  tTransform.multiply(aCamera.parent.transform.inverse())

  aCamera.transform           = tTransform
  aCamera.projectionAngle = 135.0000
end mSetCameraView
```

This places the camera as it was when the snapshot was taken. The current view might be somewhat different, because any animated elements in the 3D world might no longer be in the same place. If your snapshot was taken pointing at an animated node, that node might have moved.

Animating the Camera

You can set seven parameters for a still camera: the x, y, and z values for the camera's `worldPosition`; the x, y, and z values for the camera's `rotation`; and the camera's `projectionAngle`. When you animate the camera, you can alter each of these seven parameters individually over time. In other words, you are working in a total of eight dimensions, with time as the eighth dimension, which makes designing the movement of a camera extremely complex.

One of the simplest ways of reducing this complexity is to allow the user to do the work for you. A subjective camera sees the world from the hero's eyes (cf. *Citizen Kane*). An over-the-shoulder camera sees the hero and what the hero sees. If the users control the hero, they also control the camera. Regardless of whether you control the camera directly or give control to the user, the same principles apply. You need to keep the camera upright and move it steadily. The gForce.dir movie in the 3D\Cameras\ folder on the CD-ROM allows you to experiment with different types of movement.

The gForce.dir movie illustrates several techniques for animating a camera. You can use the `mMakeCameraPath()` method to build a path for the camera the same way you might fit the stretches of track of a model railway together. You can use the Record button at the bottom of the movie to create a freeform path, piloted by the mouse and a couple of keys. You can place the camera at the center of the path you've recorded, in a first-person view; or you can use it as a guide for any number of variations on the over-the-shoulder type of shot. You also can place the camera at a fixed point and follow a point as it moves along the path. You can even zoom in on the point as it moves.

Programming a Path

Let's start by programming a path. The path is already visible; we'll use the path defined by the square gates that mark out the race track. To get an idea of the shape of the path, run the gForce.dir movie; then use the pop-up menu at the bottom right to choose the Overview, EndView, and TopView fixed camera positions. It also might help to click the Play button and to toggle between the Spectator and the Hi Mom views. (In Windows, you can toggle between these views by pressing the `S` and `H` keys.) The Spectator view follows the course of the spacecraft from a fixed position; the Hi Mom view looks back at the Spectator camera position from the moving spacecraft.

Using One Script to Create Another

The position of the gates is determined by the Sample Track script in cast slot 9. This consists of a single repetitive handler that starts like this:

```
on mMakeTrack(me, a3DWorld)
  tResource = a3DWorld.modelResource("Gate")
  tShader   = a3DWorld.shader("Gate")
```

```
-- Start of straight section
 tTransform = transform()
 tTransform.position = vector( 0.00000, 0.00000, -1.60000e2 )
 tTransform.rotation = vector( 0.00000, 0.00000, 0.00000 )
 tGate = a3DWorld.newModel("0", tResource)
 tGate.transform = tTransform
 tGate.rotate(90, 0, 45)
 tGate.shader      = tShader
```

and then repeats the second block of code with minor but significant variations another 165 times. Each block creates a new gate model at a new world position.

The tedious script here was created automatically by a more interesting one. You'll find the Make Tracks Parent Script in the Utilities cast. This script creates another script with a single mMakeTrack() method like the preceding code extract. The generator script contains eight handlers, as you can see in Figure 12-11.

The mAddStraight, mAddCurve, and mAddLoop() handlers act like stretches of model railway track, designing the shape of the curve. Each of these handlers regularly calls the mAddGate() handler, which writes out the blocks of code needed to create each transform into a string variable. The recipe for the shape

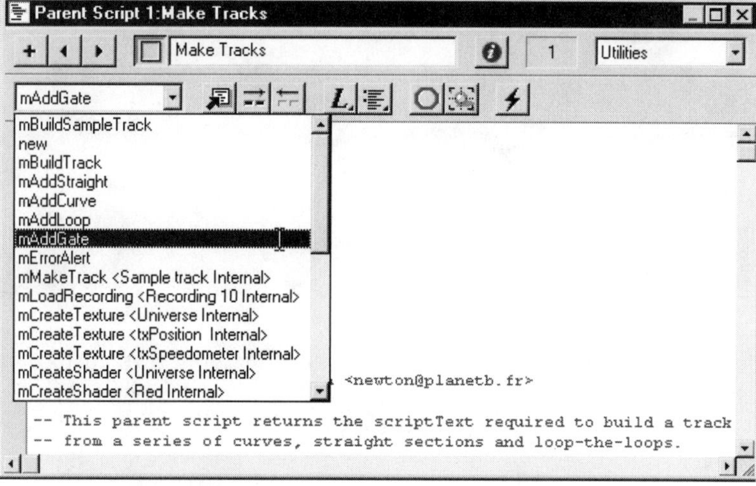

Figure 12-11 *The Make Tracks parent script*

of the track is given by the `mBuildSampleTrack()` handler. Figure 12-11 is a condensed version of it.

```
on mBuildSampleTrack(me)
  tInstance = me.new()

  tAxis   = vector(1, 0, 0) -- axis of rotation for curves (x-axis)
  tAngle  = 180.0           -- angle for a curved section
  tOffset = 4               -- lateral distance between entrance and
  --                           exit of a loop

  tInstance.mAddStraight(8) -- adds gates over a distance of 8 units
  tInstance.mAddCurve(8, tAxis, tAngle) -- curve radius = 8 units
  tAxis   = vector(0, -1, 0) -- -y-axis
  tAngle  = 90.0
  tInstance.mAddCurve(8, tAxis, tAngle)
  tAxis   = vector(0, 0, 1) -- -z-axis
  tInstance.mAddLoop(8, tAxis, tOffset)
  tAxis   = vector(0, 1, 0) -- y-axis
  tInstance.mAddCurve(8, tAxis, tAngle)
  tAxis   = vector(1, 0, 0) -- x-axis
  tInstance.mAddCurve(8, tAxis, tAngle)
  tInstance.mAddStraight(4)
  tAxis   = vector(0, 0, 1) -- z-axis
  tInstance.mAddCurve(4, tAxis, tAngle) -- curve radius = 4 units
  tInstance.mAddStraight(8)
  tAxis   = vector(0, 1, 0) -- y-axis
  tInstance.mAddCurve(4, tAxis, tAngle)
  tInstance.mAddStraight(16)

  return tInstance.mBuildTrack()
end mBuildSampleTrack
```

Of course, you can build your own track by connecting your own custom sequence of straight and curved sections together. This would be a good exercise in visualizing shapes in 3D space.

Paving the Way for the Camera

Before you try designing your own path, why don't you create a series of camera positions that matches the gate positions? The second script in the Utilities cast is called Make Camera Path; it contains a similar set of handlers. Indeed, the `mAddStraight`, `mAddCurve`, and `mAddLoop()` handlers are almost identical, and the `mBuildSamplePath()` handler is different only in name. The path it creates is the same as the one created by the `mBuildSampleTrack()` handler. The main difference is that an `mAddView()` handler replaces the `mAddGate()` handler. This handler builds a string variable, `pScriptText`, which starts…

```
on mGetDataList(me)
  tDataList = []
```

…and ends…

```
  return tDataList
end mGetDataList
```

Here is the `mAddView()` handler that adds blocks of code for each camera position to the `pScriptText` string:

```
property pScriptText

on mAddView(me, aTransform)
put \
"  tPropList = [:]"&RETURN&\
"  tPropList[#worldPosition]    = "&aTransform.position&RETURN&\
"  tPropList[#rotation]         = "&aTransform.rotation&RETURN&\
"  tPropList[#projectionAngle] = 30"&RETURN&\
"  tDataList.append(tPropList)"&RETURN&RETURN\
after pScriptText
end mAddView
```

In this version, the camera's `projectionAngle` remains constant, but you could extend the idea to deal with progressive zooms. To create a script from this template, type the following in the Message window:

```
scriptMember = new(#script, member(5, 3)) -- at end of Utilities cast
pathScript= script("Make Camera Path")
ScriptMember.scriptText=pathScript.m.BuildSamplePath()
scriptMember.scriptType = #parent
scriptMember.name = "Custom Camera Path"
```

Now launch the gForce.dir movie; then type

```
script(scriptMember).new(sprite 1)
```

Figure 12-12 shows the steps described here.

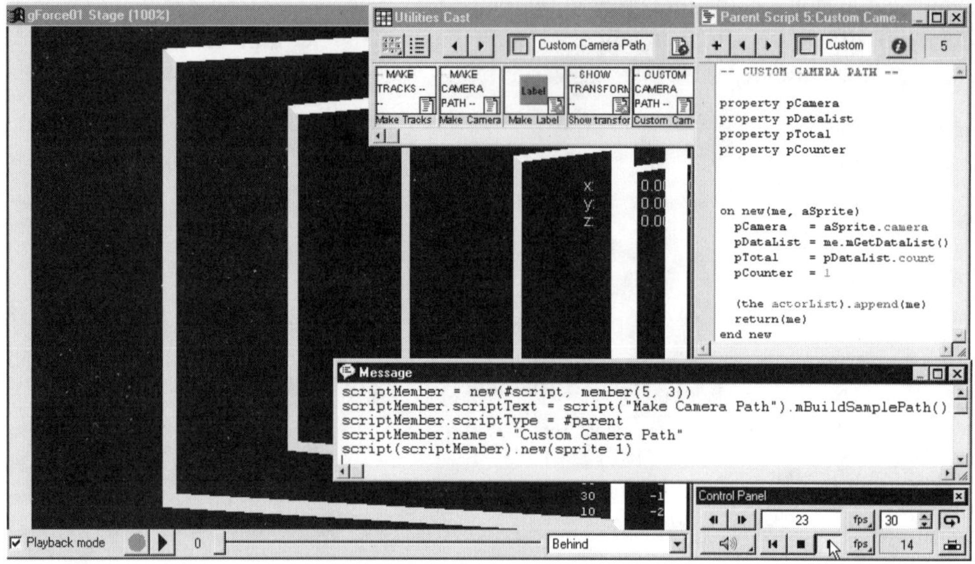

Figure 12-12 *Making a custom path for the camera*

The camera will start moving at a rapid pace along the path marked out by the square gates. At times, the gates will seem not to move because the camera jumps forward one gate at a time. You can tell the camera is moving, though, because the color of the sky behind changes constantly.

Studying the Code

So how does the script work? Here is the beginning of the scriptText you created:

```
-- CUSTOM CAMERA PATH --

property pCamera
property pDataList
property pTotal
property pCounter


on new(me, aSprite)
  pCamera    = aSprite.camera
  pDataList = me.mGetDataList()
  pTotal     = pDataList.count
```

```
  pCounter  = 1
  (the actorList).append(me)
  return(me)
end new


on stepFrame(me)
  if pCounter > pTotal then
    exit
  end if
  me.mSetCameraView(pDataList[pCounter])
  pCounter = pCounter + 1
end stepFrame


on mSetCameraView(me, aDataList)
  tTransform              = transform()
  tTransform.position     = aDataList[#worldPosition]
  tTransform.rotation     = aDataList[#rotation]
  tTransform.rotation     = tTransform.rotation

  tParentTransform        = pCamera.parent.getWorldTransform()
  tTransform.multiply(tParentTransform.inverse())

  pCamera.transform       = tTransform
  pCamera.projectionAngle = aDataList[#projectionAngle]
end mSetCameraView


on mGetDataList(me)
  tDataList = []

 -- Start of straight section
  tPropList = [:]
  tPropList[#worldPosition]   = vector(0.00000, 0.00000, -1.60000e2)
  tPropList[#rotation]        = vector(0.00000, 0.00000, 0.00000)
  tPropList[#projectionAngle] = 30
  tDataList.append(tPropList)
  -- etc
  return tDataList
end mInitialize
```

When you create an instance of the script, it builds a list of camera positions using the `mGetDataList()` handler. The instance then places itself on `the actorList`, so that it will receive `#stepFrame` events. On each `stepFrame`, it moves one step down the list of camera positions and sets the transform of the camera appropriately. The `on mSetCameraView()` handler used here is a variant of the one you saw earlier in the Snapshot movie.

Extending the Idea

The scriptText created in this example is fairly simple. It makes the camera move at a steady pace with a fixed `projectionAngle`, facing along its path at all times. A more sophisticated version would allow you to create a movement that accelerates and decelerates gradually, tracks a fixed or a moving point, and alters the `projectionAngle` smoothly as the camera advances.

You might like to add these features to the existing Make Camera Path script. Don't be tempted to create scripts with more than one acceleration/deceleration, more than one change of `pointAt` target or direction, or more than one zoom. Not only would this make the programming overly complex, it also would lead to overly fussy camera movements.

Piloting the Camera

The gForce.dir movie provides a second method for creating a path: piloting the camera through the 3D world and recording its flight path. The best technique for piloting the camera will depend on the type of movement you want to create. In the gForce.dir movie, I have used the metaphor of space flight: the camera can move in any direction at any speed. If you are working on a walk-through of an architecture project, you will want to make the camera more pedestrian.

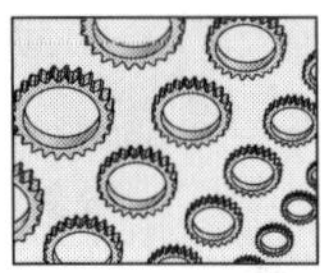

NOTE

Close the Snapshot window before proceeding, or deselect the Intercept Mouse button. If you do not do so, the Snapshot movie will take control of the camera.

Accelerating

To take the camera for a spin, deselect the Playback Mode button. If you now press the A key ("a" for accelerate), the camera will start to move forward at an ever-increasing pace, following the spacecraft that you see in the center of the screen. A yellow column at the bottom right of the sprite indicates your speed. A purple column indicates your acceleration. Press the D key ("d" for decelerate) to slow down. If you press D for long enough (or if you start by pressing D), the spacecraft will start moving backward. When this happens, pressing A slows down the backward movement and eventually starts accelerating you forward again.

Steering

To steer the spacecraft, click anywhere on the Shockwave 3D sprite and drag the mouse in the direction you want to turn. A 3D compass at the top right indicates the direction of the world's x, y, and z axes. When you release the mouse, the spacecraft and the camera will gradually right themselves, so that the camera's y axis points upward. You'll see the green y axis arrow of the compass rotate to point more or less upward when you do so.

Self-Righting

The self-righting feature is quite simple. The spacecraft is made to point temporarily at a point 1 unit in front of itself. The resulting upright transform then is stored and the spacecraft's original position is restored. The difference between the original and the upright transform is calculated and then applied incrementally over the next few frames. In the Pilot script in cast slot 17, the `mRightShip()` handler calculates the incremental transform to apply and the following extract of the `mMoveShip()` handler applies it:

```
property pCraft     -- group("spacecraft")
property pSteering  -- TRUE if the mouse is being dragged
property pFrames    -- number of frames left for righting craft
property pTransform -- incremental transform to apply

on mMoveShip(me)
  if pSteering then
    -- More code
  else if pFrames then
    -- pTransform is being used to right the ship
    pCraft.transform.preMultiply(pTransform)
    pFrames = pFrames - 1
    if not pFrames then
      -- The ship is now fully upright
      pTransform.identity()
    end if
  end if
  -- More code
end mMoveShip
```

Compass

Look at the Compass script in cast slot 20 to see how the compass works. In short, on each `stepFrame`, the compass group is set to the same relative position with respect to the camera. Its rotation then is set so that it aligns with the world's axes (or rather, so that it appears to do so, because its angle must be adjusted relative to the camera).

Sky

The sky is created from a sphere primitive with a radius of 16 384 world units. The race track is at the center of the sphere. The distance between two gates is 160 world units, so there is plenty of space between the race track and the sky. If the sky goes black, it indicates you have flown outside the sphere. If a hole appears in the center of the sky, you probably are outside the sphere looking in. Only the inside surface of the sphere is visible: the hole appears where the inside surface on the opposite side of the sphere is too far from the camera to be rendered.

No Collisions

Flying through the sphere or through a gate has no impact on the spacecraft. There is no collision. We'll be looking at collision detection in Chapter 14. In most projects, camera movements need to be constrained by walls and other solid objects. In a virtual world, by default, all objects are as thin as dreams.

Recording Your Flight

Practice flying without constraint until you feel you can control the spacecraft; then click the red Record button. The spacecraft will return to its original position and the recording slider will start to move. (Press the A key before you release the mouse over the Record button to start accelerating immediately.) Accelerate cautiously; then try to keep the spacecraft on track between gates. If you move too far off course, the recording will stop and you will find yourself back in playback mode. To try again, deselect the Playback Mode button and then click Record.

If you complete the course, you will have the chance to save your recording. (You also can cheat by clicking the Record button again before you reach the end. Alternatively, you can start by cheating: If you hold the SHIFT key down as you click the Record button, you will be able to record an unrestricted flight. Click the Record button again to stop your recording.) The new script created by your recording will be saved to the Utilities cast. The beginning and end of your script will look something like this:

```
on mLoadRecording()
  tList = []

  tTransform = transform()
  tTransform.position = vector( 0.0000, 0.0000, -0.2646 )
  tTransform.rotation = vector( -90.0000, 0.0000, 0.0000 )
  tList.append(tTransform)

  tTransform = transform()
  tTransform.position = vector( 0.0000, 0.0000, -0.8120 )
  tTransform.rotation = vector( -90.0000, 0.0000, 0.0000 )
  tList.append(tTransform)

  -- and so on for many lines

  return tList
end mLoadRecording
```

In other words, the generated script reproduces the list of world transforms that the camera passed through during your flight. During recording, the original transforms are simply added to a linear list. Here is a highly condensed version of the Pilot parent script (member 17):

```
property pCraft      -- Group of models representing spacecraft
property pRecordList -- List of transforms on current path

on stepFrame(me)
  me.mMoveShip()
end stepFrame

on mMoveShip(me)
  -- Code to steer the spacecraft
  -- Code to accelerate/decelerate the spacecraft
  pRecordList.append(pCraft.getWorldTransform())
end mMoveShip
```

When the recording is over, the `mSaveRecording()` handler in the Pilot script is called to save the list of transforms as a script in its own right. Here is an edited version:

```
on mSaveRecording(me)
  tScriptText = \
"on mLoadRecording()"&RETURN&\
```

```
"  tList = []"&RETURN&RETURN

  tCounter = pRecordList.count
  repeat with i = 1 to tCounter
    tTransform = pRecordList[i]
    tRotation  = tTransform.rotation
    tString = \
"  tTransform = transform()"&RETURN&\
"  tTransform.position = "&tTransform.position&RETURN&\
"  tTransform.rotation = "&tRotation&RETURN

    -- Workaround for vector(x, -90, z) bug in Director 8.5
    if tRotation.y > -90.015 and tRotation.y < -89.985 then
      put \
"  tTransform.rotation = tTransform.rotation"&RETURN after tString
    endif

    put "  tList.append(tTransform)"&RETURN&RETURN after tString

    put tString after tScriptText
  end repeat

  put "  return tList"&RETURN&"end mLoadRecording" after tScriptText

  new(#script).scriptText = tScriptText
end mSaveRecording
```

DEBUGGING TIP

As the preceding code implies, Director 8.5 mishandles transforms when you apply a y rotation of around –90° or any angle that can be expressed as –90°, such as 270° or –450°. The workaround is to apply the rotation and then reset the transform's rotation to its resulting value. The bug will thus apply itself twice and cancel itself out.

As a point of interest, you can find the script that I sent to wish-director@macromedia.com as part of my bug report on the CD-ROM at Bugs\yAxisBug.ls. Import the script into a new movie; then type "rotateTest()" (without the quotes) in the Message window. Press the RETURN key. After a moment, a text member will be created to show a series of rotation values that are not treated correctly.

Taking time to isolate a bug in this way helps in two ways: understanding what causes it helps you discover a workaround (if there is one), and helping the Director engineers understand what causes it ensures that there will be a fix in the next release of Director.

Varying the Camera Position

Once you have recorded your flight, you can play it back. If necessary, click the Playback Mode button; then click the Play button. Although you recorded your flight path using an over-the-shoulder (or over-the-thruster) camera view, you can exploit the list of transforms in a number of ways. Choose any of the prepositioned cameras from the pop-up menu at the bottom right. There are three main types of camera:

On-board cameras travel with the spacecraft at a greater or lesser distance from the pilot's seat (Behind, Upright, Monitor, Pilot, Hi Mom). These cameras all are children of group("spacecraft"), and thus travel with it. The cameras' transforms define the relative position and orientation of the camera relative to the parent.

Fixed view cameras give you an idea of where the spacecraft is along the track (Overview, EndView, and TopView). These cameras are all children of a nonmoving node—group("World"), as it happens.

Pivoting cameras follow the movement of the spacecraft from a fixed position (Spectator, Zoom, RootNode, Fog). These cameras are also children of group("World"), but they are programmed to point at the spacecraft.

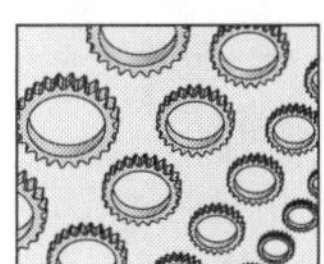

NOTE

Although the gForce.dir movie gives no example of this, it is quite possible to make the camera the child of one moving node and set the camera to point at another moving node.

As far as the camera itself is concerned, the spacecraft is just a convenience. It embodies a movement; it gives you something to look at so that you can judge relative positions and distances. The camera movement does not require such a physical manifestation. If you like, you can remove the spacecraft from the scene by typing the following line in the Message window:

```
member("3D world").group("spaceCraft").removeFromWorld()
```

To show the spacecraft again, either restart the movie or type the following line:

```
member("3D world").group("spaceCraft").addToWorld()
```

A Single Script for All the Cameras

Despite their differences, all the cameras are controlled by an instance of the same script. You will find this in the member Camera in cast slot 15. This script has three public methods: `new()`, `mUseCamera()`, and `mSetProperties()`. The `new()` handler accepts a property list as a parameter, which is used to initialize the instance. This is shown in Figure 12-13. The camera defined by the instance then

Parent Script 15:Camera

```
-- PUBLIC METHODS --

on new(me, aDataList) -----------------------------------------------
  -- Called by the mCreateCameras() handler of the "Cameras" instance
  --
  -- PARAMETER:
  -- <aDataList> is a property list with one or more of the following
  --  properties (only the first two properties are essential):
  --   [#sprite:   <shockwave3D sprite>,
  --    #name:     <string>,
  --    #position: <vector>,
  --    #rotation: <vector>,
  --    #pointAt:  <vector or node>,
  --    #parent:   <node>,
  --    #zoom:     <float between 0 and 1>,
  --    #rootNode: <node>,
  --    #fog:      <property list>]
  --------------------------------------------------------------------

  me.mInitialize(aDataList)
  return me
end new



on mUseCamera(me, aSprite) ------------------------------------------
  -- Sent by the update() handler of the "Cameras" owner instance
  -- when the user chooses a new camera in the popup menu.
```

Figure 12-13 *The parameters that you can set for the Camera script*

remains passive until the `mUseCamera()` method is called. This sets the camera of the sprite to the chosen camera until the `mUseCamera()` method of a different "Camera" instance is called.

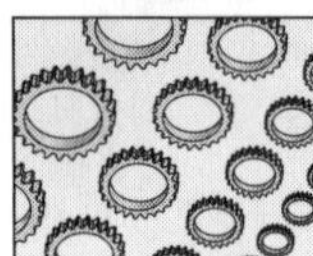

NOTE

Unlike other OOP languages, Lingo does not respect the notion of privacy; in fact, all methods and properties of an instance are public. The distinction between public and private methods in Lingo is de facto rather than de jure: a method can be considered private only to the extent that you don't call it from outside the instance.

Defining the Behavior of a Camera

For the Camera script, the behavior of a camera is determined by the property list passed as a parameter to the `new()` method. All the Camera instances are created by the `mCreateCameras()` handler of the Cameras script (member 14), which is activated by the Interaction behavior attached to the Shockwave 3D sprite. Here is an extract of the `mCreateCameras()` handler:

```
property plCameras

on mCreateCameras(me, aSprite)
  plCameras     = [:]
  tCameraScript = script("Camera")

  -- Definitions of other cameras

  tCameraData = [ \
#sprite:   aSprite, \
#name:     "Fog", \
#position: vector(100, 0, 80), \
#pointAt:  aSpacecraft, \
#fog:      [ \
 #near:        200.0,  \
 #far:       10000.0, \
 #color:     rgb(64, 64, 80), \
 #decayMode: #exponential], \
#zoom:      0.3 \
]
  plCameras[tName] = tCameraScript.new(tCameraData)
end mCreateCameras
```

This defines a camera named "Fog," which is placed near the center of the world. No `#parent` property is included in the `tCameraData` list, so the camera will be in a fixed world position.

Tracking a Node

The `#pointAt` property is set, so the camera will constantly turn to point at the spacecraft. A value of `#zoom` between 0.0 and 1.0 makes the camera change its `projectionAngle` as the distance between it and the spacecraft changes. The "Camera" instance deals with both tracking and zooming by placing itself on `the actorList` whenever it is the active camera for the sprite. This means the instance's `stepFrame()` handler is called once per frame. It is worth looking at the handler in detail, because it introduces some important ideas:

```
property pSprite -- sprite to be used with this camera
property pCamera -- pointer to the camera used by this instance
property pTarget -- pointAt target (vector or node) for camera
property pZoom   -- float (0 - 1) for zooming when target is distant
property pHeight -- "ideal" height of target when zooming
```

```
on stepFrame(me) --------------------------------------------------------
  -- Sent while this instance is on the actorList to enable the camera
  -- to track pTarget
  ------------------------------------------------------------------------

  if pSprite.camera <> pCamera then
    -- This camera is no longer being used
    me.mRemoveFromActorList()

  else -- point at target and zoom in on it if required
    case ilk(pTarget) of
      #camera, #group, #light, #model:
        tPosition = pTarget.worldPosition
      #vector:
        tPosition = pTarget
    end case
   -- Track pointAt node or vector
    if tPosition <> pCamera.worldPosition then
      pCamera.pointAt(tPosition)
    end if

    if pZoom <> 0 then
      -- Adjust projectionAngle
      tDistance = tPosition.distanceTo(pCamera.worldPosition)
      tDistance = power(tDistance, pZoom)
      tAngle    = atan(pHeight / tDistance) * 180 / pi
      pCamera.projectionAngle = tAngle
    end if
  end if
end stepFrame
```

First of all, being on `the actorList` has an overhead: before each frame is displayed, the `stepFrame()` handler (if there is one) of all instances on `the actorList` is called. It makes sense to remove an instance from `the actorList` when it is no longer required. Using the `stepFrame()` handler itself to do this is rather tricky.

Director sends the `#stepFrame` event to each instance on `the actorList` in turn. Suppose instance *n* receives the event and uses it to remove itself from `the actorList`; the following instance on `the actorList` becomes instance *n*. However, Director has already sent the event to instance *n*, so it now sends a `#stepFrame` event to instance *n*+1, unwittingly missing an instance as it does so. The `mRemoveFromActorList()` handler makes up for this: it tests whether the next instance on the `actorList` (if one exists) has a `stepFrame()` handler, and if so, sends it a personal #stepFrame of its own. Thanks to Jakob Hede Madsen for bringing this issue to my attention.

Having dealt with that little particularity, the handler then determines at which point in the world to point the camera. As I mentioned earlier, you can't point a node at itself; if you do, you cause a script error. It is therefore important to check that the camera and its target are at different locations before using pointAt().

Zoom

The way zooming works is fairly simple, if rather abstruse. If you define a #zoom property in the parameter list for the new() handler, the following lines of code will be executed:

```
on mSetProperties(me, aDataList)
  -- Other code
  tTarget = aDataList[#pointAt]
  -- Other code
  pZoom = aDataList[#zoom]
  if pZoom <> 0 then
    tDistance = tTarget.distanceTo(pCamera.worldPosition)
    tDistance = power(tDistance, pZoom)
    pHeight   = tan(pCamera.projectionAngle * pi / 180) * tDistance
  end if
end mSetProperties
```

The pZoom property is most realistic in the range 0.0 to 1.0. Any number to the power 0 is equal to 1. Any number to the power 1 is equal to itself. Raising a number to the power 0.5 is the same as taking its square root. As a general rule, raising a number to the power 1/*n* is the same as taking its *n*th root. Thus, setting the local variable tDistance to the distance between the camera and the target raised to some power between 0.0 and 1.0 has the effect of selecting a point some way between the camera and its target.

Using this point as a guide, I calculate a benchmark height; at the current projectionAngle, an object with a dimension of pHeight at a distance of tDistance would fill half the sprite. In the stepFrame() handler I work in the opposite direction: I calculate a new value for tDistance based on the current distance between the camera and its target, raised to the same power, and then work out what projectionAngle would be required at that distance to make pHeight equivalent to half the height of the sprite.

If pZoom has a value of 1.0, the target object will always appear the same size because the projectionAngle will adjust to compensate for the entire distance. If pZoom is 0.0, there will be no compensation at all; the camera's projectionAngle will not change. If pZoom is between these two limits, the camera will compensate more or less for the distance.

To judge the effect, run the gForce.dir movie and type **400** in the editable text member to the right of the Play button; then press the RETURN key. Now use the pop-up menu to select from the following cameras:

- **Spectator** No zoom (pZoom = 0.0)
- **Fog** pZoom = 0.3
- **RootNode** pZoom = 0.7
- **Zoom** pZoom = 1.0

Fog

The fog property of a camera is used to produce a heightened sense of distance. In the real world, if you look out over a landscape, the minute particles of dust in the air reduce the proportion of light that reaches your eyes from a distant object. Distant hills seem paler than close ones. The effect is even more obvious when diving in murky water.

Calculating fog requires a certain amount of processing time. On each frame, for each pixel, Director has to calculate how far the model under that pixel is from the camera. Certain officially supported renderer drivers do not support fog, so you cannot be certain that the end user will see the effect that you intend. The software renderer does support it, but animation might be unacceptably slow on many machines.

RootNode

One interesting feature of Shockwave 3D is that you can select what is visible to the eye. A camera's rootNode property is set by default to group("World"), which means, by default, a camera sees everything in front of it. If you set the rootNode property of a camera to some other node, only that node and all its children will be visible. The visible nodes will be lit only by the lights that are children of the rootNode. The node in question does not even have to be in the world. If you switch to the RootNode camera you will see only the spacecraft. You can remove the spacecraft from the world by typing

```
member("3D world").group("spaceCraft").removeFromWorld()
```

However, the RootNode camera will continue to see it, but the spacecraft will not appear so bright as in the other camera views because `group("spacecraft")` contains no lights in its children. The various models are visible only because their shaders have an `emissive` color (see Chapter 10). If you type the following in the Message window,

```
model("Cone").shader.emissive = rgb(0, 0, 0)
```

the body of the spacecraft will disappear from the RootNode view, but it will still block the view of the fins if it is between them and the camera. Viewed from other cameras, the body will still be visible (but dark gray) as it reflects ambient light from the world.

Alternatives to Creating a Script

The camera path generated by the Make Camera Path script is very pure, but it lacks excitement. Although it moves at more than four times the speed of the default recording, the camera remains perfectly aligned with the gates, and all sense of danger is lost.

However, the automatically generated list of camera positions has a major advantage of the recorded list: file size. The Make Camera Path script weighs in at just over 10K. With a minor modification, it could simply return a list of transform data instead of creating a Script member that does this. The handler that defines the camera path is only a small part of the script. Other handlers could be added to create a range of paths at little extra cost.

Recording a fairly rapid flight might yield more than 700 camera positions and require a script of over 120K to define them all. Even once the script has been stripped of its scriptText during the process of publishing the movie as a *.dcr, the weight of the script member is still important. Each transform requires 45 bytes of memory when stored on disk, so a list of 700 transforms contains a good deal of information that cannot be compressed: over 30K, in fact. Creating additional camera paths would require saving additional transforms, and the cost in file size would increase in direct proportion.

In low-bandwidth situations, it would make sense to generate the list of transforms on-the-fly instead of building a specific script. Are there ways of making smooth camera movements that look less as if they were created with a straight edge and a compass? The answer is yes, but the mathematical concepts are more complex.

Bézier curves, splines, and NURBs all can be used to define a path for a camera; in a nutshell, these techniques use quadratic, cubic, and quartic equations to define curves in space, given a number of fixed points.

Unfortunately, there is not space here to cover these concepts. Fortunately, Barry Swan provides an excellent tutorial on the use of Catmull-Rom splines, plus a demonstration movie, at http://www.theburrow.co.uk/d85/index.htm.

Backdrops, Overlays, and the colorBuffer

The gForce.dir movie demonstrates another powerful feature of the camera object: The possibility of displaying a texture either in front of all other models, as if stuck on the lens of the camera (overlay), or behind all other models as if the texture were stuck to the Stage behind the sprite (backdrop). The following examples all deal with overlays, but the principles are identical for backdrops. The `colorBuffer` property allows you to set an individual background color for each camera; it can also provide an interesting trails effect.

Manipulating Overlays and Backdrops

Overlays and backdrops are properties of individual cameras. In the gForce.dir movie, I assign the same overlays to all cameras to give a homogenous feel to the movie, but this need not be the case. Indeed, as you will see, creating duplicate overlays or backdrops for separate cameras multiplies the internal assets of the Shockwave 3D member.

Overlays and backdrops do not have names like nodes do. Instead, you must refer to them by index number, which makes them more akin to sprites, and, indeed, they are rendered in the same order as sprites: the lowest numbered backdrop appears behind all others; the highest numbered overlay appears on top of everything else.

Like sprites, overlays and backdrops have a `loc` property. Like bitmap members, they also have a `regPoint` property. By default, this is `point(0, 0)`, or the top-left corner. Together, the `loc` and `regPoint` define where the overlay or backdrop will appear with respect to the top-left corner of the sprite.

Setting the `rotation` property rotates the overlay or backdrop around its center, not around its `regPoint`. Setting the `scale` property alters the height and width of the overlay or backdrop proportionately. You cannot alter the height and width separately. Scaling is calculated from the top-left corner of the overlay or backdrop, not from the center or the `regPoint`. Modifying the `blend` property might not have any effect with certain renderers.

The appearance of an overlay or backdrop is determined by its source property. This must be a texture object. The source, loc, and rotation all must be specified when you create a new overlay or backdrop.

Static Textures

Simplest to create is a static texture. The speedometer displays the image of a text member in an overlay. The technique is simple, so why not create your own demonstration from scratch? Here's how:

1. Create a new movie
2. Create a Shockwave 3D member in cast slot 1.
3. Name it "3D World" and drag it onto the Stage.
4. In cast slot 2, create a Text member and type some text into it. (You also could use a Vector Shape member or import a Flash member.)
5. Set the text to a light color, so that it will show up on the black background of the Shockwave 3D member.
6. Run your movie.
7. In the Message window, type

```
tTexture  = member(1).newTexture("Test", #fromImageObject, member(2).image)
tTopLeft  = point(10, 10)
tRotation = 0
sprite(1).camera.addOverlay(tTexture, tTopLeft, tRotation)
```

The text in the overlay will probably not look as sharp as the original text. Can you think why? As a clue, type the following into the Message window:

```
put tTexture.width
put tTexture.height
```

Figure 12-14 should give you a further clue.

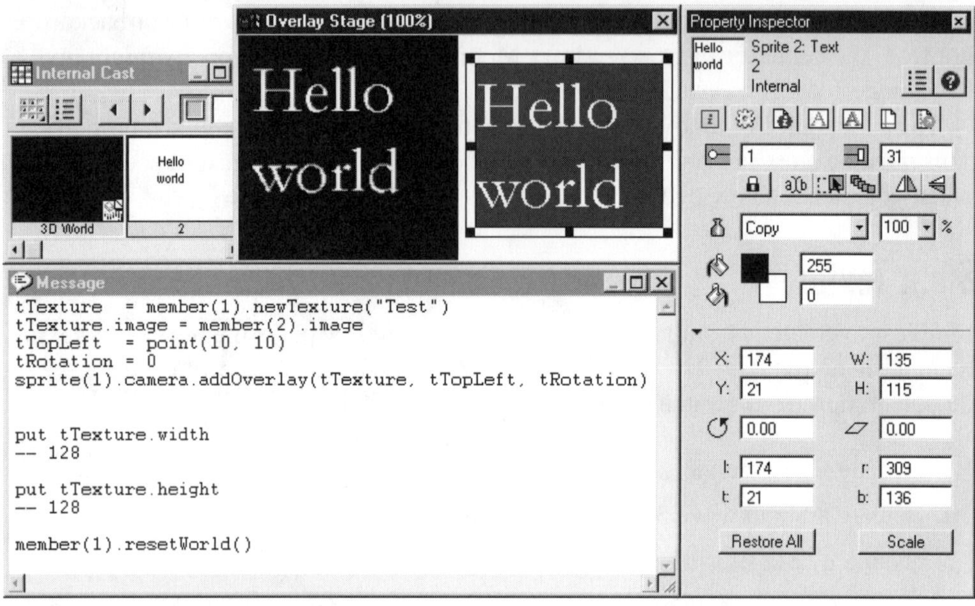

Figure 12-14 *Creating an overlay*

As you saw in Chapter 10, textures are always created with dimensions that are a power of 2. To get the best resolution, you should set the dimensions of your Text member to powers of 2. A quick way of doing this is to drag the Text member onto the Stage, set its framing (`#boxType`) to Fixed using the Property Inspector, and then adjust the size of the sprite. In the Message window, type

```
member(1).resetWorld()
```

and then try again.

Overlay and Backdrop Trivia

Now that you have created an overlay, you can carry out a number of experiments to see how Director treats them. Director will create a model object for each backdrop and overlay. These will have names such as `model("Overlay-copy1")` and `model("Backdrop-copy2")`. In the Message window, type

```
put member(1).model(1)
-- model("Overlay-copy1")
```

Overlay and background models use the default plane resource (whose name is, strangely, "DefaultModel"):

```
put member(1).model(1).resource
-- plane("DefaultModel")
```

Perhaps for this very reason, models created from the default plane resource cannot be made visible in the 3D sprite. Try it and see (or not, as the case may be).

Each camera possesses two nameless groups: one for its overlays and one for its backdrops. Despite sharing the same (lack of) name, these groups seem to coexist peacefully.

```
put member(1).model(1).parent
-- group("")

sprite(1).camera.addBackdrop(tTexture, tTopLeft, tRotation)
put member(1).model(2)
-- model("Backdrop-copy2")
put member(1).model(2).parent
-- group("")
put member(1).model(2).parent.child.count
-- 1
```

These groups are not accessible through a standard query:

```
put member(1).group.count
-- 1

put member(1).group(1)
-- group("World")
```

The overlay and backdrop models have their own set of coordinates:

```
put member(1).model(1).worldPosition
-- vector( -2.5000, 12.5000, 0.0000 )

sprite(1).camera.overlay[1].scale = 2
put member(1).model(1).worldPosition
-- vector( 65.0000, -45.0000, 0.0000 )
```

However, this seems to be divorced from the rest of the world:

```
put member(1).model(1).transform
-- transform(
1.00000,0.00000,0.00000,0.00000,
0.00000,1.00000,0.00000,0.00000,
0.00000,0.00000,1.00000,0.00000,
0.00000,0.00000,0.00000,1.00000)

put member(1).model(1).parent.transform
-- transform(
1.00000,0.00000,0.00000,0.00000,
0.00000,1.00000,0.00000,0.00000,
0.00000,0.00000,1.00000,0.00000,
0.00000,0.00000,0.00000,1.00000)

put member(1).model(1).parent.parent
-- <Void>
```

If you create the same overlay for two different cameras, this will create two separate models:

```
camera2 = member(1).newCamera("Camera 2")
camera2.addOverlay(tTexture, tTopLeft, tRotation)

put member(1).model.count
-- 3
put member(1).model(3)
-- model("Overlay-copy3")
```

Each new backdrop or overlay also creates a new shader named "OverlayShader-copy*X*," where *X* is a number that increments for each new backdrop or shader added to the member.

The main point to note from all this is that the Shockwave 3D might contain more models and shaders than you expect. If you have a routine that acts on all models in turn (as the Snapshot.dir movie does), it should filter for models whose names start "Overlay-copy…" and "Backdrop-copy…." These models cannot be displayed as such, because they are invisible except as overlays or backdrops.

Dynamic Textures

Because you can change the image or the member of a texture at any time, it is a simple matter to create dynamic overlays and backdrops. The gForce.dir movie has two examples of this:

- The height of the columns indicating the spacecraft's speed and acceleration change as you press and release the A and D keys.
- The x, y, and z positions of the spacecraft are updated regularly.

These appear on the right side of the movie, as you can see in Figure 12-15.

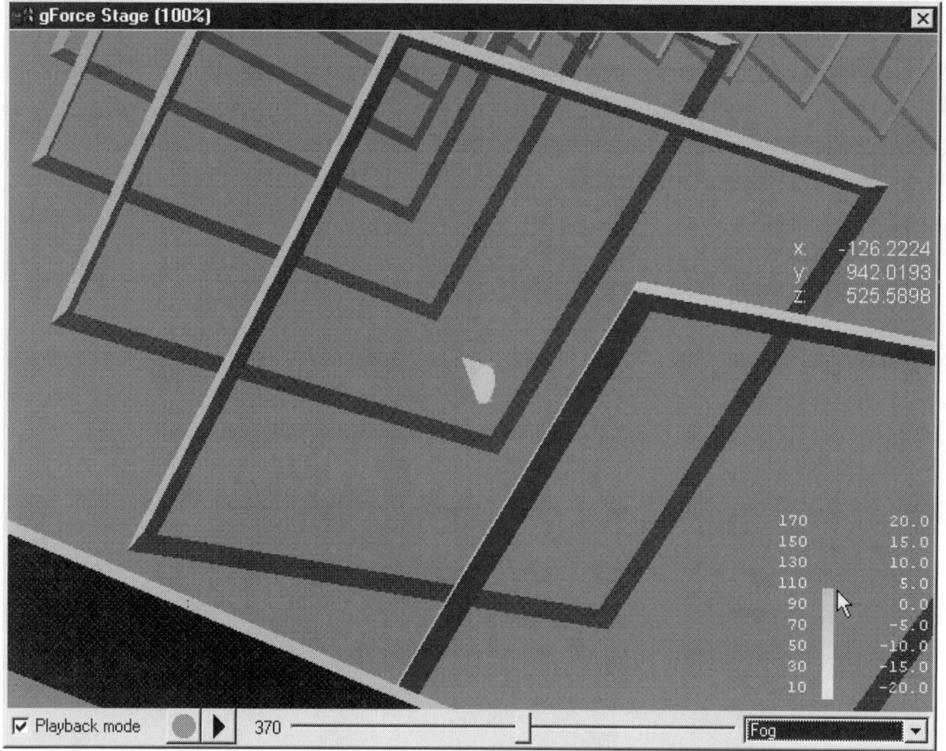

Figure 12-15 *The dynamic overlays for speed, acceleration, and position*

Using Imaging Lingo

Imaging Lingo provides a very rapid means of updating an image used by a texture. This is treated in depth in Chapters 1 through 5. The main point to note is that, after every modification, you will need to reset the `image` property of a texture: the texture's `image` property and the source image are kept at separate memory locations.

In this particular case, the speedometer images are a fixed shape, color, and size: the display changes because the alpha channel of the image is edited. See the `mShowSpeed()` handler of the gForce script in cast slot 18 for details.

Using Text Members

Grabbing the image of a text member takes a little time because you create a new 32-bit image each time. In certain circumstances, you could check if the text has changed before grabbing the new image. In the gForce.dir movie, the text will change constantly, as long as the spacecraft is moving. To prevent this from slowing the movie down too much, I update the text and its associated texture only once every three frames. It also seems to help slightly to set the member of the texture rather than the image, but this might not be significant:

```
property myNode     -- the group("spacecraft")
property myCounter -- used to check for every third frame
property myMember   -- text member used for its image
property myTexture -- overlay texture
property myIndex    -- number of this overlay


on stepFrame(me)
  myCounter = myCounter + 1
  if myCounter mod 3 then
    exit
  end if

  tPosition = myNode.worldPosition
  tString = \
"x: "&TAB&tPosition.x&RETURN&\
"y: "&TAB&tPosition.y&RETURN&\
"z: "&TAB&tPosition.z
```

```
  myMember.text    = tString
  myTexture.member = myMember
end stepFrame
```

The colorBuffer

Each camera has a `colorBuffer` property, which determines what appears in any empty space behind the models, and between the overlays and backdrops. In Director 8.5 you cannot access this color buffer directly, but you can get and set two of its properties: `clearAtRender` and `clearValue`.

clearAtRender

For Chapter 8, I provided the movie Interpol.dir to show how to interpolate between two transforms. This instruction,

```
sprite(1).camera.colorBuffer.clearAtRender = 0
```

makes the moving box model leave a trail behind it, so that the intermediate positions remain visible (see Figure 12-16). Setting the camera's `colorBuffer.clearAtRender` property to 1 wipes the sprite clean before each new view of the model is rendered.

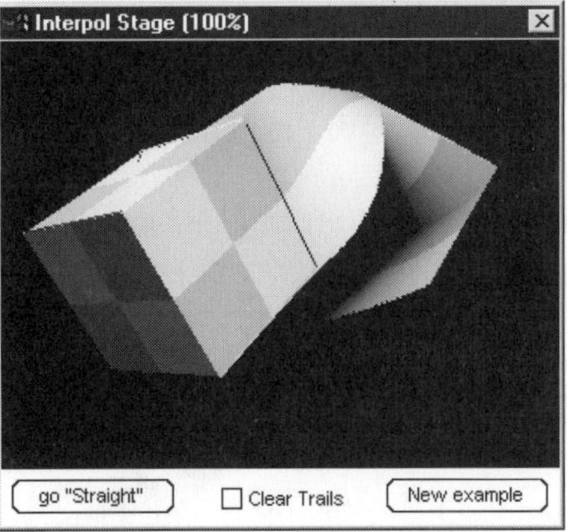

Figure 12-16 *The effect of setting the clearAtRender property to FALSE*

clearValue

If the sprite is cleared before each render, what color should be used for the background? Up until now I have used `member("3D World").bgColor = <color object>`. This sets the default background color for all cameras. To create a different background color for a specific camera, you can use

```
member("3D World").camera(2).colorBuffer.clearValue = <color object>
```

Possible uses for this are

- **Debugging** If each camera has a distinctive background color, you can tell immediately which camera is active.
- **Characterization** A subjective camera used for a wolf character might use a different background color from that used for a human's subjective camera. This will have an effect only where no models are visible. It will not tint the models in any way. (You can use colored lighting to tint the models; see Chapter 13.)
- **Team identification** You can set the `clearValue` to yellow for the cameras that show the Yellow Team in action, and use blue for the cameras that follow the Blue Team.

Adapting the gForce Movie

There are a number of ways to improve the gForce movie:

- You could use your own spacecraft and gate models instead of the simple models provided.
- You could add models for a grandstand and other scenery.
- You could use the Make Tracks script to build your own circuits.
- You could modify the number of laps required to complete the race.
- You could add a stopwatch overlay for timing a lap.

- You could include a fuel consumption gauge and limit the amount of fuel available.
- You could add a multiuser interface so that several players can race at the same time.

Conclusion

This chapter showed a number of basic camera techniques, and provided tools and handlers to help you create interesting camera views and movements. The main camera movements are illustrated by the different views in the gForce.dir movie. You've seen all the properties and methods of the camera object, including overlays, backdrops, and the color buffer.

The way you use the camera determines the atmosphere of your scene. Imagine a scene where your main character enters a vast hall. A subjective view (first person or over the shoulder) gives a sense of mastery and control: the character dominates the scene. A view from high above crushes the character; it emphasizes the dimensions of the hall and the power of the person who owns it. A rapid series of views from low down (perhaps accompanied by the sound of rats scuttling and squeaking) creates a sense of unease.

Multimedia implies interaction and user control. Atmospheric camera work implies some passivity as far as the spectator is concerned. As the sophistication of multimedia increases, so audiences are going to expect developers to provide more imaginative solutions to these two conflicting demands. If you want to make your mark, don't content yourself with utilitarian camera work.

In Chapter 14, we'll be looking at collision detection. You'll be able to use techniques from that chapter to make the gates "solid"; you could add code to the gForce.dir movie so a collision between the spacecraft and a gate results in a particle-primitive explosion.

CHAPTER

13

Lights

IN THIS CHAPTER:

At night, all cats are gray.

—French proverb

Until now, we have made only limited use of lights, relying for the most part on those provided by default; however, in fact, lights are not essential. In Chapters 10 and 11, you saw how to make models visible without using lights, by setting the `emissive` property of the models' shader or by using the `diffuseLightMap` property of a shader layer. The RootNode camera in the gForce.dir movie in Chapter 12 provides an example of an unlit view.

Director 8.5 proposes four types of light: ambient lights, directional lights, point lights, and spot lights. These virtual lights are very different from those in the real world:

- They have no physical size.
- They do not shine.
- They do not cast shadows.
- Their rays pass through solid objects.
- No cone is visible where the rays pass through semitransparent objects.
- Rays are not necessarily reflected from shiny objects.
- Their effect does not necessarily diminish with distance.

If you are used to working with rendering software that produces high-quality images at less than real-time rates, you might be surprised at this lack of realism. Director provides such simple light objects to provide acceptable real-time performance. For instance, to calculate shadows, you would need to look at the scene from each light source in turn and determine, for the whole of the visible scene area, which is the first model on which the light shines. If that model were partially transparent, you would have to diminish the light quality, alter its color and direction, and seek out the next model—and so on. Such complex ray tracing calculations can take several seconds per image, even on expensive custom-designed machines. Even if processing speed continues to double every 18 months, as it has done in the past, real-time ray tracing is still many years away.

Shockwave 3D renders scenes much more succinctly, but many times per second. There is time left over from the rendering process to accept input from the user. The simplicity of the light objects allows you to provide interaction and pace on off-the-shelf machines. So what do Shockwave 3D lights have to offer? In short, they add color, shading, shininess, and the capability to focus attention on a particular spot.

Types of Lights

Gallery.dir

To allow you to reconcile image quality and performance, Director 8.5 proposes 4 different types of light. These are listed here in order of complexity, starting with the simplest. In a project where performance is critical, directional lights give an acceptable sense of three-dimensionality. Use the more complex lights to create a more studied atmosphere.

You'll find the movie Gallery.dir in the 3D\Lights\ folder on the CD-ROM that accompanies the book; it illustrates the four different types of lights. To move through the Gallery, click the 3D sprite and drag the mouse. Dragging horizontally turns the camera; dragging vertically moves it forward or backward. You have to move at least 20 pixels vertically for this to have any effect. You can switch individual lights on or off via check boxes. All the lights used in the movie are set to the same color value: `rgb(255, 255, 255)`.

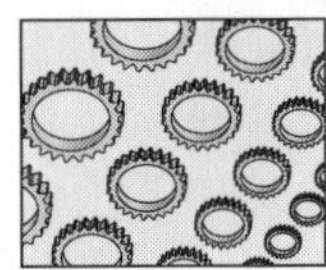

NOTE

In this version of Gallery.dir, you can move the camera through the walls. You'll find out how to prevent this from happening in the next chapter.

- **Ambient lights** Ambient lights fill the whole world evenly with light. Ambient light is like sunlight on a cloudy day: it comes from all directions at once, even the floor. You need only one such light, and it doesn't matter where you put it or which way you point it. You can set the color and brightness of this light by using the Shockwave 3D member's `ambientColor` property. You also can use the Director Light Ambient color chip on the Shockwave 3D member tab of the Property Inspector to set this property. Ambient lighting makes models visible, but it creates no shading information; models appear to be flat because no sides appear darker than others. Ambient light is the fastest light to apply, as it affects all surfaces uniformly. The specular property of ambient light does not have any effect; ambient light does not create reflected highlights on shiny surfaces, such as the picture frames in Figure 13-1.

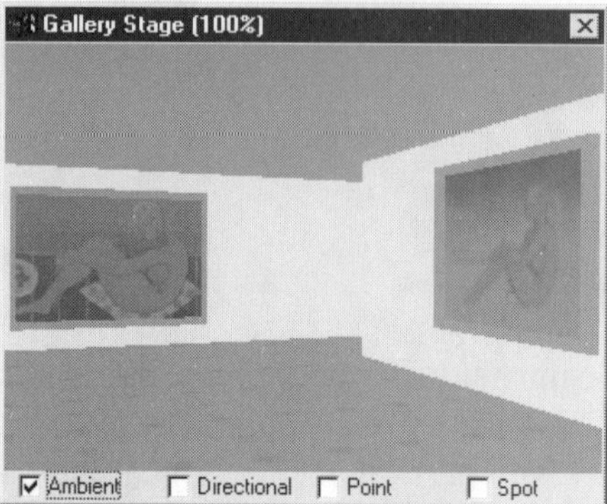

Figure 13-1 *An example of ambient light*

- **Directional lights** A directional light is like sunlight on a clear day. It provides parallel rays of light from an apparently infinite distance. Directional light will shine on surfaces that face it, but not on those that face away; so surfaces with the same color are shaded differently according to their orientation. This provides a basic sense of three dimensionality. The position of a directional light is not important—wherever you place it, the light appears to come from beyond the edge of the world. Directional light is the second fastest light to apply, as it affects all surfaces at a constant angle. In Figure 13-2, note the effect of specular directional light on the shiny picture frame: a highlight appears at the top right of the left-hand frame.

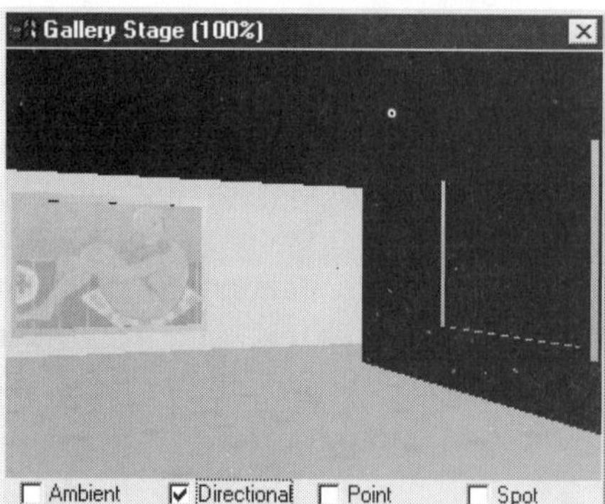

Figure 13-2 *An example of directional light*

- **Point lights** A point light shines in all directions from a particular position, like a bare light bulb. Light from a point light falls on all surfaces that face toward the light source. A point light inside a room will light all the walls, whereas a directional light will not light two of the walls. If you move the light source, the angle at which its rays are reflected from the surrounding surfaces will change. Like the two previous lights, but unlike a light bulb, its effect does not diminish with distance. Point light is slower to apply, because the faces to which it is applied and the angle from which it falls on them varies according to the respective positions of the light and the models. See Figure 13-3.
- **Spot lights** Spot lights have both position and direction, and they also can have an intensity that varies with distance. They give an effect that is reminiscent of theatrical spot lights. The angle of the cone of light can be varied so it lights a greater or a smaller area. A spot light in a room will illuminate only the area in front of it. These are the slowest lights to calculate, because their effect is so complex. See Figure 13-4.

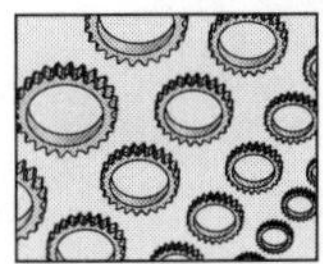

NOTE

To reproduce these images, use the Property Inspector to set the Directional light to Top Left; then run the movie (in that order). Use the Xtras menu to open the Snapshot window and select KeyView in the pop-up View menu. Use the 3DPI window to move the Point light to `vector(0, 50, -140)`*. This is the same position as the spot light: in the center of the ceiling for this room.*

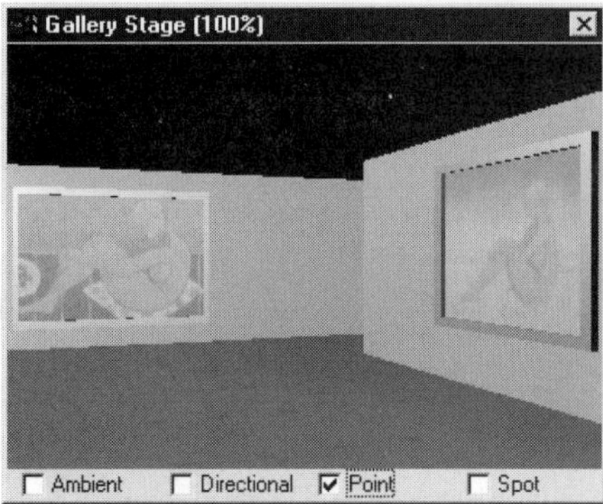

Figure 13-3 *An example of a point light*

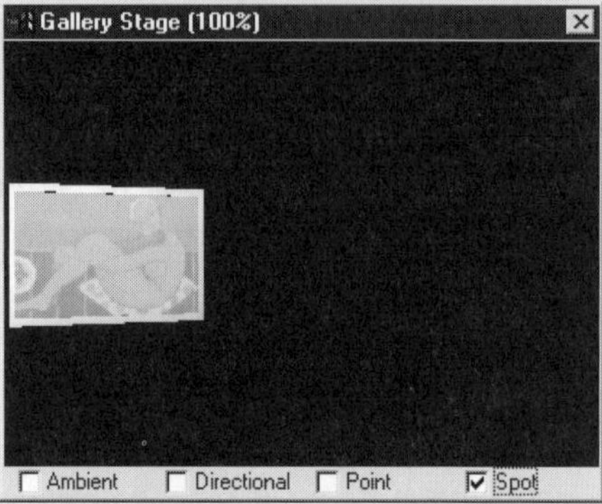

Figure 13-4 *An example of a spot light*

Understanding the Mathematical Model for Shockwave 3D's Virtual Lights

I am grateful to Sébastien Portebois for the following description of the lighting model used in Director 8.5.

Shockwave 3D breaks lighting down into three categories: ambient, specular, and diffuse. Although the results might appear natural at first glance, a little investigation shows that, for example, the notion of ambient light is a pure fiction. The definition of ambient light suggests that every surface reflects the same quantity of light toward the observer's eye, regardless of the orientation of the surface or its distance from the observer. Ambient light exists in the absence of any light sources. You also might be wondering why the light model chosen for Shockwave 3D ignores both shadows and mirrors—but let's begin at the beginning.

The human eye perceives objects as a result of the light signals that they emit (in the case of light sources) or reflect (in the case of solid objects) in the direction of the observer. In a virtual 3D world, these light signals need to be expressed as equations. Different sets of equations lead to different models of how light acts in the real world. The model adopted—and thus the complexity of the equations—depends on the user's requirements. Game enthusiasts want real-time simulation, and; thus fast equations that can calculate images many times a second. Architects prefer to study photorealistic images of the spaces they intend to create; therefore, they need a much more complex set of equations, which takes longer to render the final image. Between these two extremes, there is room for compromise. These two extremes lead to two distinct lighting models: the *global* model and the *local* model.

The color of an object as seen by the eye depends on the sum of the different light waves that fall on the object, either directly from light sources or indirectly from light reflected off other objects. A global model takes into consideration the full interplay of all the lights and all the reflecting objects in the given scene. The result, produced by tracing the path of individual light rays, is photorealistic but requires an immense amount of calculation.

A local model is designed to reduce the calculation time. Why is such a model called "local"? This model considers interaction only between a single light source and a single surface at a time. Each surface is treated once for each light source; only the reflections local to the surface itself are considered.

What exactly is meant by "reflection"? A reflection depends on the nature of the surface. To take a concrete example, try shining the light from your desk lamp onto concrete, glass, or cloth. Reflected light can be broken down into two components:

- **Specular** In this case, the light rays are reflected in a symmetrical manner, like a billiard ball bouncing off the edge of a billiard table.
- **Diffuse** The light energy is scattered in all directions, like children running out into a school playground.

To take a couple of visual examples: reflection from a glass table is almost entirely specular, whereas reflection from a table cloth is almost entirely diffuse. All surfaces have a mixture of specular and diffuse reflection, although in extreme cases one of the components might be negligible.

It is thus possible to break the color of any given point of a given surface down into two components: a diffuse value and a specular value. The diffuse value depends on an interaction between the color of the object itself and the color of the light source; the diffuse value depends on the angle from which the light source falls on the surface but it is independent of the position of the observer. The specular value depends on both the angle from which the light falls on the surface and the angle from which the observer is looking at the surface.

The light model used in Shockwave 3D is based on the sum of these two components, plus a constant due to the ambient lighting.

```
Light intensity at a given point
=   Ambient intensity
  + Incident energy * ((diffuse coeffiecient * cosine of the incident angle)
                     + (specular coefficient * cosine of the difference
                                               between the angle of
                                               observation and the angle
                                               of reflection))
```

Why introduce a fictional ambient constant? In reality, light is reflected off each object in a scene onto each of the others. In the preceding equation, the effect of this multiply-reflected light is simplified to its extreme: it is expressed by the value for ambient light. This blanket approximation accelerates the calculations dramatically. Lighting can be determined from a single calculation for each light source and each surface; other objects in the scene can be ignored.

The down side is that this same approximation makes the model unrealistic. Reflection in a mirror is impossible, because it depends entirely on the other objects in the scene. For the same reason, one object will not throw a shadow on another.

Shockwave 3D uses two different rendering techniques: *Gouraud Shading* (used by default) and *Lambert Shading* (used to improve performance)

In Gouraud Shading, lighting for each triangular surface is calculated in three steps. First, the total light energy falling on each of the summits of the triangle from each light source is determined. Then these values are interpolated along each edge of the triangle. Finally, the surface of the triangle is filled by interpolating the values for the edges. Interpolation of the color data is thus performed twice, in a linear manner each time—a bilinear interpolation.

As far as lighting is concerned, the surface is deemed to curve smoothly. As far as the profile of the model is concerned, each surface is flat. If there are few polygons in a given curved surface, the difference between the angles of adjacent surfaces might be significant. This has a greater effect on the specular component than on the diffuse component, because the value of the specular depends both on the angle of incidence of the light and the angle of observation.

Using the #smooth parameter with the `meshResource.generateNormals()` command and setting the `flat` property of the shader to `FALSE` tells Director to use the Gouraud Shading technique. If you generate the normals of a mesh using the `#flat` parameter, or if you set the `flat` property of the shader to `TRUE`, the simpler technique known as Lambert Shading is used and the faces will appear as distinct facets. Instead of bilinear interpolation for each pixel, the average color of the three vertices of a given face is used over the whole area of that face. This improves performance at the expense of quality.

To create as realistic an image as is possible with this model, the value for ambient should be kept low (darker colors), ambient and diffuse lighting should use the same hue, and a pure color (typically, white) should be used for specular light.

Using Multiple Light Sources

fpsMeter.dir

As Figure 13-5 shows, using more than one light allows you to combine the effects described in the preceding. However, lights consume processor power; it is important to switch them off when they are not required. In this section, we will be looking at the performance and memory issues associated with lights.

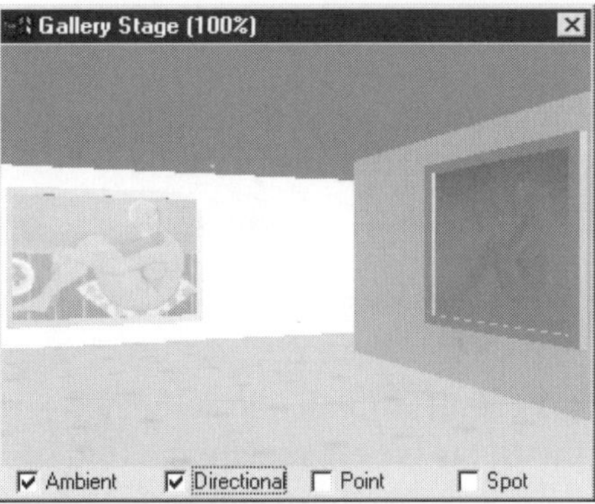

Figure 13-5 *Combining two types of light object*

Testing Performance

You can test this for yourself by opening the Gallery.dir movie on the Stage, and then opening the fpsMeter movie in a window. If you run the AddXtras.exe projector, which you will find on the CD-ROM, you should find the fpsMeter movie is placed in your Xtras folder. You can open it in a window by selecting the menu Xtras | fpsMeter.

Restart the Gallery.dir movie, so that you see the lighthouse photo at the entrance. Now switch off all the lights and check the reading in the fpsMeter window. To get the most accurate result, close all Director windows that need to update as the movie runs, such as the Score window and the Tool Panel. Now switch on the spot light and see how this affects the reading, as shown here.

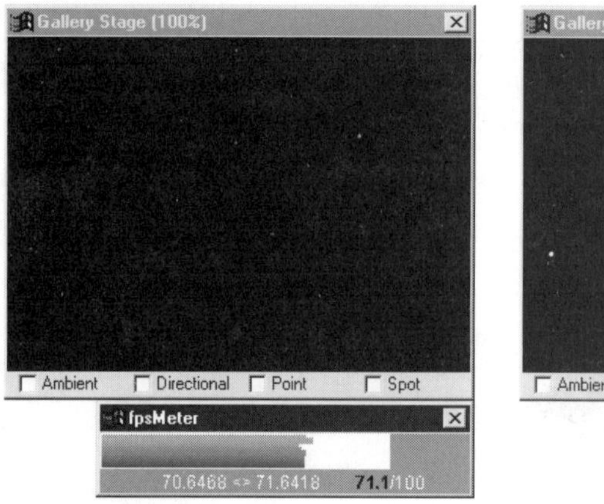

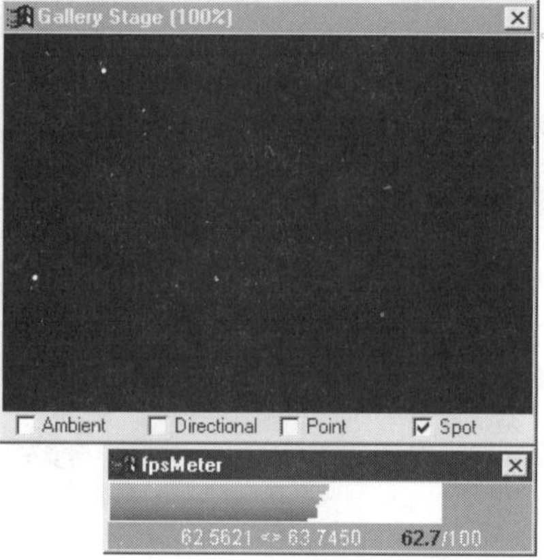

The spot light is two rooms away and points toward the right. Its effect cannot be seen from the initial camera position. Nonetheless, the performance of the movie drops noticeably. In the test illustrated in the preceding, the difference is more than 10 percent. The fpsMeter movie is dealt with in more detail in the following section.

Switching Lights On and Off

The easiest way to switch a light off is to use the command `removeFromWorld()`. In the Gallery.dir movie, the lights are created by the Initialize Lights script in cast slot 11. This simply sets the color of the two default lights UIAmbient and UIDirectional to white—`rgb(255, 255, 255)`. It also creates two new lights, which also are set to white:

- `light("Point")`, which is placed at the center of the ceiling in the second room, behind the wall that appears in front of you when you start the movie
- `light("Spot")`, which is placed at the center of the ceiling in the third room, pointing at the painting to the right.

```
on mInitializeNode(me, a3DMember)
  a3DMember.light("UIAmbient").color = rgb(255, 255, 255)
  a3DMember.light("UIAmbient").color = rgb(255, 255, 255)

  -- Create and place two new lights
  tName = "Point"
  tLight = a3DMember.newLight("Point", #point)
  tLight.color = rgb(255, 255, 255)
  tLight.worldPosition = vector(0, 50, 0)

  tLight = a3DMember.newLight("Spot", #spot)
  tLight.color = rgb(255, 255, 255)
  tLight.spotAngle = 21
  tLight.worldPosition = vector(0, 50, -140)
  tLight.pointAt(100, 21, -140)
end mInitializeNode
```

The buttons at the foot of the movie are controlled by the Light Switch behavior, which you will find in cast slot 7:

```
property mySprite
property myLight

on beginSprite(me)
  mySprite = sprite(me.spriteNum)
  tName    = mySprite.member.name
  myLight  = member("Gallery").light(tName)
  mySprite.value = myLight.isInWorld()
end beginSprite

on mouseUp(me)
  if mySprite.value then
   myLight.addToWorld()
  else
    myLight.removeFromWorld()
  end if
end mouseUp
```

Memory Consumption

There is little or no performance hit if you simply create a light and then remove it from the world. It will be where you want it when you need it. Of course, holding unused lights in memory will take up space. You can test how much by creating a new movie and writing a Movie Script handler like this:

```
on testLight(a3DMember, aLightType)
  tBytes = the freeBytes
  repeat with i = 1 to 1000
    tLight = a3DMember.newLight("light "&i, aLightType)
  end repeat
  tUsedBytes = (tBytes - the freeBytes) / 1000
  tBytes = the freeBytes

  repeat with i = 1 to 1000
    a3DMember.deleteLight("light "&i)
  end repeat
  tFreedBytes = (the freeBytes - tBytes) / 1000

  put "Bytes used by a single "&aLightType&" light:"&tUsedBytes
  put "Bytes freed by a single "&aLightType&" light:"&tFreedBytes
end
```

Here's how you could call this handler from the Message window:

```
t3DMember = new(#shockwave3D)
testLight(t3DMember, #spot)
-- "Bytes used by a single spot light:763"
-- "Bytes freed by a single spot light:763"
```

The values you get might vary slightly, depending on how Director has purged its memory. Try the `testLight()` command a few times and the results should settle down. At less than 1K per light, you can afford to have a few unused lights available.

Manipulating Lights with Lingo

The lights in the Gallery.dir movie are static. You can move them around using the Ullala's 3DPI window, as shown in Figure 13-6. You also can test the effect of changing the colors and other properties. Use the New… button to create additional

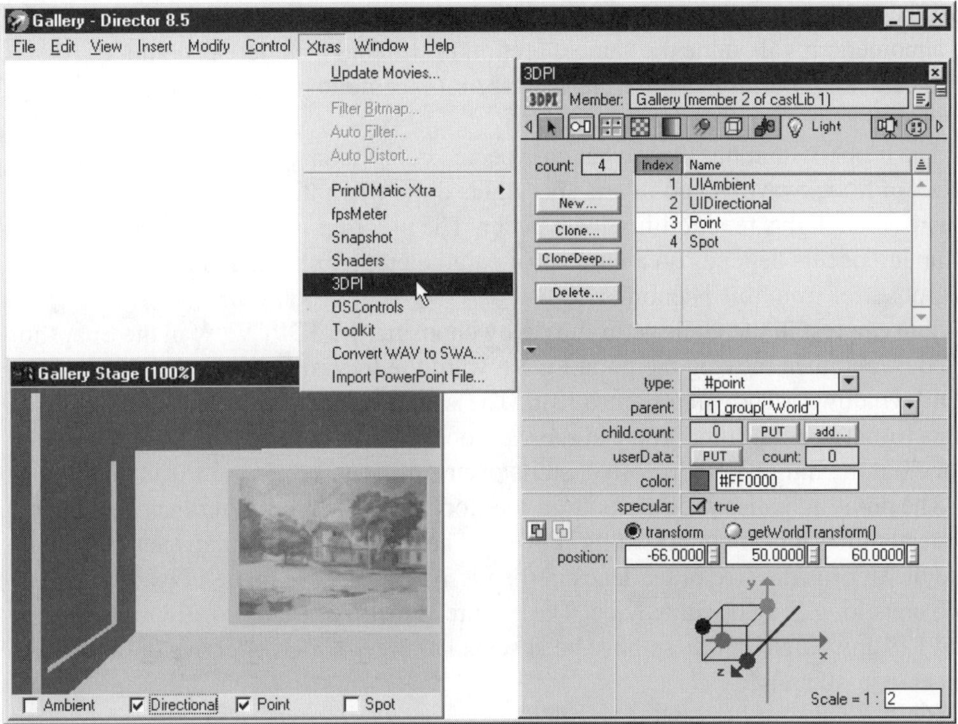

Figure 13-6 *Manipulating light using the 3DPI*

lights. If you want to switch one of your own lights off, you can set its parent to VOID, which has the same effect as `removeFromWorld()`. Use the spaces and models in the Gallery to experiment with the possibilities of each type of light.

position, rotation, and scale

Like models, cameras, and groups, lights have a `transform` property that defines their `position`, `rotation`, and `scale`. For `ambient` and `directional` lights, changing the `position` of the light has no effect on the way it illuminates the world; for ambient and point lights, changing the `rotation` of the light has no effect either. For all types of light, changing the `scale` of a light has no effect on the light itself. However, all these properties do have an effect on the light's children, if it has any.

For `directional` and `spot` lights, the `rotation` property acts as you would expect. Lights shine down their negative z axis, just as cameras look down their negative z axis. If you make a spot light the child of the camera, as we shall do in a moment, it will shine the same direction in which the camera is pointing. As with cameras, you also can use the `pointAt()` command to set the rotation implicitly.

The property that has somewhat unexpected consequences is `position`. The effect of Shockwave 3D point and spot lights dims when they get close to a model, whereas real lights tend to illuminate better. The precise distance at which the dimming occurs depends on a number of parameters. (Ambient and directional lights do not suffer from this phenomenon.)

You can test in the Gallery.dir movie by choosing the 3DPI View in the Snapshot window and then moving the point light toward the left using the Light tab of the 3DPI window, as shown in Figure 13-6. The wall on which the painting is hung is 50 units from the point light (you can see the floor plan for the museum in member 29). This is at the limit where the effect starts occurring.

The point light also is 50 units from the floor, but it will not illuminate the floor correctly until it is about 300 units above it. The main difference between the picture and the floor is the size of the faces in the mesh. The floor is made of two triangles 400 units long and 200 units wide. The picture is made of triangles 128 units long and 128 units high, but these have been scaled to 30%, so the effective dimension is fewer than 40 units.

TIP

To make lights work more effectively, you can break large surfaces up into many smaller faces. To do this, use the `resolution` property of sphere and cylinder primitives and the `lengthVertices` and `heightVertices` properties of box and plane primitives. For mesh primitives, you need to add more vertices by hand.

Just as surprising is the fact that the effect of Shockwave 3D lights does not dim with distance. Once it has passed the critical distance from a given face, a light will shine just as strongly, regardless of its distance. The exception, as you shall see in the upcoming section "spotDecay and attenuation," is spot lights. Even so, you have to make a deliberate choice.

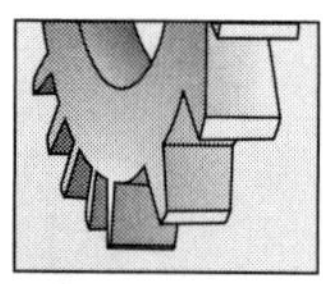

TIP

When the Snapshot window is open, it will intercept the mouse input to the Stage. To stop the Snapshot window from taking control of the camera, deselect the Intercept Mouse button.

color

Lights do not have to be white; the default color of a new light is a pale gray: `rgb( 191, 191, 191 )`. When a light falls on a shader, the separate red, green, and blue values in the light combine with the color of the shader at each point. Using a light value of 255 for a given color channel makes the pixel at that point in the shader reflect the full value for that color channel. Using a light value less than 255 makes the shader reflect a lower value for that color channel. For example, using a uniform gray light makes the shaders appear uniformly dim. Using a pure blue light makes the shader reflect only blue values.

Shining more than one light on the same mesh of a model has a cumulative effect: the maximum value for each color channel will be used. Therefore, you cannot bleach the colors of a shader by adding more and more light; you only make the colors brighter until they reach their full value. It's as if you lived in a world where the maximum quantity of sunlight was fixed by statute.

Use the 3DPI window to set the UIAmbient light to red, the UIDirectional light to green, and the Point light to blue. The resulting mix of colors will give you a clear idea of where each light shines strongest. For example, the ceiling will be dull red, due to the UIAmbient light, whereas the floor will be pale green under the effect of the UIDirectional light with a touch of UIAmbient. The different walls will be various violent shades ranging from muddy yellow to purple. Only the painting lit by the white spot light will retain its true colors.

Deliberately mixing colors in this way can help while debugging, or if you are simulating disco lighting. You are likely to want to use more subtle shades to create an atmosphere.

specular Light

As you saw in Chapter 10, all lights have a `specular` property that can be set to `TRUE` or `FALSE`. This adds a further layer of complexity to lights: it makes them reflect in surfaces where the shader has a `specularLightMap` or a `shininess` value. This is more fully addressed in Chapter 10.

spotAngle

The `spotAngle` property is recognized only by spot lights. Think of it as the angle that the reflector of the spot light makes with the light's z axis. The default `spotAngle` is 90.0, meaning 90°. With this `spotAngle`, the spot light will illuminate everything that is in front of it. Decreasing the `spotAngle` narrows the beam (you can't increase it beyond 90°).

Run the Gallery.dir movie, and then switch off all the lights. In the Message window, type the following:

```
tTorch = member("Gallery").newLight("Torch", #spot)
put tTorch.spotAngle
-- 90.0000
```

Now set the spot light up as a headlight for your camera:

```
sprite(1).camera.addChild(tTorch, #preserveParent)
tTorch.color = rgb( 255, 255, 255 )
```

You now should be able to move about using the mouse, and the surface in front of you will always be lit. Even if you get close up to a painting or a photograph, you can still see the details.

Now open the 3DPI window, select the Gallery member, and click the Lights tab. Restart your movie, switch all the lights off again, and re-create your torch. (Notice how the Torch light is automatically selected in the 3DPI window.)

In the Message window, type

```
tTorch.spotAngle = 16
```

The beam narrows so that only the photograph of the lighthouse is lit.

Click the Shockwave 3D sprite and move the mouse upward to advance. Before you reach the lighthouse photograph, the light from the spot light will fail. For me, this happened when the spot light was still 97 units along the z axis from the photograph. (In the Snapshot window, you can choose the Torchlight view to reproduce the same position.)

```
put tTorch.worldPosition
-- vector( 20.0000, 25.0000, 178.0000 )
put member("Gallery").model("Lighthouse").worldPosition
-- vector( 20.0000, 42.0000, 81.0000 )
```

Use the spotAngle control in the 3DPI window to increase the `spotAngle` of the Torch spot light until the photograph appears again, as shown in Figure 13-7.

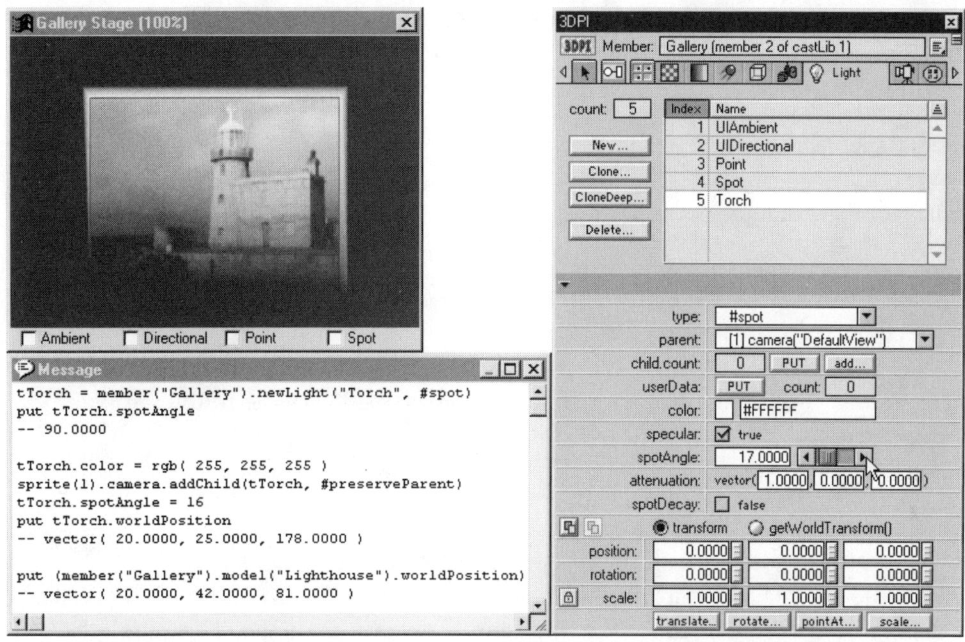

Figure 13-7 *Exploring how a spot light dims when used close up*

It would appear from this experiment that, if the rays from the spot light do not touch any of the edges of a particular shader on a model, the entire shader will not be lit. Unfortunately, there is no built-in method of determining when this occurs.

The comparison between a Director spot light and a torch is rather tenuous: the spot light does not produce the characteristic circle of light that a torch does. Increasing the number of polygons used to create a given surface can help make the effect more natural, at the expense of extra processing time. You might like to investigate the use of the Sub-Division Surfaces Modifier (SDS), which adds polygons on-the-fly if there is sufficient processor time to spare.

spotDecay and attenuation

The other two properties unique to spot lights are `spotDecay` and `attenuation`. The `attenuation` property has no effect unless `spotDecay` is `TRUE`; `spotDecay` is `FALSE` by default. In the Message window, type the following:

```
tTorch.spotAngle = 90
tTorch.spotDecay = TRUE
```

Do you see how the illumination from the Torch light dims slightly? The default value for `attenuation` is `vector(1.0, 0.0, 0,0)`. The use of a vector here is purely utilitarian. The meaning of this is (pseudo-Lingo)

```
spotAttenuation = 1.0 + (0.0 * distance) + (0.0 * distanceSquared)
```

Or, more accurately (but also more obscurely):

```
spotAttenuation =  attenuation.x \
                + (attenuation.y * distance) \
                + (attenuation.z * distance * distance)
```

The values you use in the vector should be very small. Try the following in the Message window:

```
tTorch.attenuation = vector(10.0, 0, 0)
```

The lighthouse photograph all but disappears. (Look closely.)

Reset the attenuation to its initial value; then dolly backward until you are outside the gallery or choose Outside in the Snapshot View pop-up menu. The amount of light that falls on the photograph does not change with distance. Now type the following in the Message window:

```
tTorch.attenuation = vector(0.0, 0.01, 0.0)
```

Darkness falls. Use the Dolly bar in the Snapshot window to move forward, as shown in Figure 13-8. Do you see how the walls grow brighter as you approach with your torch? Setting the `y` value of the attenuation property makes the effect of the spot light diminish in proportion to the distance.

In the real world, light from a source diminishes as the square of the distance. Imagine two spheres: one with twice the radius of the other; each with a light source at its center. The same amount of light will be spread out over the surface of two spheres. The surface of each sphere depends on the square of its radius; a square inch on the smaller sphere will receive as much light as four square inches on the larger one. Or, to put it another way: any area on the larger sphere will receive a quarter of the amount of light of the same area on the smaller sphere.

To simulate this in Shockwave 3D, you can set the `z` value for the attenuation property. Unless you want the range of your spot light to fall off very sharply, you should make this value very small indeed. Try this in the Message window:

```
tTorch.attenuation = vector(0.0, 0.0, 0.0001)
```

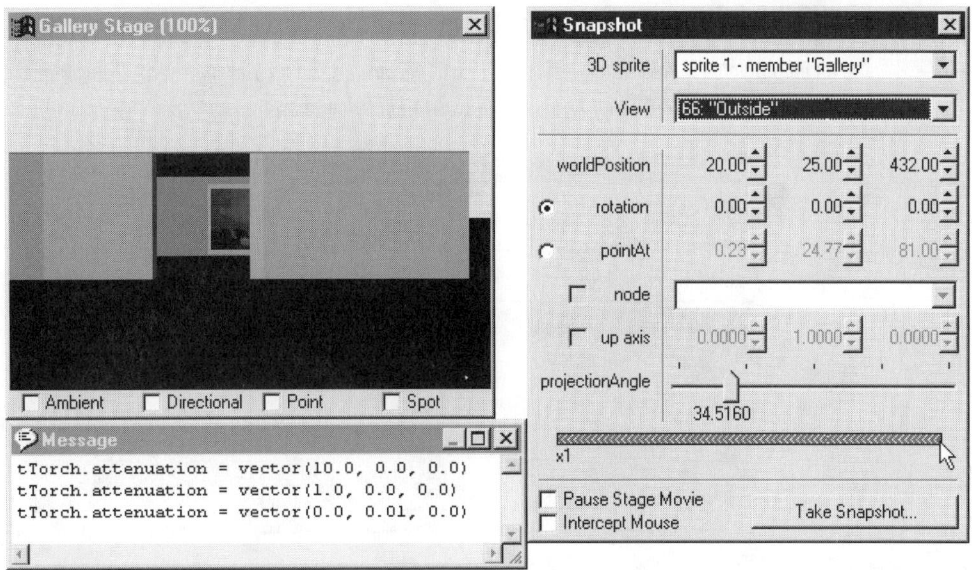

Figure 13-8 *Testing the attenuation property of a spot light*

Now, dolly back and watch how the effect of the torch light falls off rapidly, as shown in Figure 13-9.

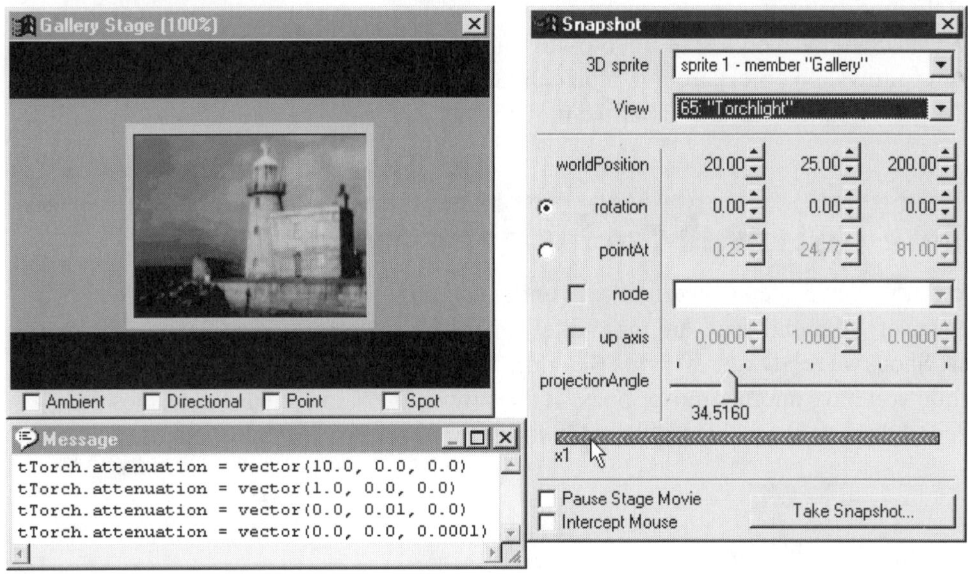

Figure 13-9 *Using realistic attenuation for a spot light*

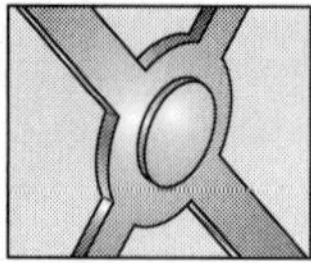

DEBUGGING TIP

The minimum value in the `attenuation` *vector must be greater than zero. If this is not the case, you will invoke a Script Error, as the illustration below shows.*

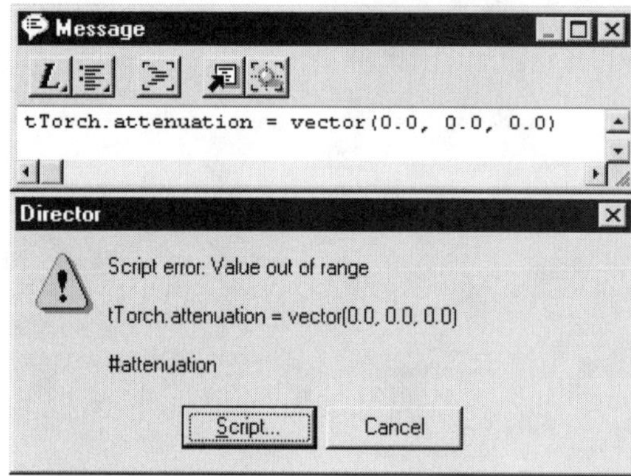

Moving Lights

The techniques for moving and orienting the camera you saw in the gForce.dir movie in Chapter 12 can be used for lights, too. You can use commands such as `pointAt()` to direct a light in a given direction, or to track a moving object. Unlike with cameras, the Up direction of lights has no visual impact, so you can safely ignore it.You can also make a light a child of another object, as you did when you attached the Torch spot light to the camera in the preceding section, so that the light follows the object around. You can turn the light on the object itself. See Chapter 12 for further details of the movements you can use.

More Tests with the fpsMeter Movie

So far, we have been concerned with understanding the concepts of the 3D world. However, your end users are more likely to prioritize performance. So let's see how fast Shockwave 3D runs.The fpsMeter.dir movie is designed to run in a window while you have another movie open. It does much the same job as the frames per second display in the Control Panel, but it is more sensitive. It has a double display;

at the top are a series of red bars, which indicate the average frame rate achieved by the movie on the Stage over increasingly longer periods. The bar at the top shows the instantaneous frame rate, or the speed of the last frame. The second bar shows the average of the last two frames, and the third shows the average of the last four. Each successive bar shows the average frame rate over twice the number of frames: the last bar is the average of 1,024 frames.

Below this graphic display is a digital one. At the far right, you see the target frame rate for the Stage. The current frame rate appears in bold black just beside this. To the left, you have the minimum and maximum frame rates over the past two seconds.

The results might not tally with those shown in the Control Panel. Unlike the Control Panel, you can check the source code and see exactly how the values are calculated.

Testing an Empty World

To test the fpsMeter tool, create a new movie, click the Script Channel of the score at (say) the 20th frame, and create the following Frame Script:

```
on exitFrame
  go 2
end
```

Add a Shockwave 3D sprite to your movie, and place it on the Stage. In the Control Panel, set the target `frameTempo` to the maximum 999 frames per second; then launch the movie, as shown in Figure 13-10. Now select fpsMeter in the Xtras menu and watch the readings it gives.

For clarity, Figure 13-10 shows the Score window and the Control Panel open. However, updating the position of the playback head in the Score window and changing the frame number displayed in the Control Panel steals cycles from the movie itself. To get the fastest possible reading, close all Director windows that are not strictly needed.

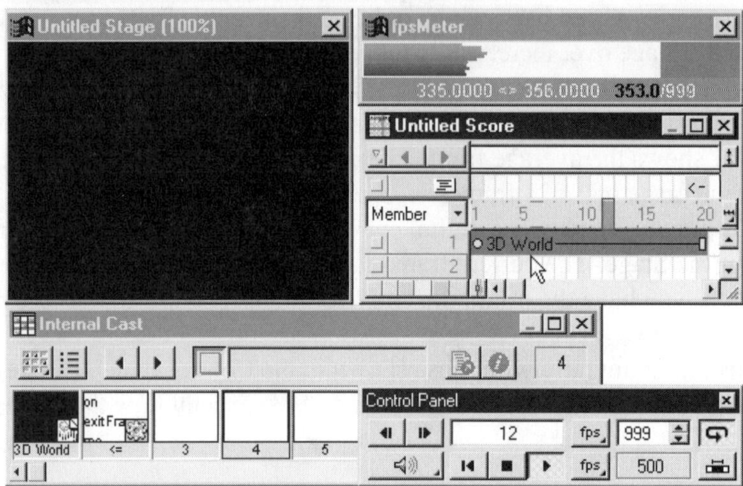

Figure 13-10 *Benchmarking a barebones movie with an empty Shockwave 3D member*

To see how an empty Shockwave 3D sprite slows down performance, click the button that disables the sprite channel and watch how the playback speed suddenly increases.

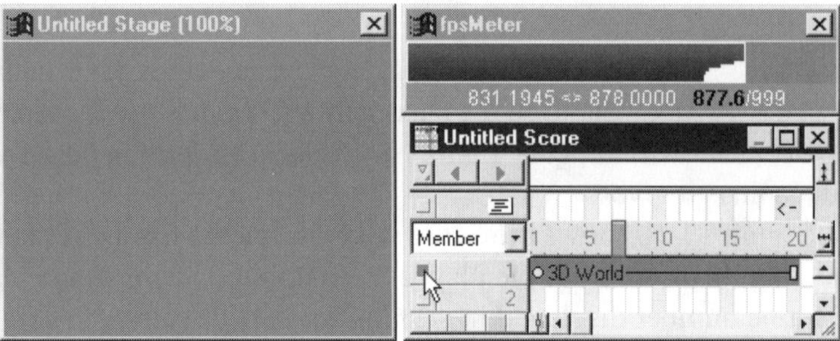

Try the same test using a single Text member on Stage; and then use the Property Inspector to convert the `displayMode` of the Text member to `#mode3d`, as shown in Figure 13-11. The playback head slows even further than with a Shockwave 3D member.

Conclusion: 3D takes a heavy toll on the processor, even when there is nothing to show.

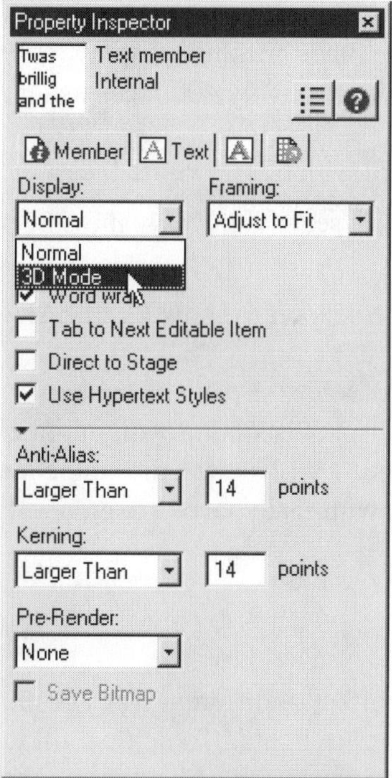

Figure 13-11 *Setting the #displayMode of a Text member to #mode3D*

Testing Primitives

Lightest.dir

The Lightest.dir movie, which you can find in the 3D\Lights\ folder on the CD-ROM, is designed as a benchmarking tool. It allows you to create as many as 100 models of a given primitive and 100 lights of each of the four types. Open the Lightest.dir movie on the Stage and the fpsMeter movie in a window. Open the Control Panel and set the frameTempo of the Lightest.dir movie slightly faster than Director can play it back. In other words, make sure the tempo bars stretch almost—but not quite—to the right edge of the light rectangle. Consider this to be the movie's top speed.

Now use the sliders to alter the number of models. Try different types of primitives and note which ones slow the movie most. Spheres are made of a large number of faces treated with `#smooth` shading. Planes are made of a small number of flat faces. Understandably, spheres are much slower than planes.

Choosing the mesh primitive has a somewhat different effect: instead of creating a number of models, it creates a single model with a controllable number of faces. To bring the mesh into the same league as the other primitives, I have chosen to make six times as many faces as the other primitive display models.

For example, you can produce roughly 400 faces using any of these techniques:

- Displaying a single mesh with 67 × 6 = 402 faces
- Displaying 33 box models set to show only the `#front` faces (33 × 12 = 396 faces)
- Displaying 100 plane models set to show `#both` sides (100 × 4 = 400 faces)

Remember that each face of a box or plane is made of two triangular faces. Since the number of faces in each display is similar, you might expect comparable performance. In fact, as Figure 13-12 shows, the single mesh is by far the fastest.

Conclusion: a few models with many faces are more efficient than many models with few faces.

Testing Lights

Now that we have tested the effect of different types of models on performance, let's test the effect of different types of lights. To do this, fill the display with the largest possible mesh, and then experiment with adding more lights of different types.

The Effect of Different Types of Light

How many lights of each type does it take to illuminate the scene? Stop adding lights when adding a new light has no further effect. Test each type of light individually. These lights all have the default color value of `rgb( 191, 191, 191 )`: a light gray. Does it make sense to have more than half a dozen lights? How much does a small number of a given type of light slow the movie down? Does changing the type of primitive change the results?

Adding ambient lights has little effect on the speed of playback. Adding a single spot light can cause a significant dip in speed. Point lights also have a visible effect. Conclusions: The cumulative effect of lights puts a limit on the number that usefully can be deployed at any one time. Spot lights and (to a lesser extent) point lights should be used with caution.

The Effect of Shiny Shaders

The `specular` property of lights interacts with the `shininess` property of shaders. Try setting the `specular` property to `TRUE` and the `shininess` to `1` (the value that has the greatest effect). Note the maximum and minimum values displayed by the

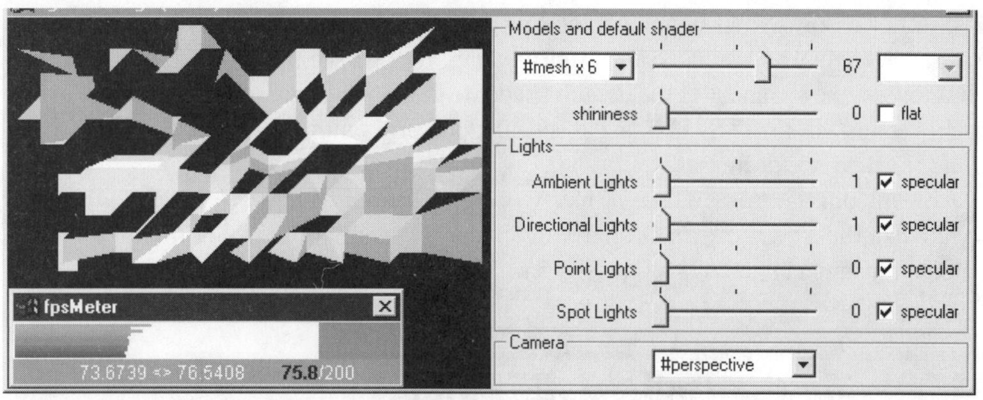

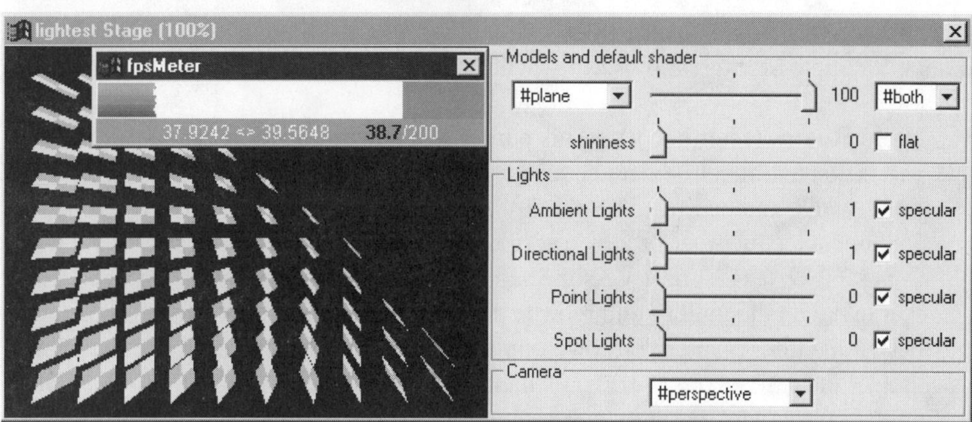

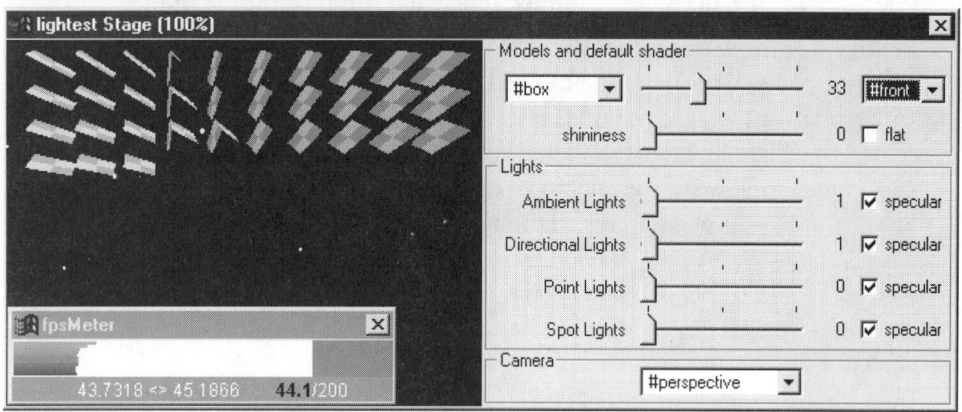

Figure 13-12 *Comparing the performance of a single model with many faces to the performance of many models with few faces*

fpsMeter window. Now, switch off the `specular` property. The models or models in the Shockwave 3D sprite no longer appear shiny. Do you see the frame rate improve at all? Now set the shininess of the default shader to 0. Do you see a significant improvement this time? Switch on the specular property for the lights again. Does it look as if the frame rate decreases?

Conclusion: the `specular` property of lights has much less effect on playback speed than the `shininess` property of shaders. Presumably, the additional calculations are carried out by the shader object rather than by the light.

Modifying the Gallery.dir Movie

Apart from giving you a chance to experiment with lights, the Gallery.dir movie contains a couple of interesting scripts, which build meshes from a template:

- **Build Rooms (member 9)** This parent script is designed to create the 3D vertexList and faceList data needed to create a mesh resource consisting of floor, walls, and ceiling. The plan for the room or rooms can be provided by a Vector Shape member or a by a script that returns a list with the same structure as the 2D vertexList of a Vector Shape member. The script builds the models that make up the gallery and returns them as the children of a group. You can design the floor plan of your own one-story building in a Vector Shape member and let the `mGetRoomGroup()` handler deal with all the rest. You'll have to apply any shaders to the models manually. See the Initialize Gallery script (member 28) for an example of how to use the Build Rooms script.
- **Picture in Frame (member 10)** This parent script creates a model resembling a framed painting or photograph. The image in the frame is provided by a shader with a non-void texture. It builds a mesh in two parts: a couple of triangles in the center, to which the image shader is applied, and a further 28 triangles, which make up the frame and the backing. A separate frame shader is applied to these. See any of the script members starting at member 36 for examples.

Using these scripts, you should be able to build your own art gallery with the architecture designed to fit the works. I am most grateful to Charlotte Thibault, Karina Steffens, and Mike Chausovsky, all of whom have allowed me to use their original artwork for the Gallery.dir movie.

Toward More Realistic Lights

As mentioned at the beginning of this chapter, Shockwave 3D lights provide shading but they do not cast shadows. A computer screen provides a two-dimensional view of a three-dimensional world; the missing dimension means missing information. Shadows provide important visual clues on the relative depth and height of objects. Without shadows, it can be impossible to tell whether an object is placed on a surface some distance to the camera, or whether it is hovering in space closer to the camera.

One technique, pioneered by Barry Swan, is to create additional models, give them a flat, shadow-colored shader, and skew them according to the position of the light source. This technique will work only for shadows projected onto flat surfaces. Barry has made the source code for his technique available at http://www.theburrow.co.uk/d85/index.htm. You also will find other interesting 3D demonstrations and tutorials here.

Conclusion

Shockwave 3D has to provide a trade-off between realism and performance. You will need to design your project in such a way that the user is not hampered by the necessary omissions.

This chapter has explained what aspects of realism have been sacrificed for performance, and it has also examined how you can optimize performance of your own movies by making intelligent choices in the use of models, shaders, and lights. The lesson to keep in mind is that Shockwave 3D is by nature processor intensive, so managing performance is a key issue.

In the next chapter, you will be looking at the performance issues raised by collision detection.

CHAPTER

14

Collision Detection

IN THIS CHAPTER:

The human psyche would not have evolved in a world dominated by truth-telling.
—Richard D. Alexander

In the previous chapter, you may have noticed that it was possible to walk through walls in the Gallery.dir movie. In the gForce.dir movie in Chapter 12, it was possible to fly through the "solid" part of the square gates that lined the race track. Such ghostly activity undermines the illusion of realism that you need to foster. In this chapter, I will describe three different ways to make virtual objects aware of each other:

- A callback technique that relies on the built-in Collision Modifier
- A technique that exploits the solid body physics of the Havok Xtra
- A custom-built technique that uses vector mathematics

In Chapter 7, you saw a fourth technique, using `modelsUnderRay()`, that you could adapt for collision-detection purposes. I won't be dealing with this technique here.

Each of these techniques has its advantages and drawbacks. Understanding all four will help you choose the one that best suits your work style, your project, and the features that you need to implement.

In Director 8.5, a number of features of the Collision Modifier are idiosyncratic, to say the least. Rather than throwing the baby out with the bathwater, this chapter shows you how to determine which features are reliable and which require workarounds. The approach described here can be applied to any Director feature or Xtra, not just to the Collision Modifier. In other words, this chapter provides a practical example of discovering the potential of third-party code. You will be carrying out experiments to determine how the Collision Modifier works and how best to use it. In the process, you will see how to isolate any bugs, how to avoid them, and how to provide the feedback necessary for ensuring that these bugs are fixed.

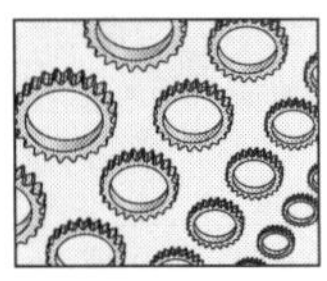

NOTE

I have good reason to believe that the bugs described in this chapter will be fixed in the next version of Director. This chapter is concerned more with the general process of isolating bugs than with any particular short-lived bugs in the Collision Modifier. If, by the time you read this chapter, a new version of Director is available, you might wish to check whether all the quirks described here have been dealt with. In doing so, you will likely be running some of the same tests as the Director Quality Assessment engineers.

The Concept of Collision

All three collision-detection methods are based on a set of multiple calculations. The more solid objects there are, and the more complex their geometry, the greater will be the number of calculations that need to be carried out, and therefore the slower the playback. What is simple geometry for collision detection is not necessarily simple for the renderer. For example, spheres are collision-detection friendly, but take a while to render. A shape like that of the square gates in gForce.dir is easy on the renderer, but complex when it comes to collision detection because it contains holes and concave spaces. The spacecraft can pass through the hole, and two such gate shapes could interlock, like links in a chain, without actually touching. A comprehensive collision-detection algorithm would have to test for such cases.

To optimize performance, you should avoid comprehensive collision detection whenever possible, and use approximations instead. Consider using one shape for the model and a completely different one for collision detection. Another useful technique is to reduce the number of potential collisions that are checked for at any given time.

An Example of Distance Detection

The gForce.dir movie, which you can find in the 3D\Cameras\ folder on the CD-ROM that accompanies the book, provides a simple example of optimized distance detection. When you record a flight, the recording stops if you move too far from the track. In other words, to remain in recording mode, the spacecraft must "collide" in some way with the track at all times. Rather than calculating the intersection between the spacecraft and the track, I calculate the distance between them.

The track can be imagined as a series of points, each one at the center of one of the square gates. Each square gate is surrounded by a hypothetical sphere: the model's `boundingSphere`. You can visualize this sphere by setting the model's `debug` property to `TRUE`, as shown in Figure 14-1.

Consecutive gates are placed at a distance of one `boundingSphere` radius. This means that each gate's `boundingSphere` is completely within a second sphere that has twice the radius and whose center is at the center of the next gate.

Figure 14-1 *Visualizing the bounding sphere of the gate under the mouse*

Consequently, as diagrammed in Figure 14-2, if the spacecraft moves into the `boundingSphere` of a given gate A, it must also have entered the double-sized sphere centered on the following gate B.

If the spacecraft now leaves the double-sized sphere around gate B without entering gate B's `boundingSphere`, it cannot have passed through the gate itself. (To be exact, only the corners of the gate touch the bounding sphere. It is therefore possible to enter the next bounding sphere by flying low over the top of a gate.) To detect

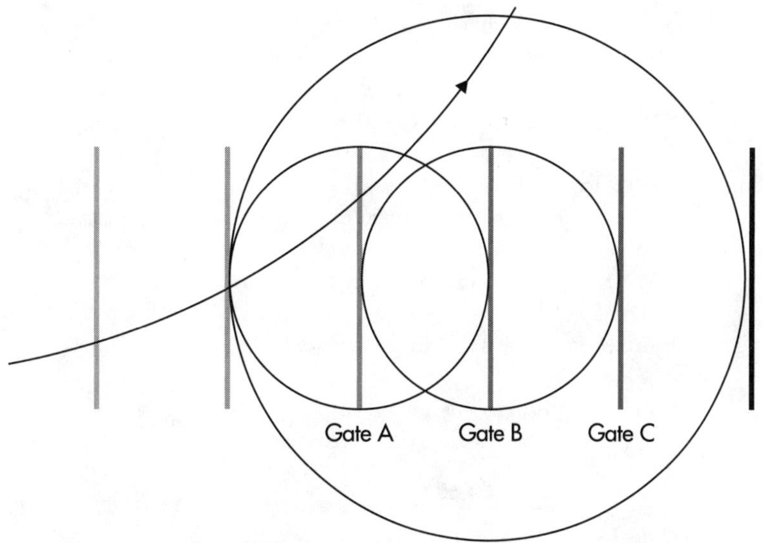

Figure 14-2 *Detecting when the spacecraft misses a gate*

whether the spacecraft is still on track, we need make only two simple calculations at any given time:

- Has the spacecraft entered the `boundingSphere` for the next gate? If so, it is on course, and we can move our attention (and the center of the double-sized sphere) to the following gate.
- Has the spacecraft left the current double-sized sphere? If so, it is off course.

Because, in this case, we can accurately predict the path that the user should take, it is easy to minimize the number of distance detection calculations. In the gForce.dir movie, these calculations are carried out by the Pilot script in cast member slot 17. The relevant fragments of code are shown here:

```
property pmWorld -- Shockwave 3D member
property pCraft  -- model("spacecraft")
property pGate   -- the number of the next gate to pass through
property pRadius -- radius of gate model boundingSphere
property pCenter -- center of model(pGate)
property pRecord -- TRUE if recording is in progress
```

```
on mCheckNextGate(me) -- sent by stepFrame()
  -- Determine how far we are from the next gate
  tPosition = pCraft.worldPosition
  tDistance = tPosition.distanceTo(pCenter)

  if tDistance < pRadius then
    -- The spacecraft has moved into the next gate's bounding sphere
    pGate = pGate + 1
    tGate = pmWorld.model(string(pGate))
    -- Aim for the following gate
    pCenter = tGate.worldPosition

  else if tDistance > pRadius * 2 then
    -- The user missed the next gate: stop recording
    pRecord = 0
  end if
end mCheckNextGate
```

The Collision Modifier

Director 8.5 provides a built-in collision-detection feature. This is provided via the Collision Modifier. Modifiers are optional components that give you fine control over your models. You can attach a custom selection of modifiers to individual models and, thus, manage processor time in an optimal manner, depending on the role of each model. Director 8.5 provides eight modifiers in all:

- Two animation modifiers: BonesPlayer and KeyframePlayer. These let you control the animation data included in models that have been created with third-party software. The animation modifiers cannot, however, be used with any of the models created from scratch in Director.
- Two appearance modifiers: Toon and Inker. These provide additional features similar to those you can obtain through the `#painter` shader.
- Two display modifiers: Level of Detail (LOD) and Sub-Division Surfaces (SDS). These are mutually exclusive. You can use the LOD Modifier to reduce the number of visible polygons, thus reducing the amount of required processing time, in situations where performance is a priority. You can use the SDS Modifier to create extra polygons, thus increasing the image quality, in situations where looks take priority.

- Mesh Deform. This modifier allows you to treat any model as you might treat a mesh. It lets you move individual vertices in the modelResource used by the model that the modifier is attached to. All models that share the same modelResource will be deformed in the same way.
- Collision. This modifier sends you notification when the relative movement of two models would result in an intersection, and gives you options for stopping the movement before the intersection occurs.

I shall only deal with the Collision Modifier here. The techniques you will meet, such as adding the modifier to a model as required and setting its properties, will stand you in good stead for exploring the other modifiers on your own. For projects created entirely in Director, the effect of solidity that can be imparted by the Collision Modifier is a basic requirement.

What the Collision Modifier Can Do

Collide.dir

Before we look at the code, let's look at the effect of the Collision Modifier. In the 3D\Collide\ folder on the CD-ROM that accompanies the book, you'll find the movie Collide.dir. This movie shows two L-shaped mesh models, which are placed so that their boundingSpheres are not touching. There are several options for viewing the models:

- Orthographic views along the x, y, and z axes
- A perspective cavalier view, which you can alter with the arrow keys

In all sprites, you can use the mouse to drag the models around in the same plane as the camera.

You can attach the Collision Modifier to the light and dark models separately, via the pop-up menus in the right-hand column. If a collision is detected, an asterisk will appear in the lower right-hand corner, and a list of property values will appear in the `collisionData` display at the lower left of the box, as shown in Figure 14-3.

If you select the Resolve check box for one model and then drag that model toward the other, the model will stop moving as soon as a collision is detected.

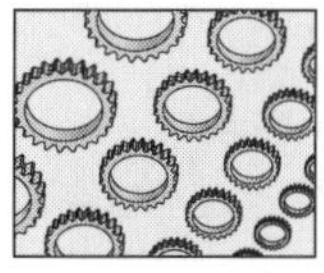

NOTE

The model that you drag will not slide along the edge of the static model: you'll need to back off so that the two models are not in collision, and then drag your model sideways.

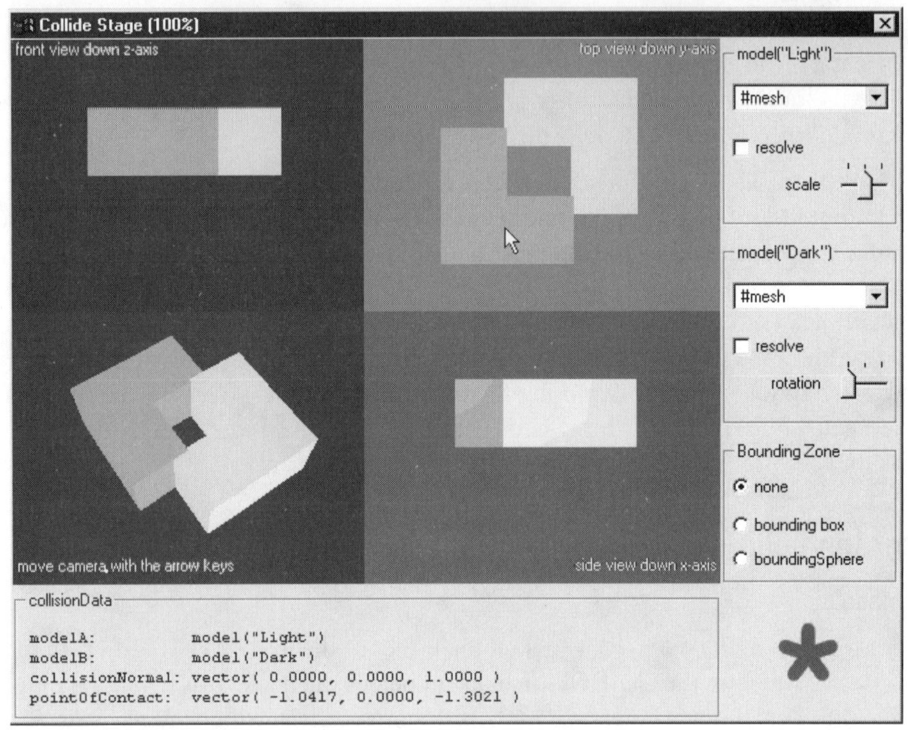

Figure 14-3 *Experimenting with model intersections using the Collide.dir movie*

There are four possible settings for the Collision Modifier:

- **`none`** No modifier is attached, so no collisions are detected. Alternatively, you can set the `collision.enabled` property to `FALSE` for a given model. This allows you to have the modifier attached to the model, but not active. (To simplify the interface, I have provided no buttons for toggling the `collision.enabled` property; if you wish to interrupt collision detection, select None from the pop-up menu.)
- **`#sphere`** Each model is hypothetically surrounded by the smallest sphere that contains all the vertex points. A collision is detected if the `boundingSphere` of both models touch at any point. Calculating an object's `boundingSphere` is a straightforward business (as you'll see in the following section). The `boundingSphere` can be described as a center point and a radius length. A collision is detected if the distance between the center of each `boundingSphere` is less than the sum of the two radii.

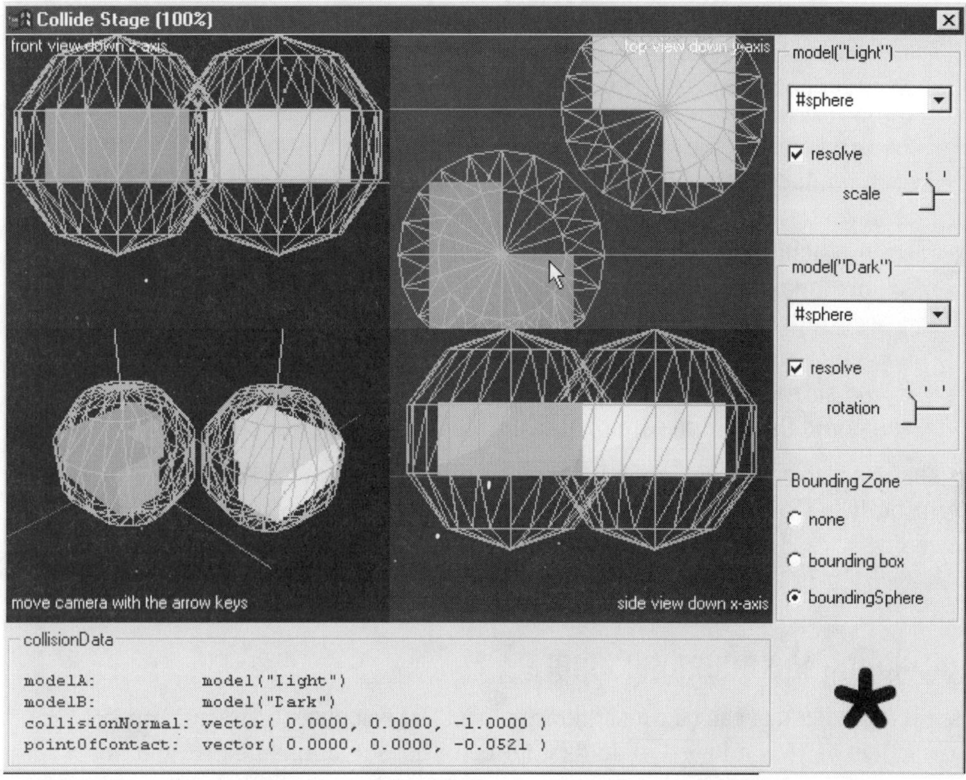

Figure 14-4 *Bounding spheres may appear not to touch when a collision occurs*

You can visualize the `boundingSphere` for both models by clicking the `boundingSphere` radio button. You may find that the wire frame spheres do not seem to touch even when a collision is detected, as shown in the top view in Figure 14-4. This is because only the vertex points of the shape displayed are actually located on the *surface* of the `boundingSphere`: the edges of the faces cut across the inside of the sphere.

- **`#box`** Each model is hypothetically surrounded by the smallest box that contains all the vertex points, and whose faces are perpendicular to the x, y, and z axes of the model's resource. Such a box is usually smaller than the `boundingSphere`, although, in the case of a model that is itself almost spherical, this will not be the case. A collision is detected if a part of the bounding box of one model intersects the bounding box of the other.

  You can visualize the bounding box for both models by clicking the Bounding Box radio button. Unlike the `debug` property, this feature is not built into

Director. The bounding boxes that you see are, in fact, separate models, which are only visible when they are children of the L-shaped models. They use a shader whose `renderStyle` property is set to `#wire`.

- **#mesh** This is the most precise collision test. In this example, the mesh of each model is very simple: 12 vertex points and 18 triangular faces. In a model representing a realistic human figure, the number of polygons can run from several hundred to tens of thousands. Using the mesh mode to detect a collision requires making a separate calculation for each face: more faces means slower processing. If you need to detect contact between human figures, for example, it would make sense to create an invisible model with a low polygon count that would surround the higher-polygon visible figure. To increase performance, you could then use the simpler, invisible model to detect collisions.

There is also a fifth choice in the pop-up menus: #Lingo sphere. This is not part of the built-in Collision Modifier. Instead, it provides a Lingo-only solution for detecting `boundingSphere` collisions. Surprisingly, this option may be faster than the built-in `#sphere` mode. We'll look at this in more detail shortly.

Calculating the boundingSphere

Here's a handler that can take an arbitrary model and calculate its `boundingSphere`. In practice, there is no need to do this: Director does it automatically, and much faster than Lingo can. The handler simply demonstrates what Director must be doing under the hood, and it also gives you a little practice with the Mesh Deform modifier. You can find a fuller version of this handler in the Collide.dir movie.

```
on mGetBoundingSphere(aModel)
  tCenter    = vector(0, 0, 0)
  tRadius    = 0
  tTransform = aModel.getWorldTransform()

  -- Add Mesh Deform Modifier to gain access to vertex point data
  aModel.addModifier(#meshDeform)
  tMeshCount = aModel.meshDeform.mesh.count

  -- Calculate the average of all the vertex points
  tVertexTotal = 0
  repeat with i = 1 to tMeshCount
    tVertexList = aModel.meshDeform.mesh[i].vertexList
    tCount = tVertexList.count
    tVertexTotal = tVertexTotal + tCount
    repeat with j = 1 to tCount
```

```
      tVertex = tTransform * tVertexList[j]
      tCenter = tCenter + tVertex
    end repeat
  end repeat
  tCenter = tCenter / tVertexTotal

  -- Find distance to vertex point furthest from center
  repeat with i = 1 to tMeshCount
    tVertexList = aModel.meshDeform.mesh[i].vertexList
    tCount = tVertexList.count
    repeat with j = 1 to tCount
      tVertex = tTransform * tVertexList[j]
      tRadius = max(tRadius, (tCenter - tVertex).magnitude)
    end repeat
  end repeat

  aModel.removeModifier(#meshDeform)

  return [tCenter, tRadius]
end mGetBoundingSphere
```

DEBUGGING TIP

Due to rounding errors in 32-bit calculations, you may find slight differences between the results of this handler and those returned by Director. Even Director's native method may not be exact. With the Collide.dir movie open, try entering the following in the Message window:

```
tResource = member(2).newModelResource("sphere", #sphere)
tModel    = member(2).newModel("sphere", tResource)
put tModel.worldPosition -- should be identical to center of boundingSphere
-- vector( 0.0000, 0.0000, 0.0000 )
put tModel.boundingSphere
-- [vector( 0.0000, 0.0000, 0.1164 ), 25.1153] -- z value and radius incorrect
put mGetBoundingSphere(tModel)
-- [vector( 0.0000, 0.0000, 0.6303 ), 25.6245] -- ditto in spades
```

The Mesh Deform modifier returns a list of vertex points with a separate point for each corner of each triangular face. Your mesh models might use the same vertex point for several faces, but the Mesh Deform modifier will not take this into account. The list returned by `aModel.meshDeform.mesh[index].vertexList` may therefore contain many duplicate points.

Calculating the Bounding Box

The #box mode is the one that raises the most questions. How is the bounding box for #box mode calculated? What happens if you rotate the model? Is the box calculated with reference to the model or to the world? The Collide.dir movie lets you test this for yourself.

The Bounding Box Rotates with the Model

Run the Collide.dir movie, and choose the #box collision-detection mode for both models. Select the Bounding Box radio button so that the bounding box is displayed. Use the slider to rotate model("Dark"). The bounding box will rotate with it. Now move model("Dark") toward model("Light"), and check to confirm that collisions are detected whenever the bounding boxes intersect.

The Bounding Box Is Orthogonal to modelResource Space

The L-shaped model fits neatly inside its bounding box. Is this because the orientation is chosen to fit the model as closely as possible, or is it because the faces of the model are perpendicular to its x, y, and z axes?

To test this, you need to build a model whose faces are not perpendicular to its axes. I have made this easy for you. In the Create World behavior, you will find the mCreateWorld() handler. This includes the following line:

```
tAngle = 0
```

If you alter this to, say,

```
tAngle = 45
```

then the vertex points in the mesh will be rotated by 45° around the y axis before the build() method is applied to the mesh resource. Restart the movie. The models will appear in the same initial position, since the handler has compensated for the rotation by rotating the models by –45° around the y axis.

Select the Bounding Box check box. This will show you how the model sits inside the modelResource space. Now add the collision modifier in #box mode to both models. Move one model toward the other, and check to confirm that collisions are detected whenever the bounding boxes intersect, as shown in Figure 14-5.

Consequences of the Way the Bounding Box Fits the Model

The #box mode for the collision modifier provides a rapid technique for approximating collisions. The closer the bounding box fits around the model, the less approximate the

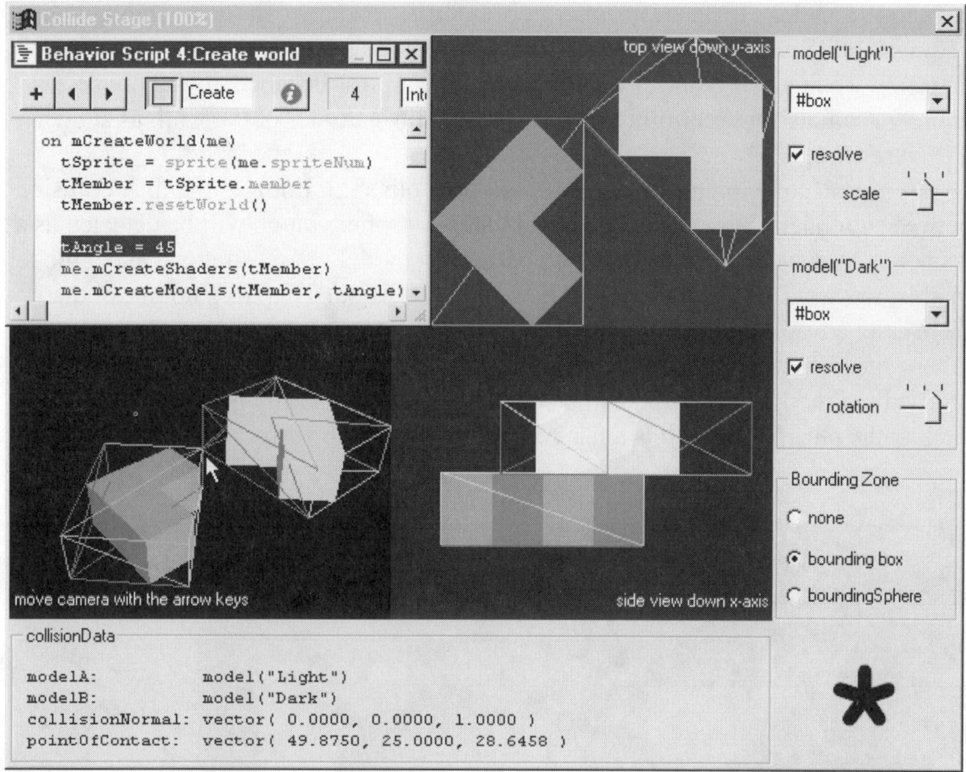

Figure 14-5 *The bounding box is calculated in the frame of reference of the model resource*

method becomes. It therefore makes sense to design mesh resources in such a way that the resulting shape sits square to the modelResource's axes, minimizing the empty space between the model and its bounding box.

Collisions are detected only between models. Other nodes (groups, cameras and lights) are not affected by collision detection. This means that if you build a figure from a set of roughly box-shaped models, which you then group together to form the full complex shape, the #box collision mode can give very satisfactory results.

As you saw in the preceding chapter, a single, complex mesh is rendered more rapidly than a number of simple meshes. To get the best results, you would have to find a happy medium: more models can lead to faster collision detection but slower rendering.

Mixing Modes

You can set the `collision.mode` of one model to #sphere and the other to #box. Director will use a hybrid technique to determine whether there is a collision. This technique may lead to a certain amount of intersection between the bounding zones before a collision is reported. While this mixed-mode technique works well for detecting when a ball bounces off the face of a wall, for instance, it will not be entirely accurate for determining when the ball hits a corner of the wall, as shown in Figure 14-6.

The #mesh collision mode does not mix with others: it imitates them. A collision between a model in #mesh mode and a model in #sphere mode will be detected as a #sphere-#sphere collision. A collision between a model in #mesh mode and a model in #box mode will be detected as a #box -#box collision. This does not mean that there is no advantage to using the #mesh collision mode on some models but not on others; the performance hit due to #mesh-#mesh collision detections is very much reduced in #mesh-other collision detections, and the model in #mesh mode adapts itself to the other. The result is a fair compromise between performance and precision.

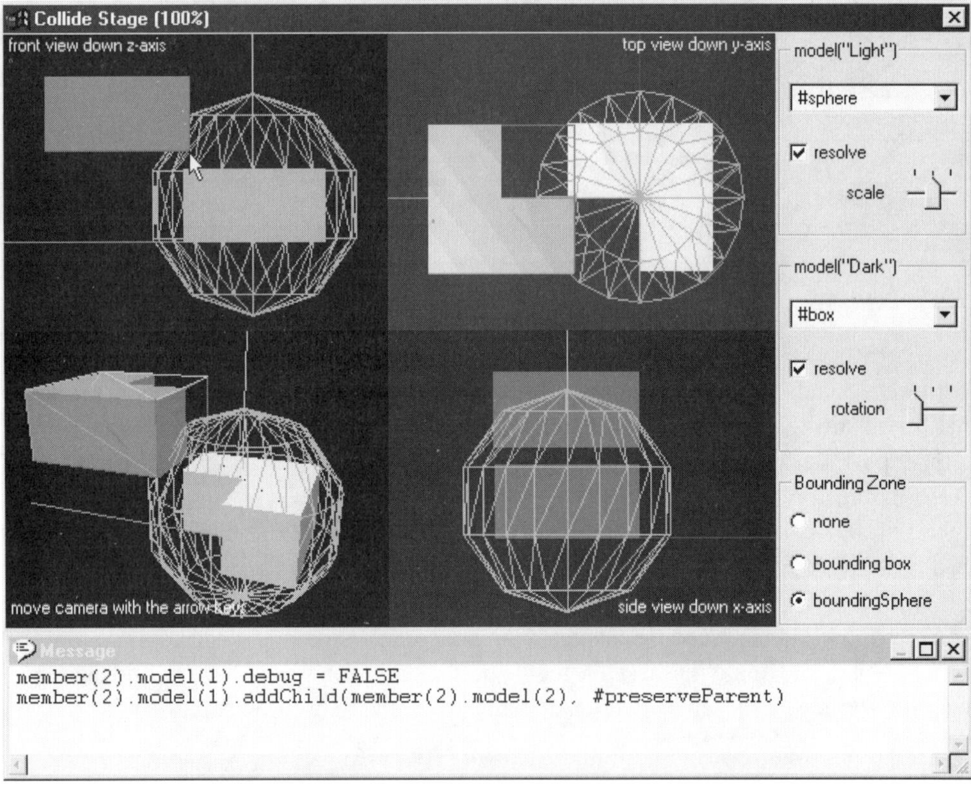

Figure 14-6 *Using #sphere and #box collision mode detection together*

Working with the Collision Modifier

Now that you have an idea of what the Collision Modifier can do, let's look at how to make it work.

Applying the Collision Modifier to a Model

Vector7.dir

As with all modifiers, you need to add the Collision Modifier explicitly to each model that is to use it:

```
tModel = member("3D World").model(1)
tModel.addModifier(#collision)
```

The Collision Modifier gives the model four new properties and sets their default values as follows:

```
put tModel.collision.enabled
-- 1
put tModel.collision.resolve
-- 1
put tModel.collision.immovable
-- 0
put tModel.collision.mode
-- #sphere
```

The `collision.enabled` property is straightforward: it lets you temporarily suspend collision detection for the model in question. I treat the performance implications of this property later in this chapter. (See "Taking Advantage of the enabled Property.")

If the `collision.resolve` property is set to `TRUE`, as it is by default, the model's bounding zone will not enter the bounding zone of any other model to which the Collision Modifier is attached. It will not bounce off the other model, nor slide around it; it will simply not move. Director tests for collisions once per frame, just before the new frame is displayed. Resolution occurs if the paths of two models cross each other in the time between the two frames, or if the bounding zones of the models intersect at the end of the period. You can see a simple 2D demonstration of this in the Vector7.dir movie that you will find in the 3D\Collide\ folder on the CD-ROM. In the pop-up menu, choose Point Of Impact. You can drag the start and end points for each ball to create different paths. When you click the Calculate Impact button, the position of the balls is resolved (see Figure 14-7).

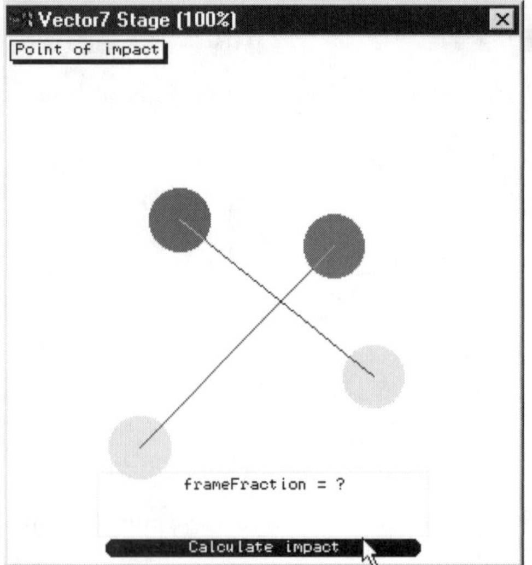

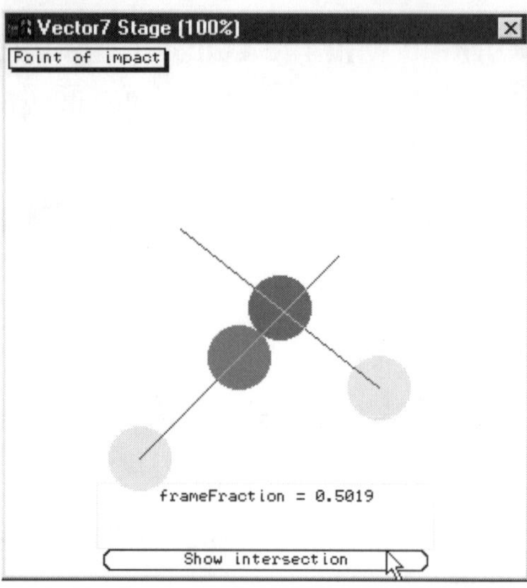

Figure 14-7 *A 2D representation of how collisions are resolved*

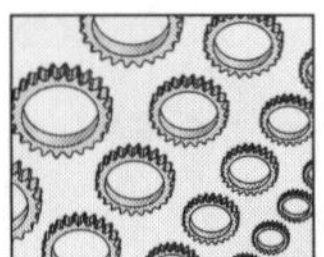

NOTE

Vector7.dir was originally written in Director 6 and last modified in Director 7. This explains its verbose syntax.

Director 8.5 takes care of all the necessary calculations. You don't have to work these out for yourself, as you would have done in previous versions of Director, and you get the third dimension as a bonus.

Despite its name, the `collision.immovable` property does not lock a model to a given world position or orientation. It is perfectly possible to set the `collision.immovable` property of a model to `TRUE`, and then move it. If it collides with an object whose `collision.resolve` property is `TRUE`, then only the position of the other model will be resolved. In other words, setting the `collision.immovable` property to `TRUE` has the same effect as setting the `collision.resolve` property to `FALSE`.

Preventing the Camera from Walking Through Walls

Gallery.dir

Director checks for collisions between all models that have the Collision Modifier. With the default settings, this is enough to make such models mutually solid. In certain circumstances, this may be all you need to do. For example, to prevent a camera from moving through walls, you can make the camera a child of an invisible model, and place the Collision Modifier on both the walls and the invisible model.

In the Gallery.dir movie that you saw in Chapter 13, a slight modification to a couple of scripts will prevent the camera from walking through the walls. You could change the `beginSprite()` handler in the Walkabout Camera Behavior script (member 5) to this:

```
property pCamera -- small invisible box to which the camera is attached

on beginSprite(me) -------------------------------------------------------
  -- ACTION: Make the camera the child of a small invisible box model,
  -- to which the collision modifier is attached in #mesh mode
  ---------------------------------------------------------------------

  tSprite             = sprite(me.spriteNum)
  tMember             = tSprite.member
  tName               = string(me) -- unique name
  tResource           = tMember.newModelResource(tName, #box)

  -- Make the box big enough for collision detection
  tResource.width     = 4
  tResource.height    = 4
  tResource.length    = 4

  -- Create an invisible model at the same position as the camera
  pCamera             = tMember.newModel(tName, tResource)
  pCamera.visibility = #none -- No faces of the model will be visible
  pCamera.transform  = tSprite.camera.transform
  pCamera.addChild(tSprite.camera, #preserveWorld)

  -- Add the collision modifier in #mesh mode
  pCamera.addModifier(#collision) -- resolve = TRUE, enabled = TRUE
  pCamera.collision.mode = #mesh

  pfPixelAngle = 360.0 / tSprite.width
end beginSprite
```

You'll also need to add the Collision Modifier to the walls. In the Initialize Gallery script (member 28), you should add three lines in the middle of the `mInitializeNode()` handler:

```
on mInitializeNode(me, a3DMember)
-- <more code>

  tShaderName = "Walls"
```

```
  tShader = a3DMember.shader(tShaderName)
  if ilk(tShader, #shader) then
    tNode.child[2].shader = tShader -- model("Gallery walls")
    -- Add the collision modifier in #mesh mode to prevent the camera
    -- from walking through the walls
    tNode.child[2].addModifier(#collision) -- ADDED LINE
    tNode.child[2].collision.mode    = #mesh  -- ADDED LINE
    tNode.child[2].collision.resolve = FALSE  -- ADDED LINE
  end if

  -- <more code>
end mInitializeNode
```

The #mesh mode is essential here, since the invisible model to which the camera is attached is inside both the `boundingSphere` and the bounding box of the model for the outside walls. With this modification, you will no longer be able to walk through walls, but you will find the paint on them sticky. If you run into a wall, you have to back off before you can move again. Setting `collision.immovable` to `TRUE` would have the same effect as setting `collision.resolve` to `FALSE`. You can use either technique.

Using an invisible box model with sides 4 units long means that the camera cannot get nearer to any wall than 2 units. The paintings hang one unit away from the walls: the camera can thus not pass through the paintings, either. There is therefore no need to attach the Collision Modifier to the paintings themselves. Doing so would mean that more collisions had to be tested for on each frame, and this would slow the movie down.

You may find that a very fast mouse movement will still allow the camera to pass through the walls. If so, you can increase the size of the box model around the camera. If you make it too big, however, you won't be able to move through the door or along the corridors.

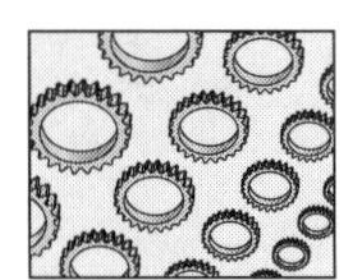

NOTE

If you use the Snapshot window to move the camera in your modified version of the Gallery.dir movie, you will still be able to walk through walls. This is because the Snapshot window controls the camera directly, without moving its box model parent. It is best to close the Snapshot window and restart the Gallery.dir movie if this occurs.

setCollisionCallback()

In many cases, you will want your models to react to a collision. One model may bounce off another, or slide along it, or you may want to play a sound or create an explosion on impact. This means that you need to be informed when a collision occurs. There are three different techniques for ensuring this, or rather, three methods for applying the same technique:

- `aModel.collision.setCollisionCallback()`
- `aNode.registerScript()`
- `aMember.registerForEvent()`

The `collision.setCollisionCallback()` method is the simplest. The other two are important in that they can also be used with the BonesPlayer and KeyframePlayer modifiers, as well as for sending custom events to a 3D member or node. We will look at the `setCollisionCallback()` method here.

To make sure that you know when a given model enters into collision with any other model to which the Collision Modifier is attached, you can create a behavior with handlers such as these:

```
on mRegisterForCollisions(me)
  tModel = member("3D World").model("model name")
  tModel.addModifier(#collision)
  tModel.collision.setCollisionCallback(#mCollisionHandler, me)
end

on mCollisionHandler(me, collisionData)
  -- Treat collision here
end
```

The `collision.setCollisionCallback()` tells the Collision Modifier what handler to call in which script or script instance. Here, the `me` keyword identifies the behavior instance itself as the location of the `mCollisionHandler()` callback handler. You can use `0` instead to indicate that the handler is to be found in a Movie Script, or you can provide a reference to any other script member or script instance. You can set more than one collision callback handler for any given model. You can also set the same collision callback handler for any number of models.

It is not enough, however, to know that a collision has occurred. Your callback handler will also need to know where the collision happened, and what the model in question has collided with.

The collisionData Parameter

When the callback handler is activated by a collision, an object is passed as a parameter. By convention, the name `collisionData` is used as the variable name for this object, but that name is not obligatory. The `collisionData` object is not a list, but it acts like a property list in many ways. It provides the following information:

- **`collisionData.modelA`** A pointer to the model that the collision callback is attached to
- **`collisionData.modelB`** A pointer to the model that `modelA` has collided with
- **`collisionData.pointOfContact`** The world position of the point where the impact has occurred
- **`collisionData.collisionNormal`** A direction vector that represents the direction in which the force of impact was applied to `modelA`.

The Collide.dir movie shows the properties of the `collisionData` object in the bottom panel. This information remains visible even when no further collisions are detected; a flashing asterisk, however, indicates that a collision is taking place.

There is only one `collisionData` object. For each collision, the values reported by the object change. You cannot apply the `duplicate()` method to make a copy of the `collisionData` object. In other words, the `collisionData` object is permanent, but the data it contains is ephemeral. Here's a test:

Uncomment the following lines in the `mCollisionDetected()` handler of the Collision Object script (member 15):

```
if collisionData.modelA.name = "Dark" then
  (the globals)[#collisionDataDark] = collisionData
else
  (the globals)[#collisionDataLight] = collisionData
end if
put "Frame "&the frame&":"&reportCollision(collisionData)
```

This will save the values of `collisionData` in two globals named `collisionDataDark` and `collisionDataLight`, depending on which model is considered to be `modelA`. It will also print the current values of the various properties in the Message window. Now restart the Collide.dir movie, add the Collision Modifier to both models, set the `resolve` property to `TRUE` (so that the Message window doesn't flood), and drag one toward the other to provoke a collision.

In the Message window, type the following two lines:

```
put reportCollision(collisionDataDark)
put reportCollision(collisionDataLight)
```

The results of my test are shown in Figure 14-8.

Your results may be slightly different. Notice that both global variables contain the same information. In other words, they both point to a single `collisionData` object somewhere in RAM space, whose values have been updated. Notice also that the values are not those printed out into the Message window during the last `mCollisionDetected()` event: they have been updated since, presumably when Director checked to ensure that the collision had finished. The last time the `mCollisionDetected()` handler was called, `modelA` was considered to be `model("Light")`. The current value of `modelA` is `model("Dark")`. The direction of the `collisionNormal` is also inverted.

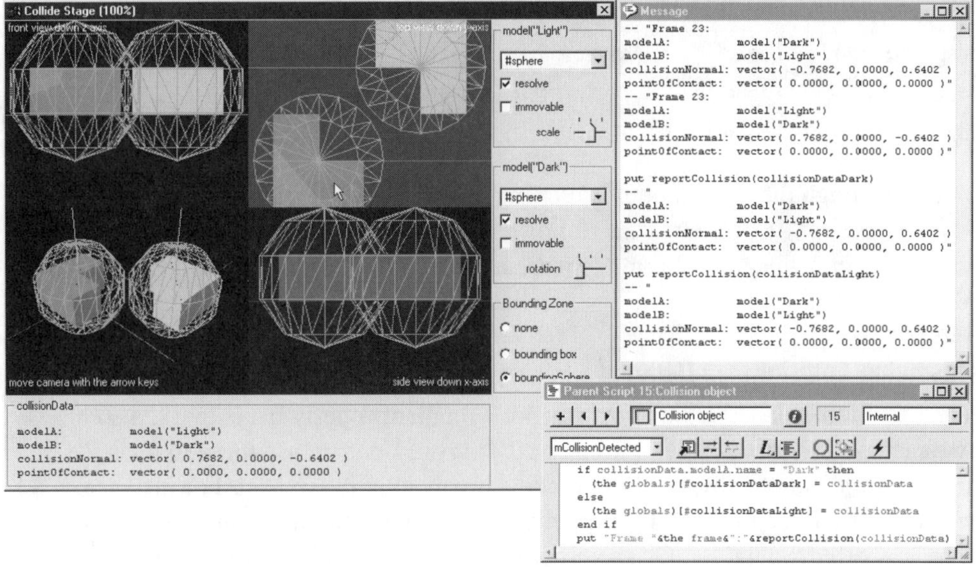

Figure 14-8 *Exploring how the collisionData object functions*

I find that, in Director 8.5, the `collisionNormal` value is not reliable. If your dragging movement has been short and straight, you'll probably find that you have the data for more than one collision printed into the Message window. While the `pointOfContact` vector may be the same, the `collisionNormal` may be different.

Try this test. Restart the Collide.dir movie, and then type the following in the Message window:

```
member(2).model("Light").worldPosition = vector(28, 0, 0)
member(2).model("Dark").worldPosition = vector(-48, 0, 0)
```

Now set the `collision.mode` for both models to #sphere, and select the Resolve check box for both. In the Message window, create a collision by typing

```
member(2).model("Dark").worldPosition = vector(28, 0, 0)
```

Note, as shown in the following table, the values for `collisionData.modelA` and for `collisionData.collisionNormal`. Now set the `collision.mode` for both models to #box and execute the last line again. Note the new `modelA` and `collisionNormal` values. Finally, set the `collision.mode` to #mesh and try a third time. Here are my results. Again, yours may differ.

Mode	collisionData.modelA	collisionData.collisionNormal	collisionData.pointOfContact
#sphere	model("Light")	vector(1.0, 0.0, 0.0)	vector(-10.0, 0.0, 0.0)
#box	model("Light")	vector(0.0, 0.0, 0.0)	vector(53.0, -25.0, 25.0)
#mesh	model("Light")	vector(-1.0, 0.0, 0,0)	vector(-0.27, 10.71, 7.14)

Even though the same model is moving in the same direction in all cases, the value of `collisionData.collisionNormal` is different. Not only that, but the values for both `collisionNormal` and `pointOfContact` are invalid for the #box mode test.

Resolving Collisions on Demand

The reason that `collisionData` is not a regular property list is that it also has two methods: `resolveA()` and `resolveB()`. You can use these to override the `resolve` setting for either of the models involved in the impact. For instance, if `modelA` is a fly, and `modelB` is a tennis racket, you may not want the collision to have any effect on the fly. On the other hand, if `modelB` is a fly swatter, then you will want the impact to have an effect. The `resolve...()` methods allow you to choose how the collision should be treated on a case-by-case basis. Confusingly, in Director 8.5, `resolveA()` is applied to `modelB`, and vice versa, despite what the documentation and your own logic might say.

We'll use this shortly, in a practical example involving a simple Pong game. The following section gives you a brief glimpse of some of the code we'll be using in that game.

Collisions Are Detected If One Model Moves Right Through Another

PassThru.dir

You can find the movie PassThru.dir in the 3D\Collide\ folder on the CD-ROM. This demonstrates a simple situation: four box models are used as walls, while a fifth sphere model is used as a ball that bounces off the walls. The ball starts off in a random direction. Normally, the ball appears as a shade of gray, except when a collision with one of the walls is detected. In this case, the ball takes on the color of the wall for that one frame. Each time the ball hits a wall, its speed increases by 5 percent. The main camera's `colorBuffer.clearAtRender` property is set to `FALSE` so that the ball leaves trails.

The ball's diameter is 10 units. It starts moving at a speed of 8 units per frame, and collisions are detected using a simple technique. As soon as the ball's speed moves over 10 units per frame, collision detection needs to use a different technique. The ball may not intersect with any other model either at the start or at the end of its displacement for a given frame, but it may have passed through a model on the way.

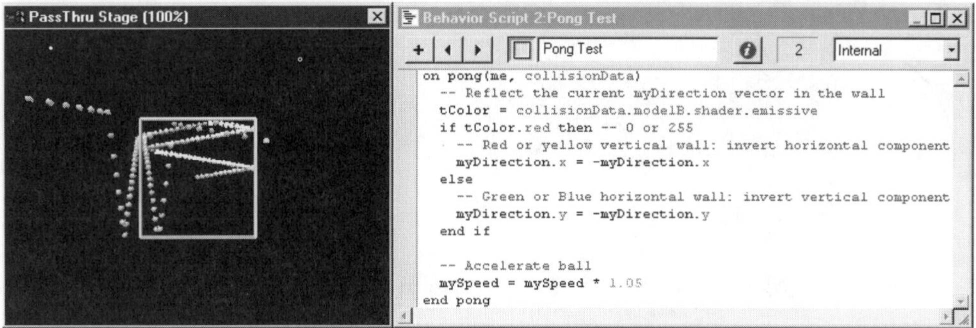

When this happens, the trail of colored ball positions indicates that collisions are detected even when the ball is not touching any wall. This is because the `resolve` property is not used to halt the ball at the point where it first touched the wall. The ball passes clean through the wall to a new position on the other side.

The `mCollisionDetected()` handler then reacts to this collision by changing the direction of the ball's motion. . .which makes it pass back through the wall again, provoking a new collision. The trail is double: it appears on both sides of the wall the collision was detected with. The result is that the ball oscillates on either side of the wall, traveling faster all the time.

This example does not make clear how the collision path is determined. As it happens, an error creeps into the calculations. Figure 14-9 shows two similar situations. In both, the position of a ball is shown in two successive frames. In both cases, the ball starts in collision with a wall. In both, the ball no longer intersects the wall in the second frame. In one case, the ball moves by less than its own diameter. No collision is detected on the second frame. In the second, the ball moves more than its own diameter. Since the path followed by the center of the ball passes through the wall, a collision is detected. If the `resolve` property for the ball were set to `TRUE`, in the first case the ball would escape from the wall, while in the second it would remain stuck.

In a Pong type of game, we need to be prepared for this situation. Limiting the speed of the model could ensure that only the first type of collision detection is used.

Timing of Collision Callbacks

Events.dir

The collision callback handler is called between `exitFrame` on frame *n* and `stepFrame` on frame *n*+1. In other words, collision detection takes place before any other action on a given frame.

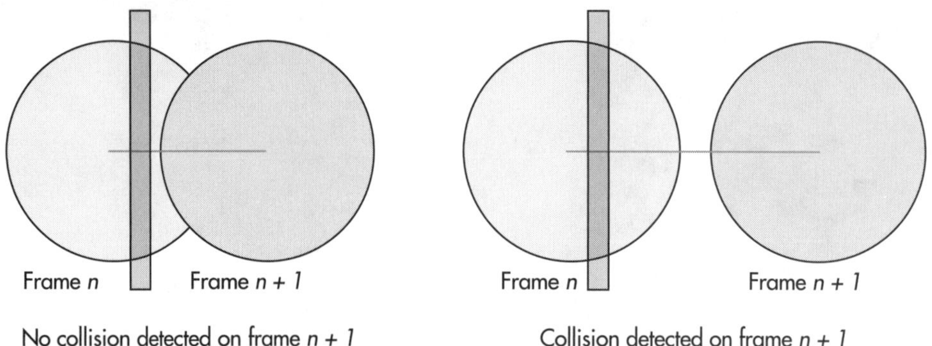

Figure 14-9 *Detection of a collision may depend on speed of movement.*

But it's not quite as simple as that, as you can see in the following table. When you use the `go` command to make the playback head jump to a different frame, the collision callback handler will be called twice: once before `stepFrame`, and once before `enterFrame`. If you are using a `go to the frame` loop, you will get two collision callback events on every frame. You can test this for yourself by running the Events.dir movie and watching the printout in the Message window.

Frame 1	Frame 2	Frame 3	Frame 2	Frame 3
#beginSprite	**#collision**	**#collision**	**#collision**	**#collision**
#stepFrame	#stepFrame	#stepFrame	#stepFrame	#stepFrame
#prepareFrame	#prepareFrame	#prepareFrame	#prepareFrame	#prepareFrame
#enterFrame	#enterFrame	#enterFrame	**#collision**	#enterFrame
#exitFrame	#exitFrame	#exitFrame	#enterFrame	#exitFrame
		<go frame 2>	#exitFrame	<etc.>

Figure 14-10 shows how the collision callback handler is apparently executed during an `#exitFrame` event subsequent to the command `go 2` in the frame script of frame 3.

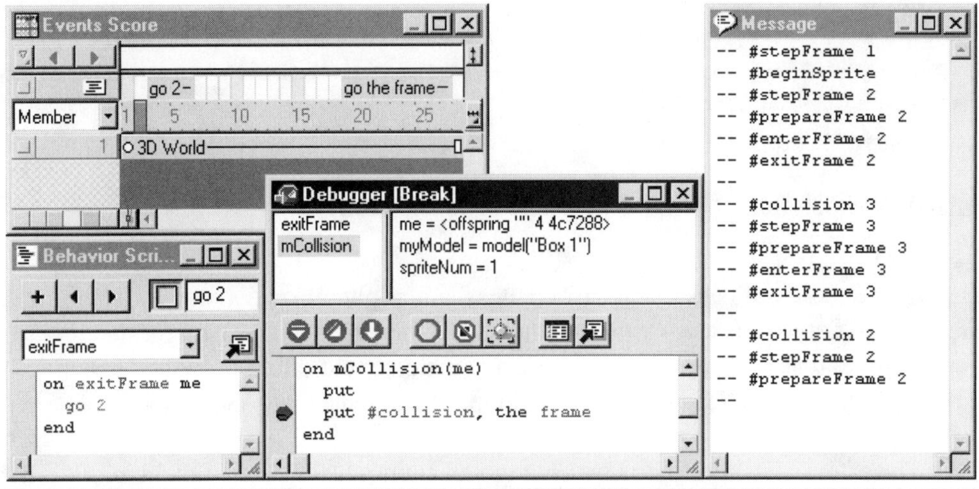

Figure 14-10 *Isolating the "go frame" quirk in the collision callback*

DEBUGGING TIP

The extra collision callback generated by a `go` *command may or may not be eliminated in a future version of Director. Your Director 8.5 code should allow for either eventuality. One way you could deal with this issue would be to use a behavior with handlers based on the following:*

```
property myFrame, otherProperties

on collisionCallback(me, collisionData)
  if myFrame = the frame then
    -- The collisionCallback() handler was called twice in
    -- succession due to a "go frame" command: ignore second call
    exit
  end if
  myFrame = the frame

  -- <More code>
end collisionCallback


on exitFrame(me)
  -- Set myFrame to zero so that the collisionCallback handler will
  -- execute fully the first time it is called in the next frame.
  myFrame = 0
end exitFrame
```

Model Manipulations During a Collision Callback Event

resolveB.dir

During a collision callback event, any changes you might make to a node's transform are reverted to their previous values at the end of the event. The reason for this appears to be that moving a model inside a collision event might provoke further collisions, which may lead to an infinite loop. This means that

- The effect of using `resolve` on a model cannot be determined within the collision callback handler itself. Inside the collision callback handler, expressions such as `collision.modelA.worldPosition` and `collision.modelB.worldPosition` will always reflect the unresolved position.
- If you need to move models as the result of a collision, you will have to calculate any changes during the collision event, store them in a property, and apply them in a subsequent `stepFrame()` or `prepareFrame()` handler.

This last issue is more awkward than it may at first appear. Although you can move models at any time after the collision-detection handler, the next round of collision detection compares the position `on exitFrame` with the position at the previous `exitFrame`. You cannot therefore pretend that a collision never happened. Even if you move the model out of striking distance on `prepareFrame()`, before the new frame is drawn, when collisions are tested after the next `exitFrame`, Director will check the whole path traveled since the collision, and will detect the point where the model moved free of the collision. That point will be considered as a new impact point, as illustrated in Figure 14-9.

You can see a demonstration of this if you study the movie resolveB.dir. We shall see the implications of this later.

Frame Rate and the Collision Modifier

Lightest.dir

Adding a modifier slows the movie. You can get an idea of how much the Collision Modifier slows the movie by trying the following test. Open the Lightest.dir movie that you saw in Chapter 13, create a new Movie Script member, and add the following handler:

```
on collisionTest(anAction)
  i = member(2).model.count
  case anAction of
   #add, VOID:
     repeat while i
       member(2).model(i).addModifier(#collision)
       i = i - 1
     end repeat
   #remove:
     repeat while i
       member(2).model(i).removeModifier(#collision)
       i = i - 1
     end repeat
  end case
end collisionTest
```

Now choose fpsMeter in the Xtras menu to open the fpsMeter movie in a window. Run the Lightest.dir movie, and use the slider at the top to create a number of box models. The more models you create, the more marked an effect you will see. Create enough models to reduce the frame rate to a round figure, such as 50fps. If you have a good hardware accelerator, you may need to choose a much faster frame rate. Remember, though, that end users may not have such powerful machines.

Now, in the Message window, type the following:

```
collisionTest()
```

The Collision Modifier will be added to each of the box models you created. Do you see how the frame rate of the Lightest movie decreases? In my test, with 31 box models, the speed dropped from just over 50 to under 43 frames per second: a drop of about 15 percent. (See Figure 14-11.)

This slowdown occurs even if none of the models intersect: on each frame, all the models must be checked for intersection. With *n* models, there need to be `(n * (n - 1)) / 2` collision tests. In other words, the number of tests varies with the square of the number of models concerned. It therefore makes sense to apply the Collision Modifier to as few models as you can get away with.

Taking Advantage of the enabled Property

You may have a situation where a large number of models enter into collision at different times. The gForce.dir movie is an example of this. You can attach the

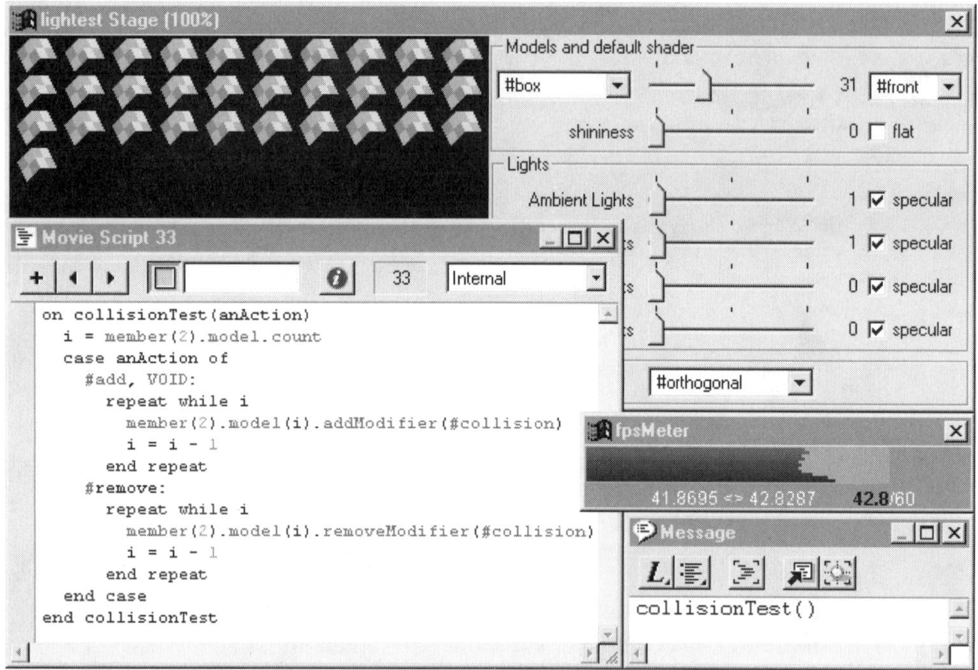

Figure 14-11 *Testing how the collision modifier affects performance*

Collision Modifier to all of the models at the beginning, and then set the `collision.enabled` property of the models to `FALSE`. As the movie progresses, you can switch the `collision.enabled` property of certain models to `TRUE`, and then revert it to `FALSE` again as soon as the danger of collision is passed.

Switching the `collision.enabled` property on and off is slightly slower than adding and removing the Collision Modifier with default property values. However, the chances are that you will also need to set at least one property value each time you add the Collision Modifier. This additional action makes switching the `collision.enabled` property more efficient. To test this for yourself, run the gForce.dir movie, and type the following into the Message window:

```
enabledTest()
```

My results for this test are shown in Figure 14-12. You can find the test code in member Test in cast slot 13.

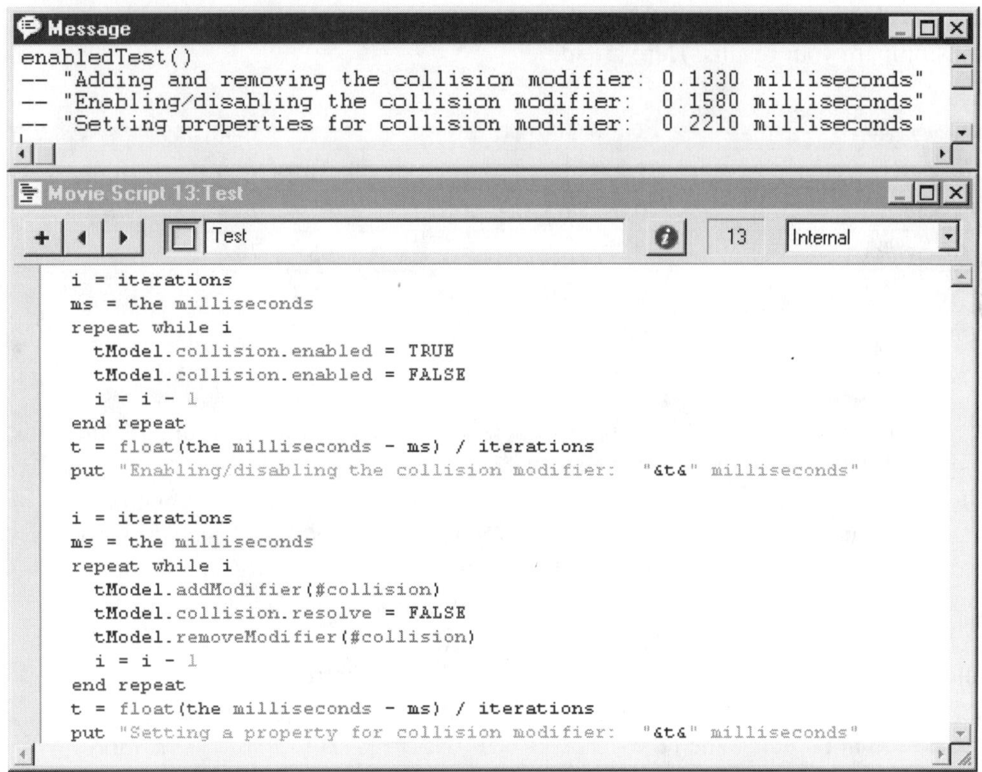

Figure 14-12 *Exploring how to optimize the use of the Collision Modifier*

Performance Differences Between Collision Modes

The collision mode does not affect the frame rate, at least not until collisions are detected. To test this, you'll first need to disable all the display activity that occurs in the Collide.dir movie when a collision is detected. When a collision is detected, the handler `mCollisionDetected()` in the Collision Object script (member 15) is called. Short-circuit this by uncommenting the first line:

```
on mCollisionDetected(me, collisionData)
  exit -- Uncomment when testing collision.mode performance
  -- <more code which slows performance>
end mCollisionDetected
```

Restart the Collide.dir movie, and open the fpsMeter window. With the models in their initial positions, none of the `collision.mode` values will detect a collision. Notice the frame rate with no Collision Modifier added, and then with each of the Collision Modifier modes. Now place the models directly on top of each other, so that a collision will be detected in all modes. Test each of the different modes again and compare your results. Here are mine:

collision.mode	No Intersection	Complete Intersection
None	71.2 – 73.7	71.5 – 72.9
#sphere	70.0 – 72.3	67.9 – 70.6
#sphere/#box	70.2 – 72.1	68.4 – 70.6
#box	70.4 – 72.0	68.1 – 70.3
#mesh	70.2 – 72.2	61.4 – 63.3

As you can see from the No Intersection column, the effect of adding the Collision Modifier is the same regardless of the collision.mode, as long as the models do not collide even in `#sphere` mode. The Complete Intersection column shows that, when a collision is detected, the difference between collision modes is more obvious. The slowest frame rate occurs when a collision is detected in #mesh mode. The differences between the other values is not statistically significant.

Collision detection using `boundingSphere` mode gives a first approximation as to whether two objects intersect. If the `boundingSphere` of two models do not intersect, the meshes of the models do not intersect. The reverse is not true: the `boundingSphere` of the two models may intersect, even though the model meshes do not touch. When the `collision.mode` is set to `#mesh`, the more exhaustive mesh calculations are only carried out after a preliminary boundingSphere check. The difference between the collision modes is thus only felt when the models concerned are within striking distance of one another.

Comment out the exit instruction at the beginning of the mCollisionDetected() handler, then restart your movie and set the Collision Modifier on both models to #mesh mode. Now drag one model toward the other, a little at a time, and observe how the frame rate drops progressively. As the distance between the models decreases, so the Collision Modifier needs to perform more calculations, and more precise ones, to ensure that a potential collision is not overlooked.

Shortcomings of the Collision Modifier

As you may have noticed, in Director 8.5, the Collision Modifier displays a number of quirks. These may be resolved in future versions of Director. Nonetheless, you might wish to carry out the following tests to make sure. (We've already looked at two quirks: the reliability of the collisionData object and the generation of extra collision callback events.)

Surface Collisions Are Not Properly Detected

The Collision Modifier in Director 8.5 suffers from a bug whereby collisions that make two models intersect only very slightly are not properly detected.

Restart the Collide.dir movie; then try this test in the Message window:

```
member(2).model("Light").worldPosition = vector(28, 0, 0)
member(2).model("Dark").worldPosition = vector(-48, 0, 0)
```

Now add the Collision Modifier to both models, in #sphere mode. Select the Resolve check box for both models. In the Message window, type

```
member(2).model("Dark").worldPosition = vector(-46, 0, 0)
put member(2).model("Dark").worldPosition
-- vector( -47.2000, 0.0000, 0.0000 )
```

This moves the model("Dark") a short distance to the right. The movement is resolved, so that the two boundingSpheres are just (not) touching. From this position, try to move the model("Dark") so that its center coincides with that of the model("Light"):

```
member(2).model("Dark").worldPosition = vector(28, 0, 0)
put member(2).model("Dark").worldPosition
-- vector( -47.2000, 0.0000, 0.0000 )
```

As expected, model("Dark") does not move. Now try moving it only a very short distance, so that the `boundingSphere` of the two models are only barely intersecting:

```
member(2).model("Dark").worldPosition = vector(-47, 0, 0)
put member(2).model("Dark").worldPosition
-- vector( -47.0000, 0.0000, 0.0000 )
```

The model("Dark") moves. The two boundingSpheres now intersect, but no collision is detected. From this new position, try to make the centers of the two models coincide:

```
member(2).model("Dark").worldPosition = vector(28, 0, 0)
put member(2).model("Dark").worldPosition
-- vector( -47.0000, 0.0000, 0.0000 )
```

As you might expect, the model does not move. The difference is that this time Director cannot resolve the movement correctly, since the movement started from an undetected collision situation. A whole series of collision events are now detected, and the model("Dark") is stuck.

The problem arises when the intersection is superficial. It does not matter how far the model has traveled since the previous frame: what matters is that the bounding zone of one model should only lightly graze that of the other.

A Model's Resolved Position Is Not Consistent

Run the Collide.dir movie. Use the two pop-up menus to add the Collision Modifier to both models in #sphere mode. Select the Resolve check boxes for both models. In the Message window, type the following lines:

```
member(2).model("Dark").worldPosition = vector(-50, 0, 0)
member(2).model("Light").worldPosition = vector(50, 0, 0)
member(2).model("Dark").worldPosition = vector(0, 0, 0)
put member(2).model("Dark").worldPosition
-- vector( -30.0000, 0.0000, 0.0000 )

member(2).model("Dark").worldPosition = vector(-27, 0, 0)
put member(2).model("Dark").worldPosition
-- vector( -27.0000, 0.0000, 0.0000 )

member(2).model("Dark").worldPosition = vector(-24, 0, 0)
put member(2).model("Dark").worldPosition
-- vector( -25.2000, 0.0000, 0.0000 )
```

The result is that the resolved position of the moving model will now depend on its impact position. Let's move the model("Dark") back and try again:

```
member(2).model("Dark").worldPosition = vector(-50, 0, 0)
member(2).model("Dark").worldPosition = vector(-24, 0, 0)
put member(2).model("Dark").worldPosition
-- vector( -29.2000, 0.0000, 0.0000 )

member(2).model("Dark").worldPosition = vector(-24, 0, 0)
put member(2).model("Dark").worldPosition
-- vector( -25.0400, 0.0000, 0.0000 )
```

This shows that the resolved position of the moving model also depends on its initial position. The direction of movement is identical in all these cases, so it seems reasonable to expect that the collision should be resolved to the same position, regardless of the start or end points of the motion.

resolveA() and resolveB() May Be Applied to the Wrong Model

resolveA.dir

You can at any time modify the `collision.resolve` property for a given model. This will take effect the next time a collision is detected. You may need to modify the property during a collision callback. In this case, according to the documentation, you can use the `collisionData.resolveA(trueOrFalse)` method to override the current value for `collision.resolve` for `collision.modelA`., and the corresponding `resolveB` method on `modelB`. If you use the `collision.setCollisionCallback()` method on a given model, that model is considered to be `modelA`, and the model it hits is considered to be `modelB`.

Unfortunately, in Director 8.5, the `collisionData.resolveA()` method is applied to `collisionData.modelB`, and vice versa. The resolveA.dir movie illustrates this (see Figure 14-13).

The movie consists of two models: a wall and a ball. The Collision Modifier is attached to both, and a collision callback is set for model("Ball"). The ball is then fired at the wall. At the moment that it collides with the wall, the ball model's `collision.resolve` property is `TRUE` (the default value). The ball should thus stop at the left-hand side of the wall. In the callback handler, `collisionData.modelA` is model("Ball"). The command `collisionData.resolveB(TRUE)` should have no effect on the ball whatsoever.

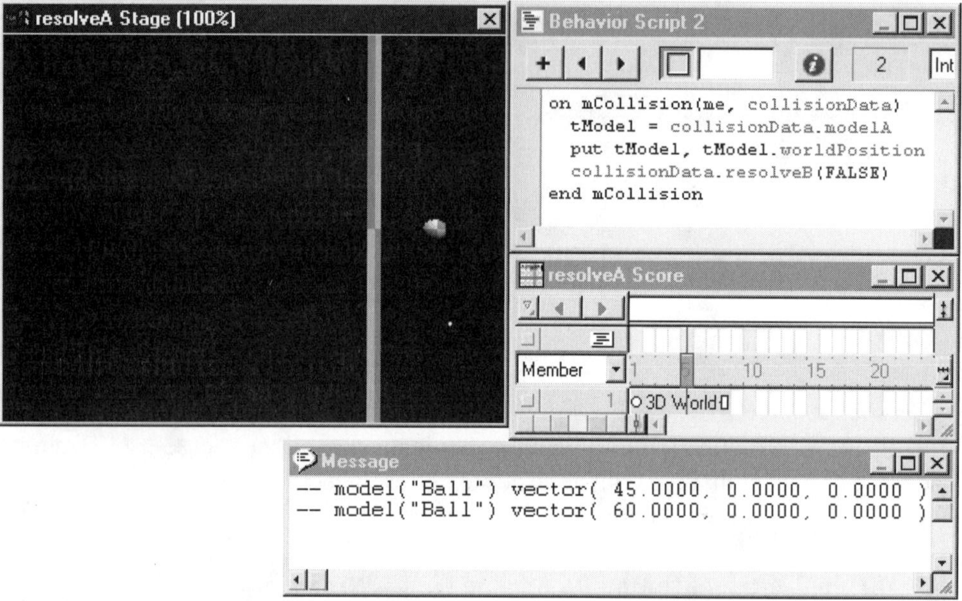

Figure 14-13 *Testing resolveA and resolveB*

It does, however. Run the movie and see. The ball passes through the wall as if the `collisionData.resolveA(FALSE)` had been used. Director 8.5 is at least consistent in its errors: the `resolveA()` method has no effect on `modelA`, but does affect `modelB`. Try changing the `mCollision()` method as follows; then try again.

```
on mCollision(me, collisionData)
  tModel = collisionData.modelA
  put tModel, tModel.worldPosition
  collisionData.resolveA(FALSE) -- B becomes A
end mCollision
```

The ball is stopped by the wall, since, despite appearances, the `resolve` property on `modelA` is not changed.

This seems to be a consistent inversion. However, if it is fixed in future versions of Director, then any code relying on the inversion will break, and Director 8.5 movies played on future versions of Shockwave will not perform as expected. Be sure to keep an editable copy of any Director 8.5 movies that use this feature, so that you can update them when the next version of Director is released.

Scaling Models

The Collision Modifier assumes that the model it is attached to is not deformed. As long as you maintain the proportions of the model, you can scale its size up or down. You can test this by using the Scale slider to change the scale of the model("Light") in the Collide.dir movie. If you change the proportions of a model while scaling, however, you may find that it no longer responds as you would expect.

Instead of using the Collision Modifier on models that have been stretched or squeezed, you will get more reliable performance if you create appropriate modelResources at the required size.

Lingo Versus the Collision Modifier

Here's an experiment that you can do to compare the speed of the #sphere mode of the built-in Collision Modifier, and a similar but simpler feature coded in Lingo.

Run the Collide.dir movie on the Stage. In the Xtras menu, choose the fpsMeter movie. (If it is not available, run the AddXtras.exe projector on the CD-ROM first.) In the Control Panel, adjust the target `frameTempo` to the fastest speed that the movie seems capable of: the red bars in the fpsMeter window should almost reach the right-hand side of the light rectangle.

Choose #Lingo Sphere as the collision-detection method for both models. Make sure that the Resolve check box is not selected for either model. Drag one model toward the other. The asterisk at the bottom right-hand corner should start blinking when a collision is detected. Note the frame rate detected by the fpsMeter window. Now, without moving the models, choose #sphere as the collision-detection method for both. Do you see that the frame rate drops significantly? And yet the detection is no more accurate.

The resolve technique I use with the Lingo `boundingSphere` detection is simplified: it assumes that only one of the models has moved. However, the slowdown is due to the collision detection itself, not to its resolution, so this simplification should have little effect.

The difference in speed occurs mainly because the Lingo technique assumes that the moving model will not move by more than its own diameter in a given frame. The Lingo technique does not test whether the path of the moving model passes through the static one between two collision-detection checks. If it did, a collision would result, even if there were no intersection with the moving model in its new position. Adding such path detection would slow the Lingo technique down below that of the Collision Modifier technique. Since the Collision Modifier's path detection is unreliable in any case, there seems to be little justification for its being slower than the simpler Lingo technique.

The #mesh Mode May Need a Jump Start

When using the #mesh mode, collision detection should be on a mesh-by-mesh basis. In certain circumstances, Director 8.5 will erroneously use the simpler #sphere mode instead. Here are the steps to reproduce this:

1. Restart the Collide.dir movie.
2. Select #mesh mode for both models.
3. In the green y axis view sprite, move one model toward the other. A collision is detected, even though the meshes are not touching.
4. In any of the other views, change the vertical position of one of the models so that they no longer share the same horizontal space.
5. Move the model back to its previous level. The #mesh mode detection now works as it should.

A Simple Implementation: Single-Player Pong

Pong4One.dir

Now that you are aware of the pitfalls you might encounter with the Collision Modifier, let's create a simple game of Pong. We can base this on the PassThru.dir movie that you saw earlier. Here is what we'll need to do:

- Switch off the trails (or rather, stop switching them on).
- Adjust the position of the walls and the projectionAngle so that the play zone fills the sprite.
- Make one of the walls shorter, so that the ball can escape from the square.
- Make the shorter wall moveable, so that the user can use it as a paddle.
- Give the ball a slower initial speed.
- Use resolve to ensure that the ball does not pass through any of the walls or the paddle.
- Modify the direction that the ball will take when it bounces off a moving paddle.
- Detect when the ball is too far from the center to be in the play zone.
- You may also want to remove the code that changes the color of the ball and use the same shader for all the walls.

These changes are not too hard. Perhaps you could try them on your own before you open Pong4One.dir, where it's all done for you. Here are some more changes that are necessary, but that might need more careful consideration:

- Relaunch the ball from the center of the world if the player misses it.
- Ensure that the ball does not get stuck in the wall due to an undetected collision.

I have deliberately kept the game simple: the ball only moves in two dimensions. This reduces our need for complex concepts and mathematics. It allows you to compare these techniques described with those you may have used in the past for creating any 2D Pong game.

Tips for the Easy Part

I've chosen to place the paddle at the bottom. This means that, when the ball bounces off the paddle, the *y* component of its direction vector will be positive.

Modifying the Direction of the Ball When It Hits the Paddle

When the ball hits the paddle, the *y* component of its direction vector is negative. To make the ball bounce upward, the following line could suffice:

```
myDirection.y = abs(myDirection.y)
```

This would lead to a perfectly symmetrical bounce. The ball would bounce at the same angle every time. To make the bounce more realistic and the game more interesting, I change the angle of the bounce depending on the way the paddle is moving. If the paddle is moving, the reflection angle is changed by between 5° and 15°.

Suppose the angle is already almost horizontal. Changing the angle may be enough to make the ball move upward. In this case, the *y* component of the direction vector will already be positive. I therefore apply the `abs()` function to the *y* component after I change the angle:

```
property myDirection  -- unit direction vector for movement of ball
property myPaddleMove -- -1 if paddle is moving left, 1 if moving right

on mCollisionDetected(me, collisionData)
  -- <Code we'll look at in a moment>
  tWall = collisionData.modelB.name --"paddle", "left", "top", "right"

  case tWall of
```

```
    "Paddle":
      tTransform = transform()
      tTransform.rotate(0, 0, (4 + random(11)) * myPaddleMove)
      myDirection = tTransform * myDirection
      myDirection.y = abs(myDirection.y)

  -- <Other cases and the code that treats them>
  end case
end mCollisionDetected
```

Detecting When the Player Misses the Ball

Adding the Collision Modifier to a model and using `collision.setCollisionCallback()` allows you to detect when a collision occurs. But how do you detect when a collision does not occur? The answer is—you can't.

You could provide a model below the visible part of the sprite, rather like the stop-netting around a ball park. If the ball collides with that, the player must have missed it. In other words, you detect a lack of collision in one place by detecting a collision elsewhere.

The technique I have used is different: on each `exitFrame`, I test whether the ball is farther from the center than it could possibly be if it were still in the play zone. Here's an extract:

```
property myBall        -- model("Ball")
property myDirection   -- unit direction vector for movement of ball
property mySpeed       -- floating point number indicating its speed

on exitFrame(me)
  myBall.translate(myDirection * mySpeed)
  if myBall.transform.position.magnitude > 150 then
    -- The ball is out of sight
    me.mLaunchBall() -- replaces ball in center of play zone
  end if
end exitFrame
```

Using resolveB( )

Pong0.dir, PongGlue.dir

Why is relaunching the ball tricky? If the player misses the ball, it passes outside the playing zone. If you use Lingo to place it inside the playing zone, there is a chance that its path will cross that of the paddle. If this should happen, you don't want to resolve the collision; if you do resolve it, the ball will remain outside the playing zone.

If a collision is reported when the ball is placed in the center of the world, then it must have passed through a wall or a paddle, moving inward. Such a collision could not be reported if the ball were moving outward. In other words, the ball may not be able to get to the center of the world if collisions are resolved automatically because there may be another model in the way. The solution is to resolve collisions only if the ball is not in the center of the world.

The following code extracts will deal with collisions on a case-by-case basis:

```
property myBall -- model("ball")

on mCreateWorld(me)
  -- <Code to create the paddle and walls: collision.mode for all of
  -- these is set to #box, collision.resolve is set to FALSE>

  tResource          = tMember.newModelResource("Ball", #sphere)
  tResource.radius   = 5
  myBall             = tMember.newModel("Ball", tResource)
  -- Add collision modifier
  myBall.addModifier(#collision) -- default collision.mode = #sphere
  myBall.collision.resolve = FALSE -- Treated on a case-by-case basis
  myBall.collision.setCollisionCallback(#mCollisionDetected, me)
end mCreateWorld

on mCollisionDetected(me, collisionData)
  if myBall.worldPosition = vector(0, 0, 0) then
    -- The player missed the ball and it has been placed in the center
    exit -- don't stop the ball in its path or bounce it
  else
    -- The ball will be modelA: we need to use resolveB to control it
    collisionData.resolveB(TRUE) -- stop the ball at the wall or paddle
    -- <More code to make the ball bounce>
  end if
end mCollisionDetected
```

This technique is used in the Pong0.dir movie. You may find that, in this movie, the ball gets stuck in the walls or the paddle when the ball reaches a critical speed. If the ball travels more than its own diameter in a single frame, or if a collision with a wall occurs on the frame immediately after a `go frame` command, the ball might get stuck. It might also stick to the sides of the paddle for a time, before flying off again in a random direction.

Fortunately, this is unlikely to occur unless the player is a true champion who never misses the ball, even at high speed. You can force the situation, however, by making the paddle so wide that the ball cannot escape, and by setting the initial speed of the ball to 10, so that it starts out at the critical speed (its diameter is 10 units). The movie PongGlue.dir has been modified in this way.

Using the Havok Xtra for Collision Detection

The Havok Xtra provides an alternative approach to collision detection. The Havok Xtra allows you to treat chosen models as solid objects, or *rigid bodies* in the Havok terminology. Such bodies can have mass and momentum, and as a result, they can be made to bounce off of each other in a realistic way.

The Havok Xtra is completely independent of the Collision Modifier. Indeed, the two features should not be used together; you should adopt one or the other for a given 3D world.

The Havok Xtra provides much more than collision detection: it allows you to simulate real-time physical interactions. A full description of Havok would require a second book the size of this one, so I will limit myself to a simple Havok version of the Pong game for now. This will let you compare the two techniques on an equal footing.

Installing the Havok Xtra

The Havok Xtra is installed by default when you install Director 8.5. It is not, however, included by default in the Shockwave plug-in. If you are planning to use Havok with content to be played back in a browser, keep in mind that it will entail an additional 500+K download for the first-time user. Remember to set the Xtra to download, if needed, via the menu Modify | Movie | Xtras.

The library of behaviors to use with the Havok Xtra is not installed by default when Director is installed. You will find it in the Havok\ folder on the Director 8.5 CD-ROM, along with two Acrobat manuals and an HTML tutorial.

Open the folder that contains your Director application, and find the Libs folder located inside it. Open the Libs folder, and create a new subfolder; name this one Havok Behaviors. Copy the Control.cst and the Setup.cst files from the Havok\ Behaviors\ folder on the Director 8.5 CD-ROM, and paste them into the folder you have just created. Finally, restart Director 8.5. If you use the menu Window | Library Palette to open the Library Palette window, you should now find the Havok behaviors available (see Figure 14-14).

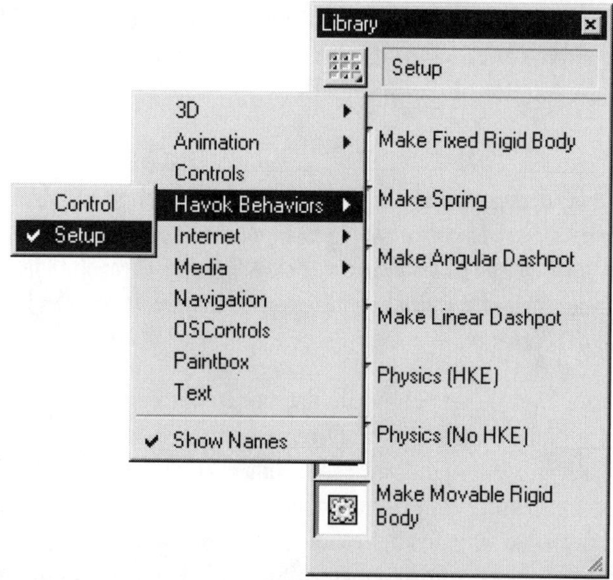

Figure 14-14 *The Library Palette after installing the Havok behaviors*

How the Havok Xtra Works

To use the Havok Xtra, you need to add a new Havok member to your movie. To do so, select Insert | Media Element | Havok Physics Scene. The code inside this new member can be used to control the models in any Shockwave 3D member as if they were rigid bodies. Before the code can work, however, you have to give it a few clues about the world it is going to work on:

- **Time step** This determines how often the physics scene should be updated. In most cases, you will want the time step to be equal to your target frame rate.
- **Time sub-steps** These divide time into even finer steps. Sub-steps are executed between `enterFrame` and `exitFrame`, but the screen is not updated at this time.
- **Tolerance** This indicates how close two models should be before a collision is detected.
- **World scale** This tells the Havok member how big a world unit is. The default is one meter. Calculations of speed and acceleration are affected by this parameter.

The easiest way to connect the Havok member to the Shockwave 3D member, and to provide the Havok member with the data indicated here, is to use one of the Physics behaviors in the Havok Setup palette.

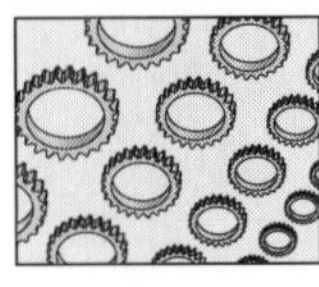

NOTE

If you are using a scene created in a third-party 3D design package, the values for tolerance and world scale will already be defined. In this case, you should use the Physics (HKE) behavior. If you are using a scene created on-the-fly in Lingo, either from primitives or via the `loadFile()` *command, you will need to define both tolerance and world scale: you should therefore use the Physics (No HKE) behavior.*

One of the reasons that these behaviors are not installed along with Director itself is that they have not passed through the Director engineering team's own Quality Assessment process. You may find, like me, that you prefer to tweak them before use, or that you prefer writing your own scripts based upon them. One minor example of this is that, if you drop a Physics behavior on a Shockwave 3D sprite before you add a Havok member to your internal cast, a Script Error will occur. For this reason, I have rewritten parts of the Physics (No HKE) behavior that I use in the HvkPong.dir movie. In particular:

- The choice of Havok member is more user friendly, especially if you move the member to a different cast slot after applying the behavior.
- If you choose the default value of `0.0` for the time step, the behavior will automatically calculate the time step that fits your target frame rate.
- A tolerance of 1 is used by default, as, in the HvkPong.dir example, this gives the best results.
- Unused handlers have been removed.

You must call the `havok.initialize()` method before you can use any of the other functions of the Havok member. The easiest way to ensure that this happens is to make the Havok Physics behavior the first behavior on the sprite (see Figure 14-15).

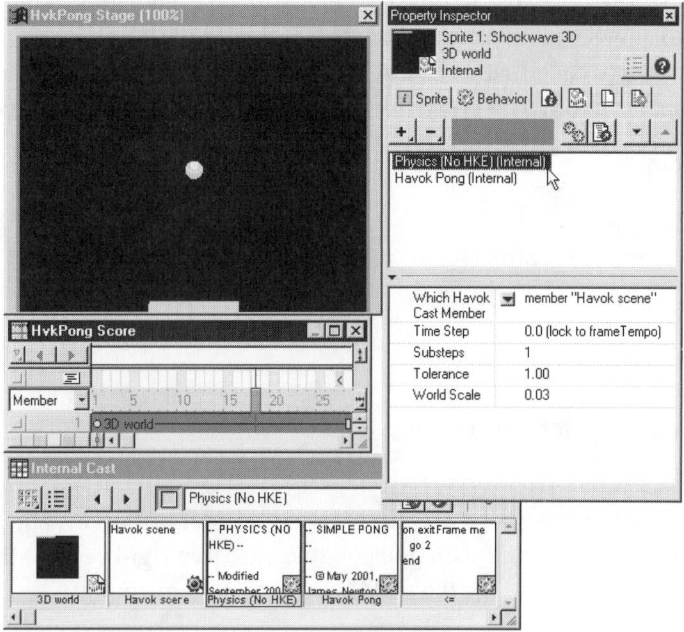

Figure 14-15 *Ensuring that the modified Havok Physics behavior is the first behavior on the sprite*

Differences Between Havok Collision Detection and the Collision Modifier

The Havok Xtra only acts on models that have been used to create Havok Rigid Bodies. There are two types of rigid body: fixed and movable. In our Pong movie, the walls will be fixed, and the ball and paddle will be movable.

Fixed bodies are considered to have infinite mass. They therefore do not budge when any movable rigid bodies collide with them. While you can move the model that a fixed rigid body is based on, the Havok Xtra will ignore the model's new position, and will continue to behave as if the fixed rigid body were still in the same place.

This illustrates an important point: the Havok Xtra creates and maintains a parallel universe. You must choose whether to control your 3D world through standard Lingo calls or through calls to the Havok member. If you try to mix both types of control, the visual display may no longer correspond to the physical world simulation; this will cause incoherence.

Declaring the Havok Member

When you drop one of the Havok Physics behaviors on a Shockwave 3D sprite, you will be asked to choose a Havok member. The behavior will save a pointer to this member in a property called `pHavok`. All other behaviors on the same sprite can access this property in order to create their own pointers to the same Havok member:

```
property havok

on beginSprite(me)
  tSprite = sprite(me.spriteNum)
  havok   = tSprite.pHavok -- declared + set in Havok Physics behavior
  -- etc
end beginSprite
```

Using Rigid Bodies Instead of Models

HukPong.dir

The HvkPong.dir movie starts by creating shaders, model resources, and models, just as the Pong0.dir movie does. It then goes on to create five rigid bodies: three fixed for the wall and two movable for the paddle and ball. For example:

```
tResource = tMember.newModelResource("Wall", #box)
tModel    = tMember.newModel("Left", tResource)
tModel.addModifier(#meshdeform)
havok.makeFixedRigidBody("Left")

tResource = tMember.newModelResource("Ball", #sphere)
tModel    = tMember.newModel("Ball", tResource)
tModel.addModifier(#meshdeform)
myBall    = havok.makeMovableRigidBody("Ball", 0.1) -- 100 grams
```

There are four points to note:

- Since all models must have a unique name, the name of a model is enough to identify it. A model must exist with the given name; that is the model that Havok will convert to a rigid body.
- You must have the Mesh Deform Modifier attached to any models that you want to use as rigid bodies. As you saw earlier in the "Calculating the boundingSphere" section, the Mesh Deform Modifier makes the geometry of the model available, both to Lingo and to the Havok member.

- You must provide a mass for each movable body. Fixed bodies are considered to have an infinite mass, so there is no need for you to provide them with mass. The weight of a movable rigid body determines how its trajectory is affected when struck by another movable rigid body. The unit of mass is the kilogram, but this is merely a convention. All that matters is that the relative mass of each body is correct in relation to the relative mass of all the others.
- Once you have created your rigid bodies, you should manipulate these, rather than the models that they are based upon. For example, instead of manipulating `myModel.worldPosition`, you would need to manipulate `myHavokRigidBody.position`.

Default Gravity

The Havok physics scene will automatically assign a gravity value for all the movable rigid bodies. If you leave this value as it is, all rigid bodies will start falling down the z axis, unless they collide with a fixed rigid body on the way. You may want to alter gravity so that it acts down the y axis instead of down the z axis. In the HvkPong.dir movie, we do not want gravity to affect the models at all. The simplest solution in this case is to set gravity to zero:

```
havok.gravity = vector(0, 0, 0)
```

Creating a Collision Callback Using the Havok Member

Just as you used `aModel.collision.setCollisionCallback()` to tell the Collision Modifier to check for collisions for a given model, so you must use a similar instruction to get the Havok Member to deal with collisions. The simplest is to get the ball rigid body to bounce off of all the others:

```
havok.registerInterest("Ball", #all, 0, 0, #mBounce, me)
```

The syntax is more complex. In this instruction, there are two arguments set to zero: frequency and threshold. Setting these to zero ensures that all collisions, no matter how insignificant, provoke a callback to the `mBounce()` handler of the current instance.

Exploiting Your Knowledge of the Physics of Motion

The physical approach to manipulating models with the Havok Xtra is quite different from the purely mathematical approach that I have been using so far. In this example, I have tried to make the transition as easy as possible; but in doing so, I have not exploited the full range of possibilities that the Havok Xtra provides. If you have a good grounding in the physics of motion, you should find it easy to create more complex examples. See the Havok Xtra Lingo Reference.pdf file inside the Havok\pdf docs\ folder on the Director 8.5 CD-ROM for details of all the keywords recognized by the Havok Xtra.

A Custom Lingo-Only Collision-Detection Solution

LingPong.dir

Learning the power of the Havok Xtra and the idiosyncrasies of the Collision Modifier can take time. Both of these approaches are generic: they can cover a multitude of situations. This is both a strength and a weakness. These features can simplify the development of a given solution, but there is also a chance that they will fail to deliver if your situation is slightly off-beat.

In such situations, a customized Lingo can often provide a better answer. You maintain control of the quality of your Lingo at all stages, and can adapt it to suit your particular case. A one-off Lingo solution can be tuned to perform faster, and with lower memory requirements.

I provide such a solution in the LingPong.dir movie. This includes an `mResolve()` handler. The parameters of this handler are

- The current position of the ball, assuming that there are no walls
- The position of the ball on the last frame
- The position of any walls that the ball has crossed, or the paddle, as the case may be

It returns the position of the ball at the moment when it first touched the nearest wall, or the symbol #miss if the ball misses the paddle. Figure 14-16 shows the meanings of the various variables in the handler.

Here is a simplified version of the `mResolve()` handler, which assumes that the path of the ball intersects with a single two-dimensional wall:

```
on mResolve(me, aLastPosition, aPositionNow, aSegment)
  tMotion = aPositionNow - aLastPosition
```

```
  tPoint  = aSegment[1]
  tVector = aSegment[2] - tPoint
  -- Create a vector perpendicular to tVector
  tPerp   = vector(tVector.y, -tVector.x, 0)

  -- Lines intersect where:
  --     aLastPosition + (iSect * tMotion) = tPoint + (a * tVector)
  -- => (iSect * tMotion) = (tPoint - aLastPosition) + (a * tVector)
  -- Take the dot product of both sides, using tPerp.

  -- tPerp * tVector will be zero since the vectors are perpendicular
  -- => (iSect * tMotion) * tPerp = (tPoint - aLastPosition) * tPerp

  iSect = (tPoint - aLastPosition) * tPerp / (tMotion * tPerp)
  -- No need to consider the case where tMotion * tPerp = 0, since
  -- we already know that the lines cross

  return aLastPosition + (iSect * tMotion)
end mResolve
```

This movie runs faster than either of the other two. Its failure rate for collision detection is zero. It does not require a 500+K Xtra download over the Internet. The main disadvantage is that the technique is not generic: it makes specific assumptions

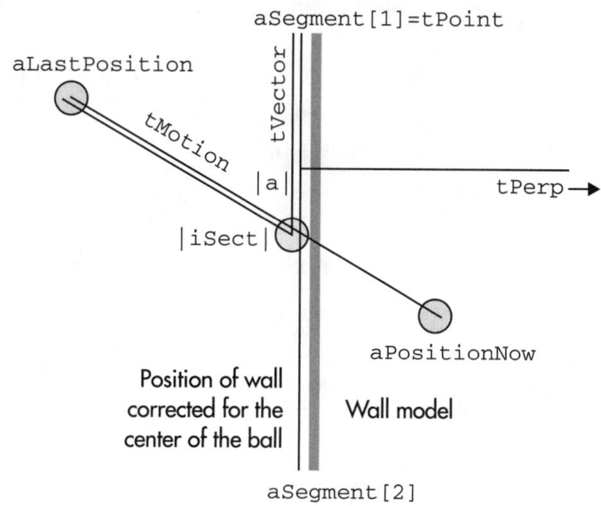

Figure 14-16 *Variables used in the mResolve( ) handler*

about the collision situation. For a different situation, you would probably need to rewrite the handler completely.

Improving the Movie

The LingPong.dir movie is still not perfect: if the ball does not hit the paddle squarely, it returns to its start position. A more complete version would both handle the way the ball bounces off the sides of the paddle and let the ball disappear from the sprite before it replaces it at the center.

You can also improve the movie in other ways:

- Change the way the ball bounces off the top of the paddle so that the user has more precise control. For example, you could use a spherical paddle. The angle of the bounce would then depend on which part of the paddle the ball hits.
- Elaborate on LingPong.dir, or on the Pong movie of your choice, by transforming it into a game of BrickBats.
- Add overlays to provide a score, using the techniques you saw in the gForce.dir movie in Chapter 12.
- Make the movie you choose to work on fully three-dimensional.

Over to You

In this chapter, you have seen three different ways for detecting collisions between models. You have also seen the performance implications of collision detection. Choosing which technique you use depends on a variety of factors, including

- The complexity of the collisions that you need to handle
- The maximum speed of any of the models involved in a collision
- Your familiarity with vector mathematics
- Your familiarity with the physics of motion
- Whether your project needs to run in Shockwave

As far as I can tell, the shortcomings of the Collision Modifier mentioned in this chapter should be fixed in the next major release of Director. If you come across others, be sure to let Macromedia know. Fill in the bug report form at http://www.macromedia.com/support/director/ts/documents/bug_submit.htm. In the meantime, cultivate the art of creative workarounds.

CHAPTER

15

Exploring Director Shockwave Studio on Your Own

IN THIS CHAPTER:

Any attempt to teach Enlightenment is like throwing pebbles at a minnow in the shallows. Whatever path you predict a student will take causes the student to choose another.

—Koan

You have now almost reached the end of the book, and many of your questions on Director still go unanswered. I have not touched upon a number of Shockwave 3D features:

- Working with modifiers
- Importing files created in third-party 3D design packages
- Using motion objects
- Working with 3D Text members

In the second part of this chapter, I'll describe what each of these features can enable you to do and give you suggestions on how to investigate them. However, before I deal with specific issues, I'd like to provide a general approach to exploring the potential of Director. In the first part of this chapter, I will draw your attention to the techniques I have used throughout the book to work out how Director works. Of course, sometimes Director doesn't work, or at least not the way you expect it to. I'll provide guidelines on how to determine whether there is a bug in the software or your own understanding.

Pioneering Tactics

Each new version of Director brings new features. Dealing in detail with Director's entire range of possibilities is an endless task. Where should you find the information you need? There are many excellent online sources (you'll find a list at the end of this chapter). You can use these to keep abreast of the techniques that other developers are using. But what if you have to strike out into uncharted territory?

Solving a problem is not a case of finding a solution; it is a case of finding a set of easier problems you already know how to solve. When you tackle a new Director feature, you should use divide-and-conquer tactics.

Understanding the Keywords

My first port of call is always the "Lingo by Feature" section of the *Lingo Dictionary*. This gives a list of the keywords associated with a particular feature. I then check each entry in the *Lingo Dictionary* to see how each of these keywords is described.

Like most Director developers, I do not take the Lingo Dictionary entirely on trust. The manuals included with any software package are prepared while the software is at the beta trial; Director is no exception. The process of printing the manuals takes longer than engraving the final CD-ROMs. This means bug fixing and code tweaking continues after the manuals are sent to press. Very rarely, one bug fix breaks another piece of code and the secondary bug slips through the Quality Assessment net. More often, a feature is modified slightly after the manuals are finalized. In other words, all software manuals are already slightly out of date even before they ship. This, unfortunately, is a fact of life.

Experimenting with the Syntax

Once I have an idea of how a feature is supposed to work, I start creating little snippets of code. These might be a short sequence of one-line commands in the Message window, a short handler in a Movie Script, or a simple behavior. This helps me understand and remember the syntax.

I will often deliberately try to use the wrong syntax to see what happens. Nine times out of ten, I end up with a script error. My experiments are not random, though. I compare the syntax for similar commands to detect patterns. For example, the `translate()` command can be used either on a node or on the node's transform. The result is a change in the node's `position` property, which is a vector. According to the documentation, the first argument of the `pointAt()` command must be a position vector. Would it work if I used a node instead? Indeed it does. I annotate my paper copy of the 3D Lingo Dictionary; in the online help, I modify the HTML file associated with the `pointAt()` command and carry on with my tests.

Testing Cross-Platform

Once I have an idea of how the syntax works, I create a simple movie. In some cases, my movie will be designed to test borderline cases: very small and very large values, ambiguities in the syntax, behavior at the edge of a sprite or the edge of the stage, and so on. In other cases, I create a movie that can be used to experiment with each value of a given parameter. The InkTest.dir movie in Chapter 3 is an example of this.

I then test the movie on both MacOS and Windows. Sometimes, the movie behaves quite differently on the other platform. An example of this is the `anImageObject.draw()` command when used to draw a line. I described the differences in detail in Chapter 3.

Building Reference Movies and a Code Library

Writing isolated commands gives a very fragmented picture of how a feature works as a whole. If the feature is simple, this might be enough. For more complex concepts,

I find it helps to build a reference movie. You have seen examples of these in the preceding chapters: Copyxels.dir, Shaders.dir, and a number of simpler movies. These movies have a double role: creating them is as informative as using them.

As I work on the code, I am forced to use all the keywords for a given feature in a disciplined way. Specific problems will arise. I might notice there are two or more ways of achieving an identical result: which is the most efficient? I run a quick test, annotate my Lingo Dictionary, and create a code snippet for my library that demonstrates the fastest method. I might find that a technique I had planned to use does not produce the results I anticipated. Is this due to a lack of understanding on my part or a bug in Director? Nine times out of ten, Director is innocent.

Reference movies are a great time saver in three ways. I build such movies in time that I have set aside for exploratory work, not in time that I charge to a client. Although I might run into dead ends while I am doing this, I am not under any pressure. When I do implement the features in contracted work, I can run a test in seconds to find the right parameters to use. Not only that, I already have a body of working code that I can cut and paste into other movies.

However, building a reference movie takes time. Is the time it saves greater than the time spent creating it? In the cases of the movies included on the CD-ROM that accompanies this book, the answer is definitely No. Because these were developed for other people such as you to use, I have spent much longer creating a simple interface, tidying the code, and tracking bugs unconnected with the feature under study than I would normally do. When making such movies for my own use, I tend to leave them in a state where they are usable but rather ramshackle. I will polish and fully comment only the code that deals with the feature itself.

Creating Useful Behaviors for a Feature

During the process of writing a reference movie, I most likely will identify the need for a number of generic behaviors. This also might happen at an earlier stage, or while I am working on a contract. Quite often, the idea of making a process generic comes with hindsight: I find that I could reuse a piece of code that I have written for a particular situation. Inevitably, the piece of existing code doesn't fit neatly into my current project, so I try to generalize it. When I try to reuse the generalized behavior later, I may find that it needs a tweak. I store the latest version of any behavior or useful handler in a special library cast, which I keep in the Xtras folder.

I prefer the Xtras folder to the Libs folder, because it gives me immediate access to the scripts. I can open a script, copy the appropriate handler, and paste it into my movie. I can drag a script into my movie, revise it to handle the specific issues of the current movie, and then paste the revised script back into my library cast. If you like, you can keep your own library cast in the Libs file and place an alias to it in the Xtras folder. That lets you open it from both places.

On the CD-ROM, you will find a copy of all the scripts from my code library that are relevant to the subjects treated in this book. This is in the Toolkit8.cst. My own code library actually includes many more snippets of code, written when I first explored an idea, and later forgotten. The process of researching the best way of doing something and storing an example often is enough in itself. Later I find it takes me less time to rewrite a few lines of code than it does to find the original example. The scripts I have included here are those I have reused at least once. I arrange them by category and often identify individual scripts with a thumbnail, which helps me quickly find them again when I need them. I use the thumbnail view for my code library because I find I remember the positions of the scripts much better than I remember their names.

If you look closely at the movies I have created for the book, you might notice this process at work. You will find different versions of the same behavior in different movies. You should find the most up-to-date version in the Toolkit8.cst on the CD-ROM. If you use the thumbnail view, as I do, for this cast you will notice that some of the scripts in the Toolkit cast have icons and others don't. I create thumbnails for behaviors to indicate that they have become pretty stable and that I have commented them correctly.

I recommend that you use the Toolkit8 cast library as a guide rather than a source. The scripts all were originally written for a specific purpose, which might correspond only distantly to your current aims. Rather than trying to bend my scripts to fit your projects (or worse, bending your projects to fit around my scripts), I suggest that you build a toolkit library of your own.

Distinguishing Software and Wetware Bugs

Often, code I have written to explore a new feature does not work. Is it my fault or Director's, or an error in the documentation? Despite rumors to the contrary, I find that bugs in Director itself are pretty rare. Director engineers on the receiving end of my messages to wish-director@macromedia.com might find that a surprising statement, given the number of bug reports I have submitted over the years.

Isolating the Problem Area

The truth is that, especially at early stages in investigation, my code does not work because it contains errors. There might be a number of reasons for this: my knowledge of the topic might be shaky, my understanding of the way Director implements the feature could be wrong, my syntax might be influenced by that of other programming languages I use, and so on.

So when I find that my code does not work, my first reaction is to consult the official documentation. If I believe I am using the keywords and the concepts in the right way, I will try a set of basic debugging techniques:

- Stepping through my code line by line in the Debugger window, watching the values of each variable change, following key expressions in the Watcher, and looking for discrepancies.
- Rewriting my code so that a single operation is performed on each line and each result is stored in a separate variable.
- Cutting a copy of my current movie back to a minimum so that it is testing the problem issue and nothing else.
- Testing individual lines of code in the Message window.
- Writing *meta-Lingo*, Lingo code that highlights how Lingo code works (or doesn't).

You can see snapshots of this process at various places in the book, and notably in the section on the Collision Modifier in Chapter 14. Mostly what you see is the final result, not all the dead ends that I might have followed to reach that result. At times, I do deliberately take you up a dead end, because I feel it helps to understand how a feature works if you first see what makes it fail. For every dead end I mention, I must have followed at least 10 others. There is no high road to understanding—only painstaking effort.

Providing Evidence of a Bug

At the end of this phase, I might have discovered the error of my ways. If so, the process stops here and I apply my newfound knowledge to the movie I originally was working on. In other cases, I may by now be tempted to use the word "bug." It is not enough to submit a bug report using wish-director@macromedia or http://www.macromedia.com/support/director/ts/documents/bug_submit.htm, which says "There's a bug in feature X." Director engineers are not omniscient—and they are busy.

The ideal bug report consists of six items:

- A single-line description of the bug
- A detailed description of the minimal steps to reproduce the bug
- An explanation of what happens when you perform these steps
- An explanation of what should happen (but doesn't)
- A tiny Director movie that performs the minimal steps automatically when the Director engineer runs it.

- A description of the version of Director used (including build number), the platform (OS), the runMode, and some information about the hardware if this appears to be useful (especially the graphic accelerator board model and driver version for 3D rendering problems, for instance).

Bugs are tricky things and few fit the mold of the ideal bug report. The important point to note is that a bug that can't be reproduced cannot be fixed; a description of the bug alone is not enough.

Crying "Bug"

Even after I have amassed damning evidence of a bug, there is still a chance that the bug is a figment of my imagination. When I first started, I believe I was right only half of the time. Over the years, my ratio of valid bug reports has increased, which means the number of reports I send in has diminished. It also means I take longer to create my bug demonstration movies. If, as a result, the Director engineers need to spend less time understanding what the issue is, my time is well spent.

Exploration Is a Nonlinear Process

In the preceding description, I might have given the impression that I follow a steady progression from simple through systematic to a synthesis. This is only partially true: In actual practice, the process contains a lot of subsidiary loops. While working on the interface for a reference movie, I might find myself exploring a different feature altogether. While trying to isolate what I think is a bug, I might find that my understanding of a feature changes, and I need to go back and simplify code that I have already written.

Exploration is time consuming and unpredictable. It is not best done under pressure. You might want to reserve a group of hours every week for researching new features. Such research would include reading new articles on Director-oriented sites, reading interesting messages on mailing lists, and saving them by theme for later reference. It should be clearly understood by all—you, your boss, and your colleagues—that this time is reserved for learning. Alternatively, you may like to arrange groups of days during any slack periods when you can work undisturbed on an area of your choice.

Sharing Your Discoveries

There is no better way to learn a subject than to teach it to others. If you find that no information on the feature you are exploring is available, why not consider writing an article on it for a site such as Director-Online.com? Not only will this save others the effort of following the same dead ends, it can earn you a reputation as an expert in that particular field. Others working on the subject will write to you and share their insights, and the whole Director community will benefit.

Tips for Exploring the Remaining 3D Features

Here are some suggestions for how you could investigate the Shockwave 3D topics I have not had the space to cover. A number of these topics require either access to *.w3D files created in third-party 3D design packages, or access to the design packages themselves. You can find information on each feature in several separate places in the *What's New in Director Shockwave Studio* manual. The hyperlinked HTML Help often can be easier to use in the first instance. Ullala's 3D Property Inspector (3DPI) is always a great help.

Working with 3D Text Members

You can use Text members in two ways in Director 8.5. By setting the `displayMode` of a Text member to `#Mode3D`, you can display extruded text directly inside a Text member. You also can create an `extruder` resource for use inside a Shockwave 3D member, in which case the extruded text can interact with other elements in a 3D world.

You'll find a short tutorial on Using 3D Text in the manual *What's New in Director Shockwave Studio*, which is included in the box with Director 8.5. You can find the same information in HTML form by choosing the menu Help | Director Help, and clicking the links What's New in Director 8.5 and Using 3D Text. This tutorial ends with a list of new keywords for 3D text, which you can also look up in the 3D Lingo Dictionary chapter.

You might like to use the fpsMeter movie in a window to test the relative performance of 3D Text members and Shockwave 3D members with extruder resources. You also could try using an extruder resource instead of an overlay made using the image of a Text member. If the text needs to change, is an extruder resource faster or slower than an overlay? Which uses more memory? Visit Tom Higgins's site, http://www.shockwavemovies.com/, for undocumented techniques on how to use an `extruder` resource in conjunction with a Vector Shape member to create custom extruded models.

Modifiers

Shockwave 3D proposes eight modifiers. These are objects that add functionality to your models, at the price of performance. You can attach modifiers to models on a need-to-use basis and remove them when they are no longer needed. This means you can exploit the possibilities they provide while limiting their effect of the speed of playback.

You saw the Collision Modifier in Chapter 14. In the following section, I've grouped the remaining modifiers together by family.

Mesh Deform

The work you did in Chapter 9 should have prepared you for most of the possibilities of the Mesh Deform Modifier. This allows you to deal with any model as if it were created from a mesh resource. Try adding the Mesh Deform Modifier to a mesh to see if there are any differences in the way it works. One difference is the additional `neighbor[]` property. Can you imagine a situation in which this could be useful?

You might like to create a simple movie with a model based on a sphere modelResource. Could you use the Mesh Deform Modifier together with the detailed information provided by `modelsUnderLoc()` to change the color of the face the user clicks? Could you get this color to spread gradually over the whole sphere, using the `neighbor[]` property? How about deforming the sphere if the user clicks a given point and drags it?

Level of Detail (LOD) and Sub-Division Surfaces (SDS)

The Level of Detail Modifier is used to reduce the number of polygons in a scene to improve performance. What sort of scenes are going to require this modifier? Where in the scene would the reduction of polygons be the least noticeable? Try building such a scene. Use the 3DPI tool to test which settings give you the best results. Use the fpsMeter movie in a window to give you an idea of how performance is improved.

The Sub-Division Surfaces Modifier increases the number of polygons. This improves the quality of models, both in terms of shape and in terms of lighting effects. Note that it is incompatible with both the LOD Modifier and the Toon Modifier. Open the Gallery.dir movie (Chapter 13) and test it on the walls lit by the spotlight. Test it also on the various pictures. The effect can be surprising. Open the Lightest.dir movie (also Chapter 13), choose the #mesh x 6 model in the pop-up menu, create a multifaceted mesh model, and then apply the SDS Modifier to it. What settings are required to get it to work? Does the effect correspond to your expectations? How does use of the SDS Modifier affect performance? Is this surprising? Based on your observations, try to create a simple movie that uses the SDS Modifier effectively.

Toon and Inker

You can find a movie named DoNotPush.dir in the folder Intel 3D Examples\DoNotPush\DSWMedia on the Director 8.5 CD-ROM. This provides an example of the Toon Modifier in use. Could you adapt it so that it also uses the Inker Modifier? How about creating a simple movie and using the 3DPI movie in a window to test the various properties? Once you understand the workings of each modifier, could you write a behavior for your simple movie that makes you use the appropriate syntax?

BonesPlayer and KeyframePlayer

The DoNotPush.dir movie mentioned in the preceding section also demonstrates the BonesPlayer Modifier. You can use the 3DPI movie in a window to watch the different keywords at work. Look up these keywords (you'll find a full list in the "Animation Modifiers" section of the "Working with Models and Model Resources" chapter of *What's New in Director Shockwave Studio*). Use the entries in the 3D Lingo Dictionary to give you an image of the possibilities. Create a sketch of a simple *.w3D file you could create to demonstrate those possibilities.

Import the file and place it on the Stage. Run the movie and try to control the models from the Message window. Create a simple behavior that runs the same commands automatically.

Look at the `registerForEvent()` and `registerScript()` commands. How do these compare with the programming language or plug-ins of your 3D design package? How easy is it to transfer your existing knowledge to Director? How does the callback feature provided by these commands compare to the way you already use scripts and behaviors in 2D Director?

Using Motion Objects

You can extend your investigation of the BonesPlayer and KeyframePlayer Modifiers by combining existing Motion Objects into groups. Perhaps you could create a movie with a human figure, where users can test a variety of separate dance movements and combine them to create their own personalized dance style.

Importing Files Created in Third-Party 3D Design Packages

Just as you can combine Motions created in the third-party 3D design packages, so can you add the models contained in one *.w3D file to the world created in another file. Look into the `loadFile()` command and the various `clone...()` commands. The various files available in the 3DModels\ folder on the Director 8.5 CD-ROM can serve as guinea pigs. Try to get the different human characters to meet each other, or create a car showroom.

Useful Director-Oriented Sites

The community of Director users worldwide provides a great deal of mutual support; the lion's share of this help is free. Following are some useful addresses to bookmark.

In English:

- **http://www.macromedia.com/support/director/**
  This is the official web site for Director. Use it to search for information on supported features, access the technotes, and link to other major Director sites.
- **http://www.directordev.com/**
  Another official site with a more hands-on approach. Content is provided by both Director engineers and power users.
- **http://mcli.dist.maricopa.edu/director/**
  Home of the most active Director-oriented mailing list, this site provides an impressive set of archives for questions asked on the list.
- **http://www.director-online.com/**
  Started by Zachary Belado, Alex Zavatone, and Pat McLellan, and now edited by Darrel Plant, this dynamic site hosts a series of well-informed articles on a wide variety of Director topics.
- **http://www.updateStage.com/**
  Gretchen Macdowall's provides three important services at this site: the Quirk List, which gives details on a great many bugs, their workarounds and the versions in which the fix appears; her regular column on her latest Director discoveries; and a centralized source of many excellent xtra extensions.
- **http://www.penworks.com/**
  Run by Tab Julius, who also runs the popular Lingo-L mailing list.
- **http://www.trevimedia.com/**
  Terry Schussler's site with information on his latest seminars and links to the work of many leading Director users.
- **http://www.mediamacros.com/**
  Source of a wide variety of behaviors and other scripts from many different contributors.
- **http://www.ullala.at/**
  This is where you can find the invaluable 3DPI shareware movie.
- **http://www.theburrow.co.uk**
  Barry Swan is one of the most active developers of games in Director. His site contains demonstrations and tutorials of many advanced concepts.
- **http://www.shockwavemovies.com/**
  An unofficial site run by Tom Higgins, an official Director engineer. Full of undocumented tricks and insider's insights.

- **http://www.duguk.org/**
  Home of the British Director Users' Group.
- **http://perso.planetb.fr/newton/**
  My own collection of behaviors and other useful scripts. The vast majority of movies were written in response to questions on various mailing lists, and are working demonstrations in unprotected format that you can download and study.

In French:

- **http://www.director-fr.com/**
  Run by Emmanual Beuque and Florian de Joannès, with active participation of other subscribers to the French-language Pistes-L mailing list.

In German:

- **http://www.lingopark.com/**
- **http://www.startmovie.net/**
- **http://www.score.de/**
- **http://www.3d-lingo.de** (Shockwave 3D only)

In Spanish:

- **http://www.listadirector.cjb.net/**
- **http://www.mmug-ar.com.ar/director/**

Director-Oriented Mailing Lists

You're likely to find me and many other helpful Director users on the mailing lists shown in Table 15-1. You're more likely to learn from these lists if you follow these guidelines:

- Participate. Actively asking and answering questions means others will notice your strengths and help you with your weaknesses. The more you offer, the more you will receive. I will often go out of my way to write code to answer a specific question. When I do, I learn something new. I always test code before I send it—that's when most of the learning occurs.

- Be brief. Quote only those extracts from the previous message that are essential. Identifying the key points in the discussion is a key social skill. Hone your answers so that you gain a reputation for neat solutions. Don't send messages in HTML. Don't ever send attachments to a mailing list; post an example on your web site and provide a URL.
- Ask questions only as a last resort. Most mailing lists have archives where you can find previous answers to questions similar to your own. All copies of Director are sold with a manual (online or hard copy) that contains the answers to many questions.
- Be polite. Use a self-explanatory subject for your messages. Wait patiently for others to answer. Do not get upset if they do not answer. You have no claim on other developers' time.

Name	Center of Interest	To Subscribe, Send a Message to	Text of Your Subscription Message	Web Site for List
Direct-L	All Director-related topics	listserv@uafsysb.uark.edu	subscribe DIRECT-L	http://mcli.dist.maricopa.edu/director/ index.html
Lingo-L	Only topics directly related to the use of Lingo	majordomo@cyberportal.net	subscribe lingo	http://www.penworks.com/lingo-l.cgi
DUG	General multimedia mailing list with specific interest in Director (British)	Majordomo@obsolete.com	subscribe dug	http://www.duguk.org
3DDirector-L	Shockwave 3D	listserv@trevimedia.com	SUB 3DDIRECTOR-L	http://www.trevimedia.com/
Multiuser-L	Multiuser Server and Xtra	listserv@trevimedia.com	SUB MULTIUSER-L	http://www.trevimedia.com/
DirGames	Advanced discussions on programming games			http://nuttybar.drama.uga.edu/mailman/listinfo/dirgames-l/

Table 15-1 *Director-Oriented Mailing Lists*

There also are a number of lists in languages other than English:

Mailing List	Language and Center of Interest	Where to Subscribe
Pistes-L	French language list for all Director-related topics	http://www.director-fr.com/mailman/listinfo/pistes-l
LingoPark-L	German language list	http://www.lingopark.com/
3D-Lingo	German language list dealing specifically with Shockwave 3D	http://www.startmovie.net/
Director	Spanish	http://www.listadirector.cjb.net/
Sala Multimedia	Spanish	http://www.mmug-ar.com.ar/salas/salamulti_inscr.html

Many xtras developers also run their own mailing lists to help users and would-be users to get the most out of their products:

- **OSControls from PegHole <http://www.peghole.com/xtras/>** Send a message to majordomo@peghole.com with the text SUBSCRIBE osc-xtra-list.
- **Integration New Media <integration.qc.ca>** A variety of lists exist for each of their products. Visit the site for more details.

After You Close This Book

This book doesn't answer all your questions, but I hope that it has opened your eyes to new possibilities. Come and visit the book's web site at http://nonlinear.openspark.com/, where you will be able to find updates to the tool and reference movies, extracts from chapters forthcoming in the next edition, and examples provided by other readers.

This book doesn't answer all your questions, but perhaps I or some of the other readers can. At the nonlinear web site, you can join the nonlinear-l mailing list and discuss the issues raised in this book. Your participation can help us all learn to use Director better.

See you there.

Index

Note: Page numbers in *italics* refer to illustrations or charts.

B

C

D

drawText( ) command, 81–84

G

J

K

L

M

N

Q

R

S

U

V

INTERNATIONAL CONTACT INFORMATION

AUSTRALIA
McGraw-Hill Book Company Australia Pty. Ltd.
TEL +61-2-9417-9899
FAX +61-2-9417-5687
http://www.mcgraw-hill.com.au
books-it_sydney@mcgraw-hill.com

CANADA
McGraw-Hill Ryerson Ltd.
TEL +905-430-5000
FAX +905-430-5020
http://www.mcgrawhill.ca

GREECE, MIDDLE EAST, NORTHERN AFRICA
McGraw-Hill Hellas
TEL +30-1-656-0990-3-4
FAX +30-1-654-5525

MEXICO (Also serving Latin America)
McGraw-Hill Interamericana Editores S.A. de C.V.
TEL +525-117-1583
FAX +525-117-1589
http://www.mcgraw-hill.com.mx
fernando_castellanos@mcgraw-hill.com

SINGAPORE (Serving Asia)
McGraw-Hill Book Company
TEL +65-863-1580
FAX +65-862-3354
http://www.mcgraw-hill.com.sg
mghasia@mcgraw-hill.com

SOUTH AFRICA
McGraw-Hill South Africa
TEL +27-11-622-7512
FAX +27-11-622-9045
robyn_swanepoel@mcgraw-hill.com

UNITED KINGDOM & EUROPE (Excluding Southern Europe)
McGraw-Hill Education Europe
TEL +44-1-628-502500
FAX +44-1-628-770224
http://www.mcgraw-hill.co.uk
computing_neurope@mcgraw-hill.com

ALL OTHER INQUIRIES Contact:
Osborne/McGraw-Hill
TEL +1-510-549-6600
FAX +1-510-883-7600
http://www.osborne.com
omg_international@mcgraw-hill.com

About the CD

The CD-ROM contains:

- All the source files mentioned in the book
- A number of tool movies to use in a window to help you while you are authoring your own movies on the Stage
- The demo version of a number of third-party xtras, some of which are required by the source files
- A projector that allows you to install the required xtras into the Xtras folder of all copies of Director on your hard disk

If you do not yet have a copy of Director Shockwave Studio, you can download a 30-day trial of the latest version from http://www.macromedia.com/software/director/trial/.

File Organization

The source files are arranged in two folders, with the following structure:

Imaging

- Concepts (Chapter 1)
- Colors (Chapter 2)
- Commands (Chapter 3)
- Members (Chapter 4)
- Timing (Chapter 5)

3D

- Space (Chapter 6)
- Physics (Chapter 7)
- Dragging (Chapter 8)
- Meshes (Chapter 9)
- Surface1 (Chapter 10)
- Surface2 (Chapter 11)
- Cameras (Chapter 12)
- Lights (Chapter 13)
- Collide (Chapter 14)

AddXtras Folder

In the AddXtras folder you will find a projector for each platform (Macintosh and Windows). The AddXtras projector enables you to install the following files into your Xtras folder:

- The demo version of OSControls Xtra 1.2. The full version is available from http://www.peghole.com/xtras/osc_xtra/downloads/. This xtra is used by many of the source movies. It provides system-specific controls such as scrollbars, sliders, pop-up menus, and so on. Please install this xtra unless you already have a newer version.
- A demo version of Ullala's 3D Property Inspector 3.9. The latest version is available from http://www.ullala.at/3DPI/. This gives you visual feedback on the state of your 3D members.
- Toolkit8.cst, a Director 8 castlib containing over 120 reusable behaviors, movie scripts, and parent scripts
- fpsMeter.dir, a Director 8 movie that helps you test the performance of your own movies
- Copyxels.dir, a Director 8 movie that gives you real-time feedback on how the many parameters of the `copyPixels()` command works
- Shaders.dir, a Director 8.5 movie that provides a visual interface for designing textures and shaders for Shockwave 3D members
- SnapShot.dir, a Director 8.5 movie that enables you to find the best vantage point for your 3D cameras
- Demonstration versions of a selection of powerful xtra extensions for Director, provided by Integration New Media and updateStage. You will find these in the appropriate folders.

LICENSE AGREEMENT

THIS PRODUCT (THE "PRODUCT") CONTAINS PROPRIETARY SOFTWARE, DATA AND INFORMATION (INCLUDING DOCUMENTATION) OWNED BY THE McGRAW-HILL COMPANIES, INC. ("McGRAW-HILL") AND ITS LICENSORS. YOUR RIGHT TO USE THE PRODUCT IS GOVERNED BY THE TERMS AND CONDITIONS OF THIS AGREEMENT.

LICENSE: Throughout this License Agreement, "you" shall mean either the individual or the entity whose agent opens this package. You are granted a non-exclusive and non-transferable license to use the Product subject to the following terms:
(i) If you have licensed a single user version of the Product, the Product may only be used on a single computer (i.e., a single CPU). If you licensed and paid the fee applicable to a local area network or wide area network version of the Product, you are subject to the terms of the following subparagraph (ii).
(ii) If you have licensed a local area network version, you may use the Product on unlimited workstations located in one single building selected by you that is served by such local area network. If you have licensed a wide area network version, you may use the Product on unlimited workstations located in multiple buildings on the same site selected by you that is served by such wide area network; provided, however, that any building will not be considered located in the same site if it is more than five (5) miles away from any building included in such site. In addition, you may only use a local area or wide area network version of the Product on one single server. If you wish to use the Product on more than one server, you must obtain written authorization from McGraw-Hill and pay additional fees.
(iii) You may make one copy of the Product for back-up purposes only and you must maintain an accurate record as to the location of the back-up at all times.

COPYRIGHT; RESTRICTIONS ON USE AND TRANSFER: All rights (including copyright) in and to the Product are owned by McGraw-Hill and its licensors. You are the owner of the enclosed disc on which the Product is recorded. You may not use, copy, decompile, disassemble, reverse engineer, modify, reproduce, create derivative works, transmit, distribute, sublicense, store in a database or retrieval system of any kind, rent or transfer the Product, or any portion thereof, in any form or by any means (including electronically or otherwise) except as expressly provided for in this License Agreement. You must reproduce the copyright notices, trademark notices, legends and logos of McGraw-Hill and its licensors that appear on the Product on the back-up copy of the Product which you are permitted to make hereunder. All rights in the Product not expressly granted herein are reserved by McGraw-Hill and its licensors.

TERM: This License Agreement is effective until terminated. It will terminate if you fail to comply with any term or condition of this License Agreement. Upon termination, you are obligated to return to McGraw-Hill the Product together with all copies thereof and to purge all copies of the Product included in any and all servers and computer facilities.

DISCLAIMER OF WARRANTY: THE PRODUCT AND THE BACK-UP COPY ARE LICENSED "AS IS." McGRAW-HILL, ITS LICENSORS AND THE AUTHORS MAKE NO WARRANTIES, EXPRESS OR IMPLIED, AS TO THE RESULTS TO BE OBTAINED BY ANY PERSON OR ENTITY FROM USE OF THE PRODUCT, ANY INFORMATION OR DATA INCLUDED THEREIN AND/OR ANY TECHNICAL SUPPORT SERVICES PROVIDED HEREUNDER, IF ANY ("TECHNICAL SUPPORT SERVICES"). McGRAW-HILL, ITS LICENSORS AND THE AUTHORS MAKE NO EXPRESS OR IMPLIED WARRANTIES OF MERCHANTABILITY OR FITNESS FOR A PARTICULAR PURPOSE OR USE WITH RESPECT TO THE PRODUCT. McGRAW-HILL, ITS LICENSORS, AND THE AUTHORS MAKE NO GUARANTEE THAT YOU WILL PASS ANY CERTIFICATION EXAM WHATSOEVER BY USING THIS PRODUCT. NEITHER McGRAW-HILL, ANY OF ITS LICENSORS NOR THE AUTHORS WARRANT THAT THE FUNCTIONS CONTAINED IN THE PRODUCT WILL MEET YOUR REQUIREMENTS OR THAT THE OPERATION OF THE PRODUCT WILL BE UNINTERRUPTED OR ERROR FREE. YOU ASSUME THE ENTIRE RISK WITH RESPECT TO THE QUALITY AND PERFORMANCE OF THE PRODUCT.

LIMITED WARRANTY FOR DISC: To the original licensee only, McGraw-Hill warrants that the enclosed disc on which the Product is recorded is free from defects in materials and workmanship under normal use and service for a period of ninety (90) days from the date of purchase. In the event of a defect in the disc covered by the foregoing warranty, McGraw-Hill will replace the disc.

LIMITATION OF LIABILITY: NEITHER McGRAW-HILL, ITS LICENSORS NOR THE AUTHORS SHALL BE LIABLE FOR ANY INDIRECT, SPECIAL OR CONSEQUENTIAL DAMAGES, SUCH AS BUT NOT LIMITED TO, LOSS OF ANTICIPATED PROFITS OR BENEFITS, RESULTING FROM THE USE OR INABILITY TO USE THE PRODUCT EVEN IF ANY OF THEM HAS BEEN ADVISED OF THE POSSIBILITY OF SUCH DAMAGES. THIS LIMITATION OF LIABILITY SHALL APPLY TO ANY CLAIM OR CAUSE WHATSOEVER WHETHER SUCH CLAIM OR CAUSE ARISES IN CONTRACT, TORT, OR OTHERWISE. Some states do not allow the exclusion or limitation of indirect, special or consequential damages, so the above limitation may not apply to you.

U.S. GOVERNMENT RESTRICTED RIGHTS: Any software included in the Product is provided with restricted rights subject to subparagraphs (c), (1) and (2) of the Commercial Computer Software-Restricted Rights clause at 48 C.F.R. 52.227-19. The terms of this Agreement applicable to the use of the data in the Product are those under which the data are generally made available to the general public by McGraw-Hill. Except as provided herein, no reproduction, use, or disclosure rights are granted with respect to the data included in the Product and no right to modify or create derivative works from any such data is hereby granted.

GENERAL: This License Agreement constitutes the entire agreement between the parties relating to the Product. The terms of any Purchase Order shall have no effect on the terms of this License Agreement. Failure of McGraw-Hill to insist at any time on strict compliance with this License Agreement shall not constitute a waiver of any rights under this License Agreement. This License Agreement shall be construed and governed in accordance with the laws of the State of New York. If any provision of this License Agreement is held to be contrary to law, that provision will be enforced to the maximum extent permissible and the remaining provisions will remain in full force and effect.